COMPARATIVE POLITICS

SECOND EDITION

Now in a completely updated second edition, this textbook has become a favorite for the introductory undergraduate course in comparative politics. It features ten theoretically and historically grounded country studies that show how the three major concepts of comparative analysis – interests, identities, and institutions – shape the politics of nations. Throughout the presentation, countries appear in the context of a changing global order that creates challenges to each country's path of development. These challenges frequently alter domestic interests and identities and force countries to find new institutional solutions to the problems of modern politics. Written in a style free of heavy-handed jargon and organized to address the concerns of contemporary comparativists, this textbook provides students with the conceptual tools and historical background they need to understand the politics of our complex world.

Jeffrey Kopstein is the author of *The Politics of Economic Decline in East Germany, 1945–1989* (1997). He has published more than 40 articles in scholarly journals and books. He is currently Director of the Institute of European Studies at the University of Toronto.

Mark Lichbach is Professor and Chair of Government and Politics at the University of Maryland, College Park. He is the author or editor of many books, including the award-winning *The Rebel's Dilemma*, and of numerous articles that have appeared in scholarly journals in political science, economics, and sociology.

COMPARATIVE POLITICS

INTERESTS, IDENTITIES, AND INSTITUTIONS IN A CHANGING GLOBAL ORDER

SECOND EDITION

Edited by

JEFFREY KOPSTEIN
University of Toronto

MARK LICHBACH
University of Maryland, College Park

CAMBRIDGE
UNIVERSITY PRESS

CAMBRIDGE UNIVERSITY PRESS
Cambridge, New York, Melbourne, Madrid, Cape Town, Singapore, São Paulo

Cambridge University Press
40 West 20th Street, New York, NY 10011-4211, USA

www.cambridge.org
Information on this title: www.cambridge.org/9780521843164

First edition published 2000
Second edition first published 2005

Printed in the United States of America

A catalog record for this publication is available from the British Library.

Library of Congress Cataloging in Publication Data

Comparative politics : interests, identities, and institutions in a changing global order /
edited by Jeffrey Kopstein, Mark Lichbach. – 2nd ed.
    p. cm.
ISBN 0-521-84316-2 (hb) – ISBN 0-521-60395-1 (pb)
1. Comparative government.   I. Kopstein, Jeffrey.   II. Lichbach, Mark Irving, 1951–
III. Title.
JF51.C6235   2006
320.3 – dc22   2005006516

ISBN-13   978-0-521-84316-4 hardback
ISBN-10   0-521-84316-2 hardback

ISBN-13   978-0-521-60395-9 paperback
ISBN-10   0-521-60395-1 paperback

To Max and Isaac Kopstein and to Sammi Jo and Yossi Lichbach

May they someday help repair our world.

Contents

PART FOUR. EXPERIMENTAL DEVELOPERS

Maps

Preface to the Second Edition

This book originated during many hours of pleasant conversation about teaching comparative politics at the University of Colorado at Boulder. Out of these conversations emerged the idea of an introductory textbook that would convey to students the main currents in contemporary comparative politics. These currents are summed up here under three rubrics: interests, identities, and institutions. We decided to illustrate this framework through a series of country studies cast in world-historical perspective. At the same time, we wanted to avoid weighing down the country studies with a heavy-handed or outdated theoretical apparatus that inevitably discourages even the hardiest of students. The result, we hope, has struck an acceptable balance between conceptual rigor and flexibility.

To the extent that we have accomplished this, most of the credit is due to our contributors, who have cheerfully taken on our framework without losing what is interesting and distinctive about their country's experience. We are also grateful to the staff of Cambridge University Press and especially Ed Parsons for his professionalism, enthusiasm, and common sense.

As in the first edition, editing this book has been a collaborative act. It represents the tangible result of a long friendship. The order of our names on the cover reflects only the order of the alphabet. Our efforts have been equal in every way. Although both of us have moved on to different universities, this book has allowed us to continue the conversation that started over coffee and ice cream fourteen years ago.

Contributors

Michael Bratton, Michigan State University

Arista Maria Cirtautas, University of Virginia

Anthony Gill, University of Washington

Andrew C. Gould, University of Notre Dame

Stephen E. Hanson, University of Washington

Jeffrey Kopstein, University of Toronto

Mark Lichbach, University of Maryland, College Park

Vali Nasr, Naval Post-Graduate School

Peter Rutland, Wesleyan University

Miranda A. Schreurs, University of Maryland, College Park

Rudra Sil, University of Pennsylvania

Yu-Shan Wu, Academia Sinica

CHAPTER ONE

What Is Comparative Politics?

Jeffrey Kopstein and Mark Lichbach

Introduction

Imagine that you could design the political order (e.g., democracy in the United States, Communist Party dominance in China) for a country of your choosing. Where would you start? Who would get to rule? What rules for political life would you choose? Could you make rules that would be fair to everyone? If not, whom would these rules favor and whom would they disadvantage? Would they be rules that even those at the "bottom" of the social order, the poorest and least powerful people, would agree to? What would be the rules for changing the rules? These are difficult questions because to answer them in a meaningful way requires an understanding of why and how different countries of the world are governed differently. With so many choices to make, it is easy to see why the job of designing a constitution would be such a difficult one.

It could, however, be made easier. One might start by evaluating the existing possibilities as exemplified by the various forms of government in the states of the world. The state is an organization that possesses sovereignty over a territory and its people. Yet, within our world of states, no two are ruled in exactly the same way. Why should this be the case? Why are societies run, and political orders designed, in so many different ways? What consequences do these differences hold for a people's well-being?

Comparativists (i.e., political scientists who study and compare the politics of different countries) believe that it is possible to provide answers to these questions, and in this book students will begin to understand the craft of comparative politics. Even if it is not possible to design a country as one sees fit, it is possible to understand why countries develop the way they do and why they are ruled as they are. By comparing the range of possible political responses to global opportunities and constraints, we can begin to offer explanations for why countries develop as they do and evaluations about the trade-offs

1

involved under different political orders. Understanding and explaining the differences among the politics of countries are really the core concerns of comparative politics.

COMPARATIVE POLITICS AND POLITICAL SCIENCE

Within political science, comparative politics is considered one of the major "subfields." How is it situated in relation to the other subfields? Let us consider two that are among the most closely related: political theory and international relations.

In some ways, the first comparativists were political theorists. Two thousand years ago, the ancient Greek political theorists Plato and Aristotle identified different kinds of political orders – such as aristocracy (literally "the rule of the best"), oligarchy ("the rule of the few"), democracy ("the rule of the people"), and tyranny (the rule of the tyrant) – and wrote carefully argued treatises on which form of government is the best. Although they offered basic explanations for why one type of government changed into another, they were more interested in justifying what is the right kind of government than in telling us systematically why we get the kind of government that we do. Contemporary political theorists within political science continue this venerable tradition. They continue to write about different kinds of political orders and analyze the structure of ideas about those orders primarily to make judgments about them.

Comparativists, by contrast, tend to suspend their normative evaluation of the world in favor of describing the political world and explaining why it is the way it is. It is important to remember that comparativists do this not because they lack preferences or are unwilling to make normative judgments but rather because as social scientists they are committed first to offering systematic explanations for the world as it is. A comparativist may not like fascism or communism (or even democracy!) but usually considers it challenging enough to answer the question of why some countries become fascist, communist, or democratic in the first place. Comparativists may disagree about whether the acquired knowledge may help make the world a better place or help us make better moral judgments about politics, but they usually agree that the job of describing and explaining is big enough, and perhaps some of the deeper philosophical meanings of our findings can be left to the political theorists. So, for example, rather than evaluating whether democracy is good or not, comparativists spend a great deal of time trying to understand and identify the general conditions – social, economic, ideological, institutional, and international – under which democracies initially appear, become unstable, collapse into dictatorship, and sometimes reemerge as democracies.

What is the relationship between comparative politics and international relations? Like comparativists, most students of international relations consider themselves to be social scientists. Additionally, like comparative politics, the subfield of international relations can also trace its roots to ancient Greek political theory. In this case, the person of interest is Thucydides, who attempted to understand the origins and consequences of the Peloponnesian Wars between the Greek city-states. War, as we all know, is unfortunately an important part of the human condition. Modern scholars of international relations understandably devote a great deal of time and energy to explaining why states go to war with each other. Of course, peoples of different states do not only fight with each other. They also trade goods and services with each other. It is not surprising then that scholars of international relations also study trade between countries.

Comparativists, although acknowledging the importance of war and international trade, concentrate on the politics within countries rather than the politics that occurs between them. This intellectual division of labor between comparativists, who study "domestic politics," and international-relations specialists, who study the "foreign politics" of states, has long characterized political science. With so much to learn, it seemed to be a sensible way of dividing up the discipline.

In the last quarter of the twentieth century, this began to change. For one thing, most scholars of international relations now recognize that what happens within a country may determine whether it wages war or makes peace. Would there have been a Second World War without the election of Hitler's Nazi Party in Germany in 1932? It is difficult to say for certain but it is much less likely that the politics *between* the European states during the 1930s would have developed the way they did if the politics *within* one of them, Germany, had been different.

Comparativists also understand the huge impact that international relations has upon the politics of almost every country in the world. War and preparing for war have always influenced domestic politics. So has international trade. Today, the ease with which goods and services, people and the ideas they espouse, and, perhaps most importantly, weaponry move around the world have made our planet a much smaller place. Clearly, what transpires between countries influences what happens within them.

Rather than sustain an artificial division between comparative politics and international relations, in this book we explicitly take account of the global context in which the politics of a country takes shape. The international environment often provides a political challenge to which countries have no choice but to respond. In responding as they do, however, they may introduce a new kind of domestic institutional order that other countries find appealing or threatening and to which they in turn also feel compelled to respond. There is an intimate connection between international and domestic politics, and in the next chapter we offer a framework for thinking about this connection.

How Comparativists Practice Their Craft: Concepts and Methods

REGIME TYPES

Although comparativists think about a broad range of questions, they are most frequently interested in the origins and impact of different kinds of government, or what they refer to as "regime type." That is, if we accept that there are different kinds of political orders in the world, what are the main characteristics of those orders, and why do they appear where and when they do? For example, all of the country chapters in this book consider why democracy took root or did not take root with the country in question.

Before inquiring into the origins of democracy, however, one must have a fairly clear concept of what democracy is and what it is not. The classification of countries into regime types is tricky. Most comparativists do not simply accept the word of the rulers of a country that its political institutions are democratic. Instead, they operate with a definition of democracy that contains certain traits: competitive, multiparty elections, freedom of speech and assembly, and the rule of law are the minimum that most comparativists require for a country to be classified as a democracy.

Similarly, when comparativists classify a country as communist, they usually mean that it is ruled by a communist party that seeks to transform the society it rules according to the tenets of Marxist-Leninist ideology. Real countries, of course, never practice perfectly all of the traits of any regime type. They are never perfectly democratic, communist, fascist, or Islamist. Democracies sometimes violate their own laws or conduct elections that are not perfectly free and fair. Beyond a certain point, however, it makes little sense to categorize a country as democratic if it prohibits free speech or falsifies election results. Or, to take an example from this book, if a communist country, such as China today, allows markets to determine economic life, at what point do we cease categorizing it as communist? Comparativists do not agree on the answer to this question, but clearly it is an important one because before we can understand why certain regime types exist in one place and not in another, we have to agree on what that regime type looks like.

TOOLS OF ANALYSIS: INTERESTS, IDENTITIES, AND INSTITUTIONS

Even once they have agreed on the important differences between democratic, communist, fascist, and Islamic states, comparativists frequently disagree on how best to evaluate the conditions that produce the political regime types in question. This is also a very tricky question. Let us say that you were parachuted into a country and had to figure out quickly what the most important facts about that country were for determining its politics. On what would you choose to concentrate? Comparativists do not always agree on this either.

A first group of comparativists maintain that what matters most is material interests. People are rational calculators. They organize politically when it serves their interests and support political regime types that maximize their life chances. They are rational in the sense that they minimize their losses and maximize their gains. If you accept this assumption, then to get a handle on the politics of a given country, what you should be studying is the structure of material interests in its society and how those interests organize themselves to gain power.

The major interests seen in democratic states are usually organized into interest groups, trade unions, social movements, and political parties. In non-democratic states, it may be illegal for individuals to come together in interest groups or competing political parties, but even in communist and fascist states, political scientists have identified many ways in which people pursue their interests to get the kinds of public policies that benefit them the most.

A second group of comparativists maintain that there is no such thing as "objective" interests outside of some set of values or ideas that defines your interests. Who you think you are – your identity – determines what you really want. Yes, all people require food and shelter, but beyond this minimum what people value most in this world may have very little to do with maximizing their material lot. In fact, it is all too easy to find people who are willing to die for what they believe in (that is, to act against the most important material interest of all – physical survival). Instead, what people demand out of their rulers and what rulers do is to pursue the ideals that they most cherish and enact policies that are consistent with their identities. So, rather than focusing on material interests, to understand politics you are much better off concentrating on the dominant identity of a given society.

Religion and ethnicity are two of the most common forms that identity takes. In democracies, political scientists have consistently shown that religion and ethnicity are very good (though not perfect) predictors of how people vote and what kinds of policies they favor. In the United States, for example, most Jews vote for the Democratic Party and most Southern Baptists vote Republican because these respective parties are considered by both religious groups as having ideas similar to their own on important issues. In India, a state that consists of a multitude of nationalities and religions, parties based primarily on particular ethnic and religious groups have successfully competed against parties that run on a nonethnic platform. And it is not only minority groups that engage in identity politics. The success of anti-immigrant parties throughout Europe and Hindu nationalist parties in India shows that majorities engage in identity politics, too.

Modern societies constantly generate new identities not only on religion and ethnic belonging but also on gender, sexual orientation, and care for the environment. Democratic societies now have strong and important women's rights, gay rights, and environmental movements. And, of course, identity politics matters not only in democratic settings but also in nondemocratic ones. Communist revolutionaries hoped that if they built a better society, people would begin to define themselves in new ways and that a new "socialist man" would appear who would subordinate his selfish desires to the greater needs of society as a whole. Part of what makes the study of politics so interesting is the constant proliferation of new identities and the myriad ways in which these new identities are either accommodated or rejected by the political order or can undermine the existing order.

A third set of comparativists maintain that both material interests and identities do not really determine on their own how a country's politics works. What matters most are institutions, the long-term, authoritative rules and procedures that structure how power flows. People may deeply desire a certain kind of policy (a new health care system, for example) and have an identity that would support this (say, a widely spread ethic of care that reflects the simple maxim "I am my brother's keeper"), but the rules of the political game may be structured in such a way that numerical minorities can easily block all attempts to change the policy. So, if you want to get a quick analysis of a country's politics, what you should concentrate on are the authoritative rules of the game – the institutions.

Political life is teeming with institutions. Democracies have institutions for electing their leaders, for channeling the flow of legislation, and for determining whether the laws are just or "constitutional." Some of these institutions are so important, such as regularly held free and fair elections, that they are part of what we mean by democracy. Other institutions, such as the rules for electing leaders, have a great impact on the politics of a country, but no single set of electoral rules can be held to be more "democratic" than another. In Great Britain, parliamentary leaders are elected much as in the United States, in a single-member district, "first-past-the-post" election. In Germany, members of the Parliament – the Bundestag – are elected primarily in a multi-member district, "proportional representation" contest in which parties are represented in the legislature according to their share of the popular vote. Both systems have strengths and weaknesses but are equally democratic.

Of course, nondemocratic countries have institutions, too. The most important institution in a communist state is the Communist Party, which has small party cells at all political levels spread throughout the society. Communist states also have elaborate institutions for economic planning and administration. And, of course, there is the institution of the secret police. Iran, as an Islamic republic, not only has an elected parliament but standing over this parliament is an unelected Supreme Revolutionary Council of religious leaders that possesses the right to declare invalid legislation that contradicts its interpretation of Islamic law. As in democratic countries, the institutions of nondemocratic countries shape the political arena and influence what kinds of policies are enacted.

These three ways of studying the determinants of politics – interests, identities, and institutions – represent the dominant concepts in comparative politics, and some admixture of them is present in just about every study, including the chapters in this book. They give us a powerful set of tools for grappling with some of the most important questions that comparativists think about.

Consider again the question of why some countries (or "cases," as comparativists often refer to them) are democratic and others are not. Scholars who stress the importance of interests point to the size of a country's middle class on the assumption that poorer countries have smaller middle classes and diminished chances for sustaining democracy. Comparativists who study identities and values explain the presence or absence of democracy by the strength of a population's commitment to representative government and democratic participation. Institutionalists, by contrast, focus on which kinds of political arrangements (U.S.-style presidentialism or British-style parliamentary government, for example) best ensure that elections, freedom of speech, and the rule of law will continue to be practiced.

Comparativists apply the tools of interests, identities, and institutions not only to the determinants of regime type; that is, why countries are democratic or nondemocratic. They also use these concepts to understand why countries have the kinds of public policies that they do. Even among democracies, one finds important differences. For example, some have large and extensive welfare states – systems to equalize socioeconomic benefits. Others have much smaller ones. Consider the issue of publicly financed health insurance. It is generally acknowledged that most industrialized democratic countries have universal systems of government-funded health insurance and tightly controlled regulations for the provision of medical services. The big exception to this rule is the United States, where health insurance and service provision remain mostly private. Why is this the case? What accounts for this American exceptionalism? An analysis based on interests might point to the influence of powerful groups, such as insurance companies and doctors, who oppose government interference in the market for health care. An analysis based on identities would stress the value most Americans place on individual responsibility and the suspicion that they generally harbor toward governmental intervention in the market. An institutional analysis of this question would point to the structure of political institutions in the United States in order to show how health care legislation can be blocked relatively easily by a determined minority of legislators at several points along its way to passage. Which of these different approaches to the question yields the most powerful insights is, of course, a matter of debate. What comparativists believe is that the answer to the question of U.S. exceptionalism can only be found by comparing U.S. interests, identities, and institutions with those of other countries.

In fact, the concepts of interests, identities, and institutions can be used to assess a broad range of themes that comparativists study. Why do some democratic countries have only two parties, whereas others have three, four, or more? Why do minority ethnic groups mobilize politically in some countries and during some eras but not in others? Why do some people enter politics using parties and elections, whereas others turn to street demonstrations, protest, or even terrorism?

A question that many comparativists have studied using interests, identities, and institutions is that of when revolutions occur. This is an especially fascinating question for students of comparative politics because political change does not always occur slowly and peacefully. Some of the truly momentous changes in political life in countries throughout the world occur quickly and entail a great deal of violence. Notice, for example, that most of the countries in this book have experienced political revolutions at some time in their history. Their political orders, especially in those countries that became democratic early in their history, were born as much through violent revolutionary conflict as through peaceful compromise. Comparativists frequently deploy the concepts of interests, identities, and institutions in order to identify the conditions under which revolutions occur.

Using these tools and the cases they study, comparativists often establish explanations for general families of events such as revolutions, elections, and the onset of democracy itself. When the explanation works well (that is, when it can account for the same phenomenon across a sufficiently large range of cases) and the family of events is general enough, comparativists will use the term "theory" to describe what they are talking about. Theories are important because they help us discover new facts about new cases, and cases are important because they help us build new and more powerful theories.

Comparative Politics and Developmental Paths

A CHANGING FIELD

Comparative politics developed as a subdiscipline in the United States after World War II. At that time, Americans suddenly found themselves in a position of leadership, with a need for deep knowledge about a huge number of countries. The Cold War between the United States and the Soviet Union raised the question of whether countries around the world would become increasingly democratic and capitalist or whether some version of communism would be more appealing. Comparativists initially provided an answer to this question by maintaining that over time most countries would look more and more alike; they would "converge" with each other. Especially as they became wealthier, industrialized, educated, and less bound by unquestioned tradition, states throughout the world would become more democratic. As society changed, "political development" would occur. This approach to comparative politics was called modernization theory.

Even though it yielded important insights and inspired a great deal of research throughout the world, by the late 1960s modernization theory confronted withering criticism on a number of fronts. First, it universalized the particular experience of the West into a model that all countries, independent of time or place, would also follow. Political scientists doing field research in other areas of the world maintained that this was simply not happening. Especially in poorer countries, democracies often collapsed into dictatorships. Second, and more important, political scientists working in poorer regions of the world argued that even if the history of Europe and North America (the "West") did represent a shift from traditional to modern society, the fact of the West's existence changed the context in which poorer countries had to develop. Some political scientists maintained that the poorer nations of the world lived in a condition of "dependence" on the West. Large Western corporations, so the argument of the "dependency theorists" ran, supported by their governments at home and by the regimes they controlled in the poorer countries of the world, economically exploited these countries. As long as this relationship existed, the people of these poorer countries (called the "developing world") would remain poor and would live in undemocratic conditions. Even those who did not share this view came to believe that the notion of a unilinear path to the modern world was not supported by the facts and that the West's existence at a minimum changed the context in which the poorer countries of the world had to live. In the face of these trenchant criticisms, most comparativists backed away from thinking in such broad terms and began to concentrate on "smaller" and more tractable questions such as those we have outlined here.

During the 1970s, however, a new wave of democratization began and dozens of countries that had been dictatorships for decades or that had never known democracy at all became democratic. Rather than return to modernization theory, with its sweeping generalizations about the intimate tie between industrial and capitalist society on the one hand and democracy on the other, comparativists have attempted to develop theories that were more sensitive to historical and geographic context. That is the point of departure in our book. Although we share the long-term interest of comparativists in the conditions that produce and sustain democracy, our approach acknowledges the uniqueness of the experience of the West and the huge impact that this experience has had and continues to exercise on the political development of the rest of the world.

Our approach is thus "developmental" in that we place the analysis of each country within the context not only of its own history but also within a broader global history of political development. The initial breakthrough of the West into industrial capitalism and political democracy set out a challenge for the rest of the world. The responses to this challenge sometimes took a democratic form, as in the case of France's response to Great Britain's power in the nineteenth century, but sometimes they did not, as in the cases of communism and fascism. In fact, all of the nondemocratic regime types that we examine in this book were responses to the challenge posed by the most powerful capitalist and democratic countries. The international context provides the impetus through which domestic interests and identities create new institutions.

Not every comparativist will agree with our approach. Some maintain that the perspective emphasizing the Western developmental challenge to the rest of the world is too focused on the "West" and ignores indigenous developments that have little to do with the West. Others contend that it is best to leave these larger questions aside altogether because they are basically unanswerable and that the purpose of comparative politics is to approach matters of the "middle range" (that is, questions that are amenable to neat generalizations). Although we acknowledge the hazards of starting with the West and proceeding to the frequently poorer and less democratic areas of the world – the "East" and "South," the West's impact is too important to ignore. Equally, although we understand that theorizing about such large questions as why countries have the political orders they do is asking a great deal, comparative politics has never shied away from asking big questions about the origins of regime types and their impact on world history. Furthermore, as the country chapters make clear, there is no reason why smaller and more tractable questions cannot be pursued within our framework of interests, identities, and institutions.

PATHS OF DEVELOPMENT

We divide our country chapters into four groups. Each group represents a distinct developmental path. The first group we term "early developers," and we use the examples of Great Britain and France to illustrate what is distinctive about this group. We could also have chosen other Northern and Western European cases such as the Netherlands, Sweden, and Switzerland, as well as the United States and Canada. Great Britain and France, however, offer important features that make them worth studying. In both cases, long-term economic changes created urban middle classes who used their new social power to demand a greater say in the affairs of government. In the case of Great Britain, the economic growth that produced the new middle classes was so rapid and decisive that it has been termed by economic historians an "industrial revolution" and caused Britain to become the most powerful country in the world and remain so for over a century. France, too, became very powerful and created an overseas empire that competed with Great Britain's. In both cases, however, democracy became firmly rooted. In Great Britain, it was never questioned. In France, where the struggle for democracy was much more intense, the proponents of democratic government time and again gained the upper hand.

A second group of countries took a different developmental path. We term them "middle developers." We include in this group Germany and Japan, although we could also have included Italy, Spain, Austria, and several other countries of Central Europe. The key feature of this pattern of development is that these countries all got a "late start" in economic development and had to catch up with the early developers if they were to compete militarily and satisfy the material desires of their people. In all cases, the state played a much larger role in fostering economic development, the traditional agrarian nobility did not really leave the political scene until well into the twentieth century, the military wielded a great deal of influence, and the middle classes were socially far weaker and politically more timid than in the early developers. This combination of external pressure to develop, the dominance of traditional social classes in the modern political world, and the relative weakness of the middle classes laid the groundwork for uncertain democratic politics and authoritarian rule. In the twentieth century, both Germany and Japan developed indigenous responses to the early developers that political scientists have termed "fascist." Fascism offered an alternative way of looking at the world compared with the liberal democracy of the early developers. It stressed ethnic and racial hierarchy over equality, dictatorship over democracy, and military conquest over international trade. Although the fascist response to the challenge of the West was largely defeated in World War II, and both Germany and Japan subsequently entered the family of democratic states, fascist rulers remained in power for much longer in Spain, and fascist ideology continues to attract support in parts of Europe and Asia (e.g., postcommunist Hungary and Slovakia and India).

Our third group of countries we term "late developers." We include here Russia and China, although we could also have included other countries in Eastern Europe and Southeast Asia. In both Russia and China, economic development occurred so late after its initial breakthrough in the West that the state was forced to play the dominant role. As both societies entered the twentieth century, the middle class was tiny and weak. The industrial working class was also small, deeply disaffected, and lived in horrible conditions. The majority of both societies consisted of illiterate and landless peasants. The response in both cases was a communist revolution based on an intellectual elite leading the mass peasantry in the name of a yet to be created industrial working class. Communism promised a world based on material equality and a nonmarket planned economy under the leadership of a communist party that supposedly understood the scientific "laws" of historical development. At the beginning of the twenty-first century, the late developers cast off their communist economies and China (but not Russia) experienced rapid economic growth. Both, however, remained less than democratic – China was still formally ruled by a communist one-party dictatorship – and both were still attempting to close the economic gap between their own country and the more advanced West.

The countries in our fourth developmental path we term "experimental developers." We have chosen as our cases Mexico, India, Iran, and South Africa. These countries are faced with unique developmental problems characteristic of their respective continents. Mexico's grand experiment is independence. Is it possible for a country to be autonomous when its northern neighbor happens to be the most powerful country in the world? Until the mid-1990s, Mexico's postrevolutionary political development was characterized by a one-party state and an autarkic economy. These features of Mexico's political development have changed dramatically since the mid-1990s. India's grand experiment is nonrevolutionary democracy. Is it possible for a large post-colonial country to be a democracy when it has had a major independence movement but not a social revolution? It is interesting to note that India's one-party dominance and autarkic development have also been strongly challenged by both domestic and international pressures for change. Iran's grand experiment is Islam. Is it possible for a country to be economically and politically powerful and thrive in the modern world after an Islamic revolution? Is there an Islamic path into the modern world? Iran seeks a distinctive path of development that combines political participation and markets in ways that accommodate local religious traditions. One finds here a struggle between pro-Western and anti-Western forces. Finally, South Africa's grand experiment is multiracial democracy. Is it possible for ethnoconstitutional democracy in which power is shared along ethnic lines to survive in a country that made a relatively peaceful transition from colonialism and apartheid?

These four grand experiments remind us that political development is open-ended. It is by no means inevitable that countries will become democracies. Because new challenges to development exist in today's small world, undiscovered paths may still emerge. It is true that during the 1990s the end of the Cold War and the demise of communism diminished the pride in being part of the "developing world" and hence encouraged the search for alternative paths to development. Many countries that were formerly considered part of the "developing" world began to redefine their interests, identities, and institutions to compete globally via democracy and markets. This redefinition was not always easy or genuine, and some countries did not stay democratic for long or were democratic on paper only. Still, there is no doubt that, during the 1990s, the global hegemony of democracy and capitalism seemed unchallengeable.

The terrorist attacks of September 11, 2001, and their aftermath brought much of this into doubt. The intention of Osama bin Laden's Al Qaeda network was to launch a global holy war against the world's democracies in the hope of creating Islamic states throughout the Muslim world. Whether this latest challenger to the global hegemony of democracy and markets will be able to translate its ideas into policies that appeal to significant numbers of people and whether it will be able to translate its dogma into a concrete institutional framework in any state of the Middle East remains an open question. What is clear then is that challengers to liberal democracy have not disappeared.

WHY STUDY COMPARATIVE POLITICS?

Even once we have agreed on the main questions that we care about and the main concepts used in our analysis, we still have the question of how exactly we should go about studying politics. It will not surprise you to read that comparativists are deeply committed to *comparing* and believe that a great deal can be learned by comparisons of just about anything. Not only can we compare but we *must* compare in order to get an accurate picture of political life. Just think about why we take pictures of giant redwood trees with people or even automobiles next to them. We do this because it is impossible to understand just how large a redwood is in the absence of something of known size against which we can compare it. So, too, for political life. We compare political orders in order to understand what we are looking at in each one.

All governments grapple with complex global issues: the need to accommodate diverse ethnic and religious identities, the struggle to improve economic security and growth, the quest to provide a strong basis for national citizenship, and the effort to cope with demands for democracy and participation. The world is a laboratory in which countries engage in grand experiments in development. There are a variety of such experiments: many different forms of culture, civil society (informal networks of citizens), economic markets, political democracy, state bureaucracies, and public policies. The comparativist compares and contrasts how two or more countries conduct these experiments. Much of this book involves describing and explaining the similarities and differences among countries.

Why, for example, are political parties different in Britain and Germany? Perhaps they are different because of institutions: The British electoral rules, as in the United States, are a "first-past-the-post system" that normally leads to two dominant parties. The French electoral system, by contrast, is based on a plurality system that encourages the formation of minority parties. On the other hand, perhaps the differences in parties can be attributed to differences in identities. France's tradition is one of radical revolution and Great Britain's one of slow and evolutionary change. To take another example, why did Britain and Germany react differently to the oil shocks and budget crises of the 1970s and then the highly competitive international economy of the 1990s and the beginning of the twenty-first century? Perhaps they reacted differently because of the configuration of interests. Interest groups work more closely with government in Germany than in Britain. On the other hand, perhaps the differences can be attributed to identities. German workers value more highly the protections offered by the state against the ups and downs of the market and were therefore less willing to accept cuts in their benefits (employment security, duration and size of payment from the state in case of unemployment, health and disability insurance) than were their British counterparts. We try, in other words, to construct plausible explanations for the variations we observe. Comparison thus allows us to test our ideas about comparative politics. When done well, this sort of comparison provides us with a powerful set of explanations and theories that can help us understand not only the countries from which we developed them but also new countries that we have yet to consider.

The purpose of this book is therefore not to cram your head with information about politics in faraway places and times long ago. Comparing cases and explanations helps us to do comparative politics because it forces us to think in a rigorous way. It forces us to think theoretically. It also forces us to confront in a particularly acute way the problem of applying theories to reality. Recall our example of the absence of universal public health insurance in the United States. It is quite common to read that it does not exist because of powerful interest groups who oppose it. But did not powerful interest groups oppose its introduction in other countries? It will not surprise you to learn that Canadian doctors and insurance companies were just as opposed to universal public health insurance as their U.S. counterparts. Yet Canada enacted universal publicly funded health insurance as far back as 1963. By helping us to eliminate wrong answers, this small comparison of two cases illustrates how powerful a tool comparison is for helping us zero in on the correct answer to an important question.

You are not likely to become a social scientist, however. As policymakers and advisers, or simply as citizens wishing to participate in politics, we have two reasons for comparing countries. First, comparison encourages us to broaden our knowledge of political alternatives and possibilities. It also allows us to recognize diversity. Such knowledge permits us to make informed judgments about our leaders and political life. Second, the laboratory of political experiences may be transferable. Nations can learn from one another. They can locate ideas for solving their own problems. They can borrow foreign models or adapt their acquired knowledge to perfect their own institutions. In short, comparison allows us to draw positive lessons from successful experiments and negative lessons from failed experiments.

Comparison, in sum, allows social scientists to describe and explain and allows policymakers to understand and choose. There are, however, many obstacles to comparing countries that differ in language, size, culture, and organization. The end result of our comparisons might be to recognize the differences rather than the similarities of experiences and experiments. Comparing the problems of two or more countries might lead us to conclude that each country is importantly unique. The dimensions of this uniqueness, however – the precise way in which each country is unique – can only be discovered through comparison.

Americans, for example, might conclude that they are very different from the rest of the world. As we have seen, American exceptionalism is a major theme of comparative politics. Americans need to recognize, however, how big, important, rich, and powerful the United States is compared with the rest of the world. In order to understand the United States itself – to describe, explain, and evaluate U.S. politics – Americans must consider circumstances different from their own. When they do so, they gain perspective on their own society.

Comparison, therefore, has always been used by scholars, students, and citizens to produce a better-informed and more critical understanding of the political world in which we live.

CHAPTER TWO

The Framework of Analysis

Jeffrey Kopstein and Mark Lichbach

Introduction

The core idea of this book is simple: three important aspects of domestic politics – interests, identities, and institutions – are explored in a set of country studies cast in world-historical and developmental perspective. We teach, in short, the following framework.

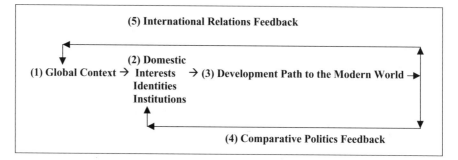

To put it in words: (1) The global context influences (2) domestic interests, identities, and institutions, which produce (3) developmental paths to the modern world, which, in turn, generate (4) comparative-politics feedback effects on domestic interest identities and institutions and (5) international-relations feedback effects on the global context. Our approach allows us to raise important empirical questions about comparing governments and significant normative concerns about evaluating good and bad governments. Let us turn to each of the five parts of our framework.

Global Context

Today's world is small. Our book therefore has a "globalist" slant. The global context for comparative politics involves tensions between nations and states,

contradictions between global homogenization and local diversity, and conflict among states at particular points in history.

NATIONS AND STATES

The first thing to understand about the world is that it is divided into nations
and states and that nations and states are often in tension with one another.
What are these two sets of things that dominate the globe, and why are they
in tension?

When we speak of modern states, we mean first that states have external
independence. Political scientists call this external independence sovereignty.
Governments have armies, navies, and air forces to maintain their external
security. They send and receive ambassadors to other states and belong to the
global club of states, the United Nations. Sovereignty also has a second, internal dimension. The international community of states generally recognizes
and accepts the right and power of the government to make laws and monopolize force within its boundaries. This means that states have internal control
over their populations. They maintain internal order, collect taxes, regulate
economic life, confine people in prisons, and conscript or recruit citizens
into the armed forces. States vary, however, in how much external independence and internal control they in fact exert. Some states, such as the United
States and Great Britain, possess independence that is widely accepted exter-
nally, and they also exercise significant control over their populations. Other
states, such as Afghanistan or Sudan, enjoy much less external independence
and exercise so little control over their populations that political scientists
argue about whether they actually have a state.

States are populated by "peoples." Peoples are often called nations. The
origins of nations and their defining characteristic may be linguistic, religious,
racial, or the perception of a common history or shared fate. Nationhood is
largely a subjective category. If a people considers itself to be a nation, then
we must at least begin to think of it as a nation.

Global society is thus divided into states that are defined organizationally
and nations that are defined culturally. Because a state is a set of governing institutions and a nation a community of people, some – especially nationalists –
argue that the two should coincide in a nation-state. Nationalists maintain
that the only proper form of government is one in which the boundaries of
the state correspond with the boundaries of the nation. They claim that only
in a nation-state, where people identify with the state because the rulers of
the state are also members of the nation, will people accept the government
as the legitimate representative of their community that is entitled to make
laws on their behalf.

Although nationalists believe that national identity should coincide with
state boundaries, when we look at a map of the world we quickly discover
that the relationship between state and nation is highly imperfect. In fact,

they rarely coincide. Very few states are composed of a single national group. Some states, such as Russia and India, are composed of several or even many nations. Some nations, such as the Kurds, are spread out over many states and have never governed themselves. Finally, there are some nations, such as the Jews and the Armenians, that are spread out over many states and that have one central governing state more or less serving as a focal point for their nationalist aspirations.

State and nation often do not coincide because of history. "State-building" (the formation of a state) frequently did not coincide with "nation-building" (the formation of a sense of national unity). It may surprise you to learn, for example, that late into the nineteenth century, many people in large parts of France did not even speak French as their first language. These people had to be "made" into French men and women. It may also surprise you to learn that more than two centuries ago, when the United States gained its independence, there were fewer than 20 governments in the world that we would designate today as states. Most political entities were principalities, city-states, empires, and tribal areas without fixed and legally recognized boundaries. Today, the entire surface of the globe is divided into independent states that make claims to control national territories and their populations.

GLOBALIZATION AND HETEROGENEITIES

The second thing to understand about the world is that it is a whole and that the whole and the parts are also often in conflict with one another. Consider, first of all, the world as a whole. Regional and global forces respond to and shape a set of common and converging global interests, identities, and institutions. Markets, cultures, and institutions operate not only within countries but among them as well.

Interests, identities, and institutions have all become global. Trade, finance, and production are now global activities. Global markets exist not only for land and capital but also, increasingly, for labor. Economic problems are consequently global problems. Growth and prosperity are global problems. Inequality and poverty are global problems. The gap in political and social equality and economic prosperity between those living in the Northern and Southern hemispheres is a global problem. Diseases and epidemics are global problems. Environmental problems are also now global. And, of course, so is terrorism. In sum, it is not possible for a country to isolate itself from global economic trends, cycles, and shocks.

Examples abound of the ways in which Western values dominate and define social and cultural identities throughout the world. For instance, English is the international language used in business, politics, the arts, and the sciences. Innumerable technical standards derived from the West define the global business culture. The notion of universal human rights derives from Western ideas of justice. At a more mundane level, consumer culture itself has become global. People throughout the world increasingly wear the same kinds of clothing, eat many of the same kinds of food, listen to the same music, and watch the same television programs. The global masses who consume Coca-Cola soft drinks and McDonalds hamburgers, wear Nike sneakers and Levis blue jeans, and watch Stephen Spielberg films attempt to move up the material and status hierarchy and enter the world of Armani apparel, Chanel perfume, Dom Perignon champagne, and Perrier mineral water. Much of the upwardly mobile global middle class, in turn, strives to acquire the lifestyle of Lear Jets, Porsche cars, and the transnational managerial elites' Rolex watches. These aspirations, at each level, are the same around the world.

Not only have interests and identities become global but institutions have also. Examples of regional or continent-wide institutions include the European Union and the North American Free Trade Agreement (the comprehensive regional trade agreement signed by the United States, Canada, and Mexico in 1994). Global actors such as the United Nations, the World Bank, the International Monetary Fund, and the World Trade Organization issue extensive supranational regulations and exert an extraordinary amount of influence. International nongovernmental organizations such as the Roman Catholic Church, the International Red Cross, Greenpeace, and Amnesty International affect the lives of ordinary people in large and small ways.

Global markets, Western values, and international institutions exercise an important common, one might even say homogenizing, influence across borders. In some ways, the world has partially converged, and the result is diminished diversity of political and economic institutions. And the more states and societies begin to resemble each other, the more pressure there is on nonconforming states to change their ways to fit in.

LOCAL HETEROGENEITIES

The worldwide movement toward variations on a common theme of democracy and markets, a theme originally developed in the West, has generated its own antithesis. Notwithstanding global trends, there persist important and interesting differences. States attempt to develop distinctive national policies to deal with the global economy and evolve institutional variations of democracies and markets. In some market economies such as those in Great Britain and the United States, the state plays a primarily regulatory role, setting out the rules of the game in which people and companies compete. In Germany and Japan, in contrast, the state has a much stronger hand in guiding the market, frequently involving itself in such areas as finance and wage negotiations. Despite some global convergence, the idea of different paths to the modern world – for example, variations on democracy, authoritarianism, and communism – is still relevant. Since the 1980s, political scientists have debated whether global economic competition will force all advanced industrial economies to adopt similar social policies and levels of taxation.

There is little evidence at the dawn of the twenty-first century that this is actually occurring, and in fact the pressures of economic competition have intensified the search within different countries for ways to adapt that preserve their national identities, unique structures of domestic interests, and distinctive institutional orders. Similarly, although the states of the democratic West exerted a great deal of pressure on the states of the Middle East to democratize, especially after September 11, 2001, this pressure has been strenuously resisted and the search by the people of this region for a distinctive Islamic path to the modern world has intensified.

Comparativists often ask whether the principle of sovereignty will remain globally dominant in the twenty-first century. It is too early to answer this question definitively, but there are several challenges to sovereignty from society itself that are turning up in many countries at the same time:

- Various kinds of subnationalism involving territorially based minorities have attempted to separate nations from states. Whether it be Scots in Great Britain, Quebecois in Canada, the Baltic peoples of the Soviet Union, or the Sikhs in India, ethnic and cultural groups have sought with varying degrees of success to crown their own sense of separateness with a state of their own.
- Religious fundamentalism in Judaism, Christianity, and Islam challenges the individualism, materialism, and secularism of the Western state.
- The rise of gender and sexuality in politics – the struggle for political representation of women, gays, lesbians, and the transgendered – also challenges the nation-state from below by questioning dominant definitions of political membership.
- The authority of the state is also challenged from below by libertarians – who want deregulation of markets, privatization of state services, severe cutbacks in welfare-state expenditures and public-sector taxes – and by environmentalists, who seek to control the effects of economic growth.

Comparativists often study these challenges to the state under the rubric of social movements and revolutions. Student revolts, terrorism, and fascist and Marxist revolutions have come in waves that affect many countries at the same time. Why? Herein lies another paradox of globalization – the increasing interdependence of the world – and heterogeneity: The source of globalization, the West, is also frequently the source of the challenges to it, and thus of heterogeneity. Democracy, fascism, and communism, for example, were all conceived in the West.

In your reading you will find contradictory globalist and localist forces that characterize the current community of nations and states. Although since the 1800s there has been a consolidation of the world into nation-states, there has also been a set of challenges to the state: those from below, which challenge the state through the growing independence of civil society; and those from above, which challenge the state through the growth of regional and supranational forces that put into question these global trends in global ways.

WORLD-HISTORICAL TIME AND CONFLICTS AMONG STATES

Modern sovereign states developed in response to the experiences and challenges of other states. Our historical point of departure in this book is the profound and irreversible changes that occurred in the northwest part of Europe, and especially Great Britain, approximately 250 years ago. This most important critical juncture in modern history is often subsumed under the rubric of the Industrial Revolution, which ran its course roughly from 1780 to 1850. In a very short period, new technologies of mass production, the creation of large urban areas containing a growing proportion of the population, the commercialization of agriculture, the increasing ability to manipulate nature due to rapid advances in scientific knowledge, and new methods of organizing people in administrative bureaucracies combined in Great Britain and a few other countries to generate a new society of unprecedented power that succeeded during the nineteenth century in conquering much of the rest of the planet.

The rest of the world had to respond to the British challenge. Comparativists have spent much time documenting and explaining these responses. To take just one example, once Great Britain became *the* major power in the world, Germany felt pressure to catch up. In responding, however, Germany could not simply repeat the British experience because that would have taken, many Germans believed, far too long. Instead, Germany developed its own set of political and economic institutions that exercised an important impact on its subsequent political and economic history. In fact, as we will see later, Germany still lives with the institutional legacies of its initial response to the British "challenge."

Any global order thus involves competition in world-historical space and time that affects the evolution of states. Here are the questions comparativists ask: What was the competitive international situation in which a state found itself when it attempted to modernize and industrialize? Who are its principal rivals and competitors among sovereign states? In other words, who developed first, had a head start, and could serve as a benchmark? And who developed later, had to play catch-up in order not to be left behind, and hence looked for negative and positive role models?

The developmental logic of countries thus differs partly because the countries began their development during different world-historical eras. Great Britain, for example, embarked on the path to development before any of the other states and thus laid down the political, economic, and military challenge to which other states responded. In Europe, France, Germany, and Russia responded to the British challenge out of fear of being considered backward as a country and fear of political humiliation, but they did so in their own ways, and hence their developmental histories differ from Britain's and from each other's. Outside of Europe, Japan, China, Mexico, India, Iran, and South Africa, the other countries studied in this book, attempted to find their own ways into the modern world of competitive sovereign states. Each used the resources – human, institutional, and economic – available at the time it responded to the challenges that came from the outside world.

To understand the way states are today, it is crucial to look at the strategic and defensive modernization that these states undertook to preserve their national interests, identities, and institutions. Global political competition affects all countries of the world. Late development brought challenges in the form of malevolent Western colonialism and imperialism. It also brought opportunities in the form of benevolent liberal democratic hegemons and positive and negative models of development that permitted the late and experimental developers to learn from the positive experiences and avoid the negative experiences of countries that preceded them historically.

In sum, we stress that domestic politics must be understood in world-historical perspective; that our descriptions and explanations must take into account particular historical situations; and that domestic economies, cultures, and politics are invariably affected by the competitive international environment of states.

Domestic Interests, Identities, and Institutions

What aspects of domestic politics are affected by the global context of development? We advance three concepts that are relatively simple but very powerful. First, people are rational beings who pursue their interests. Second, people are meaning-seeking beings who are defined by their identities. Third, people's interests and identities are shaped by and pursued within institutions. Interests, identities, and institutions are all, in turn, shaped, as shown in our country chapters, by the global context of development. The global context of development, therefore, matters to comparativists because it produces certain patterns of interests, identities, and institutions that persist over time and shape the countries in which we live.

INTERESTS

Politics is partly about the pursuit of interests. One reason that people become involved in politics is to get the things they want from the government and to ensure that the state enacts laws and policies that advance their interests. Of course, what people want varies greatly. Still, there is no denying that a large part of politics in any society revolves around the question of who gets what. I may want a higher economic standard of living and you may want a cleaner environment. How these differences in interests are resolved tells us much about a country's politics.

We therefore assume that individuals have preferences, goals, and objectives. They also face temporally fixed constraints, limitations, and resources. People are problem solvers who try to optimize their gains and minimize their losses. They therefore make choices among available alternatives in order to reach their goals. In politics, what this means is that material interests determine policy preferences. People react to the incentives they face and devise strategies and tactics to pick the alternative that best enables them to satisfy their material self-interest.

Material interests are often pursued not only by individuals but also collectively. People who share an interest attempt to act as if they were a single individual. It is not easy to do this because of what political scientists call the collective-action problem: People who want to act as a unified group often find that individuals are narrowly focused on their own personal situation and refuse to contribute their time or resources to collective causes. Yet, people do band together in pursuit of their common concerns and join political parties, interest groups, and social movements that become important bodies. Professional associations, trade unions, health lobbies, and environmental organizations are but a few of the many kinds of interest groups that people join in order to pursue their interests.

Comparativists frequently focus on a particular category of collective interest that they term "class." For example, when they write of the "working class," they are referring to the large group of people who make their living by selling their labor. Of course, with such a large group it is unlikely that they will speak with a single voice or act as if they all had the same interest. The concept of class therefore can be a very tricky one to use.

Comparativists also note that interest groups are more powerful in some countries than in others. More than a century ago, Alexis de Tocqueville observed the propensity among the inhabitants of the United States to join groups and participate in associational life. Since then, other comparativists have painted a more complex picture. In some countries, such as Germany and Japan, large numbers of people join trade unions. In others, such as the United States and Canada, this number is much smaller. In dictatorial countries such as Russia under Joseph Stalin or China under Mao Zedong, it may be very difficult for interest groups to form because the leaders have the power and will to prevent them from coming into existence. One measure of whether a country is becoming more democratic then is whether the people have the right to form interest groups and through these groups to influence political decisions. The kinds of interest groups and their strength determine much about the politics of a country.

So many interest groups are often at work in a country that its politics become gridlocked. All too often such is the case in the United States. In countries such as India and South Africa, ethnic interest groups frequently alter the legislative agendas of ruling coalitions and presidents. Another focus for comparativists therefore is how conflict and cooperation among interest groups get worked out in different societies. In Great Britain, as in the United States, politics revolves around the intense competition among interest groups that comparativists call "pluralism." In Japan and Germany, on the other hand, social groups often seek to cooperate and avoid conflict, even of the peaceful kind, through institutionalized bargaining arrangements called "corporatism."

Comparativists doing interest-based analyses typically ask: What is the distribution of resources in society? What are the major interest groups in a society? What are their political preferences? What are the obstacles to collective action, and which groups have managed to overcome the obstacles to acting collectively? Are there coalitions between well-endowed or poorly endowed groups that can tilt the balance in the case of conflict? Who are the winners and losers of conflicts?

In sum, the pursuit of material interests through interest-group politics is affected by the global context and, in turn, interest groups battle over alternative paths of development. The pursuit of material interests thereby affects the distribution of economic rewards in society and consequently represents one important way of approaching comparative politics.

IDENTITIES

Politics is also about identity. Although evidence shows that people all over the world often pursue common goals, and thus can be said to share certain interests, people also frequently define what is in their interest differently. Based on particular sets of beliefs and values that we often refer to as culture, they will even define their material interests differently. What people are willing to give their life for, how much hardship they will bear during war, or how many hours on weekends they are willing to work varies across societies. Likewise, the kinds of ideas, political language, and even physical demeanor that people expect from their politicians also vary greatly across nations and states.

Think, for example, how religion and ethnicity influence politics. If people define their identity in religious terms – that is, if they say to themselves, "We are primarily Jewish, Christian, or Muslim, and not German, French, or Iranian" – they will define their interests differently from people who do not tend to define their identity on the basis of religion. In turn, they will support different kinds of governmental policies toward religion, schooling, and popular culture. Ethnicity and national sentiments have a similar kind of influence on how people define themselves. If someone defines herself primarily in ethnic terms, she will tend to care most about how many people of her own ethnic group or nation are in politics. She will tend to define her interests in ethnic terms. It is common, for example, for people of an ethnic group to want a state that will defend its rights to schooling in their language and cultural traditions and to want politics and administration to be controlled by people of their ethnic group.

Just as people with different economic or material interests can clash over their differences, people with different identities also frequently disagree on politics. Although the Soviet Union was a single country, it consisted of many different ethnic groups that never managed to transcend their own particular identities. One contributing factor to the breakup of the Soviet Union was the failure of the Communist Party to create a unifying "Soviet" identity among the many ethnic groups in the country. Often, however, the results of identity politics can be tragic. During the Yugoslav civil wars of the 1990s, people who speak basically the same language began to define their identities so differently (often in terms of religious and "ethnic" differences) that they were willing to kill one another in order to live in areas that were ethnically "pure."

Of course, people may possess not simply one identity but several competing identities, and it is not obvious which one will dominate or how people will ultimately act based on their identities. Someone might be, for example, a woman and black and feel equally strongly about both of these identities. Political leaders often play an important role in mobilizing some identities and neutralizing others. In France, for example, right-wing politicians have tried since the 1990s to convince the French that their traditional notions of who is French – someone born on French soil – should be changed and that the true French are those who have been born into the French culture. The idea here is to exclude as many immigrants from citizenship and public life as possible. On the other hand, at the same time, German politicians have been working to alter the notion of who is a German, an idea that to this day remains based on blood ties to other Germans, in order to make German identity more inclusive. Similarly, successive Indian governments have worked very hard at catering to the various subnational identities within the country while simultaneously carving out a distinctive "Indian" national identity that will be more important to people than all of their other identities.

Religion and ethnicity are only two of the more important kinds of identities. One can easily point to a politics of gender, environmental, and regional identities. Each of these identities informs what people want out of politics, what they are willing to do, and how they define their interests.

The subject can be made even broader, however. Comparativists frequently study attitudes in society toward such issues as the role of government, the kinds of institutions that people want, and the degree of their commitment to democracy. Such studies may take the form of quantitative public-opinion surveys about attitudes and opinions or may be microlevel ethnographic studies of civic associations, such as Greenpeace, the National Rifle Association, or the Parent-Teacher Association.

Material interests frequently trump social identities. In 1992, for example, Bill Clinton won the U.S. presidential election with the slogan "It's the economy, stupid." But it is easy to be cynical and think that people care only about money. In fact, many types of social identities can trump material interests, allowing identity politics to prevail. For example, in Iran, Ayatollah Khomeini thought that "economics is for donkeys." The world has seen a revival of traditional communities, religious fundamentalism, ethnic and racial identities, and gender identifications that have not been washed away by (and have actually been strengthened as a reaction against) Western materialism.

In fact, social identities can even influence what people think their material interests are. The great German social scientist Max Weber showed how the early Protestants' concern about the fate of their immortal souls caused them to work as efficiently as they could and consume as little as possible in the hope that their worldly success would be a sign that they were members of the "elect" and not the "damned." This work ethic, the Protestant ethic, as Weber termed it, created a huge increase in productivity and savings and laid the foundation for modern capitalism. The impact of identities on material life, however, extends well beyond the West. Because identity can discipline a labor force for economic development, authoritarian states often try to impose ideas on societies in order to promote economic growth. Stalin in the Soviet Union and Mao in China were ideologically committed to socialism. They sought to create a dedicated population of true believers who would suspend their own material desires in the present in order to build utopian, egalitarian societies in the future. In Iran at the beginning of the twentieth century, secular nationalism replaced Islam in part to encourage economic development. Now that secular nationalism has been replaced by Islam, many hope that it, too, will encourage economic development.

Comparativists doing identity-based analyses of politics will ask: What are the dominant ideas of a society? What do people value most? How do these values shape political behavior? What ideals do people expect their leaders to share? Why do some identity groups conflict and others live in relative harmony? How do leaders use identities to mobilize their populations for projects they deem important?

INSTITUTIONS

We now turn from interests and identities to institutions. Institutions provide an important arena in which politics takes place. When comparativists speak of institutions, they usually mean the authoritative rules and organizations that structure political life. We first explore how the global context influences domestic institutions and how these institutions, in turn, affect developmental paths by influencing identities and interests. We then explain why many comparativists consider the study of politics to be synonymous with the study of institutions.

INSTITUTIONS AS CONSEQUENCES (OF THE GLOBAL CONTEXT) AND AS CAUSES (OF INTERESTS AND IDENTITIES)

Comparativists often start their analysis by examining the state. The state is an organization that maintains control over a particular territorial jurisdiction. It is important to note, however, that this control may be stronger or weaker depending upon a great number of circumstances. An important factor affecting how societal interests and identities influence politics and public policy is whether the state is strong or weak. But what do we mean by a "strong" or "weak" state? Comparativists usually think of state strength as being determined by two factors: autonomy and capacity.

Consider autonomy. The state may be autonomous from the interests and identities of civil society. This means that it cannot be easily influenced by specific groups in society – business associations, working-class unions, or religious identity groups, for example – that try to penetrate and capture the state to use it to pursue their narrow concerns rather than to pursue the broader public good. The state's political and administrative leaders in a strong state are capable of formulating and defining their own preferences for what they would like to see the state do. Hence, the state could be autonomous in the sense of making its own decisions.

Now consider capacity. The state might also have great power and capacity in relation to the interests and identities of society. That is, a strong state will have the resources and the ability to use those resources effectively to implement its decisions and strategies in order to address the problems, challenges, and crises of development, in spite of what class interests and religious identities might prefer.

Many late developers believe that a strong – autonomous and capable – state is good for economic development. A strong state can pursue the general good of all society. It does not have to follow the narrow interests or identities of a single subnational group that has selfish reasons for not contributing to the public welfare.

Of course, strong states need not always be democratic ones. In fact, there is a certain amount of tension between strong states and democracy. A strong state does not have to accept the notion that the public good is the sum of the interests and identities that emerge from voting and lobbying. Rather, a strong state can pursue the "true" public good of the entire nation. In other words, some argue that a strong state can rectify the selfishness found in society. The Japanese state, for example, embodied in the persons of its bureaucrats and civil servants, has often operated autonomously of business and labor interests and has had the capacity to implement its choices over the opposition of both groups.

Such common variations of democratic institutions as divided government, checks and balances, federalism, and weak political parties were therefore avoided by states that followed the early developers because they were thought to decrease state power and promote political fragmentation, insta-bility, and gridlock. Many late developers have come to believe, however, on the basis of recent experience, that a strong state *hinders* economic develop-ment because it burdens society with high taxes and other policies that are designed to feather the beds of the bureaucrats that constitute the strong state rather than foster economic growth for the population as a whole.

Ironically, former totalitarian states such as the Soviet Union proved weaker than the supposedly weak democracies, such as the United States. Democ-racies, especially those with a powerful president or prime minister, can be strong because the state power they wield is considered legitimate by most people. Under these circumstances, democratic states may even reinforce na-tional unity and provide the key to resolving political conflicts over interests and identities.

INTERESTS AND IDENTITIES, AND THE STRUGGLE OVER INSTITUTIONS

We have maintained that the competitive geopolitical context generates the demand for economic development that, in turn, generates individuals and groups with material interests and social identities. Interest groups and iden-tity groups with different preferences about development then come into conflict with each other.

We have also argued that political institutions empower some groups and constrain others, thereby transforming interests and identities into public policies. Bureaucratic and democratic institutions thus influence the forma-tion of interests and identities, restrict and promote their expression, and finally mold them into policies associated with paths of development.

Interest groups and identity groups realize that institutions influence the outcome of their policy struggles over a path of development and therefore seek to retain or change institutions in order to gain the political power needed to satisfy their own interests and identities. An important part of politics thus involves generally unequal groups fighting over the making and remaking of political institutions. As we will see in the chapter on Russia, for example, the struggle over the rules of the game after the collapse of communism was especially intense. But this is, in fact, an age-old part of politics. In Britain during the eighteenth and nineteenth centuries, middle-class inter-ests fought against monarchs and aristocrats. They sought a parliament to limit the king and enhance their own status and power. In Germany dur-ing the nineteenth and early twentieth centuries, urban industrial and rural landowning elites fought against lower-class workers' and peasants' interests. They sought a strong state that would preserve their influence. In both cases, democratic and bureaucratic institutions were the outcomes of interest- and identity-driven political struggles. Hard bargains were struck. In some cases, elections were introduced, but the right to vote was extended to the lower classes only gradually. In other cases, landowning and urban elites enjoyed disproportional representation in Parliament. Although some believed that the bargains made everyone in the country better off by permitting economic development, others believed that the bargains bestowed much greater advantages on some than others.

Because institutions are so central to politics, they stand at a pivotal point in our framework. Although the global context influences domestic interests, identities, and institutions, the institutions, which are often contested, shape and filter interests and identities into developmental paths.

Developmental Paths to the Modern World

Global competition forces countries to adopt a developmental path. States and societies choose domestic and foreign policies in politics and economics to compete in the global order. What do such policies, paths, and regime types entail?

With respect to domestic policy, states do many things. Governments pursue extractive policies. They take goods and services from their citizens in the form of money (taxes) and time (military service). Governments also pursue distributive policies in which they return goods and services to their citizens, for example, roads and social security payments. Governments organize and pay for systems of public education. Governments also pursue regulatory policies in which they set the rules for property rights, human rights, and occupational safety. Finally, governments sometimes attempt to shape the equality of opportunity and/or the equality of results.

Governments also pursue foreign policies. Some states expend a great deal of energy on preserving the global status quo. Others are "revolutionary" and attempt to change the global order. Some states pursue war as a tool of statecraft. Others remain relatively peaceful, except under the most extreme circumstances.

The domestic and foreign policy choices often combine into what is called a *development strategy* or *grand strategy*, as shown in Table 2.1. Different

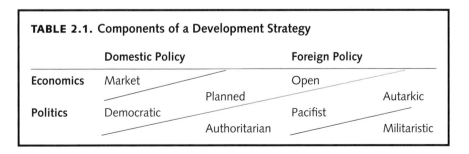

TABLE 2.1. Components of a Development Strategy

	Domestic Policy		Foreign Policy	
Economics	Market		Open	
		Planned		Autarkic
Politics	Democratic		Pacifist	
		Authoritarian		Militaristic

world-historical circumstances favor certain grand strategies over others. Take, for example, economic policy. During the Cold War, Japan developed its export-oriented consumer goods industries and India chose to develop its nascent industries by protecting them from foreign competition. The global trading system may influence whether nations adopt import-substitution industrialization, as in India's case during the Cold War, or export-led industrialization, as in Japan's attempt to compete in the world automobile market. World markets might influence whether states are free-traders or protectionist, whether they institute a laissez-faire market economy or a statist one, and whether they pursue peaceful or aggressive foreign policies.

A major theme of this book is therefore democratic capitalism and its alternatives. *There is no single developmental path to the modern world.* States can and do make their own developmental choices and often evolve local institutional variations of globally or regionally dominant political economies. Theories suggesting that all states move through common stages and converge in the end, such as some versions of modernization theory, are wrong. Looked at historically, there have been multiple paths to the modern world. There has been no inevitable triumph of democracy, markets, and peace. Domestic interests, identities, and institutions have combined in the past and continue to combine today with the global context to support undemocratic, anticapitalist, closed, and militaristic paths. And a key source of local variation in institutions today is the existence of alternatives to and variations on democracy, markets, and peace.

We therefore need to develop a comparative and historical understanding of the alternative paths to the modern world adopted in different international environments. We offer four sets of country studies that have been chosen to exemplify the different developmental logics of countries that began their journey into the modern world during different world-historical eras.

- Early Developers: Britain and France
- Middle Developers: Germany and Japan
- Late Developers: Russia and China
- Experimental Developers: Mexico, India, Iran, and South Africa

These cases should remind us that development is open-ended. Because new challenges to development exist in today's small world, undiscovered paths may still emerge.

You should note three things about our choice of cases. First, our global and developmental perspective allows us to choose states on theoretical and substantive grounds and thus to set contemporary issues of policy and performance in a larger setting. Second, we have chosen cases that are today's engines of development for the Western, Middle Eastern, Asian, African, and Latin American regions of the world. Third, all of our cases have had revolutions of one type or another rooted in world-historical problems of development, which, in turn, influence country-specific patterns of development.

You should also note two features of developmental paths. First, paths are competing political alternatives. People always debate the choice of a developmental path, and these debates inevitably involve a power struggle among competing interests and identities. In early twentieth-century China, for example, the urban intelligentsia advocated a liberal path based on urban middle-class interests, Western liberal values, and democratic institutions. The nationalists pushed an authoritarian path rooted in conservative, rural elite interests, a strong nationalist ideology, and statist institutions. The communists advocated a communist path based on peasant interests, Marxist ideology, and totalitarian institutions controlling civil society. Similar debates among liberals, conservatives, and socialists can be located in every Western country during the 1930s. Fascist, communist, and liberal movements that vied for political power also can be found in Russia during the late nineteenth and early twenty-first centuries.

Second, the debate among proponents of various paths leads to governing or developmental coalitions, combining state and societal actors, that form behind grand strategies of development, and these coalitions attempt to implement their development strategies using institutions designed for that purpose. Under fascism, rural and urban elites used the state to repress workers, peasants, and groups defined as ethnically "alien." Under post–World War II "corporatist" systems in Europe, business, labor, and government worked together. During the 1990s, and in many parts of the world at the beginning of the twenty-first century, market-oriented (or what are sometimes called neo-liberal) development coalitions became dominant in many countries. Such policy coalitions, however, face formidable problems. They are vulnerable to shifts in global context and can be quite unstable. Some members leave voluntarily and others are purged. Many, for example, have traced the failure of democracy in Weimar Germany to cabinet instability, and others have traced cabinet instability to the failure of the democrats to put together a viable developmental coalition. Hitler and the Nazi Party then seized power and proposed a new grand strategy of conquest and genocide for Germany and Europe. This example teaches us that although state–society coalitions are difficult to construct, their success defines development – for better or worse.

In sum, comparativists believe that the world-historical time in which countries modernized or industrialized has influenced their development strategy. This book therefore chooses its cases based on the international situation within which states found themselves when they first attempted to develop.

Comparative-Politics Feedback

A particular developmental policy backed by a specific regime coalition may or may not be successful. Based on the rule of thumb, "If it ain't broke, don't fix it," one would expect that when development is working well for everyone in the country, regimes would want to consolidate their developmental path.

Often, a developmental path performs poorly everywhere and for nearly everyone except a very small group of beneficiaries. A path such as the creation of a predatory, nondevelopmental state could produce little economic growth, wasteful and inefficient allocation of resources, crime and violence, corruption, worker absenteeism, and alcoholism. Moreover, developmental strategies can produce misdevelopment, uneven development, or exploitative development. For example, the British approach to colonial development in India involved a divide-and-rule strategy that produced distorted development: interests, identities, and institutions were constructed to favor Britain and not India. And, more generally, developmental experiments can fail and result in either stagnant or collapsed states. Although some regimes are by definition interim, transitional, and provisional, there are dead-end developmental paths that did not look so dead-end at the time they were adopted. The dustbin of history is littered with colonial administrations, world empires, principalities, city-states, tribal areas without fixed territorial boundaries, bureaucratic authoritarianism, feudalism, slave states, apartheid systems, and fascist and communist regimes.

Poor economic performance in failed and misshapen development experiments lead to uncertainty, poverty, and social tensions: civil disorder and political anarchy, leadership succession crises, illegitimacy, and alienation. Developmental models are thus constantly being rethought. For example, until 1990, countries throughout the world sought to emulate the Japanese economic "miracle"; when Japan sank into a prolonged recession, it was no longer considered a "model." The result of such new thinking can be evolutionary or revolutionary change of domestic interests, identities, and institutions in order to pursue new developmental paths.

Failed developmental paths also can be altered by revolutionary changes of interests, identities, and institutions from above. National elites can coalesce into a new regime whose purpose is to resist the global order. For example, German and Japanese "revolutions from above" during the nineteenth century and first half of the twentieth century remade social classes, solidified national identities, and created militant and strong states that sought to reshape the global order rather than adapt to it.

Of equal importance, failed developmental paths are sometimes changed by revolution from below, often after failed attempts at revolution from above. For example, economic and political liberalization under Soviet President

Mikhail Gorbachev created new interests, identities, and institutions that brought about the collapse of the Soviet Union. It appears that certain developmental paths and the coalitions behind them run their course wherever and whenever they are tried and therefore contain the seeds of their own revolutionary demise. Not long ago, for example, many academics and policymakers believed that late-developing countries needed strong states to mobilize resources for industrialization, assure territorial integrity, collect taxes, and staff bureaucracies. As resistance movements began to think otherwise and toppled many such states, global thought shifted. It is now widely argued that strong populist authoritarian regimes, military/bureaucratic absolutisms, patrimonial states that concentrate power in rulers and their families, and corporatist and state-led industrialization generate problems, such as bloated public sectors, mismanagement, corruption, waste, and inefficiency, that result in such economic imbalances as inflation, currency overvaluation, and balance-of-payments crises. Neo-liberal regimes based on expanded free markets that have been created in turn have also generated severe problems.

At the same time, however, some comparativists now believe that "shock-therapy" policies of rapid marketization, advocated for many states by the World Bank and International Monetary Fund, can also produce instability and the possibility of revolution. If strong states provide too much control, weak states provide no framework at all for capitalist development. Different developmental regimes, in short, contain different flaws that eventually lead to the appearance of resistance movements in a set of similarly situated countries.

International-Relations Feedback

National development also influences the global context within which a regime finds itself. Consider some examples. British power helped define the eighteenth- and nineteenth-century worlds. In the aftermath of World War II, the United States imposed its own vision on the global economic order. The decision by the U.S. Federal Reserve Bank to raise interest rates from 1979 to 1982 contributed to the world debt crisis by increasing the amount that debtor states in poorer regions of the world had to pay for borrowed money. German authoritarianism and fascism plunged the world into global war. Japanese authoritarianism had the same result. The Soviet Union's and China's internal patterns of development led them to try to export communist regimes to the rest of the world. During the Cold War, Mexico and India legitimized and encouraged a third way of development for a large number of states. Iran's decision, along with the rest of the major oil-producing states, to raise oil prices in the 1970s shook the developed world. Its Islamic Revolution shook regimes throughout the Arab and Muslim worlds. And, finally, South

Africa's bold experiment in multiracial democracy has important implications for other deeply divided states.

In sum, developmental paths may contribute to global peace and prosperity. They also contribute to global war and poverty. A nation's development can thus have an impact far beyond a single nation's borders.

The two feedback loops of our framework – comparative-politics feedback and international-relations feedback – yield a path-dependent view of history. Once a state starts down a developmental path, where it goes next is affected by where it has been. Choices made at critical junctures in a state's history not only set a state down a certain path but also preclude alternative paths. A state's contemporary problems thus originate in the historical crises and challenges it has faced. The developmental choices a country makes today are partly a result of the choices that were put in place when it began to develop in a particular world-historical context.

For example, interests, identities, and institutions can persist even through revolutions. First, economic markets and the interests they define show continuity. Today's close connection between interest groups and government in Germany, for example, can be traced to the developmental choices of Germany's nineteenth-century rulers. Second, cultural identities and the values and beliefs that people cherish are resilient. Religion and ethnicity often reemerge after a revolution and affect developmental priorities and choices. Fundamentalist Islam in today's Iran, for example, survived the Shah's regime and was shaped by his industrialization policies. Finally, institutions that define and resolve conflicts among different interests and identities in a country can also survive revolution. Contemporary Russia's interests, identities, and institutions are part of the historical legacy of communism.

The two feedback loops also offer a "punctuated-equilibrium" view of how the present is shaped by the past. What comparativists mean by this is that countries have developmental regimes, supported by developmental coalitions, that are separated by identifiable political crises or critical junctures that produce breakpoints and turning points in a country's history. In other words, a country's global context, its domestic interests, identities, and institutions, and, most significantly, its developmental path to the modern world can change and lead to a new developmental regime. Germany, for example, made the transition from empire, to the democratic Weimar Republic, to two states divided by capitalism and communism, and finally to a new united and democratic Germany. Regime changes are often closely identified with leadership changes. Thus, the change of leadership from Gorbachev to that of Boris Yeltsin in Moscow involved a redefinition of Russian state institutions and national identity. Our country chapters are chronologically organized to take account of the historical changes in regimes associated with changing global contexts; domestic interests, identities, and institutions; and developmental paths.

Our Approach to Comparison

Comparison is essential to comparative politics, and we have made it central to this book. Our approach to comparison involves, first, a common set of tools with which we fashion country studies that reveal distinctive paths of development, and second, explicit comparisons among two or more cases designed to establish the causes and consequences of the significant differences among countries.

First, we have provided a set of tools to study substantive problems rather than a blueprint to develop a theory of comparative politics. Because politics in Britain is interestingly different from politics in France, which is interestingly different from politics in Germany, we have not forced the chapters into a common, encyclopedia-like framework. That is, for each country we have not devoted three pages to interests, four to identity, and five to institutions. Rather, we have allowed our authors to use our common tools to bring out what is unique and significant about each country. This approach gives students a better sense of British politics, French politics, and South African politics than would be possible if every country's politics were forced through a homogenizing boilerplate framework that drains the countries of their uniqueness. Our framework permits authors to tell the story of their own country in their own way and hence makes for more interesting reading.

Second, after each part of the book – divided into early developers, middle developers, late developers, and experimental developers – we include a section called "stop and compare." These sections should really be called "stop and think" because we ask students to use the comparative method to draw empirical and moral lessons from the country studies by establishing the similarities and differences within and between each of our four sets of cases.

Here are the sorts of questions we ask: How are Britain and France variations of early development, and how are they different from the United States? How are Germany and Japan variations of middle development, which are different from the early developers? How do our two late developers, Russia and China, differ from one another, and how are they different from the early and middle developers? Finally, what are the similarities and differences among contemporary experimental developers – Mexico, India, Iran, and South Africa – and what sorts of contrasts do they make with the early, middle, and late developers we have studied?

By alternating country studies with explicit sections on comparison, we demonstrate how comparativists think. Comparativists mix the specific and the general. They begin with cases, turn to theory, and then return to the cases in a never-ending sequence of induction and deduction.

Conclusion

This book guides the beginning political science student through the master concepts, dominant theories, and substantive problems of comparative politics. The country chapters that you are about to read take you on a journey through space and time. Why would you, a college student, be interested in joining this tour through the countries of today's small world?

Our global framework implies that what happens in other countries is important to you, no matter where you live. Take the United States, for example. Although the United States is large, important, and rich, and spans a continent separated from the rest of the world by oceans, Americans are dependent on the economics and the politics of countries around the world. Our political and economic security, our material welfare, and the well-being of our environment are wrapped up with political change and development in the rest of the world. The transportation and communication revolutions that have contracted time and space have created global interdependence. The process is accelerating: It is only since the 1960s that we have had pictures of the globe as a "whole" world, and it is only since the 1990s that the Internet has provided instant multimedia communication to people around the world. In short, a state – even a powerful one such as the United States – that seeks to be isolated, autonomous, and sheltered from global forces is doomed to fail. A state that accepts the inevitability of contacts between different societies, and hence attempts to integrate itself into today's small and interdependent world, can potentially succeed. Americans thus need to know and understand what is going on elsewhere. Citizens in the United States and in other countries must be aware of the world in which they live. They need to be cognizant of the potential dangers and challenges, as well as the possible opportunities, that will confront them in the decades ahead. The same would apply to any student reading this book in any country of the world.

Our approach allows you to be exposed to the theoretically and substantively important currents in contemporary comparative politics. Moreover, we do not expect you to be interested in names and dates for their own sake but because understanding the contemporary world is made easier by knowing some of the more important ones.

At critical points along our journey, we will stop and make comparisons in order to explain and evaluate what we see. Let us repeat our framework: (1) The global context influences (2) domestic interests, identities, and institutions that produce (3) developmental paths to the modern world, that in turn, generate (4) comparative-politics feedback effects on domestic interests, identities, and institutions and (5) international-relations feedback effects on the global context. Let us begin.

PART ONE

EARLY DEVELOPERS

CASES

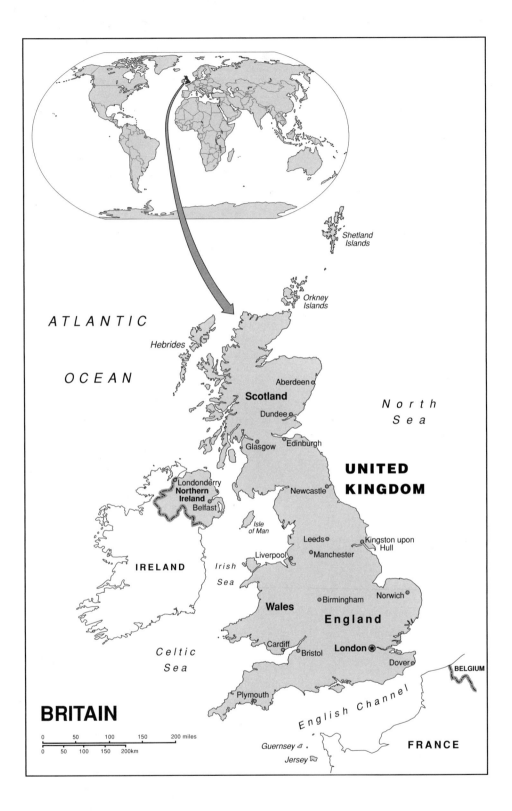

ATLANTIC

OCEAN

Shetland Islands

Hebrides

Orkney Islands

Aberdeen

Scotland

North Sea

Dundee

Glasgow ○ Edinburgh

Londonderry
Northern Ireland
Belfast

UNITED KINGDOM

Newcastle

Isle of Man

IRELAND

Irish Sea

Leeds

Kingston upon Hull

Liverpool ○ Manchester

○ Birmingham   Norwich ○

Wales

England

Celtic Sea

Cardiff

Bristol

London ✪

Dover

BELGIUM

Plymouth

English Channel

BRITAIN

| 0 | 50 | 100 | 150 | 200 miles |
| 0 | 50 | 100 | 150 | 200km |

Guernsey ◁   **FRANCE**

Jersey

CHAPTER THREE

Britain

Peter Rutland

Introduction

Britain is the usual starting point for comparative politics textbooks because its political system has some similarities with the U.S. system, but it also has some important differences. Furthermore, most people believe that Britain has a successful political system and therefore is worthy of study and emulation. Britain is seen as having strong and stable political institutions that have endured for centuries. Britain has a firmly established national identity, and, in British society, economic and social interests are clearly defined and vigorously defended.

All of these things are true, but only half true. There are serious contradictions within the British model that undermine the image of stability and that have provoked a sense of profound political malaise and even crisis. Up until World War II, Britain ruled an empire that extended over one-quarter of the globe. This means that, for older generations, British national identity is still overshadowed by the legacy of empire. This has made it psychologically difficult for Britain to become an active and committed member of the European Union (EU). The division between Europhiles, those who support Britain's membership in the EU, and Euroskeptics, those who oppose it, is the most important rift in British politics today. Meanwhile, back at home, Britain is grappling with constitutional reforms to satisfy the demands of nationalists in Scotland, Wales, and Northern Ireland for greater autonomy and even independence. Hence, British identity is still very much a work in progress.

Moving from identity to interests, one finds that Britain's entrenched social hierarchy led to a century of class warfare between labor and capital. This struggle polarized the political system, paralyzed public policy making, and hampered Britain's ability to adapt to a changing global economy. Only since Prime Minister Tony Blair's Labour Party gave up its struggle to transform market capitalism in the mid 1990s has the country managed to shake off this legacy of social confrontation. In contrast with most of continental Europe, Britain has embraced U.S. style capitalism, with a lower level of social protection from the state. But prosperity remains elusive for a large and growing underclass.

Britain does indeed enjoy highly stable political institutions that have been in place for centuries. Britain's basic political structures have remained largely unchanged since the turn of the twentieth century, and this stability has inhibited much-needed structural reform. Britain is headed into the twenty-first century with nineteenth-century political institutions. Constitutional reforms introduced in the 1990s include the reform of the House of Lords (the upper house of Parliament), and the introduction of parliaments for Scotland and Wales for the first time in 300 years. Britain has come under increasing pressure to integrate British institutions with those of the European Union, which it joined in 1973.

THE BRITISH MODEL

Over the course of the twentieth century, Britain's prominence as a world power steadily eroded. Britain pioneered the system of liberal democracy that has now spread in some form or other to most of the world's countries. Its political institutions – especially its legal tradition – had a very strong influence on the political system that was created in the United States.

The United States sees itself as the most pristine model of democracy because it introduced the first written constitution in 1787 and has lived under that same constitution for more than 200 years. Britain lacks a formal written constitution, so it is hard to put a date on the introduction of liberal democracy to that country. The story usually begins with the **Magna Carta** of 1215, when powerful regional lords forced King John to sign a charter respecting their feudal rights in return for the taxes and troops they provided the king. Parliament emerged as the institution through which the lords, and later common citizens, could negotiate their rights with the king. Under the leadership of Oliver Cromwell, the Parliament fought a civil war with the king in defense of these rights from 1642 to 1648, culminating in the execution of King Charles I. In the subsequent **Glorious Revolution** of 1688, the Protestant William of Orange deposed the Catholic king James II, and took office as a constitutional monarch who accepted that ultimate sovereignty rested with the Parliament. Since then, there have been no violent political upheavals in Britain.

One of the main virtues of the British model is its capacity to adapt gradually over time. The British model is not based on a set of ideas captured in a single document but in an evolving set of social conventions. Many of these practices, such as the system of common law (a legal system based on judicial decision rather than legislation), jury trials, freedom of speech, a bill of rights, and the notion of popular sovereignty – were already established by the seventeenth century and formed the bedrock upon which the U.S. Constitution itself was based. But many of the features of the contemporary British model, such as **parliamentary sovereignty**, a system in which most political decisions are made by Parliament, constitutional monarchy, and an ideologically polarized party system, stand in contrast with the American model.

The British political system is a product of that country's unique history. There is an old story about the Oxford college gardener who, when asked how he kept the lawn so immaculate, replied: "That's easy, you just roll it every day...for 300 years." This continuity argument raises the question of whether Britain's democratic experience can be "exported" elsewhere, or whether other countries are merely supposed to marvel at the unique virtues of the "**Westminster model**" of parliamentary sovereignty.

The U.S. model of democracy comes more ready for export. Its essence is captured in a short document, based on a fairly simple set of principles: that all men are equal in the eyes of the law, the rule of law, and the separation of powers, an institutional system of checks and balances. This has enabled the United States to play the leading role in the spread of democracy around the world since the end of World War II. It was U.S. advisers who oversaw the writing of new constitutions in postwar Germany and Japan.

But the British model is no less important than the U.S. model in understanding the global spread of democracy. As the British Empire shrank after 1945, it left a series of democratic political systems modeled along British lines in its former colonies. The white-settler colonies of Australia, New Zealand, and Canada were granted their independence from 1867–1907. Then came decolonization in India (1947), Africa (the 1950s), and the Caribbean islands (the 1960s). Cross-national analysis shows that countries that were formerly British colonies such as India are more likely to be stable democracies than are other countries. In part, this is because they are parliamentary democracies, which are generally more stable than presidential systems. No such correlation can be found for ex-colonies of other European powers. India, the jewel in the imperial crown, has remained a democracy (the world's largest) for half a century despite a very low level of economic development, which is usually seen as an obstacle to democracy. The British ex-colonies in Africa do not fit this pattern, however. With the exception of Botswana, they have all slipped into periods of military or one-party rule since independence.

The Long Road from Empire to Europe

AN ISLAND NATION

If you ask someone from England the most important date in English history, they will almost certainly say 1066. That was when the invading Norman army of William the Conqueror defeated the Anglo-Saxon forces of King Harold at the Battle of Hastings. The French-speaking Norman aristocracy took over England and started the long and bloody process of welding it into a unified state. Britain has not been invaded since 1066. The Spanish Armada was repulsed in 1588, as were Hitler's forces in 1940. The Britons are proud of having preserved their sovereignty against foreign invasion for more than 900 years. This feeds British patriotism and a feeling that Britain is fundamentally distinct from the rest of Europe.

The fact that Britain is an island meant that it relied on the Royal Navy for its security. Unlike the states of continental Europe, it did not require a large standing army to protect itself from its neighbors. Author George Orwell once suggested that this reliance on the navy is the reason that Britain became a democracy. Unlike the absolutist monarchs of Europe, Britain's rulers did not have a large army that they could also use to put down social unrest. Instead, they had to meet popular discontent with compromise. (The United States, like Britain, never had a standing army and relied on its navy for defense.) Whereas all of the powers in continental Europe introduced compulsory military service during the nineteenth century, Britain continued to rely on a small, professional, volunteer army (most of which was stationed overseas). Only in the middle of World War I was the military draft introduced, and it was dropped immediately thereafter. It was reintroduced in 1940 and finally abolished in 1960. Most other European countries still have compulsory military service.

THE END OF EMPIRE

By the nineteenth century, Britain's global naval power and advanced manufacturing industry made it the dominant imperial power. Conquest and trade were constitutive of British national identity. Its pantheon of heroes included pirates who robbed Spanish galleons laden with silver (Francis Drake) and the clerk who rose to be the conqueror of India (Robert Clive). British colonies covered one-quarter of the planet in an empire on which "the sun never set."

After World War I, Britain lost its economic leadership to the United States. Its empire was challenged by growing independence movements in its colonies. Britain lacked the manpower, and ultimately the political will, to fight these colonial wars. After World War II, Britain granted independence to India and Palestine, then Malaya, and then its possessions in East and West Africa. As U.S. Secretary of State Dean Acheson observed in 1963, Britain "had lost an empire but not yet found a role." Most former British colonies joined the **British Commonwealth**, a loose association of 53 countries (founded in 1931) that now has a largely ceremonial role, organizing cultural exchanges. Seventeen Commonwealth countries still have the British House of Lords as their final court of appeal. Britain initially clung to a network of smaller colonial possessions around the globe, but these, too, were slowly jettisoned. In 1968, to save money, Britain decided to close all of its military bases east of the Suez canal, with the exception of Hong Kong.

Just as memories of empire were fading, in 1982, Argentina's military rulers decided to seize the Falkland Islands, a worthless British territory a few hundred miles off the Argentine coast. Prime Minister Margaret Thatcher sent a naval task force to liberate the islands, which was accomplished at the cost of 5,000 Argentine and 125 British lives. The **Falklands War** boosted Thatcher's waning popularity ratings and helped her win a second term as prime minister in 1983.

The British Empire achieved symbolic closure in July 1997 when Britain returned Hong Kong to the People's Republic of China on the expiration of its ninety-nine-year lease on the territory. China promised to preserve a special status for Hong Kong for fifty years and respect its economic and political rights. These rights did not include democratic government: Only in the last few years of its lease had Britain made half-hearted efforts to introduce democratic elections to Hong Kong.

Most Britons look back at the empire with unembarrassed nostalgia, clinging to the myth that British rule brought civilization (from railways to the rule of law) to the more primitive corners of the globe. The uglier side of imperial rule was edited out of collective memory. There was no guilt over Britain's role in the transatlantic slave trade, or the 1842 war with China, the purpose of which was to force China's rulers to allow the import of opium. Visions of empire are sustained in the British imagination by a steady flow of movies and TV dramas.

Although Britain slipped from its dominant role in the international order, it held onto a place at the table of leading powers. As one of the "big three" allied nations that won World War II, it was given one of the five permanent seats on the United Nations Security Council in 1945. It acquired nuclear weapons in the 1950s. The Labour Party advocated unilateral nuclear disarmament in the 1980s, a policy that won little public support.

Britain owes its prominent role in world affairs since 1945 to its "special relationship" with the United States. This began with Franklin Roosevelt and Winston Churchill during World War II and was carried over into the Cold War. As part of the U.S.-led NATO (North Atlantic Treaty Organization) alliance, Britain kept 50,000 troops in West Germany until the end of the Cold War. Britain sent troops to support U.S.-led military actions in Korea in 1950 and Iraq in 1990 and 2003. There have been some rocky periods in the relationship, however. The United States blocked the Anglo-French seizure of the Suez Canal in 1956, and Britain refused the U.S. request to send troops to Vietnam in 1965.

The close partnership between Britain and the United States continued under Prime Minister Margaret Thatcher and U.S. President Ronald Reagan in the 1980s (united against the Soviet "evil empire"). After the Cold War, British Prime Minister Tony Blair and U.S. President Bill Clinton forged close ties, both seeking an elusive, centrist "**Third Way**" in their domestic reforms while cooperating in humanitarian intervention in the former Yugoslavia. The socialist Tony Blair gave strong support to the conservative U.S. President George W. Bush in the war on terror that was launched after terrorists attacked the United States on September 11, 2001.

Britain often put the special relationship with Washington ahead of closer integration with Europe. For example, Britain's decision to use U.S. Polaris submarine missiles to provide its nuclear deterrent in 1962 encouraged France to veto the United Kingdom's (UK) application to join the European Economic Community, the forerunner of the European Union (EU). (France had been hoping to jointly develop a European submarine missile system.) In 2003, France and Germany, Britain's European partners, refused to support the U.S.-led war in Iraq, but Tony Blair persuaded Parliament to send 45,000 British troops to take part in the invasion.

THE RELUCTANT EUROPEAN

Britain was the dominant European power in 1945, but as the victor in the Second World War it did not feel obliged to become involved in building a new political structure on the shattered continent. In 1952, it refused to join the European Coal and Steel Community, an early forerunner of the European Union, fearing that plans for a common industrial policy would infringe upon its national sovereignty. The European Economic Community (EEC, a broader European economic regional alliance launched in 1957) emerged as Britain's major trading partner, and its economic growth outpaced that of Britain. Twice during the 1960s, Britain tried to join the EEC but was rejected, mainly because Paris feared that British entry would weaken France's influence.

It was not until 1973 that Britain entered the renamed European Community. Much of the next decade was spent haggling over the terms of Britain's membership. In 1984, the Euroskeptic Margaret Thatcher won a reduction in Britain's high contribution to the common budget, half of which went to support inefficient European farmers through the Common Agricultural Policy, a policy aimed at integrating and regulating agricultural production in member countries. Thatcher warily signed the Single European Act (1986), which promoted the free flow of goods, labor, and capital but also introduced qualified majority voting in place of the veto that the larger countries formerly enjoyed. Thatcher favored free trade but opposed EU-mandated labor and welfare programs. She wanted a Europe of nation-states rather than one ruled by supranational institutions that lacked democratic accountability. Many conservatives object to the fact that the European Court of Justice has the power to invalidate British laws that contradict EU law. Thatcher's resistance to European integration caused splits within the Conservative Party and led to her removal as prime minister in 1990.

Britain, together with the Scandinavian EU member countries, declined to enter the economic and monetary union that was agreed to at Maastricht in 1991 when the EC renamed itself the European Union. Britain did not adopt the single European currency (the Euro), which was introduced in stages beginning in 1999. Britain's links to Europe grew closer with the opening of the Eurotunnel for trains under the English Channel in 1995. Even as economic ties between Britain and the Continent deepen, Britain is reluctant to pursue political integration with Europe. Britain was a strong supporter of "widening" the EU to include the former communist countries of Eastern Europe, in part because this might delay a political "deepening" of the union; that is, a deeper penetration of European Union regulations into the political systems of member countries. (Ten more countries joined the EU in May 2004, raising the membership to 25.)

Closer political union would weaken Britain's strategic alliance with the United States and undermine its ability to run an independent, liberal economic policy. A "federal Europe" would challenge the principle of parliamentary sovereignty, which lies at the very heart of the British political tradition.

Who Are the British? Contested Identities

We all have an image of who the British are: Lady Diana, the Beatles, Austin Powers. The British seem to be confident and self-assured, even complacent. But this image of comfortable homogeneity is an illusion. Britain was always riven by deep social-class divisions at home and doubts over the viability and morality of its overseas empire. Britain's political identity as the country entered the twenty-first century was more fragile than outsiders usually suppose.

The political identity of many older Britons is tied to the lost empire that disappeared from the world atlas more than half a century ago. Britain's reluctance to join its neighbors in European integration stems from the fear that such a step would undermine British identity. The Scots, Irish, and Welsh are still there to remind us that the "British" should not be conflated with "English." The Celtic periphery makes up 10 million of Britain's population of 59 million and has won increased political autonomy in the last quarter of the twentieth century. Despite 900 years of continuous self-rule, Britain's ethnic identity remains curiously ill-defined.

FORGING A BRITISH NATION

"Britain" and "Great Britain" are synonyms, referring to the main island that includes England, Scotland, and Wales. The United Kingdom is the political unit that includes Great Britain and Northern Ireland. The 59 million inhabitants of the United Kingdom have a complex and shifting hierarchy of identities. They identify themselves as English, Scots, Welsh, or Irish, and at the same time they are aware of themselves as British subjects.

Regional identities are quite strong, with many counties and cities having distinct dialects and proud traditions. The contemporary United Kingdom is an ethnically diverse society with strong national communities in Wales, Scotland, and Northern Ireland. While the empire existed, the four peoples of the British Isles were united in a common endeavor of mutual enrichment through global conquest. With the end of the empire, that powerful practical and ideological cohesive force is now lacking. Since the 1990s, an emergent "European" identity has been added to the mix.

The south of England was occupied by Angles and Saxons who crossed from the European continent during the sixth to ninth centuries, while Vikings conquered the North. The French-speaking Normans displaced the Anglo-Saxon rulers in 1066 and set about creating a unified kingdom. By the end of the sixteenth century, a notion of the English people was quite firmly established – as reflected in the patriotic plays of William Shakespeare. Through the stick of conquest and the carrot of commerce, the English absorbed the Celtic peoples of Wales (1535), Ireland (1649), and Scotland (1707). Local parliaments were dissolved, and a unitary state was created and run from London.

The process of absorption was different in each of the three Celtic regions. English lords moved into Wales and took over the land, but the peasantry maintained their distinct Welsh identity. Today, about one-fifth of the three million residents of Wales still speak the distinctive Welsh language at home. In Scotland, the indigenous feudal elite was divided. Most of the lowland lords sided with London and helped subjugate the recalcitrant Highlanders. This culminated in the defeat of the Jacobite rebels at Culloden (1745), the last battle fought on British soil. Most of the rebellious clans were deported to America. The Scottish elite played a leading role in the forging of the British nation and the expansion of its empire. During the eighteenth century, Edinburgh, the Scottish capital, rivaled London as an intellectual center. It was there that Adam Smith developed the conceptual framework of liberal capitalism.

Like the Welsh, the five million Scots still maintain a strong sense of national identity, although the Gaelic language has almost disappeared. Scotland preserved its own legal and educational systems, independent from the English model. The Scottish National Party (SNP) believes that Scotland's identity would be best preserved through the creation of an independent Scottish state. Their cause was boosted during the 1960s by the discovery of oil and gas in the North Sea off eastern Scotland. Even so, Scotland remained a net recipient of subsidies from the British national budget.

Also during the 1960s, a nationalist movement, **Plaid Cymru**, arose in Wales. Its main goal was the preservation of Welsh language and culture. The nationalists won concessions from London in language policy: Welsh road signs, a Welsh TV station, and the teaching of the Welsh language in schools. Plaid Cymru routinely wins around 10 percent of the vote in Wales in elections.

Whereas the focus of Welsh nationalism is culture, the Scottish movement is broader, with economic and political goals. As a result, its support fluctuates, depending on the level of voter disaffection with the mainstream parties. The SNP usually wins between 12 and 20 percent of the vote but managed to garner 30 percent in 1974. This led the Labour government to steer more public spending into the Celtic regions. Under the 1974 Barrett formula, Scotland, Wales, and Northern Ireland get 15, 10, and 5 percent of the spending in England – more than their share of the total population in the United Kingdom. The Labour Party also promised to create regional assemblies in each country with the power to pass laws and raise taxes, a reform known as "**devolution**." Scots were split on the idea because the SNP still wanted outright independence. A referendum was held in 1979, and only 12 percent of Welsh and 33 percent of Scots voted in favor of a regional assembly.

The idea of devolution was dropped, but it was revived during the 1990s by the Labour Party under its new leader, Tony Blair. The new Labour government held referenda on devolution in September 1997. Seventy-four percent of Scots voted in favor of a new Scottish parliament, and 64 percent approved giving the body tax-raising powers in the form of an extra 3 percent income tax (the "tartan tax"). The Welsh were rather lukewarm about self-government. Their referendum backed a Welsh parliament by the slimmest of margins (50.3 percent to 49.7 percent), on voter turnout of only 50 percent.

Many Britons fear (or hope) that the creation of the Scottish parliament will lead ineluctably to full independence for Scotland. Despite a number of scandals since they started work in 1999, the two new regional parliaments have been moderately successful, broadening the range of political participation. The new Welsh executive became the first government anywhere in the world to have a majority of female ministers.

THE IRISH QUESTION

Catholic Ireland was brought under British control only after brutal military campaigns by Oliver Cromwell (1649) and William of Orange (1689). English lords moved in to take over the land, while Scottish Protestants established a colony in Ulster (present-day Northern Ireland). The English banned the

Irish language, which survived only in the more remote regions. Unscrupulous landlords, cheap food imports from the United States, and the failure of the potato crop resulted in famine in the 1840s and a mass exodus from the Irish countryside. A growing movement for Irish independence was met with proposals for autonomy ("home rule") from London. These plans foundered initially over land reform and later because of opposition from the Ulster Protestants.

The year 1916 saw an abortive nationalist uprising in Dublin. In the wake of World War I, as Ireland sank into civil war, the British decided to cut their losses. In 1921, London granted independence to the southern Republic of Ireland while maintaining Northern Ireland as part of the United Kingdom. Northern Ireland was granted its own parliament (Stormont), which was controlled by the 1.6 million strong Protestant majority. The 800,000 Catholics of the province lived in segregated housing estates and went to separate (Catholic) schools. The Protestants controlled the police force and steered jobs and public spending to their own community.

In 1968, a civil rights movement sprang up, demanding equal treatment for the Catholics and borrowing the tactics of the U.S. civil rights movement. Its peaceful protests were brutally dispersed by the Protestant police. The Irish Republican Army (IRA), a long-dormant terrorist group, mobilized to defend the Catholics, but their goal was a united Ireland. In 1969, 16,000 British troops were sent to take over the job of policing the province from the discredited Ulster constabulary. Over the next three decades, Northern Ireland was wracked by a three-way "low-intensity" conflict among the British army, the IRA, and sundry Protestant paramilitaries. Riots, bombings, and assassinations became part of everyday life. The British government fought back with special courts and internment without trial. From time to time, the IRA planted bombs on the British mainland, and they managed to kill several top British officials. All told, the conflict claimed about 3,200 lives. At least the British army managed to prevent the conflict from escalating into open civil war or Bosnian-style ethnic cleansing. On occasion, human rights went by the board. Six Irishmen accused of planting a bomb in Birmingham, England, in 1975 were imprisoned for 16 years before they were declared innocent and released.

The British abolished the Stormont parliament in 1972, but efforts to introduce power sharing between Catholics and Protestants foundered on opposition from hard-line Protestant **Unionists**, who staunchly defended remaining part of the United Kingdom. The Protestants were living in a seventeenth-century time warp, adhering to values of God, queen, and country that had long been forgotten in mainland Britain. The Protestants feared the exchange of their majority status in Ulster for minority status in a united Ireland – particularly because the Irish Republic's laws were still based on the Catholic faith (banning divorce and abortion, for example).

Britain and Ireland drew closer through integration into the European Union, and in 1985, London agreed to grant Dublin a direct role in any future peace settlement for the North. London promised the Unionists that Ulster would only join a united Ireland if a majority in the North voted in favor of it. Peace talks resumed in 1993, and a complex peace deal was agreed upon, under the chairmanship of former U.S. senator George Mitchell, in 1998. The IRA and Protestant paramilitaries were supposed to disarm, and their convicted comrades would be released from prison. Protestant and Catholic politicians in the North agreed to share power in an assembly elected by proportional representation. The "Good Friday" accord was approved in a referendum, winning 71 percent support in the North. Despite some continuing violence from renegade extremists, hopes for peace were high. The leaders of the main Protestant and Catholic parties, David Trimble and John Hume, were awarded the Nobel Peace Prize in 1998. Prisoner releases began, but the IRA refused to disarm and Protestant leaders balked at sharing power with their Catholic counterparts. In the June 2001 British parliamentary elections, extremist parties hostile to the accord won more support than the centrist parties on both the Unionist and Catholic sides.

After the September 11, 2001, terrorist attacks in the United States, the IRA sensed that world opinion was turning against terrorism, and they started to give up (or "decommission") some of their weapons caches under the supervision of an independent commission headed by a retired Canadian general. However, low-level sectarian violence continued, and the IRA refused to disband. In October 2002, the London government suspended the Northern Ireland Assembly and Executive for the fourth time since 1998 as relations between the leaders of the two communities broke down. Elections to the Assembly in November 2003 saw losses for the moderate parties that had championed the peace process (the Ulster Unionists and the mainly Catholic Social Democratic and Labour Party) at the expense of the hard-line Democratic Unionists and republican Sinn Fein.

Ireland was the first – and last – British colony. The Northern Ireland "troubles" are a blot on British democracy and the most painful reminder of the legacy of empire.

BRITISH – AND BLACK

Another important echo of empire was the appearance in the 1960s of a community of immigrants from Asia and the West Indies. These Asians and blacks broke the image of social homogeneity that had prevailed in Britain for decades.

Facing a labor squeeze, as early as 1948, Britain started to recruit workers from Jamaica and Trinidad, former British colonies in the West Indies. These black workers were joined by a flow of migrants from India and Pakistan, a process accelerated by the expulsion of Asians from Kenya and Uganda in

1965. More restrictive immigration laws were introduced, which slowed but did not halt the flow. By 2001, there were 1.5 million blacks (half African, and half from the Caribbean), 1.1 million Indians, one million Pakistanis and Bangladeshis, and 500,000 other Asians, mainly Chinese. This meant that 7.9 percent of the population belonged to nonwhite minorities. (White immigrants accounted for another 4 percent.) Race was not the only issue. The South Asian migrants were Hindus and Muslims, who posed a challenge to Britain's avowed status as a Christian nation.

Few Americans realize that the Church of England is the established state religion, with the queen as its official head. Anglican religious education used to be legally compulsory for all pupils in state schools, with separate (state-funded) schools for Roman Catholics and Jews. With the appearance of Muslim and Hindu pupils in the 1970s, most state schools stopped teaching religion. In practice, less than 10 percent of the British population are regular churchgoers. The new immigrants forced Britain to acknowledge the fact that it was in reality a secular, urban, individualist culture and that its old self-images of queen, church, and empire were sorely outdated.

Immigration was also a political challenge. Many older Britons harbored racist attitudes from the days of empire, and some young workers saw the immigrants as a threat to their jobs and state housing. The racist National Front Party arose in the late 1960s, and there were occasional street battles between racist skinheads and immigrant youths throughout the 1970s and 1980s. The situation began to change as the first cohort of British-born blacks and Asians passed through the educational system and entered the professions. Whereas their parents had kept a low social and political profile, the second generation was more assertive in demanding a full and equal place in British society. It took several decades before the new immigrant communities won political representation. In 1987, four minority candidates won seats in Parliament, rising to 10 in 1997 (all but one for the Labour Party). Tony Blair subsequently appointed the first black minister, and he named a black woman to head the House of Lords.

London is now a relaxed, multicultural city. Intermarriage rates across racial lines are high (in comparison with the United States): around 50 percent for both blacks and Asians. The media deserve much of the credit for helping to redefine Britain as a multiracial community. However, accusations of racism in the police force were highlighted by the failure to prosecute the skinheads who killed a black youth, Stephen Lawrence, in London in 1997. In May 2001, race riots broke out in several northern cities, highlighting the tension in poor white and immigrant communities competing for scarce jobs and housing.

During the 1990s, attention focused on the problems posed by an influx of asylum seekers, mainly from Eastern Europe and countries as far-flung as Afghanistan and Somalia. More than 500,000 entered the United Kingdom from 1991 to 2001, with 100,000 arriving in 2002 alone. Four out of five applicants were rejected, but housing and processing them caused public outrage. The Conservatives attacked the Labour government for allegedly liberal asylum policies that were encouraging refugees to head for Britain, and the government responded by tightening border controls.

British Political Institutions

The British political system is characterized by a high level of stability. Its main strength has been institutions able to defuse the deep conflicts in British society before they turn violent. The core features of what is known as the Westminster model – parliamentary sovereignty, prime ministerial government, and two parties alternating in power – have remained basically unchanged for more than a hundred years. (Westminster is the district of London where the Houses of Parliament are located.)

THE PATH TO PARLIAMENTARY DEMOCRACY

The U.S. political system is based on the idea of a written constitution, a contract among the founders to form a new state based on certain principles. In contrast, the linchpin of the British system is the notion of parliamentary sovereignty. The Parliament, representing the people, has the power to enact any law it chooses, unrestrained by a written constitution or the separation of powers. Another difference is that the U.S. system strives for a separation of powers among the executive, legislative, and judicial branches. In contrast, the British system of parliamentary sovereignty fuses the executive with the legislature, while the House of Lords also serves as the nation's highest court.

The notion of popular sovereignty, where voters get to choose their leaders through frequent direct elections, is the essence of British democracy. At first, in the eighteenth century, the number of voters who got to participate was very small, perhaps 2 percent of the population. It took 200 years of social conflict before the franchise spread to the majority of citizens. It is remarkable that an institution designed to protect the interests of medieval nobles – the parliament – also came to be accepted by industrial workers in the twentieth century as a vital instrument for the protection of their interests.

Regional *parlements* emerged in France as a forum for nobles to resolve disputes. (The word *parlement* means "talking place" in French, the language also used by the British nobility at the time.) The institution spread to England in the late thirteenth century, providing a forum for the monarch to persuade the nobles to pay taxes. Over time, the monarch grew more powerful and came to be seen as the divinely chosen ruler of the kingdom (whose right to rule was subject to approval by the pope). In 1534, King Henry VIII broke with the Church of Rome and established a separate Church of England, with himself as head. This removed an important external prop to the legitimacy claims of the British monarch. The rhetoric of king and Parliament gradually shifted from divine right to that of serving the interests of the people and nation. However, there remained many fierce disputes over economic interests, political power, and religious identity.

The upper chamber of Parliament (the House of Lords) consisted of **hereditary peers**, lords appointed by the monarch, whose title automatically passes down to their eldest sons. The lower chamber (the House of Commons) consisted of representatives elected by property owners in the public at large.

Conflict between king and Parliament over the right to raise taxes erupted into civil war (1642–1648). After 30 years of military-theocratic rule by Oliver Cromwell, in the Glorious Revolution of 1688, the Parliament welcomed back William of Orange as a constitutional monarch with limited powers. In the eighteenth century, the Parliament's role developed into what has come to be known as the Westminster model. One of its most important features was its division into two parties – Her Majesty's Government on one side and **Her Majesty's Opposition** on the other. The idea that one can disagree with the government without being considered a traitor was novel. This was the source of the two-party system that became a structural feature of British democracy.

In his classic 1971 book *Polyarchy*, Robert Dahl argued that liberal democracy develops along two dimensions: contestation and participation. "Contestation" means that rival groups of leaders compete for the top state positions; "participation" refers to the proportion of the adult population who play an active role in this process through elections. Over the course of the twentieth century, many countries have made an abrupt transition from closed authoritarian regimes to competitive, democratic regimes. In these cases, contestation and participation develop in parallel. In the British case, however, the politics of contestation were firmly established long before mass participation appeared on the scene. Prior to the nineteenth century, property requirements meant that only 2 percent of the adult population had the right to vote. Parliamentarism, initially reflecting the interests of landed elites, preceded popular democracy by several centuries.

THE HOUSE OF COMMONS

The centerpiece of the British political system is the House of Commons. The House of Commons consists of 659 members of Parliament (MPs) elected from single-member constituencies. Although a handful of members sit as Independents, the vast majority of MPs run for election as members of a political party. The Commons must submit itself for election at least once every five years in what is called a General Election. (If an MP dies or resigns between elections, an individual by-election is held for that seat.) The leader of the party with a majority of MPs is invited by the queen to form a government. If no single party has an absolute majority, party leaders negotiate and the monarch appoints a coalition government. That has not happened since 1935 because the winner-take-all electoral system typically throws up two strong parties.

The best example of British democracy in action is **Prime Minister's Question Time**. For thirty minutes once a week, the prime minister stands before the Commons and answers questions, largely unscripted, from members of parliament of both parties. The ritual often strikes foreign observers as rather silly. The questions are not really intended to solicit information but to score political points and make the other side look foolish. Members of Parliament from both parties shout, whistle, laugh, and jeer to express their encouragement or displeasure. The drama is enhanced by the fact that the two main parties sit on ranked benches facing each other, just yards apart. (Since 1989, Question Time has been televised.)

The spectacle seems juvenile, more akin to a college debating competition than a legislative assembly. However, the game has a serious purpose: public accountability. Week after week, the members of the government have to take the stand and defend their policies. It is a kind of collective lie-detector test in which the failings of government policy are ruthlessly exposed to ridicule by the opposition. Problems or scandals are speedily brought to light: A controversial newspaper article will stimulate questions in Parliament within days. And a minister who is caught lying to the Commons must immediately resign.

Question Time illustrates the radical difference between the U.S. and British legislatures. A sitting U.S. president never has to confront his political adversaries face to face. (The televised debates once every four years are between presidential *candidates*.) The president's communications with the public are carefully managed through public statements, photo-ops, and the occasional press conference.

FROM CABINET TO PRIME MINISTERIAL GOVERNMENT

The head of the government is known as the prime minister (PM). The PM nominates a cabinet of about 20 ministers, who are appointed by the queen to form Her Majesty's Government. There are another 70 to 90 ministers and deputy ministers without cabinet rank. Whereas U.S. cabinet members work for the president, their British counterparts are accountable to Parliament. All ministers are members of Parliament, either from the Commons or the Lords, and they must account for their actions, individual and collective, to that body. The PM can pick whom he or she wants to be a minister, although a Labour PM is slightly constrained by the fact that the parliamentary party elects a "shadow cabinet," a group of senior MPs whose members track their counterparts in ministerial positions when their own party is in opposition.

Individual ministers are not confirmed by the legislature as in the United States.

The cabinet meets weekly in the PM's residence, **No. 10 Downing Street**. The PM chairs and directs cabinet meetings, and votes are usually not taken. The most senior ministers are those heading the foreign office, the treasury, and the home office (dealing with police, prisons, etc.). The ministers rely on the permanent civil service to run their departments, with only one or two personal advisers brought in from outside. The total number of outside appointees when a new government takes power is fewer than 50, compared with more than 2,000 political appointees in the United States.

There is no separation of powers between the executive and legislative branches under the British system. On the contrary, the two are fused together. The public elects the House of Commons knowing that the majority party will form the executive branch. The PM comes from the party with a majority in the Commons, and this majority always votes according to party instructions. This means that the legislative program of the ruling party is almost always implemented. The government rules as long as it can sustain its majority in the Commons. A government will resign after defeat in the Commons on what it deems to be a vote of confidence.

This system gives the prime minister tremendous power, in what **Tory** (a member of the Conservative Party) Lord Hailsham called "an elective dictatorship." The power of the prime minister is augmented by the fact that he or she chooses when to call an election. The Commons can vote to dissolve itself at any time, leading to a general election just six weeks later. Thanks to having control over the majority party in the Commons, the prime minister can choose when to face the electorate. This gives a tremendous political advantage to the incumbent government. The PM carefully monitors opinion polls and economic data, and calls an election when support is at a peak (although an election must be called no later than five years after the previous election).

If the U.S. Congress is a policy-*making* legislature, Westminster is at best a policy-*influencing* legislature. In Britain, the government is responsible for introducing virtually all legislation: It is extremely rare for a bill proposed by an individual MP to make it into law. Members of Parliament are expected to vote in accordance with party instructions (the party "whip"), except when a vote is declared a matter of personal conscience. An MP who defies the whip may be expelled from the party and denied its endorsement at the next election, which will usually prevent her or his reelection. Even so, in about 10 to 20 percent of votes in the Commons, a small number of rebels defy the party whip. The parliaments of 1974–1979 and 1992–1997 saw frequent revolts by dissident MPs from the ruling party, but they had only a marginal effect on the government's capacity to enact its program. In an attempt to bolster the Parliament's powers, 14 new committees giving MPs oversight over ministry activities were introduced in 1979.

During the 1980s, when Margaret Thatcher was PM, there were complaints that the PM was becoming too powerful, even "presidential," in her ability to dictate policy to the cabinet and ministers. In particular, Thatcher took over direct control of foreign policy, at the expense of the foreign secretary. These complaints returned after Tony Blair became PM in 1997. After his reelection in 2001, Blair created special units for European and foreign/defense affairs inside the prime minister's office, further undercutting the role of the foreign office and defense ministry.

The upper chamber of Parliament, the House of Lords, has a limited capacity to block or delay government legislation. The judicial branch has only a limited ability to interfere with the government's actions because there is no written constitution to which they can appeal to declare a law invalid. Any act that is passed in three readings by the Commons and Lords and signed into law by the queen supersedes all preceding laws and precedents and must be implemented by the judiciary. The lack of a bill of rights has troubled many liberal observers.

Britain has a unitary system of government. There is no federal system that can block the powers of the Westminster Parliament. There are separate ministries for Scotland, Wales, and Northern Ireland, the main task of which is spending regional development funds. Local governments have very limited powers, and the national government sets the rules by which they raise and spend money. Eighty percent of the funding for local councils comes from the national government, and there are strict rules over how it can be spent. Margaret Thatcher was so annoyed by the policies of the Labour-controlled Greater London Council that she had Parliament abolish the council in 1986. (It had been created only in 1964.) The New Labour government of Tony Blair set about reversing the centralization of the Thatcher years, creating a new Greater London Authority in 1999 and moving ahead with plans for the introduction of new parliaments in Wales and Scotland.

THE ELECTORAL SYSTEM

Britain operates a first-past-the-post, or winner-take-all, electoral system, similar to that in the United States. This produces clear winners and strong alternating majority parties in the House of Commons. However, it is criticized for offering voters an exceptionally narrow range of alternatives (two) and denying third parties adequate representation.

Each of the 659 members of Parliament is elected from a single-member constituency in which the candidate with the highest number of votes wins. This first-past-the-post electoral system works to the advantage of the two leading parties, which tend to finish first and second in every race. Britain's third-largest party, the Liberal Democrats, has 15 to 25 percent support in nearly every constituency in the country, but this is not enough to displace a Labour or Tory incumbent with 40 to 60 percent support. Hence, the Liberal Democrats win very few parliamentary seats.

Also, because several candidates compete for each seat, the winner may not have an absolute majority of the votes cast. Similarly, at the national level, there is no guarantee that the party that wins the most seats will have won a majority of the votes. In fact, no government since the coalition that won in 1935 has gained more than 50 percent of the votes cast in a British election – yet this did not prevent those governments from having absolute control of the Commons and pursuing an aggressive legislative program.

The first-past-the-post system is unpredictable in the degree to which voter preferences are translated into parliamentary seats. Table 3.1 shows the results of the 1992 and 1997 elections (excluding Northern Ireland). The third column illustrates a hypothetical case: how many seats each party would have won if they had been allocated in strict proportion to the share of total votes cast – a system of proportional representation, or PR. Note how small differences in the votes gained by the rival parties produce huge differences in the number of seats won.

In 1992, both Labour and Tories won more seats than they would have had under a PR system, whereas the Liberal Democrats got only one-fifth of the seats they would have had under PR. In 1997, the Liberal Democrats won twice as many seats as they did in 1992, although they garnered fewer votes than in the previous election. The Conservatives (Tories) did worse in 1997 than they would have under PR, whereas Labour scooped up two-thirds of the seats with only 44 percent of the national vote.

In June 2001, Labour scored a second consecutive victory in national elections. They won 413 seats (6 fewer than in 1997), while their share of the vote slipped by 2.5 percent to 40.7 percent. The Conservatives polled 31.7 percent of the vote but garnered only 166 seats, and the Liberal Democrats increased their seats by 6 to 52, with 18.5 percent of the vote. (Other parties won 9.3 percent of the total vote and 28 seats.) In May 2005 Tony Blair won an unprecedented third term. Labour narrowly led the conservatives, by 35.2 percent to 32.3 percent of the popular vote – but this translated into 355 seats for Labour and 197 for the Tories. The Liberal Democrats, with 22.0 percent of the vote, picked up 62 seats.

The unequal relationship between votes and seats is exacerbated by the unequal geographical concentration of voters and the economic divide between the prosperous Southeast and the depressed North and West. Labour does well in London and in northern cities but usually wins few seats in the southern suburbs and rural areas. (An exception was in 1997, when Labour did well even in the South.) The gap in regional voting patterns actually increased during the 1970s and 1980s. As a result of this pattern, four out of five constituencies are "safe seats" that rarely change hands between parties in an election. Despite this, voter turnout was relatively high, usually around

80 percent, although it slipped to 69 percent in 1997 and 57 percent in 2001, recovering to 61 percent in 2005.

Under the first-past-the-post system, minor parties with a regional concentration, such as the Scottish and Welsh nationalists, can win seats on their home turf. The third-largest party in Britain, formerly the Liberals and now called the Liberal Democrats, wins seats mainly in the alienated periphery where their supporters are concentrated: Scotland, Wales, and the southwest of England. Elsewhere, they win few seats.

There are growing calls for a reform of the British electoral system in order to make the results more representative of voter opinion. The Liberal Democrats have the most to gain from the introduction of European-style proportional representation. Most advocates of PR suggest a compromise system, such as that operating in Germany, where half the seats are reserved for single-member races (to ensure that there is an MP responsible for each district) and half for party lists (to ensure proportional representation). Britain now has some experience with the PR system. Elections to the European Parliament using the PR system took place in Britain in 1999. The two new parliaments in Scotland and Wales are elected by PR (single-seat constituencies, topped up by additional members from a national party list to ensure proportionality).

Proponents of the existing British system argue that it produces a strong government with the power to implement its legislative program. Proportional representation would spread power among three or more parties, which would require coalition governments of more than one party. This may be undemocratic because in most countries coalition governments are usually formed in backroom deals that take place after the election. Neither Labour nor Tories are likely to introduce PR because this would undermine their capacity to form single-party governments. The Liberal Democrats hope that if a future Parliament is equally split between Labour and Conservatives, the Labour Party might introduce PR in return for Liberal Democratic support. In its 1997 election manifesto, Labour promised to hold a referendum on electoral reform, but it dropped the idea after the election.

POLITICAL BEHAVIOR

Voter loyalty to political parties is quite high in Britain, although it has fallen since the Second World War. During the 1990s, the fierce partisan loyalties and "tribal" divisions of previous decades gave way to more centrist, middle-class politics. In 1950, 40 percent of those polled "strongly identified" with a single party, but this figure had halved by 1992. In the 1950s, social class and income level were good predictors of voting behavior, although even then one-quarter of industrial workers voted Conservative and not Labour (which was attributed to deferential or patriotic values). The protracted economic crisis of the 1960s and 1970s eroded party loyalties as voters started to shop around for new ideas. Social-class origin could explain 70 percent of voting behavior in the 1950s but only 50 percent by the 1970s. Voting became less a matter of habit and more a matter of choice. Voter behavior became more volatile, harder to predict, and more likely to be swayed by party campaigns. Voter turnout fell, especially among young people.

Given the large number of "safe" seats, the parties pour their efforts into winning the "marginal" seats, those that may change hands at every election. In **marginal seats**, the parties canvas every household and record the voting intentions of each family member. On election day, party volunteers stand outside polling stations to record voters' registration numbers. The data are collated at party headquarters, and supporters who have not voted are reminded to go to the polls.

Tight limits on campaign spending have mostly prevented the spread of U.S.-style money politics in Britain. There are no limits on donations to national parties, however, which has fueled repeated scandals. It is the role of the media, rather than money, that is the main source of controversy in British politics. The British are avid newspaper readers (average daily circulation is 14 million). In contrast with those in the United States, most British papers are not politically neutral but actively campaign for one of the parties. The papers are not controlled by political parties, as in much of Europe, but are owned by quixotic business magnates who enjoy playing politics. In 1997, the *Observer* newspaper concluded that the second most influential man after Prime Minister Tony Blair was **Rupert Murdoch**, the Australian who owns one-third of Britain's newspapers. Two-thirds of the newspapers usually back the Tories, but in 1997 most papers switched to Labour, which helps to explain Labour's dramatic victory that year. Most newspapers are hostile to Europe, which has caused problems for Europhile Tony Blair. Unlike the press, the television stations are required to be politically neutral and are generally valued for their objectivity. The BBC is state-financed, whereas the three other broadcast stations are commercially owned and depend on advertising for their financing.

Civil society is deeply rooted in Britain, with a broad range of interest groups. Such groups expanded during the 1970s as voters became disillusioned with the mainstream political parties and turned toward "postmaterialist" values. The environmentalist group **Greenpeace** saw its membership swell tenfold to more than 400,000, in part thanks to media coverage of their spectacular protests. Groups protesting new road construction and defending animal rights continued to be active throughout the 1990s. However, environmental issues did not really transform the agendas of the mainstream political parties.

THE DIGNIFIED CONSTITUTION

Queen Elizabeth II ascended to the throne in 1953. She is the head of state but has only limited influence over the affairs of government. The queen meets the prime minister each week for a private chat over tea. The most important function of the monarch is to invite a prime minister to form a government, usually after a general election. If that government wins majority support in the Commons, the monarch's effective role is at an end.

The last time the monarch played a significant role in British politics was in 1910. The House of Lords blocked a high-spending welfare budget passed by the House of Commons. Liberal Prime Minister Herbert Henry Asquith called an election, which he won, and he asked the king to create enough new peers to tip the voting in the upper chamber. The Lords gave in and accepted a new law abolishing its right to delay bills involving public spending. They retained the right to return nonspending bills to the Commons, although if passed a second time by the Commons, such bills become law after a two-year delay (reduced to one year in 1949).

The House of Lords is a bizarre anachronism. In a democracy, it does not make sense to give a legislative role to the descendants of medieval knights. The Lords consisted of 750 hereditary peers and 600 life peers. Hereditary peers are exclusively male, and they pass their title to their first sons. The system of life peers was introduced in 1958. They are mostly retired politicians, men and women, who are nominated by the PM and appointed by the queen. Their heirs do not inherit their seat in the House of Lords.

The ultraconservative hereditary peers gave the Tories a guaranteed majority in the upper chamber, so Labour had a strong interest in reforming the House of Lords. However, reform of the Lords proved difficult because the House of Commons did not want to create a new elected second chamber that could rival its power. But a second chamber is useful in scrutinizing laws passed on party lines in the Commons. In 1998, the Blair government announced its intention to phase out the hereditary peers but was unable to come up with an acceptable plan for an elected component to the Lords. Proposals to have an upper chamber composed of elected representatives from the nations and regions of Britain were seen as too much of a threat to the legitimacy of the Commons. In 2003, the final group of hereditary peers was abolished, leaving the Lords full of politically appointed life peers (with an average age of 68).

The idea of reforming the monarchy is not on the agenda. Having a ceremonial, nonpolitical head of state preserves the authority of Parliament, and few people advocate abolishing the monarchy in favor of an elected or appointed president. The main argument is over money. Each year, the Commons votes a budget for the queen and her extended family in recognition of their public duties. During the 1990s, as the royal family fell prey to divorce and scandal, the public began to wonder whether they were getting value for their money. The queen's vast personal wealth is exempt from tax, but in response to public criticism in 1995, she voluntarily started to pay income tax. Defenders of the monarchy often fall back on the argument that royal pageantry is good for the tourism industry.

The life of the royals is a reality TV soap opera that provides endless copy for the tabloid press in Britain and throughout the world. Princess Diana, the wife of Prince Charles, was probably the most well-known woman on the planet. Her dramatic divorce and subsequent untimely death in a car accident in August 1997 produced an extraordinary outpouring of emotion in Britain, equivalent to that following the death of President John F. Kennedy in the United States. Diana, whom Blair called the "people's princess," had come to represent the new England, breaking down barriers of class, gender, and race through her charity work.

RIVAL INTERESTS AND THE EVOLUTION OF BRITISH DEMOCRACY

The British political system revolves around strong, well-organized social groups defending their respective economic and political interests. Over the course of history, these rival interest groups developed a set of political institutions to defend and broker their competing interests. Social interests and political institutions evolved in a parallel and intertwined process. By the seventeenth century, British thinkers were describing the emergence of a "civil society" consisting of a dense network of independent social actors linked through mutual respect, accepted social norms, and the rule of law.

In class terms, British history was dominated by the legendary landowning aristocracy, which was later joined by a resilient and rapacious commercial bourgeoisie. The rising capitalist class, along with elements of the landed aristocracy, went to war against the king and his aristocratic supporters in the middle of the seventeenth century to decide which institution would rule – the monarch or the elected Parliament. The institutions that emerged as a compromise in the wake of the civil war (parliamentary sovereignty and constitutional monarchy) have persisted to the present day.

Many social groups, such as the peasantry, religious minorities, and women, were shut out from civil society and struggled to find a political voice. But during the nineteenth century, the rising class of industrial workers forged a powerful trade-union movement and later a parliamentary political party to defend its interests. Each of these social classes (lords, peasants, capitalists, and workers) lived a different life, went to different schools, and even spoke different dialects.

Despite this highly stratified social system, Britain emerged as a peaceful, stable democracy. Strong political institutions emerged that were able to express and absorb these competing class interests. Stability is the most widely praised attribute of the British political system. The general level of social unrest and political violence (Northern Ireland excepted) has been quite low. Britain has functioned with the same set of political institutions, without coups or revolutions, since 1689. There are few nations in continental Europe that can make such a claim. Germany has gone through four regimes since its formation in 1871; France is on its fifth republic since 1815.

Britain's institutions emerged gradually over time and were the product of experience rather than design. The operating principle was Anglo-Saxon pragmatism (what works) as opposed to French rationalism (what is best).

This stable set of political institutions was embedded in a broad consensus of political values. This consensus was particularly strong among the tightly knit ruling elite, who have shown a high degree of cohesiveness over the years. Prominent among these consensus values was the notion of loyalty to the monarch, church, and empire. The very strength of the divisive social-class system was also, ironically, a source of stability. Everyone was fully aware of the existence of the class system and their family's location within it. They all "knew their place."

THE RIGHTS TRADITION

An important part of Britain's consensus values was the recognition of individual rights and the notion of limited government. Over the centuries, medieval England built up a body of common law: the accumulated decisions of court cases that defined and protected individual rights. Such rights included the right to trial by jury and habeas corpus, meaning protection against arrest without a court hearing (literally, the right to one's own body). Such rights to personal liberty and private property were spelled out in the Magna Carta, a contract that was presented to King John in 1215 by a few dozen leading nobles. That document was designed to protect the privileges of a narrow and oppressive aristocracy, but it set the precedent for the sovereign's power being negotiated and conditional. Over the ensuing centuries, the same rights were slowly extended to broader sections of the population.

The rights to personal liberty and property did not initially extend to religion. Although the 1689 Act of Toleration granted freedom of worship to those outside the Church of England, it was not until the 1820s that bans on Catholics and Jews serving in the military or in public office were lifted. Unlike the United States, Britain does not have a formal bill of rights guaranteeing individual rights. Despite the absence of a bill of rights, the individualist, rights-oriented tradition ran deep in British political life. For example, in contrast with Europe, there is still no national identity card system in Britain (or in the United States).

In 1951, Britain ratified the European Convention on Human Rights, which created a supranational European Court of Human Rights in Strasbourg, France. Since 1966, British citizens have been able to appeal to that court (and the court has reversed British legal decisions in some fifty cases). In 1998, the Blair government introduced the Human Rights Act, which formally incorporated the European Convention on Human Rights into domestic law. This moved the United Kingdom closer to U.S.-style judicial review.

An important difference from the United States is that the right to bear arms was not part of the British tradition. On the contrary, British monarchs were keen to keep a monopoly of force in their own hands, systematically tearing down nearly all of the castles of the aristocracy in the sixteenth century. Restrictions on personal gun ownership are very tight. British police usually patrol unarmed, and guns are used in fewer than 100 murders per year in Britain (compared with some 10,000 in the United States). After the massacre of sixteen children by a deranged gunman in Dunblane, Scotland, in 1996, private possession of handguns was completely banned.

THE IMPACT OF INDUSTRIALIZATION

From the seventeenth century on, Britain emerged as the preeminent maritime power, pulling ahead of Holland, Spain, and finally France. This was due to the skill, enterprise, and ruthlessness of its sailors in trade and in war. Napoleon described England as a "nation of merchants" (often mistranslated as "a nation of shopkeepers"). Trade was the main source of England's wealth, and it generated a new capitalist class that gradually merged with the old landed aristocracy.

Britain was the first country to experience the agricultural revolution. Peasants were driven from their subsistence plots to make way for extensive farming methods. These peasants had a very limited range of political and economic opportunities. Many opted for emigration. About one-quarter of the population left the British Isles (some unwillingly, as convicts) for America, Canada, Australia, and other outposts of the empire. This provided an important safety valve, reducing the surplus population and easing social discontent. In a TV interview, singer Mick Jagger was asked why there had never been a revolution in England. He replied that it was because all the people who did not like the place had left. Whereas the United States was formed as a nation of immigrants, Britain was a nation of emigrants.

Britain was also the first country to experience the Industrial Revolution, in the first decades of the nineteenth century. Industry and empire grew together. Britain became "the workshop of the world," selling its manufactured goods throughout its global trading network. However, the governing coalition of old landlords and new bourgeoisie was terrified that the example of the 1789 French Revolution could be replicated in Britain. Growing protests from the expanding working class were met with a mixture of repression and reform. The 1832 Reform Act loosened the property requirements for voting, but even then only 5 percent of the adult population were enfranchised. A two-party system emerged in the House of Commons, with reformist and reactionary elements grouping themselves into the parties of Liberals and Conservatives (also known as Tories). Further Reform Acts in 1867 and 1884 gave the vote to 20 percent and then 40 percent of the population.

It was the arrival of organized labor that forced open the doors of Parliament to the mass electorate. Faced with mounting labor unrest, Britain's ruling class opted for compromise rather than confrontation. By giving most adult men the right to vote, they provided an outlet for workers' political frustrations and turned them away from industrial violence. Trade unions had started to form on a craft basis in the 1840s, and by the 1880s they were expanding to the masses of unskilled workers. Heavily influenced by the Methodist revival, a Protestant movement, British workers were generally deferential to their masters and accepting of the status quo. Their initial focus was on improving wages and conditions rather than gaining political rights. For decades, they had precious little to show for their loyalty, as they were crowded into Dickensian slums and labored long hours in the "dark satanic mills" of the Industrial Revolution.

In 1900, the unions formed the Labour Representation Committee (LRC) to advance their interests in Parliament. They realized that they needed legislative protection after a court case had threatened severe civil penalties for strike action. The LRC renamed itself the Labour Party and won 50 seats in the 1906 parliamentary election in alliance with the Liberal Party.

The Liberal government that ruled from 1906 to 1914 introduced some elements of a **welfare state**, such as rudimentary public health care, school meals, and public pensions. These measures were not merely a response to the rise of labor. They were also prompted by the shocking discovery that one-third of the recruits for the British army in the Boer War between British and Dutch interests in South Africa (1899–1902) were medically unfit to serve. To match the mass armies of Germany and Russia, Britain would have to start looking after its workers. Joseph Chamberlain, the reform-minded cabinet minister who served as Colonial Secretary during the Boer War, advanced the philosophy of "social imperialism" – welfare spending in return for the workers' political loyalty in imperial ventures. This was clearly an echo of Otto von Bismarck's model of welfare capitalism in Germany. The program did not include equal rights for women. The Liberal government resisted a vigorous protest movement for the woman's right to vote (the Suffragettes). It would take the shock of World War I to change public opinion on the issue.

The British elite came through the Industrial Revolution with its medieval institutions remarkably intact. The aristocracy went from country house to royal court to London club, educating their sons at Oxford and Cambridge and sending them off to fight in the colonies in the family regiment. There were a few innovations during the nineteenth century. The new Harry Potter-style "public" schools (in theory open to anyone who could pay the stiff fees) were designed to forge a new elite of like-minded young men by means of a rigid regimen of sport and Latin. In 1854, officials in government service were organized into a politically neutral career civil service in which recruitment and promotion were to be based on merit rather than political connections.

LABOUR'S RISE TO POWER

The bloodbath of World War I was a major challenge to the integrity of the British state. Britain would have lost the war had the United States not intervened. The conflict killed one in ten of the adult male population, drained the economy, and sapped the enthusiasm of the British state for foreign ventures. Still, Britain got off lightly: The war caused the complete collapse of the political systems of Germany, Russia, Austria-Hungary, and Turkey. In recognition of the people's sacrifices for the war effort, in 1918 all adult males were given the vote, irrespective of their property holdings, as were women over the age of 28. (The "flappers" – 18- to 28-year-old women – were enfranchised 10 years later.) Thus, it was not until 1929 that "one person, one vote" became the law in Britain, showing that democracy is a quite recent historical development.

The Labour Party fought the 1918 election as coequal of the Conservatives and Liberals and came out of the 1924 election as the largest single party. Although they did not control a majority of seats in the House of Commons, they formed a minority government. It had taken the trade unions only two decades to ascend from the political wilderness to the pinnacle of power. The euphoria was not to last, however. The 1924 government fell within a year, and economic recession triggered a decade of poverty and industrial conflict.

It was not until World War II that a major shift could be seen in the distribution of power within the British political system. British patriotism blossomed in 1939–1941, when the nation fought alone against Nazi-occupied Europe under a coalition government headed by Conservative Prime Minister Winston Churchill. In return, the people demanded a brighter future once the war was won. In 1942, the government released the Beveridge Report, promising full employment and state-provided health care, insurance, and pensions. This was not enough to satisfy the voters. In 1945, they turned out Churchill and for the first time in history elected a majority Labour government, although Labour won only 48 percent of the vote.

That government introduced a radical socialist program, including the nationalization (taking into state ownership) of large sections of private industry. They introduced the basic institutions of the "welfare state": a National Health Service, state pensions, and state-funded higher education. They expanded state-subsidized housing (called council housing because it was provided by local councils). Health care, jobs, and housing were seen as social rights to which everyone was entitled. (In 1945, one-third of Britons were still living in houses without bathrooms.) Laws were passed taking about one-quarter of private industry into public ownership, including coal mines, electric and gas utilities, steel mills, docks, railways, and long-distance trucking. The expropriated private owners, who were paid modest compensation, opposed nationalization but were powerless in the face of Labour's parliamentary majority. The postwar government also granted independence to such colonies as India and Palestine. But the Labour government did support the United States in forming NATO to oppose Soviet expansionism and reintroduced the draft to help fight the Cold War. The new commitment to socialism at home and the Cold War abroad provided a double anesthetic to dull the pain caused by the loss of empire.

THE POSTWAR CONSENSUS

During the 1950s, British politics slipped into a familiar pattern that would last until 1979. The Labour and Conservative parties alternated in power, and both accepted the basic institutions of postwar Britain. The Tories acquiesced in the retreat from empire and realized that it would be political suicide to try to dismantle the welfare state. Labour knew that the British public did not want more nationalization, not least because problems soon emerged in the management of state-owned industry. Both parties accepted **Keynesianism**, the economic analysis of John Maynard Keynes, who argued that state intervention with public spending could have prevented the Great Depression of the 1930s.

This consensus left little for the two parties to debate. It is ironic that a political system built around two-party adversarial politics should have produced such a consensus. Anthony Downs offered one explanation for this in his 1957 book *An Economic Theory of Democracy*. In a two-party system, Downs reasoned, leaders will compete for the "median voter" in the middle of the policy spectrum. Hence, both party programs will tend to converge.

During the 1950s and 1960s, successive governments managed to avoid another depression. However, they were too ambitious in trying to "fine-tune" the economy by adjusting interest rates and the money supply to ensure simultaneous economic growth, low inflation, and full employment. The country fell into a debilitating "political business cycle." Attempts by Conservative governments to lower inflation typically led to a recession and a rise in unemployment, causing a surge of support for Labour. In turn, Labour efforts to boost economic growth would cause inflation, and on occasion caused embarrassing financial crises when international investors deserted the British pound sterling (in 1967 and 1976).

Despite the introduction of the welfare state, relations between labor and management were tense and confrontational. Unlike in Germany or Scandinavia, after the war there was no attempt to introduce corporatist institutions, such as works councils, to give labor a say in the management of private industry. With unemployment held at 3 to 4 percent, workers were able to threaten strike action to push for better wages and conditions. The economy was plagued by waves of strikes, which came to be known as the "**British disease**." British industry was slow to adopt the latest technology, and Britain was overtaken in industrial output by Germany, France, Japan, and even Italy. London was still a major center of international finance, however. The easy profits from banking, or the prestige of a career in the civil service, tended to draw the "brightest and best" away from careers in industry.

The 1960s were not all gloom and doom. While industry was rusting, London was "swinging." A new youth subculture was invented in Britain and exported to the rest of the world. Music and the arts flourished, putting Britain back on the world map as a cultural superpower. By the end of the 1970s, Britain was earning more from exports of rock music than it was from steel.

The 1964–1970 Labour government tried to address the problem of industrial stagnation by promoting tripartite negotiations among the state, employers, and unions to set prices and incomes. But Labour could not challenge the power of the unions. The unions financed the Labour Party, and their 10 to 12 million members dominated the 250,000 individual party members in elections to choose parliamentary candidates and the party's National Executive Committee.

Industrial unrest led to the Labour Party's defeat in 1970, and a prolonged strike by coal miners brought down the Tory government in 1974. The 1974–1979 Labour government was undermined by a wave of strikes by garbage collectors, railway workers, and nurses that culminated in the 1978 "winter of discontent."

Exasperated by the dominant role of unionists and left-wing radicals in their party, a group of centrist Labour leaders broke away to form a new **Social Democratic Party** (**SDP**). Their centrist program appeared to reflect the views of the majority of voters. However, the winner-take-all party system (see Table 3.1) makes it very difficult for third parties to gain a foothold in Parliament. In the 1983 election, the SDP–Liberal alliance won 26 percent of the votes (only 2 percent less than Labour) but won only 23 of the 635 seats in the House of Commons at that time. The SDP eventually merged with the Liberal Party to form the Liberal Democrats.

By the end of the 1970s, the British model seemed to be in irreversible decline. The economy stagnated, while inflation hit double figures. Journalists began to write about the "ungovernability" of Britain and a system "overloaded" with the demands of competing interest groups.

THATCHER TO THE RESCUE?

At this point, change came from an unexpected source – the Conservative Party. In 1975, the Conservatives selected Margaret Thatcher as their new leader. Thatcher was an aggressive intellectual with an iron will and razor-sharp debating skills. Unusual for a Tory leader, she came from humble social origins – her father was a grocer. She earned a Ph.D. in organic chemistry at Oxford before switching to a legal career to have more time to raise her children.

Thatcher was influenced by the writings of the libertarian Friedrich Hayek and the monetarist Milton Friedman. Her philosophy of popular capitalism drew heavily upon U.S. ideas of rugged individualism and free-market economics. Thatcher concluded that the British model was not working, and her solution was to try to minimize state interference in the economy and society. "Thatcherism" had a profound impact on the British political system, shattering the postwar consensus on the welfare state and locking Labour out of power for 18 years.

Thatcher's bracing New Right rhetoric caught the attention of the British public and gave the Conservatives a clear victory in the 1979 election. She had ambitious plans to deregulate the economy and to privatize large chunks of state-owned industry, and she pledged to follow a tight monetary policy in order to control inflation, whatever the effect on unemployment. Unlike in the United States, the New Right in Britain did not have a social agenda (abortion had been legal since 1967), although they promised to be tough on crime.

Thatcher's first task was to break the power of the trade unions. She introduced new legislation to make it more difficult to call strikes (requiring pre-strike ballots and cooling-off periods). She doubled spending on police and equipped them with riot gear so that they could take on rock-throwing strikers. Thatcher used the courts to seize the assets of the coal miners' union when they mounted an **illegal strike in 1984**, and she went on to shut down most of the state-owned coal mines. By 1990, the number of coal miners had fallen from 300,000 to 50,000. Thatcher broke the back of organized labor, and labor unrest shrank to historically unprecedented levels and was lower than in almost any other country in Europe.

Economic growth was sluggish during Thatcher's first term, and it was probably only her victory in the 1982 Falklands War that won her reelection in 1984. One of the most successful elements of her "popular capitalism" was allowing tenants to buy public housing with low-cost mortgages. From 1979 to 1989, home ownership leapt from 52 percent to 66 percent of all households. Thatcher also sold off many of the nationalized industries: British Telecom, British Gas, and the electric and water utilities. Privatization generated cash for the budget and profits for the millions of citizens who applied for shares in the new companies. Tax rates were cut: The top personal income tax rate fell from 90 percent to 40 percent. Workers were encouraged to opt out of the state pension system and invest some of their payroll taxes in a private retirement account, a measure that was expected to cut state pension spending to a projected 6 percent of Gross Domestic Product (GDP) by 2030, compared with 14–17 percent in continental Europe. A deregulatory program for the financial markets in 1983–1986, called the "Big Bang," enabled London to reinforce its position as the world's leading international financial center.

By the late 1980s, the economy was growing, living standards were rising, and productivity and profits were booming. However, inequality was rising. Average incomes rose 37 percent during 1979–1993, but the earnings of the top 10 percent of the population leaped by 61 percent while those of the bottom decile fell 18 percent. Unemployment climbed to 10 percent from a level of 5 percent in the 1970s, but fell again to 5 percent by 1989. Still, one-third of the population lived in poverty, and there arose a large underclass of jobless youth, which led to a surge in drug use and crime. Ironically, demographic changes and the rise in unemployment caused state welfare spending to rise during the Thatcher years despite her intention to cut public spending.

In 1988, Thatcher introduced an ambitious **"New Steps" program** to change the way state services were delivered. This reform provided much of the intellectual inspiration for the "reinventing government" movement in the United States. State agencies had to introduce independent cost accounting for each stage of their operations. State services were contracted out to private companies or voluntary agencies through competitive tendering. Many state offices were turned into independent agencies, which then bid to provide government services, from sewage to prisons. Local governments, the National Health Service, and the education system were forced to adopt these reforms. Individual schools were encouraged to opt out of local-authority financing and receive direct grant funding. From 1979 to 1993, the number of civil servants was slashed by 30 percent, and about 150 new semi-independent government agencies were created. This reform created more than 40,000 new patronage positions for central ministers. The reforms increased efficiency and cut costs but led to increased corruption. They triggered widespread protests, especially over the unpopular "poll tax," introduced in 1988, that replaced the former local property tax with a flat per capita tax.

THE FALL OF THATCHER

Thatcher secured reelection to an unprecedented third successive term in 1989. However, after 10 years under the "Leaderene," strains were beginning to show in the upper ranks of the Conservative Party. Many traditional conservatives disliked Thatcher's radical reforms, and her authoritarian style alienated many colleagues. Her vocal opposition to further European integration, such as the introduction of a single currency, lost her the support of the internationalist wing of the party. Between 1979 and 1992, membership in the Conservative Party slumped from 1.5 million to 500,000.

Thatcher's departure came not with a bang but with an uncharacteristic whimper. Her popularity steadily eroded throughout the 1980s, dipping to 29 percent in 1990, and she came to be seen as an electoral liability. At that time, the Conservative leader was selected by an annual ballot of members of Parliament (MPs). Usually, no candidates ran against the incumbent, but in 1989 an obscure MP came forward to challenge Thatcher, winning 33 votes. The next year, she faced a serious opponent in the form of ex-Defense Minister Michael Heseltine. Thatcher beat Heseltine in the first round by 204 votes to 152 (with 16 abstentions). Under party rules, a candidate winning less than two-thirds of the vote has to face a second round. Even though she would almost certainly have won, Thatcher chose to resign, partly in order to clear the way for her chosen successor, **John Major**.

Major, like Thatcher, came from humble origins. His father was a circus trapeze artist turned garden-gnome manufacturer. Major left school at 16 to be a bus-ticket collector and later worked his way up from bank teller to bank director before entering politics. Major was reasonably popular, but he lacked Thatcher's charisma. Despite a deep recession that began in 1990 in which GDP fell by 3.6 percent, Major won the 1992 election, thanks mainly to the inept Labour campaign.

Major pressed ahead with privatization of British Rail and the nuclear power and coal industries. But the Conservative Party was badly split over Europe, with a hard-core right wing opposing further integration. The British public was skeptical about the Brussels bureaucracy but generally favored EU membership. (In a 1996 poll, 42 percent approved and 24 percent disapproved.) In 1990, Britain joined the **Exchange Rate Mechanism (ERM)**, the precursor to the single European currency. But in 1991 Britain opted out of the "social chapter" of the Maastricht treaty on European integration. This would have introduced the EU's generous labor legislation to Britain (longer vacations, shorter working hours) and was opposed by employers.

The key turning point in the Major administration was September 1992, when the British pound came under attack from international speculators. Despite desperate government efforts, including spending $5 billion (U.S.) to defend the exchange rate, the pound was forced to leave the ERM. This was a major humiliation and left the government's financial strategy in ruins. Major's approval rating plummeted from 49 percent to 25 percent after the devaluation crisis, and it never recovered.

Conservative Party credibility was further battered by a series of sex and corruption scandals. Tory MPs were caught taking cash to ask questions in the Commons, and government officials were implicated in illegal arms sales to Iraq and Malaysia. The biggest policy disaster came with the 1996 discovery that **"mad cow" disease** (BSE), an incurable disease that attacks the brain stem, had spread from cattle to humans, killing 14 people. The government initially downplayed the problem and delayed ordering the mass slaughter of cattle. (A government minister even appeared on TV feeding hamburgers to his daughter.) Major protested a subsequent EU ban on British beef by blocking all EU business for several weeks, bringing UK–EU relations to an all-time low. Eventually all of Britain's cattle had to be killed and burned. And to this day British people are not allowed to give blood in the United States.

Dissent over relations with the EU was ravaging the Conservative Party, and John Major found it increasingly difficult to control his MPs. In 1995, Tory rebels defeated a government proposal to introduce an extra tax on heating fuel, a measure that would have hurt the poor. The same year, 89

Tory MPs voted against Major's reappointment as their leader. Clearly, the Tories had been in power for too long. But was Labour in a fit state to replace them?

THE RISE OF NEW LABOUR

After the 1992 election, the Labour Party feared that it would never be able to defeat the Tories and might even be overtaken by the Liberal Democrats as the main opposition party. In 1994, the party selected the young, charismatic Tony Blair as its new leader. Blair set about fashioning a new Labour Party that would recapture the middle-class and working-class voters who had defected to the Tories.

Following their defeat in 1979, the Labour Party was split between parliamentary leaders anxious to improve the party's electoral chances and trade-union bosses keen to retain their control over the party. The party's 1918 constitution had given Labour MPs the right to choose the party leader, but in 1981 an electoral college was introduced, with 40 percent of the votes in the hands of the trade unions. In 1983, **Neil Kinnock** became the Labour leader, and he waged a vigorous campaign to diminish union power and expel left-wing militants from the party.

After their defeat in 1987, the Labour leadership started to expunge leftist policies from the party program, dropping their commitment to reverse Thatcher's privatizations, to strengthen union power, and to give up Britain's nuclear weapons. Intraparty reforms shifted the balance of power away from union bosses toward the parliamentary leadership. The union vote at the annual party conference was cut from 90 percent to 50 percent, while the share of union contributions in the party budget fell from 80 percent to 40 percent thanks in part to an influx of cash from sympathetic business interests. The unions had been weakened by Thatcher's defeat of the miners and by changes in the economy. The share of manufacturing in total employment fell from 38 percent in 1956 to 19 percent in 1990, and the proportion of the workforce in unions fell from a peak of 53 percent in 1978 to 30 percent in 1995.

Kinnock resigned following the humiliating 1992 electoral defeat. After the untimely death of Kinnock's successor, John Smith, in 1994 Tony Blair took over as party leader. Blair, a deeply religious, 41-year-old lawyer from a middle-class background, sought to turn Labour into a modern, European, social-democratic party of the center. He wanted to redefine Labour's identity in order to convince the middle-class voter that Labour no longer favored the redistributive, "tax and spend" policies of the past. Britain had become a society of "two-thirds haves and one-third have-nots," and Labour would never get back into power by appealing to the "have nots" alone.

But what would "New Labour" stand for? It would not be enough simply to steal Thatcher's reform agenda. Blair used focus groups to try out ideas, such as communitarianism and the "stakeholder society," before hitting on the formula of the "**Third Way**." As Andrew Marr explained (*The Observer*, August 9, 1998): "The Third Way can be described, so far, by what it is not. It isn't messianic, high spending old socialism and it isn't ideologically driven, individualist conservatism. What is it? It's mostly an isn't." Many of the planks of Blair's new program were pulled straight from nineteenth-century liberalism. The state should stay out of economic management while providing moral leadership, investing in education and welfare, and devolving power to the regions. The centrist Third Way was encapsulated in the Labour slogan "Tough on crime, tough on the causes of crime." New Labour agreed with Margaret Thatcher that free markets are the best way to create prosperity, and they even accepted her reforms of public-sector management. In 1995, the Labour Party finally removed from its constitution Clause IV (put there in 1918), which called for state ownership of industry. All of this change was anathema to old-style socialists in the party.

Tony Blair described New Labour as a "pro-business, pro-enterprise" party, albeit one with a compassionate face. He stressed the values of community and moral responsibility in contrast with Thatcher's brazen individualism. (Famously, the "Iron Lady" had once said, "There is no such thing as 'society.'") Blair also appealed to British patriotism. He even said in May 1998: "I know it is not very PC [politically correct] to say this, but I am really proud of the British Empire."

New Labour was also more open to women. In 1993, the party decided that half of the new candidates selected by local parties for the next parliamentary election must be chosen from women-only short lists. (In 1996, a court struck down this rule as discriminatory.) As a result of these efforts, in the 1997 election 102 women were elected as Labour MPs. The total number of woman MPs from all parties rose from 60 in 1992 to 120 in 1997 before dropping to 118 in 2001 (18 percent of the total).

Tony Blair turned to an expensive and sophisticated U.S.-style media campaign to sell the New Labour image to the public. Along with a New Labour, there was to be a New Britain: sophisticated, multicultural, and hip (from "Rule Britannia" to "Cool Britannia"). Labour's main slogan was the patriotic "Britain Deserves Better." Campaign innovations included posters above urinals in pubs, saying "Now wash your hands of the Tories." In a bid to reassure the voters that their tax-and-spend policies were behind them, Labour pledged to maintain the Conservative government's spending limits for at least two years after the election. No new welfare initiatives were planned beyond a new scheme to make 250,000 unemployed youths take up government-sponsored jobs as a condition to qualify for welfare benefits, paid for by a tax on the windfall profits of the recently privatized utility companies.

Labour won a landslide victory in the May 1997 election. The Conservatives lost half their seats, and 10 percent of voters switched from Tory to Labour – the largest swing in the past century. Major went down to defeat despite a strong economic recovery, scotching the widely held notion that British election results are driven by economic performance. In June 1997, he was replaced as party leader by the uncharismatic 36-year-old **William Hague**.

Voters did not choose Labour because they preferred their program to that of the Tories, as their policies were nearly identical. Rather, the Tories were seen as divided, corrupt, and inept, whereas New Labour was trusted to do a more competent job of governing the country.

The only significant policy difference between the two parties was over Europe. Most Tories were skeptical about European integration. Prime Minister Major pursued a vague "wait and see" line, but two-thirds of Tory candidates spoke out against the EU. As recently as 1983, the Labour Party had called for Britain's withdrawal from the EU, which it saw as a capitalist plot. In contrast, Blair was adamantly pro-Europe, although he promised to hold a referendum before taking Britain into the single European currency.

One of the first acts of the new Labour government was the granting of independence to the Bank of England, a striking example of their rejection of the old policies of Keynesian demand management. Since its founding in 1694, the Bank of England had followed government advice in setting interest rates. From now on, like the U.S. Federal Reserve, the independent board of directors could fix rates as they pleased in order to prevent a rise in inflation. The head of the treasury, Gordon Brown, followed a tight monetary and fiscal policy, although he borrowed heavily to fund higher spending on health, education, and welfare.

BLAIR'S SECOND TERM

On June 7, 2001, the Labour government won a second consecutive landslide victory, while the Conservative Party scrambled to hold onto second place. People started to wonder whether the Conservatives, once the "natural party of government," would ever manage to win an election again. William Hague resigned as Conservative Party leader in the wake of the electoral defeat. Previously, Tory leaders had been elected by Tory MPs. In 2001, for the first time, the MPs picked the two leading contenders, and the party's 320,000 members selected the final winner. The pro-European Kenneth Clarke lost to former army officer Iain Duncan Smith. The Conservative Party remained deeply divided over European integration, and was split between modernizers and traditionalists.

In September 2003, Labour lost the Brent by-election, the first such loss since Tony Blair became party leader in 1994, but the Conservatives finished third behind the Liberal Democrats. In October 2003, the Conservative Party congress removed the ineffective Duncan Smith as leader and replaced him with the centrist Michael Howard.

Tony Blair proved to be a skillful political leader, asserting strong control over the Labour Party and steering public opinion in what David Goodhart has called a "media driven popular democracy." Blair used this power to pursue an ambitious agenda of domestic and foreign reform, with mixed results.

On the home front, Blair's New Labour has forged ahead with the most ambitious constitutional reforms that Britain has seen in the past one hundred years. First, there was the decentralization of power through the creation of Scottish and Welsh parliaments. Second was the abolition of hereditary peers in the House of Lords. Third was the introduction of a bill of rights and judicial review through the European Court of Human Rights. Finally, in 2003, a new department for constitutional affairs was introduced that will take over the judicial appointment process, although the final decision will still rest with the minister of justice (choosing from a list of nominees). This means the abolition of the post of lord chancellor, who formerly served as head judge, speaker of the House of Lords, and member of the cabinet, fusing all three branches of government in a single individual. There are plans to remove the law lords from the House of Lords and create a separate supreme court.

Some complained that Blair had introduced these reforms in a top-down manner, without extensive public comment. Constitutional expert Vernon Bogdanor explained (in *Prospect*, April 20, 2004): "We are transforming an uncodified constitution into a codified one, but in a piecemeal and pragmatic way."

Blair's biggest gamble was his resolute support for U.S. President George W. Bush in pursuing the war in Iraq. Blair had developed a close partnership with Bush's predecessor, Bill Clinton, whose views matched Blair's own, and had ambitious goals for Britain in helping to shape a new, more just world order at America's side. Such a vision was expressed in the speech Blair delivered in Chicago on April 22, 1999, in the midst of the NATO war to force Yugoslav troops out of Kosovo.

Blair followed the same strategy when Clinton was replaced as U.S. president by the conservative and initially isolationist George W. Bush. Blair even supported Bush's plan to build a missile-defense system, which led to the U.S. withdrawing from the 1972 treaty barring such a system's deployment. After the September 11, 2001, terrorist attacks in the United States, Blair expressed unequivocal support for the war on terror, mounting a diplomatic crusade to line up allies for the U.S. campaign. British troops took part in the war in Afghanistan. In return, Blair hoped to persuade Bush to tackle the roots of terror by restarting the peace process between Israelis and Palestinians and launching a war on poverty in Africa. Alas, such hopes were sadly misplaced, as Bush failed to act on any of these suggestions.

Things came to a head with the Iraq war. Blair persuaded the British Parliament that Iraq was in possession of weapons of mass destruction that could be launched at 45 minutes notice, according to an intelligence report released in September 2002 (later known as the "dodgy dossier"). Blair encouraged Bush to go through the United Nations, first sending in UN weapons inspectors into Iraq in August 2002 and then going back to the United Nations for endorsement of military action in February 2003 – when the UN inspectors were still asking for more time. Blair failed to foresee the strong Franco-German resistance, which forced the United States to go ahead with the invasion without UN support. British public opinion was against going to war without UN support but rallied behind the troops after the Parliament approved military action on March 18, 2003.

British participation in the Iraq war led to the resignation of two senior Labour ministers and the largest public protest demonstrations in decades. Criticism focused on the "45 minutes" chemical weapons claim contained in the "dodgy dossier." Reporter Andrew Gilligan of the BBC said that Blair's advisers had "sexed up" the intelligence claims in the dossier. A defense-ministry weapons expert, David Kelly, admitted that he was Gilligan's source and committed suicide on July 17, 2003. The subsequent **inquiry by Lord Hutton**, a senior judge, exonerated the government of any wrongdoing but led to the resignation of the two top BBC executives. The subsequent insurgency in Iraq, and obviously inadequate planning for postwar reconstruction, added to the criticism heaped on Blair. But he had managed to survive the biggest political crisis of his career.

Meanwhile, relations between the United Kingdom and Europe were in the doldrums. In October 2002, France and Germany rejected the British plan to reform the Common Agricultural Policy. Tony Blair welcomed the draft EU constitution in July 2003, having successfully resisted attempts by some EU members to extend majority voting to foreign affairs and taxation, which would have threatened Britain's capacity to pursue independent policies in these areas. Back in 1997, Blair had promised to hold a referendum to take Britain into the Euro zone if five economic conditions were met. Public skepticism about abandoning the pound sterling for the **Euro** caused Blair to postpone the referendum.

Blair's government displays at times an unstable mix of cynical populism and lofty idealism, explains David Goodhard, editor of *Prospect* magazine (June 19, 2003). New Labour moved away from the collective interest politics of previous decades toward identity politics and a focus on the individual citizen and consumer. Blair distanced himself from the traditional ideology and activist base of the Labour Party, and this left him vulnerable when political crises flared up, such as the outbreak of foot and mouth disease in May 2001, or the war in Iraq. Labour Party membership fell from

405,000 in 1997 to 280,000 in 2002, and the trade unions started cutting their financial contributions to the party to protest continuing privatization.

New Labour has had only limited success in delivering the promised improvements in public services through decentralization and increased competition. The public remains very dissatisfied over the quality of the health and education services, not to mention the accident-prone railways. (In October 2001, the privatized Railtrack collapsed and was taken back into public ownership.) Globalization of the economy means that the British state, like all states, now has less discretion in national economic policy than it did during the 1950s and 1960s. Increasingly, British policy is driven by informal networks of transnational corporate elites, not represented in the institutional structures of the Westminster model.

Despite discontent with the war in Iraq and poor public services, Blair was able to win a third term in the election he called in May 2005. Tory leader Michael Howard closed the gap with Labour by campaigning for tougher immigration rules, but the divisions in his party prevented him from attacking Blair's pro-European policies. Blair was now seen as a liability rather than an asset, and he said he would not stay on as Labour Party leader for another election.

Conclusion

Britain has a robust and successful political system that seems to have recovered from the economic stagnation and class warfare of the 1970s and 1980s. The Westminster model is no longer the "envy of the world," as was complacently assumed by many Britons during the nineteenth century. But the parliamentary system, with strong parties competing for office, has proved its mettle in producing strong governments capable of exercising leadership to tackle Britain's social and economic problems. The experience of countries in the "third wave" of democratization, during the 1970s and 1980s, seems to confirm that parliamentary systems are more successful than presidential systems in reconciling conflicting interests in society and, hence, promoting less violence and greater stability.

The major challenge facing Britain is the same one that confronts the other European countries: crafting transnational institutions to manage the global economy while maintaining the capacity to tackle social problems that arise at the national and regional levels, and also preserving national and subnational identities. Britain has been a follower rather than a leader in this process of international institution-building (such as the European Union), which is a reflection of its diminished role in the international system since the end of its empire.

TABLE 3.1. Key Phases in Britain's Development

Time Period	Regime	Global Context	Interests/ Identities/ Institutions	Developmental Path
1688–1832	constitutional monarchy, parliamentary sovereignty	imperial expansion	elite consensus on values, interests	capitalism, limited state
1832–1914	parliamentary sovereignty, electoral democracy	global hegemony based on naval power	extension of franchise	industrialization, free trade, gold standard
1918–1945	rise of Labour Party, three-party system, coalition governments	hegemony weakened, struggling to retain empire	intense social conflict	defensive
1945–1973	two-party competition	retreat from Empire, Cold War, U.S. alliance, exclusion from Europe	Keynesianism, welfare-state consensus	slow growth
1973–1979	two-party deadlock	entry into European Union, global recession	severe labor unrest, N. Ireland conflict	crisis
1979–1987	Margaret Thatcher dominant	economic globalization, second Cold War	organized labor crushed	neoliberalism: deregulation, privatization
1987–2004	Tony Blair's New Labour dominant, constitutional reform	economic globalization, European integration, war on terror	growth for middle class, business boom, Scots and Welsh devolution, role of immigrants	neoliberalism plus reformed welfare state multiculturalism

BIBLIOGRAPHY

Butler, David, and Denis Kavanagh. *The British General Election of 1997*. New York: St. Martin's Press, 1998.

Dunleavy, Patrick, Andrew Gamble, Ian Holliday, and Gillian Peele, eds. *Developments in British Politics No. 5*. New York: St. Martin's Press, 1997.

Foley, Michael. *The British Presidency: Tony Blair and the Politics of Public Leadership*. New York: Manchester University Press, 2001.

Geddes, Andrew, and Jonathan Tonge, eds. *Labour's Landslide*. New York: Manchester University Press, 1997.

Hutton, Will. *The State We're In*. London: Jonathan Cape, 1995.

Kavanagh, Denis. *Thatcherism and British Politics: The End of Consensus?* New York: Oxford University Press, 1990.

King, Anthony, et al., eds. *Britain at the Polls 1992*. London: Chatham House, 1993.

Marquand, David, and Anthony Seldon. *The Ideas That Shaped Modern Britain*. London: Fontana Press, 1996.

Robins, Lynton, and Bill Jones, eds. *Half a Century of British Politics*. New York: Manchester University Press, 1997.

Seldon, Anthony. *Major: A Political Life*. London: Trafalgar Square, 1998.

Seldon, Anthony, ed. *Blair Effect: The Blair Government 1997–2001*. New York: Little, Brown, 2001.

Stephens, Philip. *Tony Blair: The Making of a World Leader*. New York: Viking, 2004.

Stothard, Peter. *Thirty Days: Tony Blair and the Test of History*. New York: Harper Collins, 2003.

Thatcher, Margaret. *The Downing Street Years*. New York: Harper Collins, 1993.

IMPORTANT TERMS

British Commonwealth cultural association linking 53 former colonies of Britain.

"British disease" a high level of strike activity caused by powerful trade unions taking advantage of low unemployment to push for higher wages.

devolution the creation of regional assemblies in Wales and Scotland, debated since the 1970s and introduced in 1999.

Euro currency unit introduced in January 1999 for Germany and the 10 other members of the European Monetary Union. The German mark is now officially just a denomination of the euro, which fully replaced all national member currencies except for the British pound, in July 2002.

European Union (EU) now an organization of 25 European countries, in which West Germany or Germany has always played a key role. It originated as the six-member European Coal and Steel Community in 1951 and became the European Economic Community in 1958, gradually enlarging its membership and becoming known as the European Community (EC) until the Maastricht treaty of 1991 came into effect in 1993 and enlarged its authority and changed its name for most purposes to the EU.

Exchange Rate Mechanism (ERM) the common currency band of European Union currencies, which Britain joined in 1990 and was forced to leave in 1992.

Falklands War the 1982 conflict that resulted after Argentina had seized the British-owned Falkland Islands and a British naval task force was sent to recapture them.

Glorious Revolution the 1688 removal of the Catholic king James II by Protestant William of Orange, who accepted the principle of parliamentary sovereignty.

Greenpeace an environmental action group that saw its membership expand during the 1980s.

William Hague the leader of the Conservative Party, who replaced John Major in 1997 and who resigned after losing the 2001 election.

hereditary peers members of the House of Lords appointed by the monarch and whose title automatically passes down to their sons.

Her Majesty's Opposition the second-largest party in the House of Commons, which is critical of the government but loyal to the British state as symbolized by the monarch.

Hutton inquiry investigation into the government's actions leading Britain into the 2003 war with Iraq.

Keynesianism a philosophy of state intervention in the economy derived from the work of John Maynard Keynes, who argued that the Great Depression could have been avoided by increasing state spending.

Neil Kinnock the Labour Party leader during the 1980s who introduced reforms to decrease the power of trade unions in the party.

"mad-cow disease" scandal a political scandal in 1996 that followed the Conservative government's delay in taking urgent measures to stop the spread of the BSE disease, which was infecting humans.

Magna Carta the contract guaranteeing the rights of noble families that King John agreed to sign in 1215.

John Major Conservative Party leader who replaced Margaret Thatcher as prime minister in 1990 and resigned after losing the 1997 election.

"marginal" seats seats in the House of Commons that are closely contested and are likely to change hands between parties in an election (the opposite of "safe" seats).

Rupert Murdoch the Australian-born magnate who owns one-third of Britain's newspapers and has considerable political influence.

1984 miners' strike the coal miners' strike that was defeated by Margaret Thatcher, clearing the way for legislation limiting the power of trade unions.

"New Steps" program Margaret Thatcher's program to cut state bureaucracy and make it more responsive to citizens' interests.

No. 10 Downing Street the prime minister's residence and the place where the cabinet meets.

parliamentary sovereignty the power of Parliament, representing the people, to enact any law it chooses, unrestrained by a written constitution or the separation of powers.

Plaid Cymru the nationalist party in Wales that advocates more rights for the Welsh people, including use of the Welsh language.

Prime Minister's Question Time the thirty-minute period once a week during which the prime minister stands before the House of Commons and answers questions from MPs.

Social Democratic Party (SDP) a group of moderate socialists who broke away from the Labour Party in the early 1980s.

"Third Way" the new, moderate philosophy introduced by Tony Blair after he became Labour Party leader in 1994.

Tory the colloquial name for a member of the Conservative Party.

Unionists the Protestant majority in Northern Ireland, who want to keep the province part of the United Kingdom.

welfare state the program of state-provided social benefits introduced by the Labour Government of 1945–1951, including the National Health Service, state pensions, and state-funded higher education.

Westminster model the British system of parliamentary sovereignty, prime ministerial government, and two parties alternating in power.

STUDY QUESTIONS

1. What were the main features of the bipartisan consensus in British politics that lasted from the 1950s to the late 1970s?

2. Why did some observers argue that Britain was "ungovernable" in the 1970s?

3. Which aspects of British society were the targets of Margaret Thatcher's "revolution"?

4. Why did Margaret Thatcher fall from power in 1990?

5. What does Tony Blair mean by the "third way"?

6. What factors have been holding Britain back from greater participation in the European Union?

7. When did most British citizens get the right to vote, and why?

8. Why did Labour defeat the Conservatives so soundly in 1997?

9. How does the power of the prime minister compare with that of the U.S. president?

10. What are the strengths and weaknesses of the first-past-the-post electoral system compared with proportional representation? Is Britain likely to introduce PR in the near future?

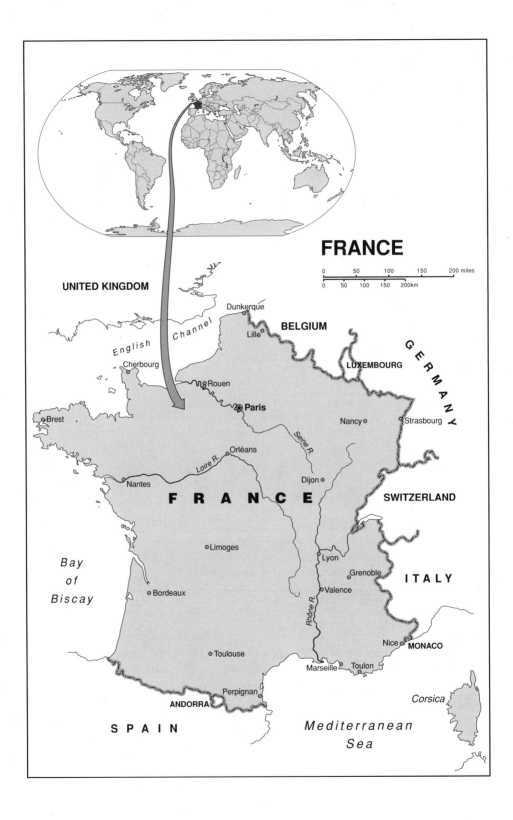

FRANCE

UNITED KINGDOM

English Channel

Dunkerque

BELGIUM

Lille

G E R M A N Y

Cherbourg

LUXEMBOURG

Rouen

Paris

Nancy

Strasbourg

Brest

Loire R.

Orléans

Seine R.

Nantes

F R A N C E

Dijon

SWITZERLAND

Limoges

Lyon

*Bay
of
Biscay*

Grenoble

I T A L Y

Valence

Bordeaux

Rhône R.

Nice

MONACO

Toulouse

Marseille

Toulon

Perpignan

Corsica

ANDORRA

S P A I N

*Mediterranean
Sea*

CHAPTER FOUR

France

Arista Maria Cirtautas

Introduction

If a new epoch of global politics is evolving in the first years of the twenty-first century, shaped by new forms of contestation and competition in "world-historical space and time," then France has been very much in the forefront of such developments both in the international arena of state competition and cooperation and in the domestic arena of state–society relations. Arguably, not since the revolutionary era of the eighteenth century has France played such a prominent role in reacting to competitive global pressures by attempting to recast not just domestic but also Europe-wide policies and institutions, all while playing an assertive international role as the most vocal Western critic of U.S. *hyperpuissance*, or hyperpower. Although the means may have changed – France is no longer launching revolutionary armies across Europe but has instead played an instrumental role in writing and then rejecting the new **European Union** constitution – the objectives of preserving not just French prestige but also the French concept of just government, as a viable alternative to prevailing orthodoxies, remains the same. Anglo-American liberal capitalism and U.S. military hegemony have simply replaced **monarchical absolutism** as the contested orthodoxy. At the same time, however, contemporary French society is almost as deeply divided as its historical predecessor over what exactly just government and a good society might entail in these uncertain times.

The central historic division between a progressive vision of an enlightened, universalizing civic order sustained by the "one and indivisible" republic on the one side and a reactionary conservative vision of a traditional, particularizing cultural order embodied by a paternalistic nation-state on the other side (with various radical interpretations of both visions on the far left and extreme right thrown in for good measure) has again emerged as a decisive fault line ordering political and social identities. Interestingly, not too long ago, in 1988, leading French historians, including Francois Furet, proclaimed an end to this type of French "exceptionalism," believing that the dramas, passions, and distinctive forms of French "political theatre" born out of the revolution had been replaced by a convergence of all major ideologies toward centrist, mutually tolerant, pragmatic, and technocratic positions similar to those of other Western European democracies. However, in the aftermath of the 2002 presidential election, when Jean-Marie Le Pen, the leader of the far right, anti-immigrant party, the **National Front**, garnered sufficient votes to challenge the front runner, **Jacques Chirac** (center-right), in the second ballot of the runoff election, the hope that France had ultimately crystal-lized around a moderate, normal *république du centre* (centrist republic) is clearly on much weaker ground. Instead, political scientists now analyze the French political system in terms of a "tripartite ideological space" character-ized by far-right, center-right, and center-left political identities and parties. Nor has the radical left departed the political scene, as France is home to a very active antiglobalization movement, producing, in the form of small farmer Jose Bové, one of antiglobalization's most heroic protest figures. When Bové stormed McDonalds (in France in 1999) and Monsanto (in Brazil in 2001) in defense of natural farming methods and national culinary traditions against the homogenizing juggernaut of globalizing agribusiness, even Pres-ident Chirac professed his admiration for the underlying values if not for the protest actions themselves. In hindsight, the *république du centre* of the 1980s and its convergence around a two-bloc (center-left versus center-right) political party system appears to have been a brief departure from the his-torical norm. Among Western democracies, France has always been notable for the range of often mutually antagonistic ideological positions represented in public life. In the contemporary context, for example, opinion polls reveal the French to be more openly racist than other Europeans. In an oft-cited 1999 poll, two-fifths of the respondents said that they were racist, while 51 percent were of the opinion that there were "too many Arabs" in France. At the same time, however, France also has numerous nongovernmental organi-zations, with large followings, dedicated to eradicating racism and promoting integration in French society.

The French Model: Continuity, Change, and Ambiguity

One can identify significant historical continuities in the contemporary era of French politics. Most dramatically, divisive political and social identities have been reinvigorated at the same time that France is again simultane-ously challenged by external pressures and challenger to the existing global order. Thus, even when participation in the international system has placed considerable strain on the French economy, in turn calling domestic political institutions and policies into question, French political elites have consistently sought and often found the means to play a central role in shaping or reshaping that system. Although the terms of international competition may have changed over time, from military competition in the eighteenth century to competition for global markets in the twenty-first century, the French response has been broadly similar: domestic reform or retrenchment combined with an international offensive to maintain France's position as a global or regional leader. Although the means may not always have been adequate to the ambitions, French civilization, state-building achievements, and intellectual and ideological traditions have all been considered exemplary of the modern nation-state and have thus had a powerful global impact both directly through the imposition of French imperial rule and indirectly through efforts at emulation or rejection. Similarly, today, France's longtime resistance to globalization (often understood as Americanization in France) and long-standing efforts to maintain a distinctive French-led European trajectory in international affairs have become increasingly salient (largely as a counterweight to American influence) to a broader international audience concerned about the instabilities of the post–Cold War world.

There is, however, an important difference from the past in that the governing institutions of the **Fifth Republic**, unlike the monarchy of Louis XVI, are largely seen as viable and appropriate vehicles for channeling domestic responses to external pressures and for defending France's international position. The basic institutional arrangements of the Fifth Republic are therefore not in question even as ideologically driven positions are taken on specific policies and reform proposals. Without a doubt, the strength and stability of France's post–World War II governing institutions represent a remarkable achievement, as France has experienced one of the most turbulent, complex, and contradictory paths of development toward democratic government of any state. Since the **French Revolution** (1789), democracy in France has been challenged and modified, attacked and replaced, and, ultimately, fully stabilized only after 1958 in the form of the current Fifth Republic. Whereas the United States has had only one constitution with 26 amendments in two hundred years, France has experimented with three monarchies, two empires, and five republics, as well as 13 written constitutions, during the same time period. Against this backdrop, the enduring legitimacy of the Fifth Republic represents an important disjuncture in the evolution of French politics, even as the enduring nature of ideologically cast "identity politics" represents an important element of continuity in French political history.

To gain a better understanding of these outcomes, three questions in particular logically follow as orienting points for our overview of French politics. First, why has the tendency toward intense ideological polarization become such a prominent and permanent legacy of the French Revolution? Elsewhere, in Britain and the United States, for example, the historical trend has been toward convergence around one central view of democracy, namely liberal-ism, under which different groups can claim rights and representation. In contrast, French politics has more often revolved around conflicts over the very nature of the polity, not just the opening of a broadly accepted polity to previously excluded groups. Second, how was the tendency toward exper-imentation with political institutions and regime types, another legacy of the Revolution, finally overcome with the post–World War II stabilization of a particular set of democratic institutions and practices even if a consensual view of democracy itself was never quite achieved? Third, how has France managed to project its domestic experiments onto a global scale while be-ing both vulnerable to international pressures and caught up in domestic contestations?

Put in terms of the analytical framework of this textbook, these questions focus our attention on the permanence of a particular type of identity-formation process, namely the tendency to subsume both social identities and material interests under the rubric of political ideologies. French liberalism, for example, has been supported by middle and professional class inter-ests but also by social identities constructed around urban, secular, and en-lightenment cultures. Conservatism, in turn, was supported by monarchical-aristocratic interests but also by social identities constructed on the basis of regional and/or religious affiliations. Radical socialism was logically sup-ported by the urban working classes but also by regional, workplace, and intellectual solidarities. Ideological convictions thus become central to po-litical life, inhibiting interest-based bargaining and promoting zero-sum ar-guments over what constitutes an appropriate and desirable polity. In this context, how do political institutions achieve stability? What are the enabling conditions for successful institutional engineering under conditions of ideo-logically driven polarization? Finally, how are national interests defined in a competitive international arena and in a tumultuous domestic arena? What enables the successful mobilization of available resources in the pursuit of these interests? Answering these questions as fully as possible requires both a historical perspective and a contemporary focus, as the specific mix of cre-ative (re)invention, stubborn persistence, and international assertiveness that characterizes French politics today is as much a product of historically rooted processes as of contemporary developments.

In a preliminary fashion, however, certain answers already suggest them-selves when we keep in mind France's ambiguous developmental position. As the birthplace of continental European democracy, France is clearly a case of early democratic development that set the terms for later developers through-out Europe just as the French monarchy had earlier set the terms for ratio-nalizing absolutism. In addition to the resources inherited from monarchical reforms (for example, a centralized administrative state and a modernized military), the French revolutionaries were subsequently able to mobilize unprecedented numbers of soldiers through their own innovations such as the *levée en masse* (the mobilization of all available human and material resources for wartime purposes, initiated in 1793), thereby enabling the revolution to sweep well across France's borders. Although France's economic base has historically been more fragile than Britain's, in other realms (state administrative capacity, military capabilities, and nation-building processes, for example) France has kept pace with its neighbor.

Endowments of early development can thus be seen as enabling conditions facilitating French abilities to project power and influence abroad. However, France is also the country that first experienced tremendous difficulties in institutionalizing a stable democracy when competing ideologies and interests mobilized to resist this new form of government both internally and abroad. These difficulties render France much more akin to later-developing countries that have faced similar challenges when the constellation of class interests and the proliferation of ideologies have prevented stable outcomes of any kind, let alone the institutionalization of democracy. Liberalism, reactionary conservatism, and radical socialism all emerged out of the crucible of the French Revolution and were carried forward in time both in France and elsewhere as reoccurring combinations of social identities and material interests mobilized politically according to the principles articulated by these ideologies.

Not surprisingly, given the antithetical principles of these three ideologies and the inability of any one social group or class to monopolize political life for too long, governing institutions were often only sustainable not on the basis of liberal democracy but on the basis of some variant of **nationalism** as a developmental ideology capable of unifying disparate interests and social identities around the shared goal of state-building and economic growth. In short, the French experience of attempting to promote developmental objectives in order to compete effectively in the international arena, often under the auspices of tenuous, nondemocratic regimes, represents the earliest manifestation of a pattern of political development that later-developing countries would find themselves replicating in part, if not in whole. Whereas the British pattern of institution-building has often been held up as the developmental model to emulate, it is French turbulence rather than British gradualism that is more exemplary of actual modernizing efforts around the world.

From Revolution to Republic

In a certain sense, of course, France remains an unambiguous early developer (see Table 4.1) in that many of the ideologies that have informed contemporary political conflicts around the world had their point of origin in the French Revolution and its aftermath. However, the privileged status or structural position of early development alone was clearly not sufficient in the French case to produce British-style domestic outcomes even if the resources generated by early development can be seen as a sufficient explanation for France's ability to shape global outcomes alongside of and in competition with Britain. Instead, we have to look to the particularities of French history in order to understand France's rather different trajectory of domestic development.

In this section, we will examine the historical factors that account for the problematic French experience with democratic institution-building even as French power and influence continued to be projected globally. Because the French Revolution is generally held to be the founding moment of modern France, it also represents the point of departure for our historic overview. Two crucial aspects of this "fundamental event," in the words of the historian Ernest Renan, will be addressed briefly: how it came to be such an extraordinary occurrence and how it came to have such a profound effect on French politics.

The analytical focus of this overview will be on demonstrating how the interplay among international pressures and domestic identities, interests, and institutions produced specific outcomes. Because no single factor is adequate in and of itself to explain a trajectory as complex as the French Revolution's, we have to consider the cumulative impact of the interactions among key variables. Normally social scientists strive for explanations that are as parsimonious as possible (by linking outcomes solely to material interests or to levels of socioeconomic development, for example). But an interactive approach places greater weight on combinatorial dynamics. From this perspective, how and when important factors interact is more important than isolating a single causal variable.

THE MAKING OF A SOCIAL REVOLUTION: DOMESTIC RESPONSES TO INTERNATIONAL CONDITIONS

Over the centuries, much has been written about the French Revolution. Indeed, it is one of the most studied of historical phenomena, a remarkable example of the collapse of a regime considered to be among the most powerful of European monarchies. From the reign of Louis XIV (1643–1715) on, the French monarchy had undertaken a highly successful program of consolidating the king's rule. Over time, the powers of the nobility to rule their lands as miniature kings had been broken, providing for the greater stability of the monarchy's borders and ensuring that the king's decrees would be followed from one end of the land to the other. Monarchical authority was thus increasingly centralized and rendered more absolute.

Although the autonomy of the nobility undoubtedly suffered in this process, ordinary French subjects benefited, as the monarchs were able to provide higher levels of law and order, freeing the countryside from bandits and improving the transportation infrastructure. As a result, the country as a whole grew more prosperous. Between 1713 and 1789, for example, French foreign trade increased fivefold. According to some accounts, half of the gold coins circulating in Europe on the eve of the Revolution were French. Moreover, France was the center of the intellectual movement of the Enlightenment. Throughout Europe, French was considered the principal language of the educated and aristocratic circles, allowing French literature, science, and philosophy to be read and followed far beyond French borders. In light of these successes and the resources at its command, how could the monarchy fail in its ongoing efforts to rationalize and modernize monarchical rule? How could the French Revolution, unlike the Russian or Chinese revolutions of the twentieth century, take place in what was perhaps the most admired and most advanced country of its day?

Most often, the decline of the monarchy and the turn to revolution have been explained in terms of class interests and, indeed, there is a general consensus in the literature that the Revolution was the by-product, if not the direct product, of an emerging middle class of professionals and entrepreneurs who felt disadvantaged by existing feudal institutions that privileged the monarchy and the aristocracy at their expense. By the middle of the eighteenth century, ordinary farmers and peasants, small craftsmen, and shopkeepers also became increasingly restive under their constrained living conditions and limited opportunities for advancement. For example, Alexis de Tocqueville, one of the first great historians to study the Revolution and the collapse of the ancien régime (the old regime), has emphasized the extent to which French peasants especially felt their interests and their dignity violated by old feudal obligations owed to the nobility and to the Catholic clergy. But, presumably, these material interests had been present for some time. What, then, accounts for the fact that they were successfully mobilized only in the late 1700s? Here, domestic responses to international competitive pressures enter into the picture. As Furet points out, the need of the French monarchy for money was "immense" as the necessary means for conducting the "interminable war for supremacy" waged not only against the Habsburgs (the royal house that ruled the Austrian empire of the time) but also against the British in such far-flung places as the American colonies. Successive efforts of the French rulers throughout the eighteenth century to rationalize the operations of the state to enhance efficiency and productivity had, however, fallen short of the desired effects. By mid-century, the monarchy was growing ever more incapacitated and unable to manage the complexities of the bureaucratic machinery of the state – including raising sufficient tax revenues to offset costs such as the financial assistance given to the American revolutionaries. Financial strain brought on by international commitments is clearly the context under which the immediate crisis of the ancien régime occurred, but similar revenue crises had been weathered before without leading to widespread social unrest. This time, however, the cumulative impact of monarchical reform efforts conducted during the past decades combined with this particular revenue crisis to produce the setting, the means, and the motives around which class interests could mobilize.

One might note here the irony of unintended consequences. As the French monarchs developed an absolutist regime to strengthen their rule, they also set in motion the very social, political, and economic forces that would undermine that rule. Economic prosperity and the decline of feudal institutions, both encouraged by the monarchy, created the conditions for the development of new propertied interests, both small and large, that by the late 1770s had greater material means to defend themselves against any perceived abuses of monarchical authority. The fact that this authority was increasingly seen as abusive is due also to previous monarchical policies that had raised levels of popular frustration. Thus, for example, the monarch had for a brief period of time opened higher offices in the state administration and military to men of talent in the middle class, only to close these opportunities in the wake of aristocratic protest. Frustrated ambitions on the part of an increasingly wealthy and educated social group ultimately provided the motive and legitimation for antimonarchical protest.

Additionally, had the French peasants never experienced the freedom of owning their own lands – if they had remained fully dependent on the nobility – they might not have so greatly resented the restrictions under which they lived. The erosion of feudal institutions, encouraged in part by monarchs interested in limiting the privileges of the nobility, had enabled wealthier peasants to acquire land rights, which, in turn, made poorer peasants increasingly restive and desirous of acquiring land of their own. Finally, even the nobility was frustrated by the reform efforts designed largely to curtail or abolish their privileges, such as exemption from taxation. An "aristocratic resurgence" was the result as members of the nobility in turn began to contemplate reforms that would limit the powers of the monarchy by giving the aristocracy and the clergy the right to rule alongside the king. According to the historian R. R. Palmer, widespread social discontent with the existing state of affairs had, by the 1760s, developed into a "revolutionary situation" characterized by the existing regime's loss of legitimacy and credibility. Previously accepted social, political, and economic circumstances were no longer considered valid, just, or reasonable given the degree to which the monarchy's own policies had promoted the transformation of latent interests into collectively held grievances against a common adversary, the old order itself.

Yet, why were British- (1688) or U.S.-style (1776) outcomes precluded in the ensuing efforts to do away with the ancien régime? Certainly, various social groups put forward ideas that replicated these earlier revolutions, demonstrating that "world-historical time and space" should be considered not only from the perspective of competitive pressures but also from the perspective of the global transmission of ideas and practices rooted as often in emulative diffusion as in coercive enforcement. The reform-minded nobility, for example, envisioned something like a constitutional monarchy that would guarantee certain crucial rights such as "personal liberty for all, freedom of speech and press, freedom from arbitrary arrest and confinement." The king would henceforth have to share authority with a permanent parliamentary body with the aristocracy as its most powerful component. In order to achieve this vision of a new community, numerous members of the aristocracy were even willing to give up their privileges and become more equal members of society. By and large, a constitutional monarchy along these lines would have been quite similar to the English model of government, and French nobles were no doubt influenced by what the English had achieved.

Unfortunately for the aristocracy in France, the world had changed since 1688, when the English nobility had successfully limited monarchical powers in favor of parliamentary authority. Significantly, the Enlightenment had transformed the world of ideas. French philosophers such as Voltaire, Diderot, Rousseau, and Montesquieu provided the philosophical and moral basis upon which the French middle classes, and quite a few nobles as well, began to contemplate an entirely new community – one that would be founded on the fundamental equality of all men, that could do without the monarchy entirely, that would reanimate the ancient republican traditions of self-government and civic virtue, and that would preserve and protect the inalienable rights of all citizens. Most importantly, the American Revolution, which had just taken place across the Atlantic, proved to many Frenchmen that these ideals of the Enlightenment could be given concrete form and substance in the creation of an entirely new form of government. Accordingly, the middle classes called for a parliament that would represent all the people (ultimately understood as the propertied men) of France equally without giving undo weight and power to the nobility. Such a parliament would serve to protect the fundamental equalities demanded by those of non-noble birth: equality in the state, equality in taxation, and equal access to public office and to the civil service. No longer would men of talent and merit be held back by hereditary privileges that denied them the right to pursue their interests and objectives. The type of community they envisioned, rooted in individual rights and liberties, is not too far distant from what was achieved in the United States. The fact that this program for revolutionary change failed to replicate the success of the U.S. case is, in large part, because of the range and intensity of lower-class mobilization that accompanied the downfall of the monarchy.

So far, we have seen that a financial crisis brought about by international pressures had combined with the cumulative effects of domestic reform efforts and the transnational diffusion of democratic ideas and practices to galvanize various nascent class interests into contesting the monarchy. Why that mobilization turned out to be so widespread, animated by such distinct ideological visions, and resistant to the restoration of any form of postmonarchical public order or authority is again usually explained simply with reference to socioeconomic conditions and material interests. Seen from this perspective, disparities in livelihood prompted not just a representation of class interests in the political arena but the subsequent, often literal, conflict of these interests as nobility, bourgeoisie, peasants, and the urban poor all sought to achieve their specific objectives after the collapse of the monarchy. However, levels of mobilization capable of producing sustained conflict are not just an automatic consequence of collectively held material interests and frustrated ambitions. Lower-class revolts, in particular, tend to subside rather quickly, as they did in the English and American revolutions.

In order for such revolts to be sustained, as they most remarkably were in the French case, additional barriers to lower-class collective action needed to be overcome, including a breakdown of the coercive apparatus of the state, the achievement of a degree of autonomy from overlords, and a breakdown of hierarchical worldviews, often religiously mandated, that function psychologically to keep people "in their place." In France, these barriers were substantially eroded, the first most rapidly and dramatically during the crisis months leading up to the revolution itself, when visible uncertainty characterized monarchical responses to social unrest, the second more gradually during prior generations as urbanization and the erosion of feudal privileges freed people from direct dependence on the nobility. Most importantly, however, the general political culture of French society had been changing in those years as well. Fueled unintentionally by the monarchy's own efforts to repress them, pamphlets denouncing the king and sexually ridiculing the queen found ever broader audiences as both literacy and cheaper printing technologies spread. Although the historian Roger Chartier warns that this "massive distribution of an aggressively disrespectful pamphlet literature" cannot be directly linked with the progressive delegitimation of the monarchy, it doubtlessly had an indirect impact on mobilization propensities by showing that open protest was possible. First the monarch's authority and subsequently all forms of public authority simply became less awe-inspiring and hence more susceptible not just to rumor and denunciation but to overthrow. As C. A. Bayly argues, "popular culture, beliefs, and representations of politics give us an important middle stage in a 'model' of revolution, standing between social tension and radical political breakdown." Most dramatically in the context of the French Revolution, "they acted as a kind of conceptual 'accelerator,' which brought fundamental political and social conflicts to the point of chaos." Significantly, the chaotic effects of these "conceptual accelerators" were enhanced in the French case by the degree to which different social audiences often drew different conclusions from very similar readings – readings that were perceived through the prism of specific social identities and material interests.

The vocabulary of citizenship and the rights of man may have been shared, as were the writings of Rousseau, but the inferences drawn were radically different. These differences can most clearly be seen in the contrast between middle-class revolutionaries and the impoverished urban laboring classes. With much passion, and often quite violently, urban groups demanded both basic economic necessities, such as lower bread prices, and political representation on their own terms. They, too, wished to have an active voice in governing the new political community – one that they envisioned in terms of universal economic and social rights, not just in terms of civil and political rights. In other words, their ideal community would provide for both equality of outcome and equality of opportunity. Centuries of economic oppression and deeply ingrained social, cultural, and institutional patterns had relegated peasants and wage laborers permanently to the lowest positions in the social hierarchy. It is therefore not surprising that their vision of the new republic called for the most complete level of equality. In this vision, they were supported by radical members of the more privileged classes, who interpreted Rousseau's writings, in particular, as a call to arms not just for a political revolution but also for a profound social revolution – a precursor to Marx's communism, in effect.

Additionally, the widespread political mobilization of the lower classes was again unintentionally facilitated by the degree to which France had been unified into one state under the monarchy. Events in one region were relatively rapidly transmitted throughout the country by publications and by word of mouth. Violent uprisings, whether in Paris or in the provinces, were therefore difficult to contain and to localize because of the administrative successes of the French monarchy in unifying a diverse and far-flung population. Unfortunately, the "proto-parliamentary" bodies, the **Estates-Général** (called up by King Louis XVI in 1788 to address his reform proposals) and subsequent revolutionary conventions, proved to be incapable of channeling or diffusing such discontent, as the orders in need of direct representation, the peasants and the urban *sans-culottes*, were not present. Unlike the British case, therefore, the institution of Parliament could not serve as a stabilizing factor given the degree to which political radicalization had made the indirect representation of the lower classes by their social "betters" inherently unstable. A combination of mutually reinforcing cultural and institutional factors thus adds to our understanding of how the French Revolution came to be characterized by an historically unprecedented social explosion of democratic claims-making that could not be readily controlled by the newly emerging elites (the middle classes) and their preferred system of government (parliamentary sovereignty).

When counterrevolutionary groups mobilized as well (led by members of the aristocracy and assisted by foreign monarchs) to protect and preserve hierarchical worldviews and traditional institutions such as the Catholic Church and the monarchy itself, civil war ensued. Not surprisingly, the First Republic is mainly associated with the years of **the Terror**, 1793–1795, when the unrest and violence of the laboring classes, along with armed conflict against the enemies of the Revolution, created a momentum that influenced the new legislature, the National Convention, to undertake extreme measures against internal and external enemies. Under the leadership of Maximilien-François-Marie-Isodore de Robespierre, head of the radical Jacobin group, the dominant force in the Convention, about 40,000 people from all social backgrounds were killed as enemies of the Republic. At the height of the Terror, even members of the Convention were put to death, including, ultimately, Robespierre himself. Order was only restored when **Napoleon Bonaparte**, fresh from his successes on the battlefields, acquired the prestige and the manpower he needed to take over the government in 1799.

In short, this is one dimension of what makes the French Revolution extraordinary, namely the actual unfolding of events in which democratic principles, widespread social mobilization, violence, institutional instability, and an eleventh-hour "rescue" by a singular leader all combined with unprecedented force. Another dimension, however, of what gives this revolution its enduring resonance lies less in the events themselves, remarkable though they may be, and more in their impact on future developments – specifically, how the Revolution structured future outcomes by reconfiguring the political, cultural, and socioeconomic landscape of France. Having seen how international factors, domestic interests, identities, and institutions converged to produce a social revolution in France, we now consider how that revolution, in turn, effected the subsequent formation of identities, interests, and institutions as well as France's ability to remain competitive internationally.

IN PURSUIT OF THE REPUBLIC: POSTREVOLUTIONARY IDENTITIES, INTERESTS, AND INSTITUTIONS

During the course of the Revolution, new political identities, such as citizens and republicans, and new political ideologies, such as liberalism, **nationalism**, **conservatism**, and proto-socialism, were given form and substance. As the Revolution receded into the past, these ideologies continued to represent, in the words of Maurice Agulhon, "particular and incompatible attachments inspired by passions" not readily tempered by existing institutions or by popular acceptance of a more or less unified national community. A general recognition of common Frenchness, in other words, did very little to mitigate the "moral civil war" between secular **republicanism** ("liberty, equality, and fraternity") and religious conservatism ("authority, hierarchy, order") that came to define French political culture in the aftermath of the

Revolution. As Agulhon goes on to note, the fault lines between the two sides were so deep that "each was the embodiment of evil for the other." In addition to this central line of demarcation, each side was also split between a radical or revolutionary tradition and a more moderate tradition oriented toward the rule of law.

So, how exactly did the Revolution give rise to both polarization and fragmentation? Clearly, the decision of the initial revolutionary regime to subordinate the Catholic Church to its power and authority played an important role in setting clerical and anticlerical forces into motion. During the first years of the Revolution, the revolutionary assembly (the provisional representative body after 1789) dispossessed the Church of its lands and its role in public education (then largely in Church hands), decreed that bishops were to be elected by all citizens, not appointed by Rome, and finally demanded that priests take an oath of loyalty to the new constitution. Inevitably, the pope condemned the entire Revolution and all it stood for in 1790, thereby initiating a "war of religion" that would divide French society for generations. Although the assembly's effort to control the church has been called the "greatest tactical blunder of the Revolution," the effort itself was consistent with enlightenment principles and the belief in a universal form of republicanism that is loath to recognize any particularism, be it religious, regional, or social. To this day, the French government (and a large portion of French society) reacts negatively to the intrusion of religious symbols in public life not just as a defense of the separation of church and state but as a defense of the "one and indivisible" secular republic.

Paradoxically, the focus on universal morality, principles, and values fostered during the course of the Revolution served to enhance tendencies toward ideological fragmentation as well. Because the particularisms of **feudalism** (specific privileges, rights, duties, and obligations linked to social standing) were under attack on all sides, all sides consequently attempted to cast their views of what should replace the monarchy in terms of the general good, not specific or particular rights and interests. Thus, even though the various political orientations were clearly reinforced by particular social identities and material interests, the principles put forward were likely to be universal in scope and ambition. Working-class radicalism, for example, was clearly class-based but also fueled by the conviction that a social and political order founded on the interests of the working class would be of universal benefit. In this context, sustaining a comprehensive revolutionary agenda for political transformation can appear tenable to a minority of adherents even in the face of evident objective difficulties in actually coming to power. The resulting continuity of extremisms on both sides of the political spectrum did much to fuel the class hatreds that further served to divide French society. Even as late as the 1930s, these hatreds played a consequential role in the French collapse against Hitler's invasion. According to Agulhon, for example, "one of the most sinister and enigmatic moments in French history" is rendered more explicable when one remembers that for substantial numbers of property owners a fate under Hitler was preferable to the continued political advancement of their own radical working class.

Although class hatreds may have been tempered over time, substantial continuities remain evident in contemporary French politics given the degree to which French public opinion still supports, as Elgie points out, a "huge" list of competitive political parties ranging from radical Trotskyites (followers of Russian Communist leader Leon Trotsky) on the left to counterrevolutionary reactionaries on the right, many of which can be traced back to distinct historical traditions and precursors. In large part, the sustainability of these political traditions over time can be explained by the extent to which they became actual subcultures in their own right capable of reproducing themselves through socialization and institutionalization. Fostered by the extreme politicization of social, cultural, and intellectual realms in the aftermath of the Revolution as all spheres of life attempted to address the ongoing "crisis of meaning and authority," and carried forward by an active press and associational life, the original interests and social identities mobilized during the Revolution fused into more permanent cultures with their own organizations, media, symbols, heroes, rituals, and repertoires of political action. As postrevolutionary French political development provided ample crises and struggles around which mobilization could take place, the collective memories of the Revolution itself were constantly reinforced, and these memories acted as a further transmission belt linking past and present. Against this background, it is not surprising that political identities remain highly salient in structuring French responses to new socioeconomic and cultural realities. For example, the predominant responses to the problems of integrating the largest Muslim population in Europe have fallen neatly along secular republican (enhanced civic education efforts combined with the banning of religious symbols, such as Muslim headscarves or Jewish skullcaps, from display in state schools – a controversial ban that was enacted in March 2004) and reactionary conservative lines (calls to ban immigration).

Turning from identities to the interests and institutions shaped by the Revolution, we see that sociologist Barrington Moore's famous dictum "no bourgeoisie, no democracy" needs to be qualified. The presence of substantial middle-class interests may be a necessary condition for early forms of democratic institution-building, but it was hardly sufficient, as the French case demonstrates. Although the Revolution, in fact, promoted middle-class interests almost exclusively, by enacting numerous laws that promoted "free economic individualism" for example, this was not enough to guarantee the support of the bourgeoisie for a democratic Republic. Basically, the Revolution created both winners and losers that were unwilling to support a fully democratic, representative form of government in subsequent years. Instead, clear losers such as the royal family (although Louis XVI was beheaded in 1792 for treason against the revolutionary authorities, he left behind a brother who would continue struggling from abroad to restore the throne), the nobility, and the clergy wished to overturn the Revolution and return to the past. Moreover, the newly enriched property owners and the wealthier peasants, although they would not endorse a full restoration of monarchical powers, did ultimately come to support any form of government that could restore order and guarantee the rights and properties they had already obtained.

Given this pattern of interests, and the violent excesses and weaknesses of the First Republic, it is not surprising that considerable social support existed for Napoleon's seizure of power and for all of the restorationist regimes that followed. Memories of the Terror, in particular, frightened propertied France with nightmare images of lower-class rebellion and radicalism, rendering the upper classes more susceptible to authoritarian rule. In effect, during all of the **restorationist regimes**, a majority of French citizens were willing to sacrifice extensive political rights, such as universal suffrage and truly representative government, for the guaranteed maintenance of their civil rights and their property rights. This willingness was enhanced by the extent to which these regimes, from Napoleon on, actually did carry out the Revolution's objective of abolishing the remnants of feudal privilege on behalf of a liberal middle-class reform agenda that assured universal legal equality, property rights, and opportunities for advancement for the bourgeoisie. As R. R. Palmer notes, the Napoleonic codes (the body of law instituted by Napoleon) in particular "set the character of France as it has been ever since, socially bourgeois, legally equalitarian, and administratively bureaucratic."

In addition to interests, institutional factors also generated support for alternatives to the republican forms of government initiated during the Revolution. The constitution of 1791, in particular, began the French democratic tradition of vesting all powers in a unicameral elected assembly. The tendency of French republicans to associate proper democratic governance with a preponderance of powers given to the legislature – a tendency overcome only after World War II – originated in the revolutionary struggles against the executive powers of the French monarchy. From that time on, the executive component of government came to be associated with antirevolutionary, antirepublican forces. However, governing without a strong executive branch led to problems that pushed French moderates, conservatives, and reactionaries alike to support the reintroduction of "strong man" rule. Consequently, for almost the next one hundred years, French governments oscillated between the soft authoritarianism of the executive-based restorationist regimes and efforts to return to republican (i.e., legislative) rule, efforts that led eventually to the establishment of the **Third Republic**, which, in the French context, lasted a remarkably long time, from 1870 until 1940 and the outbreak of World War II.

Given the extent to which restorationist regimes supported middle-class interests, offered effective governing institutions, and legitimated themselves, often quite successfully, as transcending the "moral civil war" in French society by embodying the French nation in the person of the ruler, it seems surprising that republican government ever returned. Explaining this remarkable transition is again best accomplished through a combinatorial lens that takes a number of factors into consideration: the impact of the Revolution on state-sponsored socioeconomic development, the subsequent ascent of pro-republican interests and identities, and the facilitating context of particular international conditions.

Fundamentally, the Revolution had succeeded in legitimating and, indeed, mandating the emergence of a more modern France, as exemplified by a progressive, rationalized state administration staffed by men of talent and merit rather than of birth and breeding, and by a more uniformly prosperous society. Because even the restorationist regimes promoted modernization under liberal auspices, they, too, fostered the Revolution's developmental objectives, albeit under antirevolutionary forms of government. Their successes ultimately empowered the social groups and individuals that had remained committed to republican values, just as the monarchy's reforms had once unintentionally empowered precisely those classes that would rise against the king. Thus, the intensity of postrevolutionary political cleavages, which tended to be reinforced by socioeconomic cleavages, began to diminish in the late 1800s as the economic well-being and social security of all levels of French society were enhanced.

Under conditions of increasing prosperity, republican supporters were able to gain the resources needed to pursue their interests and implement their vision of just government. Importantly, in spite of the benefits of the restoration regimes, significant groups in French society, especially the lower middle classes, the growing working class, and peasant families that had benefited from the land redistributions of the revolutionary era, had remained republican in both political and cultural orientation. In their eyes, socioeconomic development was, in and of itself, insufficient and incomplete if unaccompanied by political democracy. This belief represents perhaps the most significant positive legacy of the Revolution, a legacy that would set France apart from other modernizing European states, such as Germany, that were content to pursue development without democracy. As we have seen, based on a combination of material interest and heroic republican identity forged originally during the Revolution, and subsequently carried forward in new periods of conflict and contestation, an enduring commitment to republicanism had been maintained over time among these groups. Republican beliefs therefore again acted as a "conceptual accelerator" linking socioeconomic development and material interests to particular political outcomes.

Domestic realignments of identities and interests in the course of socioeconomic development do not, however, fully explain the transition to the Third Republic in 1870. International factors also played a significant role. In general, when military defeats, such as Napoleon's famous downfall at Waterloo, are added to the inability of the postrevolutionary French economy to compete in the emerging global markets on equal terms with the British and German industrial sectors and with U.S. agricultural production, continued French vulnerability to international pressures is clearly evident. French defeat in the Franco-Prussian war of 1870, in particular, fundamentally discredited the restorationist regime of Louis-Napoléon (Napoléon III), thereby paving the way for a greater acceptance of alternative forms of government just as diminished economic differences had shifted social support toward republicanism.

Hence, even conservative nationalists were willing to give the Third Republic a chance to redeem French pride and prestige, especially after the new government demonstrated its willingness to use force to ensure stability by brutally crushing a radical republican uprising in Paris in the earliest months of its existence. International competitive pressures did not just facilitate domestic changes, however. They also fueled French efforts to exert influence on the international system. From the days of the Revolution onward, France had attempted to maintain a global presence commensurate with Britain's, regardless of cost. Thus, even when the country's economic base was inadequate to support sustained military campaigns against competing powers in Europe itself, less costly colonies were pursued abroad. The Third Republic also succumbed to this tradition as imperial expansion was propelled forward by a potent synthesis of nationalism, republican universalism, economic interests in protecting key markets and access to raw materials, and military-bureaucratic interests in promoting opportunities for career advancement abroad.

Although never as globally dominant (or as profitable) as the British Empire, postrevolutionary French empires did have a powerful impact not only on their colonies, where French policies of direct rule and attempted cultural assimilation left behind profoundly altered societies, but on Europe itself, where Napoleon's short-lived empire changed the course of European history as struggles for or against French political innovations took deep root across the continent, playing themselves out in pro- and antidemocratic conflicts that would last well into the twentieth century. With an inadequate economic resource base and a deeply divided society, how was France able to project so much power on a global scale in the aftermath of the Revolution? A combination of capacity and necessity provides something of an answer – the capacity generated by a strong administrative state, a popular, well-endowed army, and a deeply felt loyalty to *la grande nation*, and the necessity generated by domestic divisions that could often only be bridged by the shared objective of promoting French glory and prestige abroad.

By the end of World War II, however, imperial overreach had rendered this form of projecting French power and influence abroad untenable. The resulting decolonization crisis again set in motion both profound domestic changes (the birth of the Fifth Republic in 1958) and the pursuit of international influence by different means (most significantly partnership with Germany in the evolving structure of what is now known as the European Union). As in the case of the Third Republic, political outcomes (in this case, the institutional innovations of the current republic) were sustained and legitimated by a convergence of identities and interests as well. Importantly, the founders of the Fifth Republic used the powers of the state to ensure the permanence of this convergence by fostering economic and social policies that would tie all social groups as strongly to the republic as possible. If the levels of socioeconomic development conducive to the evolution of the Third Republic had once been produced accidentally or unintentionally by restorationist regimes, they would now be pursued most vigorously and consciously by the agents of the republican state. In the process, a republican identity rooted in the ideals of equality and fraternity was reinforced over time to the point where even in a 2001 poll, 56 percent of the respondents said that their idea of France was a "country of solidarity and social justice."

Contemporary Politics

THE INTERPLAY OF INTERESTS AND IDENTITIES
IN THE FIFTH REPUBLIC

Founded in 1958 by General **Charles de Gaulle**, leader of the Free French (non-occupied France) during World War II, the Fifth Republic experienced a tumultuous and inauspicious beginning. Many observers at the time believed that this latest republic would be as short-lived as the postwar Fourth Republic, which had survived only thirteen years (1945–1958) before succumbing to parliamentary paralysis in the face of numerous postwar crises. Among these crises, the most significant was the inability of the French government to manage a peaceful process of decolonization. Instead, wars raged in Indochina and in **Algeria** as the French colonial presence was violently resented and resisted. The war in Algeria proved to be especially costly, as members of the French armed forces, dissatisfied with the conduct of the war, staged a putsch in Algeria that brought down the Fourth Republic, thereby paving the way for de Gaulle's ascent to office. Although this means of coming to power awakened fears of a return to one-man rule in the tradition of the Bonapartes, the political and military impasse was so great that existing political parties and the general public were willing to entrust de Gaulle with the formation of a new government. Remarkably, de Gaulle did preside over the creation of a lasting republic, giving it constitutional and institutional form and substance. In the process, de Gaulle also established the basic parameters of the crucial policy domains – foreign, economic, and social – that remain in effect to this day. Following a brief overview of these policies, the remainder of this chapter will focus on the contemporary institutions and policy-making mechanisms of the Fifth Republic.

Under de Gaulle's leadership, the new republic withdrew from Algeria and provided a new purpose for the military in establishing France as a nuclear power. Although the price of Algerian withdrawal was high – another attempted military putsch in 1961, an attempt on de Gaulle's life in 1962, and, ultimately, a reanimation of ultraconservative right-wing nationalist forces – de Gaulle had the support of the vast majority of the French population, which favored decolonization. Although fraught with fewer dangers, developing an independent nuclear arms capacity also came at a price – diplomatic conflict with the United States and withdrawal from NATO command structures. In spite of these difficulties, de Gaulle persisted in his policies because he believed they were crucial prerequisites to the attainment of the active international role he envisioned for France. For de Gaulle, even in a bipolar Cold War world, France, as a unique source of universal culture, rights, and freedoms, had to retain its historic position of aloof grandeur, succumbing neither to the patronage of the United States nor to the blandishments of the Soviet Union. Overall, French foreign policy adheres, to this day, to the course set by de Gaulle: alliance with the West while maintaining independent maneuverability in the pursuit of national objectives. In order to sustain this maneuverability since the collapse of the Soviet Union and the return to a more unipolar international system dominated by the United States, France has reverted to the policy of competitive balancing it once maintained vis-á-vis the British when Britain was the dominant global power.

To further restore France's international position, as well as strengthen the republic's domestic support, a state-led program of economic development and recovery was initiated after World War II in order to enhance the competitiveness of French industries. Again under de Gaulle's leadership, state control over crucial sectors such as energy, transportation, insurance, and banking was established, while key companies such as Renault were nationalized. For the next thirty-odd years, until the mid-1970s, the payoffs of this **"directed" economy *(l'économie dirigée)*** were notable. France had the highest annual growth rate, 5.8 percent on average, of all industrialized nations, including the United States. By the mid-1980s, after a second wave of nationalizations initiated by the Socialist government of President François-Maurice Mitterand (1981–1995), state control extended over 24 percent of the French economy.

Although the process of nationalization has come to an end, and many firms were even reprivatized during the late 1980s, state control over the economy remains considerable. State-controlled financial institutions, for example, still distribute two-thirds of French credit, while as many as 1,500 companies remain under state control. Even a growing awareness of the extent to which planning might impede competitiveness and growth has, for the time being, failed to produce a sustained rollback of the state's involvement in the economy. Nor have European Union policies, designed to create a level playing field across the single market, served to curb French enthusiasm for giving state support and subsidies to firms and industries designated as "national champions." In fact, French state-led, *dirigiste* policies are increasingly at odds with EU competition and monetary policies and increasingly out of step with global liberalizing market trends.

The reason for this failure to adapt to international norms lies in the political and social benefits that are thought to accrue from the policies of state-regulated capitalism. De Gaulle himself clearly believed that the state provided the best means, as he put it in a 1944 speech, "to direct the economic struggle of the whole nation for the benefit of all, to improve the life of every Frenchman and every Frenchwoman." In France, trust in the state's ability to transcend narrow sectoral and individual interests in pursuit of the greater general interest, a trust that goes back to the days of the French revolution, obviously outweighs any faith in the self-regulating forces of the free market (the "invisible hand").

In addition to state-led economic planning, de Gaulle and other French postwar leaders, such as Robert Schuman and Jean Monnet (principal architects of what was to become the European Union), recognized the value of European economic integration as a means to assert French influence in a new forum. In its earlier phases, European economic integration also dovetailed quite nicely with French economic policies, providing additional resources with which to target specific sectors for growth and development while protecting threatened, but politically essential, sectors such as French agriculture from unacceptable levels of decline.

To assure the success of integration efforts, French postwar leaders were even willing to reconcile with Germany. Indeed, this reconciliation possibly represents de Gaulle's greatest foreign policy accomplishment, as the Franco-German relationship provided a vital guarantee for peace in postwar Europe, as well as becoming the pivotal decision-making axis determining the course of European integration. As one pundit put it, "European officials in Brussels spoke French, and West Germany's economic strength was a perfect fit with French political leadership." Although de Gaulle's emphasis on maintaining national sovereignty rights within the context of increased cooperation and integration has been replaced by a focus on the merits of strengthening the EU's supranational institutions and joint, policy-making capabilities, the relationship with Germany remains pivotal given a shared interest in further developing the integrationist project so that the EU can serve more adequately as a counterbalance to U.S. power and as a means of preserving the models of managed capitalism that both countries value over unrestricted free-market policies.

Even if the EU that France initially helped to create is currently more liberal (in the sense of being too free-market-oriented) than the French would like, French elites (unlike their British peers) remain committed to using all of the policy instruments, institutional resources, and informal mechanisms of influence at their disposal within the context of the EU to promote and pursue national objectives. As the Minister of the Interior, and later Prime Minister, Dominique de Villepin, stated succinctly: "France needs Europe and Europe needs France." Thus, French leaders have been at the forefront of EU developments: former president Valéry Giscard d'Estaing flamboyantly (and not uncontroversially) steered the convention that produced the EU's first constitution (largely in keeping with French interests), while current president Chirac has been abrasively instrumental in getting the member states to approve the document in principle. (Actual promulgation will have to wait until each member state ratifies the constitution either by parliamentary vote or popular referendum.) Unfortunately for French political elites, French citizens did not support the new constitution for Europe given the extent to which de Gaulle's emphasis on maintaining the independent ability of the French state to act on behalf of the French nation (not just internationally but domestically via welfare policies that are now threatened by EU policies) has retained its popular appeal.

In social policy, de Gaulle's government initiated a state-led program of welfare measures designed to enhance the living conditions of postwar French society. At the time, France was in the midst of a population boom that required specific measures above and beyond the typical characteristics of the European welfare state such as guaranteed health care and pensions, and greater job security. For example, the government embarked on an extensive project of constructing subsidized housing throughout France. To this day, 13 million people in France, almost one-quarter of the population, live in such housing projects. Since the late 1990s the government has allocated substantial funds to renovate the worst of the projects, especially those that house almost exclusively immigrant populations, where the conditions of life have deteriorated to the point of becoming a national policy priority. More successfully, the state developed an extensive network of child care facilities (French nursery schools are deemed to be among the best in the world), as well as providing direct financial subsidies to families with children. France currently devotes nearly 4.5 percent of its GDP to family policy – more than any other country in Europe. Not surprisingly, birth rates in France are stable, and the country is not facing the same type of demographic crisis as its neighbors Germany and Italy, where declining birth rates are rapidly becoming a public-policy obsession. In health care as well, an extensive state-sponsored system was established that currently takes up 10 percent of GDP, the highest level of spending in the European Union. In general, investment in infrastructure has been high, leading one British observer to note that although France breaks the rules of Anglo-Saxon economics, the country works: "its health system is the world's best, its public transport is outstanding and its towns and cities are tidier, better-organized places than their UK counterparts."

Although these provisions failed to diminish all sources of social discontent, as de Gaulle himself ultimately resigned the presidency in the wake of student uprisings in 1968, they did ensure that postwar economic recovery was not limited to too narrow a section of French society. Indeed, most observers are struck by the rapid pace of change in French society since World War II. From a tradition-bound, rural, Catholic, peasant-based society, France has been transformed into a postindustrial society where all classes can, in theory at least, share similar lifestyles and consumption patterns. The reduction of the work week to 35 hours (mandatory since January 2000, down from 39 hours, with no loss of pay) for full-time employees of large and medium-sized firms, making France the only EU country to initiate a sizable reduction in working hours, represents a further step to equalize lifestyles – while also encouraging more part-time employment as a means of cutting back the stubbornly high unemployment rate of 10 percent on average.

The success of de Gaulle's government in overcoming both its early problems and in laying the policy groundwork for all subsequent governments of the Fifth Republic, whether under Gaullist or Socialist leadership, can be explained with reference to three major factors: the leadership abilities of de Gaulle himself, the impact of World War II on France, and the novel institutional arrangements of the republic. First and foremost, the Fifth Republic was a product of what one historian has called de Gaulle's "inexhaustible originality." Drawing on considerable resources of intelligence, courage, and a not insignificant amount of self-confidence, de Gaulle was capable of envisioning a completely new form of government for his beloved France, while his practical skills as a politician ensured that he would have sufficient support to carry out his plans. In forming his own political party/movement in the late 1950s (the Gaullists), which still exists in today's political arena, de Gaulle was able to rally to his cause a significant number of center-right political interests, ranging from republicans to nationalists to Christian Democrats. Mindful of the limits of sectarian party politics, however, de Gaulle made every effort to appeal to the population at large for his mandate. The birth of the Fifth Republic was therefore validated and legitimated by a series of referenda beginning with a vote on the new Constitution (approved in September 1958 by 80 percent of the voters in a turnout of 85 percent) and ending with a vote on the direct election of the president (approved in October 1962 by almost 62 percent of the voters). In this context, de Gaulle was one of the first political figures to use the new medium of television with remarkable effectiveness. His physical stature, his voice, and his use of language and song to convey his message all resonated quite powerfully with the wide new audience that television could provide. Quite simply, de Gaulle was the right man at the right time.

However, even though de Gaulle did not turn out to be a twentieth-century Bonaparte, he remains a controversial figure. For some critics, he was too much the populist demagogue, whereas for others he was too much the high-handed autocrat; but both sides agree that he was not a republican in the traditional French understanding of the term. His disdain for conventional party politics and for parliamentary government as practiced by the first four French republics was quite apparent. Yet had de Gaulle been alone in this disdain, he would not have succeeded in his objectives no matter how much talent and charisma he possessed. The fact that de Gaulle's attitudes were representative of broader social and political opinions and interests in the aftermath of World War II represents an additional factor that promoted both his career and the rise of the Fifth Republic.

In many ways, the impact of World War II on French political culture had been a positive one, allowing old conflicts to be overcome and paving the way for a new consensus to emerge in the aftermath of the war. In the interests of promoting national survival, long-standing conflicts between classes, between political camps, and between clerical and anticlerical groups were set aside, if not entirely forgotten. A consensus emerged that France, in order to survive after the war, would have to reform both its economy and its polity in order to enhance competitiveness and efficiency. France could clearly no longer afford the luxury of its chaotic parliamentary-based republics. Nor, having just fought a reactionary fascist regime – Nazi Germany – did the soft authoritarianism of France's own conservative governments seem attractive any longer. The only solution was a strong liberal government that could ensure national survival. Such a government was not just desired on instrumental grounds, however. A new consensual identity, based on the commonalities inherent in both Christian and socialist humanism, had also emerged. In the face of the Nazi regime, French Catholics and socialists in particular, old antagonists since the days of the Revolution, discovered that the values they held in common far outweighed their differences. Consequently, the political ideals (a fusion of patriotism, liberalism, and humanism) and the interests that underlaid the founding of the Fifth Republic, although most clearly articulated by de Gaulle, were widely shared in the aftermath of World War II.

The time was accordingly right for a new type of republic that would be based not on legislative supremacy but on a strong executive branch capable of providing efficient and timely leadership. The institutional innovation of the Fifth Republic was therefore to rehabilitate executive leadership (which had, since Napoleon's regime, been associated with undemocratic, conservative forms of government) by embedding it in a constitutional context. The role of the presidency in the new republic thereby took on tremendous significance. Like the U.S. president, the French president is empowered to provide national leadership – initiating legislation, conducting foreign policy, and overseeing military and strategic concerns. Beyond this, however, the French president, like the British monarch, also serves as a national symbol of unity, transcending political interests and conflicts. To facilitate this transcendent role, the constitution of the Fifth Republic provides for a prime minister (drawn from the parliamentary majority) as well, whose role it is to conduct the daily affairs of government. In addition to removing the presidency from the wear and tear of mundane politics, this semipresidential system, characterized by a **dual executive system** wherein the president is head of the state and the prime minister is head of the government, was designed by de Gaulle to promote two kinds of leadership, innovation and implementation. The president innovates, whereas the prime minister implements.

For all of its complexity, this system has generated able leadership since the republic's founding and has survived several crucial challenges: the first when de Gaulle resigned and a successor was successfully elected, thereby alleviating concerns that the republic's institutions were too closely linked to their founder; the second when a Socialist, François Mitterand, was elected president in 1981, thereby alleviating concerns that the institutions were somehow rigged to exclude the left permanently from power; and the third when the presidency under Mitterand had to come to terms for the first time with a prime minister from another party. (In 1986, Jacques Chirac became prime minister when his center-right party won a parliamentary majority in that year's election.) This so-called **co-habitation** situation did in fact alter the balance of power between the two executives without, however, fundamentally destabilizing the system. Nonetheless, co-habitation increasingly produced policy stalemates during the 1990s as presidents and prime ministers from different parties competed for power and electoral influence, and hence it was targeted for reform. The fourth challenge to the French republic came in 2000 when the original seven-year term of the presidency was reduced to five years in a popular referendum. Presidential and parliamentary votes now correspond more closely in time in order to reduce co-habitation outcomes.

In short, establishing a strong but adaptable presidency, a "republican monarchy" that fused traditional and democratic bases of authority, was the vital, if not entirely uncontroversial, institutional ingredient needed to stabilize the postwar French republic. In conjunction with the convergence of identities and interests produced by World War II and sustained by de Gaulle's postwar policies, the successful institutional design of the Fifth Republic has finally overcome the postrevolutionary pattern of experimenting with different regime types.

INSTITUTIONS OF THE FIFTH REPUBLIC

All liberal-democratic governments are based on an institutional separation of powers, often accompanied by a territorial separation of powers between the federal and state levels of government. Whereas the United States represents the most extreme case of separating and offsetting the three branches of government (executive, legislative, and judiciary) with the checks-and-balances system, Western European democracies follow suit by distinguishing between the rights and responsibilities of the executive and the legislative branches, even if the judiciary does not always retain an independent role. In France, however, the executive branch has been given such extensive powers that a considerable institutional imbalance exists, leading some observers to claim that the French presidency has resulted in a "quasi-monarchical system." Indeed, given the specific need to stabilize the French republic after World War II with strong executive leadership, the constitution does grant the president substantial formal powers in the area of "high politics" (e.g., guaranteeing the continuity of the state, negotiating treaties, defending the nation and the constitution), which have been supplemented over time by the authority and prestige that have accrued to the office. Indeed, these informal dimensions of presidential power are quite extensive, leading one analyst to conclude that the current state of the presidency represents an act of "political self-levitation."

Additionally, however, the means whereby the president is elected serve to reinforce the powers of the office. The French president is elected by direct universal suffrage for a five-year term. The electoral mechanism itself was designed to confer maximum legitimacy upon the winner because he or she must receive an absolute majority of votes cast – either in a first round of ballots (which no one ever has achieved to date) or in a second runoff round of ballots where voters must choose between the top two candidates produced in the first round. Such an electoral mandate tends to invest the presidency with even greater legitimacy than the popularly elected **National Assembly** (the lower chamber of Parliament), which can too readily be seen as the result of 577 local elections. In contrast, presidential campaigns are national in focus, articulating a universal vision and a comprehensive policy agenda. Although presidential candidates initially come out of the party system, representing a particular party, the electoral mechanism encourages the notion that the elected candidate represents more than just his party – that he or she represents the nation at large. Consequently, even committed party activists such as François Mitterand, a longtime leader of the Socialist Party, acted, once in office, counter to the interests and program of his own party. Although presidents obviously have the greatest room to maneuver when their own party controls a majority in the Assembly, consequently determining the prime minister and the cabinet, even periods of co-habitation have strengthened the perception that the presidency stands above party politics, as it is the prime minister who is most often held accountable by the electorate for immediate government policies.

In terms of his formal powers, the French president appoints the prime minister, presides over the Council of Ministers (the cabinet), often determining the agenda of the Council's meetings, signs decrees and ordinances, and appoints three members of the **Constitutional Council** (the French counterpart to the U.S. Supreme Court), including its President, as well as appointing senior-level civil servants. Additionally, the president can call for a referendum, dissolve the National Assembly, and during crisis periods exercise extraordinary powers for as long as he deems necessary. More conventionally, the president is also the commander in chief of the armed forces and head of the Diplomatic Service. By and large, given these powers, the president sets the agenda for the government as a whole, except during periods of co-habitation. During these periods, policy leadership and innovation, especially in domestic affairs, reverts to the prime minister, who can, when backed by a solid parliamentary majority, successfully replace presidential legislative initiatives with his own. Because the government, under the leadership of the prime minister, determines the agenda for the legislature, the powers of this "junior" executive are quite extensive as well, further adding to the fundamental imbalance in the governing institutions of the Fifth Republic.

If the general functions of a democratic parliament are to play a major role in initiating legislation, to oversee the executive branch, and to represent its given constituencies, then the French legislative branch tends to fall short on all counts. In formal, constitutional terms, the Fifth Republic has transformed what was once one of the world's strongest parliaments (under the Third and Fourth Republics) into one of the weakest. For example, the French Parliament's ability to initiate legislation is severely restricted, as over 90 percent of all laws start out as government bills. Although this trend is not unknown in other Western European democracies, what is unusual in France is the extent to which the government can manipulate the lawmaking process in its favor. For example, during the period in which the upper chamber (the Senate, elected for nine years by an electoral college comprised mostly of municipal councillors under a complex, mixed voting procedure: a **two-ballot majority–plurality system** for départements electing one or two senators, and a proportional system for those electing more deputies with party lists that must alternate male and female candidates) and the lower chamber (the National Assembly, elected for five years by direct popular vote in a two-ballot majority–plurality system based on single-member districts) attempt to reconcile their respective drafts, the government more or less dictates the outcome either by using the upper house to block the lower house or by ignoring the upper house altogether because, in the case of a failure to agree on a compromise draft, the government can ask the Assembly to vote on whichever draft is favored by the government – the joint committee's or the Assembly's. If all else fails, the government can bypass the lawmaking process altogether and simply promulgate a decree, ordinance, or regulation. Although certain key areas of legislation are constitutionally reserved for the Parliament – areas such as budget and tax matters, civil liberties, and penal law – the constitution also gives the government the authority to ask the Parliament to delegate its powers in these specific areas to the government, which is then free again to legislate by decree.

In terms of oversight as well, the Parliament is hampered by the constitution, which allows it only six permanent committees. Oversight committees can therefore be constituted only on a temporary basis and, because membership is determined by a proportional representation of the parties, committees are dominated by the majority party, which determines the cabinet as well. Minority or dissenting reports are not allowed, effectively ruling out an unbiased inquiry or control procedure. High levels of absenteeism also hinder the legislature's ability to monitor and/or question the government's actions and policies even in the traditional "question-and-answer" setting. Although the French Parliament is not quite a rubber-stamping body (debates and disagreements with the government do arise), its ability to act efficiently and to carry out even the duties and responsibilities allocated to it by the constitution are impeded by further problems in the realm of representation.

First and foremost, the unique French practice of allowing elected officials to hold more than one office at a time (*le cumul des mandats*, or **accumulation of elected offices**) has meant that members of both the upper and lower chambers also hold local or regional offices, usually as a mayor or member of a municipal council, which, although not making them less representative of their communities, does tend to diminish their ability to represent their constituency effectively at the national level because their time and attention are divided between two offices. Although recent reform efforts (in 1985 and 2000) attempted to diminish the practice, 97 percent of all deputies in the 1997–2002 legislature still held multiple offices. In addition, problems of actual representativeness do plague the Senate, which, in the eyes of its critics, is not directly elected, serves for too long, and gives too much weight to conservative, rural interests.

Evidently, to see how executive powers might be balanced in the absence of a strong legislature, we must look elsewhere. Although the judiciary in France does not constitute a fully independent branch of government, much as in England, a 1974 constitutional reform has given expanded powers to the Constitutional Council (comprised of nine appointees: three appointed by the president, three by the president of the National Assembly, and three by the president of the Senate, serving nine-year nonrenewable terms), a body roughly analogous to the U.S. Supreme Court that has the authority to review proposed legislation for its constitutionality. However, the right to review is restricted to the period before a law is actually enacted and is only activated once a bill or law has been submitted for review either by the government or by the legislature (individual citizens do not have the right to petition), rendering the Council much weaker than its U.S. or German counterparts. Because the republican tradition in France was hostile to the judiciary as agents first of the monarchy and then of counterrevolutionary regimes, the judicial branch has on the whole been subordinated to the executive branch, as exemplified by the fact that the courts are placed under the Ministry of Justice, which has the authority to determine the career advancement of judges and prosecutors and the extent to which cases will be prosecuted. If it were not for the existence of the Council of State, a court with jurisdiction over matters concerning the state administration, and the Constitutional Council, the executive branch in particular and the state administration in general would be completely free from judicial oversight. Grave concerns, however have been raised about the relationship between the executive branch and the Constitutional Council. In 1999, the Constitutional Council declared, unsolicitedly, that the president was immune from all prosecution (including criminal) during his term in office. Because the head of the Constitutional Council at the time was facing corruption charges (he was later convicted and forced to resign), as was President Chirac himself (who is now immune and likely to run for a third term to evade pending charges), public suspicions of collusion do not appear too far-fetched.

An additional, and not insignificant, check on executive powers does, however, exist in the form of popular opinion and the willingness of disgruntled groups to contest the government's policies through strikes and protests. In this context, the French Revolution has provided both a legacy of and a model for popular protest that continues to animate contemporary French citizens, be they workers, students, civil servants, or farmers, all of whom have vehemently protested government policies. In 2001, in Paris alone, 800 political demonstrations took place in addition to the 1,461 job-oriented protests. Even before protests reach the streets, popular opinion can constitute a barrier to executive intentions. De Gaulle, for example, resigned the presidency in 1969 when a referendum he initiated failed to pass. In the absence of a strong legislature and an independent judiciary, the final check on the government, that of popular pressure, remains true to a pattern established in the past when powerful executives ruling in the name of the people ultimately succumbed to the will of the people, most notably in 1830 and 1848, when restorationist rulers were forced out of office.

POLICY MAKING IN THE FIFTH REPUBLIC

Given the preponderance of powers given to the executive branch in the interests of efficient leadership, it is not surprising that the state administration, as embodied by both appointed civil servants and career bureaucrats, plays the predominant role in policy making as well as in policy implementation. The scope and reach of the French bureaucracy is, of course, also consistent with the historic pattern of a strong, centralized, unitary, as opposed to federal, state administration dating back to the days of the monarchy. In crucial ways, the administration of today is quite like past administrations of notables, leading one observer to apply the label "modern nobility" to the upper ranks of the civil service. In other ways, however, the administration is much more democratic, encompassing not just the elite levels of French society centered around civil-service careers in Paris but also regional and local-level state employees from a multiplicity of backgrounds performing their jobs in diverse settings across the country. Close to five million people are employed in the state bureaucracy, clearly not all of whom correspond to the prevailing images of elite French civil servants. Moreover, 57 percent of the adult population are either civil servants themselves or are the child, parent, or spouse of civil servants.

At the highest levels, the bureaucracy is, in fact, represented by a closed and elite group of specially educated and usually well-born or well-connected men and, to a far lesser extent, women, who move easily from one management position to the next, regardless of whether it is in the public domain or in the private domain. The resulting interpenetration of elites (administrative, political, and economic) is the most extensive in Western Europe, which is perhaps, in turn, the result of the *grandes écoles* system, wherein future civil servants and managers are trained at very prestigious and highly competitive national schools – again a system without a counterpart in Western Europe.

Although this background has certainly produced a state administration characterized by efficiency, stability, and expertise, it is not a system designed to promote equal opportunity, transparency, or democratic accountability. For example, data indicate that two-thirds of the chairmen of the top 40 French companies are graduates of this system, while two of the past three presidents, six of the past eight prime ministers, and over half of the current cabinet are all graduates of just one of the top schools – the prestigious École Nationale d'Administration, established by de Gaulle in 1945 to train a new generation of civil servants untainted by collaboration with the **Vichy regime**.

Nor is the state bureaucracy an impartial one, designed to stand aside from politics like the British civil service. Instead, the level of interpenetration has produced a bureaucracy that fully serves the government even to the extent of failing to implement and enforce laws enacted by the legislature. It has also produced an increasingly corrupt interplay among business interests, elected officials, and state administrators. As a dramatic example of how high these levels of corruption reach, former prime minister and Chirac's heir apparent, Alain Juppé, was forced to withdraw from public life after his conviction on corruption charges in 2004.

In spite of such drawbacks, the centrality of the state administration is unlikely to be contested given the extent to which political parties, interest groups, and popular opinion are all invested in the continuity of the republican state – just as the founders of the Fifth Republic intended. Whereas political parties in a democracy are generally responsible for producing coherent policy initiatives, agendas, and objectives, even when sitting in the opposition, as well as mobilizing popular opinion in support of their initiatives, French political parties tend to be too tied to party leaders, too focused on presidential elections (at the expense of consistent grassroots organization), and too fragmented organizationally to fulfill these functions fully. Certainly, the major French parties are spread across a conventional left-center-right spectrum, with the Communists (the Parti Communiste Français, or PCF) and Socialists (the Parti Socialiste, or PS) located on the left, the smaller Christian Democrats and old-style republicans (the UDF – Union pour la Démocratie Française; Union for French Democracy) in the center, and the Gaullists (the UMP – Union pour un Movement Populaire; Union for a Popular Movement) on the right, with Le Pen's National Front (an ultraconservative, anti-immigration party) located on the far right. However, party leaders rather than party platforms tend to stand out in the mobilization process, as well as in the party-formation process. Indeed, all of the parties on the right and far right were founded on the personalities of particular leaders. This degree of personalism is perhaps a logical outcome of the example set by de Gaulle himself when he created a party or movement in his own image. In general, de Gaulle adhered to a political tradition dating back to Rousseau that views parties with deep suspicion – as divisive and particularistic bodies that are incapable of transcending their narrow interests. Therefore, they are only palatable when they serve immediate, instrumental objectives such as getting exemplary leaders elected to the presidency. This degree of instrumentalization, where loyalty to the leader and not a programmatic adherence to the party platform dictates careers, limits the role that parties can play in the political system.

A further limitation on the role of parties lies in the sheer number of political parties, which dilutes their ability to promote viable policy alternatives backed by a substantial number of voters. Here, the institutions of the Fifth Republic clearly serve to perpetuate a situation that benefits the state administration, given the extent to which electoral mechanisms and state financial support provide incentives for small parties to continue catering to the diversity of political opinions and identities present in French public life. Most notably, the two-ballot system for electing the president gives small parties an incentive to run on the first ballot in order to then play a role in the jockeying for political support that takes place prior to the casting of the second ballot. Additionally, voting by proportional representation in regional and European elections does give candidates from smaller parties a legitimate chance at winning office.

Whereas diverse groups in French society may feel themselves to be better represented by these small parties, the political party system as a whole is not able to serve as a counterweight to the unelected powers of the bureaucracy. Given France's history of extremist political parties, currently embodied by the National Front, de Gaulle's efforts to elevate the bureaucracy at the expense of the party system are not surprising. In this context, equally unsurprising are the results of a 2002 poll that show 63 percent of respondents declaring their confidence in civil servants and only 18 percent finding politicians worthy of the public trust.

The impact and influence of interest groups also tend to be supportive of the state. Rather than acting as independent monitoring or watchdog organizations, French interest groups prefer to attain more institutionalized and cooperative relationships with relevant state ministries. In turn, state actors have been happy to delegate the provision of key public goods and services to social partners in relationships of "mutually beneficial cooperation." Although this stance would seem to guarantee interest groups a considerable voice in the policy-making process, the outcomes are more variable. Because the cooperative relationship is at the discretion of the state, not all groups have equal access. Trade unions that are dominated by Communist Party radicalism are not likely to have the same influence as their more conservative peers, for example. In general, the fragmentation of private-sector trade unions, which are the weakest in Europe, with a combined membership of only 2.5 million, has hampered their ability to influence public policy directly. Public-sector trade unions, in contrast, are far more powerful, comprising 26 percent of those employed in the public sector, and therefore capable of mounting serious challenges to government policies. Farmers' associations also have historically been granted a considerable voice in policy making ("an empire within the state," according to one analyst), influence that they still maintain even as the actual numbers of those employed in the agricultural sector are declining (in 1999 the figure was 627,000, down 38 percent from 1989). It is important to remember, however, that even when these more powerful interest groups mobilize in protest, which they often do, their grievances are likely to focus on specific policies, not the state itself, whereas their demands are more than likely to reinforce the role of the state in maintaining the provision of benefits to their constituencies.

In short, the state administration has been able to acquire considerable power and prestige as the predominant player in the policy process that represents and indeed is held to embody the public's general interest as opposed to all other players, which represent only narrow sectoral or ideological interests. Even the "public–private partnerships" that have evolved to provide public goods more efficiently tend to reinforce the prestige of the state as the key actor enabling the "mobilization of private interests in the service of public ambitions." Although this perception clearly obscures the extent to which special interests are actually involved, even at the state level, and the extent to which civil servants might pursue their own specific interests, it is consistent with French political traditions that allow the state administration to appropriate, as it were, the definition of the public good without allowing that good to emerge from an interplay of interests and public debates. Although a preference for state-based leadership and a correspondingly weak concept of pluralism is not novel in the context of continental European traditions, what renders France unique is the extent to which this preference is validated by democratic ideals (the state as reflection of the general will) as opposed to simply conservative traditions or an instrumental need to overcome economic backwardness by using the agency of the state.

As a result of this particular path of development, the sheer size and influence of the French state remains remarkable – even as the United States and Great Britain attempt to minimize the impact of their own state bureaucracies. Because the French state today employs one in four workers, endowing them with very substantial benefits, the state is responsible for spending 54 percent of GDP, one of the highest rates of public spending in the European Union. As one observer has noted, the state in France is "regulator, educator, protector and planner," a multiplicity of roles that the French have come to expect from their state. Consequently, although the powers of the state and the executive branch represent a considerable deviation from the liberal democratic norm, they are consistent with French democratic traditions and have been highly functional throughout the postwar era.

Conclusion: Current Challenges

Currently, the scope and nature of state policies are becoming a cause for concern in French political life even if the powers of the state per se are not contested. Three problems in particular have combined to generate a formidable series of challenges to the republic created in de Gaulle's image. First, in the economic realm, remaining competitive in global markets and adhering to the EU's monetary policies require scaling back the state's public expenditures. Second, in the social realm, newly emerging inequalities in French society, "*la fracture sociale*" as President Chirac labeled it, require both socioeconomic redress and political measures to integrate excluded social groups into mainstream social life. Third, in the political realm, a "**crisis of representation**" is emerging as the gap between establishment political elites and French voters is growing, leaving the future stability of the political system open to question.

Responses to these challenges have been, according to a 2002 survey by Britain's *The Economist*, "muddled" because the French remain uncertain both over the nature of the challenges and over the degree to which change is actually necessary. There are ongoing confusions, therefore, "over France's place in Europe, over the impact of globalization and, at root, over what it means to be French. In their hearts they want precious little to change; in their heads they suspect change is inevitable." Adding to the image of confusion, at least from the perspective of British observers, are the positions of international assertiveness undertaken by the French government: on the one hand, a prominent player in Western organizations such as the G8 group of advanced industrial nations, and on the other hand, a critic both of globalization and of U.S. leadership. When viewed against the backdrop of French history, however, there is greater "method" to the "muddle" than is apparent at first glance. Significantly, public policies and public debate, more generally, have crystallized around the familiar fault lines of French political culture (progressive versus reactionary), which inevitably endorse different, often contradictory, responses. At the same time, domestic preoccupations and conflicts have never precluded, and indeed have in some ways even necessitated, taking aggressive foreign policy positions designed to maximize French influence and maneuverability abroad. Thus, the fact that France has sent twice as many official representatives to the World Social Forum in Brazil (an antiglobalization summit) as to the annual meeting of the World Economic Forum (also called the Davos group after its meetingplace in Davos, Switzerland) may be ideologically inconsistent given the degree to which the French economy is dependent on globalization but entirely pragmatic given French foreign policy objectives.

French dependence on global markets and U.S. economic health is clearly evident in the country's recent decline in key indicators: from a respectable 3.3 percent annual economic growth rate in the late 1990s, for example, to only 1 percent in 2002, with a parallel drop in per capita economic output from eighth in the world in the early 1990s to eighteenth in 2004. France has thereby been challenged in the first years of the twenty-first century to maintain competitiveness during a downturn in U.S. economic growth, a challenge made more difficult no doubt by the high taxes, social charges, and administrative red tape that French firms must contend with. The impact of Europeanization, especially the fiscal and monetary stability pact that undergirded the common currency in its first years, has been equally problematic in that the pact mandates a budgetary deficit of no more than 3 percent of GDP. In the face of conflicting pressures, however, France and Germany both violated the pact in 2003 and 2004, helping to pave the way for serious reconsideration of what it really takes to have a common currency.

In terms of French social dynamics, there is an ever-expanding divide between "the haves," those who are a part of the working population, well paid and well endowed with state-mandated benefits, and "the have-nots," those who are jobless and dependent on government handouts. Unemployment levels in the late 1990s remained stubbornly high at about 11.5 percent, rising to almost 21 percent unemployed in the under 25 age group, with structural unemployment (long-term unemployment resulting from a decline in industry or other systemic problems) estimated at between 9 and 10 percent. Moreover, 12 percent of the population is estimated to live in poverty. As a consequence, social problems are growing, especially in the housing projects where young people without work and without prospects are becoming increasingly restive. Basically, the French *économie dirigée* has failed to create a flexible job market that would allow younger, unskilled, or part-time workers to find a place in the economy. As a result, the level of jobs created in the private-sector services in France falls far below that of the United States and Britain. Logically, employers overburdened by the benefits they must provide to their existing employees are extremely reluctant to hire new workers. As *The Economist* concluded in 1999, "because the government taxes employment so heavily, joblessness remains high, which in turn means the government has to keep on taxing heavily to pay for it."

It would appear obvious, at least to English and U.S. analysts, that the French state must fundamentally alter its relationship with the economy and the society by reducing its public spending, freeing the labor market from current burdens and restrictions, and transferring responsibility for many social programs, such as pension funds, to the private sector. Without reforms, for example, state pensions could comprise up to 20 percent of GDP by 2040, up from 12 percent during the late 1990s.

Although the situation is clearly urgent, progress to date in reforming the scope and nature of state policies has been slow, hindered in large part by public resistance, political stalemate, and ideological reluctance to change. President Chirac, upon assuming office in 1995, attempted to initiate a reform agenda and almost immediately faced a massive strike of public-sector employees that brought the country to a standstill. The understandable reluctance of these employees to give up substantial benefits, including secure lifelong employment and earlier retirement, longer holidays, and higher pensions than private-sector workers, is further compounded by the extent to which these benefits are seen not as privileges but as accustomed rights. Although public-sector reforms are still on the table during Chirac's current second term, the government is likely to face continued resistance to any substantial curtailment of existing benefits. Furthermore, every effort undertaken by the center-right to cut back state expenses has fueled a voter backlash to the benefit of the major opposition party, the center-left Socialists, who are then placed in a position to implement their own public-policy agenda. Most strikingly, in 1997, Chirac's call for early parliamentary elections led to the election of a Socialist majority, which then, under the leadership of former Socialist Prime Minister Lionel Jospin, introduced the 35-hour work week, a reform that, while doubtlessly progressive, adds to France's competitive burden by imposing additional costs on employers, including the French state.

A further barrier to reforms designed to roll back the state is represented by ideological reluctance on all sides of the political spectrum to exchange France's unique republican model of development, which is based as much on social development as on economic development, for the Anglo-American liberal model. As Jospin declared, "Yes to the market economy, no to the market society." From this perspective, creating a quantity of low-quality, low-paid jobs is just as disruptive to social solidarity as are persistently high levels of unemployment. From a historical perspective, French republics are strongest when socioeconomic inequalities are kept to a minimum, thereby limiting social support for alternative forms of government. State-sponsored social solidarity has thus become a defining attribute of the Fifth Republic. French policy makers are currently caught in a bind between accepting the necessity of responding to a changed global context in which the Anglo-American model dominates, a model that threatens to increase socioeconomic inequalities, which, in turn, risks fueling political instability, and a desire to maintain the distinct quality of social life in their country – even as that social life is increasingly threatened by internal divisions.

Most importantly, in this context, a tense and highly problematic division has emerged between (white European) French and the immigrant population of Arab and North African Muslims, many of whom are French citizens from the former colony of Algeria, who wish to retain their culture and traditions. In the past, France has readily granted equal citizenship rights as long as immigrants became French and accepted a French identity based in large part on the republican myth, born during the revolutionary era, of a single, united, and unified French nation. This image of a uniform nation and the indivisible republic representing it continues to color official responses to the question of how such a different population of between four and five million (an estimated 20 percent of which are religiously active) can be treated equally both legally and socially without falling into the *communautarisme* (separate communities claiming rights on behalf of specific racial, ethnic, or cultural identities) characteristic of Anglo-American political evolution. Most remarkably, it has been difficult even to gain the data required to make intelligent public-policy choices given the government's reluctance to categorize population groups according to particular characteristics such as religious or ethnic affiliation, categorizations that go against republican values that enshrine universal equality. Public-policy responses have consequently been filtered through the prism of republican secularism and reactionary conservativism, often without an adequate factual basis for public debate and decision making. For example, because the effects of introducing the ban on Muslim head scarves in state schools were not systematically studied or evaluated (leading critics to point out that the ban may actually inflame Islamic fundamentalism – the opposite of the law's intent), the parliamentary debate centered entirely and abstractly on the need to preserve the secular republic. On the reactionary side of the political spectrum, high levels of unemployment and problems of assimilation have all too easily turned into problems of blatant hatred and racist exclusion. Such sentiments are, unfortunately, nothing unusual in Europe today, as these traditionally homogeneous countries are struggling to come to terms with multiculturalism.

France, however, is unique in fielding the most significant right-wing extremist party in Europe, the National Front, which can draw on a long tradition of reactionary conservatism that has never been discredited to the same extent as have similar traditions in Germany and Italy. Not surprisingly, the Front managed to achieve 15 percent of the vote in national elections during the mid-1990s, culminating in almost 17 percent of the vote in the presidential election of 2002, a large percentage of which (close to 68 percent) was drawn from blue-collar workers and the unemployed. In fact, support for the National Front's simplistic remedies (keep out foreigners, produce more French children, build more prisons, cut taxes, and leave the EU) has been so considerable that the government has implemented a number of policies in keeping with the Front's agenda, including making naturalization more difficult (children of immigrants born in France are no longer automatically French citizens), building more prisons, and devoting more funding to law-and-order measures.

The fact that the government has attempted to straddle both progressive and reactionary policy responses to the problem of immigration is perhaps less surprising when we consider the third challenge faced by French political elites, namely the "crisis of representation." Since the 1990s, record levels of abstentions, spoiled ballots, protest votes (in the 2002 presidential election, for example, the 13 "no-hope" candidates received a total of 47 percent of the vote in the first round), and low support for incumbents have been consistently registered in every election, and even in the most recent referendum (2000) to limit the presidential term, only 30 percent of eligible voters took part. In this context, the success of the National Front has been deemed the "vengeance of the people" as corruption scandals and continuing social and economic problems have discredited existing elites and the privileged system that produces and protects them. The exclusive *grandes écoles* system has been called into question, as has the educational system in general, with its blatant advantages for the better-off members of society. Additionally, the taxation system, which contains parallel privileges, has come under increasingly critical scrutiny. For many ordinary French citizens, these privileges no longer seem just or warranted. Neither social nor official responses to this gap between the governed and the elites have been entirely cast in a reactionary mold, however.

The progressive traditions of the French revolution have been manifest as well over the last twenty years. Socially, for example, there has been a sharp rise in civic activism and associational life, with 60,000 new associations registered annually, bringing citizens together for a range of political, cultural, and leisure activities. Although French membership rates in such associations remain below those of other Western democracies, the turn to associational life represents a positive development for the strength of civil society. Additionally, the decentralization reforms of the late 1980s have, over time, served to activate and energize local governments that now have more decision-making authority, making local politics a more viable locus for civic engagement. Finally, and most dramatically, a gender-parity law was enacted in 2000 that requires all political parties to nominate an equal number of men and women for public office. The law has already been carried through in municipal (2001) and legislative elections (2002), with the result that women are on the brink, almost overnight and after a long history of discrimination (having only gained the right to vote in 1945), of achieving equal representation in all representative institutions. This achievement will place France at the forefront of all Western democracies.

The long-term consequences of these responses, both progressive and reactionary, to the loss of faith in the existing political system remain to be seen. What does seem certain, however, is that French political leaders will continue to pursue an assertive foreign policy, even in the midst of domestic contestations, both to restore public confidence in the capabilities of French elites as they maintain French prestige abroad and to promote French interests in all relevant international forums in order to maintain the viability of France's distinct political, economic, and social traditions for as long as possible. The best defense, as they say, is a good offense.

BIBLIOGRAPHY

Agulhon, Maurice. *The French Republic, 1879–1992*. Oxford: Blackwell, 1990.

Bayly, C. A. *The Birth of the Modern World, 1780–1914: Global Connections and Comparisons*. Malden, MA: Blackwell, 2004.

Bell, David S. *French Politics Today*. Manchester: Manchester University Press, 2002.

Chartier, Roger. *The Cultural Origins of the French Revolution*. Durham, NC: Duke University Press, 1991.

Corbett, James. *Through French Windows: An Introduction to France in the Nineties*. Ann Arbor: University of Michigan Press, 1994.

Denomme, Robert T., and Roland H. Simon. *Unfinished Revolutions: Legacies of Upheaval in Modern French Culture*. University Park: Pennsylvania State University Press, 1998.

The Economist. Country Survey, France, June 5, 1999.

The Economist. Country Survey, France, November 16, 2002.

Elgie, Robert. *Political Institutions in France*. Oxford: Oxford University Press, 2003.

Furet, Francois. *La République du Centre: La fin de l'exception française*. Paris: Calmann-Levy, 1998.

Furet, Francois. *Revolutionary France 1770–1880*. Oxford: Blackwell, 1988.

Gaspard, Françoise. *A Small City in France: A Socialist Mayor Confronts Neofascism*. Cambridge, MA: Harvard University Press, 1995.

Gerson, Stephane. *The Pride of Place: Local Memories and Political Culture in Nineteenth Century France*. Ithaca, NY: Cornell University Press, 2003.

Goux, Jean-Joseph, and Philip R. Wood, eds. *Terror and Consensus: Vicissitudes of French Thought*. Stanford, CA: Stanford University Press, 1998.

Hoffmann, Stanley, et al. *In Search of France: The Economy, Society and Political System in the 20th Century*. New York: Harper Torchbooks, 1963.

Lefebvre, Georges. *The Coming of the French Revolution*. Princeton, NJ: Princeton University Press, 1989.

Lewis-Beck, Michael S. *The French Voter: Before and After the 2002 Elections*. New York: Palgrave Macmillan, 2004.

Meny, Yves, and Andrew Knapp. *Government and Politics in Western Europe*. London: Oxford University Press, 1998.

Palmer, R. R., and Joel Colton. *A History of the Modern World*. New York: McGraw-Hill, 1992.

Rydgren, Jens. *The Populist Challenge: Political Protest and Ethno-Nationalist Mobilization in France*. New York: Berghahn Books, 2004.

Skocpol, Theda. *Social Revolutions in the Modern World*. Cambridge: Cambridge University Press, 1994.

Soboul, Albert. *The Sans-Culottes*. Princeton, NJ: Princeton University Press, 1980.

Tocqueville, Alexis de. *The Old Regime and the French Revolution*. Translated by Stuart Gilbert. New York: Anchor Books, 1983.

Tombs, Robert. *France 1814–1914*. London and New York: Longmans, 1996.

Willis, F. Roy. *France, Germany and the New Europe 1945–1967*. London: Oxford University Press, 1968.

Wright, Gordon. *France in Modern Times*. Fourth Edition. New York: W.W. Norton & Co., 1987.

TABLE 4.1. Key Phases in France's Development

Time Period	Regime	Global Context	Interests/Indentities/ Institutions	Developmental Path
1789–1804	revolution	monarchical absolutism challenged; Enlightenment	rising middle classes and mobilizing lower classes, republicanism vs. conservatism, parliamentary sovereignty vs. one-man rule	state-building
1804–1870	restoration	Industrial Revolution	propertied classes, conservatism vs. republicanism, executive supremacy	state-sponsored economic development
1870–1940	Third Republic	imperialism	small and medium propertied classes, moderate vs. radical republicanism, parliamentary sovereignty	state-protected economic stability
1958–present	Fifth Republic	decolonization; globalization	middle and professional classes, Gaullism (center-right)-socialism (center-left)-conservative populism (radical right), presidential democracy	state-led socioeconomic development

IMPORTANT TERMS

accumulation of elected offices the practice whereby elected officials are allowed to hold more than one office at a time, which tends to diminish the role of the National Assembly.

Algeria France's most significant colony. The number of French living in Algeria and considering it their home made the process of decolonization a long and conflict-ridden one. Currently, Algerians living in France are the focus of considerable anti-immigration sentiment.

Jacques Chirac the current president of the Fifth Republic, who is faced with the challenge of fundamentally restructuring the French welfare state and furthering the process of market liberalization. At the same time, Chirac faces pending charges on the corrupt misuse of public office once he is no longer president.

co-habitation the term used to describe the situation when the president and the prime minister represent different political parties. At first, it was feared that this situation would lead to political deadlock, but it has proven to be much more manageable than originally thought. During these periods, the prime minister logically has a greater range of maneuverability vis-á-vis the president.

conservatism in the French case, an ideology that emerged in the wake of the French Revolution, rooted in the conviction that traditional customs and institutions should be protected at all costs against the onslaught of modern republican thought. Although often compatible with economic liberalism in its more moderate guises, French conservatism also manifests a radical-extremist face that has periodically been expressed in populist movements hostile not just to republicanism but to the "strangers within" (i. e., French Jews or immigrant communities).

Constitutional Council a judicial body roughly analogous to the U.S. Supreme Court. However, the Council can only review laws before they are enacted, which considerably weakens its powers of judicial oversight.

crisis of representation although the causes are still being debated by political commentators and analysts, there is an emerging consensus that the French presidential election of 2002, in particular, represents a "crisis" of sorts given the number of protest votes and the electoral support given to Le Pen's National Front.

Charles de Gaulle military leader of the Free French during World War II and subsequently the first president of the Fifth Republic, de Gaulle had immense influence in shaping the institutions and policies of the contemporary French government.

directed economy (*l'économie dirigée*) because of the degree of state involvement in economic planning and direct state ownership and control of critical sectors of the economy after World War II, the French economy represents a different path of development from that of the Anglo-American "free" market economy.

dual executive system as established by de Gaulle, the executive branch of the French government is divided between a directly elected president and a prime minister selected from the winning majority in Parliament. Within this division, the president has more authority and influence than the prime minister, especially in regard to foreign policy.

Estates-Général a proto-parliament originally divided into the three basic orders of society – the aristocracy, the clergy, and the middle orders – that was convened by Louis XVI in a last effort to save his throne on the eve of the Revolution.

European Union a complex set of intergovernmental and supranational institutions that, in addition to regulating the single market, increasingly sets the policy parameters for domestic policy making in member states. These growing restrictions have challenged France in particular. On the one hand, as a founding member state, France is greatly invested in the EU and exercises considerable influence within it, but on the other hand, the much-valued autonomy of French policy making has been severely circumscribed. The resulting tensions became more visible as France held its referendum on the new EU constitution in May 2005.

feudalism a social and political order that developed during the Middle Ages and was based on hierarchies of power and authority that linked peasant to lord and lord to king in a network of duties and obligations.

Fifth Republic the current government of France, characterized by a dual-executive system in which the president traditionally wields considerable authority and the state administration in general holds the preponderance of power.

French Revolution next to the American Revolution, the most consequential democratic revolution, paving the way for the expansion of democracy throughout continental Europe. However, whereas the American Revolution is often seen as primarily a political revolution aimed at changing the institutions of government to more suitably reflect already existing socioeconomic and cultural conditions, the French Revolution is held to have been a social revolution, profoundly altering not just political institutions but social, economic, and cultural domains as well.

grandes écoles the elite universities of the French educational system that train professionals for careers in the state administration, business management, and politics. Without a degree from one of these universities, it is virtually impossible to reach the top ranks of one's chosen profession.

"la fracture sociale," or social fracture President Chirac's labeling of the current social divisions in French society between employed and unemployed and between "native" and immigrant populations.

François Mitterand the first Socialist president of the Fifth Republic, Mitterand's regal manner of leadership further solidified the authority of the office of the president.

monarchical absolutism a form of government, best exemplified in the reign of Louis XIV, in which the monarch's powers are supreme, as opposed to constitutional monarchy, in which his powers are limited and shared by a representative body.

Napoleon Bonaparte while exercising dictatorial powers as the first of a series of postrevolutionary one-man-rule regimes, Napoleon also acted constructively to stabilize France after the turmoil of the revolutionary era and even consolidated a significant number of the republican gains made during the Revolution.

National Assembly the lower chamber of the French Parliament, elected for five years by direct popular vote in single-member districts. Constitutionally not as powerful as the executive branch, its powers are further diminished by high levels of absenteeism and, in general, unassertive leadership.

National Front the most significant radical right-wing party in Europe, representing an anti-immigration nativist platform.

nationalism another ideology that emerged in the context of the French Revolution, it was designed to promote patriotism and loyalty to the nation and the state that protects it. Subsequently, forms of nationalism were used by both restorationist and republican governments to help solidify their domestic support.

Republicanism what might be called the French form of liberalism is an ideology committed to representative government, broad-based suffrage, and equal protection under the state. But unlike liberalism, French republicanism is more oriented toward the attainment of political, civil, and social rights than the preservation of economic rights as enshrined in the Anglo-American liberal tradition.

restorationist regimes beginning with Napoleon's takeover of power in the wake of the Terror and ending with the rule of Louis Bonaparte (Louis-Napoléon), a series of postrevolutionary governments based on executive powers supported by social groups hostile to republicanism.

the Terror the phase of the Revolution under the leadership of Jacobin extremists such as Robespierre that has come to be equated with revolutionary excess because both innocent members of the aristocracy and moderate revolutionaries were put to death as enemies of the newly proclaimed Republic.

Third Republic in spite of its scandals and rotating parliamentary coalitions, the regime that was finally able to overcome the negative legacies of the Revolution and firmly consolidate republican government.

two-ballot majority–plurality system this electoral system has prevailed for much of the Fifth Republic's history and, although based on a majority as opposed to proportional representation system, differs from the Anglo-American, first-past-the-post tradition in that a second, runoff election between the frontrunners must be held if the first election fails to generate a clear majority winner.

Vichy regime the government of Nazi-occupied France. The extent to which Vichy leaders and the French in general collaborated with the occupying forces is currently a contested subject in France.

STUDY QUESTIONS

1. Compare the French and British models of institutional development. What are the major similarities and differences? Given the extensive differences, does it still make sense to place both countries in the same category of "early development"?

2. Identify the most significant legacies of the French Revolution. Consider especially the extent to which material interests and social identities have converged around particular political identities. Is this an important and long-lasting legacy? In general, what, in your opinion, accounts for the tenacity of the revolutionary legacies over time?

3. One of the basic arguments of this chapter is that complex phenomena such as the French Revolution have complex causes. Considering the interplay of multiple factors presented, what are the strengths and weaknesses of such an approach? For example, do we really need to consider the cumulative interaction of various factors to explain pertinent outcomes, or can we prioritize one causal factor, such as class interests or international competitive pressures, as being the most salient?

4. Turbulent domestic politics combined with aggressive international policies would appear to be an enduring characteristic of French political development. How can this apparent paradox be explained? Will France continue to manifest both tendencies in the future?

5. What are the costs and benefits associated with the strong state as it has evolved in France?

6. Discuss the role of Charles de Gaulle in the founding of the Fifth Republic. Does any other modern democracy owe its existence to such a personalized form of institutional crafting and design?

7. What are the costs and benefits associated with the dual-executive system? Is the French presidency too powerful, in your opinion?

8. How can the imbalance between the extensive powers of the state administration and the very limited powers of political parties and interest groups best be explained?

9. What are the costs and benefits associated with the Fifth Republic's model of directed economic growth and development?

10. In your opinion, is France today a "normal" European democracy or does it remain more of an exception – an enduringly unique case of democratic development?

STOP AND COMPARE

EARLY DEVELOPERS: BRITAIN AND FRANCE

An important part of democracy is the role of parliaments. Much of Great Britain's history has been a constant refinement of the principle of representative parliamentary government. Through a long series of struggles and reforms, British parliamentary government emerged triumphant over the rule of kings and queens. In the course of these changes, the monarchy remained a symbol of national integration and historical continuity, but the real political power came to reside in the prime minister and his or her cabinet of ministers. Of course, even in Britain, parliamentary and cabinet government did not necessarily mean the same thing as democracy: The right to vote – the franchise – was only gradually extended to the lower classes and women, and the final reforms came about during the twentieth century.

Despite the important upheavals in British history, political scientists continue to view the British experience as one of successful gradualism, of a gradual extension of the freedoms of liberal democracy to ever-larger groups of people. In the creation of liberal democracy, the British were undoubtedly aided by the simultaneous and successful rise of a commercial and capitalist economy during the eighteenth and nineteenth centuries. This was the age of the Industrial Revolution. Although the transition to a new kind of economy was not easy, for the first time in history, an economy generated large amounts of goods that could be consumed by a large number of people. To be sure, at first these goods were enjoyed only by the new "middle" classes, but over time the new lifestyle spread to the working class as well. Accompanying these changes in material living standards came changes in the way people thought about their place in the world. One's position and life chances were no longer set in stone from birth. Upward mobility was now a possibility for people who never would have thought such a world possible a mere century earlier. It was in this context that common people could begin to demand a political voice

125

commensurate with their contribution to the public good. The argument was a powerful one, and gradually the old feudal/aristocratic oligarchy gave way to wider sections of society in search of political representation.

Of course, a further important feature of the British experience was the creation of a global empire between the seventeenth and the nineteenth centuries. Industrialization both contributed to and was assisted by the military, economic, and political conquest of large parts of Africa and Asia. The empire provided raw materials for manufacture, markets for export, a "playground" for military elites, and a source of national pride that made it easier for the British to try to universalize their particular experience. As other countries in Europe began to compete economically and militarily, however, and as locally subjected peoples from Ghana to India recognized the incongruity of British ideals of parliamentary democracy and law with continued imperial domination, the costs of empire began to rise. By the beginning of the twentieth century, Britain had clearly fallen from the imperial heights it had once occupied, and domestic discussion began to focus on issues of economic decline and how to extricate the country from costly imperial commitments. With Britain divested of its empire, its economy continued to decline throughout the twentieth century relative to other European countries, and much of contemporary British politics has concerned ways to reverse this decline. In Britain's (mostly) two-party system, both parties have proposed cures for what ails the economy, but neither has been able to offer recipes for regaining the national confidence (indeed, some say arrogance) that was once taken for granted.

Notwithstanding such troubles, the British experience continues to be the benchmark against which comparativists think about the developmental experience of other countries. The British (or what is sometimes called the Westminster) model of government became the standard against which other countries measure their own progress.

Britain's experience could not be duplicated, however. Even France, the country whose experience we pair with Britain's, initially developed in Britain's shadow and bridged early and late developmental paths. The logic of pairing France and Britain is, nevertheless, compelling. Like Britain, France's history is largely one of the people emerging victorious over kings. The difference is that, in France, the monarchy and the old feudal oligarchy were displaced not through a long series of conflicts and compromises but largely through a major revolution in 1789 in which the monarch was executed and the aristocracy hounded out of political life. Over the course of the next century, French political history was tumultuous, the political pendulum swinging back and forth between democratic development and periods of authoritarian or populist regimes. Despite these changes, what remained a constant in French political life was the notion that power ultimately resided with the people. Even such populist demagogues as Napoleon and, later, his nephew

Louis Bonaparte (Louis-Napoléon) never managed to depart fully from the notion of popular sovereignty. Indeed, they could not, if only because postrevolutionary France depended on its people to serve in its armies and mobilize for war.

If the British political experience is one of subjugating monarchical power to representative institutions, the French democratic experience is one of regulating a strong centralized state through plebiscitary mandate. War was a staple of political life on the European continent and preparing for it an important part of what states did. The French state was no exception; in fact, it became a model for others to emulate (and eventually surpass). Even before the French Revolution, French monarchs and their states played an important part in encouraging economic development and collecting taxes for the purposes of military preparation. The revolution did little to change this and in many ways intensified the power of the French state. In fact, one way of thinking about the revolution is in terms of a rebellion against the taxing power of the French monarchy and its resurrection in the form of more or less democratically elected heads of state who, because of their popular mandate, had more power to draw on private resources for public goals than ever before. Given its pattern of development, it is perhaps not surprising for us to learn that after much experimentation with various forms of representative government in the latter part of the nineteenth century and first part of the twentieth, France has settled on a strong, popularly elected presidency with a five-year term of office.

This contrast between parliamentary rule in Britain and presidential rule in France has become a model one for political scientists. Such differences in democratic institutions have important long-term effects on politics and policies. Given the importance and centralized nature of the French state, it is natural that the state became highly involved in economic development during the twentieth century. French economic planning, a subtle and highly developed system of state guidelines and state-induced market incentives, has often been contrasted with the heavy-handed Soviet communist model, not merely in the differences in style but also because for a very long time the French model seemed to work so well. More recently, however, the impacts of European integration and increased global trade have brought the feasibility of the model under question and led to a debate in France on the future of French-style economic planning and whether it will have to adapt to the competing model of Anglo-American capitalism. Britain has also experienced a debate between Euroskeptics and Europhiles.

Finally, globalization has also meant that both Britain and France are now home to large numbers of people born in other countries. Right-wing sentiment against "foreigners" has emerged, and politicians have raised questions about national identity. Questions of identity are nothing new to Britain and France. British identity has always been contested – the Celtic periphery of Scots, Irish, and Welsh have frequently challenged the hegemony of the English. French identity has long been split between a Catholic and conservative France rooted in the rural peasantry and a secular and progressive France rooted in the urban classes. Yet, for both Britain and France, the presence of so many "non-Europeans" in their midst is something quite new. How democracies, especially two of the oldest and most stable ones, manage the tensions among multiculturalism, national unity, and democratic politics is a topic that will capture the interest of comparativists for years to come.

PART TWO

MIDDLE
DEVELOPERS

CASES

GERMANY

0   50   100 miles
0   50   100km

DENMARK

North Sea

Baltic Sea

Kiel

Rostock

Lübeck

Hamburg

Emden

Bremerhaven

Elbe R.

Bremen

POLAND

NETHERLANDS

Hannover

⊛ Berlin

Magdeburg

Duisburg   Essen

Kassel

Leipzig

Düsseldorf

Cologne

Dresden

Bonn

GERMANY

BELGIUM

Wiesbaden   Frankfurt am Main

CZECH

LUXEMBOURG

REPUBLIC

Rhine R.

Mannheim

FRANCE

Stuttgart

Danube R.

Munich

SWITZERLAND

LIECHTENSTEIN   A U S T R I A

CHAPTER FIVE

Germany

Andrew C. Gould

Introduction

In October 1990, the East German state (the **German Democratic Repub-lic – GDR**) collapsed, losing control of its territory and people to the West German state (the **Federal Republic of Germany – FRG**), even though just over a year earlier almost no one had expected this to happen. Yet, the collapse of East Germany makes sense as part of Germany's path through the modern world, which has been influenced strongly by the surrounding political and economic conditions. A precarious military-strategic position in Europe made it difficult for one German polity to rule over everyone who is in one way or another conceivably German. As a result, German political organizations frequently competed with one another for people and territory. Thus, only rarely did one king, emperor, or chancellor succeed in dominating all other German rulers. Even today, millions of German-speaking people and considerable territories that were formerly ruled by various German polities remain outside of a unified Germany.

The challenges and opportunities that Germans faced were characteristic of their "middle path" through political and economic development. Falling behind the early developers put Germany at a disadvantage. In politics, German rulers could not match French rulers in establishing strong central authority over their vast territory. In economics, German industrial develop-ment lagged behind Britain's. Apart from these strategic and economic dis-advantages, however, the rapid diffusion of new ideas into Germany offered certain opportunities. Germany's newer bureaucracies skipped over tradi-tional practices and instead adopted only the latest organizational techniques. German industries, unimpeded by false starts, implemented advanced tech-nology on a massive scale. In the struggle with the early developers, Germany developed powerful institutions (the army and an authoritarian monar-chy), identities (nationalism and anti-Semitism), and interests (protectionist industry and labor-repressive agriculture) that fought against liberalism and democracy.

The German experience demonstrates that backwardness compared with early developers has powerful and wide-ranging effects on a country's path to development. When Germany was attempting to catch up, its industries modernized, its state engineered massive social and economic changes, and its leading political ideologies emphasized power, obedience, and material well-being over political freedom. But with the failure of the fascist regime of Adolf Hitler's Nazi Party to deliver its promises of victory, social order, and prosperity atop a new world order in World War II, and once two new superpowers emerged in virtually unassailable positions, German elites no longer sought to remake their country into the world's greatest power. Under these conditions, postwar Germany was a medium-sized power almost entirely dependent upon the United States for its security, without any significant offensive military capability of its own. Its economy grew to become the world's third largest, and democracy, freedom, and the rule of law flourished in the heart of the European continent.

Contemporary interests, identities, and institutions in Germany stem from Germany's path through the modern world. With regard to interests, the reliance of major German industrialists on the state and big banks for funding during the nineteenth and twentieth centuries, and the struggles of many small- and medium-sized firms to stay afloat, stemmed from Germany's economic position and attempts to catch up with France and Britain. In the early twenty-first century, the German government is seeking to transform the state's intricate involvement in the market, especially in the labor market, a difficult reform process that does not win strong support even from leading firms, much less labor unions. The almost bewildering variety of contemporary German identities – from right-wing nationalism, to ecological activism, to recent immigrants seeking a new status – also flows from previous episodes of identity formation and reformulation. Some of the key institutional features of the contemporary German state, including the relocation of the capital from **Bonn** back to **Berlin** after reunification, show the pull of past practice. Other political institutions, notably the **Basic Law (Grundgesetz)** of 1949, are explicitly crafted to prevent any reemergence of authoritarianism. In this chapter, we explore how Germany's particular sequence of development created international and domestic legacies that strongly influence the country today.

Origins of a Middle Developer, 100 B.C. – A.D. 1800

If you place key moments in German history, even familiar ones, in the analytic framework of this text, then you can see just how much influence the global context has on the development of a given country. To start the analysis, and in contrast with nationalist myths of a pure beginning, the origins of modern Germany did not lie uniquely within German lands but instead in the contact between two societies. Early German and Roman cultures blended and grew together during the expansions and contractions of the Roman Empire across Europe. Roman influence, starting in the first century B.C., brought a common culture of Christianity, a common elite language of Latin, and a common experience of the Roman legal code. As the Roman Empire declined during the fifth century, Germanic warriors reinvigorated their practice of honor-based pacts of loyalty to provide a political foundation for new feudal kingdoms.

Germany at this time resembled the rest of Europe. As in the rest of Europe from the eighth through the twelfth centuries, aspiring German kings were usually at war with one another. As in other parts of Europe, strong cities emerged during the thirteenth through sixteenth centuries, especially along the Rhine River and the Baltic Sea. In contrast with the personalistic and custom-bound rule in feudal kingdoms, cities governed themselves through written laws and representative institutions for various social groups. Also during the sixteenth century, a wave of religious revival swept across Europe and Germany; the Catholic and Protestant Reformations left German territories religiously divided.

Germany became a middle developer during the seventeenth and eighteenth centuries because this is when German rulers could not match the successes of monarchs in France and England. Whereas each of the early developers became unified under absolutist or would-be absolutist rulers, Germany remained politically divided. For instance, starting in 1618, the Thirty Years' War devastated the population and economy of many German states; it ended with the 1648 Peace of Westphalia, which marked the ascendancy of France under Louis XIV as a European power and the inability of Germany's nominal imperial ruler (Habsburg Emperor Ferdinand III in Vienna) to stem the growing sovereignty of the many different and competing German states and principalities. The weakness of pan-German political institutions and the persistence of political divisions accentuated other differences within the German lands, such as the cleavage between Protestants and Catholics and the contrast between economically advanced regions in western and southern Germany and the backward agricultural economies and social structures east of the Elbe River.

Competing Modern States, 1800–1871

German polities were middle developers in building a modern state; that is, in the task of building a political organization that could successfully claim to be the only organization with the right to use violence over the German territory and its people. The two most powerful political units were

Austria-Hungary in the southeast and **Prussia** in the northeast. They competed with each other and with dozens of other would-be states in what is now modern Germany. The winnowing down of German states accelerated under the renewed military conquests of an early developer. In 1806, the French emperor Napoleon Bonaparte invaded, consolidated many German states into larger units, and imposed a common legal code. German leaders sought both to imitate and resist Napoleon by rationalizing their own bureaucracies and building stronger armies. When the allies finally defeated France in 1815, Prussia and Austria emerged even stronger than before over the other German states. As an eastern power, Prussian military might was centered on its capital in Berlin, but the peace treaty agreed to at the **Congress of Vienna** awarded Prussia control over many economically advanced territories in the west along the Rhine River.

Two main social and political groups contended for influence in Germany during the nineteenth century. The first group included many people energized by the broader European liberal movements for nationalism and constitutionalism. They were liberals in the nineteenth-century meaning of the term: They favored large and free markets, the separation of church and state, and constitutional representative government. German liberals sought to build a German nation that encompassed all of the people then divided into various polities; they wanted a national market unhindered by internal boundaries; and they wanted to limit monarchical power by building new political institutions, such as a national electoral system, a parliament, and a written constitution. Leading intellectuals, professors, government officials, industrialists, professionals, and various members of the middle classes played key roles in the liberal movement.

The second group contending for influence was the landed elite (**Junkers**) of eastern Prussia. These owners of large tracts of land employed agricultural labor in conditions of near servitude to produce grain for world markets. They were deeply conservative politically and sought to forestall any political change that threatened their control over land and people, including any changes in the system of German states, in the ways the various states were governed internally, and in the harsh conditions of life for their agricultural workers. Their estates produced grain for the world market at very competitive prices, but their approval of market economics did not extend to the conditions of production for their workers. In fact, their economic success rested on political power and economic exploitation.

German monarchs successfully resisted most of the political demands of the liberal group and allied themselves with the landed elite. For example, in 1830, liberal revolutions took place in France, Belgium, and Switzerland. Liberalism was strong in the Rhineland as well, but the Prussian king in Berlin avoided changes by taking advantage of his government's physical separation from most of the revolutionary action and his additional military resources based in the east. Even less change occurred in Austria-Hungary than in Prussia.

During 1848, important political reforms again engulfed many countries of Europe. Widespread revolutionary activity in the Rhineland, Berlin, and Vienna led to a call for the election of a national assembly of delegates. Elections were held in all of the German states, from Prussia to Austria-Hungary and the many other states. The delegates met in Frankfurt to draw up a new constitution for a unified German state, but the Prussian and Austrian monarchs used force to preserve their rule, and the **Frankfurt Parliament**, unable to reform, overthrow, or unify the conservative states, disbanded without achieving any of its intended aims.

The rejection of liberalism had the unintended consequence of setting in motion future revolutionary movements. In the spring of 1841, **Karl Marx** was a 23-year-old student whose dissertation was accepted by the University of Jena. Marx had planned for a career as an academic philosopher, but the Prussian government's imposition of strict controls on university appointments meant that he had to write for a different audience. His new job as the editor of a newspaper financed by liberals and run by radicals, the *Rheinische Zeitung*, ended abruptly when the Prussian censor closed the paper for being too critical. Unable to find work in Germany, Marx left for France in 1843, where he met his lifelong collaborator, Friedrich Engels. In 1848, he and Engels wrote the *Communist Manifesto*, closing with the statement: "The proletarians have nothing to lose but their chains. They have a world to win. Working men of all countries, unite!" Marx returned to Germany during the revolutionary movements of 1848 and advocated an alliance with liberal reformers, but the failure of this revolution finally convinced him and many other activists and supporters that real reform was impossible without more fundamental changes in the economy and society.

In the battle for supremacy among the German powers, the Prussian monarchy adopted the economic dimension of the liberal program but used its military strength both to dominate the smaller German states and reject the political dimensions of liberalism. Prussia sponsored a growing free-trade zone among the German states, and the size of its own market made it costly for other states to avoid joining. Prussia defeated Austria-Hungary in war in 1866, paving the way for the formation of the North German Confederation under Prussian leadership in 1867. The final steps in Germany's first modern unification required that France be forced to accept the change in the German situation. The Franco-Prussian War of 1870 matched two nondemocratic rulers – France's emperor Louis-Napoléon (Napoleon Bonaparte's nephew) against the king of Prussia, Wilhelm I. The war had widely divergent consequences. Louis-Napoléon lost the war and was replaced by a democratic regime, the Third Republic (1870–1940). Prussia won the war and used its victory to consolidate a larger German state under authoritarian rule.

The Prussian king – advised by his chancellor, Otto von Bismarck – had himself crowned the emperor of Germany while at the French palace of Versailles in 1871. The military victory established the new German borders. Unified

Germany encompassed Prussia (including its eastern territories along the Baltic in what is now Poland and Russia) and virtually all of the non-Austrian German states. It also included territory taken from France, the economically advanced provinces of Alsace and Lorraine. Austria and Switzerland remained outside of the new German empire as independent countries.

Unification under Authoritarian Leadership, 1871–1919

Germany's late unification gave its newly constructed state institutions a great deal of influence over society. The state's initiative played a crucial role in changing Germany, even if the state was not always successful in its efforts. In other words, the developmental path of relatively late state-building in Germany gave the German state, compared with early state-building in Britain and France, an opportunity to attempt to reshape society, the economy, and politics.

The leaders of the German state reshaped society in unintended ways when they set about recasting institutions and reformulating identities. First, the mainly Protestant leaders attacked Catholicism. In the early 1870s, the state leaders pursued a cultural struggle (**Kulturkampf**) with laws and regulations to make it difficult for Catholic priests to carry out their work. Political activists responded by founding a political party, the **Center Party (Zentrumspartei)**. The party's top decision makers were Catholic lay leaders, and Center Party candidates received the implicit and explicit aid of the church. The long-term effects of the Kulturkampf, however, were neither what the German political elite wanted nor what the Catholic Church expected. Instead of a retreat from politics, the struggle against Catholicism induced Catholics to mobilize in their own political party. Instead of increasing the power of the Catholic Church in politics and society, as the Catholic hierarchy would have preferred, the Kulturkampf brought about the emergence of professional party leaders who were not priests, even though they were Catholic. The state reconciled with the church during the 1870s, but the Center Party remained to represent German Catholics, and it went on to become one of Germany's largest political parties.

As the regime made its peace with a recast Catholic community, the leaders next turned their attention to the emerging political movements among the working classes. The Socialist Worker's Party was formed in 1875 from various radical groups, and it won only 9 percent of the vote in 1877. Bismarck, however, blamed the party for Germany's economic situation: "As long as we fail to stamp on this communist ant-hill with domestic legislation," he said, "we shall not see any revival in the economy." In 1878, Bismarck won majority support in the Reichstag (parliament) for severe antisocialist legislation. The government closed Socialist Party offices and publications, prohibited its meetings, and generally harassed its organizers. Many left-wing activists fled from Germany, especially to Switzerland, and sought to keep their efforts alive in exile.

Despite the repression, many workers and other supporters continued to identify themselves as working class and to support the Socialist Party. Most of the antisocialist laws lapsed in 1890, and the party reemerged under a new name as the **Social Democratic Party** (Sozialdemokratische Partei Deutschlands, SPD). The Socialists climbed at the polls in 1898 with 27 percent of the vote. In the final elections under the empire in 1912, the Social Democratic Party won even more – 35 percent of the vote. The typical Socialist voter was a young, urban worker who was Protestant but did not go to church, and who was German rather than a member of the Polish or another minority group. The party attracted little support from Catholics or people living in rural areas. Still, the Social Democrats had almost a million members in 1912, a substantial accomplishment, as its members were expected to pay regular dues as in many other European parties. Like other mass parties in Europe, the Social Democrats reached beyond the purely political realm to organize funeral societies, buying cooperatives, book-lending libraries, gymnastic societies, choral clubs, bicycling clubs, soccer teams, Sunday schools, and dance courses.

The new German state had to foster economic development in difficult circumstances. Most importantly, from 1873 to 1896 there was a Europewide depression. Agricultural prices fell with the introduction of inexpensive Russian and midwestern American grain on world markets; industrial prices also fell, employment figures were unstable, production rose, and profits decreased. One response to these difficult conditions lay beyond state control: Many Germans emigrated from Europe to North and South America.

German firms enjoyed some "advantages of backwardness." They could adopt advanced machinery and industrial organization from British examples without having to devise these things themselves. But there were also disadvantages of backwardness. In order to acquire expensive technology and survive early competition with established businesses, many German firms relied on large banks and the state for the necessary capital funds. From 1875 to 1890, both the eastern German grain growers (the Junkers) and the big industrialists sought and won state protection from imports in the form of high tariffs; Germany's relatively large working class would have preferred free trade and cheaper food.

One can argue that the German empire's institutions were on their way to becoming more democratic during the early twentieth century. The Social Democratic Party and the Center Party were gaining in strength, and liberal industrialists were gaining in influence over the old Junker elite. As the success of industrialization began to materialize in the 1890s, for example, many leading industrialists saw that they could compete on the world market and broke with the Junkers to seek lower tariff barriers. Industrialists, like workers, now favored low tariffs and the resulting lower prices on food. Several shifts in cabinet formation resulted, followed by a victory for low-tariff delegates in the Reichstag election of 1912.

For all of the democratic gains at the ballot box under the empire, however, Germany's position within the global context made a transition to democracy problematic. German leaders ruled over a middle developer and felt threatened by the early developers. Frustrated in their ambitions to challenge Britain and France as leading imperial powers, the German elite responded to a crisis in southeastern Europe and opted for war in 1914. Their basic hope was for a quick victory to expand Germany's base from which to challenge the established powers. But the quick German victory did not materialize. Instead, the forces of Germany and its ally in this war, Austria-Hungary, bogged down in trench warfare against those of the Triple Entente (Britain, France, and Russia). The German high command's next gamble to win the war quickly – by introducing submarine warfare in the Atlantic – did not weaken Britain and France sufficiently before the feared and ultimately decisive intervention of American troops and resources.

As in other countries affected by the Great War, as World War I was called, massive mobilization had political consequences for Germany. Eleven million men, amounting to 18 percent of the population, were in uniform. Workers and families scrambled to support the war effort. Massive propaganda campaigns encouraged a strong national feeling and the sense that every German person was a valuable member of the nation. Similar campaigns in the other great powers boosted the feelings of national belonging in every state and increased the pressure for political reform to give every member of the nation an equal set of citizenship rights.

Although there was a gradual democratization of political life under the empire, the transition to a full democracy came abruptly. As it became clear that Germany was losing the war, several navy and army units mutinied. This was followed by uprisings in Berlin and the abdication of the kaiser. As in France at the end of Emperor Louis-Napoléon's rule, loss in war combined with military defections and domestic uprising sparked the transition from authoritarianism to democracy.

Democracy and Competitive Capitalism, 1919–1933

With the fall of the Second Empire, a democratic, constitutional regime took command of the German state. Under the **Weimar Republic**, all adult men and women had the right to vote in elections to the parliament (Reichstag). Elections were also held to select a president. In turn, the president usually requested the leader of the strongest parliamentary party to serve as the chancellor, form a cabinet, and lead the government. If the chancellor's party could not form a majority on its own, the chancellor had to put together a coalition of parties in the Reichstag in order to govern. Given the absence of a single party that could command a majority, most governments were coalition governments composed of several parties. Not all coalition governments are weak, but in the case of Weimar Germany many were.

Adherents of the empire retained considerable influence even under the new regime. The new democratic leaders never purged reactionary officers from the army or police. Instead, the democrats relied on the old authoritarians. For example, the Social Democratic leaders of the new German government called on the army to suppress demonstrations in a bid to restore order to rioting cities, quell the threat of a communist revolution, and prevent a German example of the recently successful 1917 revolution in Russia. In addition, most of the judges had received their legal training under the empire and continued to interpret the law in an antidemocratic fashion. Many of the highly trained and well-placed civil servants were holdovers from the previous era. Whereas the first president was a leading Socialist, **Friedrich Ebert**, the second and only other president, **Otto von Hindenburg**, was a Junker and former army officer. It was Hindenburg who appointed Hitler as chancellor in 1933.

If the usual distribution of vote shares had been sustained as the country moved into the early 1930s, the Weimar Republic might well have survived. The leading parties in the regime during the 1920s were the Social Democratic Party, which usually received about 25 percent of the vote, and the Center Party, which usually received about 15 percent of the vote. Further to the left, the Communist Party also polled steadily in the 15 percent range. On the center-right, various bourgeois, liberal, and traditional-nationalist parties accounted for most of the remaining 45 percent of the vote. The governments worked reasonably well, as long as parties in the center of the political spectrum remained strong.

Important aspects of the Weimar Republic's demise were the increasing strength of extreme left-wing and right-wing parties committed to the destruction of the republic and the failure of the center-right parties to retain their constituencies. Beginning with the election of 1930, the new **National Socialist German Workers' Party (Nazi Party)** started to capture a substantial share of the vote, mostly from the old center-right, bourgeois, and liberal parties. In 1933, in the last democratic election, for example, the Socialists received almost their typical amount at 20 percent, and the Center Party won its usual 15 percent. The Communists received a somewhat higher than normal 17 percent. It was the collapsing center-right and right-wing parties that provided the Nazis with a plurality of 33 percent of the vote, paving the way for Hitler to be named chancellor.

Our perspective on global contexts and paths to development illuminates important causes of the democratic collapse and fascist takeover that stand up to comparative analysis. First, Germany's size and middle-developer status interacted in ways dangerous for democracy. Germany was a big country, and many of its people had seemingly reasonable expectations that Germany would become the next great power. Yet, years of competition with the early developers, especially Britain and its ex-colony, the United States, and now added competition with a late developer, the Soviet Union, seemed to leave Germany lagging behind. For many people in Germany and in other populous middle developers (such as Japan and Italy), one temptation was to change the nature of the competition and embark on a military strategy to remake the world order with their nation on top. The temptation had already faded in the countries that had suffered serious defeats in attempts to use force and authoritarianism to improve their global position (Sweden in 1648; France in 1815 and 1870); the temptation was also weak in smaller countries with no realistic hope of a military path to greatness. Thus, one can see World War I, World War II, and the authoritarian regimes that pushed them forward as part of a common tendency among large middle developers to seek to improve their global position by military means. It is interesting to note that this tendency remains even today in several other large countries with frustrated developmental ambitions such as India, Pakistan, and Argentina.

Second, Germany's middle-developer status allowed an antidemocratic class at the top of its social structure to exercise considerable influence. Although Germany's rapid industrial development helped to produce a substantial middle class and working class, both of which are frequently in favor of democratic regimes in other states, there also remained a small but powerful class of landed elites who used labor-repressive modes of agriculture on their estates. These Junkers were also highly placed in the German state and could use their position to maintain their social and economic status. As we have noted, it was Hindenburg, a Junker president of the Weimar Republic, who appointed Hitler as chancellor. Although most Junkers certainly preferred more traditional conservatives to the Nazis, the Nazis had a better hold on mass support and were seen as useful tools in the larger struggle against communism. Other landed elites using labor-repressive modes of agriculture (such as plantation owners in the southern United States) had fought against full democracy; in these and similar cases, it seemed to require a major military defeat to force these small but powerful groups to relinquish key aspects of their authority.

Third, Germany's path to development set up political institutions that made it more difficult to reach agreements among social and political forces. Other middle-developing democratic regimes (in Sweden, Norway, Denmark, and Czechoslovakia) survived the interwar years without succumbing to domestic fascist movements. These liberal democracies survived at least in part because their democratic regimes were supported by strong coalitions between socialist and agrarian parties. Such a democratic urban–rural coalition did not form in Germany, nor did one form in the two other Western European countries that succumbed to fascist movements (Italy and Spain). Thus, it may be that the inability of predominantly urban socialists and predominantly rural agrarian parties to reach agreement fatally weakened the German, Italian, and Spanish democracies during the interwar years. Taken together, all three reasons imply that Germany's global position and domestic institutions tended to undermine attempts at democracy and competitive capitalism.

Nazism in Power, 1933–1945

Germany's Nazi regime was similar to other fascist regimes in several key organizational aspects. Hitler used his legal appointment as chancellor of the Weimar Republic to consolidate his command of the Nazi Party and put his party in control of the state. Within weeks, Hitler took advantage of communist resistance as a pretext to prohibit and suppress the Communist Party. During the rest of 1933, other parties were strongly encouraged to dissolve and allow their members to join the Nazi Party; for the remainder of the regime's rule, the Nazi Party was the only legal party in Germany. In principle, Nazis sought to enroll all Germans from every social class in various party-affiliated organizations. With these steps toward constructing a one-party, mobilizing, authoritarian regime, German Nazism can be seen as similar to the fascism in Italy under Benito Mussolini and, to a lesser degree, Spain under Francisco Franco.

What separates Nazi Germany from other cases of fascism, however, is the world war it initiated and the genocide it committed. Widespread support for militarism and expansionism, especially to the east, were part of Hitler's initial program and appeal. Hitler prepared for war from the start and successfully annexed Austria in 1938 and the Sudetenland in Czechoslovakia in 1939 without provoking a military response. There is evidence that Hitler hoped to avoid having to fight until the middle 1940s, and many Germans believed that war, when it did come, would be short. Nevertheless, the German invasion of Poland in September 1939 led the British and French to declare war. When German forces entered Paris in 1940, many Germans hoped for both victory and peace, but as the fighting dragged on over Britain and deep in Soviet Russia, this combined outcome became unlikely. From 1939 until the Nazi regime's fall in 1945, Germany, Europe, and the rest of the world's major powers were at war.

The Nazi regime undertook a brutal and virtually unique policy, the mass murder of civilians based on beliefs about their racial background, that both demands and evades explanation. The **Holocaust**, as the Nazi destruction of European Jewry is called, could not have gone forward without a combination of (1) racist beliefs, (2) the organizational capabilities of a modern state, (3) a fascist political regime, and (4) a leader who favored killing not just as a means to another end but also as a major policy objective in its own right. Of the three major fascist regimes of the period, only the Nazi regime carried out a campaign to exterminate all European Jews and people belonging to many other groups (Sinti and Roma, homosexuals, psychiatric patients, and the handicapped). In Italy, for example, the early fascist leadership openly included some people of Jewish descent, and Mussolini did not seek a campaign against Jews. Prior to the Holocaust, traditional forms of anti-Semitism were influential in Germany (but also throughout much of predominantly Christian Europe), as were modern, scientific forms of racism and population theories (these, too, were present elsewhere in Europe and in the United States). Other demagogues sought power in all of the major Western countries, but these potential leaders were less successful than Hitler. Taken alone or in various partial combinations, racist ideas, modern states, nondemocratic regimes, and murderous leaders have contributed to terrible outcomes throughout history and around the world, but the full combination of all four has so far come together only under Hitler's regime.

The choices made in the 1930s and early 1940s carried unintended consequences. Whereas many Junkers welcomed Hitler, at arm's length, in a bid to bring order to their rapidly changing society, the result of Nazism and its failure was the Junkers' elimination from a role in German politics. Germany lost its eastern territories, and the landed elite lost their grip on military and political power. World War II weakened all of the European powers, including Germany, and left two other powers at the top of the global military system: the Soviet Union and the United States. The global context of a bipolar, Cold War world was thus ushered into being by the developmental path and choices taken by Germany's political leaders.

Occupation (1945–1949), Division (1949–1990), and Unification (1990–)

Germany today is strongly democratic, capitalist, and internationally cooperative with other democratic, capitalist states. The radical transformation from its past took place in three basic steps. The victorious Allied powers occupied and administered Germany in four zones with virtually no central state apparatus from 1945 to 1949. Two new German states then emerged from the occupation: the Federal Republic of Germany (FRG), based on the American, British, and French zones in western Germany, and the German Democratic Republic (GDR), based on the Soviet zone in the east. The two-Germanys situation seemed destined to last for generations, yet a third period began with the fall of Soviet communism in Central Europe in 1989, the rapid collapse of the GDR, and the unification of the German states in 1990.

Germany's place in the global arena changed decisively. During the Cold War, each of the German states was tied to one of the major powers. The FRG became one of the world's leading economic developers, albeit without its own offensive military capabilities. The economy of the GDR languished and remained tied to the less successful command economies of the Soviet bloc. The collapse of the Soviet Union sparked the final decay of the GDR. Reunited Germany now occupies a leading position among the nations of the world and within Europe. Like all other major powers in the early twenty-first century, however, Germany lags far behind the United States in military power, especially in the ability to conduct large-scale military operations out-side of its home territory. As we shall see, these changes in the global context influence the makeup of Germany's current interests, identities, and institu-tions, as well as its overall development path.

Interests in Contemporary Germany

Germany's economy ranks at the very top of industrialized economies. Germany had the world's third-largest economy as measured by its Gross National Income (GNI) of $1.9 trillion (all figures in U.S. dollars) in 2002 (only the United States and Japan had larger economies); it had Europe's largest economy. (France had Europe's second largest with $1.3 trillion.) The economy yielded a per capita gross GNI (adjusted for purchasing-power parity – the relative cost of identical items) of $27,000, virtually the same as in Japan, France, and the United Kingdom. This average income per person is impressive, especially considering that Germany's population is 82 million people; if East Germany had not been annexed in 1990, Germany's produc-tion would be almost as high but with a smaller population of only about 65 million people. Only the United States has both a larger population (288 million) and a higher per capita GNI ($36,000).

Germany today benefits greatly from competing economically within the current system rather than attempting to subvert it through military force as it had attempted to do earlier. Germany is the world's second-leading exporter of goods and services. German exports in 2002 were valued at $704 billion (U.S.); only the United States had more ($1,020 billion), while Japan trailed significantly behind in third place ($445 billion). Whereas, prior to World War II, Germany had achieved impressive economic growth but still lacked the imperial success of Great Britain, now German economic and political ambitions seem well served by the current distribution of power. Germany is a member of the Organization for Economic Cooperation and Development (OECD) and a leader in the Group of Eight (G8), which is composed of the leaders from the world's eight largest economies. Several constraints on German sovereignty have been lifted since 1990 as a result of unification. The German-Polish border was finally settled at the **Oder-Neisse line**; the old allies from World War II no longer occupy Berlin. Although Germany is a member of the United Nations, it still lacks a seat on the powerful Security Council, which includes, by contrast, Great Britain and France.

Within Europe, Germany is, along with France, one of the key states pushing for greater economic and political cooperation in the European Union. In contrast with its own past, Germany adopted a radically new stance toward other European states. In order to avoid future military conflicts and to guide growing intra-European trade, West German leaders supported the drive for closer economic and political cooperation among European countries. The FRG was one of the six founding members of the European Coal and Steel Community in 1951, and it was a major supporter of the Rome Treaties of 1957 that built the European Economic Community and related institutions of cooperation. During the 1970s and 1980s, the U.S. and Japanese economies put severe pressure on European industries. In response, West Germany took the lead, along with France, in pushing for a stronger European cooperation, notably in the Single European Act, which went into effect in 1987 and significantly reduced barriers to trade and institutional obstacles to Europe-wide political cooperation. Unified Germany in the 1990s supported the Treaty on European Union of 1992, which strengthened the EEC and other institutions, transforming them into the European Union. Germany also pushed for European Monetary Union (EMU) in 1999 and EU expansion in 2004, so that the EU now includes 25 member countries, including most of the former communist countries in Central Europe.

As a whole, Germany's material interests lie in maintaining and working within the current world economic system. But that does not mean that all Germans have exactly the same interests. What are the various interests in Germany? Which interests emerged as dominant, and how do they seek to position Germany in the world economy? How do they add up to produce a national political outcome?

One way to divide up the economy is to look at the major factors of production: land, labor, and capital. As you might expect, these factors generate different interests. Owners of land favor low costs for the inputs – labor and industrial products – that they use in agricultural production and high prices for their agricultural products. Owners of labor – that is, workers – favor low food prices and high wages. Owners of capital – such as factory owners – favor low food prices, low wages, and high prices for their own products.

Since the end of World War II, the impact of the generally expanding world trade on these different interests has helped to sustain democratic and capitalist institutions in Germany. Productive labor and capital are both relatively abundant in Germany. The German workforce is highly skilled and productive. Germany imported more workers as immigrants, especially during the 1960s, and the German workforce remains one of the world's strongest. One problem is relatively high unemployment; it reached 10 percent in 1997, remained at 8 or 9 percent through 2002, and has been a major challenge for the government of Chancellor Gerhard Schröder. With regard to capital, Germany possesses a massive industrial base, some of which survived from before World War II but much of which was built after the war along highly efficient lines. To take one measure of Germany's capital abundance, in 1953 West Germany was the seventh most-industrialized country in the world, measured by industrialization per capita, and by 1980 it was the third most-industrialized country (behind only the United States and Sweden). German industry relies on being able to sell its goods in European and other foreign markets.

Germany, however, has a relatively scarce supply of agriculturally productive land; there are too many people and too small a territory. In West Germany, there were fully 414 people per square kilometer of arable land. By contrast, for example, in the land-abundant United States, there are only about 41 people per square kilometer of arable land. Agriculture adds just 1 percent to German GDP (whereas it adds 2 percent to U.S. GDP and 3 percent to that of France); agriculture produces just 1 percent of Germany's merchandise exports (compared with 2 percent of U.S. merchandise exports). Thus, unlike industry and labor, most of German agriculture was not in a position to produce on a global scale at competitive prices; Germany cannot meet its demand for agricultural products from domestic sources.

One can see the practical political effects of these economic interests in at least two ways. First, the major political parties agree on the basic outlines of economic policy. Industry and labor have won the fight with agriculture to put Germany in the free-trade camp. German industry and labor now have strong interests in an open international trading system in which they use their strength to compete on a world market and avoid flooding their own market with too many goods. Given the size of these two sectors in Germany, their joint interests overrode those of the opposing agriculturalists, who would have preferred trade restrictions and higher food prices. The Social Democratic Party, with a stronghold in the working class, favors free-trade industrialization. The **Christian Democrats** (composed of the allied parties of the Christian Democratic Union and the Christian Social Union), with strong support from industrialists, also favor free-trade industrialization. Both have pushed for the reduction of trade barriers on a global scale and within the European Union.

The second political impact of interests is that the main parties advocate even greater economic free trade and are willing to compensate the losers under this policy. Even during the late 1990s, when world financial crises unsettled global markets, the major political parties remained strongly in favor of the continued economic integration of Europe, including monetary union with ten other European countries. A major concession that the government regularly has to make in order to deepen European integration is to its farmers. As compensation to landowners and farmers for the losses caused by economic integration and free trade, to this day the European Union spends the bulk of its budget on support for farmers. Both of Germany's two main political parties have supported the relatively generous welfare provisions of the German state that cushion the blows of international economic competition and allow the employed workforce to maintain its high level of technical skills, albeit at the cost of relatively high unemployment rates and pension costs.

The social classes that make up German society come out of a tradition of stark class distinctions. However, the experiences of fascism, the post–World War II economic success, and now the transition to a service-oriented economy have dulled long-standing divisions. One can take the occupational composition of the workforce as a measure of changes in Germany's class structure. In 1950, 28 percent of workers were in agriculture or self-employed, 51 percent were manual workers (mostly in industry), and 21 percent were salaried, nonmanual workers (so-called white-collar and service workers). By 1994, only 10 percent were in agriculture or self-employed and only 38 percent were manual workers, whereas fully 52 percent were salaried, nonmanual workers. Thus, as in the rest of the industrialized world, Germany has developed a combined industrial and postindustrial social structure.

Identities in Contemporary Germany

Gradually, after World War II, antidemocratic values weakened. The failure to win world domination shook many people's faith in the fascist alternative to democracy. After the war, many Germans avoided overt politics and turned inward – toward family, work, and the pursuit of personal well-being – and abandoned a belief in grander political ends. The relative economic success of the West German economy during the 1950s and 1960s reinforced the value placed on the pursuit of prosperity.

Support for democracy has grown. In a 1950 survey, German respondents were asked about political competition. Fully 25 percent said that it is better for a country to have only one political party, and another 22 percent were undecided about this question or gave no response. A bare majority, just 53 percent, said that it is better for a country to have several parties. It would be hard to say that a political culture is democratic if such a slight majority of people believe that political competition among parties is a good idea. Things have changed, however. In a 1990 survey, just 3 percent of respondents said that it is better to have only one party, and only 8 percent were undecided or gave no response. Now, the overwhelming preponderance of respondents, 89 percent, state that it is better for a country to have several political parties.

Today, a strong faith in democracy can be seen at the elite and mass levels. The German political philosopher Jürgen Habermas has described "constitutional patriotism" as the ultimate political value. Support for democracy is also reflected in public-opinion polls. According to a survey carried out in the 1990s, 50 percent of respondents in Germany state that they are "very satisfied" or "fairly satisfied" with the way democracy is working in Germany; 37 percent say they are "not very satisfied," and only 11 percent are "not at all satisfied." Although this measure of support for democracy is not as high as in the United Kingdom – where 61 percent report that they are "very satisfied" or "fairly satisfied" – the distribution of responses to this question in Germany is about average among EU countries. Still, there are important differences between the former East Germany and West Germany: only 30 percent of East German respondents state that they are "very" or "fairly satisfied," compared with 55 percent in the West. The indicators of public opinion suggest that there is widespread support for human rights as a basic value and broad support for the current version of democratic institutions in Germany.

Still, the more than 82 million people living in Germany do not share a single identity. One dimension on which Germans differ is how they situate themselves with respect to the rest of Europe and the possibility of a European identification that transcends national identifications. In a survey conducted in the late 1990s, 49 percent of respondents said that they consider themselves to be "German only." Another 35 percent of respondents said that they considered themselves to be "German and European." Seven percent said that they considered themselves "European and German," and 5 percent chose "European only." The distribution of national versus European identity in Germany is about average for the 15 European Union countries. Among the bigger countries, German national identity is located halfway between the weak national identity in France (where just 31 percent chose "French only") and the strong national identity in the United Kingdom (where 60 percent chose "British only").

Many Germans are relatively new residents of the German state. In the post–World War II period from 1949 to 1989, when Germany was divided, approximately 13 million refugees whom the state identified as German migrated to the FRG from Poland, the Soviet Union, and the GDR. The territory of the GDR in 1948 was home to about 19 million people. The GDR's population shrank during the decades of division, mostly because of legal and illegal migration to the FRG. In 1989 alone, some 344,000 people from the GDR left for the FRG, along with 376,000 "ethnic" Germans from the Soviet Union and elsewhere in Eastern Europe. As mentioned earlier, what was left of the GDR's population, 16 million people, came under FRG control in 1990.

Many people who live in Germany are considered by the German state to be foreigners – about 7.3 million people, the largest group of foreigners in any European country. People from Turkey and southern Europe (the former Yugoslavia, Greece, and Italy) arrived in large numbers during the 1960s under the government's policy of encouraging the temporary migration of foreigners to work in German industries that needed more labor. Almost a million people from these groups left Germany during the 1970s when the government provided incentives for foreign workers and their families to leave Germany, yet most of the immigrants did not leave. The single largest group of foreigners in Germany are from Turkey (in 1997, there were about 2.1 million people whom the state identified as from Turkey, 1.3 million from the former Yugoslavia, 600,000 from Italy, 400,000 from Greece, 300,000 from Poland, 200,000 from Austria, and 100,000 from the United States). By 2002, foreigners comprised 9 percent of Germany's total population (somewhat below the 11 percent figure for the United States but well above the typical 4 percent figure for other European countries).

Although there are signs of change toward a more permanent official status, the conventional term for foreign workers, "**guest workers**" (**Gastarbeiter**), underscores the state's attempt to emphasize the temporary nature of their stay in Germany, despite their deep involvement in the German economy and society. Many of the hardships faced by these immigrant groups are common to the experience of immigrant laborers in other industrialized countries: low wages, dangerous employment, few opportunities for advancement, racism, victimization by crime, discrimination in housing and employment, and the near-constant threat of legal deportation. The difficult situation of many immigrants defined as nonethnic Germans is exacerbated by their exclusion from the political process. It was virtually impossible for foreign workers, or even their children, to earn the right to vote, become a citizen, or run for public office. The still-strong German legal tradition of defining citizenship by descent, rather than by place of birth, lies at the core of the problem. After assuming power in 1998, Chancellor Schröder's government introduced legislation to ease citizenship requirements but was forced to postpone and moderate its plan in the face of widespread opposition.

With the absorption of the former East Germany, the long-standing predominance of Protestantism in the population has been renewed, along with a new injection of people not affiliated with any religion. Protestants comprise 45 percent of the population, Roman Catholics 37 percent, Muslims 3 percent, and those unaffiliated or members of other faiths a total of 15 percent. In the former West Germany just before the transition, in 1987, Roman Catholics comprised 43 percent of the population, and Protestants (Lutheran-Reformed and Lutheran) comprised an almost identical 42 percent. In addition to these two main groups, there were Muslims (2.7 percent),

Reformed tradition (0.6 percent), Jews (0.1 percent), and others, including those officially without religion (12 percent). Meanwhile, in the former East Germany (in 1990), Protestants comprised fully 47 percent of the population and Roman Catholics just 7 percent. Most of the rest were officially unaffiliated – about 46 percent (a figure that also includes a very small proportion of "other"). Just several thousand German Jews survived the Holocaust, and only about 30,000 Jewish people live in Germany today, predominantly in Berlin.

The identities of men and women are changing, too. Germany emerged from World War II with gender identities rooted in the past. In the FRG, the law still reflected greater rights for men than for women, especially in regard to marriage and property. In the GDR, strict legal equality was undermined by pervasive informal occupational segregation by gender. A movement for women's rights developed during the 1970s in the FRG, as in virtually all Western democracies. By force of example, this movement has changed how men and women think of themselves. Institutional changes have reinforced these new conditions, although not as dramatically as in some other countries. Abortion laws were almost liberalized in the 1970s but were turned back by a conservative majority on the Constitutional Court. After unification, the differences in abortion laws between West and East proved to be a difficult political issue: The liberal abortion law for the East expired in 1992, and a moderately pro-choice, all-German law was declared unconstitutional in 1993. Nearly 90 percent of women in the communist East had worked outside of the home, whereas not even half of women did in the West. Pay and working conditions were better in the West, but the advancement of women into the higher ranks of important professions remained slow.

Institutions in Contemporary Germany

The founding document of the Federal Republic of Germany is the Basic Law (Grundgesetz). Although political actors use it much like a constitution, it is usually not called a constitution, given the prominent role that the occupying Western powers had in its formulation and given the reluctance to recognize as permanent the division of Germany into two parts. Under the Western occupation, political life began to reemerge mainly at the regional rather than the national level. In September 1948, the Allied military governors and provincial leaders convened a constituent assembly of 65 delegates to draft a provisional constitution. The aims of the framers were to avoid the perceived weaknesses of the Weimar system, to prevent a renewed fascist movement, and to lock western Germany into the Western alliance. The resulting document strengthened the chancellor and the legislature over the bureaucracy and army, and it decentralized power to the various regional governments. The framers placed the rule of law and basic liberal institutions at the very heart of the system. Their proposed Basic Law was ratified by regional parliaments in May 1949. It has been amended several times, and its provisional character has faded; it was not replaced during unification, but rather its terms were used to incorporate the former East Germany into the FRG.

The two largest political parties in post–World War II West Germany grew out of the Christian Democratic and Socialist camps from the Weimar era in radically new ways. The Christian Democratic Union (Christlich-Demokratische Union, CDU) and the Christian Social Union (Christlich-Soziale Union, CSU) comprise the Christian Democratic camp. Although officially two parties, most political scientists consider them to function as one party for they do not nominate candidates to compete in the same district; the CSU contests elections in predominantly Catholic Bavaria, whereas the CDU contests them in the rest of the FRG. The two parties are often referred to collectively as the CDU/CSU. A major transformation is that the CDU explicitly sought support from Protestants as well as Catholics. Various Christian Democratic parties won local elections in the occupied zones after World War II, and many of them came together once CDU leader Konrad Adenauer became chancellor with the support of the CSU. The CDU/CSU supporters were not just former Center Party voters but also those who had supported liberal and socialist parties in the past. A second major transformation was that the party, especially Economics Minister Ludwig Erhard, who later became chancellor himself, strongly championed free-market economics. The CDU/CSU has been a center-right party, advocating capitalism with strong social protections, close ties to the United States and other Western powers, and strong anticommunism.

The Social Democratic Party (Sozialdemokratische Partei Deutschlands, SPD) was transformed by the unexpected successes of the CDU/CSU and the SPD's long years in opposition until 1966. The party emerged from under the Nazi-era ban on its activities as the best-organized party in occupied Germany. Yet its failure to win elections during the 1950s convinced its leading figures, such as future chancellors Willy Brandt and Helmut Schmidt, of the need to break from its overdependence on orthodox Marxist rhetoric and almost exclusively working-class support. With major reforms at the 1959 Bad Godesberg party conference, the SPD officially stated its policy of reaching out to religious believers and to middle-class voters, changes that gradually began to have their effect on voters, who gave them increasing support in the early 1960s. The successful participation of the SPD in the Grand Coalition government with the CDU from 1966 to 1969 demonstrated the ability of its leading figures to manage the economy and politics in pro-democratic and pro-capitalist ways and paved the way for its electoral success in 1969 and the formation of its own governing coalition with the Free Democratic Party through 1982.

Two medium-sized parties have played pivotal roles in modern German politics as well. The Free Democratic Party (Freie Demokratische Partei, FDP) stands for individualism and free economic competition. In the immediate post–World War II years, the party was formed by Weimar-era liberals, although the anticlerical emphasis of German liberalism was pared away to leave the focus on free-market economics. Although the FDP has never polled more than 13 percent of the vote in national elections, it has frequently been able to give one of the two larger parties the necessary support to form a government. With roots in the environmentalist and antinuclear social movements in the 1970s, another party, the Greens, first won parliamentary representation in the 1983 elections. For much of the 1980s, the party was divided into a more fundamentalist faction that advocated far-reaching reforms to reject capitalist development and to protect the environment, and a more realist faction advocating less drastic reform while working within the system. After reunification in 1990, the Greens joined with Bündnis90, former East German counterparts who had been leading dissidents under the GDR, but the alliance between the wealthier and poorer partners has not been smooth. The Greens have been in government as a junior coalition partner with the SPD following the 1998 and 2002 elections. Some small parties have won seats in the **Bundestag** (the lower house of parliament), although not participation in the formation of a government, most recently the Party of Democratic Socialism (PDS), which was formed by leading figures from the former Communist Party of the GDR such as Gregor Gysi. It was able to win districts in the former East Germany, mainly with support from older voters dissatisfied with the rapid pace of postunification change; it performed poorly in the 1998 and 2002 elections.

In part because of the Basic Law's well-crafted institutional design, Germany has sustained its political democracy since 1949. At the most basic level, Germany qualifies as a political democracy because all of the major actors in German society expect that elections for the highest offices in the state will be held on a regular basis into the foreseeable future. This situation contrasts with the Weimar Republic, where many leading political actors either sought to end the practice of elections or at least reasonably expected that elections would be suspended at some point. Although not a guarantee, it is certainly important that free and fair national elections in the Federal Republic were held in 1949 and regularly thereafter, including the elections of 1998 that ended 17 years of Christian Democratic rule under Chancellor Helmut Kohl and brought the Socialist Party to power under Gerhard Schröder. According to the Basic Law of 1949, elections to the national legislature are held every four years. (The Basic Law's exceptions to this rule occur when the legislature is deadlocked. If this happens, it provides for the **federal president (Bundespräsident)** to call early elections. So far, this has happened only twice, in 1972 and 1982.) The intervals between German national elections are not quite as regularly spaced as election intervals in presidential systems, such as the United States, but they are more regular than in other parliamentary systems, such as that of the United Kingdom.

For the most part, the powers of the president are severely restricted compared with the relatively powerful role for the president under the Weimar system. Although the president is the official head of state, the president's powers are mainly restricted to the calling of elections and ceremonial functions, and one person can serve for no more than two terms as president. The president can pardon criminals and receives and visits other heads of state. The president promulgates all federal laws with a signature (the authority to refuse to sign is disputed, and presidents have signed all but perhaps five laws). The president is not popularly elected. According to the Basic Law, every five years a special federal convention convenes for the sole purpose of selecting the president; it is composed of the delegates to the legislature, an equal number of representatives from the state assemblies, and several other prominent persons. The selection by the federal convention has so far led to presidents with moderate views, at the end of distinguished careers, and well respected by the political elite. Johannes Rau began serving his presidential term in July 1999 at the age of 68; he had previously served as the Deputy National Chairman of the Socialist Party and as prime minister of Germany's largest state, North-Rhine-Westphalia. His 2004 successor, 61-year-old Horst Köhler, was chosen by the majority in the federal convention held by parties in opposition to the SPD-Green government – the CDU/CSU and the FDP. Trained as an economist and political scientist, Köhler served in the economics and finance ministries of CDU governments, rising to Deputy Minister of Finance from 1990 to 1993, during which time he helped to negotiate the Maastricht treaty on European Economic and Monetary Union and undertook major responsibilities for the process of German unification. Some presidents have been able to influence national debates by means of skillful speech making, as when Richard von Weizsäcker (president 1984–1994; CDU) gave a 1985 speech commemorating the fortieth anniversary of the end of World War II that cautioned Germans not to forget the nation's past and to guard against a revival of nationalist sentiment.

The **federal chancellor (Bundeskanzler)** is the real executive power in the German system. Although the chancellor is responsible to the legislature, as in other parliamentary systems, he or she may appoint and dismiss other cabinet ministers at will, rather like U.S. presidents. The relatively regular interval between elections gives the chancellor a somewhat firm idea about the political struggles that lie ahead and enhances the authority of the legislature and the chancellor over that of the president. Another source of the chancellor's authority is Article 67 of the Basic Law, the so-called **constructive vote of no confidence**, which states that the legislature may dismiss the chancellor only when a majority of the members simultaneously elects a successor. This brake on the authority of the legislature helps prevent weak

TABLE 5.1. German Chancellors since World War II

1949–1963	Konrad Adenauer (CDU)
1963–1966	Ludwig Erhard (CDU)
1966–1969	Kurt Georg Kiesinger (CDU)
1969–1974	Willy Brandt (SPD)
1974–1982	Helmut Schmidt (SPD)
1982–1998	Helmut Kohl (CDU)
1998–	Gerhard Schröder (SPD)

chancellors from emerging. For example, the only time that a constructive vote of no confidence succeeded was in 1982, when the Free Democratic Party (FDP) withdrew from the ruling coalition and went along with a vote of no confidence regarding Social Democratic Party (SPD) Chancellor Helmut Schmidt. A new FDP and CDU/CSU coalition in the legislature selected Helmut Kohl as chancellor. With a majority behind him from the beginning and with several election victories thereafter, Kohl served as chancellor from 1982 until 1998. In other parliamentary governments, legislatures can agree to dismiss a sitting government but then may fail to agree on a strong successor, agreeing instead only to select weak figures unable to take real initiatives on their own.

The lower house (Bundestag) of the bicameral legislature produces the executive. The lower house is directly elected, whereas the upper house (**Bundesrat**) is composed of delegates chosen by the 16 federal states (each state is called a Land). The leader of the largest party in the lower house usually puts together a two-party coalition (neither of the two largest parties controls a majority of seats alone); the coalition in turn supports the party leader as chancellor. The chancellor must maintain a legislative majority in order to stay in power. With majority support, however, the chancellor has a relatively free hand in appointing and dismissing members of the cabinet. For example, the Social Democratic Party won the single largest block of seats in the 1998 and 2002 elections; after each election, its leader, Gerhard Schröder, formed a coalition with the Green Party to control a majority of seats. His cabinet is dominated by SPD politicians, but as it is a coalition government some key posts were given to Green Party politicians, notably the post of foreign minister to Joschka Fischer.

The rules for translating votes into seats comprise a crucial institution in any democracy. Germany employs a mixed-member proportional formula (a subtype of proportional representation). Each voter makes **two ballot choices** in a national German election for representatives in the lower house. One choice is for a candidate to represent the voter's district. The winning candidates in each district take half the seats in the lower house. A voter's second choice is for a national party overall in the lower house. The other half of the seats are awarded such that the proportion of seats per party matches the votes per party on the second ballot choice. The two types of representatives give the system its mixed-member label; once in place, however, the two types of members behave the same and have identical powers in the legislature.

Germany's mixed-member proportional system preserves the influence of medium-sized and large parties and minimizes the impact of small parties with widely dispersed supporters. Germany's medium-sized parties gain national representation via the second ballot choice more easily than under a plurality electoral system, in which the voter makes only one choice for a given office and the top vote-getter in a district wins the office (as is the case in the United States and United Kingdom). Most notably, two German parties have won seats in the legislature by securing a national vote of more than 5 percent on the second ballot choice, even though their candidates did not win any districts on the first ballot choice. The Free Democrats have been a crucial player in legislative politics since 1949, while typically winning about 10 percent of the popular vote. Similarly, the Greens have become almost as influential since the 1980s although securing only around 10 percent to 5 percent of the popular vote. There was a Grand Coalition government of the SPD and the CDU/CSU from 1966 to 1969, but all of the other coalition governments have involved one of the big parties with one of the medium-sized parties.

The big winners in the electoral system are the two largest parties. Germany's electoral system includes three special rules, two of which aid the largest parties. One is the "5 percent rule": A party must win at least 5 percent of the national vote on the second ballot choice in order to get a matching share of seats. Thus, small parties with support distributed across many districts are eliminated from gaining representation (for instance, the extreme right-wing Republican Party won 3 percent of the national second-choice vote but no seats in 1994; similar results emerged in 1998 and 2002). Even the medium-sized Free Democrats and the Greens are perennially concerned about falling below the 5 percent threshold; their coalition partners in government have periodically advocated strategic voting in order to ensure that the medium-sized parties do not fall below that mark. During the SPD–FDP coalition of 1969–1982, SPD supporters offered crucial support to the FDP on their second ballot choice; in 1998, the FDP relied upon second ballot choices of CDU supporters, while the Greens relied upon second ballot choices of SPD supporters. The 5 percent threshold thus increases the reliance of the medium-sized parties on their larger partners. A second important rule is the "three-district waiver" exception to the 5 percent rule: If a party wins a seat in at least three districts, then the national 5 percent rule is waived, and the party is also awarded seats according to its share of the total vote on the second ballot choice. This second modification permitted the former East German Communist Party, campaigning as the Party of Democratic Socialism, to win national representation after unification in the elections of the 1990s based on its victories in the former East Berlin, despite its very small national vote share. This second modification is the only one that aids very small parties, and it comes into play only if the small party's supporters are concentrated in a few districts. In 2002, however, the PDS won only two districts and thus did not qualify for additional seats by the three-district waiver. Finally, the "excess mandate provision" holds that if a party wins more district mandates than the proportion of the popular vote on the second choice would otherwise award the party, then the party gets to retain any extra seats, and the size of the legislature is increased accordingly. Although of relatively little consequence for most of the Federal Republic's electoral history, this third rule during the 1990s helped the big parties that can win seats in many districts; it gave the CDU 6 extra seats in 1990, and then in 1994 gave the CDU 12 extra seats and the SPD 4.

All of these rules, combined with the way voters actually cast their ballots, produce governments. To take a specific example, the 2002 elections gave five parties seats in the lower house: Social Democratic Party (SPD), 251 seats; Christian Democratic Union (CDU)/Christian Social Union (CSU), 248 seats; Bündnis90/Greens, 55 seats; Free Democratic Party (FDP), 47 seats; Party of Democratic Socialism (PDS) – socialist, former communist, 2 seats. Over a dozen other parties were on ballots in one or more states but did not qualify for national representation. As in previous elections, the extreme right-wing parties were fragmented and ineffectual at the national level. These seat totals for the five parties in the legislature produced an 11-seat majority for the SPD-Green alliance, so Chancellor Schröder remained in power, although he shuffled some individual cabinet posts. As we have seen, Germany's bicameral system can provide other opportunities for the opposition and their supporters despite a government's majority in the lower house. The opposition was able to play a strong role in influencing Schröder's sweeping economic reform plans in 2003 after elections in the states of Hesse and Lower Saxony in February of that year gave victories to the CDU; with the CDU in power in those states, their delegates to the Bundesrat gave a majority to opposition parties. The final legislation agreed to in December 2003 required the government to compromise from its original proposals.

Germany's federal structure gives the republic's constituent units a great deal of power. Sixteen states (*Länder*) make up the republic. The combination of federalism in the state and bicameralism in the legislature gives Germany a substantial amount of institutional overlap that differs both from unitary systems (such as in the United Kingdom and France) and from other federal systems that have sharper federal–state distinctions (such as in the United States). Compared with regional governments in Europe, the states possess a good deal of power in relation to the central government. Each state has a premier and a legislature. The state legislatures send delegates to the assembly that elects the president and also send delegates to the national legislature's upper house (the Bundesrat). The Basic Law reserves certain powers for the states, including education, police and internal security, administration of justice, and the regulation of mass media. The states are also responsible for administering federal laws and collecting most taxes. Changes since the Basic Law of 1949 have been designed to enhance or at least preserve the states' powers. They now have at least a joint role in higher education, regional economic development, and agricultural reform. Reforms in 1994 were designed to give the various states a voice in policy making at the European level; until then, the federal government had a larger role to play.

The economy itself can be seen as an institution, especially because its key actors are linked in stable relationships that go beyond mere monetary exchange. Many terms have been used to describe the economy of the Federal Republic of Germany: neocorporatism, social democracy, and coordinated market economy, to name three important ones. These terms seek to capture Germany's blend of social and market institutions in a single economy. In fact, a term that Germans commonly use to describe their economic order is a "social market economy." A social market economy rests not only on market principles of supply and demand but also on extensive involvement by the state and societal institutions. Germany has institutions that are designed to ensure the smooth functioning of free economic exchange. Prior to the European Monetary Union, Germany's central bank, for example, was for a long time one of the most independent and powerful central banks in the world. In fact, Germany's central bank was the main model for the European Central Bank. Germany's bank sought to keep interest rates and inflation low and the currency stable. There is no purer example of a firm commitment to market principles than a central bank free of political influence. On the social side of the equation, the German state guarantees a free university education for all who qualify academically, and basic health care and adequate income for all its citizens. In addition, the state supports organized representation in the workplace and vocational training for workers, rather than letting these matters be handled by firms or unions alone.

At the heart of Germany's social market economy is the "social partnership" of business and labor. According to the political scientist Lowell Turner, social partnership is defined as "the nexus – and central political and economic importance – of bargaining relationships between strongly organized employers (in employer associations) and employees (in unions and works councils) that range from comprehensive collective bargaining and plant-level co-determination to vocational training and federal, state and local economic policy discussions." In addition to labor and business, there are also important "framing and negotiating roles" for two other actors, large banks and the government. In this kind of system, negotiated agreements between the social partners of business and labor shape politics and economics at all levels: national, regional, and local. As an example of national peak agreements, one could point to the Concerted Action of 1967 or the Solidarity Pact in 1993. There are also industry-wide or simply firm-level agreements regarding, for example, vocational training and industrial policy.

The Solidarity Pact of 1993 nicely illustrates a peak bargain under social partnership. The federal government agreed not to let old industries in the former East Germany simply wither away. Instead, it sought an active role for itself in industrial restructuring. Eastern industries benefited from temporary assistance, as did labor, because employment was protected. Western industrialists were also given opportunities for developing infrastructure (such as roads, railroads, and government offices), while they promised to invest in the old eastern industrial core rather than simply dismantling it and confining their production to the already developed western regions. Unions, in return, promised to hold back wage demands in both the East and West and promised to support the program of adjustment in the East rather than adopt a posture of militant opposition. Although this bargain worked to the benefit of all sides, it was the product of institutionalized negotiation, not simple economic logic.

Scholars and policymakers do not agree on the future of German social partnership. In the view of many, the Solidarity Pact of 1993 was just an isolated episode in a period more noted for conflicting interests. The early 1990s witnessed a new phase of economic globalization: Would the institutions of social partnership survive the neoliberal economic policy atmosphere? Would they hold up against rapid financial movements across international borders? Could they be maintained in the face of widening international economic competition as the costs of communication and transportation continued to fall? During the early 1990s, it was plausible that Germany's more moderate social partnership would succumb to the new conditions. Unemployment rose to over 10 percent in late 1995 and grew to over 12 percent in early 1997. Because unions typically find it difficult to maintain their bargaining position in the face of persistent joblessness among workers, German unions will likely find it hard to sustain their influential role. Furthermore, the increasing integration of European economies weakens the position of national-level actors, especially labor unions. Finally, the prospect of extending the European Union to the east introduces the possibility that employers will use low-cost labor in less-developed member countries rather than continue to invest in the developed core.

Others are more optimistic that German social partnership may be resilient after all. Although recognizing the difficulties facing partnership, especially the challenges facing organized labor, one can point to more positive signs. In the first place, the eastern decay has not spread to the West; instead Western institutions have spread to the former East Germany. Employer associations, industrial unions, comprehensive collective-bargaining arrangements, elected works councils, and legally mandated codetermination have all taken root in the old East. The economic integration of the East, although not complete and not as painless as Chancellor Helmut Kohl argued it would be in 1990, certainly has not led to an economic collapse. According to these optimists, few companies actually relocated to low-wage countries during the 1980s. They further maintain that there will likely be little relocation to the East during the next few decades. Investment in the East, moreover, may serve to stimulate demand for exports from Germany and may also open up even more markets for German goods. In addition to these favorable trends, the international financial crises of the late 1990s – first in Asia, then in Russia, and then in Latin America – dampened enthusiasm for unregulated free markets, even among global investors. In times of uncertainty, many international financial decision makers sought the greater security provided by more institutionalized forms of industrial organization. European Union institutions leave a great deal of leeway to national-level institutions, by the principle of "subsidiarity" (the notion that decisions should be made at the most local level possible), and because each individual government, especially governments of big countries such as Germany, has a major say in what happens at the European level. Finally, Germany's major firms have actually sought to preserve key elements of its social market economy, such as their successful efforts to maintain policies of generously supported early retirement for workers.

Persistent unemployment (reaching levels above 11 percent) and poor economic performance were cited by the Schröder government as the reasons for major cuts in social spending and labor-market reforms in 2003. Although key reforms did pass, making it easier for firms to hire workers without providing them protections against firing, for example, two key features of the German labor market did not change: sectorwide wage agreements and workers' codetermination. Both of these institutions involve businesses, labor unions, workers' elected representatives, and the state in managing change on the shop floors of Germany's leading industries. Thus, even as Germany's Social Democratic and Green coalition governing parties attempt to put forward major changes in the state and the economy, the core features of social partnership continue to play key roles.

The new German judiciary and the legal philosophy of the state is the product of a deliberate attempt by post–Nazi era political actors to transform radically an institution that had not protected basic civil and human rights. On the side of institutional redesign, the Basic Law created a Federal Constitutional Court with the power of judicial review. The practice of judges reviewing state actions for conformity with a higher law – in this case, the Basic Law – was completely foreign to the German legal tradition before 1949. The change was strongly championed by the U.S. occupiers, who had at their disposal the model of the U.S. Supreme Court and who were clearly thinking of the old German judiciary that did not strike down any of the Nazi government's decrees.

A distinctive and controversial aspect of German law and legal institutions, however, concerns what Americans would call freedom of speech. Unlike in the United States, "hate speech" is unconstitutional in Germany, and the organizations that promote it are banned after being investigated by the Office of Constitutional Protection (Verfassungsschutz). It is illegal, for example, to organize a Nazi Party, to deny publicly the historical fact of the Holocaust, or to sell or distribute Nazi propaganda. How does the German state justify actions and policies that Americans would consider unacceptable, and even unconstitutional, departures from liberal democratic practices? Germans view their democracy as a "militant democracy" that is unwilling to permit antidemocratic forces to use the protections of the liberal state to help undermine it. These ideas and the institutions that are in place to back them up are one obvious reaction to Germany's authoritarian past.

The German judiciary nevertheless also shows some continuity in its institutional practices. On the side of persistence, German judges are closely integrated with the state bureaucracy, and their posts are like those of high bureaucrats. They are rarely former politicians, prosecutors, or other types of attorneys, as is often the case in the United States. Instead, aspiring jurists begin their careers as apprentices to sitting judges; they then rise through the hierarchy and, if they are successful, never leave the judicial branch. The dominant institutional philosophy of judging puts the judge in the role of actively applying the law to individual cases in a deliberate pursuit of the truth, unlike U.S. judges, who more commonly see themselves as impartial arbiters between two conflicting parties. German judges do not set precedents as do their Anglo-American counterparts; the job of German judges is simply to apply the law correctly, not interpret it or adapt it to circumstances unforeseen by the framers of a statute. Despite the otherwise federal structure of the judiciary, the German legal code is uniform across all of the various state governments.

Germany's Post–World War II Developmental Path

Whereas Germany had relied upon state-led development for most of its unified history, the post–World War II German state acted as a cooperative partner in social and economic development. The FRG itself led much of the world's post–World War II economic growth, partly financed internationally by the U.S. Marshall Plan for European recovery. Germany's economic development was grounded domestically in its close cooperation among top businesses, organized labor unions, and the state. The state still influences Germany's society and economy through institutions similar to those found in many other European countries. The economic slowdown in the early twenty-first century presents challenges for its governments that are seeking to streamline the state and energize economic growth, yet Germany today is still a model for those seeking to strike a new balance between the strengths of the free market and the support of significant social protections. In its foreign economic policy, Germany promotes deep economic integration with world markets and especially within an expanded European Union. In foreign security policy, Cold War Germany was the forward base of U.S. power in Europe. Germany remains a key U.S. ally in the early twenty-first century, although it advocates greater multilateralism in the use of force to fight terror and rogue states around the world.

Germany's path of political development was profoundly shaped by its long period as a middle developer (see Table 5.2 at the end of the chapter). Germany began much like the rest of Europe. Yet, compared with England and France, Germany's lateness in developing a single territorial state and a strong industrial base, and then new challenges from even later developers, such as Russia, put Germany in a difficult position. Germany was also a relatively large middle developer, like Japan, and thus it acquired domestic interests, identities, and institutions different from smaller middle developers, such as Sweden and Denmark. The temptation to use a massive state apparatus for military conquest in a bid to improve its global position did not disappear in Germany until after World War II. Germany's persistent reliance on the state to address many important tasks fostered a distinctive set of interests, identities, and institutions that made it hard to develop or sustain democratic political institutions. As a result, for much of its history, Germany's economic development was state-led, and its political order was authoritarian.

Germany's global context predisposed it to adopt the state-led path to development. The Second Empire rose by facing challenges from its military rivals. With a heavy reliance on its army and bureaucracy, the state then aided the growth of heavy industry in a bid to catch up with leading industries in Britain. In politics, the state strongly discouraged dissent and refused to permit elections to the highest public offices. The empire never became a democracy. The Weimar Republic departed from this pattern to adopt competitive capitalism and democratic, constitutional government. In stark contrast with the preceding regime, the two political parties at the core of most of its coalition governments were the Socialist Party and the Catholic Center Party. The global context, however, remained unfavorable for capitalist democracy in Germany. In addition to the burden of reparations payments to France and Britain after World War I, Germany still faced stiff industrial competition from its Western rivals. After the establishment of communist rule in Russia during the 1920s, Germany felt threatened and discriminated against, both from the West and the East. The economic crisis brought on by the Great Depression was the final blow to the Weimar Republic. In the end, the Nazi Party offered Germans a chance to take a new version of antiliberal state-led development. Thus, the durability of the Second Empire, the experiment with democracy under Weimar, and the reversion to state-led development under Nazi rule all point to the importance of the state for much of Germany's existence.

The path of state-led development was difficult to change because of the feedback effect through domestic institutions. The legacies of the Second Empire, including strong authoritarian enclaves in the army, bureaucracy, and presidency, made the survival of the Weimar Republic precarious. The Second Empire's support for Protestant nationalism against Catholicism and class-based sentiments left contradictory legacies. On the one hand, Catholic and working-class identities and institutions developed in opposition to the regime and then went on to be bulwarks of the Weimar Republic. On the other hand, the legacy of strong nationalism and the experience of stigmatizing various groups as unpatriotic and non-German fed into support for the Nazi Party and the overthrow of the democratic system.

Germany's state-led development also fed back into the international system itself. German militarism provoked Soviet defensive action and the fortress mentality of communist regimes, and it also provoked the established Western powers to use force in defense of the liberal international order. The defeat of Nazi Germany in World War II laid the groundwork for a new global rivalry between the United States and the Soviet Union. These two main powers occupied and divided Germany. The U.S. and international support for West Germany's reindustrialization and reintegration into the world economic and political systems helped to set Germany down a new path.

Germany's new global position as one of the world's leading economic powers supports a revised set of interests, identities, and institutions and a kind of democratic capitalism that can be described as embedded liberalism. Germany stands for strongly liberal economic policies, and its industries are fiercely competitive in the international marketplace. Its institutions are a firmly democratic regime with a constitutional framework. The market is combined with the social partnership of strong labor unions, business leaders, and key administrative agencies. Germany's political parties, labor unions, and federal institutions all consistently support the basic practices of constitutional, parliamentary democracy. As for identities, most political scientists agree that Germany is as solidly democratic today as any country in Europe.

The continuing globalization of the economy presents a new set of challenges and opportunities for Germany. With the collapse of the Soviet Union, a unified Germany is exercising even greater influence in European and world politics, especially through its leading role in the strengthened European Union. The German social welfare system so far remains more or less intact, despite some cuts in recent years. Germany also maintains a high level of wage equality and keeps government budgets largely in balance, but the price has been a relatively high level of unemployment. The question of how Germany's distinctive set of interests, identities, and institutions will respond to new global challenges remains an exciting issue to follow in the coming years.

BIBLIOGRAPHY

Bairoch, Paul. "International Industrialization Levels From 1750 to 1980." *Journal of Economic History* 11, no. 2 (Fall 1982): 269–333.

Conradt, David P. *The German Polity*. Seventh edition. White Plains, NY: Longmans, 2001.

Dahrendorf, Ralf. *Society and Democracy in Germany*. New York: Norton, 1967.

Ertman, Thomas. *Birth of the Leviathan: Building States and Regimes in Medieval and Early Modern Europe*. Cambridge: Cambridge University Press, 1997.

Eurobarometer Surveys of public opinion. Recent Eurobarometer Surveys can be accessed at http://europa.eu.int.

Gerschenkron, Alexander. *Economic Backwardness in Historical Perspective: A Book of Essays*. Cambridge, MA: Harvard University Press, 1962.

Gould, Andrew C. *Origins of Liberal Dominance: State, Church, and Party in Nineteenth Century Europe*. Ann Arbor: University of Michigan Press, 1999.

Iversen, Torben, and Anne Wren. "Equality, Employment, and Budgetary Restraint: The Trilemma of the Service Economy." *World Politics* 50, no. 4 (July 1998): 507–546.

Janos, Andrew C. "The Politics of Backwardness in Continental Europe, 1780–1945." *World Politics* 41, no. 3 (April 1989): 325–358.

Luebbert, Gregory M. *Liberalism, Fascism, or Social Democracy: Social Classes and the Political Origins of Regimes in Interwar Europe*. New York: Oxford University Press, 1991.

Maddison, Angus. *Monitoring the World Economy, 1820–1992*. Paris: Development Centre of the OECD, 1995.

Moore, Barrington. *The Social Origins of Dictatorship and Democracy: Lord and Peasant in the Making of the Modern World*. Boston: Beacon, 1966.

Rogowski, Ronald. *Commerce and Coalitions: How Trade Affects Domestic Political Alignments*. Princeton, NJ: Princeton University Press, 1989.

Suval, Stanley. *Electoral Politics in Wilhelmine Germany*. Chapel Hill: University of North Carolina Press, 1985.

Turner, Lowell. "Introduction. Up Against the Fallen Wall: The Crisis of Social Partnership in Unified Germany." In Lowell Turner, ed. *Negotiating the New Germany: Can Social Partnership Survive?* Ithaca, NY: Cornell University Press, 1997.

Wehler, Hans-Ulrich. *The German Empire, 1871–1918*. Leamington Spa: Berg Publishers, 1985.

World Bank. World Development Indicators 2004. http://devdata.worldbank.org/dataonline/

TABLE 5.2. Key Phases in German Political Development

Time Period	Regime	Global Context	Interests/ Identities/ Institutions	Developmental Path
1800–1870	competing monarchies (authoritarian)	industrial and political revolutions	strong landed elite Protestant nationalism and Catholic resistance authoritarian institutions evade reform	state-building
1871–1918	second empire (authoritarian)	European imperialism	industry and landed elite strong nationalism and working-class and Catholic subcultures authoritarian with elections	state-building
1919–1933	Weimar Republic (democratic)	rise of U.S. economic power; communist revolution in Russia	strong industry socialism, Catholicism, nationalism, weak democratic values, and fear of communism democracy with powerful reserved domains for authoritarian office-holders in army and bureaucracy	competitive capitalism
1933–1945	third empire (authoritarian)	great power rivalry and global depression	strong industry fascism and anti-Semitism authoritarian	totalitarian overthrow of world order
1945–1949	foreign occupation (military)	U.S. and Soviet military dominance	reindustrialization fascism discredited parties, unions, and local governments rebuild	international aid
1949–1990	Federal Republic of Germany (democratic)	Cold War and economic growth in capitalist countries	automobiles and high-technology industry democratic values grow, new immigrants, feminism, and environmentalism parties, unions, federal state	embedded liberalism
		German Democratic Republic (authoritarian)	heavy industry communist indoctrination but increasing disaffection one-party state	Leninism
1990–	Federal Republic of Germany (democratic)	U.S. as sole superpower and globalization	advanced industry and services strong democratic values, feminism, environmentalism parties, unions, federal state, EU	embedded liberalism

IMPORTANT TERMS

Basic Law (Grundgesetz) founding 1949 document of the Federal Republic of Germany that serves as its constitution. Originally designed to be replaced by "a constitution adopted by a free decision of the German people," it has never been replaced but has been amended several times, including to incorporate the new states from the East in 1990.

Berlin city in northeastern Germany, capital of reunified Germany since 1990. It was earlier the capital of the kingdom of Prussia, the Second Empire, the Weimar Republic, and the Third Reich. It was occupied and divided after World War II. The support of the United States during the Berlin airlift (1948–1949) kept Soviet forces from taking the western sector. The Berlin wall (1961–1989) kept easterners from leaving for the West. Berlin's eastern half was the capital of the German Democratic Republic.

Bonn city on the Rhine River in western Germany, from 1949 to 1990 the provisional capital of West Germany. After 1990, it continued to house many federal offices during the move back to Berlin. It was occupied by French revolutionary forces in 1794 and was awarded to Prussia in 1815.

Bundesrat (Federal Council) the second, or upper, house of the Parliament. It represents the 16 federal states and is composed of 69 delegates chosen by state governments, usually ministers in state governments. Each state receives at least three delegates; larger states receive up to three additional delegates based on population; the five former Eastern states were also granted more delegates as a ratio of their population. Delegates vote in state blocs according to state government instructions. The Bundesrat's approval is required in about two-thirds of legislation, where the states' powers are involved. Secondary in power to the Bundestag but important when different parties control the two houses.

Bundestag (Federal Diet) the primary, or lower, house of the Parliament. Its delegates are chosen by popular vote, with all seats up for election normally every four years. The Bundestag's approval is required for all legislation, as in most parliamentary systems, and it exercises more oversight of government than do most parliaments. Its majority party or a coalition selects the chancellor. A total of 603 delegates won seats in the 2002 election; the exact number of delegates can vary slightly from one election to another because of the "excess mandate provision" and the "three-district waiver" electoral rules.

Center Party (Zentrumspartei) the political party that emerged in defense of Catholic interests in the 1870s under the Second Empire. It was the second-largest party for much of the Weimar Republic (with 15 percent to 20 percent of the vote), and it frequently was in the governing coalition. Its predominantly Catholic supporters for the most part did not defect to the Nazi Party during the early 1930s, but its deputies voted for the Enabling Act that gave Hitler dictatorial powers in 1933.

Christian Democrats the Christian Democratic Union (CDU) and the Christian Social Union (CSU), allied parties that campaign together and form one parliamentary grouping (CDU/CSU). The CDU operates in all states except Bavaria, where it is allied with the more conservative CSU. The CDU's founding in the post–World War II era broke from tradition by including Protestants as well as Catholics. The two parties usually win 40 percent to 50 percent of the second ballot choice.

Congress of Vienna the 1815 great-powers conference after the defeat of French Emperor Napoleon Bonaparte. The powers agreed to give Prussia control over most of the Rhine territories in order to keep France in check, greatly expanding Prussia's role in Germany overall.

constructive vote of no confidence requirement in the Basic Law that the Bundestag, in order to dismiss the chancellor, must simultaneously agree on a new chancellor. It was designed to limit the power of the Parliament and strengthen the chancellor. Attempted twice but successful only once, it has generally had the intended effect.

Friedrich Ebert leader of the moderate wing of the Social Democratic Party and first president of the Weimar Republic.

federal chancellor (Bundeskanzler) head of the government, usually the head of the leading political party. Once the chancellor is selected by the Bundestag, he or she can count on majority support most of the time. The chancellor has more authority than prime ministers in most parliamentary systems.

federal president (Bundespräsident) head of state with largely ceremonial authority. The president is selected by a federal convention of all Bundestag deputies and an equal number of delegates selected by the state legislatures. The position has a five-year term and is usually filled by senior politicians; activist presidents can use the office to influence public opinion.

Federal Republic of Germany (FRG) Bundesrepublikdeutschland (BRD), the current German state. Founded in 1949 and based on the U.S., British, and French zones of occupation, it was often known as West Germany until 1990. It acquired the states of the German Democratic Republic (GDR) in the unification of 1990.

Frankfurt Parliament (1848–1849) the all-German Parliament elected in 1848 that met in the city of Frankfurt and attempted to unify and reform the many German states along more liberal or democratic principles. Its inability to do so began a long period of authoritarian predominance in German states.

German Democratic Republic (GDR) Deutsche Demokratische Republik (DDR), the German state based on the Soviet zone of occupation from 1949 until 1990, often known as East Germany.

guest workers (Gastarbeiter) frequently used term for immigrant workers that underscores their temporary status in Germany.

Otto von Hindenburg the Junker former army officer who became the second president of the Weimar Republic and appointed Hitler as chancellor in 1933.

Holocaust the Nazi attempt to kill all European Jews during World War II. An estimated 5.7 million Jewish people were killed, and other so-called undesirable people – including Roma, homosexuals, psychiatric patients, and the handicapped – were also targeted for destruction. A total of between six and seven million people lost their lives. Auschwitz and Treblinka were two major death camps.

Junkers the landed nobility of eastern Prussia. Their vast estates east of the Elbe River produced grain for Germany and the world market but only by keeping agricultural laborers in near slavery. They formed the core of the Prussian state administration and the Second Empire's administration, and never fully accepted the legitimacy of the Weimar Republic.

Kulturkampf (cultural struggle) the attempt by the Second Empire to break the authority of the Catholic Church in unified Germany by means of legislation, regulation, and the harassment of priests, mainly between 1871 and 1878. It reduced the church's authority in some areas but generally sparked a revival of political Catholicism and popular religiosity.

Karl Marx founding thinker of modern socialism and communism. Born in 1818 in Trier, in the Rhine province of Prussia, he became involved in various German and French radical movements during the 1830s and 1840s. He wrote *The Communist Manifesto* (in 1848, with Friedrich Engels) and many other polemical and analytical works. The guiding personality in the Socialist International movement in the 1860s, he died in London in 1883.

National Socialist German Workers' Party (Nazi Party) the fascist party taken over by Adolph Hitler in 1920–1921. It became the largest political party in the Weimar Republic in the early 1930s, winning 38 percent of the vote in July 1932 and 33 percent in November. Hitler's appointment as chancellor in 1933 was followed by the end of the republic and the beginning of one-party Nazi rule until 1945.

Oder-Neisse line the contemporary eastern border of Germany with Poland along these two rivers.

Prussia the North German state governed from Berlin by the Hohenzollern dynasty beginning in 1701 that grew in military strength and gained control of most of what is now Germany and western Poland during the eighteenth and nineteenth centuries. It formed the core of the Second Empire in 1871. Subsequently a state within Germany, it was disbanded during the Allied occupation in 1947.

Social Democratic Party Germany's oldest political party, generally on the left but more recently similar in its political program to the Democratic Party in the United States. It emerged in the 1870s as a working-class protest party, and its main wing helped to found and frequently govern the Weimar Republic. It governed in West Germany alone or in coalition from 1966 to 1982 and returned to power in a reunified Germany in 1998. Social market economy is its term for a tempering of the free market with concern for its social consequences. It is based on a "social partnership" of business and labor, along with the state and banks, to shape politics and economics at the national, regional, and local levels in order to cushion and guide economic change.

two-vote ballot procedure the voting method to select delegates in the Bundestag. The first vote is for a candidate to represent the voter's district. Half of the seats are awarded as a result. The second vote is for a party overall. The remaining seats are distributed so that the overall share of seats for each party matches the second ballot choices.

Weimar Republic the German state and democratic regime that was formed after the fall of the Second Empire in 1919 and lasted until 1933. It was named for the city where its constitution was written. Bitter and polarized partisan competition from the communist Left to the extreme nationalist right wing made it difficult for the moderate and mostly Social Democratic and Center Party governments to operate.

STUDY QUESTIONS

1. Consider Germany in 1815. In what ways was it like the rest of Europe? How was it different?

2. Why were Germany's political institutions under the Second Empire authoritarian rather than democratic?

3. Why did the Weimar Republic fail to survive as a democracy?

4. What were the main features and policies of the Nazi regime?

5. How did the Allies reshape interests, identities, and institutions in occupied Germany from 1945 through 1949?

6. What were the major differences between the FRG and the GDR between 1949 and 1989?

7. How did Germany's interests, identities, and institutions change as a result of reunification in 1990?

8. What are the major political parties in the FRG?

9. What impact has the FRG had on Europe and the world since World War II?

10. How is the global context after 1990 affecting Germany's developmental path?

CHINA

RUSSIA

Administered
by Russia,
claimed by
Japan

Hokkaido
Sapporo

NORTH
KOREA

S e a   o f
J a p a n

Akita

Sendai

SOUTH
KOREA

JAPAN

Honshu
Tokyo ✪

Kyoto
Nagoya
Kobe
Osaka

Kitakyushu

Fukuoka
Shikoku

Kyushu

E a s t

C h i n a

S e a

P A C I F I C

O C E A N

Philippine

S e a

JAPAN

Okinawa

0	100	200	300	400	500 miles
0	100	200	300	400	500km

CHAPTER SIX

Japan

Miranda A. Schreurs

Introduction

Japan is a fascinating country for political scientists to study. In a century's time, Japan went from being an almost completely isolated feudal society to the world's second-richest country and a stable democracy (see Table 6.1).

Japan was the only imperial power in Asia, itself becoming a colonizer rather than a colonized state. Like Germany, Japan experimented with democracy during the 1920s before succumbing to militarist powers during the 1930s. Japan launched the war in the Pacific with the bombing of Pearl Harbor on December 7, 1941, and had conquered much of East and Southeast Asia before its eventual defeat with the U.S. atomic bombings of Hiroshima and Nagasaki, respectively, on August 6 and 9, 1945. Japan was occupied by the U.S.-led Allied forces from its defeat in World War II until it regained sovereignty in April 1952. The subsequent democratic transition of postwar Japan can be considered among the most successful cases of democratization that occurred during what Samuel Huntington has referred to as the Second Wave of countries to democratize.

The Japanese Constitution, which was drafted with significant U.S. influence, includes an article **(Article 9)** that renounces war as a sovereign right of the nation. Although this article is the subject of much debate, and there have been calls for constitutional revision, Japan is arguably one of the most pacifist countries in the world today. Japan's security is guaranteed by the U.S.-Japan Security Treaty, and Japan is the most important U.S. ally in Asia. Because Japan does not function as a "normal" state in the realpolitik sense of the word (that is, as a state that wields power through military strength), it has had to rely on economic and "soft" power in its foreign relations.

Japan is also of interest because of the unique form of parliamentary democracy that has taken root during the post-occupation period. Japan has been ruled by the **Liberal Democratic Party (LDP)** ever since the party's founding in 1955, except for a brief interlude during the 1990s. Although a recession has plagued the country since the bursting of Japan's economic bubble in 1989, Japan remains a state where one party is dominant. Electoral reform in 1994 was aimed at leading the state toward a two-party system, but to date no real rival to the LDP has emerged.

The Geography of Japan

Japan is a vast archipelago made up of over 3,000 islands and extending 1,300 miles from the Sea of Japan to the Pacific Ocean, the distance from New York City to Miami, Florida. There are five large islands where the majority of the population live: Honshu, the main island, where both the ancient capital of Kyoto and the modern capital of Tokyo are found; Hokkaido, the northernmost island, which today is increasingly closely tied to Russia in its trade; Okinawa, which was returned to Japan only in 1972 and is home to the largest U.S. military base in the Pacific; Kyushu; and Shikoku.

Japan's 127 million inhabitants make it the world's tenth most populated country and also one of its most densely populated. The population density is made more intense by Japan's mountainous terrain. Seventy percent of the country is mountainous, meaning that a population that is only somewhat less than half that of the United States lives in a territory about the size of California but of which only 30 percent is arable. In fact, it has been estimated that 50 percent of the Japanese population lives on just 2 percent of its land! Japan lacks much in the way of natural resources and must import virtually all of its oil and natural gas.

Japan is a largely homogeneous nation; 99.4 percent of the population is Japanese and only 0.6 percent other ethnicities, primarily Korean and some Chinese. Japan has among the highest life expectancies of any country (over 80 years for both men and women) and among the lowest infant mortality rates. Although the second-richest nation in the world, the high cost of living means that per capita income on a purchasing-power parity comparison was only roughly $28,000 (U.S.) compared with $36,000 (U.S.) for the United States in 2001.

The Historical Roots of Institutions, Identities, and Interests

To understand why Japan was able to modernize so quickly and to develop a stable democracy during the post–World War II period, it is important to examine briefly the impact of the global historical context on the development of Japanese institutions, identities, and interests.

TOKUGAWA JAPAN, 1603–1867

In 1600, Tokugawa Ieyasu succeeded in military battle to unify a country that had essentially been divided into 260 feudal fiefdoms, each headed by a

daimyo, a feudal lord. Although still technically ruled by the imperial family, Japan's emperors had become too weak to keep real power. For the next two-and-a-half centuries (1603 to 1867), the Tokugawa shogunate ruled Japan from Edo (Tokyo), while the emperor maintained his residence in Kyoto. During this time, the daimyo were required to spend every other year in Edo working on behalf of the **shogun** and to leave their families in Edo when they traveled back to their feudal lands, an extremely expensive proposition that effectively prevented rival powers from emerging. This system of alternate residency, known as *sankin kōtai*, not only helped solidify the Tokugawa clan's power but was also an important element behind the development of a relatively strong economy. The fact that the daimyo and their retainers had to travel from across the vast archipelago to Edo every other year meant that an elaborate road system developed. This road system helped to support local economies and the process of urbanization. By 1720, Edo had a population of well over one million, making it the world's largest city. Urbanization helped stimulate demand from rural areas and the development of commodity and financial markets. The Edo period is known as a time of peace when various cultural arts such as Kabuki drama and ukiyo-e art flourished. Confucianism places a high value on learning, and a large number of schools were created for the samurai (warriors in service to the daimyo) as well as for commoners. By the beginning of the Meiji period, Japan had attained a fairly high literacy rate. All of these factors were important for Japan's later rapid economic, political, and cultural transformation.

Japan was a Confucian, class-based society, with samurai at the top of the hierarchy, followed by peasants, artisans, and merchants. The only group that was considered lower than the merchants were the *eta*, the outcasts, whose professions, which included leather work, were considered impure. Although Christian (primarily Jesuit and Franciscan) missionaries attempted to spread their religion in Japan, by the late sixteenth century they had become the targets of persecution, and by the turn of the seventeenth century, Christianity was banned. Japan remained a nation of Buddhists and Shintoists.

Japan was remarkably isolated from the world during the Edo period. During the 1630s, Japan closed its ports to foreigners, except the Dutch and Chinese, who were granted permission to trade out of the port of Nagasaki in southern Kyushu. Foreign books were also banned until 1720. Given Japan's isolation, it must have been a real shock when in the summer of 1853 **Commodore Matthew Perry** steamed into Edo Bay with four armed ships carrying a letter to the Japanese emperor from U.S. President Millard Filmore requesting (and in essence demanding) that Japan open its ports to U.S. ships for trade and supplies. Recognizing the superior military power of the Americans, the shogunate acquiesced and a peace and friendship treaty that allowed for limited trade was signed. Perry's voyage was to mark the beginning of similar demands by other countries and Japan's forced acceptance of what are known as "unequal treaties." These were trade agreements that gave Westerners extraterritorial rights in Japan so that if they committed a crime on Japanese soil, they would not be subject to Japanese law but only their own country's courts.

Perry's visit also marked the beginning of a century of rapid and at times turbulent changes in Japanese politics, economics, and society as Japan sought first to prevent domination by the West, as it saw had happened in neighboring China and throughout much of Southeast Asia, and then to "catch up" economically with Europe and North America. Japan's late entry onto the world stage had fateful consequences for Japanese development and for relations between Asia and the West.

THE MEIJI ERA, 1868–1912

The shogun's acquiescence to U.S. demands was viewed by some as a betrayal of the Japanese nation and led to national uprisings under the slogan *sonno joi*, "revere the emperor, expel the barbarians." In 1868, the period of shogun rule was brought to an end in a process known as the **Meiji Restoration**. Young Prince Mutsuhito became Japan's 122nd emperor. He took the name Meiji ("enlightened government"). The Meiji era was an immensely important period of institutional and cultural transformation. The emperor moved the imperial capital to Tokyo ("eastern capital"), and a centralized government was created. A circle of oligarchs (**genro**), many of whom were from the nobility that supported the "restoration" of the emperor, advised the emperor and were the true wielders of power. They effectively used the name of the emperor to legitimize the revolutionary changes they imposed upon the country. State Shintoism was made the ideology of the country; it reified the emperor as the divine descendant of the sun goddess Amaterasu. Militarists were later to politicize state Shintoism and use it to support their expansionist quest. There was to be no bourgeois middle-class revolution from below in Japan.

During the Meiji era, profound changes were made to virtually all sectors of society. With the goal of achieving *fukoku kyohei* ("rich country, strong military"), Japan's leaders set out to modernize the country. They brought in Western advisers and teachers and sent hundreds of Japanese students abroad to study everything Western, including science and technology, the political systems and constitutions of Europe and the United States, and the concepts of universities, hospitals, and even Western dress and social customs. By the end of the Meiji era, Japan's reformists had succeeded in containing popular revolts from below while creating a modern state and world power, a new economy, and a rebuilt society, all truly remarkable feats given the short period of time in which they occurred.

The Meiji leaders in 1889 adopted a constitution based on the Prussian parliamentary model. (The U.S. constitutional model was rejected as being too liberal.) The Meiji constitution created an authoritarian parliamentary system. It provided for the establishment of an imperial **Diet** (a parliament) with a popularly elected House of Representatives. In addition, a House of Peers, composed largely of nobility (the former daimyo and court nobility) who received their title by birthright, was formed. The power of the elected House of Representatives, however, was strongly limited. Sovereignty rested with the emperor. The emperor appointed his cabinet ministers, had legislative superiority over the Diet, and could make emergency decrees and enter into treaties. Only the emperor could amend the constitution, and the military was directly responsible to him and not to the Diet. The special powers of the emperor, including emergency powers, were in reality wielded not so much directly by the emperor as by his ministers and a special Privy Council that advised him. In addition, the genro who had masterminded the Meiji constitution held much influence into the beginning of the twentieth century. Suffrage, moreover, was limited to males who held substantial property – in other words, only 1 percent of the population, most of whom were landlords.

During the Meiji period, many of Japan's most famous universities were established, including those of Tokyo, Kyoto, Keio, and Waseda. Powerful financial and industrial conglomerates known as *zaibatsu* also solidified their positions. They were usually tied to rich families that had begun to do business during the Edo era; many of their names remain familiar today, such as Mitsubishi (shipping), Mitsui (banking), and Sumitomo (mining). The zaibatsu worked closely with the government and in later periods the military.

A BRIEF INTERLUDE WITH DEMOCRACY: THE TAISHO DEMOCRACY, 1918–1932

By the Taisho era (the period of rule of the Taisho emperor, which began in 1912), the power of the oligarchs had waned and that of the political parties – of which there were many – in the House of Representatives had grown. It appeared that Japan might develop a more representative form of democracy. Indeed, during this period of **Taisho democracy**, the first commoner became prime minister, a competitive party system took root, and suffrage was extended to all males (in 1925). There was, however, considerable discontent with the government because of its failure to deal with inflation and labor unrest, and sharp ideological differences had emerged in society.

Left-wing movements and activism grew during the early part of the 1920s, influenced by developments in Russia. An illegal Communist Party formed in 1922, and socialist parties, which had existed since the early 1920s despite government suppression, became more vocal. The growing appeal of the Left at a time when suffrage had been greatly expanded was viewed by conservatives as a threat to the imperial family and the essence of the Japanese nation. In 1925, just after universal male suffrage was granted, conservatives pushed through the Peace Preservation Law, which made illegal organizations and movements that had as their goal changing the political system. A

1928 amendment by emergency imperial decree strengthened the law and made left-wing activism essentially punishable by death. A 1941 amendment went one step further and allowed for preventive arrest. The Peace Preservation Law marked the beginning of the empowerment of ultrarightists and the elimination of open political debate.

Japan as a Military Power and a Colonial Force

Japan's rapid industrialization during the Meiji era was considered critical to the strengthening of the military. Japan tested its military strength in the Sino-Japanese War of 1894–1895. Japan's victory over China attested to the success of the Meiji Restoration and was a humiliating blow to a greatly weakened China. As a result of this war, Korea was made a protectorate of Japan, and Taiwan, the Liadong Peninsula, and the Pescadores were ceded to Japan. Concerned about competition from Japan in China, however, Russia, France, and Germany forced Japan to return the Liadong Peninsula to China. This was but one of many events that were to leave Japanese feeling that they were not respected as equals by Western powers, which in turn nourished a resentful nationalism.

Japan achieved another military victory that surprised the world when it defeated Russia in the 1904–1905 Russo-Japanese War. In defeat, Russia recognized Japanese paramount political, military, and economic interests in Korea as well as Japanese control of the railways of Inner Manchuria and Port Arthur (Lüshun). Russia also ceded to Japan the southern portion of Sakhalin and the adjacent islands. (These islands are now commonly referred to as the Northern Territories or Kurile Islands.) Russia seized these islands in the closing days of World War II, but Japan has disputed Russian claims. Because of this territorial dispute, Russia and Japan have yet to sign a treaty officially ending the Second World War! Japan formally colonized Korea in 1910, joining Western countries and becoming the only Asian nation to be a colonizer.

During World War I, Japan joined the Allied powers declaring war on Germany in 1914, seizing German-leased territories in China. Although at the end of the war Japan failed to convince Western powers to include a racial-equality clause in the Treaty of Versailles, Japan was recognized as one of the "Big Five" and obtained a permanent seat in the League of Nations. Japan had become a major foreign power.

During the 1930s, ultrarightists and militarists gained the upper hand, and hopes for a democratic Japan faded. This failure was intimately related to Japan's late development in a highly competitive global order. Japan strengthened its grip on Manchuria, formally detaching it from China in 1931. In 1937, Japan attacked China, beginning the war in the Pacific that would eventually lead to an alliance between Japan, Italy, and Germany in World War II. Seeking to curb Japanese imperialism, the United States slapped economic sanctions on Japan. Japan responded by attacking Pearl Harbor and extending its sphere of influence into Southeast Asia in a quest to secure oil and to become the dominant power in Asia. Japan declared war on the United States in 1941 and capitulated on August 14, 1945.

Japan's colonization of Korea, China, and Taiwan, and its military advance into large parts of Southeast Asia, were done in the name of expelling Western imperialists from Asia and creating a Greater East Asia co-prosperity sphere, but the often brutal colonization and military rule of Japan left bitter memories in much of Asia.

Occupation of Japan

The U.S. occupation of Japan has received renewed attention as a result of the U.S.-led war in Iraq. The administration of President George W. Bush has compared the occupation of Iraq with the postwar occupations of Japan and Germany. Pulitzer Prize–winning author John Dower, a leading authority on the occupation of Japan, has argued, however, that the differences with the situation in Iraq are great. Although young Japanese soldiers during World War II were trained for suicide missions as kamikaze pilots, once the occupation of Japan began there were no serious cases of violence against the occupying forces, a major difference with Iraq.

The demilitarization and democratization of Japan, moreover, were rapid. **General Douglas MacArthur** was appointed by President Harry S. Truman to be the Supreme Commander of the Allied Powers (SCAP) and head of the Allied occupation of Japan. Although the officials who were considered the masterminds of the war were purged, imprisoned, and in a small number of cases tried by the Tokyo War Crimes Tribunal, the government was left intact; SCAP worked with and through the Japanese bureaucracy and Diet.

Two months after the occupation began, MacArthur called for the "liberalization of the constitution" and democratization in five key areas – the emancipation of women, permitting the unionization of labor, liberalizing education, establishing an effective judicial system that would protect human rights, and dismantling the *zaibatsu* to create a more liberal and democratic economic system. The democratization process happened remarkably quickly.

In February 1946, six months into the occupation, the Japanese government presented a draft constitution to SCAP headquarters. Unhappy with the Japanese draft, MacArthur had his staff prepare a more liberal model, which was then debated in the Diet. The new constitution went into effect in May 1947.

The occupation of Japan was so successful in large part because it was considered legitimate by the Japanese, who were weary of war. When the occupation began, Japan was a demoralized, exhausted, malnourished, and ravaged country. Japan's cities had been heavily bombed and much of its heavy industry destroyed. Soldiers and colonists were repatriated to a country that was too poor to provide them with work. In this context, it proved relatively easy to blame the military for Japan's ill-fated imperialism. Moreover, when the war ended, it was the emperor, considered divine by his people, who ordered that the military disarm. Rather than trying Emperor Hirohito as a war criminal as some wanted, MacArthur argued that because of his divine status in the eyes of the people and because his advisers and the military had been the ones who really decided to invade China and launch the war, he should remain as emperor. The emperor's endorsement of the occupation and its reforms helped to legitimize SCAP's activities.

It can also be argued that it was important that Japan was led by a man generally supportive of SCAP policies during most of the occupation. **Shigeru Yoshida** served as prime minister from May 1946 to May 1947 and again from October 1948 to October 1954. During his time as prime minister, he chose to align Japan with the United States politically and economically, focus Japan's political attentions on economic development, and allow the United States to take on the role of protecting Japan. His policies, commonly referred to as the Yoshida Doctrine, became the basic guiding ideologies of the conservative Liberal Democratic Party (LDP) when it formed in 1955 out of the merger of the Liberal Party and the Democratic Party.

Other reforms included the passage of an antimonopoly law and the breakup of the *zaibatsu*, which SCAP believed had played a major role in Japan's militarization. The 1946 land reform led to the redistribution of land from absentee landlords and large landowners to tenants at fixed 1945 prices. The land reform reduced rural unrest and contributed to a relatively high degree of equalization of wealth in Japanese society.

The Japanese Constitution and the Establishment of a New Political Order

The 1946 constitution remains in force in Japan today and has never been amended. It differs from the Meiji constitution in several key aspects. First, sovereignty was placed with the people rather than with the emperor as had been the case in the past. The emperor's status was changed from head of state to symbol of state, and his functions were limited to ceremonial ones. The House of Representatives (also known as the lower house) was greatly empowered. The House of Peers was abolished, and in its place an elected House of Councilors was created. The bicameral Diet was made the highest organ of state and given sole law-making authority. The constitution stipulated that the prime minister and the majority of ministers should be members of the Diet and that the prime minister should be elected by the Parliament, a major difference with the Meiji cabinet, which was a transcendental cabinet (i.e., one that was to be "above" the Parliament). The new political structure was based largely on the British parliamentary model.

Second, the new constitution emphasized respect for fundamental human rights and individual freedoms. Freedom of the press was assured. Political parties that had been banned were given the right to form, paving the way for the formation of the **Japan Socialist Party** and the Communist Party. Citizens were given the right to seek redress against unjust actions by government under a revised judicial system. The constitution also established equality of the sexes before the law (a right that is not written into the U.S. Constitution). Despite there having been a women's movement in Japan during the prewar period, women did not gain the right to vote until the occupation granted it to them, and this right was then enshrined in the new constitution. Interestingly, in the first postwar election in April 1946, women won 39 seats in the Diet, more than they have won in any election since that time. In the most recent election, in 2004, women won 35 seats, or 7.3 percent of the 480-member lower house. The age of suffrage was also reduced from 25 to 20.

Third, the Japanese constitution is pacifist. The Preamble of the constitution begins:

> We, the Japanese people, acting through our elected representatives in the National Diet, determined that we should secure for ourselves and our posterity the fruits of peaceful cooperation with all nations and the blessings of liberty all over this land, and resolved that never again shall we be visited with the horrors of war through the action of government, do proclaim that sovereign power resides with the people . . .

In addition, Article 9 explicitly denounces the right to war:

> Aspiring sincerely to an international peace based on justice and order, the Japanese people forever renounce war as a sovereign right of the nation and the threat or use of force as a means of settling international disputes. In order to accomplish [this] aim, land, sea, and air forces, as well as other war potential, will never be maintained. The right of aggression of the state will not be recognized.

These pacifist elements of the Japanese constitution have been central to defining Japan's approach to foreign policy. It remains a matter of historical debate with considerable implications for nationalism as to whether Article 9 was MacArthur's idea or whether it was proposed by Kijūrō Shidehara, who served briefly as prime minister until the first postwar election was held in 1946. The interpretation of these elements of the constitution and what they mean for Japan's ability to contribute to international peacekeeping efforts and to new security threats have been hotly debated for years.

The "Reverse Course" and Japan's Emergence as a Key U.S. Ally

The initial goals of the U.S. occupation were to demilitarize and democratize Japan and help it regain basic economic functions in order to be self-sufficient. Beyond that, Japan was of little interest to the United States. The onset of the Cold War altered U.S. thinking about Japan, which suddenly took on a new strategic significance, and a "**reverse course**" was initiated in 1947.

The reverse course slowed and on occasion reversed the democratic reforms introduced by the United States during the early phase of the occupation. Initially, for example, SCAP had encouraged labor unions as a critical element of democratic politics. Concerned about growing labor unrest and labor's ties to the Communist Party, SCAP intervened, banning a planned nationwide strike in 1947. Behind the reverse course were concerns about the spread of communism. Global politics once again conspired to intervene in Japanese politics.

The victory of Mao Zedong's communist forces over the Kuomintang (the nationalists) in 1949, the outbreak of the Korean War in 1950, and the Soviet Union's grip on Central and Eastern Europe created concern in Washington that communism could spread to a weak Japan. Japan's Communist Party, the only party to speak out against Japan's military aggression, reemerged after the war as a legal party but suffered renewed repression by SCAP, which launched its own "Red Purge" in 1950. Although the Japan Communist Party (JCP) was greatly weakened, it survived as a party. Many labor leaders were also removed as part of the Red Purge. The politics of this period created a deep-seated ideological divide between conservatives who supported the United States in most of its policy initiatives and the parties of the left and, especially, the Japan Socialist Party and the Communist Party, which opposed Japan's strong alignment with the United States.

The Cold War was instrumental in the U.S. decision to have Japan establish a National Police Reserve for the maintenance of domestic order. In 1954, the Police Reserve was turned into the Japanese Self-Defense Forces (SDF) for the protection of the country. Although the Japanese Self-Defense Forces are now one of the largest military forces in the world, because of Article 9 they are restricted to national self-defense. In the 1990s, however, a new interpretation of Article 9 has led to Japan's participation in noncombat roles in UN peacekeeping operations.

In 1951, the United States and Japan concluded the San Francisco Peace Treaty formally ending the U.S. occupation of Japan and the U.S.-Japan security treaty. The occupation formally ended on April 28, 1952, one month after the U.S. Senate had ratified the agreement. The security treaty engendered considerable opposition both within Japan from left-leaning parties and internationally, as it gave the United States the right to maintain troops in Japan and use it as a base for U.S. activity in East Asia even after the occupation ended. This is interesting to ponder in light of the U.S.-led occupation of Iraq and questions concerning the stationing of troops there after the country technically regains sovereignty. In Japan's case, the U.S. military operates independently of, but in close cooperation with, the Japanese Self-Defense Forces.

The U.S.-Japan security treaty was renewed in 1960, permitting the continued stationing of U.S. troops in Japan, but this was done over the strong objections of parties of the left, the radical *Zengakuren* student movement, and labor unions. In fact, the treaty was rammed through the Diet under highly questionable circumstances; the Socialist Party members of Parliament and their male secretaries were dragged out of the Diet by the police, which Prime Minister Nobusuke Kishi had called in so that the Liberal Democrats could vote to renew the treaty. Fearing that democracy itself was at stake, there were massive demonstrations in front of the Japanese Diet that resulted in one of Japan's most serious political crises of the postwar period and led both to the cancellation of President Dwight D. Eisenhower's planned visit to Japan to celebrate the treaty's renewal and the resignation of Prime Minister Kishi. The treaty, however, was passed and in subsequent years was generally accepted by society. The United States currently maintains approximately 53,000 troops in Japan, about half of whom are based in Okinawa. The question of whether or not U.S. troops should remain in Japan continues to be an important and divisive political question for Japan and has been especially hotly debated in Okinawa. The United States somewhat reduced its troop size in Okinawa in the wake of widespread demonstrations during the mid-1990s after the public erupted in anger when three U.S. servicemen raped a young Japanese girl. Since then, the situation has calmed somewhat, although the Iraq war engendered renewed debate about Japan's close military alliance with the United States and its implications for Japan's own security.

Understanding Japan's "Economic Miracle"

Few would ever have predicted that Japan would emerge from its war-ravaged state in 1945 to become one of the world's richest nations by the end of the 1960s. The Japanese "economic miracle" is one of the most studied aspects of Japanese politics and economics. Numerous factors contributed to Japan's economic recovery, many of which were external to Japan and can be considered circumstantial.

When World War II ended, Japan received financial and technical assistance from the United States. The American banker John Foster Dulles was sent to Japan in 1948 as an economic adviser and introduced austerity measures, including wage and price controls, balanced budgets, and currency-exchange controls, among others. The yen–dollar exchange rate was fixed at 360 yen to the dollar; this rate remained in place until the collapse of the Bretton Woods system of fixed exchange rates in 1973. It can be argued that the favorable exchange rate aided Japan's export expansion. Japan's economic recovery received a major stimulus from the demand for military and other supplies for UN troops fighting in the Korean War. The dollar purchases gave Japan a means to pay for its imports and reequip its industries. Steel and other heavy industries did especially well. Finally, it has been argued that Japan benefited enormously from being able to concentrate on economic development while leaving its defense largely to the United States. Japan's budgetary expenditures on the Self-Defense Forces remained at less than 1 percent of the national budget until well into the 1980s.

Beyond these external conditions, however, there were important domestic factors at work as well. First was the stabilization of the party system. There was a consolidation of political parties in 1955 when the conservative Liberal Democratic Party formed out of a merger of the Liberal Party and the Democratic Party. In reaction to the formation of the LDP, the socialist left also merged to form the Japan Socialist Party (JSP). The socialists, however, had historically been ideologically divided between those supportive of a radical, Marxist socialism and those supporting a more moderate socialism that worked within the system. The JSP split in 1959 when the more moderate wing of the party, in connection with the JSP's opposition to the security treaty, broke off to create the Democratic Socialist Party (DSP). In addition, the Communist Party represented a share of the left-leaning vote. As a result of the division of the left-leaning opposition, the LDP was able to maintain a majority in the lower house – even if at times a bare majority. The dominance of the LDP in postwar Japanese politics provided for a high degree of policy stability.

In 1960, Prime Minister Hayato Ikeda announced a goal for Japan to double the national income in a decade. Over the course of the decade, Japan expanded its range of export goods from textiles and low-end goods ("made in Japan" in the 1950s was a symbol often associated with cheap toys and plastic goods) to heavy industry – including steel, chemicals, shipbuilding, and automobiles – and electronic goods, such as radios, televisions, cameras, calculators, and computers. By 1967, Japan's Gross National Product (GNP) had surpassed that of Great Britain, France, and West Germany. So successful was Japan at importing technologies, improving upon them, and then reexporting new designs that Japan began to develop trade surpluses with the

United States, and trade frictions between the two countries began to grow. For much of the 1970s and 1980s, the United States worked to open Japan's economy to U.S. goods, which were often barred by protectionist policies.

Japan's economic wealth was more evenly distributed than in many developing countries, and with a growing economic pie, there was relatively limited unrest in Japan, although labor engaged in annual wage offensives. Most Japanese considered themselves to be part of the middle class even though by U.S. or European standards the average Japanese lived in a rather small home – largely an issue of space rather than wealth. In the 1970s, Prime Minister Kakuei Tanaka, one of the more colorful and controversial prime ministers of Japan, who in his later years was accused of massive corruption, decided that it was important to keep rural areas connected to the increasingly economically dominant cities of the Kantō (the area surrounding Tokyo and Yokohama) and Kansai (the areas surrounding Osaka, Kyoto, and Kobe) regions. He initiated a program called Reconstruction of the Japanese Archipelago. It was this program that led to the building of Japan's famous bullet trains, the *shinkansen*, which permit travel between Tokyo and Kyoto in as little as three hours.

One of the most intriguing informal institutional systems at play in postwar Japan is known as administrative guidance, or **gyōsei shidō** in Japanese. One of the consequences of SCAP's purging of politicians who were associated with Japan's militarism was that the bureaucracy became very influential. Many of Japan's postwar parliamentarians and prime ministers were bureaucrats who turned into politicians because of the sudden opening of electoral positions as a result of the purges. This helped create links between parliamentarians (and especially the LDP) and the bureaucracy.

Bureaucrats were highly involved in the formulation of legislation. In fact, most bills originated in the bureaucracy rather than in the House of Representatives, even though important committees in the Diet, such as the Policy Affairs Research Committee, did influence the shape of bills and the Diet had the ultimate authority to vote on legislation. More recently, politicians have begun to initiate more legislation, but the bureaucracy still remains powerful and heavily involved in policy formulation.

The influence of the Japanese bureaucracy had prewar origins, as the ministries were powerful under the old system as well, and considerable continuity between the prewar and postwar bureaucracies meant that competencies were maintained. Bureaucrats, moreover, had moral authority in a society that respects educational attainment. Entering the bureaucracy was considered a prestige track for male graduates of Japan's elite universities, although this is somewhat less true today than in the past. Japan has a career civil service, and entrance to the bureaucracy requires passing extremely difficult exams and interviews. Until the Equal Employment

Opportunity Law was passed in 1986, women were permitted to take the exams but were often screened out during the interview process. In the meantime, the doors of the bureaucracy have been opened to more women, and women are beginning to assume more powerful posts, including as bureaucratic ministers.

The **Ministry of International Trade and Industry** (renamed the Ministry of Economy, Trade, and Industry in the government reform of 2001) and the Ministry of Finance were particularly important to Japan's economic development. They used administrative guidance or what Richard Samuels called a process of negotiation or "reciprocal consent" between ministries and industries to push the economy in particular directions. The ministries had various tools in their hands to do this, including preferential tax treatment and the provision of low-interest loans.

Administrative guidance was aided by the close connections that existed between bureaucrats and especially the large corporations, where lifetime employment was quite common. Japan is a network society. Personal relationships such as those established during high school and in universities are immensely important. These networks helped to link bureaucrats with industries. In addition, because Japan's bureaucracy is a career civil service, as one ascends the ladder of hierarchy, the number of available positions diminishes. Bureaucrats who know they have hit the glass ceiling within their ministries typically retire from the ministry and take up positions either in industry or government-created institutions. This process is so well-known that it has a special name: **amakudari**, or literally "descent from heaven." The idea behind *amakudari* was that it would provide direct communication links between bureaucrats and industry officials.

The role that women played in this system should not be underestimated either. There are fairly strong gender role divisions in Japan. Throughout most of the postwar period, women could work, but they were expected to retire upon marriage or at the latest with childbirth, not to reenter the workforce until their role as mother and primary child-care giver was complete. When they did reenter the workforce, it was usually as part-timers. Women therefore provided Japanese companies with highly educated but inexpensive employees. Lifetime employment, moreover, was not a privilege conferred upon women. Employers could more easily let women go, providing companies with flexibility during economic downturns. Salaries reflected this gender-divided system as well. A male employee's wages increased upon marriage and with the birth of children, and men earned more than women. Since the 1986 Equal Employment Law went into effect, such gender discrimination is now illegal, and as a result the position of women has improved somewhat. Still, during the recession that began in the early 1990s, women, who now make up the majority of university graduates, have had a much harder time than their male counterparts in finding employment.

Opposition to the Conservative Agenda

Japan's economic success made it the envy of many countries. Yet, there were also controversial elements to Japan's rapid economic growth and the Conservative Party's approach to politics. We have already discussed the Socialist Party's opposition to the security treaty and its view that the Self-Defense Forces were unconstitutional. In comparison with the German Socialist Party, which distanced itself from Marxism at its 1959 Bad Godesburg summit, the JSP maintained its Marxist orientation and opposition to Japan's close security relationship with the United States. Interestingly, the downfall and near-total collapse of the JSP, which throughout most of the postwar period had managed to garner about one-third of the electorate's support, came when it compromised on its positions, accepted the U.S.-Japan Security alliance and the SDF, and agreed to go into a coalition government with the LDP in 1994 in exchange for the position of prime minister. The JSP paid a heavy price for its dramatic policy shift. In 1996, the party was all but wiped out by a disenchanted electorate.

Japan's conservative politics engendered criticism from various quarters for other reasons as well. During the 1960s and 1970s, there were widespread consumer movements and environmental movements. Consumer movements protested policies that favored industrial expansion at the expense of consumers, who had to pay high prices for imported goods and were paying more for televisions manufactured in Japan than Americans were paying for those same televisions. Environmental movements arose because of the severe, health-threatening pollution that resulted from the failure to enact any pollution controls. So bad was pollution in Tokyo during the 1970s that vendors sold oxygen on street corners. In the fishing community of Minamata, which had the misfortune of being selected as the site for a petrochemical complex in the 1950s, mercury poisoning resulted in severe birth defects and fatalities.

The dominance of the LDP had led to Japan being identified as a system dominated by one party. The LDP's majority was always relatively slim, however, and this gave the parties of the Left some opportunity to influence policy developments. During the early 1970s, the LDP was threatened with a loss of electoral support. Communists and Socialists had won mayoral and gubernatorial positions in Japan's major cities, and the LDP feared a similar loss at the national level. To prevent this from occurring, the LDP adopted policies that were being called for by the social movements and leftist mayors and governors. Thus, during the 1970s, the LDP expanded social programs and introduced advanced pollution controls.

Another problem with the close ties that formed among the LDP, the bureaucracy, and industry was the potential for corruption of both politicians and bureaucrats and the political apathy this generates within the public. The LDP was in power for so long that it is perhaps not so surprising that corruption scandals began to plague the party, and the influence of the bureaucracy meant that it was a target as well. One of the most riveting examples of corruption led to the arrest of Shin Kanemaru, a godfather-type politician who was the effective head of the largest faction of the LDP and mentor to Kakuei Tanaka, who also fell into disgrace. Kanemaru was arrested for accepting bribes from Sagawa Kyūbin, a delivery company, and asking the company to put him in touch with the *yakuza*, the Japanese mafia, so that they might take care of his detractors. When the police raided his homes and offices, they found over 3 billion yen in bond certificates, tens of millions in bank notes, and over 200 pounds of gold bars! The police discovered that many of the contributions came from construction companies. Tanaka was also implicated in the scandal but died before ever serving any time. The failure to apply harsh punishments commensurate with the size of the crimes committed disillusioned many in the public.

Other scandals made the public even more distrustful of the government. These included the government's inept handling of rescue efforts after the devastating 1995 Hanshin Earthquake, in which at least 4,000 in the Kobe area died; a case in which the Ministry of Health and Welfare permitted hemophiliacs to be given untreated blood and as a result thousands are now HIV-positive; numerous nuclear accidents, including one at the Tokaimura Uranium reprocessing plant, in which case poorly trained employees caused a criticality accident and died of nuclear radiation; and most recently, Naoto Kan, head of the opposition Democratic Party (newly formed in the 1990s), resigned after admitting to having failed to pay into the mandatory national pension plan. Prime Minister Jun'ichiro Koizumi subsequently also admitted to having failed to make all payments but appears to have managed to avoid calls for his resignation in part by deflecting national attention by making a visit to North Korea, a major international political move. The pension scandals have angered the public, which under planned pension reforms is being asked by politicians to pay more into the pension plan.

The Politics of Reform

ECONOMIC REFORM

In 1989, the Japanese economy was soaring. Japan's remarkable economic growth had some predicting that Japan would surpass the United States economically. Land prices had reached astronomical levels. The real estate value of land adjacent to the Imperial Palace grounds in downtown Tokyo was so high that it led to estimates that the palace grounds themselves – an area

similar in size to Central Park in New York – were worth more than the entire real estate value of California! Japan's wealth was staggering, and the
"Japanese model" became an object of study. Universities across the United
States were teaching the Japanese business model, and Japanese became one
of the most studied foreign languages in the country. Japanese individuals,
companies, and banks invested their money in real estate and development
projects at home and abroad. In Japan, a rural construction boom ensued as
golf courses and leisure facilities were built and the government instituted a
policy to promote "leisure" in response to international complaints that the
Japanese worked too hard.

But then the economic bubble burst. Real estate prices began to tum-
ble, and banks found themselves sitting upon huge sums of nonperforming
loans. The huge speculation boom, which went far beyond what would have
occurred had banks been using more stringent accounting practices, led to
many companies and banks going bankrupt. In addition, excessive public
spending produced a huge government deficit, measured at 130 percent of
Gross Domestic Product (GDP) in 2001, the highest of any industrialized
country. Concerns about Japan's aging society and the long-term viability of
its public pension system also weighed upon policymakers.

As a result of this lackluster performance of Japan's economy, various
economists both inside and outside of Japan have pushed the government to
adopt structural reform measures. Japan's previously touted economic model
involved extensive government involvement in the economy, but clearly this
involvement had produced its own unique set of pathologies. Prime Minister
Koizumi initiated efforts to decrease the size of government, reducing the
number of ministries and agencies from 22 to 13. He also created a new
Council on Economic and Fiscal Policy to advise the prime minister and
appointed Harvard-trained Heizo Takenaka as the first Minister of Financial Services, Economic and Fiscal Policy to address reform of the banking
system. The International Monetary Fund has pressured the government to
survey the extent of the bank-loan problem, which in the early 2000s still
threatened the long-term health of many of Japan's banks. Given that Japan
finances a huge percentage of the U.S. government budget deficit through
its purchase of U.S. government bonds, the health of the Japanese economy
is immensely important to the United States as well as the global economy.

The government has been urged to pursue deregulation of its 77 state-
backed corporations, many of which were involved in construction and
public works, such as the Highway Public Corporation, and transportation. Large companies have been pressured to move away from their
lifetime-employment structure and to streamline their operations. Institutional structures that functioned well during Japan's phase as a developmental state in its successful attempt to catch up to the West have proved a drag

on the economy in a more globalized economic system in which Japan is one of the most mature economies. Japan must develop a more flexible economic system if it is to remain competitive in the twenty-first century.

Given that Japan does not have a very well-developed social welfare net or unemployment system and that job mobility is more limited than in the United States, there is considerable resistance to some of the reforms, especially those that have fed rising unemployment rates. The unemployment rate in the early 2000s rose to the 5 to 6 percent range (low by U.S. and European standards but a record high by Japanese standards) as a result of layoffs and bankruptcies. The development of a welfare net to catch those who lose out in the structural reform process has not received much attention from the government, although programs are being established to help small- and medium-sized enterprises and encourage entrepreneurs.

POLITICAL REFORM

The scandals that plagued the ruling party during the late 1980s and 1990s and power struggles within the heavily factionalized LDP led to a splintering of the party in 1992. In that year, Morihiro Hosokawa and a small group of followers split off from the LDP to form a new party, which Hosokawa called the Japan New Party, promising to pursue economic, political, and social reforms. Ichiro Ozawa, another reformist politician, also abandoned the LDP and formed his own new party, the Shinseitō. In the next election, in 1993, the LDP received the largest number of votes but not a majority, and this opened the door for the first non-LDP government to form since 1948. An unwieldy eight-party coalition was formed – including all of the old opposition parties except the Communist Party, plus the two newly formed parties, and Hosokawa became prime minister. Although the coalition government did not survive for long, it marked the beginning of a new era in postwar Japanese politics of coalition governments and the beginning of the unraveling of what is commonly known as the 1955 system – a system where the LDP was in power and the Japan Socialist Party, the Democratic Socialist Party, the Japan Communist Party, and the Clean Government Party (Kōmeitō, a Buddhist Party that formed in 1964) were in perpetual opposition.

One of the real achievements of Hosokawa's government was electoral reform. Japan's electoral system had been based on a complicated medium-sized, multimember district system in which each electoral district elected, in most cases, between three and five representatives. As each voter had a single nontransferable vote, this meant that the top vote getters, sometimes getting as little as ten percent of the vote, took office. This system pitted members of the same party against each other as well as against members of other parties and was immensely expensive. The coalition government argued that the system bred corruption, was unfair (as electoral redistricting had not kept pace with Japan's rapid urbanization and as a result the weight of a rural individual's vote was much greater than that of an urban dweller's vote), worked to the advantage of the LDP as a party because of its strong rural support base, and worked against the development of party ideologies. There was interest in creating a new electoral system that might eventually lead to a two-party system similar to the British system, where control of government moves between the Labour Party and the Conservative Party, and that of the United States, where it moves between the Democratic Party and the Republican Party.

In complicated negotiations, a new electoral system was agreed upon for the House of Representatives, the more powerful of Japan's two houses. The new system adopted a combination proportional-representation system and a single-member district system. The system was modified again by changes to the Electoral Law, most recently in 2000. Under the new system, 300 seats are elected in single-seat races and another 180 seats are determined by proportional representation. Each voter gets two votes, one for a candidate and one for a party.

In the 1994 election, the LDP again failed to obtain a majority. The LDP was able to prevent another opposition coalition government from forming, however, by creating a grand coalition with the largest of the opposition parties, the Social Democratic Party of Japan (SDPJ, formerly the JSP). As noted previously, as a condition of joining the coalition, the SDPJ was given the right to choose one of their own members to be prime minister. Although Tomoiichi Murayama was able to enjoy a year as prime minister, in the next election he saw his party decimated at the polls in part because in the eyes of the voters the compromises it had made to enter the grand coalition with the LDP – withdrawing its rejection of the Self-Defense Forces and the U.S.-Japan security treaty – alienated many of its left-wing supporters.

In subsequent elections, the LDP was able to stay in power by forming coalitions with one or more of the many new smaller parties to have formed in the 1990s. Since the mid-1990s, the LDP has formed coalitions with various parties, including the greatly weakened SDPJ, the New Kōmeitō, and several relatively new parties, including New Party Sakigake, the Liberal Party, and the New Conservative Party. The largest opposition party in Japan is now the Democratic Party.

Another important aspect of political change in Japan since the 1990s has been the empowerment of civil society. There were many restrictions that hampered the formation of a vibrant civil society in Japan. The devastating 1995 Hanshin earthquake and the important role played by voluntary groups in rescuing victims fostered more favorable government attitudes about civil society. There has also been pressure on Japan to open the way for a greater role for civil society in decision making as a result of international conferences, such as the United Nations Conference on Environment and Development or the United Nations Conference on Women, where nongovernmental-organization participation is expected. Since the mid-1990s, there have been important changes to laws governing the establishment of nonprofit organizations and the creation of Freedom of Information laws. Thus, along with the changes in Japan's party structure, there has been a pluralization of decision-making institutions since the mid-1990s as new interests and identities gained a greater foothold.

Carving Out a New International Role and Vision for Japan in a Changing Global Order

The LDP also had to deal with the international consequences of its economic success. The 1970s and 1980s were dubbed the years of Japan bashing, when the United States and Europe began to feel Japan's growing economic muscle and experience large trade imbalances with Japan. Although Japan was in fact a net importer in large part because of its need to import most of its energy and raw materials, it was a net exporter to the United States, many European countries, and East and Southeast Asia. The United States in particular pushed Japan to remove formal and informal trade barriers affecting automobiles, steel, computers, and machine tools, among other products. This was not always easy for the LDP to do. The protectionist policies clearly benefited Japanese industry, which was a financial backer of the party in Japan's expensive electoral system. They also benefited Japan's small but influential agricultural sector, an important voting block for the LDP.

As in other countries, Japan's interests and identities were tied to its institutions, and the Japanese resented the outside world's effort to delink them. During the 1980s, Japan was lobbied to open its doors to citrus fruit and beef exports, which it eventually did. Efforts to push open the rice market, however, were less successful. Whereas the government argues that rice has a special cultural significance and is a necessary element of Japan's food security and therefore must be protected, there are clearly electoral reasons why the LDP is reluctant to remove tariffs on rice. Negotiations also addressed informal trade barriers that made it difficult for foreign companies to set up operations in Japan. Examples of informal trade barriers are the long-term relationships among corporations that lead firms to favor familiarity and loyalty over price. The close links between firms and suppliers that are found in Japan's **keiretsu**, the postwar version of the *zaibatsu*, have made it difficult for foreign companies to break into the Japanese market. Other examples are the close networks between Japanese companies and the bureaucracy that emerge from practices such as *amakudari*, discussed earlier. Such informal institutional factors, however, are difficult to change. It can also be argued that for many years U.S. companies ignored the Japanese market, dismissing it as too difficult to enter for linguistic and cultural reasons.

Japan has opened most of its markets under pressure from the United States and Europe and because of its accession to the World Trade Organization (WTO). Japan, moreover, is now itself concerned about other countries using protectionist barriers to block its exports – as was the case when the United States slapped import duties on steel. Thus, Japan is a strong supporter of the WTO and its free-trade policies. During the 1980s, Japanese firms also began to move more of their manufacturing overseas to be closer to the markets where their goods would be sold and where cheaper labor is available. Thus, many Japanese automobile manufacturers produce automobiles for the U.S. market in the United States and many electronics firms do parts assembly in China. This also has raised issues for Japan, as there are growing concerns about industrial flight from Japan.

As a result of its economic strength, Japan also found itself pressured to do more for international society, given its status as the world's second-largest economy. Conservative elements of the LDP used this international pressure as an opportunity to push for revisions to Japan's security policies. Yasuhiro Nakasone, who was prime minister from 1982 to 1987 and had a close relationship with both Ronald Reagan and Margaret Thatcher, pushed for an expansion of Japan's budget for the Self-Defense Forces, exceeding the de facto 1 percent limit that Prime Minister Takeo Miki had established in 1976. Japan began to pay for more of the costs of maintaining U.S. bases in Japan and agreed to defend the seas between its islands and its major sea lanes. During the 1990s, these changes to Japan's security program were pushed even further as a result of the first Persian Gulf War. Under considerable international pressure and despite strong domestic concerns, the Japanese Diet agreed to permit the use of Japanese SDF personnel in noncombat roles in UN peacekeeping operations. The Japanese population could be persuaded to accept this in part because of the extensive international criticism Japan received for not contributing more to the first Persian Gulf War even though Japan paid $13 billion (U.S.) to support the war efforts. Thus, in a major reinterpretation of Article 9, Japan has participated in UN peacekeeping operations in support roles in Angola, Cambodia, Mozambique, El Salvador, the Golan Heights, Kenya and Zaire (to aid refugees of the genocide in Rwanda), and East Timor. The International Peace Cooperation Law, which went into effect in 1992, restricts Japanese SDF involvement to cases where a cease-fire is in operation and all parties consent to Japan's involvement. Weapons can be used only for self-defense. The deployment in 2004 of Japanese troops to Iraq, a combat zone, pushes the interpretation of Article 9 yet one step further, and the deployment has been called unconstitutional by some in the opposition.

Another foreign policy area where Japan began to exert more influence was in assistance to developing countries. This has been done both through Japan's role as one of the largest contributors to multilateral development banks, including the Asian Development Bank, the International Monetary Fund, and the World Bank, and the work of the United Nations. It has also been done through overseas development assistance (ODA). Japan emerged during the 1990s as the world's largest provider of ODA, although Japan's aid figures in percentage terms of GDP are well below many other countries, and recently the United States has again surpassed Japan as the largest provider of ODA. Japanese aid has been used to develop infrastructure, including roads, schools, hospitals, dams, and energy facilities overseas. A large percentage of Japanese aid, primarily in the form of low-interest loans, went to Southeast Asia, a region where Japan has tried to strengthen its economic and political ties and overcome the negative images of its wartime past. In response to criticisms that Japanese assistance was often contributing to projects that were environmentally destructive, threatening the way of life of indigenous peoples, or lining the pockets of corrupt officials in developing countries, Japanese ODA practices have been substantially revised. Environmental protection, sustainable development, and human health are now among the primary areas for which Japan provides ODA; this includes loans for sewage construction, fresh water projects, health care, reforestation, and the like. This emphasis on environmental ODA is also a means by which the foreign ministry can continue to provide aid to China, a policy that a growing number of politicians are expressing doubts about given China's growing economic strength and its military expenditures.

Since the mid-1990s, Japan has attempted to create a foreign policy more independent from the United States and has worked to improve its relations with its Asian neighbors. Asia has not forgiven Japan for the war in the Pacific during World War II, nor has Japan been very good about apologizing to Asia for the atrocities it committed during the war. Japanese politicians continue to upset China, Korea, and other Asian states by invoking wartime memories with, for example, official visits to Yasukuni Shrine, a Shinto Shrine that memorializes and enshrines Japan's war dead, including some "class A" war criminals. Prime Minister Jun'ichiro Koizumi has made yearly visits to the shrine since 2001 inviting strong criticism from abroad. The Ministry of Education's approval of a history textbook that gave scant attention to Japan's wartime atrocities led to wide-scale riots against Japanese in China in 2005. Nevertheless, although Japan has never openly apologized to Asia for the offenses of World War II, the government has taken measures to improve ties and to put the war into the past. In 1992, in a highly symbolic visit, Emperor Akihito (who ascended to the throne upon his father's death in 1989, ending the **Shōwa** era under Emperor Hirohito and beginning the Heisei "peace" era) traveled to China and expressed regret about the past. The Japanese government also agreed to make modest compensation payments to Korean "comfort" women who were victims of institutionalized rape by the military during the war.

Despite the strong protests against Japan in both China and Korea in 2005, with the notable exception of North Korea, it can be said that relations among states in Asia are generally improving. Japan has pursued the development of stronger bilateral economic, political, and cultural ties with its Asian neighbors. Japan is intensely aware of China's growing economic strength and its already powerful military, and thus improving ties with China is deemed highly important. Japan has also agreed to greater cooperation with Russia, including the possible development of a Siberian oil pipeline, despite failure to date to reach a peace agreement over the disputed Northern Territories.

Prime Minister Koizumi also has made two widely publicized visits to North Korea, the latter of which was with the goal of making progress in relation to the utterly bizarre case of 13 Japanese kidnap victims and their North Korean families (and, in one case, an American spouse who defected from his base in the South to the North). In late 2002, North Korea surprised the world by admitting to having kidnapped 13 Japanese in the 1970s to train North Korean spies in the Japanese language and culture. Intense public interest in the case – a story that could have come straight out of a James Bond movie – placed great pressure on the Japanese government not only to get the five surviving kidnap victims back to Japan but also their children and spouses. Although this issue has been uppermost in the Japanese news, Koizumi has also tried to push forward negotiations with North Korea pertaining to its expulsion of International Atomic Energy Agency nuclear inspectors, its denunciation of the Nuclear Non-Proliferation Treaty, and its development of nuclear weapons. Japan is a member of the stalled six-party talks that also include the United States, North Korea, South Korea, China, and Russia.

Conclusion

Japan is struggling to determine what its role should be in a post–Cold War world in which alliance structures are changing and the economic situation of states is changing. Many in Japan are questioning whether Japan can continue to operate as a state with such strong restrictions on the deployment of its military. Many others in Japan are arguing that Japan should remain pacifist and make nonmilitary contributions to the global system. The rapid growth of China is of great interest and concern to Japan, and as a result Japan has been working to improve its relations with China and other countries in Asia.

Long considered a follower of U.S. foreign policy, since the mid-1990s Japan has begun to show somewhat more policy independence from the U.S., although it still closely monitors U.S. reactions to its policy positions. Japan has become an international leader in the provision of overseas development assistance and has become a more powerful international player in Asia. Still, there is a lot of questioning in Japan about what its future holds.

This sense of uncertainty also pervades the political and economic systems. Efforts to create a two-party electoral system in Japan have failed to date, and there is growing public apathy about politics. On the economic front, a decade of reform efforts may slowly be beginning to pay off, but many uncertainties remain.

Japan has an extremely well-educated population, low crime rates, high life expectancy, and a relatively high GNP per capita. Thus, on many of the most important indicators of a nation's well-being, Japan ranks well compared with other "rich" countries, including the United States. Maintaining this performance as Japan's society ages and its economy enters an era of slower growth will be one of the most important challenges for the Japanese government.

BIBLIOGRAPHY

Allinson, Gary D., and Yasunori Sone. *Political Dynamics in Contemporary Japan.* Ithaca, NY: Cornell University Press, 1993.

Beasley, W. G. *Rise of Modern Japan: Political, Economic, and Social Change Since 1850.* New York: St. Martin's Press, 2000.

Dower, John W. *Embracing Defeat: Japan in the Wake of World War II.* New York: Norton, 1999.

Duus, Peter. *The Rise of Modern Japan.* Boston: Houghton-Mifflin, 1976.

Gluck, Carol. *Japan's Modern Myths: Ideology in the Late Meiji Period.* Princeton, NJ: Princeton University Press, 1985.

Johnson, Chalmers. *MITI and the Japanese Miracle: The Growth of Industrial Policy, 1925–1975.* Stanford, CA: Stanford University Press, 1982.

Pempel, T. J. *Regime Shift: Comparative Dynamics of the Japanese Political Economy.* Ithaca, NY: Cornell University Press, 1998.

Richardson, Bradley. *Japanese Democracy.* New Haven, CT and London: Yale University Press, 1997.

Samuels, Richard J. *The Business of the Japanese State: Energy Markets in Comparative and Historical Perspective.* Ithaca, NY: Cornell University Press, 1987.

Schlesinger, Jacob M. *Shadow Shoguns: The Rise and Fall of Japan's Postwar Political Machine.* Stanford, CA: Stanford University Press, 1999.

Schreurs, Miranda A. *Environmental Politics in Japan, Germany, and the United States.* Cambridge: Cambridge University Press, 2002.

Schwarz, Frank, and Susan J. Pharr, eds. *The State of Civil Society in Japan.* Cambridge: Cambridge University Press, 2003.

Stockwin, J. A. A. *Governing Japan.* Third edition. Oxford: Blackwell Publishers, 1999.

TABLE 6.1. Key Phases in Japan's Political Development

Time Period	Regime	Global Context	Interests/Identities/ Institutions	Developmental Path
1603–1867	Tokugawa shogunate (military authoritarian/ imperialism)	growing foreign trade pressures, European domination of China/U.S. – forced opening of Japan	powerful shogunate/ competition among feudal daimyo/shogun-led unification of country	unification of state through dominance of feudal domains by shogunate
1868–1912	Meiji Period (oligarchy/ authoritarian/ imperialism)	European imperialism/ Asian power struggles	political and industrial elite/political and industrial reform/ authoritarian with elections	adoption of Western political institutions and capitalism
1912–1926	Taisho democracy (democratic/ imperialism)	World War I and Treaty of Versailles, failure of West to accept Japan as an equal	political and industrial elite/democracy, socialism, communism, imperialism/ democracy with powerful bureaucrats and oligarchs	capitalism and imperialism
1926–1945	militarism (authoritarian/ imperialism)	global depression, rise of fascism and communism, World War II	military elite/fascism, imperialism/ authoritarian	capitalism, imperialism, and militarism
1945–1952	foreign occupation (military/ democratic)	Start of U.S.-Soviet Cold War, Communist victory in China, Korean War	economic develop- ment/militarism discredited/ rebuilding of industry and democratic institutions	international assistance and occupation
1955–1993	one-party dominance (democratic)	Cold War, economic growth	big business/ democratic values grow, pacifism, consumerism, environmentalism/ one-party dominant democratic system	capitalism and liberalism
1994– present	coalition government (democratic)	end of Cold War, improved Asian regional relations	economic stagnation/ globalization, expanded overseas role for SDF/ pluralization, strengthening of civil society	capitalism, liberalism, and globalization

IMPORTANT TERMS

amakudari literally "descent from heaven," this term refers to the common practice whereby retiring civil servants take up positions in Japanese corporations and public-interest bodies.

Article 9 of the Japanese constitution states that "the Japanese people forever renounce war as a sovereign right of the nation and the threat or use of force as a means of settling international disputes." It has been the basis for the maintenance of a pacifist foreign policy, although over the years it has been reinterpreted to allow for the creation of the Japanese Self-Defense Forces and participation in UN peacekeeping operations.

daimyo were the lords of the 260 feudal fiefdoms of Japan. The victory in war of the Tokugawa clan in 1600 led to a system in which the daimyo were required to pay tribute to the Tokugawa government.

Diet a German word for parliament. Japan's Diet was created in 1890 and was based on the Prussian model. The Diet was weak during the pre–World War II era, but the 1946 constitution greatly strengthened its powers.

fukoku kyohei literally "rich nation, strong army," this phrase symbolized Meiji Japan's desire to catch up economically and militarily with the West.

genro were the oligarchs who advised the emperor and effectively ran Japan during the Meiji era.

gyōsei shidō translated as "administrative guidance," this term symbolizes the power of the Japanese bureaucracy and its influence in helping to steer the Japanese economy during its growth years.

Japan Socialist Party (JSP) the largest opposition party in postwar Japan from its formation in 1955 to its disastrous electoral performance in the 1995 elections to the House of Representatives. The party changed its name in English to the Social Democratic Party of Japan (SPDJ) in 1991.

keiretsu the term for the economic conglomerates that are prevalent in postwar Japan and are the successors to the prewar *zaibatsu*.

Liberal Democratic Party (LDP) the conservative governing party of Japan from its formation in 1955 until its electoral defeat in 1993. From 1994 on, the LDP has again governed in coalition with other, small parties.

General Douglas MacArthur was appointed Supreme Commander of the Allied Powers (SCAP) by President Harry S. Truman and was in charge of the occupation of Japan. He was a very powerful figure and had a hand in the writing of the Japanese constitution.

Meiji Restoration the 1868 revolt that led to the downfall of the Tokugawa clan, the revival of the position of the emperor, and the implementation of a crash course of modernization for Japan.

Ministry of International Trade and Industry (MITI) the ministry that played an important role in the economic development of Japan. Many of Japan's smartest university graduates worked for MITI. The ministry was renamed in 2001 as the Ministry of Economy, Trade, and Industry.

Commodore Matthew Perry sailed four "black ships" into Edo Bay in 1853 and demanded the opening of Japanese ports to foreign trade. Perry's voyages to Japan were behind the great political reforms of the Meiji Restoration.

reverse course a shift in the emphasis of U.S. occupation policies in Japan after the onset of the Cold War. The focus of policies shifted from the demilitarization and democratization of Japan to the limited rearming of Japan and its economic recovery.

Shigeru Yoshida Japanese prime minister from 1946 to 1947 and again from 1949 to 1954, who chose to focus on economic development and allow the United States to guarantee Japan's security. His policies are referred to as the Yoshida Doctrine and became the guiding ideology of the LDP.

shogun the military leaders and the Tokugawa clan that ruled Japan from 1603 to 1868.

Shōwa era the name of the reign of Emperor Hirohito (1926–1989), a tumultuous period in Japanese history.

Taisho democracy the brief interlude during the period from 1918 to 1932 when parties gained political influence and a more pluralist democracy began to function.

zaibatsu the family-owned financial conglomerates of the pre–World War II era.

STUDY QUESTIONS

1. How was Japan able to avoid the fate of many other Asian countries that became colonies of the West? How did Japan go from being an isolated state under the Tokugawa Shogunate, to becoming a world power during the Meiji era?

2. Was the Meiji constitution democratic? Why, or why not?

3. What explains Japan's imperialism and the rise of militarists during the 1930s?

4. What lessons can we take from the Allied occupation of Japan? Why was the occupation of Japan so successful?

5. Japan's "economic miracle" stunned the world. How can Japan's rise from postwar destitution to economic powerhouse be explained?

6. How would you characterize postwar Japanese democracy? How does the postwar constitution differ from the Meiji constitution?

7. Why was the Yoshida Doctrine so important to Japan's defense posture and economic development during the postwar period?

8. Why might one consider the 1990s as the beginning of a period of economic and political reform in Japan? What are the driving factors behind these reforms?

9. Do you think that Japan should maintain a strict interpretation of Article 9? Why, or why not?

10. What characteristics of Japanese politics would you consider to be uniquely Japanese?

STOP AND COMPARE

EARLY DEVELOPERS AND MIDDLE DEVELOPERS

Once Great Britain and France developed, all other countries were forced to respond. Germany and Japan were among the first to do so. By the middle of the nineteenth century, Germany was not yet unified and Japan faced Western imperialism. German and Japanese variations on the grand strategies of development found in the early developers are the direct result of international competition – military, economic, and cultural – between early and middle developers.

If Great Britain's and France's historical experiences are models of development and revolution from below, Germany and Japan represent instances of development and revolution from above. Compared with their predecessors, the middle and lower classes in Germany and Japan were weaker and the upper classes stronger. The state, in alliance with the upper classes, helped initiate economic development. Above all, what drove the entire process was military competition with more advanced states.

This developmental path had fateful consequences for liberal democracy and ultimately world peace. After abortive attempts at representative democracy, both Germany and Japan thus went through a period of fascism before they could participate in the world economy on an equal basis with the developed West.

MIDDLE DEVELOPERS: GERMANY AND JAPAN

French power on the European continent guaranteed throughout the first 70 years of the nineteenth century that Germany remained a fragmented group of kingdoms and principalities. Among these separate states, however, some were more powerful than others. The most militarily capable was Prussia, which, under the leadership of Chancellor Bismarck, succeeded in defeating the French in the Franco-Prussian War of 1870 and unifying the German states under Prussian leadership in 1871. From the outset, German economic and political development reflected the fact that it came in response to French and British advancement. The fact that the need for military power came in anticipation of, rather than in response to, economic development meant that the path taken by Britain and France, which was largely a story of rising middle classes gradually securing power over monarchs and nobilities, would not be a historical possibility for Germany. Unable to rely on an economically ingenious and politically assertive rising middle class, Germany industrialized by allowing capital to concentrate in relatively few large banks, permitting industrialists to reduce risk through the creation of cartels, and creating a modern military officer corps and state apparatus on the basis of premodern agrarian elites. The coalition on which power rested consisted of an alliance of "iron and rye" that had little interest in genuine parliamentary rule. The Parliament, known as the Reichstag, was neither fairly elected nor did it have sovereignty over the kaiser whose governmental ministers continued to be appointed from the ranks of the noble elite.

Although this pattern of development forestalled democracy, it succeeded quite spectacularly in military competition and economic development. By the beginning of the twentieth century, Germany could field land armies superior to those of the French and could float ships on par with those of the British. German chemical, machine-building, and metal industries were as advanced as those of its competitors. Such rapid development, occurring really in less than 40 years, had a price. German craftsmen and especially industrial workers, who were often first-generation city dwellers, lived mostly in very difficult circumstances. Radical working-class parties, such as the Social Democrats, could easily recruit the disaffected and the poor into mass politics. The ruling elite responded in two ways: first by banning the Social Democrats, and when that could not be sustained, by relying on a kind of militaristic German nationalist appeal for solidarity among classes against other nations. Unfortunately, this latter strategy worked. Perceiving the balance of forces to be temporarily on their side, and by tradition inclined toward military solutions to social and diplomatic problems, the kaiser and his advisers exploited a crisis in European security relations in 1914 to launch a continent-wide war, which ultimately became known as World War I.

Defeat in this war forced the kaiser to abdicate and led to a fundamental democratization of German politics. This first try at parliamentary democracy, known as the Weimar Republic (1920–1933), suffered from innumerable handicaps. The old elites had not been decisively replaced either in the economy or in the state bureaucracy; the victory of democracy was associated in many people's minds with a humiliating loss in war (in a country that lived by the cult of war) and an equally humiliating peace treaty signed at Versailles; the country was saddled with heavy reparations payments to the victors; and the political institutions led to a fragmented party system and the temptation to rule by emergency presidential decree. This last factor became the fateful one when Adolf Hitler's Nazi Party managed to gain a plurality of seats in the Reichstag in the 1932 elections. Hitler had revived much of the older militaristic thinking of the pre-Weimar era, but he now laced the new ideology with large doses of revenge and racism. After spending the middle of the 1930s preparing for war, in 1939 Germany initiated, for the second time in the twentieth century, a Europe-wide conflict that cost the lives of millions.

Because war emanated from Germany twice during the twentieth century, the Allied victors decided that this would not happen again. The ultimate price that Germany paid for defeat was, in some sense, to return to the situation from which it had started: national division. The Soviet zone of occupation became communist East Germany, or what was called the German Democratic Republic, and the three Western zones of occupation (those of Britain, the United States, and France) became West Germany, or the Federal Republic of Germany.

Apart from division, the Western allies and democratically minded Germans were also determined to remake Germany from the inside in order to ensure that democracy would genuinely take root there. To that end, Germany developed a set of policies, as well as constitutional and institutional innovations, designed to foster democratic stability and prevent extremist politics from ever returning. For example, although Germany continues to have a multiparty system, there are constitutional features to guarantee that it does not become too fragmented, unstable, or gridlocked in indecision. Another such arrangement is corporatism. Most Germans are organized into trade unions or employer associations. The German government through its public offices attempts to ensure that these two groups hammer out agreements that ensure just wages, low unemployment, and high growth rates. In turn, the government attempts to soften many of the rougher edges of capitalist economics through a comprehensive welfare state. The net impact of these policies is designed to ensure that economic downturns do not occur often and, when they do occur, that they do not turn public opinion against democracy. Perhaps more crucially, corporatist policies are supposed to prevent the most rancorous debates over wages, prices, and welfare and move them off the parliamentary floor and out of politics in general.

Such policies helped secure for the Federal Republic quite remarkable growth rates throughout the postwar era and also created a society that, for the first time in Germany's history, genuinely seems to value liberal democracy for its own sake. However, the challenges of reunification, European unity, and global capitalist competition have induced slower growth rates, much higher unemployment, and a new domestic debate on whether the German model can be sustained into the future. In the first years of the twenty-first century, the German government brought the entire German social market model into question by tinkering with such bedrocks of the

STOP AND COMPARE

German model as health care, unemployment insurance, and state employment. Such questioning of the German model and initial moves to alter it are indeed troubling to most Germans precisely because it was this model that brought the country affluence and, after 1989, national unity – two things that had eluded Germany for the previous century.

Although Japan lies thousands of miles away from the European continent, grouping it together with Germany makes a great deal of sense to comparativists. For one thing, like Germany, Japan confronted external challenges to its sovereignty that forced it into rapid economic development in order to compete militarily. For another, the responses to these challenges were remarkably similar. Finally, the long-term path on which these responses set Japan led it to a similar form of militarism that also could only be overcome by fundamental restructuring after World War II.

Japan entered the early modern period a fragmented country dominated by alliances of local feudal lords (called daimyo), several of whom tried for over a century to gain control over the country. Under the leadership of the Tokugawa family (1603–1868), however, Japan at the start of the seventeenth century overcame its feudal fragmentation. Through concentration of power in the hands of the shogun, the institution of a rigid class system in which the warrior samurai nobility were given the lion's share of privileges, and the isolation of the island through a prohibition on foreign travel and a ban on the practice of Christianity, successive Tokugawa rulers succeeded in crafting out a distinctive Japanese identity and a unified Japanese state.

As effective as this system was in solving the problems of political unification – and the fact that it lasted for 250 years suggests that it was effective – the arrival of U.S. Commodore Perry's "black ships" in 1853, with the purpose of forcing Japan to open its borders to trade and foreign influence, posed challenges that the Tokugawa order was not equipped to confront. In the mid-1860s, a series of rebellions among low-level samurai, who incorporated nonprofessional soldiers and even peasants into their army under a nationalist banner of expelling the foreign "barbarians," succeeded in overthrowing the last Tokugawa shogun from office and replaced him in 1868 with an emperor whom they considered to be the true emperor of Japan, the 15-year-old Meiji.

The Meiji Restoration, as historians have subsequently dubbed it, set Japan down a course of economic and military modernization with the purpose of securing the country from foreign control. The slogan of the time "rich country, strong military" captured the essence of what the Meiji Restoration was about. As in Germany, our other middle developer, industrial modernization occurred primarily in the form of a "revolution from above." A modern army and navy were created, feudal-style control over localities was replaced with a modern local government, and class privileges were formally abolished, thus reducing the power of the old samurai class, in theory, to that of the commoners. As in Germany, industrialization was accomplished at break-neck speed under the guidance of a national bureaucracy and with capital controlled by large, family-owned industrial conglomerates called *zaibatsu*. Also as in Germany, the Japanese Meiji elite sought a political model that could accommodate the kinds of changes that were taking place. The constitutional model they settled on, not surprisingly, was that of imperial Germany, with its parliamentary electoral rules that favored the landed elite and a government that remained dominated by military institutions and values.

Fundamental democratization occurred in Japan for the first time only in 1925 with a series of electoral reforms. Unfortunately, the old Meiji ruling elites who remained on the political scene, especially within the officer corps, never fully supported democracy. When the political and economic crises of the 1930s hit, consistent pressure from right-wing extremists and the military high command constrained the actions of civilian government. The ideas of the far Right and the military about what Japan needed were somewhat diffuse, but they can be summarized relatively easily: Solve Japan's economic and domestic problems through the colonization and economic domination of continental Asia. To achieve these goals, starting in 1936 Japan engaged in a series of wars in China that yielded even more power to the military. The military viewed the United States as the main obstacle to Japan's plans for Asia, and it finally pushed Japan to attack Pearl Harbor in 1941 as a preemptive strike against U.S. might.

The devastating end of the war was the U.S. decision to drop the atomic bomb twice on Japan, after which the U.S. occupation inaugurated a series of political and economic reforms that changed life in Japan. A new constitution that forbade foreign military involvement, the complete removal of the emperor from political life, and a series of new institutions and political rules designed to bring constitutional democracy all brought about fundamental change. Japan lives with the result to this day.

Despite these changes, the nature of the Japanese political and economic model shows considerable continuities, or at least influences, from the past that remain a constant source of fascination for comparativists. Government and business continue to work closely together (although Japan's government is the "smallest" in the industrialized world), and capital remains far more concentrated than in the Anglo-American model. Furthermore, Japan continues to use a combination of hierarchy in political and social culture and a remarkable degree of equality in salaries and living standards. Japanese workers are highly unionized but almost never go on strike. Japan's trade tariffs are among the lowest in the world, but it continues to be a country that foreign businesses have trouble penetrating. Finally, Japan's Parliament, although democratically elected, continues in many ways to "pass" laws drafted in ministries rather than craft the laws itself. The latest round of globalization, however, has brought about considerable rethinking among the Japanese, who have started to question seriously whether these long-term character-istics of the Japanese model will be able to continue on into the future. As in Germany, where the fundamental democratization of the postwar period was accompanied by a selective retention of important aspects of the ear-lier model that seemed to work, the need to rethink the postwar political-economic model has led to considerable unease within Japan.

PART THREE

LATE DEVELOPERS

CASES

RUSSIA

CHAPTER SEVEN

Russia

Stephen E. Hanson

Introduction

Russia has long puzzled and surprised observers of international politics. For seven decades, Russia was at the center of a communist regime – the Union of Soviet Socialist Republics, or USSR – that competed with the United States for global supremacy (see Table 7.1). After the collapse of the USSR in 1991, Russia suffered a prolonged period of political, military, and economic decay. During the first term of President **Vladimir Putin**, the Russian economy rebounded strongly, but there were growing indications of a return to political authoritarianism. There is no consensus among specialists about how this one-time superpower became so weak so quickly; nor do scholars agree in their evaluations of Putin's efforts to revive the country. Indeed, it seems that Russia simply does not fit conventional analytic categories.

Geographically, Russia is the biggest country in the world, spanning 11 time zones. Most of its population is in Europe; most of its territory is in Asia. Although about four-fifths of its population are ethnically Russian, the Russian Federation contains hundreds of other ethnic groups, some of which are now struggling for greater autonomy or – in the case of **Chechnya** – full independence. Should we call Russia a European, an Asian, or a "Eurasian" state? Is Russia a nation or an empire? Will Russia eventually break up into smaller regional units? Or will it emerge again as a revitalized great power in world politics?

Economically, Russia is largely industrialized and urbanized, with only about one-fifth of its population living in rural areas. Its population is highly educated. Yet many of its factories are inefficient, technologically backward, and environmentally unsafe; its villages still often lack paved roads, sewage systems, and basic services; and its gross domestic product during the first decade of the twenty-first century was approximately the same as that of the Netherlands. Should we call Russia an advanced, a developing, or an underdeveloped state? Or does Russia's misdeveloped economy deserve some new theoretical category of its own?

Culturally, Russia has played a key role in European intellectual and artistic history, producing such well-known writers and composers as Lev Tolstoy, Fyodor Dostoevsky, and Pyotr Tchaikovsky. Yet for centuries – and even today – prominent Russian thinkers have claimed that their country can never be truly "Westernized" because of what they claim is the essential mysticism, communalism, and idealism of the Russian "soul." Should we call Russia's culture Western, non-Western, or something else entirely?

Neither Western analysts nor Russians themselves have come up with consistent answers to these questions. Indeed, since the collapse of the communist empire in 1991, life in Russia has become even more unpredictable and confusing. As the twenty-first century dawns, Russians are engaged in a seemingly endless debate about their country's identity. Early hopes for a rapid transition to democracy and capitalism have been dashed, and although the public mood has improved with the stabilization of the economy under Putin, there remains a pervasive anxiety about Russia's future.

Faced with the paradoxical nature of Russia's geography, economy, politics, and culture, many political scientists have been tempted to agree with Winston Churchill that Russia is "a riddle wrapped in a mystery inside an enigma." Detailed descriptions of Russian institutions seem to become outdated almost as soon as they are written. However, the comparative and theoretical approach to political analysis presented in this book can help us explain Russia's unfortunate history.

This chapter argues that contemporary Russian interest groups have been decisively shaped by the ideological identity and distinctive institutions imposed on the country by **Vladimir Lenin** and his followers from 1917 to 1991 in an effort to catch up with and overtake the West. In short, the USSR was a failed ideological experiment to design an alternative anticapitalist model of industrial society. Ironically, the collapse of Soviet institutions has left Russia once again on the periphery of the global capitalist system, facing similar challenges of economic backwardness, ethnic conflict, and international insecurity. This time, however, there is no consensual or coherent ideology to organize Russia's response to these challenges. Thus, an analysis of the rise and fall of the Soviet Union is crucial for understanding Russian politics today.

The Rise and Fall of the USSR

FROM MARX TO LENIN

What did "communism" mean to the founders of the Soviet regime and their heirs? To answer this question, we must begin with an examination of the Western European theorist who originally invented the idea of communism – **Karl Marx**. To be clear, Marx himself did not provide a "blueprint" for the Soviet system. Indeed, he died 34 years before the Russian Revolution of 1917. Those who wish to blame Marx for Soviet tyranny forget how little control philosophers and theorists have over the ways in which their ideas are interpreted decades or centuries later. Still, the Soviet leaders all considered themselves Marx's faithful disciples. We therefore need to understand Marx's ideas in order to make sense of the rise and fall of the Soviet Empire.

Karl Marx was born in 1818 in what is now Germany. When Marx was growing up, the vast majority of German-speakers, like the vast majority of human beings elsewhere, lived in small peasant villages governed by various local lords and princes. The Industrial Revolution that had already transformed England and the United States had yet to reach Germany, where merchant activity was largely confined to the larger cities and towns. Thus, Marx wrote about capitalism as it was first being developed on the European continent.

When Marx was just 29 years old, he and his best friend, Friedrich Engels, composed the most influential revolutionary essay ever written: the *Communist Manifesto*. The starting point for the analysis contained in the *Manifesto* – and indeed for all of Marx's later works – is a theoretical approach that later became known as historical materialism, which asserts that economic forces have ultimately determined the course of human social history. Politicians and philosophers may think that they are battling over principles, but in Marx's view they are really always fighting over the question of which groups get which shares of a society's overall wealth. The ruling ideas in each historical period, according to Marx, are always the ideas of a particular society's ruling class.

Marx argued that every stage of history has been marked by class struggle. Society has always been divided into two main classes: those who own property, and those who are forced to work to survive. The ruling class, Marx claimed, takes all the wealth that is left over once people's basic survival needs are met – what Marx called surplus value. However, the oppressed class always struggles to regain this surplus, which, after all, the workers themselves produced. Eventually, class struggle ignites a full-scale social revolution against the old order, leading to the emergence of a new and more advanced form of economic organization.

According to Marx, three main types of class society have shaped human history to date: slavery, feudalism, and capitalism. Slavery was the dominant "mode of production" in the earliest human civilizations, such as those of ancient Greece, Egypt, and Rome. After the fall of the Roman Empire, slavery in Europe gave way to feudalism, in which the main class struggle was between the ruling aristocracy and the oppressed peasantry.

After 1500 or so, this mode of production also began to weaken and finally disintegrate.

The third and final type of class society, capitalism, emerged in its full-fledged form in England and the United States during the 1700s. In the *Communist Manifesto*, Marx predicted – correctly, as we now know – that it would eventually encompass the entire globe. Capitalists themselves naturally argue that this new mode of production promotes individual freedom and wealth. In reality, Marx insisted, capitalism is simply another form of class exploitation with its own distinct type of class struggle. The ruling class under capitalism, the bourgeoisie, consists of those who hire workers for wages and/or own the factories, banks, and housing upon which workers are dependent. The oppressed class, the proletariat, consists of all those who own nothing more than their own labor power and are therefore forced to compete for a job in order to survive – that is, the vast majority of people. Surplus value, in the form of capitalist profits, goes straight into the pockets of the ruling class, whereas the proletariat must continually struggle to raise their wages above a very low level.

Marx was convinced that the capitalist system, like slavery and feudalism before it, would eventually be destroyed in a social revolution – this time eliminating class divisions among human beings altogether and ushering in an era of global human harmony and abundance. Marx argued that the experience of working together under the dehumanizing conditions of capitalism would serve to strip the proletariat of all forms of identity that had previously divided it. Subjected to the same forms of underpaid, repetitive, mechanized labor, workers would stop caring about one another's race, ethnicity, religion, or nationality and recognize their common humanity. The proletarian revolution, then, would be a revolution of the vast majority of human beings, united as one, to take control over the global economic system. Freed from the tyranny of wage slavery and the terror of unemployment, workers would henceforth work together in conditions of free, creative cooperation. The *Communist Manifesto* concludes: "The proletarians have nothing to lose but their chains! They have a world to win! Working men of all countries, unite!"

Yet there was a central paradox in Marx's thinking. On the one hand, Marx called for workers to unite and struggle for better conditions and wages in order to build proletarian solidarity and learn to exploit the vulnerabilities of the bourgeois system. On the other hand, Marx expected that workers under capitalism would become increasingly miserable over time, making revolution inevitable. What should communists do, then, if every successful workers' struggle against the bosses made workers less miserable and more satisfied with capitalism? Should communists support change within the existing system? Or should they continue to promote global revolution regardless of how capitalism reformed itself? Marx himself never quite resolved this strategic paradox.

In fact, no Marxist revolution has ever taken place in a developed capitalist country. Instead, communist revolution occurred first in 1917 in Russia – a country that had then only barely entered the capitalist age, with over 80 percent of its population consisting of peasants and only around 8 percent industrial workers. Why? Ironically, precisely because of Russia's underdevelopment, Marx's ideas were relatively more consistent with the interests of Russian workers and intellectuals. Although reforms had moderated the worst abuses of Western European capitalism, Russia during the early twentieth century was still suffering through the early period of industrialization, with its characteristic disregard for worker health and safety and its total lack of legal channels for worker representation. The Russian proletariat, small as it was, was thus much more revolutionary than were the better-off workers of the West. Meanwhile, many Russian intellectuals saw in Marxism a way to escape their country's economic and military backwardness without having to adopt the Western capitalist system. By achieving "socialism," it seemed, Russia could miraculously leap ahead of countries such as England and France in historical development. Finally, Marx's inspiring vision of communism proved especially powerful in a tsarist empire that had become embarrassingly weak, poor, and corrupt. Such factors help to explain the rapid spread of Marxist ideas in a feudal country – and the political evolution of the man who eventually founded a Marxist regime there, Vladimir Il'ich Lenin.

Vladimir Ulyanov – Lenin's real name – was born in the provincial town of Simbirsk, Russia, in 1870. When Lenin was 14 years old, his older brother Alexander was arrested for participating in a plot to assassinate the tsar and was later executed. This event placed the entire Ulyanov family under a cloud of suspicion. Lenin was allowed to attend law school in the capital city of St. Petersburg, but shortly after he began his legal studies, he was expelled for participating in student demonstrations against the regime. He began to read radical literature, and at the young age of 18, he became a convinced Marxist. By 1900, he had become prominent enough within Russian Marxist circles to be invited to join the leading Russian Marxists in exile in Switzerland, where they lived and worked in order to avoid harassment and arrest by the tsarist police.

In 1902, Lenin published his most famous essay, entitled *What Is To Be Done?* Lenin's ideas on party organization in this work ultimately inspired revolutionaries in China, Vietnam, Cuba, and elsewhere to create one-party regimes modeled on the "Leninist" example. Lenin's essay contained three main arguments, all of which became quite controversial among Marxists. First, Lenin bluntly insisted that the working class by itself could never make a successful anticapitalist revolution. More than 50 years after the publication of the *Communist Manifesto*, it had become clear that workers would always be satisfied with gains in local wages, benefits, and representation; in this sense, Lenin argued, workers had a kind of "trade-union consciousness"

instead of the revolutionary consciousness needed for the successful overthrow of global capitalism. Second, Lenin argued that the movement must
be led instead by Marxist intellectuals devoted at all times to revolutionary
activity. A special organization of these intellectuals – a "party of professional
revolutionaries" – was needed to guide the proletariat toward its eventual and
inevitable victory over the bourgeoisie. Finally, Lenin insisted that the party
of professional revolutionaries itself be organized as a strictly hierarchical,
disciplined, and unified body. Attempts to introduce "bourgeois" forms of
voting or legal procedure into the communist camp would only turn it into
an ineffective debating society. Instead, the party should practice what Lenin
would later term "**democratic centralism**" – meaning that debate within the
party should end the moment the party's Central Committee had made a
decision on any given issue.

It would be a long time, however, before Lenin and his followers built a
party that in reality looked anything like his original institutional proposal. Indeed, Lenin's insistence on his model of organization at a congress of Russian
Marxists in 1903 led to a split between two different factions: the Bolsheviks,
or majority – so named because of Lenin's success in getting a bare majority
of delegates present to vote to prohibit part-time party membership – and
the Mensheviks, or minority, who argued for a more decentralized and inclusive organization of Marxists and workers. By 1904, even many of those
Russian Marxists who had originally supported Lenin joined the Mensheviks
to protest what they saw as his increasingly dictatorial behavior – ironically
leaving the Bolsheviks very much a minority among Russian Marxists until
1917.

Indeed, had it not been for dramatic changes in Russia's global environment, Lenin's party might have faded into historical insignificance. However,
the outbreak of World War I in 1914 revived the Bolsheviks' fortunes. The
tsarist regime found itself hopelessly outgunned and began to disintegrate
quickly. In addition, the war's unprecedented bloodshed discredited the capitalist system. Finally, the war divided the Western European Marxist parties,
each of which voted to support its own capitalist government in a war against
their fellow proletarians.

Lenin was outraged by what he saw as the spinelessness of German, French,
and other Western socialists. He argued in his essay *Imperialism* that European Marxists had become hopelessly corrupted by payoffs from capitalist
imperial expansion. The proletarian revolution, he concluded, was therefore
more likely to begin in Russia, in the periphery of the global capitalist system, than in the developed countries of the West. Lenin made it clear, too,
that his own Bolshevik Party was ready to lead the Russian proletariat in its
revolutionary struggle. Once Russia proved to the workers of the world that
socialist revolution was possible, Lenin argued, communism would spread
like wildfire throughout the West and beyond.

The opportunity to act on this theory soon arose when the tsar, Nicholas II, suddenly abdicated in March 1917 in response to mounting losses on the battlefield, peasant uprisings in the countryside, and bread riots in the cities. This "February revolution" – so named because the old Russian calendar was then about two weeks behind the modern Western calendar – left Russia in a state of near anarchy. A **provisional government** made up of former members of the tsarist Parliament tried, with the support of the United States, Britain, and France, to revive the Russian economy and to continue the war against Germany. But this government had very little real authority, and in the cities, actual power devolved to what were called **soviets**, or councils, of workers and soldiers. Meanwhile, in the countryside, peasant revolts spread; many of the old nobility were killed or forced to flee.

Lenin did not, in any way, cause the collapse of tsarism; he had been in Switzerland for most of the war. He returned to the capital city of Petrograd (formerly St. Petersburg) in April 1917, advocating the overthrow of the provisional government, the establishment of a socialist republic based upon the soviets, and the immediate cessation of the war. Although the radicalism of these proposals at first stunned many of his own closest supporters, by the summer, mounting war casualties and the disintegrating economy rapidly turned the tide of public opinion among workers and soldiers in the Bolsheviks' favor.

On November 7 – the so-called October Revolution – Lenin and his supporters successfully seized power in Petrograd. Within a year, they had wiped out all other organized political forces within the territory they controlled. Not only were tsarist and capitalist parties banned, but socialists who disagreed with Lenin were also suppressed. A new secret police force, the Cheka – later to become the KGB – was set up to hunt down "enemies of the revolution." Even the soviets, the spontaneous organizations of the workers themselves, were reduced to little more than rubber stamps for the party's central decrees. Party organizations were set up in every factory, every school, and every public organization to help "guide" the proletariat to communism.

Lenin's theoretical expectation that Bolshevik victory would spark communist revolutions throughout the capitalist world turned out to be unfounded, however. From 1918 to 1920, Lenin and Leon Trotsky directed an enormously destructive and bloody civil war against various supporters of tsarism, liberalism, anarchism, and anti-Bolshevik socialism. But after having reconquered most of the territory of the former Russian empire, Lenin began to realize that the final global victory of the proletariat might be delayed indefinitely. Global capitalism, apparently, had stabilized.

To survive in power, then, the Bolsheviks had to revive the ruined Russian economy. In March 1921, Lenin introduced the **New Economic Policy**, which freed grain markets and allowed small-scale capitalism in the cities. Trade and agriculture began to recover soon afterward. Simultaneously, however, Lenin further strengthened one-party rule by implementing a "ban on factions" within the party's ranks. In 1922, he promoted a young disciple by the name of **Joseph Stalin** to the new position of general secretary of the Communist Party, entrusting him with the task of ensuring party discipline by control over personnel decisions.

Another vexing problem was that the new Soviet state occupied a territory containing hundreds of different religions and ethnic groups. According to Marx, of course, such identities were supposed to disappear entirely with the victory of communism over capitalism. In reality, such groups as the Ukrainians, the Georgians, and the Muslim peoples of Central Asia tended to perceive the new regime in Moscow as a continuation of the former Russian empire. Lenin appointed Stalin to be the new commissar for national-ities, expecting him to find a reasonable balance between the need for the party's central control and the concerns of non-Russians – after all, Stalin himself was an ethnic Georgian. To Lenin's dismay, Stalin immediately tried to eliminate all forms of national autonomy, even using physical violence to intimidate ethnic leaders who resisted his will. Ultimately, the new "Soviet Union" formed in 1923 did include several "national republics" for the largest and most powerful nationalities of the regime. Real political power, however, was concentrated in the Kremlin in Moscow (to which the Soviet capital had been relocated from Petrograd in 1918).

Shortly after promoting Stalin to these important positions, Lenin suffered a series of strokes that ultimately left him incapacitated. As Lenin lay on his deathbed in 1923, a fierce struggle for power broke out. In the last letter he was able to dictate, Lenin warned that such internecine battles could fatally weaken the party. In particular, his protégé Stalin had concentrated "immense power in his hands" and was "too rude" to occupy the post of general secretary. Lenin's warnings were ignored. Lenin died in January 1924. Within five years, Stalin emerged as the sole leader of the Soviet regime.

FROM LENIN TO STALIN

How did Iosef Djugashvili, the son of a poor cobbler in the small, mountain-ous country of Georgia, eventually become Joseph Stalin, one of the most powerful and brutal tyrants in history? This question is of immense historical importance because Stalin, even more than Lenin, shaped the playing field upon which Russian and other post-Soviet politicians now struggle for power. Moreover, by forging a communist bloc extending from Asia to Europe, Stalin also helped to create the basic contours of international politics in the second half of the twentieth century.

From the comparative point of view, however, the two main arguments that have been advanced to explain Stalin and Stalinism are rather unsatisfying. Some analysts argue that Stalin defeated his rivals for power and then es-tablished a tyranny simply because he was the most power-hungry, the most brutal, and the most opportunistic of any of Lenin's heirs. Although Stalin obviously wanted power and was willing to use violent means to get it, it makes little sense to accuse Stalin of simple opportunism. In order to rise within Lenin's Bolshevik Party in the first place, Stalin had to fight for 14 years for an illegal organization that until 1917 had few resources, only a few thousand loyal supporters, and a leader who lived in exile in Switzerland. During this period, the tsarist police arrested him a half-dozen times. If this was a strategy to attain future political power, it was one we can only recognize as such in retrospect. Certainly no ordinary rational politician would have chosen Stalin's early career path!

The second argument often made to explain Stalin's behavior is a psychological one: in short, that Stalin was a paranoid schizophrenic who thought that hidden enemies were always plotting against him. Again, this analysis may be clinically accurate. But this hardly explains how Stalin rose to the leadership of the world's largest state. Somehow, Stalin's personal psychology did not prevent him from convincing many intelligent men and women that he was a socialist genius and not a lunatic. How he did so must be explained in terms of the larger political, social, and global environment in which Stalin's personality was situated.

An alternative point of view, which will be defended here, is that Stalin rose to power and remained in control of the USSR until his death because he, like Lenin, was an institutional innovator within the Marxist ideological tradition. In short, Stalin was a convinced communist, as well as a staunch supporter of Lenin's ideas about party organization. Stalin was in a position to gain unprecedented political power at the head of the Leninist party only because he had identified enough with it early in life to have faith in its eventual triumph. This is why Lenin gave Stalin the crucial post of party general secretary: Stalin had proven his loyalty in times of trial, so Lenin thought he could be counted on to defend the party's interests.

Certainly, Stalin did his best to enforce Leninist norms of strict party discipline and control over a potentially hostile society, using his position to attack and purge any party member who dared disagree with the "general line" of the party leadership – within which, of course, he himself was a key figure. In this respect, however – despite Lenin's complaints about Stalin's "rude" behavior – he was only following Lenin's own principles of "democratic centralism." Shortly after Lenin's death, Stalin promoted thousands of young workers to party membership in a mass campaign called the "Lenin levy," creating an even larger base of personal supporters within the Leninist regime. None of Stalin's opponents possessed either the institutional levers or the organizational skills of the future dictator – a factor that cannot be ignored in accounting for his rise to power.

Stalin's victory was not only institutional, however; it was also ideological. Stalin, in fact, proposed a very distinct set of answers to the most troubling issue confronting Marxists in the Soviet Union in the wake of their revolutionary victory: namely, how to build "socialism" in a largely peasant country without the support of proletarian revolutions in more advanced capitalist countries. The policies that flowed from Stalin's analysis ultimately annihilated millions of people and left a burdensome economic legacy for post-Soviet Russia. Yet Stalinism was arguably the most consistent ideological response to the question of "what was to be done" after Lenin's death.

In order to see this, we must briefly examine the views of Stalin's main opponents. There were three main positions in the debate: the Left, the Right, and the Orthodox Center. The Left was led by the famous revolutionary Leon Trotsky, who had played a crucial role in the Bolshevik takeover, almost single-handedly building up the new Red Army and leading it to victory during the civil war. But after Lenin's incapacitation, Trotsky became disillusioned with what he saw as the gradual "bureaucratization" of the party and the loss of the Soviet Union's revolutionary momentum. Trotsky exhorted Soviet workers to redouble their efforts to build a strong industrial infrastructure as rapidly as possible and argued that the Bolsheviks should strive to foment revolutions throughout Western Europe. Unfortunately for Trotsky, after three years of world war, a year of revolution, and three years of civil war, most party members and ordinary workers were tired of revolutionary appeals. Some thought Trotsky might be harboring designs to take power for himself through a military coup. In the fall of 1923, the "Left opposition" was overwhelmingly outvoted in the party's Central Committee, and by 1924 Trotsky's power and influence began to decline rapidly.

The "Right opposition" in the 1920s was led by Nikolai Bukharin, a well-known Marxist theorist who edited the party's newspaper, *Pravda* (meaning "truth"). After an early alliance with Trotsky, Bukharin became convinced that the Left's proposals for continuous revolutionary advance were not feasible. Instead, Bukharin advocated a slow, evolutionary path to socialism in the USSR. Specifically, he argued that Lenin's New Economic Policy allowing small-scale capitalism should be continued "seriously and for a long time." The peasantry should be encouraged to get rich. Within factories, efficient management should be promoted – even if that meant keeping in place the same capitalist bosses as before the revolution. Eventually, Bukharin claimed, this policy would allow the Soviet people gradually to "grow into socialism." Such a policy was certainly more realistic than Trotsky's romantic leftism. Yet it failed to appeal to those who genuinely believed in the ideals of 1917. Many party members, workers, and intellectuals asked why they fought for communism if the end result was simply to establish a "New Economic Policy" that looked more like a "New Exploitation of the Proletariat."

The "Center," or Orthodox, Leninist position during the 1920s was advocated by Grigorii Zinoviev, who had been one of Lenin's most loyal supporters during the pre-1917 period. Zinoviev led the Bolshevik Party in the newly renamed city of Leningrad (formerly St. Petersburg and Petrograd). He also directed the Comintern, a global organization of communist parties loyal to Moscow, which Lenin had founded in 1919. Zinoviev argued that both the Left and the Right had gone too far: The Left called for revolution without rational analysis or professionalism, whereas the Right called for rational economic policies without any revolutionary vision. Surely, true "Leninism" – as he now began to refer to the regime's ideology – required both revolution and professionalism simultaneously! Unfortunately, Zinoviev himself had little idea of how to bring about a "Leninist" synthesis of these two concepts. His most original idea – enthusiastically supported by Stalin – was to place Lenin's mummified body on display in Moscow's Red Square so that generations of grateful proletarians could line up to see the founder of Soviet communism.

Neither Trotsky, nor Bukharin, nor Zinoviev proposed any practical policies for dealing with Russia's severe economic backwardness in a way that seemed consistent with the Soviet regime's socialist identity. Stalin did. In December 1924, Stalin proposed an alternative vision that appeared far more realistic in the context of the international isolation of the Soviet regime: "socialism in one country." The basic idea behind "socialism in one country" was simple: It was time to stop waiting for revolutions in other capitalist countries and start building socialism at home. This theoretical position contradicted Trotsky's calls for continuous revolutionary advance in Western Europe, as well as Zinoviev's hopes to inspire the world communist movement from Moscow without actually risking revolutionary changes. Bukharin, assuming that Stalin's idea of "socialism in one country" was identical to his own evolutionary socialism, threw his support behind Stalin in the power struggle against Trotsky and Zinoviev. By 1928, however, having defeated his latter two opponents, Stalin began to attack Bukharin as well, accusing him of being an opportunist who had sold out to the "bourgeois" rich peasants and industrialists. Stalin lined up large majorities to vote against the Right opposition in the Central Committee, and in 1929 he expelled Bukharin and his supporters from the party leadership.

Now the unchallenged leader of the regime, Stalin revealed that his vision of "socialism in one country" required a new revolutionary assault on Soviet society. Like Lenin, Stalin proposed to translate Marxist identity into concrete institutions that would structure the interests and incentives of millions of ordinary people – this time, in the economic and not just the political realm. Marx himself had said very little about how economic institutions should be organized in the postrevolutionary period; certainly, he had provided no guidance concerning how a single socialist state surrounded by capitalist ones could transform a largely peasant economy into an industrial power. However, Marx had indicated that he expected the "dictatorship of the proletariat" to organize state control over both the industrial and agricultural sectors of the economy, to eliminate private property wherever possible, and to organize production according to a common plan. Stalin now expanded on these principles to propose the revolutionary restructuring of the entire Soviet economy on the basis of "**five-year plans**" drawn up by the state and enforced by the Communist Party. Stalin insisted that although the Soviet economy was a century behind the West in developmental terms, that distance had to be made up in a decade – or the capitalists would "crush us."

The Stalinist planning system contained three key elements: **collectivization** of agriculture, a novel form of "planned heroism" in industry, and the creation of a huge system of prison labor camps known as **gulags**. The first of these, collectivization of agriculture, represented Stalin's "solution" to the dilemma of how to deal with the huge peasant population in forging a socialist Soviet Union: Basically, he decided to enslave or kill the entire peasantry. Again, Stalin put his argument in clear Marxist terms. The peasantry as a class, Marx had argued, was a leftover from feudalism. Capitalism was destined to destroy the peasantry and the aristocracy alike; there would be no place for peasant villages in the socialist future. Those who benefited from private property in agricultural production, Stalin reasoned, formed a sort of peasant bourgeoisie – "kulaks," meaning "the tight-fisted ones" – while the poor peasants who worked for them were essentially part of the proletariat. Proletarian revolution in the countryside required class struggle against the kulaks and eventually, as Stalin put it, "the liquidation of the kulaks as a class." In place of the old system of private peasant farming, Stalin proposed the creation of new "collective farms" (*kolkhozy*) and "state farms" (*sovkhozy*), where peasants would work for the greater good of the proletariat – under strict party supervision.

In reality, the drive to create collective farms amounted to an all-out assault on the countryside by Stalin's party supporters, by the army, and by various thugs and brigands who took advantage of the chaos to loot, steal, and rape. All over the Soviet Union, peasants battled to preserve their autonomy, even killing their own livestock rather than letting their pigs, cows, and chickens fall under party control. By 1932, the collectivization drive had generated a famine throughout the agricultural regions of the USSR during which millions of people starved to death. Even so, Stalin's goal of gaining party control over the production of food was realized. Indeed, even at the height of the famine, Stalin continued to export grain to Europe in order to earn hard currency for the regime. By the mid-1930s, most of the land in the country had been collectivized, excluding only tiny private plots where peasants were allowed to work for themselves and their families.

The second key element of Stalin's socioeconomic system was the imposition of centrally planned production targets for every manager and worker within the Soviet Union. The State Committee on Planning, or Gosplan, had been formed in the mid-1920s to provide general projections for future economic development in the USSR; in this respect, the organization acted in ways similar to planning bureaucracies in Western capitalist countries, such as France. But, in 1929, Stalin gave Gosplan officials the unprecedented task of supervising the rapid industrialization of an enormous country. The specific institutional mechanisms used to ensure this result were designed to elicit a sort of "professional revolutionary" economic activity comparable to that expected of good Leninist party members. Specifically, monthly and yearly production targets, calculated in terms of gross output, were issued for workers and state managers of every factory and collective farm in the USSR. However, the party did not promote workers or managers who simply attained these targets – in fact, just "fulfilling" the plan was held to be a "bourgeois," unrevolutionary sort of behavior. Those who consistently overfulfilled their plan targets, thus supposedly demonstrating their superior revolutionary enthusiasm and dedication – the so-called "shock workers" and "heroic managers" – were given monetary bonuses, special housing, better food, and even trips to Moscow to visit the dictator himself.

This system of incentives encouraged an atmosphere of constant, chaotic activity, as workers and managers struggled to produce higher and higher volumes of cement, coal, and steel, urged on by the state planners and party leadership. However, Soviet citizens soon learned that overfulfillment of plans by too great an amount could also sometimes get them into trouble. According to a principle known as "planning from the achieved level," Gosplan was instructed to raise plan targets to the point attained in the previous planning period. Thus, if a worker somehow produced double his or her required amount of coal in one year, he or she might be required to attain the same absurd amount of production the next – and failure to do so, again, could lead to arrest and imprisonment. Thus, Stalinist institutions encouraged individuals to overfulfill their plans, but not by too much. Managers and workers were given incentives to be "revolutionary," but in a manner that was simultaneously "disciplined and professional."

During the First Five-Year Plan, an industrial infrastructure was built in the Soviet Union in an incredibly short period of time; this result looked all the more impressive against the backdrop of the Great Depression then enveloping the capitalist West. Over time, however, the constant demands to "fulfill and overfulfill the plan" during the 1930s alienated even those groups who most benefited from Stalin's policies – the proletariat and party officials. A "final-exam economy," in which constant "cramming" to complete plan assignments before the final deadline was followed by the imposition of even greater work demands, could not but produce exhausted and exasperated managers and workers.

Thus, the third key component of Stalin's economic system, the creation of the gulag system, was vital to its overall functioning. The "gulags" – short for "state camps" – were originally set up during the civil war to incarcerate those who opposed Lenin's plans for Communist Party rule. Under Stalin, however, their scope expanded rapidly; tens of millions of people were arrested as "class enemies" of the "proletarian dictatorship." Gulag inmates were put to work building canals, paving roads, digging coal, and constructing monuments to Lenin and Stalin, often under the most brutal conditions imaginable. The contribution of the gulag system to overall Soviet production under Stalin is hard to estimate, but it clearly played a crucial role in the attainment of the ambitious industrialization targets of the 1930s. Moreover, the constant threat of the gulag undoubtedly did much to inspire ordinary people's continued efforts to overfulfill the plan.

However, the types of economic activity encouraged by Stalin's incentive structure were not conducive to the long-run performance of the system. Already during the 1930s, all sorts of dysfunctional behaviors emerged within Soviet enterprises. First, because plan targets were formulated in terms of gross quantities of output, the quality of Soviet production often suffered greatly; as a result, the basic infrastructure of Soviet industry began to crumble and decay almost as soon as it was built. The problem of quality control was even more severe in such sectors of economic production as consumer goods and services, which were given low priority by Stalin. Second, the system was poorly equipped to handle technological change. Shutting down assembly lines in order to introduce new, up-to-date machinery meant failing to meet one's monthly and annual production targets, so Soviet managers tended to rely on their existing equipment. Third, Stalinist industrialization was an environmental disaster; to fulfill and overfulfill plans mattered more than long-term concerns with people's health or the preservation of nature. Today, former Soviet factory towns are some of the most polluted places on Earth. Fourth, collectivized agriculture was enormously inefficient and wasteful. Indeed, by the late Soviet era, approximately 65 percent of all vegetables and 90 percent of all fresh fruit were produced on the mere 2 to 3 percent of the land given to peasants' private plots!

Finally, the Stalinist system was prone to rampant institutional corruption. The official banning of most forms of private property and markets meant that all kinds of buying, selling, and stealing of state resources went on in black markets and within personal networks. Managers often colluded with local party officials to lower plan targets, falsify production reports, or otherwise protect enterprises from the demands of central planners. Given the absence of either unemployment or bankruptcy procedures, the only way to curtail such behavior was to arrest the perpetrators – but because almost everyone was involved in some form of informal evasion of their official responsibilities, rooting out corruption completely was impossible.

Stalin knew full well that his vision of socioeconomic socialism was, despite its external successes, falling victim to such forms of corrosion from within. But having sacrificed decades of his life – and millions of other people's lives – to establish this system, he was not about to rethink his policies. Instead, he tried to explain the corruption of the planning system as the work of "hidden class enemies" within the USSR and "survivals of capitalist psychology" within people's minds. In 1936, Stalin began a massive blood purge of everyone he thought was conspiring with the global bourgeoisie against socialism. In Stalin's mind, this supposed conspiracy included the Right, Left, and Center oppositions of the 1920s, economists and plant managers, independent artists and intellectuals, and the entire general staff of the Red Army. Between 1936 and 1938 – the period known as the Great Terror – Stalin killed about 75 percent of the Communist Party's Central Committee, including Zinoviev and Bukharin, who were tortured and forced to testify that they were agents of capitalist intelligence services, and then executed. In 1940, one of Stalin's agents assassinated Trotsky, then living in exile in Mexico City. Meanwhile, millions more Soviet citizens were imprisoned or killed.

How did such a coercive system maintain itself? Every institutional order, no matter how oppressive, requires the allegiance of some social group whose interests it advances, and the Stalinist system is no exception. In fact, one small group did quite well within the framework of Stalinist industrialization – namely, blue-collar workers in their twenties and early thirties who had joined the party during Stalin's rise to power. Many of these men (and women, although this group was predominantly male) found themselves promoted extremely rapidly during the period of the First Five-Year Plan to positions of management and within the party hierarchy. They rose even further when their immediate supervisors were killed during the Great Terror. Some of these people ultimately became members of the post-Stalin Soviet Politburo, the highest organ of the Communist Party, including such future leaders as **Nikita Khrushchev** and **Leonid Brezhnev**. For these men, who had started their careers as ordinary workers, the Soviet Union was truly a "dictatorship of the proletariat"!

Even with the support of the communist worker elite, however, Stalin's system of planned heroism and mass terror might well have disintegrated had it not been for the enormous changes in the international environment wrought by World War II. When Adolf Hitler invaded the USSR in June 1941, Soviet forces were hardly able to resist; within months, the Nazis were at the gates of both Leningrad and Moscow. However, before the conquest of the Soviet Union was complete, the Russian winter began to set in, and the German soldiers found themselves quite unprepared for the extreme cold. Soon fresh troops from the east came to reinforce Moscow. By December, when the United States entered the war after the Japanese attack on Pearl Harbor, the pressure on the Nazis was increasing. Fighting between Soviet and Nazi troops continued for three more years, and ultimately the USSR lost more than 20 million people in the conflict. However, by the end of 1943, the tide had turned decisively against Hitler, and by 1945, Red Army troops met Allied troops in Berlin in triumph.

After the Soviet victory in World War II, Stalin insisted that his policies of the 1930s had been vindicated. After all, the giant steel mills, cement plants, and weapons factories set up in the First Five-Year Plan had played a crucial role in the Soviet war effort; without rapid industrialization, the Nazis might actually have conquered Russia. Stalin could now claim – despite his genocidal policies – that he was a great Russian patriot who had defeated an alien invader of the motherland. Finally, at the conclusion of the war, Soviet troops occupied most of Eastern and Central Europe, including the eastern portion of Germany. Within three years, Stalin had imposed both Leninist one-party rule and Stalinist collectivization and planning on these unfortunate nations. If one accepted Stalin's definition of "socialism," then, it followed that Stalin was the first person who had successfully created an "international socialist revolution," one that even included part of Marx's homeland. World War II – or, as the Russians still refer to it, the "Great Patriotic War" – thus greatly solidified the legitimacy of Stalin's regime and led many ordinary citizens to embrace a "Soviet" identity for the first time.

Until his death in 1953, Stalin continued to defend the system he had created – and to use terror to silence his real and imagined opponents. Toward the end of World War II, entire peoples whom Stalin accused of being disloyal, such as the Crimean Tatars, the Volga Germans, and the Chechens, were deported to Siberia and Central Asia. After the war was over, the arrest of supposed capitalist spies continued; even the relatives of prominent Politburo members were sent to the gulag. Meanwhile, Stalin promoted a "cult of personality" in the Soviet media and arts that constantly trumpeted the dictator's supposed genius as an architect, as a poet, as a military commander, as a linguist, and so on. Shortly before his death, Stalin was preparing to launch a new terror campaign against so-called enemies of the people – this time including Politburo doctors, who he accused of plotting to poison the leadership, and, even more ominously, Soviet Jews, who he claimed were part of a global Zionist conspiracy against him. Fortunately, Stalin died in March 1953, before he could act on these ideas.

FROM STALIN TO GORBACHEV

Stalin's successors were faced with a dual legacy. On the one hand, by 1953 the USSR was a global superpower. Its industrial production had become sufficiently large to allow it to compete militarily with the capitalist West; by 1949 it had also built its first nuclear bomb. Newly decolonized and developing countries looked to the Soviet Union as a counterweight to the power of the West and in some cases as an ally whose institutions should be emulated. The Western powers themselves had just emerged from decades of world war and global depression – phenomena Marx had predicted would result from capitalism's "inner contradictions" – and it would be some time before analysts were sure that democratic capitalism in Europe could be revived and sustained.

On the other hand, the fundamental problems of Leninist party politics and Stalinist planned economics remained. Years of dictatorship and terror had killed off whatever popular enthusiasm had once existed for heroic efforts to "build socialism." Bribe taking and black-market activity on the part of Soviet officials had already become a way of life. Problems with economic waste and inefficiency, worker absenteeism and alcoholism, and poor-quality production had become more severe. Clearly, something had to be done to address the growing cracks in the foundation of the Soviet superpower.

Again, the post-Stalin leadership analyzed and responded to these problems in a way they thought was consistent not only with their own personal interests but also with the basic outlines of the Soviet socialist identity. First, every Soviet leader after Stalin's death in 1953 agreed that the days of mass, indiscriminate terror in Soviet society must end. Stalin's last secret-police chief, Lavrenti Beria, was himself executed by the end of the year, millions of people were freed from the gulag, and the most extreme forms of Stalin worship ceased. The post-Stalin leadership also agreed that the next stage in building socialism somehow had to involve the creation of a truly socialist culture that would inspire ordinary workers and peasants to contribute their energies to the further development of Soviet institutions voluntarily. There was, however, no clear consensus on how to do this.

From 1953 until 1985, leadership struggles again centered on debates among what we can now recognize as Right, Left, and Centrist Orthodox strategies concerning how to create a "socialist way of life" without Stalinist terror. Supporters of the "right" strategy during this period, such as Georgii Malenkov, the first post-Stalin prime minister, argued that Soviet socialism must abandon revolutionary crusades in economic and foreign policy and instead promote efficiency within enterprises and high-quality production for ordinary consumers. This advice, however sensible from our perspective, struck most party officials and Stalinist planners as a direct attack on their interests and as a departure from the revolutionary ideals of Marxism and Leninism.

By 1954, Malenkov's authority had been eclipsed by Communist Party leader Nikita Khrushchev. Khrushchev advocated the opposite of Malenkov's policies, calling for a revolutionary advance toward communism as rapidly as possible. In a secret speech to the party elite in 1956, Khrushchev sought to inspire mass revolutionary sentiment by exposing the abuses of the Stalin period as "deformations" of socialism that would never be permitted again. He called on the Soviet people to participate in a whole series of economic campaigns to set records in corn planting, milk and meat production, and chemical manufacture; he even revised the party program to include a timetable according to which Marx's original vision of "full communism" would be attained in the USSR by 1980! He also pursued a risky and often reckless foreign policy, threatening the West with nuclear missile attacks if it did not agree to Soviet demands. Such "leftist" policies led to administrative chaos at home and military embarrassments, such as the Cuban missile crisis, abroad. In 1964, Khrushchev was ousted in a Politburo coup.

From 1964 until 1982, Leonid Brezhnev presided over an orthodox Marxist-Leninist Politburo that resisted any reform of Soviet institutions – and, besides supporting various pro-Soviet regimes in the developing world, did very little else. Brezhnev's leadership arrested vocal dissidents and censored open criticism of the regime, but it largely turned a blind eye to private disaffection, corruption, and black-market activity. Party officials and state bureaucrats were rarely fired, and the Soviet elite began to age, and ultimately to die, in office. The planning system, now lacking either mass enthusiasm or fear as incentives for the fulfillment of production targets, sank into stagnation and decline. By the mid-1970s, the Soviet economy became dangerously dependent upon energy exports and sales of vodka. The disastrous Soviet military intervention in Afghanistan in 1979, combined with the declaration of martial law to suppress the independent Solidarity trade union in Poland in 1981, exposed the growing vulnerabilities of the Soviet army and the Warsaw Pact alliance of Leninist regimes in Eastern Europe. Meanwhile, such leaders as Margaret Thatcher in Britain and Ronald Reagan in the United States were calling for a much more aggressive foreign policy to confront the Soviet "evil empire" (to use Reagan's term). Finally, from 1982 until 1985, a veritable parade of dying general secretaries of the Communist Party – Brezhnev, Yuri Andropov, and Konstantin Chernenko – made the USSR an international joke.

It was under these dire global and domestic circumstances that the party elite decided to entrust the key position of general secretary to the 54-year-old **Mikhail Gorbachev**. Upon his promotion to the leadership in March 1985, a furious debate ensued among Western Sovietologists. The "totalitarian" school, which insisted that the Soviet system was still in essence a regime based on terror, tended to see Gorbachev as merely a more polished representative of Soviet tyranny and warned the West to remain vigilant. "Modernization" theorists, who claimed that the USSR had become a developed, modern society not unlike the United States, saw Gorbachev's leadership as a final break with the Stalinist past and hoped for a new era of peace and cooperation between his regime and the West.

In effect, each side assumed that Gorbachev knew what he was doing but did not believe what he was saying. The totalitarian interpretation of Gorbachev assumed that he knew how to revitalize the Soviet economy in order to produce a more technologically advanced and efficient communist challenge to the West but did not believe his own promises of reform and democratization of the Soviet system. The modernization interpretation of Gorbachev assumed that he knew how to eliminate the corruption, misman- agement, and ideological rigidity of the Brezhnev period but did not believe his own constant assurances that he was a "Leninist" who hoped to revive the ideals of the October Revolution. In fact, we now know that Gorbachev believed what he was saying but did not know what he was doing. When he told the world that he was a "Leninist reformer," he meant exactly that. As for what a reformed Leninism in the Soviet Union would eventually look like in practice, however, he had no concrete idea.

How could Gorbachev really believe in Leninism as late as the 1980s? Gorbachev had been promoted his whole life for espousing this ideology. He had come of age politically during the successful and painful struggle against the Nazis and had been a teenager during the triumphant emergence of the Soviet Union as a global superpower. As a young man, he was given the Order of the Red Banner of Labor for his "heroic" work as a combine operator on a collective farm. Largely as a result of this award, he was admitted to the prestigious Moscow State University Law School. In his twenties, he became a party official, and by his thirties he had been appointed the first party secretary in Stavropol, an agricultural region in southern Russia. Because of Stavropol's strategic location on the way to various Black Sea and Caucasus mountain resorts, Gorbachev got to know almost every significant Soviet leader, including Brezhnev, Andropov, and Chernenko. By 1978, at the age of 47, he had been promoted to the Politburo as secretary of agriculture, in part because his sincere enthusiasm for Leninism and socialism had impressed his somewhat jaded elders.

Thus, by the time he became general secretary, Gorbachev was one of the few people in the USSR who still truly believed in Leninist ideology. People's enthusiasm for participation in the Communist Party and for heroic plan fulfillment, Gorbachev insisted, could be rekindled – but only if he found some way to eliminate the corrupt, petty bureaucracy that had blocked pop- ular initiative during the "years of stagnation" under Brezhnev. His first step was to purge hundreds of old party bureaucrats. By 1986, Gorbachev had already dismissed or retired almost 40 percent of the Central Committee and felt strong enough to launch his dramatic campaign for "perestroika," or restructuring.

Perestroika consisted of three basic elements: glasnost, democratization, and "new thinking" in foreign policy. "Glasnost," or openness, meant greater disclosure of people's criticisms of the Soviet past and present in newspapers, television, and films. This campaign got off to a rather ambiguous start when, in April 1986, the Chernobyl nuclear power plant in Ukraine exploded, spew- ing radioactivity over much of Eastern Europe; the Soviet government hid this information from its citizens for at least three days after the event. However, by the fall of 1986, the quantity and quality of published revelations about Soviet history and current Soviet society began to increase markedly. The release in December 1986 of the famous Soviet nuclear physicist and dissident Andrei Sakharov, who had been sent into internal exile for his public denouncement of the Soviet invasion of Afghanistan, demonstrated the seriousness of Gorbachev's break with Brezhnevite forms of censorship. After 1987, the scope of glasnost widened to include every conceivable topic, including Lenin's terror during the civil war, the horrors of collectivization, and even the dictatorial nature of Communist Party rule itself.

Democratization also began slowly, with vague calls to reinvigorate the system of soviets that had been subordinated to the party hierarchy since the Russian civil war. By 1988, however, at the Nineteenth Party Conference, Gorbachev announced that genuine multicandidate elections would be held for a new Soviet Congress of People's Deputies to replace the old rubber-stamp Supreme Soviet. To be sure, Gorbachev attempted to guarantee the continued "leading role" of the Communist Party, reserving a third of the seats in the new 2,250 seat congress for "public organizations" under direct party control. Moreover, in many electoral districts, local party bosses still ran unopposed, as in the times of Stalin and Brezhnev. Nevertheless, the national elections held in the spring of 1989 generated many serious, competitive races between "reformers" and party "conservatives" that galvanized Soviet society.

Finally, Gorbachev's campaign for "new thinking" in foreign policy announced a turn away from attempts to build client regimes in the developing world, a campaign to reduce tensions with the capitalist West, and, most significantly, an end to the Stalinist subordination of countries in the communist bloc. Since the end of World War II, Soviet leaders had been able to preserve Leninist rule in Eastern Europe only through repeated military interventions, including Khrushchev's invasion of Hungary in 1956, Brezhnev's invasion of Czechoslovakia in 1968, and the Soviet-supported declaration of martial law in Poland in 1981. Now, one of Gorbachev's spokesmen announced that the old "Brezhnev doctrine" of military intervention had been replaced by the "Sinatra doctrine": the former communist satellite states would be allowed to "do it their way." Again, early reaction to this announcement was skeptical, both in the West and in Eastern Europe. In 1989, the seriousness of new thinking was tested when Solidarity candidates won every possible seat in new elections for the Polish Parliament. When Gorbachev did nothing to prevent the creation of the first non-Leninist government in the communist bloc, liberal democrats and nationalists throughout the region moved to gain their own independence. By the end of the year, revolutions against Communist Party rule had succeeded in every single country of the former Warsaw Pact.

Gorbachev's perestroika, then, was every bit as revolutionary as its author had intended – but not with the results he had expected. Within three years of the launching of the campaign for restructuring, both the identity and the institutions at the core of Leninism had disintegrated. Instead of inspiring a new faith in socialist ideas as Gorbachev had hoped, glasnost made the history of communism appear to be a long and bloody tragedy. Democratization, designed to remove corrupt Brezhnevite bureaucrats in order to make space in the system for more enthusiastic socialists, instead destroyed Lenin's "party of professional revolutionaries" altogether. New thinking, which was supposed to allow the USSR to compete with capitalism more effectively by discarding the coercive methods of past foreign policy, resulted in the rapid disintegration of the Soviet Empire.

By 1990, the spiraling loss of party control produced two further unanticipated results: an economic crisis and a nationalist resurgence. Economically, Gorbachev's perestroika had done surprisingly little to change the fundamental elements of the Stalinist planning system other than to permit small-scale "cooperatives" in the service sector and limited "joint ventures" with foreign capitalists. The breakdown of party authority by 1990 meant that producers no longer had any reason to obey the orders of the planning bureaucracy. Those who simply hoarded raw materials or manufactured goods, then sold or traded them on the black market, could not be punished in the absence of an effective central-party dictatorship. As soon as some people stopped deliveries of goods to Gosplan, however, other enterprises found themselves without necessary supplies; they were also then forced to hoard whatever they had and barter with their former suppliers. Outright theft of enterprise resources also became commonplace; in some cases, corrupt party officials even shipped valuable minerals out of the country for hard currency and had the proceeds placed in Swiss bank accounts. As a result of the breakdown of the planning system, goods began to disappear from store shelves all over the country.

At the same time, nationalism began to fill the gap left by the discrediting of Marxism-Leninism. In many ways, it is ironic that the system of "Soviet Republics" created by Lenin and Stalin to deal with the multiethnic nature of Soviet territory had actually reinforced national identity in the USSR. Peoples living in the republics had been allowed to preserve schools, museums, and cultural institutes promoting their native traditions and languages but had been ruthlessly subordinated to Moscow politically and economically. The Baltic republics of Estonia, Latvia, and Lithuania had in fact been independent countries until 1940, when Stalin annexed them to the USSR after having made a secret deal with Hitler to divide Eastern Europe. After the revolutions of 1989 in East-Central Europe, people in the republics began to demand greater autonomy and, in the case of the Baltics, outright independence. These trends were further fueled by elections to the Supreme Soviets of the 15 republics in 1990. In each of these campaigns, advocates of greater republican autonomy outpolled representatives of the Soviet communist center; even those who did not really want full republican independence often voted for "sovereignty" as a way of protesting Gorbachev's ineffective leadership. By the end of 1990, however, the disintegration of the USSR had become a very real possibility.

That possibility became a reality because of **Boris Yeltsin**'s mobilization of a powerful movement for national independence within Russia itself. Yeltsin had originally been brought to Moscow by Gorbachev in 1986 to be the city's party boss and a candidate member of the Politburo. Yeltsin, born the same year as Gorbachev, shared the latter's belief that Soviet socialism had grown stagnant and corrupt. He won the hearts of Muscovites by criticizing party conservatives, making surprise televised visits to inspect shops suspected of profiting on the black market, and talking with ordinary people on the streets wherever he went. In October 1987, however, Yeltsin made the mistake of attacking conservative Politburo members in a party meeting – thus violating Lenin's decades-old prohibition of "factions" within the party. He was drummed out of the Politburo and given the dead-end job of USSR deputy minister of construction.

The elections for the USSR Congress of People's Deputies in the spring of 1989, however, revitalized Yeltsin's political career. Running on a platform of greater democracy and marketization, Yeltsin gained 90 percent of the votes in his Moscow electoral district. Together with Sakharov, he formed a movement of Congress deputies committed to the end of one-party rule and reintegration with the West. Such a reintegration, Yeltsin argued, could be achieved only if Russia attained greater autonomy from the Soviet Union and took control over its own political and economic life. Yeltsin's embrace of this distinctive anti-Soviet Russian nationalism attracted even some conservatives to his side, including the Afghan war hero **Alexander Rutskoi**. By the summer of 1990, Yeltsin had quit the Communist Party, and in February 1991 he called on Gorbachev to resign. In June 1991, Yeltsin, with Rutskoi as his vice-presidential candidate, easily won election to the new post of president of the Russian Federation – the first time in history that a Russian leader had been democratically elected.

Faced with the potential secession of the Soviet republics, the disintegration of the Soviet economy, and the emergence of a powerful Yeltsin-led opposition in Russia itself, Gorbachev tried desperately to hold the regime together. In May 1991, he negotiated a new "union treaty" with the newly elected leaders of those republics – or at least the nine still willing to talk to him. But on August 19, 1991, the day before the treaty was to take effect, conservative Leninists within the leadership mounted a coup against Gorbachev as he vacationed on the Black Sea. The heads of the KGB, the defense ministry, and the interior ministry announced that Gorbachev was "too sick to continue" in office and proclaimed the formation of a "State Committee for the Emergency Situation" that would lead the country for an unspecified period. However, the coup attempt was ineptly planned and executed. Gorbachev refused to cooperate with the coup plotters, as they had apparently hoped he would. Meanwhile, Yeltsin made his way to the Russian "White House," the building housing the Russian Congress, where over a hundred thousand Muscovites had gathered to protest the coup. He climbed on top of a tank and declared his uncompromising opposition to the coup plotters. At that moment, he became, in essence, the new leader of Russia.

Key units of the KGB and military defected to Yeltsin's camp. The coup unraveled shortly thereafter. Interior Minister Boris Pugo committed suicide; the other leaders of the coup were arrested. Yeltsin announced Russia's recognition of the independence of the Baltic states; he also banned the Communist Party of the Soviet Union, branding it a criminal organization. Gorbachev returned to Moscow on August 22, but he appeared to be totally out of touch with the changed situation in the country, quoting Lenin and defending the Communist Party at a televised press conference. Gorbachev continued to try to preserve what was left of the Soviet Union, but Yeltsin and other leaders of the national republics soon committed themselves to full independence. On December 1, 1991, over 90 percent of the Ukrainian population voted for national independence in a referendum; a few days later, the leaders of Russia, Ukraine, and Belarus announced the formation of a new, decentralized **Commonwealth of Independent States** to replace the USSR. On December 26, 1991, Gorbachev, bowing to the inevitable, resigned as leader of the Soviet Union, thus ending the 74-year history of the Leninist regime.

Interests, Identities, and Institutions in Post-Communist Russia

THE LENINIST LEGACY AND POST-SOVIET INTERESTS

When the Soviet Union was officially declared dead on December 31, 1991, most Western governments and many analysts understandably greeted the news with euphoria, predicting that Russia would join the prosperous, democratic West in short order. Unfortunately, Westerners tended at the time to underestimate the enormous structural problems that would inevitably face new democratic and market-oriented governments in Russia and other former Soviet republics. As we emphasize throughout this textbook, institutions inherited from the past can exert a powerful influence on politics in the present. This was especially true in the postcommunist world, which was saddled with the legacy of a particularly brutal ideological, political, and socioeconomic tyranny that had endured for decades. Moreover, former communist countries now found themselves exposed to competition from technologically advanced capitalist countries. The economic gap between Russia and the West in 1991 was, if anything, even greater than it had been in 1917.

It was extremely unlikely, then, that a rapid "transition to democracy and markets" in Russia would take place without reversals, inasmuch as the elimination of Soviet institutions often contradicted the interests of the people who had previously lived under them. It is unsurprising that those institutions most costly for individuals to abandon proved the most difficult to destroy. For this reason, Soviet institutions decayed in the same order as they were originally created: first Marxist ideology, then Leninist party politics, and finally, only very slowly, Stalin's planned economy.

Marxist ideology was the easiest to abandon, and it died soon after the collapse of the regime. Indeed, in the immediate aftermath of the August coup, popular disgust with the ideological language of the old regime was so widespread that labeling oneself a "Leninist" or even a "socialist" was tantamount to committing political suicide – as Gorbachev soon discovered. Mainstream Russian politicians strove to outdo one another with professions of opposition to communism. Even those who still called themselves "communists" largely stopped referring to Marx, Engels, and the global proletarian revolution. Even more significantly, the sudden disappearance of Marxism-Leninism left in its wake an almost total ideological vacuum; in contrast with the Soviet period, the politics of short-term material interest now blocked all efforts to articulate a new post-Soviet national identity.

In response to this situation, Yeltsin and his advisers became convinced that there was no alternative to adopting liberal capitalist ideology. However, whereas liberals in other postcommunist countries could claim – with some justification – to be returning to national traditions suppressed under Soviet rule, liberalism in post-Soviet Russia appeared to many as a capitulation to the West. As the post-Soviet crisis continued, anti-Western sentiments in Russian society understandably strengthened, and those in search of consistent ideological visions often gravitated toward radically antiliberal figures.

This brings us to the second legacy of Leninism, that of one-party rule. Again, the initial effect of Yeltsin's banning of the Communist Party of the Soviet Union (CPSU) in the days after the August coup was to encourage widespread formal defection from that organization. However, leaving the party was potentially far more costly than disavowing Marxist-Leninist ideology. Because Communist Party officials had monopolized every significant position of power in society, right down to the shop-floor level, membership in alternative political organizations could hardly deliver comparable benefits in the short run. For this reason, formal withdrawal from the CPSU was, in most cases, followed by a scramble to cement key personal ties and to maintain access to economic resources inherited from one's days as a communist functionary.

It was therefore somewhat comical to see post-Soviet Russian politicians accuse their opponents of being "communists" because almost all of them had been members of the CPSU in the recent past. This is not to deny that a very real degree of political pluralism emerged after 1991, especially compared with Soviet times. However, the legacy of one-party rule continues to be a serious obstacle to the formation of genuine, alternative grassroots organizations and mass political parties in the Russian Federation. Indeed, long after the collapse of the USSR, throughout Russia one could still find former party bureaucrats ruling over their local fiefdoms as they did under Leninist rule.

A final political legacy of Leninism was the inheritance of administrative boundaries that tended to worsen, rather than ameliorate, ethnic conflicts. The borders of the Russian Federation, like those of the other Soviet republics, had been drawn up by Stalin with little concern for nationalist sensibilities. More than 20 million ethnic Russians lived outside the new Russian state and were now suddenly inhabitants of foreign countries. Meanwhile, the Russian Federation itself contained dozens of "ethnic republics" and "autonomous districts" formally set aside for regional non-Russian ethnic groups, and although most of these regions seemed content to remain part of Russia, others, in particular Chechnya, mounted their own drives for national independence. As a result, popular acceptance of the existing boundaries of the state was weak, and several prominent opposition figures called for restoration of at least part of the old Soviet Empire.

The most burdensome institutional legacy of the Soviet system, however, was the residue of the Stalinist planned economy. All over Russia and the other former Soviet republics – indeed, all over the postcommunist region – an enormous "rust belt" of outdated factories continued to produce goods that few consumers wanted, to poison the surrounding environment, and to waste scarce energy and other resources. Enterprises that had for decades been judged solely according to their ability to overfulfill plan targets – or at least fake it – were poorly prepared to compete in a market economy, especially in the global high-tech environment of the 1990s. Unfortunately, Stalinist factories employed tens of millions of people and under the Soviet system had distributed a whole range of welfare benefits, including child care, recreational facilities, housing, and even food. The loss of one's factory job meant the loss not only of one's salary but also of one's social safety net. Blue-collar workers, former Soviet managers, and the local party officials who had formerly supervised them thus formed a natural lobby against any rapid transition to competitive capitalism.

The legacy of Stalinist collectivization of agriculture reinforced this anti-market lobby. The brutal methods used to create *kolkhozy* and *sovkhozy* during the 1930s had drained the countryside of its most knowledgeable and productive farmers; the poor services and supplies found in rural regions had inspired most young people to leave the villages for the cities. The remaining 30 million Russians living in rural areas were primarily elderly, poorly skilled, and culturally conservative. They, too, were hardly prepared for the establishment of a capitalist farming system.

Along with the sheer weight of inefficient agricultural and industrial sectors in the post-Soviet Russian economy came a more subtle problem, namely, the absence of most of the market institutions now taken for granted in advanced capitalist societies. The USSR, for example, had never created a functioning real estate market because private ownership of land was banned; a decade after the Soviet collapse, there was still no consistent legal basis for land ownership in Russia. Nor did the Soviet economy possess anything like a capitalist financial system. The Soviet ruble was never freely tradable for currencies such as the U.S. dollar or German mark; its value was set artificially by state bureaucrats. Soviet banks, instead of making careful investment and loan decisions based upon calculations of profit and loss, simply funneled resources to those enterprises the planners directed them to support. Stock and bond markets were also nonexistent under Soviet rule, and those operating in the Russian Federation have been prone to wild speculative swings. Finally, the Soviet judiciary was not trained in the enforcement of legal property rights, and it has been difficult to get post-Soviet Russian courts to uphold business contracts in a consistent manner.

Thus, decades of Leninism had generated huge institutional obstacles to a smooth reentry into the Western capitalist world. Nonetheless, Yeltsin and his supporters chose what might be termed a revolutionary, rather than evolutionary, approach to Westernizing Russia. With the support of Western political leaders and economic advisers, they launched an all-out drive to reintegrate Russia into the global economy. Predictably, the results fell far short of expectations.

YELTSIN AND THE DESIGN OF POST-SOVIET INSTITUTIONS

During the autumn of 1991, Boris Yeltsin fought successfully against conservative nationalists and supporters of Gorbachev who wished to preserve the USSR. In this struggle, he maintained the enthusiastic support of the Russian Congress of People's Deputies that had been elected in 1990. The Congress voted in November to grant Yeltsin special "emergency powers" for one year in order to deal with the extraordinary political and economic crisis resulting from the Soviet Union's collapse. On New Year's Day, 1992, the Russian Federation became, along with the rest of the former Soviet republics, an internationally recognized independent state; Yeltsin declared himself Russia's first prime minister.

Immediately, Yeltsin used his emergency powers to implement a policy of rapid marketization popularly known as "**shock therapy**." To administer this policy, he named a 35-year-old economist, Yegor Gaidar, as his deputy. The theoretical assumption behind shock therapy was that unless Russia made immediate moves toward capitalism, it would remain stuck in a hopeless halfway house between the old Stalinist system and the new global economy. In theory, shock therapy would be painful in the short run but better for Russian society in the long run. The shock-therapy plan, drawn up in close consultation with Western advisers and the International Monetary Fund (IMF), contained three key elements: price liberalization, monetary stabilization, and privatization of state property.

The argument for freeing prices was hard to refute. For decades, the Soviet planners had kept prices for energy, housing, consumer goods, and basic foodstuffs artificially low in order to prevent public protest. Such low prices made it unprofitable for anyone to produce these goods, except on the black market. Letting prices rise was arguably the only way to induce entrepreneurs to deliver food and basic goods to markets in time to prevent starvation during the cold Russian winter. But the end of price controls was bound to cause social unrest.

Price liberalization was announced on January 2, 1992. Within days, prices had doubled and even tripled; by the end of the year, they were 23 times higher. The effect was to wipe out most people's savings. An elderly person who had painstakingly saved 10,000 rubles – a significant sum in the Soviet era – by 1993 found that her fortune was worth approximately $10. On the positive side, goods did reappear in shops throughout the country; the old Soviet phenomenon of people lining up for blocks to buy scarce consumer goods was now a thing of the past.

Fighting inflation required attention to the second key element of shock therapy, monetary stabilization – controlling the money supply in order to make the ruble a strong, convertible currency like the U.S. dollar. This turned out to be easier to do in principle than in practice. By the spring of 1992, Soviet factories and collective farms everywhere were struggling to pay for supplies at vastly higher prices than before. Russian managers called up their old friends in the Congress of People's Deputies in Moscow to demand that money be sent to help enterprises pay their bills. By May, the Central Bank of Russia had begun to print new rubles day and night to subsidize failing enterprises. Instead of achieving monetary stabilization, Russia was flooded with paper money; as a result, inflation remained extremely high. The alternative, however, was to shut down an enormous number of huge factories and farms and to fire the millions of workers who worked in them.

In theory, of course, unemployed workers should have been able to find new jobs at more efficient start-up companies generated by capitalist competition. But new companies could not easily emerge in a country still owned almost entirely by the state. Thus, the third element of shock therapy, privatization of property, was seen as crucial to the entire reform effort. The privatization drive was led by Gaidar's close ally and friend, Anatoly Chubais. In late 1992, privatization "vouchers" were issued to every man, woman, and child in Russia; they could either use them to bid on state enterprises put up for sale at privatization auctions or sell them for cash. The idea was to build a mass base of support for the new capitalist economy by giving everyone at least a small share of the proceeds of the sale of Soviet properties. Unfortunately, few ordinary Russians had much of an idea of what to do with their vouchers. Many people invested them in bogus "voucher funds," the organizers of which simply cashed in all their vouchers and fled the country. An even greater problem was that much of Soviet state property was doomed to produce at a loss under market conditions – so why bid on it? After a few showcase privatization auctions, the voucher campaign bogged down.

Chubais now engineered a compromise proposal. According to a "second variant" of privatization worked out with leaders of the Russian Congress, 51 percent of the shares of a company could simply be handed over to its existing management and workers, with the rest being divided between the state and any interested outside investors. More than two-thirds of Russian enterprises chose this form of privatization – which, in effect, amounted to a simple declaration that former Stalinist factories were now "private property," although they were run by the same people, and with the same workforce, as before. In this way, Yeltsin, Chubais, and Gaidar could claim that, within two years, two-thirds of the Russian economy had been privatized; underneath the surface, however, inefficient Soviet production methods remained largely in place.

The inconsistencies and mounting social unrest associated with the shock-therapy program quickly turned a majority of Congress deputies against Yeltsin's Westernization drive. Yeltsin's own vice president, Alexander Rutskoi, now forged an alliance with the Parliament's leader, Ruslan Khasbulatov, in opposition to Yeltsin and Gaidar. At the Sixth Congress of People's Deputies in December 1992, a majority refused to confirm Gaidar's reappointment as prime minister. Yeltsin's emergency powers had by then expired, so he was forced to appoint a compromise candidate, **Viktor Chernomyrdin**. Chernomyrdin was the former head of the state natural gas monopoly, Gazprom, and shared the basic economic views of the factory managers clamoring for an end to shock therapy. At the same time, Chernomyrdin was rumored to have become a millionaire through profits from exports of gas to Western Europe. In practice, Chernomyrdin tried to be a "centrist," calling for an "end to market romanticism" but not a reversal of market reforms.

Chernomyrdin's appointment as prime minister did not end the growing tensions between Yeltsin and the Congress. Rutskoi and Khasbulatov now openly called for the creation of a new government led by the Congress itself. In April, Yeltsin turned to the public, sponsoring a nationwide referendum on his leadership and economic policies, and asking whether early elections should be held for the president and/or the Parliament. The results showed that Yeltsin's public support remained, at this stage, remarkably strong, with a majority even supporting the basic economic policies of the past year. The opposition in the Congress, however, continued to press for Yeltsin's ouster.

During the summer of 1993, a form of "dual power" emerged. Both the president and the Congress issued contradictory laws and decrees; both sides had drawn up new constitutions for the Russian state. Given the administrative chaos in Moscow, Russia's 89 regions and ethnic republics began to push for even greater autonomy, withholding taxes and resources and often insisting on the primacy of regional laws over central laws. Fears that Russia would disintegrate like the Soviet Union became increasingly widespread. In September, Yeltsin brought the crisis to a head by announcing the dismissal of the Congress of People's Deputies. The Congress responded by declaring Yeltsin's presidency null and void and declaring Rutskoi as the new Russian leader. The possibility of civil war loomed. On October 3, extremist supporters of the Congress tried to take over the main television station and mayor's office in Moscow. Yeltsin then decided to order a military assault on his enemies.

More than 150 people were killed in the attack on the Russian White House in October 1993. There was a sad symbolism in watching Yeltsin order the shelling of the same building where he had courageously defied the Soviet coup plotters just two years earlier. After October 1993, the impression that "democracy" was merely a disguise for naked presidential power became widespread among disaffected groups in Russian society.

The destruction of the Russian Congress did, however, allow Yeltsin to design and implement a new constitution in December 1993 (just barely approved by Russian voters – at least officially). The Russian constitution, like democratic constitutions elsewhere, formally divides political power among the legislative, judicial, and executive branches. The legislature is bicameral. The lower house, the **State Duma**, consists of 450 deputies. From 1993 through 2003, half of them were representatives of national parties selected on the basis of proportional representation (PR) and half were representatives of local electoral districts; beginning in the 2007 Duma election, all deputies will be selected through PR. The 178 members of the upper house, the **Federation Council**, represent the governors and regional legislatures of each of Russia's 89 federal regions. The judicial branch is led by the Constitutional Court, empowered to rule on basic constitutional issues, and the Supreme Court, the country's highest court of appeal. However, the 1993 Russian constitution gives by far the greatest share of political power to the president. The Russian president is the commander in chief of the armed forces, appoints the prime minister, and even has the right to issue presidential decrees with the force of law. Moreover, if the State Duma refuses to confirm the president's choice for prime minister three times or votes no confidence in the government twice, he can dissolve the lower house and call new elections.

Notwithstanding the overwhelming powers of the presidency, elections since 1993 have had genuine political significance. Even in the first elections to the State Duma in December 1993, Russian voters were able to express their alienation from those responsible for the shock-therapy reforms of the preceding two years. Despite highly visible state support, Gaidar's political party, Russia's Choice, attained only 15.5 percent of the party-list vote – the parliamentary seats allocated according to proportional representation. Meanwhile, the two other most successful parties were led by antiliberal ideologues. A full 23 percent of the electorate chose the Liberal Democratic Party of Russia (LDPR) farcically named, considering that it was led by **Vladimir Zhirinovsky**, a flamboyant ultranationalist who promised to lower the price of vodka, shoot criminals on the spot, and invade the Baltic states and the Middle East. An additional 12 percent of the voting public chose **Gennady Zyuganov**'s Communist Party of the Russian Federation (CPRF), which called for the resuscitation of the Soviet Union – not because of any lingering faith in Marx's communist workers' utopia but in order to rebuild Russia as a "great power." The remainder of the Duma was split among smaller parties that managed to surpass the 5 percent barrier to party-list representation, such as the more moderate pro-market party "Yabloko" (Apple), led by economist **Grigory Yavlinsky**; the Agrarian Party, representing collective farms, and the "Women of Russia" party, which emphasized problems of unemployment and abuse facing many Russian women.

A new constitution and elections did not eliminate Russia's continuing economic problems, however. The government did gradually manage to get inflation under control, primarily by stopping the printing of rubles. But factory managers throughout the country responded to the cutoff of subsidies by resorting to barter and by ceasing to pay their workers for months at a time. Eventually, mounting "wage arrears" to Russian workers, state employees, and soldiers grew into an intractable social problem. Small businesses, meanwhile, were strangled by a combination of arbitrary state taxation, corrupt bureaucrats demanding bribes, and interference by local "mafias" demanding protection money. Foreign and domestic investment remained at a very low level, and the overall gross domestic product (GDP) continued to decline. Taxation to cover government expenditures became increasingly difficult because many people (understandably) did their best to hide their incomes. The government began to rely on revenues from the privatization drive, which continued to favor well-connected elites. By 1995, a handful of billionaires – popularly known as the "**oligarchs**" – had gained control of most of the country's energy and mineral resources, banks, and mass media.

Moreover, although the new constitution contributed to a temporary stabilization in relations between Moscow and the various regional governments of the Russian Federation, the danger of state disintegration remained. Yeltsin was soon forced to conclude a series of separate treaties with restive regions, such as oil-rich Tatarstan and the diamond-producing republic of Sakha in the Far East. Then, in December 1994, hard-line advisers persuaded Yeltsin to reassert Moscow's authority over the regions by invading the rebellious republic of Chechnya. The invasion quickly escalated into a full-scale war that killed tens of thousands of ordinary citizens – many of them elderly ethnic Russians who could not escape the Chechen capital of Grozny in time. But the war only succeeded in further stiffening Chechen resistance to Russian rule. The utter failure of the campaign in Chechnya demonstrated clearly that the Russian military, like the rest of the government, was in a state of near-total demoralization and ineffectiveness.

Given Russia's continuing decline – and Yeltsin's growing health problems and increasingly erratic behavior – it is perhaps unsurprising that parliamentary elections in 1995 once again favored antiliberal forces. That voters were confronted with a long, confusing ballot listing 43 competing parties did not help matters. This time, Zyuganov's CPRF was the biggest vote-getter, attaining 22 percent of the vote. Zhirinovsky's LDPR still polled a disturbing 11 percent. The only two other parties to exceed the 5 percent barrier were Yavlinsky's Yabloko, with 7 percent, and a new pro-government party called "Our Home Is Russia," led by Prime Minister Chernomyrdin, which managed to attain only 10 percent of the party-list vote despite an expensive government-sponsored media campaign. Gaidar's party dropped below the 5 percent barrier and won just a few single-member district seats. Meanwhile, a majority of Russian voters voted for parties that did not get any Duma seats at all.

The first post-Soviet presidential campaign in Russia, in 1996, thus began with Yeltsin's political future in grave doubt. In February, polls showed that only 6 percent of Russians supported the Russian president, whereas over one-quarter supported his Communist challenger, Zyuganov. With the fate of Russia's weak democratic-capitalist regime hanging in the balance, however, Yeltsin mounted a remarkable comeback. He traveled throughout the country, energetically shaking hands, handing out money to pay late pensions and wages, and even dancing to a rock band. Yeltsin's campaign was financed by a huge infusion of cash from the IMF, which delivered the first installment of a $10 billion (U.S.) loan to Yeltsin's government, and by the oligarchs, who were terrified that their newly privatized companies would be renationalized in the event of a Communist victory. The oligarchs also flooded Russian newspapers and television with political advertising portraying Zyuganov as a tyrant who would reimpose totalitarian rule. Zyuganov, meanwhile, made such fears seem realistic by praising Stalin as a great Russian leader and declaring that the USSR still legally existed.

In the first round of the presidential elections in June 1996, Yeltsin got 35 percent of the vote to Zyuganov's 32 percent. In third place with 15 percent was General **Alexander Lebed**, who called himself a "semidemocrat" and promised to restore "truth and order." Yavlinsky managed fourth place with 7 percent of the vote, and Zhirinovsky came in fifth with 5 percent. Five other minor candidates polled less than 2 percent each – including Mikhail Gorbachev, supported by a minuscule 0.5 percent of the electorate.

Russian electoral rules require a runoff between the top two vote-getters in the first round of presidential elections if no candidate attains a majority. Thus, voters now faced a stark choice between Yeltsin and Zyuganov. The oligarchs continued their media campaign, portraying the election as a decision between freedom and totalitarianism. Lebed decided to support Yeltsin in return for an important government post. Zyuganov himself repeated his standard themes, blaming the IMF, the West, and Yeltsin for the ruin of Russia and calling for the restoration of Soviet power. In early July, Yeltsin completed his comeback, gaining 54 percent of the vote versus 40 percent for Zyuganov (with 5 percent of voters declaring themselves "against both").

Yeltsin's reelection meant that the flawed democratic-capitalist institutions he had established after 1991 in Russia would endure at least a while longer. However, powerful postcommunist interest groups, including many blue-collar workers, collective farmers, pensioners, military men, and anti-Western intellectuals, continued to oppose Yeltsin's regime. Moreover, the perpetual crises, violence, and economic decline of the early post-Soviet period had alienated even Yeltsin's own supporters among the urban, educated middle class, most of whom in 1996 had in essence voted against Zyuganov and a return to communism, rather than for the aging and erratic president. Indeed, a few days before his reelection, Yeltsin had suffered a severe heart attack; he was barely able to attend his own inauguration ceremony and was only sporadically active afterward. The president's incapacitation set the government adrift while its political, economic, and regional challenges mounted. Elections for regional governors in 1997 – though marking an important extension of Russian democracy – tended to strengthen further the power of Russia's regions as the capacity of the central government decayed.

In the spring of 1998, during one of his infrequent periods of political activity, Yeltsin made one last effort to rejuvenate market reforms. He unexpectedly fired Chernomyrdin as prime minister, replacing him with Sergei Kiriyenko, a 35-year-old ally of Gaidar, Chubais, and other liberal "young reformers." However, the underlying structural problems in the Russian economy were by this point too severe to fix. Given continued economic stagnation, decreasing confidence on the part of foreign investors, poor tax collection, declining world oil prices, and an increasingly unmanageable debt burden, Russia's budget deficit became unsustainable. The IMF tried to help Kiriyenko's government, delivering almost $5 billion (U.S.) in late July, but within a few weeks this loan had been exhausted in a vain attempt to prop up the weakening ruble.

On August 17, Kiriyenko suddenly announced a devaluation of the ruble and a 90-day moratorium on government debt payments. A deep financial crisis ensued. Inflation soared to almost 40 percent for the month of September alone, dozens of banks failed, and foreign investors left in droves. Yeltsin fired Kiriyenko but then inexplicably proposed to replace him once again with Chernomyrdin. Besides Chernomyrdin's own party, no major faction in the Russian Parliament would go along. After tense negotiations, all sides agreed to support the compromise candidacy of Foreign Minister **Yevgeny Primakov**, a Soviet academic specialist on the Middle East and former chief of Russian foreign intelligence. On September 11, 1998, Primakov was overwhelmingly confirmed as Russia's new prime minister. The constitutional order had been preserved.

Unfortunately, the endemic uncertainties of Russian politics continued. Only seven months after Primakov's promotion, another nearly disastrous battle between the president and the Parliament erupted when Zyuganov's Communist Party initiated impeachment proceedings against Yeltsin. Although more moderate political forces seemed unlikely to support some of Zyuganov's most extreme claims – for example, that Yeltsin had committed "genocide" against the Russian people by launching the shock-therapy program – the vote to impeach the president for unconstitutional actions in launching the war in Chechnya looked too close to call.

But on May 12, 1999, just three days before the impeachment vote in the Duma, Yeltsin suddenly dismissed Primakov as prime minister, proposing to replace him with Interior Minister Sergei Stepashin. Now a full-scale constitutional crisis loomed. According to the text of the 1993 Russian constitution, the Duma would be disbanded if it failed to confirm Stepashin as the new prime minister on a third vote; yet, at the same time, the constitution also forbade the president from dissolving the Duma if it voted for impeachment. Faced with the very real possibility that Yeltsin would take advantage of the constitution's ambiguity to declare a state of emergency rule – and worried that they would lose their parliamentary perks and privileges as a result – the Duma majority backed down. The vote to impeach Yeltsin failed, and Stepashin was later easily confirmed as prime minister.

Even this was not sufficient to make the increasingly isolated president feel secure, however. In early August, two new threats to Yeltsin's regime emerged. First, Primakov and the powerful mayor of Moscow, **Yuri Luzhkov**, announced the formation of a new political party supported by many of Russia's most powerful regional governors, the "Fatherland–All Russia Bloc," which would compete against parties supported by the Kremlin in the December 1999 Duma elections. Then, Chechen extremists led by Shamil Basaev and the Islamic fundamentalist Khattab invaded the neighboring ethnic republic of Dagestan, proclaiming their goal to be the creation of an Islamic state in southern Russia. Yeltsin fired Stepashin, who appeared to have been taken by surprise by these events, and replaced him with the dour, 46-year-old former KGB spy Vladimir Putin, who headed the KGB's successor organization, the Federal Security Service (FSB). Yeltsin also announced that he considered Putin to be his "heir" and that he hoped that Russians would rally around him as the 2000 presidential elections neared. Remarkably, despite Putin's almost total political obscurity at the time of his appointment, this is exactly what happened.

The key event propelling Putin into the top position in Russian politics was the outbreak of the second war in Chechnya in the fall of 1999.

Although rumors of a renewed Russian assault on the breakaway republic had been swirling for some time, the final decision to launch a full-scale invasion was reinforced by shocking events in September: terrorist bombings of apartment buildings in the suburbs of Moscow and in the southern Russian city of Volgodonsk that killed nearly 300 Russian citizens. Putin's government immediately blamed these bombings on the Chechen rebels led by Basaev and Khattab, whipping up an understandable public outcry for revenge – although suspicions about who was really responsible for them remain.

The Russian military counterattack on the Chechen rebels soon escalated into an all-out invasion of the Chechen republic. Putin now declared his intention to wipe out the Chechen "bandits" once and for all. The resulting conflict, like the first Chechen war, led to the deaths of thousands of innocent Russian and Chechen civilians and the near-total destruction of much of the region, including the capital city of Grozny, which was finally taken by Russian troops in February 2000. Once again, the Chechen resistance fighters fled to the mountainous southern part of Chechnya, from which they have launched bloody attacks on Russian forces ever since.

The emotionally charged political environment generated by the new Chechen war could not help but affect the outcome of the 1999 Duma elections. A new pro-Putin party known as "Unity," made up of various regional leaders and state bureaucrats, was hastily thrown together in October; it ended up gaining 23 percent of the party-list vote. Zyuganov's nationalist KPRF did very well, attaining 24 percent of the party-list vote and 46 seats in single-member districts. The "Union of Right-Wing Forces," including famous "young reformers" such as Gaidar, Kiriyenko, and Chubais, also received an endorsement on television from Putin; as a result, they, too, did surprisingly well, attaining 8.5 percent of the party vote. Meanwhile, pro-Kremlin television mounted a sustained mudslinging campaign against Primakov and Luzhkov; as a result, the Fatherland–All Russia Party performed well below early expectations, with just over 13 percent of the vote. Finally, Yavlinsky's Yabloko party – the one political force publicly critical of the war in Chechnya – barely squeaked past the 5 percent barrier, as did Zhirinovsky's LDPR.

This popular endorsement of Putin and his policies reassured Yeltsin that he could now leave the political stage with no fear that he or his circle of intimates would later be investigated or prosecuted, as had been continually threatened by the communists and their allies. On New Year's Eve, 1999, Yeltsin stunned the world with the sudden announcement of his early resignation as Russia's president. As specified in the Russian constitution, Prime Minister Putin now became acting president as well, and early elections for the presidency were scheduled for March 26. Given Putin's war-driven popularity and the limited time available for his opponents to campaign against him, his victory was certain.

THE PUTIN ERA

When Vladimir Putin was formally elected as Russia's president in March 2000, he inherited a corrupt government, an imbalanced economy, and a demoralized society. A new defeat in Chechnya, he claimed, might under such circumstances lead to the final disintegration of the country. Thus, the central priority for President Putin was the rebuilding of the Russian state. Pursuit of this goal would involve a reformulation of Russia's political identity and major reforms of its institutions – changes that, inevitably, had important effects on the organization of Russian social interests.

Putin's conception of Russian national identity can be summed up in one of his most frequently used slogans: *gosudarstvennost'*, or loyalty to the state. In Putin's view, a general lack of state-oriented patriotism, and a desire to pursue only short-run selfish interests, played a key role in undermining the global power of the Soviet Union and in weakening the coherence of Russia's post-Soviet institutions. His conception of *gosudarstvennost'*, designed to combat the decline of patriotism, contains three main elements. First, Putin claims that the war in Chechnya, and the final suppression of "banditry" and "terrorism" emanating from the southern borders of Russia, will lead to the resurrection of Russia as a global great power; he has even declared that the stabilization of the Caucasus is his personal "mission." Second, Putin calls for the restoration of what he calls the "vertical of power" linking Kremlin leaders to state officials throughout Russia's vast territory: dutiful obedience to one's superiors is supposed to replace the political and social free-for-all of the Yeltsin era. Third, Putin is intensely suspicious of independent social forces that oppose the Kremlin, arguing that in many cases such forces represent foreign interests trying to weaken Russia from within.

Putin's efforts to rebuild Russians' trust in the state had some positive initial impact. Public-opinion polls during Putin's first term showed that ordinary Russians were more optimistic about the country's future than at any time in the 1990s. At times, however, Putin's efforts to restore loyalty to the state, and to stifle political criticism, recalled the secrecy and political conformity of the Soviet era. In August 2000, for example, the Kursk nuclear submarine sank after a failed test of a new torpedo, killing all 118 men on board; Putin, who was on vacation at the time, remained silent about the crisis for days, while the head of the Russian navy blamed the accident on a collision with an American sub. By December 2000, Putin – over the strenuous objections of liberal lawmakers – had moved to restore the Soviet-era national anthem (with new, noncommunist lyrics) and, for the Russian military, the red flag of the USSR (without the hammer and sickle). A shadowy new youth organization called Moving Together began to organize mass pro-Putin rallies, and to criticize "unpatriotic" authors, in many Russian cities. Still, Putin's calls for state patriotism did not constitute the resurrection of any full-blown political ideology like the Marxism-Leninism of the past; indeed, Putin's political worldview remained in many respects both vague and flexible.

Along with Putin's efforts to resurrect Russian patriotism came a series of reforms designed to rebuild Russian state and economic institutions. To prevent further disintegration of central authority over the regions and republics of the Russian Federation, Putin initiated a series of federal reforms in May 2000: The 89 subjects of the Federation were now regrouped into seven new "federal districts," headed by appointed "supergovernors" answering directly to the president; regional governors and parliamentary heads were removed from their seats on the Federation Council and replaced with unelected representatives generally more supportive of the Kremlin; and new legislation allowed the Russian president to dismiss regional governors if they acted "unconstitutionally." To streamline economic policy, Putin during his first presidential term reduced the income tax to a flat rate of 13 percent and the corporate tax to 24 percent, introduced a new land code allowing – for the first time in Russia's history – the legal buying and selling of both urban and agricultural land, and introduced a new labor code weakening the power of Russia's trade unions and making it easier to hire and fire workers. The judicial system, too, was reformed: trial by jury was introduced on a limited basis; judges' salaries were raised in order to lessen the temptations of corruption; and, reversing both tsarist and Soviet-era practices, defendants were now to be considered innocent until proven guilty beyond a reasonable doubt.

Such policies convinced many analysts and business investors that Putin was at heart a Westernizer, continuing in the same basic spirit as the architects of "shock therapy" but with more decisiveness and competence than his predecessor Yeltsin. However, the antiliberal and authoritarian elements of Putin's *gosudarstvennost'* were also evident early in his presidency. In particular, Putin launched an attack on the oligarchs that seemed to focus solely on those billionaires who had the temerity to oppose the Kremlin; other pro-Putin oligarchs were allowed to keep and even expand their business empires. In June 2000, Vladimir Gusinsky, owner of the main independent television station, NTV, along with several liberal newspapers and magazines, was jailed on embezzlement charges. He was released only after pledging to give up control of NTV to Gazprom and soon fled the country. Then Putin's government opened up an investigation concerning powerful oligarch Boris Berezovsky, who had been the primary financial backer of both Yeltsin and later Putin himself during the late 1990s. Berezovsky, seeing the writing on the wall, gave up his seat in the Duma and also fled to Europe. Such attacks on oligarchs were generally quite popular among ordinary Russians, most of whom thought of these "robber barons" as thieves profiting from the poverty of the masses; simultaneously, Putin's policies sent a threatening signal to other businessmen, journalists, and opposition figures. At the same time, FSB agents also began to hassle, detain, and in some cases imprison independent journalists, scholars, and leaders of nongovernmental organizations (NGOs).

For Putin to rebuild the Russian state, however, not just identity and institutions would be important – he would have to appeal to important interest groups in Russian society as well. In this respect, Putin clearly benefited from his extraordinarily good economic timing. The post-Soviet depression of the 1990s came to an end in 1999, just as Putin entered the political arena, and Russia's GDP grew strongly every year of his first presidential term, in large part because of profits from oil and gas exports. Putin used this windfall to balance the budget, repay Western debt, and – most importantly for ordinary people – to eliminate most of the wage arrears that had accumulated under Yeltsin. Still, in order to attack the interests of oligarchs, regional governors, and opposition politicians simultaneously, Putin had to promote the interests of a more specific social group willing to back him in tough battles. Here he largely turned to friends and associates within the secret police and, to a lesser extent, the military. Five of the seven new supergovernors, for example, were FSB or military generals. In March 2001, Putin's FSB colleague and close friend Sergei Ivanov was appointed defense minister. By the end of Putin's first term, according to analysts Olga Kryshtanovskaya and Stephen White, at least one-quarter of the Russian government elite had military or security backgrounds, and their number appeared to be rising.

A final factor that has been crucial in shaping the contours of Putin's Russia is the new global context generated by the terrorist attacks on the World Trade Center and Pentagon in the United States on September 11, 2001, and the subsequent global war on terrorism launched by U.S. President George W. Bush. Surprisingly for many, 9/11 and its aftermath led initially to much closer relations between the United States and Russia; indeed, Putin was the first foreign leader to telephone the White House to express his condolences after the attacks, and he pledged his full support for the war on terror. In many respects, in fact, the U.S. response to 9/11 only reinforced Putin's general political line: He, after all, had argued all along for a more decisive and forceful response to "Islamic terrorism." Putin's position was reinforced also as Chechen rebels continued to launch major terrorist attacks throughout his first term in office – most spectacularly, the seizure of over 900 hostages at a downtown Moscow musical theater in October 2002, an event that ended in tragedy when well over a hundred hostages died from the effects of a poison gas used by the Russians to incapacitate the hostage-takers. Given the new global environment, Western official criticism of continuing Russian brutality in Chechnya became significantly more muted. In the end, the U.S.-Russian "strategic partnership" declared after 9/11 failed to live up to initial high expectations, as the two countries began to quarrel over trade issues, U.S. plans to build a missile defense system, the expansion of NATO to include the Baltic states, and, especially, the U.S. decision to invade Iraq in March 2003. But general Western support for Putin's political approach continued through the end of his first term, helping Putin maintain the backing of many liberals and Westernizers within the Russian elite.

By the end of 2003, Putin had become so dominant over his political opponents that there was little if any doubt he would win a second term. Indeed, a kind of miniature cult had emerged around the president. In one popular song, a female singer complained that she wished she could find "a man like Putin," who would not lie, drink, or break his promises. A government-sponsored Web site for children, www.uznay-prezidenta.ru, displayed photos of a smiling president Putin and his white dog. In a manner reminiscent of Soviet times, television news began to feature Putin's daily activities, no matter how trivial, as the lead story every evening. And even independent public-opinion polls continued to show Putin's popularity rating in the 70–80 percent range.

Given this political milieu – and the Kremlin's active efforts to ensure political loyalty – it is perhaps not surprising that the elections of 2003–2004 were the least competitive in Russia's postcommunist history. The campaign for the State Duma got off to a troubling start when, in October 2003, oligarch Mikhail Khodorkovsky – then Russia's richest man, and the key funder of the liberal Yabloko Party and the Union of Right-Wing Forces, as well as a backer of Zyuganov's Communists – was arrested by masked FSB police at an airport in Siberia and charged with embezzlement and tax evasion. Khodorkovsky's imprisonment not only deprived these opposition parties of crucial monetary resources but also made both the Liberals and Communists look like the pawns of an unpopular "robber baron." State-run television also did its best to promote the pro-Kremlin United Russia Party; opposition politicians found it extremely difficult to compete for news coverage. In the end, the "party of power" received 37.6 percent of the party-list vote; counting single-member district seats and defections from other parties and factions, United Russia controlled over 300 seats – that is, a two-thirds majority in the new Duma. Zhirinovsky's LDPR, capitalizing on rising nationalist sentiment, rebounded to 11.5 percent, whereas KPRF support was cut in half compared with 1999, to just 12.6 percent. The new pro-Kremlin nationalist Motherland Party, cobbled together just a few months before the election, did surprisingly well, attaining 9 percent of the vote. Meanwhile, both liberal parties failed to break the 5 percent barrier for Duma representation and won only a handful of seats, leaving their political future very much in doubt.

With Putin enjoying near-total dominance over the Parliament, and with no credible political opposition, his reelection in March 2004 was a foregone conclusion. Indeed, even a few weeks before the election itself, Putin moved to replace his prime minster, Mikhail Kasyanov – a holdover from the late Yeltsin era who had been openly critical of the Khodorkovsky arrest – with the more pliable bureaucrat Mikhail Fradkov, saying that he wanted voters to know what sort of government he planned for his second term. Both Zhirinovsky and Zyuganov refused to run against Putin at all and named obscure subordinates to campaign on their parties' behalf. Another presidential candidate even told voters that he himself favored Putin's reelection! In the end, Putin received 71.9 percent of the vote, compared with just 13.8 percent for his closest challenger, Nikolai Mikhailovich Kharitonov.

Despite Putin's increasing personal power, his second term in office got off to a very difficult start. On the first day of the new school year, September 1, 2004, Chechen rebels took hundreds of schoolchildren, parents, and teachers hostage in the southern town of Beslan; more than 340 were killed when terrorist explosives were detonated in advance of a rescue attempt by FSB troops. Putin's response to the Beslan tragedy was once again to strengthen the "power vertical": He abolished elections for regional governors, who would henceforth be appointed by the president. Soon afterward, Putin's attempts to help elect the pro-Russian candidate Viktor Yanukovich in Ukraine's November 2004 presidential elections backfired when evidence of serious electoral fraud generated massive popular demonstrations in Kiev. This "Orange Revolution" forced the Ukrainian authorities to hold new elections in December which were won by the pro-Western presidential candidate, Viktor Yushchenko. Meanwhile, the trial of oligarch Mikhail Khodorkovsky dragged on and on; after a year and a half in prison, he was formally convicted and sentenced to a nine-year term for embezzlement in May 2005. All of these developments caused deep concern in the West about the future direction of Russian politics; both Western and Russian analysts began to debate whether or not Putin would really step down at the end of his second term in office in 2008.

Institutions, Interests, and the Search for a New Russian Identity

By the end of the 1990s, it was clear to everyone that the dream of a rapid transformation of postcommunist Russia into a liberal-capitalist country like the United States was just that – a dream. From the perspective adopted in this textbook, which emphasizes the long-term impact of institutions created at critical junctures in a country's history and the specific social interests that these institutions generate, the initial failure of capitalism in Russia should not have been surprising. After all, the political and economic institutions of the Soviet Union were designed by men committed to destroying global capitalism. The all-powerful Communist Party was supposed to train new "professional revolutionaries" to conquer the world bourgeoisie, but it degenerated into a giant, corrupt bureaucracy entangled with a vast network of secret police. Those who had benefited from their positions in the party hierarchy were thus rarely interested in establishing new institutions that would strictly enforce norms of democratic citizenship and the rule of law. Soviet industrial cities were supposed to be heroic sites for revolutionary production but decayed into polluting, outmoded factory towns. They were thus ill-suited for the task of producing consumer goods according to Western standards of efficiency.

Despite the burdensome legacy of its communist past, the collapse of the Soviet Union in 1991 – like the collapse of tsarism at the beginning of the century – marked another critical juncture in Russia's history during which new institutions promoting new interests could be established (see Table 7.1). Indeed, despite all of the country's well-publicized problems, Russia did manage during the 1990s to establish the first democratic regime in its long history. Even if Russia's democracy remained rife with state corruption, undermined by abysmal economic performance, and threatened by vocal antiliberal movements, this accomplishment should not be dismissed.

The Putin era has seen both a return to economic growth and a partial restoration of the coherence of the state. At the same time, however, Putin has presided over a serious erosion of many of Russia's early democratic achievements, and even the fate of the 1993 Russian constitution itself now seems uncertain. Moreover, in the wake of 9/11, Russia finds itself in a new global context that remains highly threatening, with continued turbulence and uncertainty on nearly all of its borders. Where is Russia headed now?

Russia's future depends not only upon the nature of its institutions and interests. It depends also upon the outcome of Russia's search for a new state identity, now that both Marxism-Leninism and "revolutionary" capitalism have failed. Indeed, with the military abused and underpaid, with Chechen rebels continuing their attacks on Russian troops and civilians, and with widespread popular distrust of all political parties and movements, the Russian Federation remains an unconsolidated state prone to sudden political shocks – a terrifying prospect given Russia's substantial stockpiles of chemical, biological, and nuclear weapons. Russia's total collapse, however, appears highly unlikely, given the strong sense among almost all citizens of the Russian Federation that "Russia," in some form, must be preserved.

But which Russia? The liberal capitalist Russia originally envisioned by Gaidar and his allies has been largely discredited by the Yeltsin-era economic crisis. Zyuganov's nostalgic communist version has little appeal for younger, educated Russians, and the KPRF is a fading political force. Zhirinovsky's neoimperialism, despite the LDPR's increased support in the 2003 elections, seems unlikely to become a serious mass movement. More explicitly pro-Nazi and anti-Semitic politicians are trying to convert disgruntled youths and soldiers to their cause – but ever since Hitler's invasion in World War II, "fascism" has been deeply unpopular in Russia. Nor do any of Russia's other leading political figures – including the president himself – have a clearly developed new definition of "Russia." As long as Putin remains popular and the Russian economy continues to grow, his efforts to rebuild the Russian state might appear relatively successful. But new domestic or international challenges could quickly erode his support, and it will be difficult for him to find a capable successor. The one thing that can be predicted with confidence, then, is that we have not seen the final chapter in Russia's painful transition from Soviet rule.

BIBLIOGRAPHY

Breslauer, George. *Khrushchev and Brezhnev as Leaders: Building Authority in Soviet Politics*. London and Boston: Allen and Unwin, 1982.

Brown, Archie. *The Gorbachev Factor*. Oxford and New York: Oxford University Press, 1997.

Conquest, Robert. *The Great Terror: A Reassessment*. New York: Oxford University Press, 1991.

Conquest, Robert. *The Harvest of Sorrow: Soviet Collectivization and the Terror Famine*. New York: Oxford University Press, 1987.

Dunlop, John B. *The Rise of Russia and the Fall of the Soviet Empire*. Princeton, NJ: Princeton University Press, 1993.

Fish, M. Steven. *Democracy From Scratch: Opposition and Regime in the New Russian Revolution*. Princeton, NJ: Princeton University Press, 1995.

Fitzpatrick, Sheila. *The Russian Revolution*. Second edition. Oxford and New York: Oxford University Press, 1994.

Hanson, Stephen E. *Time and Revolution: Marxism and the Design of Soviet Institutions*. Chapel Hill: University of North Carolina Press, 1997.

Hoffmann, David. *The Oligarchs: Wealth and Power in the New Russia*. New York: Public Affairs, 2002.

Jowitt, Ken. *New World Disorder: The Leninist Extinction*. Berkeley: University of California Press, 1992.

Kotkin, Stephen. *Armageddon Averted: The Soviet Collapse, 1970–2000*. Oxford: Oxford University Press, 2001.

Kryshtanovskaya, Olga, and Stephen White. "Putin's Militocracy." *Post-Soviet Affairs* 19, no. 4 (October 2003): 289–306.

McAuley, Mary. *Russia's Politics of Uncertainty*. Cambridge: Cambridge University Press, 1997.

McFaul, Michael. *Russia's Unfinished Revolution: Political Change from Gorbachev to Putin*. Ithaca, NY: Cornell University Press, 2001.

Putin, Vladimir V., with Nataliya Gevorkyan, Natalya Timakova, and Andrei Kolesnikov. *First Person: An Astonishingly Frank Self-Portrait by Russia's President*. New York: Public Affairs, 2000.

Remnick, David. *Resurrection: The Struggle for a New Russia*. New York: Random House, 1998.

Shevtsova, Lilia. *Putin's Russia*. Washington, DC: Carnegie Endowment, 2003.

Solnick, Steven. *Stealing the State: Control and Collapse in Soviet Institutions*. Cambridge, MA: Harvard University Press, 1998.

Stoner-Weiss, Katherine. *Local Heroes: The Political Economy of Russian Regional Governance*. Princeton, NJ: Princeton University Press, 1997.

Yeltsin, Boris N. *The Struggle for Russia*. New York: Random House, 1994.

Yeltsin, Boris N. *Midnight Diaries*. New York: Public Affairs, 2000.

Zaslavsky, Viktor. *The Neo-Stalinist State: Class, Ethnicity, and Consensus in Soviet Society*. Armonk, NY: M. E. Sharpe, 1994.

TABLE 7.1. Key Phases in Russian Political Development

Date	Regime	Global Context	Interests/Identities/ Institutions	Developmental Path
1690–1917	tsarist empire	Russia as great power on periphery of capitalist West	landowning aristocracy/"divine right" monarchy/ feudal state	autocratic modernization
1917–1928	Soviet Russia/USSR	World War I, collapse of tsarist empire, civil war, postwar isolation	revolutionary intellectuals and workers/Marxist ideology/Leninist one-party rule	party control over key industries, toleration of market production
1929–1945	USSR	Great Depression, rise of Nazism in Germany, World War II	Stalinist secret police and "heroic" workers/Marxism-Leninism/planned economy	rapid industrialization, brutal collectivization, prison labor, military buildup
1945–1984	USSR	Cold War with United States, anti-Soviet rebellions in Poland and Afghanistan	corrupt party and state elites/ "superpower" socialism/stagnating planned economy	enforcement of status quo, military expansion in developing world
1985–1991	USSR	military buildup in West, disintegration of Soviet bloc and USSR	reformist intellectuals/ "socialist renewal"/ institutional disintegration	"perestroika" (unintended self-destruction of Leninism)
1991–1999	Russian Federation	Russia as fading power on periphery of triumphant capitalist global system	former party and state elites and local "mafias"/search for new Russian identity/weak democracy	"shock therapy," corrupt capitalism
1999–present	Russian Federation	Russia tries to rebuild its great power status in context of global war on terrorism	Putin loyalists and security services/pragmatic patriotism/ increasing authoritarianism	increasing state intervention in economy combined with dependence on energy exports

IMPORTANT TERMS

Leonid Brezhnev leader of the Communist Party of the Soviet Union from 1964 until his death in 1982. He presided over an "orthodox" Marxist-Leninist regime that became more and more politically corrupt and economically stagnant over time.

Chechnya An ethnic republic that declared its independence from the Russian Federation in September 1991. In December 1994, Yeltsin launched a disastrous full-scale military attack on Chechnya in which tens of thousands of Chechens and Russians were killed. This first war was settled in the summer of 1996, but the political status of the republic remained unresolved. A second Chechen war broke out in the fall of 1999.

Viktor Chernomyrdin prime minister of the Russian Federation from December 1992 until March 1998. Chernomyrdin, the former head of the Soviet natural gas ministry, was originally promoted as a compromise candidate after the refusal of the conservative Russian Congress of People's Deputies to reconfirm Yegor Gaidar as prime minister. Later, he became the leader of the pro-regime "Our Home Is Russia" Party.

collectivization Stalin's policy of creating "collective farms" (*kolkhozy*) and "state farms" (*sovkhozy*) throughout the Soviet countryside, supposedly in order to build socialist agriculture. This policy led to the deaths of millions of peasants through political violence and famine, and it created an enormously inefficient agricultural system.

Commonwealth of Independent States (CIS) the loose association of former Soviet republics formed in December 1991 to replace the USSR. It was officially created at the Belovezh Forest meeting of Boris Yeltsin, president of the Russian Federation, and the presidents of Ukraine, Belorussia (Belarus), and Kazakhstan. The CIS has been largely ineffective since the collapse of the Soviet Union.

democratic centralism the central institutional principle of Leninist political organization. According to this principle, "democratic" debates among party members are allowed only until the party leadership makes a final decision, at which point all members are obliged to implement the orders of their superiors without question.

Federation Council the upper house of the Federal Assembly. The Federation Council has 178 members and since 2001 has been made up of representatives appointed by the governors and regional legislatures of all 89 of Russia's federal regions and republics.

five-year plan the basic organizing framework of Stalinist economic institutions. Beginning with the First Five-Year Plan of 1928–1932, all industrial and agricultural production in the USSR was regulated by monthly and yearly output targets given to each manager and worker. Bonuses went to those managers and workers who overfulfilled their plan targets to demonstrate their revolutionary zeal.

Mikhail Gorbachev leader of the Communist Party of the Soviet Union from 1985 to 1991. Gorbachev tried to reverse the stagnation of the Brezhnev era by launching a policy of "revolutionary restructuring" (perestroika) that called for open criticism of the past, greater democracy, and "new thinking" in foreign policy. The result was the wholesale disintegration of Leninist political institutions and Stalinist economic organizations, leading to the collapse of the USSR.

gulag the Russian abbreviation for "state camp." The gulags were a vast network of labor camps, set up by Lenin and greatly expanded by Stalin, that were used to imprison millions of people who were suspected of opposing the Communist Party and its policies. The term actually refers to "state camp administration."

Nikita Khrushchev leader of the Communist Party of the Soviet Union from shortly after Stalin's death in 1953 until 1964. Khrushchev endeavored to reinvigorate Soviet socialism by means of a series of "revolutionary" economic campaigns in agriculture and industry and also attacked Stalin's terror. This "leftist" strategy, however, only produced general administrative chaos, and Khrushchev was ousted in a Politburo coup.

Alexander Lebed popular general who came in third in the 1996 presidential elections, after which he became the head of the Security Council. After having settled the first war in Chechnya, Lebed was fired by Yeltsin. In 1997, he was elected governor of the vast Krasnoyarsk region in Siberia. In 2002, he was killed in a helicopter crash.

Vladimir Lenin Russian revolutionary and the author of *What Is To Be Done?* Lenin insisted on strict "professional revolutionary" discipline among Marxists. In 1917, Lenin led the October Revolution and founded the Soviet regime in Russia.

Yuri Luzhkov mayor of Moscow and leader of the Fatherland Party which merged with Putin's Unity Party to form the pro-Kremlin party, United Russia. Luzhkov has built a mini-empire through his control over business activities in Russia's capital city and has become one of the country's most influential politicians.

Karl Marx nineteenth-century German intellectual, the coauthor (with Friedrich Engels) of the *Communist Manifesto* and the author of *Capital*. Marx provided the main theoretical inspiration for the later movement to create a socialist society in Europe.

New Economic Policy often abbreviated NEP, the economic program adopted by Lenin in 1921 in the wake of the social devastation caused by the Russian civil war, which he saw as a "strategic retreat" from the ultimate goal of building socialism. The NEP allowed for the reestablishment of markets for agricultural products and legalized small-scale trade in the cities, but the Soviet state retained control over the major industries, and one-party rule was strengthened.

oligarchs the group of a dozen or so bankers and industrialists who took advantage of the rapid privatization of Soviet property to amass huge personal fortunes. During the 1990s, this group controlled most of Russia's most powerful media, banks, and raw-material companies. President Putin launched a crackdown on those oligarchs who openly opposed his regime.

Yevgeny Primakov former academic adviser to Gorbachev and later head of the Foreign Intelligence Service and foreign minister. Primakov was appointed prime minister in a compromise between Yeltsin and the Communist-led Duma after the financial crisis of August 1998; he was then fired as the Communists tried to impeach Yeltsin in the spring of 1999.

provisional government the temporary government of former parliamentarians that ruled Russia after the fall of the tsarist empire in February 1917. This ineffective body failed to stabilize the revolutionary situation in the country and was overthrown by Lenin's Bolshevik Party in October.

Vladimir Putin first appointed prime minister by Yeltsin in August 1999, he was then elected as Russia's president in 2000 and 2004. Putin attained high popularity among Russians for his prosecution of the war in Chechnya, his restoration of economic and social stability, and his efforts to restore the power of the Russian state.

Alexander Rutskoi general during the Soviet war in Afghanistan, and Yeltsin's vice president from 1991 to 1993. He originally supported Yeltsin's Russian nationalism against Gorbachev's conception of "socialist reform" but later broke with Yeltsin when the president agreed to break up the USSR and tried to implement capitalism in the Russian Federation. Rutskoi was a leader of the opposition in the Russian Congress in 1993.

shock therapy policy of rapid transition to capitalism officially adopted by Boris Yeltsin in January 1992. In theory, shock therapy was supposed to involve the simultaneous liberalization of all prices, privatization of state property, and stabilization of the Russian currency. In reality, the program was implemented only haphazardly, generating disastrous economic and social results.

soviets a word that means "councils" in Russian. It refers to the spontaneous groups of workers and soldiers that formed in the chaotic social situation under the provisional government. Lenin saw these bodies as the seeds of the future communist society, and for this reason he declared the country a "soviet regime" after his party seized power. Until Gorbachev came to power, however, these councils remained politically powerless and wholly subordinate to the party.

Joseph Stalin the unrivaled leader of the Communist Party of the Soviet Union from 1928 to 1953. Stalin rose to power in a bitter and prolonged struggle with Trotsky, Bukharin, and Zinoviev after Lenin's death. He then implemented a policy of rapid industrialization and mass terror designed to build "socialism" in peasant Russia as quickly as possible – at the cost of tens of millions of lives.

State Duma the lower house of the Federal Assembly, the Russian parliament created in the constitution of 1993. The Duma has 450 members, half of whom are selected by proportional representation on party lists and half of whom are elected in single-member districts. From 2007 forward, the entire Duma will be elected by PR.

Grigory Yavlinsky leader of the "Yabloko" (Apple) movement, so named after the initials of its three founders. He argued that capitalism in Russia must be implemented by means of democratic and uncorrupted state institutions rather than via shock therapy.

Boris Yeltsin the first democratically elected president of Russia. He organized the movement to declare the "Russian Federation" an independent country and thus to destroy the USSR. In 1993, he violently disbanded the Russian Congress of People's Deputies and introduced the new Russian constitution. After winning reelection in 1996, Yeltsin experienced increasing health problems, and his power gradually diminished. He resigned on December 31, 1999.

Vladimir Zhirinovsky leader of the so-called Liberal Democratic Party of Russia (LDPR). Zhirinovsky and his party argue for an ultranationalist solution to Russia's postcommunist problems, envisioning an eventual expansion of Russia to the Indian Ocean. In practice, however, Zhirinovsky has often voted in support of the government in return for political and financial support.

Gennady Zyuganov leader of the Communist Party of the Russian Federation (CPRF). Zyuganov and his party argued for the restoration of "Soviet power," including the reconstitution of the USSR. The ideology of the party, however, is much more oriented toward great-power nationalism than toward original Marxism or Leninism.

STUDY QUESTIONS

1. Should Russia today be classified as a "developed" industrial society comparable to Britain, France, or Germany? Why or why not?

2. Was Lenin's conception of a revolutionary one-party regime consistent with Marx's vision of communism, or was it a betrayal of Marx's dream of worker liberation?

3. What were the main reasons for the rise of Stalin and his policies of mass terror? Would you blame primarily the ideals of communism, the institutions of Leninism, the interests of Stalin and his supporters, or the global context in which the Soviet Union was situated?

4. Does the failure of Gorbachev's perestroika demonstrate that the Soviet system in the 1980s was unreformable? Or could some alternative strategy for reforming communism have succeeded in revitalizing the institutions of the USSR? What is the relevance, if any, of Deng Xiaoping's reforms in China to the Soviet case?

5. Should social scientists have been able to predict the disintegration of the Soviet bloc? What explains the remarkably poor track record of Western scholars in making predictions about the future of the Soviet Union and Russia?

6. Compare and contrast the problem of ethnic conflict in the Soviet Union and in the Russian Federation. Do you think that the Russian Federation will eventually break up into smaller countries as the Soviet Union did? Or could Russia instead expand to include some of the former Soviet republics?

7. Was Russia's post-Soviet economic crisis caused by the failure of Yeltsin's shock-therapy program or was it simply the legacy of Stalinist socioeconomic institutions? Might some alternative strategy for building capitalism in post-Soviet Russia have been more successful?

8. Are capitalism and democracy in conflict in postcommunist Russia, or do they instead reinforce each other?

9. In 1917, the tsarist empire collapsed, and Lenin's radical Bolshevik Party came to power soon after. In 1918, the German empire collapsed, and within 15 years the Nazi Party came to power. Is there any chance that a radically antiliberal party like Lenin's or Hitler's will eventually triumph in post-Soviet Russia as well? Why or why not?

10. Would you expect the next generation of Russian politicians to be more successful at institution-building than was the generation reared under communism? Why or why not?

11. If you were a Russian voter, would you support or oppose President Vladimir Putin?

CHINA

0   250   500   750   1000 miles
0   250   500   750   1000km

RUSSIA

KAZAKHSTAN

L. Baikhash

KYRGYZSTAN

TAJIKISTAN

PAKISTAN

Chinese
line of control

Indian
claim

Indus R.

Lhasa

NEPAL

BHUTAN

Ganges R.

Brahmaputra R.

BANGLA-
DESH

INDIA

MYANMAR
(BURMA)

Bay of
Bengal

THAILAND

LAOS

VIETNAM

MONGOLIA

L. Baikal

Ürümqi

Amur R.

Amur R.

Harbin

Shenyang

NORTH
KOREA

Sea of
Japan

JAPAN

SOUTH
KOREA

Beijing
Tianjin

Yellow
Sea

Huang He

Lanzhou

Xi'an

Zhengzhou

Nanjing

Shanghai

Wuhan

East China
Sea

Chengdu

Chang Jiang

Chongqing

PACIFIC

Taipei

OCEAN

TAIWAN

Mekong R.

Guangzhou

Hong Kong
Macau   S.A.R.
S.A.R.

Philippine
Sea

South
China Sea

Hainan

PHILIPPINES

CHAPTER EIGHT

China

Yu-Shan Wu

Introduction

China has one of the world's most ancient civilizations, dating back more than 3,000 years. It is easy for political scientists studying China to emphasize its uniqueness, as Chinese culture, language, political thought, and history appear quite different from those of any of the major Western countries. Modern Chinese history was obviously punctuated with decisive Western impacts, but the way China responded to those impacts is often considered to be uniquely Chinese. Furthermore, Chinese political leaders themselves frequently stress that they represent movements that carry uniquely Chinese characteristics. China, it seems, can only be understood in its own light.

When put in a global and comparative context, however, China loses many of its unique features. Imperial China, or the **Qing dynasty**, was an agricultural empire when it met the first serious wave of challenges from the West during the middle of the nineteenth century. The emperor and the mandarins (high-ranking Chinese officials) were forced to give up their treasured institutions grudgingly after a series of humiliating defeats at the hands of the Westerners. This pattern resembled what occurred in many traditional political systems when confronted with aggression from the West. From that time on, the momentum for political development in China was driven by global competition and the need for national survival. China differed from other cases in the developing world mainly in the immense dimensions of the country, not in the nature of its response.

As in other developing countries, different political forces in China competed for power as the country faced international challenges. Those different political forces represented distinct interests, developed alternative identities, and proposed competing institutions (see Table 8.1). The outcome of their competition shaped the developmental path of China, and that outcome was, in turn, contingent on the international environment in which China found itself.

As previous chapters have noted, late developers tended to put more emphasis on the state's role in development. Thus, from Britain to France, Germany, and ultimately Russia, one finds an increasingly coercive state accumulating scarce capital to fuel economic growth. British liberalism was translated into strategic investment in France, state sponsorship in Germany, and total state control under the name of communism in Russia. Following this logic, one could safely predict that China would follow a development strategy that puts a much stronger emphasis on a "developmental state" than would a typical Western liberal model.

"Developmental state" in the German (and Japanese) or in the Russian sense? This is the major difference between the **Kuomintang (KMT** or nationalist) regime that ruled China from 1928 to 1949 and the Communist regime that established the **People's Republic of China (PRC)** in 1949 and has ruled the country since then. The global European and Japanese challenge forced the Chinese to adopt new institutions with greater governing capacity and, at the same time, offered models for the Chinese to emulate. The KMT opted for the German model, whereas the **Chinese Communist Party (CCP)** chose the Soviet model. The KMT and the CCP represented two different interests, upheld nationalism and communism as their respective identities, and established authoritarian and totalitarian regimes, respectively. In short, the international challenge to China brought about two distinctively different developmental models, as represented by the KMT and the CCP, and the interests, identities, and institutions of these two dominant political forces.

During the post-1949 period, mainland China experienced first **Mao Zedong**'s totalitarianism, followed by rapid economic and political reform under **Deng Xiaoping**, and then a technocratic consolidation staged by **Jiang Zemin** and **Hu Jintao**. On the island of Taiwan, to which the KMT and its followers had fled after 1949, the KMT experienced a less turbulent and more linear development toward Western liberal capitalism and an increasing attenuation of its statist model, leading ultimately to the adoption of democratic institutions. Viewed from a historical perspective, irresistible forces have compelled both the CCP and the KMT to adapt to the world market and "play by the rules." Global competition first compelled the Chinese to establish a strong state for the initial push of industrialization on both sides of the Taiwan Straits and then pressured them to tinker with the market when the state proved ineffective at sustaining growth. Markets and private property then nurtured social demands for pluralism and a shift of political culture away from the collectivism that had been vital in sustaining authoritarian rule in both mainland China and Taiwan. Taiwan has already conformed to that pressure for democracy, partly because of the strong influence of the United

States, on which Taiwan has been totally dependent, whereas mainland China remains opposed to democratic change, but with increasing difficulty.

In short, global challenges, foreign examples, and reliance on outside sponsors (in the case of Taiwan) shaped the political institutions of China. It is impossible to recognize or understand Chinese political development without first grasping the fundamental forces that influence China from outside its borders. Chinese responses to the world do carry certain characteristics that one does not easily find in other developing countries. However, the impetus and momentum for those responses and the general directions they took are quite understandable in a global and historical context. In the following discussion, we will trace the political development of China during modern times from the Qing dynasty to the Dengist reform and subsequent development. Our focus will be on mainland China, but we will also make comparative references to Taiwan, an alternative Chinese society that has taken a different developmental route.

Historical Background

Imperial China was a static system. Dynasties came and went, but the basic outlines of China's patriarchal social structure and absolutist-monarchical political institutions remained unchanged from the Han dynasty (206 B.C. to A.D. 220) until its collapse at the beginning of the twentieth century. Confucianism, a way of thought developed by the Chinese philosopher Confucius around 500 B.C. that laid emphasis on social order, was enshrined as the state ideology and emphasized filial piety and loyalty to the emperor as the ultimate virtues. A sophisticated examination system recruited intellectuals into the government based on their mastery of Confucian classics. Technological innovations and successful human organization made it possible for the Chinese dynasties to expand into great empires that often dominated neighboring tribes and nations in East Asia. Up until the Yuan dynasty (1229–1305), when China had Mongol rulers, the Middle Kingdom, as the Chinese referred to their country, was the envy of many Europeans.

China's ancient civilization, however, proved to be a mixed blessing for the Chinese people when the real challenge came in the form of the arrival of Westerners. Equipped with guns and steamers, Westerners began their exploitation of China's vast markets on a mass scale in the mid–nineteenth century, pioneered by British opium dealers. This could not have come at a worse time. China was then in the middle of the Qing (also known as the Manchu) dynasty. Following the pattern of all established dynasties, the Qing emperors during that period were not great rulers but neither were they weak enough to be overthrown easily. Had the Qing emperors at the time been as ambitious and capable as their forefathers (such as Kangxi, Yongzheng, and

Qianlong), China would have had a much better chance of rejuvenating itself while confronting the Western powers. Had they been totally weak, then the dynasty might have fallen and a new one come to power, as had happened in Chinese history more than two dozen times. Because the Manchu dynasty was in the middle of its dynastic cycle, ruled not by the vigorous founding emperors but by their mediocre successors, it could not come up with an effective response to the challenge posed by the West but was able to drag on in decline for yet another half-century before it was buried amid lost wars, unequal treaties, depleted national wealth, and a disintegrated social fabric. During this agonizing period of national humiliation and attrition, the deep-rooted sense of superiority of the Chinese elite gradually gave way to a realization that China was actually inferior to the West, not only in military might but also in institutions and even in culture.

The Manchu dynasty was ultimately overthrown in 1912 by a revolutionary movement led by **Sun Yat-sen**, a U.S.-trained doctor from the Guangdong province. The Republic of China (ROC) was then founded. Sun's ideal was to transform China into a modern, democratic, and affluent country that could repel foreign invasion and offer the Chinese people a decent life. Sun and his colleagues were at the time mainly inspired by the Western model and hoped China could evolve into a liberal democracy. However, political turmoil ensued, as no political-military force was able to prevail in China's postimperial era. Yuan Shikai, a Qing general turned president, attempted to restore imperial rule and make himself emperor. He was forced to curtail his ambition when beleaguered by defecting generals and Sun's comrades, who swore to protect the new republic.

After Yuan's death in 1916, China split into warring territories controlled by warlords of various kinds. Foremost were Zhang Zuolin in Manchuria and northern China, Wu Peifu in the Yangtzu area, and Sun Chuanfang in the southeast provinces. For his part, Sun established the KMT in 1919, expecting to rely on the support of China's urban intellectuals. He then sought Soviet support from his base in the southern province of Guangdong and accepted Moscow's advice to establish the Whampoa Military Academy for the training of an officer corps loyal to his ideas, foremost of which were the **"Three Principles of the People"** – nationalism, democracy, and people's livelihood – a kind of democratic socialism with distinct Chinese characteristics. General **Chiang Kai-shek** was then appointed commander of the academy and charged with producing a highly indoctrinated revolutionary army for the KMT. Although still holding the liberal model as the ultimate goal, Dr. Sun now envisioned a strong state to fulfill his ideal. This change of mind is important in that the KMT had opted for a nonliberal strategy in state-building. However, whether the KMT would choose a German-style statist model or a communist model was unclear at the time because the two tendencies were competing for dominance in the party.

General Chiang succeeded in building a revolutionary army committed to Sun's ideas, but only with heavy infiltration by the communists, who followed an order from Moscow to join Sun's KMT and develop the CCP's influence inside the KMT apparatus and military establishment. Sun died of liver cancer in 1925, leaving a heavily divided KMT. Chiang then launched a northern expedition to expand the KMT's territory and shed communist influence. The initial thrust north was successful, and in early 1926 the KMT army was able to control the provinces south of the Yangtze River. Chiang established his power base in Nanjing and Shanghai, on the east coast of China, while the KMT Left and their communist allies set up a separate center in Wuhan in central China. Chiang then purged the communists in territories under his control, while the left-wing elements of the KMT and the communists were finding their relations strained because they could not agree on how to deal with Chiang. Finally, the communists were forced out of the KMT and began organizing peasant riots against Chiang's government in the countryside hitherto dominated by the landowning gentry class. In the end, Chiang was able to suppress the communist uprisings, subjugate the left-wing KMT factions, and complete his conquest of northern China. He established a nationalist government in Nanjing, the capital of the Republic of China. The country was unified.

The communists became rebels in China's mountainous areas, which they called the "Soviet regions." They tried to find support in China's tenant farmers, who had long been yearning for land through a land-redistribution scheme. Moscow's influence loomed large at the time. A Chinese Soviet Republic was established in Jiangxi province and later became a target for Chiang's "annihilation campaigns." In 1934, the communists' main base in Jiangxi was attacked, and they were chased across the south and southwest provinces of China by the pursuing KMT army. This desperate retreat was what the communists would later call the "**Long March**." Ultimately, the retreating communist forces founded a new base in Yan'an, a remote town in the north of China. There the KMT offensive was finally thwarted, for the nationalist government faced a much more serious challenge from Japan's military incursions. During the Long March, Mao Zedong was able to grasp first military and then political leadership of the CCP by criticizing and ousting those Chinese communists trained in Moscow. In Yan'an, Mao firmly established his personal leadership.

The period from 1928 through 1936 is considered the golden years of the KMT's rule in China. Industry grew, commerce expanded, and foreign trade surged. China might have taken a different route from what it actually did had it not been for an all-out Japanese invasion and the ensuing Sino-Japanese War, which totally devastated the country. As it turned out, the communists were able to appeal to nationalism and generate strong support among Chinese intellectuals, who grew increasingly critical of Chiang's concentration on crushing the communist insurgency. In December 1936, Chiang was kidnapped by the son of a Manchurian warlord and although he was finally released, the nationalist government was forced to shift its priority from mopping up the communists to preparing for war with Japan.

On July 7, 1937, Japan launched an all-out attack on the Chinese army guarding Peking (Beijing). China and Japan entered into a protracted and devastating eight-year war. The Japanese had built a powerful war machine that dwarfed China's fragmented and poorly equipped army. Chiang's strategy was to "trade space for time," and the KMT troops went into a large-scale retreat. As the war dragged on and the Japanese military was spread thin in China's vast territory, the KMT army was able to hold its defense line, while the CCP found great opportunities to expand in rural China, which the KMT vacated and the Japanese failed to penetrate. As it turned out, the Sino-Japanese War decisively altered the balance of power between the KMT and the CCP so that at the end of the war the communists were in control of north China and, with the help of the Soviets, Manchuria.

The nationalist government was not prepared to fight a civil war with the communists after eight years of fighting with the Japanese. Most people simply wanted peace and were unwilling to support the KMT's war effort. Corruption and inflation cost the nationalists their traditional urban support, whereas communists were successful in mobilizing peasants with their land-reform programs. In the end, the nationalist troops were demolished in several decisive campaigns, and Chiang Kai-shek led millions of KMT loyalists to the island of Taiwan, a territory retroceded to the ROC by the Japanese after World War II. On October 1, 1949, the People's Republic of China (PRC) was formally established in Beijing, while the ROC migrated to Taiwan. There has been no peace treaty between mainland China and Taiwan since then, and the Chinese civil war technically has not ended.

The civil war was significant in shifting China's developmental strategy. During the republican period, the KMT basically pursued a statist development model, which had technocratic capitalism, authoritarian political control, and exultation of nationalism as its major components. Even though one finds traditional elements and emphasis on Confucian teachings in the KMT's ideology, the system established by Chiang was modeled on those of Germany and Japan. It was not totalitarian, as the KMT lacked the capacity to penetrate deeply into the rural grass roots, and had to share power with the gentry class, urban bourgeoisie, and international capital. Religious leaders, intellectuals, and underworld gangs also exercised great influence. The KMT attempted to monopolize the mass media but was unable to do so. Those weaknesses were fully exploited by the communists. With the defeat of the KMT, China moved into a new developmental stage characterized by Soviet-style institutions and, later on, Maoist frenetic movements, mobilization campaigns of extreme intensity.

The reason that the KMT opted for the German or Japanese model was simple. China was facing a crisis of national survival. It was only natural for the ruling elite to emphasize the importance of concentrating power in the hands of the leadership and guiding national development from the top. However, as the nationalist leaders came primarily from the middle and upper classes of Chinese society, they had no appetite for radical social revolutions as championed by the communists. The nationalists appealed to Chinese nationalism to gain legitimacy and criticized the communist notion of a "class struggle." This strategy proved successful in their initial competition with the communists, inasmuch as the latter's radical land-redistribution program antagonized the landowning class while failing to mobilize genuine peasant support. Also, it can be argued that the rise of communist power during the Sino-Japanese War was a direct result of the CCP's shift from blatant class struggle to peasant nationalism. The nationalists' social background further suggests a deep commitment to many traditional values, such as filial piety (abiding respect for parents and ancestors), and the rich cultural legacies of China. For the communists, however, those values were dispensable as long as they stood in the way of rapid modernization.

During the first half of the twentieth century, international competition and national survival forced the Chinese elite to choose an effective modernization model. The liberal, statist, and communist models, as exemplified by Britain, Japan, and the Soviet Union, were particularly appealing to the urban intellectuals, the KMT, and the CCP, respectively. These were the interests on which the identities of liberalism, nationalism, and communism were formed. Three distinctively different institutions would flow naturally from the three interests and identities. The triumph of the urban intellectuals would bring about a Western-style democracy. The victory of the KMT would install a modernizing authoritarian regime. The success of the CCP would establish a totalitarian party-state. As it turned out, the liberal intellectuals lacked the organizational means to realize their ideas. The British model never had a real chance.

China's choice, then, was narrowed down to two models: authoritarian statist or communist. When the CCP won the civil war in 1949, China's fate was sealed. There was going to be a series of stormy movements aimed at thoroughly transforming the society based on the communist model. The CCP's interest was reflected in the communist identity and a totalitarian institution – the Communist Party. On the separate island of Taiwan, however, the KMT kept the statist model alive and managed to produce an economic miracle based on private enterprise and government control of the market. The main identity on Taiwan was nationalism, and the key institution was an authoritarian state. In later years, Taiwan's statist model was attenuated by the rise of an affluent middle-class society and the hegemonic influence exercised by the United States, which preferred the liberal-democratic model.

As Taiwan gradually moved to liberalism, mainland China experienced a shift from the communist model to the statist model that Taiwan had exemplified in the past. The driving force for such a fundamental change stemmed from the inherent defects of the communist, and particularly the Maoist, developmental model, which proved inadequate in the face of economic and military competition. As we will see, the destructive Cultural Revolution transformed the minds of the party cadres and turned them into modernizing technocrats. They became keenly aware of the deficiencies and atrocities of the old model. The CCP regime began moving toward the KMT's statist model. Communism was gradually being replaced by nationalism as the national identity, and the totalitarian regime was being transformed into an authoritarian state. With the relaxation of political control, the adoption of an "open-door policy" to the outside world, and the introduction of the market and private property, reform in China has even rekindled a liberal-democratic tendency rooted in the republican period, as demonstrated in the **Tiananmen** Square protests in June 1989 when Beijing's college students allied themselves with workers and citizens in order to stage a massive, one-month sit-in for political freedoms in the heart of the capital. During that month, there were several massive demonstrations that involved more than a million participants, an unprecedented phenomenon in Communist China. However, the ease with which this pro-democracy movement was suppressed shows that liberal roots had not been thoroughly established in China. The current economic reform, however, may ultimately bring about an affluent middle-class society heavily influenced by international liberalism and eventually turn China institutionally toward liberalism, as happened earlier in Taiwan.

Some words on mainland China's relations with Taiwan are in order here. As its experience of governing mainland China gradually moved into Taiwan's past and Taiwan adopted a liberal political model, relations between the two sides remained tense and the United States found itself as involved as ever in the conflict across the Taiwan Strait. Since 1949, several armed conflicts have erupted in the Taiwan Strait, and the United States has acted as Taiwan's guardian, thwarting invasion from the mainland with a strong commitment to the security of Taiwan. In 1979, changing strategic calculations by the United States caused a shift of Washington's formal diplomatic recognition from the ROC to the PRC as the legitimate government of China. However, Taiwan still received a security guarantee from the United States through the Taiwan Relations Act, which helped the island wade through the political turbulence of the 1980s. **Chiang Ching-kuo**, Chiang Kai-shek's son, lifted martial law and allowed the formation of the opposition party, the Democratic Progressive Party, before his death in 1988. Ching-kuo was succeeded by Lee Teng-hui, who further democratized Taiwan's political system by holding a full-scale parliamentary election in 1992 and a direct presidential election in

1996. As it turned out, democratization in Taiwan produced a strong tendency toward "independence" (as demonstrated by replacing the name ROC with Republic of Taiwan and permanently separating Taiwan from mainland China) that since the mid-1990s has challenged the "one China" commitment held dearly by both the KMT and the CCP in the past. Tension ran high and threatened to engulf the United States in a cross-Strait war on several occasions, most noticeably during the 1995–1996 missile crisis, making the Taiwan Strait one of the most volatile hotspots in international politics at the turn of the twenty-first century.

Developmental Stages of the Communist Regime

Because political power in the PRC has been highly concentrated in the hands of a small group of communist leaders, and particularly in the hands of the paramount leader (Mao Zedong from 1949 to 1976 and Deng Xiaoping from 1978 to 1997), China's post-1949 political development can best be understood in terms of the ideas and policies of its top leaders. However, this does not mean that individuals determined China's political development by dint of their personalities and particular political inclinations. As strong as Mao's and Deng's influence on the political process may have been, they nevertheless reflected underlying forces that propelled a communist regime through the kinds of different developmental stages that one can also find in the Soviet Union and other communist countries. In this sense, both Mao and Deng (and Jiang Zemin and Hu Jintao, who succeeded Deng) were more representative of the underlying trend than they were creators of such a trend.

As we have seen in the Russian example from Lenin to Brezhnev, the developmental stages of a Leninist regime can be characterized as (1) the initial transformation aimed at remaking the society; (2) the reform backlash; and (3) the conservative consolidation. The logic behind these stages is simple. The communists, as true believers in their utopian ideas, tend to act on the ideology when they seize political power. This is the period of great transformation and revolutionary politics: Private property is confiscated; markets are abolished; a centrally planned economy is erected; and a forced-draft industrialization drive is launched. At this stage, one usually finds a tyrannical despot concentrating all political power in his hands and terrorizing his subjects into total subservience. Elaborate party networks, an all-powerful secret police apparatus, and gigantic state enterprises are created, and a totalitarian party-state comes into existence. However, after years of traumatic totalitarian rule, a reform period is bound to emerge. Totalitarianism traumatizes not only ordinary people but also a ruling elite whose fate is tied to the whim of the totalitarian despot, who launches repeated political campaigns to "purify" the party. The whole nation yearns for relief from economic deprivation and treacherous politics. Thus, one finds a relaxation of state control over the economy in the form of "perfecting the planning system" or "market socialism," a withdrawal of secret police from their most blatant intrusion into citizens' private lives, and a diminution of the party's omnipresent control of cultural expressions of the society. A more benign ruler succeeds the despot, but usually not until the despot dies a natural death, as in the case of Khrushchev succeeding Stalin and Deng succeeding Mao. The party-state then comes to a truce with the society.

The reform backlash does not last long, however, as the very "liberal" policies characterizing this period breed further social expectations and threaten to undermine the communist regime. What follows then is usually a conservative technocratic regime that does not embark on any major institutional initiatives or structural political reform but clings to the status quo and gives it a conservative twist. The mission is no longer radical transformation of the society or desperate redressing of the excesses of totalitarianism but rather entrenchment and consolidation. The consolidational leader might keep or even deepen certain aspects of the reform stage, particularly on the economic side, but the overall mentality is conservative and the paramount goal is stability. The elite maintained political stability, through economic performance and an all-embracing coercive apparatus. In the Soviet Union and most of Eastern Europe, this period was embodied in the rule of Leonid Brezhnev and like-minded communist leaders, such as Gustav Husak of Czechoslovakia. In the following analysis, we see that China moved into the consolidation stage with the death of Deng Xiaoping and the political ascendancy of the technocrat par excellence, Jiang Zemin, as the new top leader of the CCP in 1997 (see Table 8.3 at the end of the chapter). The partial succession of Jiang by Hu Jintao in 2002 further consolidated this trend, for the latter was a technocrat ruler just like his predecessor. It should be pointed out, however, that consolidation and stability were pursued in China through dynamic equilibrium, with periodic replacement of senior leaders and increased openness toward the world economy, whereas the Soviet and Eastern European communist regimes pursued the same goals through static equilibrium, without rejuvenation of top leadership and globalization. These are two types of consolidational leadership, although the paramount goals of political stability and regime preservation remain the same in both.

The Maoist Period: Totalitarianism

We begin our analysis with Mao Zedong, the totalitarian despot. Mao rose to power when he assumed command of the Red Army at the Zunyi conference in 1935 on the Long March. Prior to that meeting, Mao had been dominated by a group of Moscow-trained communists. Mao understood that there was no hope for the communists to establish power bases in China's cities. The size of the working class there was too small and their revolutionary consciousness too underdeveloped. Instead, the Chinese communists had to rely on the peasants. This meant that the CCP had to adopt a strategy of "encircling the cities from the countryside" and tailor its programs to the needs of the peasants; that is, redistributing land instead of creating communes. Mao's idea was in serious conflict with the Soviet experience, which relied heavily on the workers in the cities for vital support. It was not until the KMT's fifth annihilation campaign, which swept the communists from their Jiangxi base, that Mao grasped a golden opportunity to unseat his Moscow-trained rivals and assume military leadership. He then put his strategy into practice. This realistic shift of strategy, when combined with the Japanese invasion, contributed greatly to the CCP's resurgence as a serious contender for power during the post–World War II period.

Mao's greatest contribution to the communist movement was, of course, leading the party to the defeat of Chiang Kai-shek in the civil war and establishing the People's Republic of China in 1949. The 1950s witnessed a great transformation of Chinese society. The traditional gentry elite was purged. Social hierarchy in the rural areas was smashed. The business class in the cities was deprived of its properties. A Soviet-style command economy was installed with the help of Soviet advisers. The end of the civil war brought about a golden opportunity for national reconstruction. Women were given equal status with men and emancipated from their traditional subjugation in the family. One witnessed great social mobility. Although the nationalist government initiated many social reforms before 1949, its inability to penetrate into the depths of Chinese society limited the effectiveness of its reforms. Under the communists, traditional society was turned upside-down for the first time in China's multithousand-year history. All of this happened under heavy Soviet influence. In 1950, Mao paid a tribute to Stalin in Moscow when he made his first visit to a foreign country and signed a treaty of friendship between the PRC and the Soviet Union. To the outside observer, especially to politicians in the United States, it appeared as if there was now one large, unified communist bloc that extended from Berlin to Beijing.

It was only a matter of time, however, before the Chinese and the Soviets would compete for influence in the world communist movement. Mao was, after all, the leader of China, one of the five permanent members of the UN Security Council (although the seat was at that time still held by the Republic of China in Taipei), the world's most populous nation, and a country proud of its ancient civilization. It would be difficult to imagine a subservient China bowing to the interests of the Soviet Union in the name of a world communist movement. During the 1950s, Mao developed his own ideas about how to govern China and conduct Beijing's relations with other countries in the world.

This struggle for dominance in the world communist movement led to an outright acrimonious split after Stalin's death and the criticism of Stalin in the Soviet Union under Khrushchev's rule. Mao launched a series of verbal attacks on Soviet "revisionism," seeing in Nikita Khrushchev a weak, willing traitor who flirted with the world's archcapitalist nation, the United States. Determined to shed Soviet influence, Mao in the late 1950s urged the party to adopt a uniquely Chinese modernization strategy, which would prove disastrous for the nation.

Mao's experience with the Chinese civil war, in which the ill-equipped communist fighters had overpowered the KMT's huge army, convinced him that spiritual mobilization was the key to success. As China was short of capital, Mao found the abundant Chinese labor a ready substitute. Mao believed that people could be mobilized through political campaigns modeled on revolutionary action. This idea was a natural extension of Mao's wartime strategy, which had relied on China's huge peasantry. The result was a policy that Mao called the "**Great Leap Forward**." The apex of the campaign was the creation of the gigantic People's Communes, which presumably embodied the communist ideal. Communes were large in scale, collectively owned, and were composed of several production brigades, which were subdivided into production teams. They organized production activities, distributed revenues, performed governmental functions, and took care of social welfare. In the heyday of communization, rural markets were abolished, prices were set by the state, and private property was eliminated in the countryside. The Commune experience had little economic rationality and was imposed on the country at the whim of Chairman Mao. The result of this experience was a total disruption of agricultural production that ended in an unprecedented man-made famine during which some 30,000,000 Chinese people died. Mao was forced to the "second line" by his pragmatic colleagues, such as Liu Shaoqi, Deng Xiaoping, and **Chen Yun**, but the "great helmsman" refused to accept his political downfall and made a revengeful comeback by launching the Great Proletariat **Cultural Revolution** that ravaged the nation for a whole decade (1966–1976).

Mao's comeback tilted the balance between the party and the state. Prior to 1949, the CCP had an extensive party organization that performed regular government functions in the communist-controlled areas. The party was initially led by a **general secretary**, then by a chairman. The CCP practiced the "democratic centralism" of a typical Leninist party, which meant, in practice, the concentration of power in the hands of a supreme party leader. After the establishment of the People's Republic, the communists began to build a set of state institutions and gradually shifted administrative power to the newly founded government bureaucracies. This process of "normalization" coincided with Beijing's "leaning toward the Soviet Union" and demonstrated, at the time, China's earnest effort to build a society modeled on the well-established Soviet system.

In September 1949, the party began to set up a Central People's Government as the highest organ of state power. Mao was elected its chairman. Under it was the Government Administrative Council headed by **Zhou Enlai**. After the 1954 constitution was promulgated, a National People's Congress was created to serve as the Parliament. The Government Administrative Council became the **State Council** and was responsible to the people's deputies. Zhou Enlai continued to serve as the premier. This arrangement resembled the governing structure of a typical communist country. The Communist Party remained the ultimate source of power and legitimacy. The leader of the party, Chairman Mao in the Chinese case, ruled supreme. The head of government was usually the second most powerful figure in the party-state as long as that position was not taken by the party leader himself.

There was an ill-defined division of labor between the party and the government, with the party initiating policies and guaranteeing their political correctness, and the government implementing those policies. The military also played an important role at this initial stage of the People's Republic. From 1949 to 1952, military administrative committees directly controlled 20 provinces. The power of the generals, however, was curbed by Mao when the political and economic situation of China stabilized. Mao himself headed the party's Central Military Commission (CMC) and directed the People's Liberation Army in that capacity. The government's control of the military (both the People's Revolutionary Military Commission and the National Defense Council) was totally overwhelmed by the party CMC. A firmly established tradition in the PRC is for the party to "command the guns" and for the leader of the party to head the party CMC. The party's control over the military was also guaranteed by recruitment into the party of all officers above the rank of platoon commander, setting up political commissars and political departments in the army, and establishing party committees at the regiment level and above.

The party, the government, and the army are the three power pillars in the PRC. In Table 8.1, we see that it is not always easy to figure out the real paramount leader simply by looking at the official positions held by China's top politicians. The general rule seems to be that the paramount leader always controls the party CMC. This held true until Deng formally gave that position to Jiang at the end of 1989 while still running the show from behind the scenes. That anomaly did not occur during Mao's reign from 1949 to 1976, however, when he was both **chairman of the Central Committee of the Chinese Communist Party** and chairman of its Central Military Commission. That is to say, Mao directly controlled the party and the military. The government was left in the hands of Zhou Enlai, who had risen to the CCP's top leadership earlier than Mao. The 1959 promotion of Liu Shaoqi to state chairman was not an insignificant move, for even though the PRC's head of state was a titular position, Liu's advancement was widely considered to be a sign that Liu, as a moderate, was in line to be Mao's successor, which would have been

TABLE 8.1. China's Top Leaders and Their Positions

	President*	Prime Minister	Communist Party Leader	Chairman of Party CMC	Paramount Leader
1949 Oct.	Mao Zedong	Zhou Enlai	Mao Zedong	Mao Zedong	Mao Zedong
1959 Apr.	Liu Shaoqi				
1968 Oct.	Dong Biwu				
1975 Jan.	Zhu De				
1976 Feb.		Hua Guofeng (acting Feb.–Apr., 1976)			
1976 July	Song Qinglin (acting)				
1976 Oct.			Hua Guofeng	Hua Guofeng	Hua Guofeng
1978 Mar.	Ye Jianyig				
1978 Dec.					Deng Xiaoping
1980 Sept.		Zhao Ziyang			
1981 June			Hu Yaobang (Party Chairman)	Deng Xiaoping	
1982 Sept.			Hu Yaobang (General Secretary)		
1983 June	Li Xiannian				
1987 Jan.			Zhao Ziyang		
1987 Nov.		Li Peng			
1988 Apr.	Yang Shangkun				
1989 June			Jiang Zemin		
1989 Nov.				Jiang Zemin	
1993 Mar.	Jiang Zemin				
1997 Feb.					Jiang Zemin
1998 Mar.		Zhu Rongji			
2002 Nov.			Hu Jintao		
2003 Mar.	Hu Jintao	Wen Jiabao			
2004 Sept.			Hu Jintao		Hu Jintao

* The PRC's president is the state chairman when that position exists (i.e., from 1954 to 1975 and from 1983 on). In the absence of a state chairman, it was the chairman of the National People's Congress who took on the function of the head of state.

consistent with the destalinization campaign unfolding in the Soviet Union. However, Liu's assumption of the state chairmanship proved ominous in view of Mao's vengeful rearguard actions that followed his blunders in the Great Leap Forward. These kinds of power struggles, inherent in communist leadership succession, became entangled with international competition and ideological dispute within China.

Mao's rupture with Khrushchev proved fatal to China's state-building efforts, as he began to whip up local support for his Great Leap Forward and People's Communes. Mao abhorred Soviet-style technocratism and overconcentrated state planning. In 1958, Mao began to delegate very significant power to party cadres in running the economy, which set China apart from the Soviet Union and Eastern European countries, which had a more centrally controlled economy under communist rule. Even though China underwent several rounds of "decentralization-recentralization" in the following years, it never went back to the original planned-economy model that the Soviet advisers had helped China to build during the 1950s. This historical legacy of a decentralized system was later hailed as a unique Chinese advantage for implementing market reform during the 1980s. However, institutionally, the most important development during the 1958 decentralization was the shift of power from state technocrats to party cadres, which was reminiscent of the revolutionary years when they had had an important mission.

Mao's experiment proved disastrous and temporarily diminished his power. As a result, the short interlude between the Great Leap Forward and the launching of the Cultural Revolution saw a temporary revival of state institutions. The stormy politics of the Cultural Revolution, however, again dampened the vitality of government agencies and returned power to party cadres. Mao launched campaigns against the "small clique of capitalist-roaders in power" who were often found in government institutions. Revolutionary committees took the place of the local governments, and direct military control was instituted to curb the excessive infighting among "Red Guard" zealots, militaristic groups of students who had been sent to monitor and brutalize government critics and "class enemies," who Mao himself had unleashed. The normal politics of the 1950s was replaced by the stormy movements of the 1960s. State institutions were attacked, government officials were purged and sent to reeducation camps in China's remote provinces, and millions of intellectuals were humiliated and condemned to forced labor. For Mao, this was a "class struggle." The simple fact remained that Mao did his best to undermine the very institutions that he helped establish during the first decade of the People's Republic.

Even though Mao vehemently attacked the Soviet Union in the ideological battle between the two communist giants, his basic position and policies did not deviate from orthodox Stalinism. As a matter of fact, he based his attacks on Khrushchev's leadership on its betrayal of the original ideals of communism. During the decade of the Cultural Revolution, the personality cult of Mao was carried to absurd lengths. The chairman was hailed as a great hero in all walks of life. He was the greatest military genius, a brilliant and accomplished poet, and a swimmer who broke the world's record. Bountiful harvests could be assured simply by reading the "little red book"

TABLE 8.2. Share of Investment by Industries, 1953–1978

Years	Agriculture	Light Industry	Heavy Industry	Other Industries
First Five-Year Plan (1953–1957)	7.1	6.4	36.2	50.3
Second Five-Year Plan (1958–1962)	11.3	6.4	54.0	28.3
1963–1965	17.6	3.9	45.9	32.6
Third Five-Year Plan (1966–1970)	10.7	4.4	51.1	33.8
Fourth Five-Year Plan (1971–1975)	9.8	5.8	49.6	34.8
1976–1978	10.8	5.9	49.6	33.7

Source: Lin Yifu, Cai Fang, and Li Zhou, *Zhongguo de qiji: fazhan zhanlue yu jingji gaige* (China's Miracle: Developmental Strategy and Economic Reform) (Hong Kong: Chinese University Press, 1995) p. 56.

that recorded the chairman's words. Children were taught not to love their parents but to love Chairman Mao. The whole world was said to admire this great leader of China. Mao actually ruled by terror, exercising it even against his chief lieutenants (most notably State Chairman Liu Shaoqi and Party General Secretary Deng Xiaoping). Public denunciations and beatings at mass rallies were substituted for Soviet-style show trials, with equally fatal consequences for the accused. The Red Guards were Mao's invention, for he lacked organizational means to defeat his opponents in the party-state hierarchy. As a result, the chairman was able to unleash abundant social anger at the regime after the traumatic Great Leap Forward campaign and the resulting famine, directing it toward his intraparty enemies. The devastation was greater than in the Soviet Union, where purges and power struggles were conducted in a more "orderly" manner. On the economic front, Mao mercilessly mobilized China's resources to pursue heavy industrialization, and both agriculture and light industry that directly affected the livelihood of the population were severely neglected (Table 8.2). The developmental priorities were thus the same as in the Soviet Union, although Mao's strategy of spiritual mobilization and absolute egalitarianism were quite counterproductive in the long run. In short, Mao's rule in China was a classical case of totalitarianism, characterized by massive ideological indoctrination, the personality cult of the leader, rule by terror, a state-run economy geared toward heavy industrialization, and disregard of consumers' needs in economic planning. In many respects, Mao's practices were even more excessive than Stalin's.

Deng Unleashes Reform

The conflict between Mao and his political enemies in the leadership was a fight between the leftist radicals and the pro-stability technocrats, between the movement-oriented party and order-conscious state. Here one finds the conflict between two interests (cadres vs. technocrats), two identities (revolution vs. development), and two institutions (party vs. state). With the death of Mao and the political demise of the ultraleftists, a new force emerged that advocated market reform and political relaxation. Those reformers then competed with the technocrats for supremacy. This reform force was easily recognizable when one refers to the post-Stalinist Soviet Union and Eastern Europe. In China, the artificial suppression of the reform momentum during Mao's years meant that when it was finally unleashed, the reform in China came with a vengeance.

The pro-stability technocrats constituted a significant political force in the PRC after the 1950s. However, throughout the Maoist era, they were suppressed by the leftists. Their early leader was Liu Shaoqi, Mao's designated successor. Liu was an organizational man who favored orderly development of the country's economy in the manner of Soviet-style five-year plans. He abhorred the anarchy that Mao's endless campaigns brought about. With regard to basic economic policy, Mao's "red" line insisted on breathtaking growth through ideological movements, whereas the "expert" line of Liu's technocrats emphasized the need for balanced development and allowed modifications of the system in order to improve performance. This "line struggle" was elevated by Mao to the height of "class struggle," and repeated movements were launched from above to ensure that Mao's line was in command.

As the Soviet and Eastern European experiences demonstrate, "totalitarianism" is but a stage in the development of Leninist regimes. Stabilization of the political process and turning to economic reform to improve performance seem to be a natural tendency. In the PRC, however, Mao's political genius and his overwhelming prestige in the party-state artificially delayed the advent of "mature communism." In the 1960s and 1970s, Mao mustered all his vigilance to guard against having the CCP slip into Soviet-style "revisionism" as in the Khrushchev and Brezhnev eras. As a result, the Chinese communist regime delayed its reform stage until the death of its despotic ruler.

Reform was inevitable, however. Mao's revolutionary politics and stormy economic campaigns provided few benefits to either the population at large or to the ruling elite, who were in constant fear of being Mao's next target and were forbidden to enjoy a decent material life. China's economy was on the brink of collapse by the time of Mao's death, suffering from the inefficiencies and rigidities of a socialist planned economy and the irregularities of Mao's unpredictable ideological campaigns. Persistent poverty seriously undermined the regime's legitimacy, particularly when the population compared

China's economic plight with the high-speed growth of neighboring countries in East Asia. On the international front, Mao's radical politics at home antagonized the Soviet Union while forestalling a genuine rapprochement with the United States. Being at odds with both superpowers put the country in a dangerous position internationally. In these circumstances, Beijing's leaders were acutely aware of the fact that a backward economy and a predominantly rural society could not support China's ambition to compete on the world stage. The discrimination against students from the "wrong classes," the absolute demand for equality but not quality, the disdain for intellectuals, and the glorification of manual labor at the expense of formal education devastated the school system and left a whole generation of Chinese youth uneducated. Even the military was indoctrinated in the virtue of the people's war, exulting in ideological correctness and willpower at the expense of absolutely necessary military modernization. China's immense potential to become a great nation in the world was suffocated by Mao's ideology and the endless internal strife perpetuated by it. It became obvious to all but the most radical faction in the CCP elite that things had to change and that reform was necessary to save both the country and the leaders themselves. In order to survive both domestically and internationally, China had to restructure its system and shed the debilitating aspects of Mao's totalitarianism.

The fact that China resisted the advent of reform longer than most other socialist countries foretold the vengeance with which reform would ultimately come. As it turned out, Deng Xiaoping transformed the Chinese economic system much more thoroughly than did Nikita Khrushchev in the Soviet Union. In terms of politics, the personality cult and ruthless persecution of comrades were denounced in reform-era China, much as they had been during periods of reform in the Soviet Union and Eastern Europe. Obviously, this is not democratization but relaxation in a post-totalitarian society, as witnessed by Deng's continued insistence on the leading role of the Communist Party. Stability now hinged on material benefits that the communist regime delivered and on a widespread sense of improvement on the previous decades of impoverishment and rule by terror.

Mao's legacy was dismantled bit by bit. One month after Mao's death in September 1976, the **Gang of Four** (including Mao's wife, Jiang Qing, and three other ultraleftist leaders) were arrested. Two years later, at the historic **Third Plenum of the CCP's Eleventh Central Committee** held in December 1978, the interregnum leader Hua Guofeng was defeated by Deng Xiaoping, and the reform era was ushered in. With the ultraleftists dislodged from power, a schism developed in the anti-Hua coalition. The radical economic reformers, led by Deng and his handpicked lieutenants **Hu Yaobang** (general secretary of the party) and Zhao Ziyang (premier), did not see eye to eye with the technocrats, led by Chen Yun. Although Deng's reform project was a reaction to totalitarian excesses, one can nevertheless find a similar mentality between the ultraleftists and the radical reformers. They all took a pro-growth stance as opposed to the technocrats' pro-stability line. Mao, Hua, and Deng were all proponents of high growth, although they resorted to different means for achieving that same goal: Mao with his Great Leap Forward, Hua with his Great Leap Westward, and Deng with his market reform. The determination of those Chinese communist leaders to achieve super growth had a lot to do with their realization that China was backward and that extraordinary means were necessary for the country to compete effectively in the world. It was under this "surpassing mentality" that the strategic goal of doubling the PRC's industrial and agricultural production by the year 2000 was set at the Twelfth Party Congress in 1982, when the era of reform formally began.

The technocrats thought otherwise. For them, stability of the system was a paramount consideration. Led by Chen Yun in the post-Mao era, the technocrats stressed the need for balanced development, limited spending, and measured growth. After the death of Mao and the short interlude of Hua Guofeng, the technocrats' line temporarily gained dominance in Chen Yun's "adjustment" policy, designed to curb the rash and unbalanced investment surge under Hua's Ten-Year Plan. But Chen's line was in command for only five years (1979–1983). It was then swiftly replaced by Deng's pro-growth marketization drive, implemented by the new prime minister, Zhao Ziyang. With the country on the road to reform – that is, with Deng in command – the technocrats found themselves circumvented, although continuing struggles between the reformers and technocrats testified to the resilience of the latter. Vested interests were also involved in this factional conflict, as inland provinces, production ministries, planning agencies, state enterprises, and other heavily subsidized sectors of the economy naturally loathed radical market reforms, whereas coastal areas, light industries, local governments, and those sectors benefiting from reform measures supported expansion and deepening of the reforms. In this case, ideals and interests were intertwined.

Several economic cycles during the 1980s shaped the balance of power between the pro-growth reformers and the pro-stability technocrats. As a rule, the reformers fueled the economy with expansionary monetary policies and liberalization. High growth was pursued at the expense of macrostability. Under Deng, one saw the failed People's Communes farming system abolished and a realistic household-responsibility system instituted that combined compulsory state procurements with peasant discretion over above-quota produce. Prices of agricultural products increased. Rural markets revived. Township and village enterprises mushroomed. In the cities, one first saw the emergence of millions of small individual businesses (getihu) and then the rapid development of hitherto unthinkable private enterprises. The state enterprises were also reformed, first by raising the profit-retention ratio and then by a contract scheme that resembled the household-responsibility system in the countryside. A tax-for-profit reform was launched in 1983–1984 that was designed to provide level ground for healthy competition. Various kinds of ownership reforms were tested after 1986, culminating in the introduction of stock shares and their free trade in newly opened stock markets. An open-door policy invited a huge inflow of foreign capital that provided timely funding for the rapid growth of the Chinese economy. Indirect foreign investment also surged as international lenders designated China as a promising market. According to the World Bank, China's annual per capita GDP (gross domestic product) growth reached an average of 8 percent between 1978 and 1995. Only South Korea and Taiwan grew at comparable rates (at 6.9 percent and 6.3 percent, respectively).

It is not surprising that high growth brought about inflation and a trade imbalance, as happened in 1985, 1988, and 1993–1994. With wide fluctuations of the economy came episodes of political unrest, the most serious of which were the Beijing Spring of 1986–1987 and the Tiananmen prodemocracy movement of 1989. The first incident brought down the then Secretary General Hu Yaobang and the second one Hu's successor, Zhao Ziyang. The **Tiananmen incident** was a tragic confrontation between student demonstrators demanding political liberties and a communist regime heavily divided between reformers and hard-liners. It showed the destabilizing effect of Deng's reforms, the limits of which were not clearly defined by Deng himself. In an atmosphere of increasing economic liberties and political relaxation, it was only natural that young students would grow impatient with the regime's authoritarian style and demand structural political reforms. Economic mismanagement of the time provided an immediate impetus, while the signs of intraregime schism further emboldened the student activists. The Tiananmen incident was started when students memorialized the death of Hu Yaobang, a bona fide reformer in the regime, and refused to leave the Tiananmen Square in front of Beijing's Forbidden City. The stalemate between the pro-democracy students, whose numbers surged on the square, and the regime continued until Deng ordered a ruthless crackdown and soldiers fired at the unarmed demonstrators on June 4, killing hundreds or thousands of them. The picture of a brave lone man standing in front of an approaching tank column, daring them to run him over, was broadcast around the world and has become the single most powerful image of the Tiananmen suppression. It became clear that once the regime was able to mend its internal division (ousting Zhao, the sympathizer in this instance), the post-totalitarian state found it easy to quell whatever resistance and protest that the young dissidents of China were able to mount against it. However, the fact that the Tiananmen protest did happen and that tanks had to roar and shots be fired in the center of the capital city to quell it demonstrates how Deng's reforms had disturbed political stability in China. From the regime's point of view, obviously reform had gone too far, and something had to be done to prevent the recurrence of another Tiananmen protest.

In the aftermath of Tiananmen, General Secretary Zhao was replaced by Jiang Zemin, a technocrat from Shanghai. In an overall environment of regimentation, the technocrats regained some power, silencing the society with mass arrests and show trials, reimposing strict control over mass media, and launching ideological war against China's peaceful evolution into a "bourgeois democracy." Economically, they reduced investment and tightened the monetary supply, particularly against the nascent private sector. Further reform measures were put on hold. In this way, stability was restored but only at the expense of growth. Seeing his reform enterprise in a quagmire, Deng made a breakthrough tour to the south, wherefrom he relaunched a reform drive. With Deng's active intervention, the reformers resurged and snatched power from the technocrats. The economy entered a high-growth phase again, starting a new cycle.

During the course of relaunching the reform, Premier Li Peng was reprimanded by Deng for his overconservative goal of 6 percent annual growth for the Eighth Five-Year Plan period (1991–1995). After the southern tour, Deng was temporarily triumphant, and the Chinese economy registered double-digit growth rates for four consecutive years. Soon, however, the economy overheated and a new policy of "macroadjustment" came into vogue. The person in charge of this limited austerity program was **Zhu Rongji**. Zhu was widely considered Deng's favorite to succeed Li Peng as the prime minister. This should not blur the fact that there was no substantial difference between him and Li or Jiang. Jiang, Li, and Zhu are all technocrats with a good educational background, and they all consider stability a paramount goal at the PRC's current stage of development. They may belong to different power blocs and may compete vehemently for ascendancy in the post-Deng period, but they are not pro-growth zealots in the mold of the old patriarch. The desperate, extraordinary period of supergrowth has come to an end with the phasing out and, ultimately, the death of Deng. To summarize, Deng's rule in China has left a legacy of unprecedented growth that lifted the largest number of people out of poverty in human history. It also brought about unprecedented economic volatility and political instability. Unparalleled openness to the outside world and increasing influence from the West were accompanied by the creeping return of many traditional aspects of Chinese society, such as the unequal treatment of women in rural areas. Economic reform also enhanced regional disparities and inequalities between the cities and the countryside. In short, growth and openness were gained at the expense of equality and stability.

In comparative terms, Deng's strong reaction to Mao's line was, arguably, comparable with Khrushchev's reform after the death of Stalin. Both carried a movement mentality and focused on institutional innovations. Even though the economic reform of Dengist China went far beyond the scope of the limited market and reorganizational experiments of the Soviet Union under Khrushchev, the prevalent ethos and the impact of radical reform were similar in the two cases. Both the Soviet Union and the PRC were plunged into constant institutional flux by their reform leaders, and powerful technocratic interests were violated.

In the Soviet Union, Khrushchev was ultimately deposed by a rebelling technocracy led by Leonid Brezhnev, the technocrat par excellence, who then ruled with his colleagues in a self-perpetuating **Politburo** for eighteen years during the most stable and immobile period of Soviet history. In mainland China, on the other hand, Deng was able to sustain the reform's momentum through his prestige and masterful maneuvering among central and provincial interests. However, technocratization was a natural tendency for a mature communist regime, just as reform was inevitable after the rule of a revolutionary tyrant, which explains the conservative triumph during the retrenchment period of 1988–1991. And yet, the advent of the technocratic age in China was artificially thwarted by Deng, who, in his famous southern tour of 1992, single-handedly relaunched hypergrowth reform and brought mainland China out of its conservative retrenchment at one stroke, despite opposition by most of his technocratic lieutenants. That phenomenal achievement of Deng, however, should be viewed as the last gasp of radical reform rather than the beginning of a new reform era. At Deng's death, China was ready for entry into the next stage of development: technocratic consolidation.

Jiang Zemin, Hu Jintao, and Neoconservatism

In China, new developmental stages seem to await the physical death of the leader who dominated the earlier stage. For a while, Jiang was considered an opportunist who shifted his opinions to suit the political needs of the time. Thus, his various speeches made in the immediate post-Tiananmen period of 1989–1991 were characterized by the themes of "anti-peaceful evolution" and "socialism or capitalism?" These were ideological themes and were in tune with the conservative backlash of the moment. Within a few years, however, Jiang suddenly became a champion of pro-growth economic reform and stressed repeatedly the need to "prevent the resurgence of the left line." The contrast is sharp but can be explained in terms of Deng's strong pressure on him. After Deng was disabled by poor health (particularly after 1994), however, Jiang began to reveal his innate preferences. "Stability in command" became the regime's motto. Through various administrative and macroeconomic policy instruments, the overheated growth and the accompanying inflation of 1993–1994 were effectively curbed, and the leadership engineered, in 1996, a "soft landing" of the economy that successfully brought down annual inflation to 6.1 percent (from 21.7 percent in 1994 and 14.8 percent in 1995). Economic imbalances were redressed without undue austerity and loss of growth. And yet, with all the good news, Jiang still insisted on stability in early 1997, not succumbing to the temptation of raising the economic growth rate in the year of a party congress. This cautious approach suggests that stability was indeed a paramount consideration for the new secretary general.

Jiang's commitment to stability was also reflected in his insistence that politics should be in command. Initially launched in September 1995, Jiang's slogan of "mindful of politics" became a nationwide campaign in 1996, embraced first by an ardent People's Liberation Army. The purpose of this old-style political campaign was to raise party cadres' political consciousness, something that had become increasingly difficult as economic reform progressed. In this context, Jiang ordered a suppression of the Falungong religious cult, which had been attracting great numbers of practitioners within China and many believers around the world. The cult was originally approved and applauded by the communist regime for its combination of apparently innocuous religious beliefs, spiritual and body exercises, and healing techniques. Soon the ability of Falungong to recruit members from party, government, and military organizations, and to mobilize supporters to stage protests against the regime, terrified Jiang and his associates and led to a large-scale suppression that shocked the world. The underlying cause of the regime's overreaction was its obsession with absolute political control of the society. Put together, one finds that during Jiang's reign, the "soft landing" was to pursue economic stability, while the "mindful of politics" campaign and the suppression of Falungong (let alone continued repression of democracy-movement activists) were designed to ensure political stability through strict control. Both themes testified to the importance of stability in Jiang's mind.

Jiang's rule officially ended at the Sixteenth Party Congress, held in 2002. He was succeeded by Hu Jintao as secretary general. The following year, Wen Jiabao replaced Zhu Rongji as premier. Jiang still held chairmanship of the party's Central Military Commission and exercised great influence from behind the scenes until September 2004. The new Hu-Wen regime is not significantly different from the Jiang-Zhu regime in that both are dominated by technocrats with stability on the top of their agendas. Specifically, the new "fourth-echelon" leadership is keenly aware of the danger of an overheated economy and is determined to crush any political opposition. They differ from Jiang's "third-echelon" leaders only in their younger age, lesser experience, higher educational credentials, and lower prestige.

Jiang and Hu should be viewed less as unique personalities than as representatives of two generations of technocrats who rose to positions of leadership after the rule of revolutionaries (the Maoists) and radical reformers (the Dengists). The new technocratic rulers wielded much less power than their predecessors. Deng was certainly less powerful than Mao, but in many respects these two men were still comparable. The difference between Deng and his successors was much more striking. Except in the area of education, the third- and fourth-echelon leaders led by Jiang and Hu are dwarfed by Deng in all forms of power resources, such as experience, military support, charisma, will to power, vision, self-confidence, and contribution to the establishment and maintenance of the regime. As a result, the personal imprint of Jiang and Hu on Chinese politics and society is markedly lighter than that of Mao or Deng.

Declining personal authority and increasingly technocratic rule seem to be an evolutionary regularity for communist regimes. From a comparative point of view, communist regimes naturally evolved from the stage of totalitarianism, through reform, to technocratic rule. The totalitarian ruler (e.g., Stalin or Mao) launched political and economic campaigns to transform the society. The horrendous human costs that such transformation entailed forced the second-generation rulers to seek a truce with the society and terminate the rule of terror. Material improvements and political relaxation ensued. However, the reformers, in their zeal to redress the excesses of totalitarianism, often went too far, creating instability with constant institutional restructuring and risking the regime's political control over the society. The cadres' huge vested interest was also undermined. All of this prompted reactions from the technocrats.

Just as the reformers naturally acted against the extremes of revolutionary enthusiasm, the technocrats by their nature sought to bring about stability (on both the individual and regime levels and in both political and economic senses), which had been undermined by radical reform measures. In form, this seemed like a partial return to totalitarianism, but in essence the emergent technocratic rule was a conservative backlash against both revolution (the first stage) and reform (the second stage). The purpose of the regime was no longer to remold the society, or to redress the atrocities of the past and catch up with the world, but simply to keep things as they stood, particularly to keep the communist regime in power. This was what the Brezhnevite era meant in the Soviet Union.

The same development has dawned on China. The death of Deng Xiaoping and the political ascendancy of Jiang Zemin signified the advent of the technocratic era. Jiang and his colleagues of the "third-echelon leadership" had more formal and technical education than their predecessors. Hu and the "fourth-echelon leadership" in turn received even higher education than Jiang and his associates. All of those people were products of an established technocratic system and not its creators or builders. Their experience was typically concentrated on one functional area, and that usually was not military affairs. As technocrats, Jiang, Hu, and their comrades sitting on the CCP's Politburo were intrinsically more interested in preserving the status quo and pursuing stability than exploring new reform frontiers. In this sense, whether it was Jiang or any other technocrat to succeed Deng is not really important, as communist technocratic rulers basically behave in similar ways. They have a realistic understanding of the popular desire for material betterment, they loathe destruction in the name of revolution and the institutional flux brought about by radical reform, and they want to absorb Western technology and capital, but they abhor pluralistic ideas and democracy. When faced with a choice between economic development and political stability, they would overwhelmingly opt for the latter. The contrast with Russia's choice under Gorbachev of democratization before economic reform could not be more apparent.

The advent of a technocratic era has been fostered by the country's economic development. The urgency under which Deng pursued his reform programs has diminished over time. Mainland China's annual economic growth rate averaged 9.5 percent over 18 years (1979–1996), and the size of its economy is predicted to surpass that of the United States in the early twenty-first century. The desperate need to grow at breathtaking speed has been reduced. At the same time, the anxiety over the grave costs accompanying rapid growth has increased. The link between a heated economy and political disturbance has been recognized by the ruling elite, with Tiananmen serving as a vivid reminder. Because growth is more or less taken for granted, the paramount consideration is naturally stability, both economic and political. This developmental feature plays into the hands of the technocrats, who treasure stability as the primary policy goal of the regime. Thus, when Jiang outlined his blueprint for governing China, he treated stability as a precondition for development and reform, a lesson he said he had gained only with painful experience. In this regard, Hu and Wen followed in Jiang's footsteps, putting a brake on economic growth whenever there is a sign of overheating.

Besides evolutionary necessity and economic prosperity, there is a third major reason that links the Jiang and Hu regimes to stability. As has been mentioned, the new leaders were much weaker than their predecessors (Jiang being much weaker than Deng, and Hu in turn being much weaker than Jiang). This means that their ability to initiate and implement new policies against the entrenched interests – ministerial, military, regional, and others – was much smaller than when Mao or Deng ruled. Stability, then, was the default outcome, the result of inaction.

The post-Deng era is characterized by technocratic rule and stability. Power struggles increasingly take a purely factional form, in which political leaders clash not over ideological lines, or a pro-growth versus pro-stability development strategy, but over personal power and prestige. Very much like Brezhnev, Jiang was first among equals (and Hu is even less, still struggling to define his relation with Jiang, his former mentor) rather than a strongman like Mao or Deng. Certainly the PRC's economy grows much faster than its erstwhile Soviet or Eastern European counterparts, and China's political control is a bit looser, but the pro-stability technocratic mentality is the same in post-Deng China as in the Soviet Union under Brezhnev. Nothing appeals to party cadres, state officials, and managers of state enterprises more than job security, and nothing attracts communist leaders in a postideological age better than a secure political career. Here lies the appeal of stability. Communist technocrats were suppressed in both the revolutionary and reform periods, for Mao and Deng were committed to transformation of the society, albeit in opposite directions. With Jiang and Hu, technocrats par excellence, acting as the core of the leadership, pro-stability technocrats in the PRC finally have their way.

Although consolidation and technocratic rule are common to the evolution of the Soviet/Eastern European and Chinese communist regimes, there are differences in the ways in which stability was pursued in the two cases. First, the Soviet planned economy under Stalin was not as discredited as Mao's improvised economic models. Consequently, the Soviet and Eastern European economic reforms concentrated on perfecting the existing system and/or limited market socialism, whereas the Chinese reform moved beyond those schemes and embraced large-scale marketization and privatization. Those basic structures formed the background for technocratic rule in the two cases. The Soviet and Eastern European model was characterized by static equilibrium, allowing a secure political career for cadres and job security for managers. The Chinese model, on the other hand, aimed at securing reasonable growth (although not to the extent of inviting inflation) to guarantee stability or dynamic equilibrium. This means enterprises are under constant market pressure and no managers enjoy tenure. Because preservation of the communist regime is the ultimate goal, economic dynamism is coupled with tight political control. Here one finds the ostensible discrepancy of economic reform and political conservatism. These two phenomena, however, are a logical pair for preserving the rule of the Chinese party-state under technocratic rule. In order to invigorate all levels of political leadership, the Chinese even designed a system of generational replacement whereby senior leaders were retired when they reached a certain age set for specific levels of posts in the party-state hierarchy. Thus, for example, the retirement age for the provincial and ministerial cadres is set at 60, and the age limit for top party leadership is 70. There are exceptions, of course, to those rigid retirement rules, including Jiang's continued presence at the party's Central Military Commission until September 2004. However, forced rejuvenation of the ruling apparatus with the generational replacement principle has become a hallmark of Chinese technocratic rule and sets it apart from the petrification of leadership in the former Soviet and Eastern European communist regimes.

In sum, the Chinese technocratic rule that emerged from Mao's stormy revolutionary politics and Deng's precarious reformism is more open and more adaptable to changing domestic and international environments than its Soviet and Eastern European predecessors. This being said, however, one still needs to recognize that the current Chinese leadership consists of technocratic rulers who are primarily interested in preserving the party-state's monopoly of power with coercion and economic performance, just like their erstwhile European comrades. They are pragmatic, authoritarian rulers separable from the first (revolutionary) and second (reform) leaderships by great differences in age, experience, values, and educational background. Chinese communism has matured into a variant of the East Asian developmental state that is constantly shedding the communist features and adopting the statist ones. However it changes, it remains staunchly authoritarian and undemocratic.

Will China Become Democratic?

Although the communist regimes developed through concrete stages within the basic one-party structure, this does not mean that democratization is impossible in the long run. However, academic discussion on this issue is usually shaped by the current situation, thus projecting into the future a fixed picture of the present.

Discussion of China's political future after the Tiananmen Square protests of 1989 has shifted focus with the apparent increased stability of the communist regime. Although in the immediate wake of the Tiananmen crisis a complete breakdown of the system was predicted, with the consolidation of the post-1989 power structure, less dramatic scenarios have been presented. Among the latter one finds a revival of the "neoauthoritarianism" theme, which depicts mainland China's future in the light of the East Asian capitalist-authoritarian model, Taiwan and South Korea in particular. Some scholars argue that, although direct democratization is unlikely and even undesirable, a two-step transition through an intermediary phase of enlightened authoritarianism toward the ultimate destination of democracy should be welcomed. China's introduction of competitive (though not multiparty) elections at the village level is seen, from this perspective, as a particularly encouraging sign, which shows mainland China gradually evolving toward political pluralism following Taiwan's model. Since 1949, local economic and political experiments have been used as the basis from which to reorganize China. The introduction of democratically elected villagers' committees thus carries significance far beyond its immediate impact in the rural areas. A dual power structure has been created in which the villagers' committee is developing into a democratic executive apparatus to manage day-to-day politics, while the party branch has come to be responsible for general policy, and it intervenes if "necessary" by using its ties to township or county governments. Optimists predict that power would gradually migrate from the party branch to the villagers' committee and bring the countryside closer to genuine grassroots democracy. Experiments have been conducted that extend competitive elections up to the township level, a sign for further optimism. These optimistic opinions are a variant on the theme of the time-honored modern-ization theory, which predicts a universal pluralistic outcome for authoritarian systems undergoing rapid economic development.

Among the less dramatic scenarios is a reprise of the "neoconservatism" theme that popped up during the "retrenchment" period in the early 1990s. In the more rigid political and economic atmosphere after the Tiananmen protests, especially in light of the difficulties facing Russia after its demo-cratic transition, this "neoconservative" theme emphasizes order and stabil-ity and harkens back to traditional values, as opposed to the radical reforms of the previous decade. Neoconservatism argues that social progress is best accomplished through a gradual reform of society. It eschews revolution and the sudden overthrow of government. It is asserted that historically in China progress was always made gradually. Revolutionary ruptures from the past without exception begot disasters, as shown in Mao's Great Leap Forward, the Cultural Revolution, and the Tiananmen protests. Neoconservatives gen-erally support the regime and predict long-term stability under the current system. Which scenario of the three (regime breakdown, neoauthoritarian-ism, or neoconservatism) is more likely to be China's future? In order to answer this question, we have to move back to the big picture and read again the country's historical trajectory.

China's political development has always been heavily influenced by the global context in which the country found itself. The emergence of the na-tionalists and communists as the competing political forces in China was embedded in the country's desire to regain its power and rightful place in a challenging international environment. The KMT and the CCP adopted dif-ferent developmental models from abroad to revive China. Because the KMT regime lost the civil war and has been highly dependent on the United States, its development on Taiwan witnessed a gradual shedding of the statist system and an adoption of liberal-democratic institutions. The mainland moved into a comparable point in Taiwan's past when it realized that the Soviet/Maoist system was totally ineffective for China to compete in the world and for the communist regime to hold onto power. It has decisively shifted to a statist model, with authoritarian politics and developmental economic policies, and this new model has specific implications that favor the growth of liberalism.

Global competition will force China to maintain its openness to the world and sustain its market reforms. But China will not soon become a democracy. In the short run, the legitimacy of the regime will be buttressed by superb economic performance. In the long run, rapid economic development will nurture social forces that are difficult to contain in an authoritarian polit-ical environment. When China reaches a stage at which economic growth inevitably slows down while at the same time the structural changes go deep enough to arouse strong political participation for liberalization, then the pressure for democracy will greatly increase. As China is not as dependent on a liberal hegemony as Taiwan is, the route toward democratization will take much longer and will encounter greater difficulties. Nevertheless, the possibility of China's becoming a liberal, democratic system should not be dismissed under its current image of a successful, authoritarian, developmental state.

China (including Taiwan) made a historical detour away from the original pursuit of liberal democracy in the early days of the Republic of China, through the choice of statist authoritarianism (from the founding of the ROC to the mid-1980s) or communist totalitarianism (post-1949 PRC) as the major development strategy, and finally to the adoption of the liberal formula (Taiwan) or a gradual approach to it (mainland China). China's developmental trajectory has been, to a large extent, determined by a challenging international environment that forces different political actors representing different interests to respond. Urban intellectuals, the KMT, and the CCP spoke for different class interests, opted for different identities, and developed different institutional preferences. The lack of organization and power by the urban intellectuals doomed their effort to bring about a liberal democracy in China in the early years of the republican period. The authoritarian model that the KMT chose was imposed on the country before 1949 but was then transplanted to Taiwan when the KMT lost the civil war to the communists. American pressure and international competition later persuaded the KMT to embrace liberal democracy and abandon its authoritarian past. The Democratic Progressive Party's political ascendancy and the election of its presidential candidate, Chen Shui-bian, in 2000 and 2004 ended the KMT's half-century rule and testify to the democratic maturity of the ROC. On the Chinese mainland, the CCP's 1949 victory foretold the inauguration of a communist-totalitarian regime modeled on the Soviet Union. Ensuing economic disasters and the pressure of international competition prompted the leadership to embrace the authoritarian model, but not until the death of Mao Zedong. The natural tendency toward pluralism inherent in market reforms has already planted seeds of political liberalization in China, even though that tendency is now being resisted by a technocratic regime that treasures stability more than anything else and holds fast to its vested interests.

In short, as in other developing countries, different political forces in China competed for ascendancy as the country faced international challenges. Those different political forces represented distinct interests, developed alternative identities, and proposed competing institutions. The outcome of their competition shaped the developmental route of China, and that outcome was, in turn, contingent on the international environment in which China found itself. The momentum for political development in China has derived from its quest for national survival and the rigors of global competition. China differed from other cases in the developing world mainly in the immense dimensions of the country, not in the nature of its response. As such, China's political development can be best understood from a global and comparative perspective, and it is also from this perspective that one can evaluate the possibility of China becoming a democracy in the future.

BIBLIOGRAPHY

Dittmer, Lowell. *China's Continuous Revolution: The Post-Liberation Epoch, 1949–1981*. Berkeley: University of California Press, 1987.

Dittmer, Lowell, and Yu-Shan Wu. "The Modernization of Factionalism in Chinese Politics." *World Politics* 47, no. 4 (1995): 467–494.

Fewsmith, Joseph. *Dilemmas of Reform in China*. Armonk, NY: M. E. Sharpe, 1994.

Friedrich, Carl J., and Zbigniew K. Brzezinski. *Totalitarian Dictatorship and Autocracy*. New York: Praeger, 1963.

Gerschenkron, Alexander. *Economic Backwardness in Historical Perspective*. Cambridge, MA: The Belknap Press of Harvard University Press, 1962.

Gold, Thomas. *State and Society in the Taiwan Miracle*. Armonk, NY: M. E. Sharpe, 1986.

Johnson, Chalmers. *Peasant Nationalism and Communist Power*. Stanford, CA: Stanford University Press, 1962.

Jowitt, Ken. "Inclusion and Mobilization in European Leninist Regimes." *World Politics* 28, no. 1 (1975): 69–96.

Jowitt, Ken. "Soviet Neotraditionalism: The Political Corruption of a Leninist Regime." *Soviet Studies* 35, no. 3 (1983): 275–297.

Lee, Hong Yung. *From Revolutionary Cadres to Party Technocrats in Socialist China*. Berkeley: University of California Press, 1991.

Lowenthal, Richard. "Development Versus Utopia in Communist Policy." In Chalmers Johnson, ed. *Change in Communist Systems*. Stanford, CA: Stanford University Press, 1970.

Lowenthal, Richard. "The Post-Revolutionary Phase in China and Russia." *Studies in Comparative Communism* 14, no. 3 (1983): 191–201.

Meaney, Constance Squires. "Is the Soviet Present China's Future?" *World Politics* 39, no. 2 (1987): 203–230.

Nathan, Andrew. "A Factionalism Model for CCP Politics." *China Quarterly* 53 (1973): 34–66.

Shirk, Susan. *The Political Logic of Economic Reform in China*. Berkeley: University of California Press, 1993.

White, Gordon. *Riding the Tiger: The Politics of Economic Reform in Post-Mao China*. Stanford, CA: Stanford University Press, 1993.

Wu, Yu-Shan. *Comparative Economic Transformations: Mainland China, Hungary, the Soviet Union, and Taiwan*. Stanford, CA: Stanford University Press, 1994.

Wu, Yu-Shan. "Jiang and After: Technocratic Rule, Generational Replacement and Mentor Politics." In Yun-han Chu, Chih-cheng Lo, and Ramon H. Myers, eds. *The New Chinese Leadership: Challenges and Opportunities after the 16th Party Congress*. Cambridge: Cambridge University Press, 2004.

Zheng, Shiping. *Party vs. State in Post-1949 China: The Institutional Dilemma*. Cambridge: Cambridge University Press, 1997.

TABLE 8.3. Key Phases in Chinese Political Development (Rule Separates Mainland China from Taiwan)

Time Period	Regime	Global Context	Interests/Identities/ Institutions	Mode of Development
1644–1911	Qing dynasty	expansion of Western imperialism	imperial rulers vs. modernizers/ Confucianism/ traditional authoritarian institutions	sporadic reform
1912–1928	Republic of China (rise and fall of warlordism)	rising Japanese imperialism	warlords, KMT, CCP/traditionalism, nationalism, communism/warlord regimes	(country in disunity)
1929–1949	Republic of China (KMT authoritarianism)	rising Japanese imperialism and outright invasion	KMT vs. CCP/nationalism vs. communism/ authoritarian developmental state	authoritarian development
1949–1978	People's Republic of China (Maoism)	Cold War	CCP/revolutionary Marxism-Leninism-Maoism/totalitarian state	totalitarianism
1978–1997	People's Republic of China (Dengism)	end of Cold War and globalization	Reforming CCP/socialism with Chinese characteristics/ post-totalitarian party-state, provinces	authoritarian capitalist development
1997–present	People's Republic of China (Post-Deng)	globalization	neoconservative CCP/Chinese nationalism/nationalist party-state, provinces	authoritarian capitalist development
1949–1987	Republic of China (on Taiwan, party-state)	Cold War	KMT and business interests/Chinese nationalism/ authoritarian development state	authoritarian capitalist development
1987–present	Republic of China (on Taiwan, democratic)	globalization	Pro-unification and pro-independence interests, high-tech industry/liberal-democratic values, Taiwanese nativism/state and parties	liberalism and growing Taiwanese nationalism

IMPORTANT TERMS

chairman of the Central Committee of the Chinese Communist Party
the paramount leader of the CCP from the Seventh Party Congress of April
1945, when that position was instituted, to September 1982, when that position
was abolished. Three persons have assumed that position: Mao Zedong, from
April 1945 until his death in September 1976; Hua Guofeng, from October 1976
to June 1981, when he resigned at the Sixth Plenum of the Eleventh Central
Committee; and Hu Yaobang, from June 1981 to September 1982, when the
Twelfth Party Congress abolished the chairmanship.

Chen Yun an important leader in the Chinese Communist Party who was particularly powerful during the First Five-Year Plan period (1953–1957) and during
the "adjustment" period that followed Mao's disastrous Great Leap Forward.
Chen was a worker with no formal education when he joined the communist
movement. After the founding of the People's Republic of China, Chen became
the most important cadre in charge of economic construction. He was purged
during the Cultural Revolution but was rehabilitated when Deng Xiaoping came
to power in 1979. He then resumed the leading role in directing China's economic reconstruction during 1979–1983. After 1983, he quarreled seriously with
Deng and the radical market reformers, insisting on a "birdcage economy," by
which he meant that the market should be given somewhat of a free hand. Chen
represented the pro-stability technocrats.

Chiang Ching-kuo son of Chiang Kai-shek, and his successor. He was sympathetic to the communist cause when he was young and spent 12 years in the
Soviet Union. Because of his father's anticommunist policy, Ching-kuo was kept
as a hostage by Stalin and prevented from returning to China. After his eventual return in 1937, Ching-kuo became an able lieutenant to his father. After the
ROC's displacement to Taiwan, Ching-kuo headed the China Youth Corps, the
political department in the national army, and the defense ministry. He finally
became the premier in 1971 and succeeded his father as the KMT chairman in
1975 and ROC president in 1978. Ching-kuo led Taiwan through the turbulent
1970s, when the ROC faced international isolation and global economic recession. Toward the end of his rule, Ching-kuo initiated political reforms and lifted
martial law in 1987. He died in 1988.

Chiang Kai-shek the KMT's supreme leader, who succeeded Dr. Sun Yat-sen
in 1926. Chiang led the Northern Expedition to unify China in 1928 and purged
the communists from the KMT. He was forced to stop his annihilation campaign
against the communists after the Xi'an incident of December 25, 1936, when
Chiang Kai-shek was kidnapped. Chiang then led China's resistance war against
the Japanese to victory but was defeated by the communists in the civil war
that followed. He then led the nationalist government to Taiwan and ruled the
displaced ROC in the island country until his death in 1975.

Chinese Communist Party (CCP) founded in 1921 as a part of the international communist movement. From the very beginning, the CCP was heavily
influenced by the Communist International, the international organization of
Communist Parties founded by Lenin in 1919. Its organization, guidelines, and
leadership were to a great extent determined by Moscow. In 1922, the CCP
members were instructed by the Soviets to join Dr. Sun Yat-sen's KMT to form
a united front against the warlords, powerful individuals who had seized control

of land through military might. This KMT–CCP collaboration was short-lived, as the death of Sun and the launch of the Northern Expedition, the military campaign led by Chiang Kai-shek in 1927 intended to unify China under KMT rule, caused an open split between Chiang Kai-shek and the communists over leadership in the revolutionary movement. The communists then organized riots in the rural areas and saw their bases annihilated by the KMT army one by one. The incoming Japanese invasion saved the CCP, as Chiang was not able to concentrate on mopping up the communists. Under the leadership of Mao Zedong, the CCP was able to mobilize peasant nationalism, and it defeated the KMT after the surrender of Japan. The CCP then founded the People's Republic of China in 1949 and it remains the ruling party in China.

Cultural Revolution Great Proletarian Cultural Revolution, the great political upheaval in the PRC that lasted for a decade (1966–1976). Touched off by Mao's effort to regain political influence after the disastrous Great Leap Forward, the Cultural Revolution was ostensibly aimed at uprooting the traditional Chinese culture that was accused of undermining the communist revolution. The concrete targets were party cadres, state officials, and intellectuals whom Mao and the radicals found threatening to their power. Liu Shaoqi, Mao's designated heir and state chairman; Deng Xiaoping, the CCP's secretary general; and many other prominent leaders were purged. During the revolution, the state was paralyzed, the educational system destroyed, and production seriously disrupted. Young students were recruited into the "Red Guard" brigades and dubbed "rightful rebels" by Chairman Mao. They finally came into serious conflict with the army and were expelled to the countryside for correction. The Cultural Revolution brought unimaginable damage to China, but paradoxically, it also laid a solid groundwork for the post-Mao reforms, as the disrupted planned economy of China proved much more conducive to market reforms than the more rigid economic system in the Soviet Union and Eastern European socialist countries.

Deng Xiaoping paramount leader of the Chinese Communist Party from 1979 to 1997. Deng was originally a lieutenant to Mao and was appointed the CCP's general secretary in 1956. He was purged during the Cultural Revolution but rehabilitated in 1973, purged again in 1976, and rehabilitated again in 1977. Deng was a pragmatist; thus, he opposed Mao's ultraleft line, which caused his downfalls. However, with the death of Mao, Deng was able to gain political ascendancy and directed China toward a structural economic reform. The inefficient People's Communes were abolished, a limited market economy was introduced, foreign capital was invited, stock markets were opened, special economic zones were set up, industrial ownership rights were restructured, and people's living standards were significantly improved. Deng's economic liberalism, however, does not mean that he was pro-democracy, as witnessed by his order to crush the pro-democracy movement in Tiananmen Square in 1989. Deng died in 1997.

Gang of Four four ultraleftist leaders who were most prominent under Mao Zedong during the Cultural Revolution period. The four were Jiang Qing, Mao's wife and a Politburo member; Yao Wenyuan, Mao's son-in-law and a Politburo member; Vice Chairman of the CCP Wang Hongwen; and Vice Premier Zhang Chunqiao. They formed a faction against the old cadres, such as those of Liu Shaoqi, Zhou Enlai, Deng Xiaoping, and Chen Yun. After Mao's death in

September 1976, the Gang of Four attempted to seize party leadership but was thwarted by Hua Guofeng. They were arrested in October and put on trial for high treason.

general secretary the top leader of the Chinese Communist Party. From the Fourth (January 1925) to the Fifth Party Congress (April 1927), Chen Duxiu was the general secretary of the CCP. After the KMT purged the communists, Qu Qiubai, Xiang Zhongfa, Chin Bangxian, and Zhang Wentian assumed that position successively before Mao Zedong discarded it at the Seventh Party Congress in 1945 and led the CCP as chairman of its Central Committee. However, the Eighth Party Congress reinstituted the title of general secretary and elected Deng Xiaoping to fill the position, which was reduced to that of chief lieutenant to the party chairman and in charge of the secretariat, rather than that of the party's paramount leader. After Deng's purge during the Cultural Revolution, the position was again abolished. At the Twelfth Party Congress of 1982, Hu Yaobang was elected general secretary, but he was obviously beholden to Deng, who was then the paramount leader of the CCP. Finally, Zhao Ziyang (October 1987) and Jiang Zemin (June 1989) were elected general secretary under Deng's auspices. With the death of Deng, general secretary again became the most important position in the party, a situation that changed when Jiang retired at the Sixteenth Party Congress in 2002 but managed to keep the post of chairman of the party's military commission. The new secretary general, Hu Jintao, had been designated Jiang's successor by Deng when the old patriarch was still alive. With the partial succession of Jiang by Hu in 2002, the new secretary general was nevertheless still beholden to his predecessor, until Jiang's full retirement in 2004.

Great Leap Forward Mao's greatest economic adventure. During the First Five-Year Plan period (1953–1957), the PRC adopted the Soviet model and built a centrally planned economy to boost economic growth. Toward the end of that period, serious bottlenecks developed and Mao was impatient. His solution was to mobilize human labor through ideological agitation and plunge the whole population into production campaigns. The goal was to surpass Europe and the United States in industrial production. The Great Leap Forward brought unprecedented famine and the death of three million Chinese people.

Hu Jintao secretary general of the CCP since the Sixteenth Party Congress of November 2002 and president of the People's Republic of China since the Tenth National People's Congress of March 2003. Hu assumed the post of chairman of the powerful Central Military Commission of the party in September 2004. Hu was designated Jiang's successor by Deng and promoted to the all-powerful Politburo Standing Committee at the Fourteenth Party Congress in 1992 as its youngest member. Prior to his transfer to the PBSC, Hu was a graduate of the prestigious Tsinghua University and trained as a water-conservancy engineer. He spent a great amount of time serving in leading posts in China's remote provinces of Gansu, Guizhou, and Tibet, and he headed the Communist Youth League of China. He is the "core" of the fourth-echelon leadership and a technocrat par excellence.

Hu Yaobang one of Deng Xiaoping's major lieutenants during the reform era, whose death in 1989 touched off unprecedented massive demonstrations for political reform in Tiananmen Square. Hu first succeeded Hua Guofeng as the

CCP's chairman in 1981; then, at the Twelfth Party Congress in 1982, he was elected secretary general of the party. From 1982 to 1986, Hu faithfully executed Deng's reform policies and earned himself a liberal reputation. However, Hu was considered too soft toward dissident intellectuals by Deng, and in January 1987 he was removed from the position of general secretary.

Jiang Zemin former secretary general of the CCP and successor to Zhao Ziyang. Jiang was the CCP's Shanghai party secretary when the Tiananmen incident broke out in June 1989. He was chosen to replace Zhao Ziyang because he had been successful in combining economic reform with a tough political stance against "bourgeois liberalism" in both December 1986 and June 1989 without resorting to force. Jiang's strengths also included his being an outsider and not beholden to any of Beijing's entrenched factions. He took the position of chairman of the party's military commission in November 1989, and he was elected president of the PRC in 1993. After the death of Deng Xiaoping in February 1997, Jiang's leading position in the CCP became indisputable. He was replaced by Hu Jintao as secretary general at the Sixteenth Party Congress of November 2002.

Kuomintang (KMT) or Chinese Nationalist Party, the ruling party in the Republic of China until May 2000. The KMT had its precedents in *Xingzhonghui* (Society for Regenerating China) and *Tongmenghui* (Society of Common Cause), the two revolutionary organizations aimed at overthrowing the Qing dynasty. After the founding of the ROC, Dr. Sun Yat-sen first transformed *Tongmenghui* into a parliamentary party, the Nationalist Party, and then remade it into the Chinese Revolutionary Party when he saw no hope of practicing democracy in a China plagued by warlord politics. In 1919, Dr. Sun again transformed the Chinese Revolutionary Party into the Chinese Nationalist Party (Kuomintang, KMT) and then in 1924 reorganized it on the Soviet model. The new KMT was equipped with a centralized party organization, special departments targeting specific groups in the population, and the National Revolutionary Army. After the death of Dr. Sun, Chiang Kai-shek became the paramount leader of the KMT and, in that capacity, dictated politics in the ROC. When the ROC was displaced to Taiwan in 1949, Chiang continued to lead the KMT-ROC party-state until his death in 1975, after which his son Ching-kuo assumed the party's leadership. In 1988, Ching-kuo died and Lee Teng-hui took over. Lee Taiwanized the KMT and led the party to victory in all of the major elections on the national level after having successfully democratized the ROC. The March 2000 presidential election defeat by the KMT's candidate, Lien Chan, threw the party into disarray. That debacle was repeated in the March 2004 presidential election in which Lien was for a second time defeated by his DPP (Democratic Progressive Party) opponent, Chen Shui-bian. The KMT remained an opposition party in the ROC.

Long March the retreat of the communist forces of Mao Zedong from the nationalist army after the annihilation campaign of 1934. After the communists had been purged from the KMT in 1925, the CCP organized riots and set up many "Soviet regions." The KMT then launched five annihilation campaigns against them. In 1934, the largest Soviet region in Jiangxi was overrun by the KMT troops, and the communists were forced to flee from their base with the nationalist army in hot pursuit across southwest China over the most difficult terrain with the most hostile environment. After the Long March, Mao's forces ultimately settled in Yan'an of Shan'xi Province.

Mao Zedong leader of the Chinese Communist Party from 1935 until his death in 1976. Mao espoused an unorthodox strategy of revolution in China that emphasized the importance of the peasants and land reform and the need to "encircle the cities from the countryside." That strategy at first found no favor with the party leaders, but after the Moscow-sponsored leadership had failed to thwart the KMT's onslaught in 1934 and the whole party had been forced to flee, Mao captured the military leadership at the Zunyi Conference in 1935. Mao's strategy brought about the CCP's victory over the KMT, and he became the party chairman. After the founding of the People's Republic of China, Mao continued to apply his guerrilla-warfare strategy to economic development, causing the famine and destruction of the Great Leap Forward. His refusal to give up power was followed by his launch of the Cultural Revolution, which threw China into a decade of political chaos. Mao died in 1976.

People's Republic of China (PRC) the socialist country founded in 1949 and ruled by the Chinese Communist Party. The PRC has had five paramount leaders of the country and the CCP since its founding: Mao Zedong (1949–1976), Hua Guofeng (1977–1978), Deng Xiaoping (1979–1997), Jiang Zemin (1998–2004), and Hu Jintao (2005–). During Mao's rule, the PRC had a totalitarian regime. Since Deng, however, the country has gradually shifted to an authoritarian system.

Politburo the organ in the Chinese Communist Party where the real power resides. The CCP follows the Soviet model in its power structure. Ostensibly, the Party Congress is the source of ultimate power in the party. However, under the practice of Lenin's "democratic centralism," the real power migrates to the Central Committee, which the Congress elects, and then to the Politburo, which the Central Committee elects. The Politburo is headed by the general secretary and is composed of the highest-ranking officials from the party and the government. The Politburo has a Standing Committee, which assumes the power of the Politburo when it is not in session. The current (Sixteenth Party Congress) Standing Committee of the Politburo is composed of nine members: Hu Jintao, Wu Bangguo, Wen Jiabao, Jia Qinglin, Zeng Qinghong, Huang Ju, Wu Guanzheng, Li Changchun, and Luo Gan. These nine people are the most powerful leaders in the PRC.

Qing dynasty the last imperial dynasty in China (1644–1911). The Qing dynasty was founded by the Manchus, who originally lived in the northeastern part of China outside the Great Wall (Manchuria). In the middle of the seventeenth century, they invaded the Ming Empire to the south, captured the capital city of Beijing, and established their own rule all over China. The original emperors of the Qing dynasty – Kangxi, Yongzheng, and Qianlong – were able rulers who contributed greatly to the consolidation of the Manchu reign in China. When the Western powers arrived, however, the Qing dynasty was already showing signs of decline but was able to survive military defeats at the hands of foreigners, unequal treaties, domestic rebellions, and a bankrupting economy for the next 80 years. In 1911, the Qing dynasty was overthrown by a revolutionary movement led by Dr. Sun Yat-sen.

Republic of China (ROC) the country founded in 1912 by Dr. Sun Yat-sen. The ROC suffered from warlord politics and did not reach genuine political unification until after the Northern Expedition (1925–1928) led by Chiang Kai-shek. After the communists defeated the nationalists in the Chinese civil war, the ROC retreated to Taiwan, an island province off the eastern coast of China. From the 1950s to the 1980s, Taiwan was an authoritarian country with a thriving market economy. Since the late 1980s, its political system has been democratized.

State Council the central government of the People's Republic of China. The State Council's predecessor was the Government Administrative Council, headed by Zhou Enlai, which was set up in 1949. After the 1954 constitution was promulgated, the Government Administrative Council became the State Council, and Zhou remained the premier until his death in 1976. The State Council is headed by the premier, who is usually the second most important person in the PRC.

Sun Yat-sen the founding father of the Republic of China, who led a revolutionary movement to overthrow the Manchu (Qing) dynasty in 1912. When the ROC disintegrated into warring regions, Dr. Sun founded the Kuomintang (KMT), built a power base in the southern province of Guangdong, and began inviting Soviet advisers to his camp. He died in 1925 before China was unified under the KMT.

Third Plenum of the CCP's Eleventh Central Committee the historic party meeting held in December 1978 that ushered in the reform era in post-Mao China. At the meeting, Deng Xiaoping saw his political influence greatly expand as his lieutenants were elected to the Central Committee, and his line, the "four modernizations," was substituted for Mao's "treating class struggle as the major link." Hua Guofeng's authority as paramount leader was undermined with the institution of a collective leadership. The CCP's historians treat the Third Plenum as the turning point in the party's development. It signifies the shift from the totalitarian stage to the reform stage in China's post-1949 political development.

Three Principles of the People Dr. Sun Yat-sen's political philosophy of nationalism, democracy, and people's livelihood, with the last principle denoting a pragmatic program that emphasizes the combination of private entrepreneurship and active state involvement in economic development. This doctrine is by nature a liberal program for reconstructing China. It is enshrined in the constitution of the Republic of China.

Tiananmen incident the massive student pro-democracy movement of June 1989 and its brutal suppression. Deng Xiaoping's reforms during the 1980s opened up China to the world, but rapid economic growth was accompanied by omnipresent corruption and rising expectations for greater political liberties. Fluctuations in the economy fueled public dissatisfaction, and students became inspired by Western, especially U.S., democracy. Hu Yaobang's death and the visits to China by U.S. President George Bush and the Soviet communist leader Mikhail Gorbachev also came into play. The convergence of these factors in the summer of 1989 brought Beijing's college students to the streets and to Tiananmen Square, demanding fundamental political reforms. After a protracted stalemate between the students and the authorities that lasted for a month, martial law was declared and the troops moved in on June 4. Great casualties running in the thousands were reported.

Zhao Ziyang one of Deng Xiaoping's major lieutenants, who from 1983 to 1989 was mainly in charge of economic reform. Zhao succeeded Hua Guofeng as premier in 1980. After the purge of Hu Yaobang in 1987, he was promoted to general secretary of the CCP. His "soft" attitude toward the students in the summer of 1989 cost him his job. After the June 4 suppression of the pro-democracy movement, Zhao was replaced by Jiang Zemin.

Zhou Enlai China's prime minister from 1949 to January 1976. Zhou was a senior CCP leader who directed the political department at Whampoa Military Academy in 1924–1925; that is, during the first KMT–CCP collaboration. Zhou was very close to the Communist International but was wise enough to side with Mao Zedong at the Zunyi Conference, at which Mao took military leadership of the party. After 1949, Zhou became prime minister of the new government, a position he held until his death. Zhou is remembered for his restraining influence on Mao during the Cultural Revolution period and for his diplomatic sophistication outside China. In 1973, Zhou rehabilitated Deng Xiaoping, a move that later proved critical in bringing the totalitarian phase of China to an end after the death of Mao.

Zhu Rongji Chinese prime minister from 1998 to 2003. Zhu was a technocrat by training who rose in Beijing's state hierarchy until his critical tendency got him into trouble during the 1957 antirightist campaign, after which he was purged. Deng Xiaoping's political ascendancy brought Zhu back to the official arena, and he advanced rapidly until he was mayor of Shanghai. There he executed Deng's plan to build China's most important window to the world. He was promoted to vice premier during Deng's famous Tour to the South that relaunched economic reform following the conservative retrenchment period of 1988–1991. In March 1988, he was elected premier to replace Li Peng.

STUDY QUESTIONS

1. What kind of developmental strategy did the Kuomintang take on the Chinese mainland? Was it an effective response to the international challenge that China faced at that time?

2. Dr. Sun Yat-sen originally attempted to build China on the liberal model. Why and how did he abandon that model?

3. How was the first KMT–CCP collaboration formed and dissolved?

4. How did the Japanese invasion and the Chinese civil war alter China's developmental strategy?

5. Discuss the similarities and dissimilarities between political development in the PRC and in the Soviet Union.

6. Explain China's post-1949 political turbulence in terms of the conflict between the party and the state and in terms of the shift from transformation to reform.

7. How did Deng Xiaoping's reform agenda conflict with Chen Yun's emphasis on stability in the post-Mao period?

8. How do you place Taiwan's democratization in the general framework of China's political development?

9. Discuss the possibility of China's democratization.

10. Was China unique in its response to international challenges during the twentieth century?

STOP AND COMPARE

EARLY, MIDDLE, AND LATE DEVELOPERS

If it makes sense to group Britain and France as early developers and Japan and Germany together as middle developers, comparativists feel that it makes even more sense to group Russia and China together as late developers. Not only did both countries industrialize only in the twentieth century, but both also experienced communist revolutions and have lived with the long-term burdens of communist economic and institutional development. Although Russia cast off its communist political institutions and ideology in 1991, it continues to search for a viable path into the capitalist world. Moreover, after initially moving in the direction of democracy after 1991, since the late 1990s Russia's rulers have become increasingly authoritarian. China, on the other hand, has retained its communist political structures but has done so while rapidly introducing capitalist economic institutions in important parts of the economy. These are the ironies that we examine in the case of the late developers.

LATE DEVELOPERS: RUSSIA AND CHINA

Compared with its European neighbors, Russia entered the twentieth century as a politically and economically backward country. As the core region of the tsarist empire, Russia had neither a constitution nor a working national parliament. Instead, Russia's tsar, Nicholas II, ruled as his father and grandfather had – as an autocrat unchecked by the power of law or political opposition. The privileged nobility served the tsar and lived in a moral and political universe separate from that of the masses of powerless and impoverished peasants. Nor did Russia have a consolidated sense of its own nationhood; one look at a map was enough to show that the empire consisted of well over one hundred different ethnic groups and languages. Its economy was still primarily agricultural, despite some serious efforts to modernize agriculture and initiate industrialization in the latter part of the nineteenth century.

In fact, several of Russia's earlier rulers had attempted modernizing reforms. Peter the Great (1682–1725) had introduced modern technologies acquired in the West and had even built a new capital city, St. Petersburg, on the Gulf of Finland, replete with the best Italian and French architecture of the day, as a tangible symbol of Russia's Western orientation. Catherine the Great (1762–1796) had welcomed significant elements of Enlightenment rationalism and European thinking into imperial administration. Alexander II (1855–1881) had freed the peasant serfs in 1861 with the intention of unleashing the social energies of ordinary Russians in order to harness them for economic development and military competitiveness.

The problem with all of these reforms, however, was the deep ambivalence Russia's rulers felt toward them. The tsars wanted the military and technological advances that reforms and economic development might bring, but they feared the kinds of social and psychological changes in the population that occurred in France and ultimately led to revolution. Over time, as the rest of Europe was democratizing, this contradiction grew more intense: Military competitiveness required economic development; economic development entailed adopting Western technologies, methods, and ideas; but Westernization appeared to lead inexorably toward some kind of political liberalization – something that all the tsars resisted until the very end.

Even within Russian society, there was ambivalence about embracing the experience of the West. During the nineteenth century, some parts of the intelligentsia wanted to preserve distinctive Slavic traditions and were thus dubbed "Slavophiles." Others looked to the West and hoped one day to force a rupture with the nobility, who dominated political life, and the Orthodox Church, which dominated the spiritual life of Russia – and were thus labeled "Westernizers." The Westernizers themselves were split between those who wanted liberal democracy and those who wanted a distinctively socialist form of industrial modernity. Yet even among the socialists, there was a further split. The Mensheviks wanted to come to power democratically, whereas the Bolsheviks wanted a revolution and to construct a communist society. Which path Russia would ultimately take became the burning question of the nineteenth and early twentieth centuries.

The Russian Revolution of November 1917, led by Lenin and his Bolsheviks, answered this question for the better part of the twentieth century. Although the Bolsheviks wanted to build a new kind of society, they still had to build this society in a world of hostile countries, and they were thus confronted with some of the same challenges that faced their tsarist predecessors. How could a first-rate military be built on the resources of a less-than-second-rate economy? Unlike their tsarist forebears, however, the Bolsheviks faced a further dilemma. How could all of this be done without capitalist markets and be made into something called "socialism" or "communism"? Lenin died too early to deal with these questions, but his successors were forced to deal with little else.

Lenin's successor, Stalin, undertook what some comparativists have called a second revolution and created distinctive communist economic and political institutions in the successor to the Russian Empire, the Soviet Union. The Communist Party became the sole ruler of the country, agriculture was collectivized, and the economy was transformed into a command economy, planned and administered from Moscow (which, perhaps tellingly, had become the new capital after the revolution). The net result of the revolution was to create a totalitarian dictatorship that succeeded in rapidly industrializing the country and creating a huge military-industrial complex. As we now know, this could only be accomplished at a tremendous price in terms of lost lives and wasted resources. After Stalin's death, successive Soviet leaders, once again like the Russian tsars of earlier eras, sought ways to improve the economy and compete with the West without dismantling the distinctive communist political and social order.

The last Soviet leader, Mikhail Gorbachev, undertook what was perhaps the most important set of communist reforms. He, too, failed, but he implemented important political changes (his economic programs were utterly futile) that permitted society to mobilize against the Communist Party. In 1991, the Soviet Union broke up and Russia emerged as a smaller but formally democratic state. Once again, however, in some respects Russia finds itself in the position it was in before it embarked on the failed communist experiment – a country that is trying to catch up to the West using institutions, methods, and ideas not of its own design. The added burden, however, is that the legacy of the Lenin-Stalin system has made democratic and capitalist transformation exceedingly difficult for Russia's postcommunist leaders. With so many obstacles to successful transformation, Russian politicians have been tempted to cast aside democratic institutions altogether in favor of a return to more familiar hierarchical and authoritarian forms of political rule.

Like Russia, China also experienced a communist revolution. But China continues to be ruled by a Communist Party that has overseen a stop-and-go series of economic reforms since the early 1990s that have led to spectacular rates of economic growth accompanied by new social tensions. The reasons for the divergence in experience between the two countries are to be found in the very different legacies of the global past.

Comparativists are quick to point out that, unlike Russia, which had always viewed itself as being embedded within the broader European culture, China has always understood itself as culturally distinct from Europe. And for good reason, too. Chinese culture is far older than Europe's, and for centuries China remained isolated from the outside world. Under successive Confucian rulers, China had managed to create an impressive form of bureaucratic rule based on an educated elite. These rulers were not subject to democratic control, but they did face the threat of overthrow if the mandarin and gentry elite felt that they had lost the "mandate of heaven" to govern their country.

The imperial order lasted for centuries but was ultimately destabilized by its encounters with the industrialized West. Over the course of the nineteenth century, the Western powers forced China to open a number of its port cities to foreign merchants and trade. Chinese imperial bureaucrats brought this access into question in 1842, when the British were forbidden to market opium to the Chinese population. In response, the British successfully waged war and secured for the next century foreign domination of China's economically important coastal regions. British imperialism in the region ultimately paved the way for Japanese imperialism, which culminated in the Japanese invasions and atrocities of the 1930s.

Military pressures and internal fragmentation brought down the last Chinese emperor in 1911. Initially, after the emperor's departure, China was united under an alliance of the Nationalist Party (the Kuomintang) and the Chinese Communist Party (CCP), but the alliance collapsed in 1927 in a bloody rupture between the two partners. The CCP, although it was nominally a Marxist party and thus could be expected to look for support among the urban proletariat, fled to the countryside, where it worked closely with the peasant masses and perfected its unique contribution to revolutionary theory: the conduct of a guerrilla war. The leader of the CCP, Mao Zedong, established his base in the countryside among the disaffected and the outlawed. Faced with increased military pressure from the Kuomintang, in 1933 thousands of communists abandoned their base in Jiangxi to begin their Long March, a forced retreat that decimated the ranks of the party (only 28,000 of the original 100,000 arrived at the end) but also provided a formative, steeling experience for the communist elite.

At the end of World War II, in 1945, the Japanese fled the country and the civil war between the nationalists and the communists resumed. With the support of the majority of the peasants, who in fact constituted the vast majority of all Chinese, the CCP won the war in 1949, and the nationalists were forced to flee to the island of Taiwan. The People's Republic of China was proclaimed on October 1, 1949. The CCP could look to the Soviet Union for a model to emulate, but they could easily look to their own "heroic" past to justify carving out their own path. Although important aspects of the Soviet model were adopted, the CCP under Mao's leadership pursued policies that were at times much more radical than in the Soviet Union (such as the Great Leap Forward and the Cultural Revolution). After Mao's death in 1976, the reformist branch of the party emerged dominant, and under Deng Xiaoping's leadership, the CCP ushered in several waves of successful marketizing economic reforms and a broad opening to international market forces. At the same time, the party has retained tight control over political life and has forestalled any move toward democracy. The comparison with the Soviet communist experience is highly instructive. Whereas the Soviet Communist Party fell because it democratized before it marketized, part of the secret of the Chinese Communist Party's capacity to retain control has been its willingness to marketize China's economy without democratizing its politics.

PART FOUR

EXPERIMENTAL DEVELOPERS

CASES

UNITED STATES OF AMERICA

Tijuana

Ensenada

Ciudad
Juárez

Gulf of California

Guaymas

Chihuahua

Topolobampo

Nuevo Laredo

M

Monterrey

Matamoros

*Gulf of
Mexico*

E

La Paz

Durango

X

Mazatlán

San Luis Potosí

Tampico

Cancún

Mérida

Puerto Vallarta

León

Tuxpan

*Gulf of
Campeche*

I

Guadalajara

Mexico City

C

Veracrus

Manzanillo

O

Coatzacoalcos

BELIZE

PACIFIC

Lázaro Cárdenas

Oaxaca

GUATEMALA

OCEAN

Acapulco

*Gulf of
Tehuantepec*

MEXICO

```
0    100   200   300   400    500 miles
0  100 200 300 400 500km
```

CHAPTER NINE

Mexico

Anthony Gill

Introduction

January 1, 1994, will be remembered as an important date in Mexican history. As Mexicans celebrated the beginning of the new year, two events occurred that marked profound changes in the country's political development and would eventually lead to a significant shift in the country's balance of political power. First, the **North American Free Trade Agreement (NAFTA)** took effect. This treaty integrated Mexico's economy more closely with those of the United States and Canada, marking the end of a nearly seven-decade strategy of sheltering Mexico from the vagaries of global markets. Pressures from international investors and trading partners to create greater economic openness dramatically affected (and continue to affect) Mexico's domestic institutions and day-to-day politics. The day's second memorable event made this readily apparent. As Mexico's President **Carlos Salinas de Gortari** was celebrating the new year and the implementation of NAFTA at a cocktail party, he received word that a major guerrilla insurgency had erupted in the southern Mexican state of Chiapas. A revolutionary organization known as the **Zapatista National Liberation Front** (or Zapatistas) was demanding greater political participation and a solution to the dire economic plight of poor rural farmers.

That the guerrillas attacked on the same day NAFTA took effect was no accident: The Zapatistas considered Mexico's increased integration into the world economy a threat to the economic well-being of the majority of Mexico's rural population, most of whom are of indigenous origin. Once considered to be part of Mexico's national identity – a blend of pre-Columbian and Spanish heritage – the majority of Zapatista supporters asserted their ancient cultural origins as part of a subnational identity that divided Mexico along racial and ethnic lines.

The insurgency also shook the foundations of Mexico's political institutions, long considered one of the developing world's most stable polities. The Zapatista rebellion highlighted a growing trend in contemporary Mexican politics – the rise of political instability and the breakdown of one-party rule. Throughout 1994, Mexico witnessed a rash of political assassinations, including that of the ruling party's presidential candidate. Protests against the government, rare before 1980 but on the increase since the mid-1980s, became almost daily occurrences. Social turmoil alarmed many international and domestic investors, who began to withdraw their money from the country. By the end of the year, Mexico had undergone a major economic crisis that further exacerbated social tensions. The impact of this conflict was felt internationally. Fearing that other countries in Latin America would experience similar socioeconomic problems, foreign businesses scaled back their economic connections to the region, increasing unemployment and affecting the economic policies in such countries as Argentina, Brazil, and Colombia. As many Mexicans fled to the United States in the hope of finding better economic opportunities, anti-immigration pressure influenced election results in California, Texas, and other states. Clearly, the international environment has played an important role in shaping the domestic political identities, institutions, and interests of Mexico. Likewise, Mexico's developmental path has equally affected the politics of countries abroad.

To many comparative political scientists, the events of 1994 indicated a profound change in Mexican politics, culminating in the election in 2000 of the first opposition-party candidate to be elected president of Mexico. Throughout most of the twentieth century, a single party – the **Institutional Revolutionary Party (PRI)** – dominated Mexican politics. Although Mexico is technically a representative democracy with regular elections, the PRI has dominated nearly all elected offices, has tightly regulated social organizations, and has dampened real political competition. To the extent that the PRI was able to promote rapid economic growth and rising standards of living, the party retained popular support among the citizenry. This popular support translated into an unprecedented level of political stability. Whereas most other countries in Latin America were experiencing turbulent oscillations between democratic and authoritarian rule, or facing serious revolutionary challenges, Mexico had maintained a peaceful transfer of power among national and local rulers since 1920, longer than a number of European countries, such as Germany and Italy.

The socioeconomic and political turmoil of the 1990s eventually culminated in the election of **Vincente Fox**, the first candidate from an opposition party – the **National Action Party (PAN)** – to win the presidency since the 1920s. Moreover, it was Mexico's first peaceful transition of presidential power to an opposition leader since the late 1800s. And, for the first time in eight decades, the dominant Institutional Revolutionary Party (which existed under different names during its history) no longer held a clear majority in the national legislature. These results marked a crucial point in the country's political development and were hailed internationally as a major step toward a competitive, multiparty democracy. Despite this movement toward competitive democracy, most of the socioeconomic problems that beset Mexico during the last two decades of the twentieth century persist, and new political dilemmas have emerged. In a political system that in the past encouraged a strong presidency, Vincente Fox found himself constrained by a limited term in office, no clear majority in the legislature, and a bureaucracy that is still staffed by members of the PRI who have no clear interest in seeing him succeed. Whether, and how, Mexico is able to overcome these obstacles will have a profound effect on the governing institutions of Mexico for decades to come.

In light of this turbulent history, this chapter addresses the following questions: How was Mexico able to maintain such a high degree of political stability over the past century? Why did this political stability come under such intense pressure during the 1990s, and what factors led to the election of Vincente Fox? What does President Fox's victory mean for Mexico's political development? Will there continue to be a peaceful transfer of power between rival political parties at all levels of government, or will political and social chaos ensue? Answers to these questions will tell us more about Mexico's political history and help us to understand how the global context shapes domestic interests, identities, and institutions and how these give rise to varying types of developmental paths.

Historical, Social, and Ideological Origins

As seen in Chapter 1 of this text, political systems evolve from the choices and actions of earlier political actors. Previous institutional arrangements, entrenched interests, philosophical mind-sets, and the international environment help fashion a country's contemporary political institutions and social identity. Reflecting on the past is thus crucial for understanding the present. For Mexico, the obvious point of historical departure starts with the Spanish Conquest in 1521 (see Table 9.1 at the end of the chapter). This does not imply that indigenous societies had no role in shaping political and social arrangements in the Western Hemisphere. Several pre-Columbian social and political structures were adopted by the Spanish conquerors (conquistadors) to subjugate the indigenous populations. Indigenous cultures also play a complex role in shaping Mexican political identities (for example, in the way they view themselves in relation to the polity). In part, Mexicans pride themselves on a general identity that blends the country's Spanish and indigenous heritages. Yet, indigenous populations have not been fully incorporated into national life. The difficult economic problems facing these communities, particularly in southern Mexico, continue to promote social tensions. Nonetheless, when tracing the history of Mexico's contemporary political landscape, one can see that the forceful imposition and near-total dominance of Spanish institutions make the conquest a conventional starting point.

The Colonial Period

The roots of the contemporary Mexican political system date back to the sixteenth-century invasion by Spanish conquistador Hernán Cortés. With his defeat of Aztec emperor Montezuma in 1521, Spain's distinct style of colonial governance prevailed over the territory of New Spain for exactly three centuries. The colonial period had three important effects on modern Mexican political life. First, it laid the ideological bedrock of **corporatism**, the core philosophical framework guiding Mexican political life. Second, the centralized and top-heavy political structures established by the Spanish monarchy provided comparatively little opportunity for self-governance in the colonies, resulting in political instability and an all-out war for power following independence in 1821. Third, labor relations and landholding patterns established during the colonial era set the stage for future economic and political problems.

The cultural framework that came to dominate Mexico's national political identity emanated from the intersection of a strong religious tradition (Catholicism) and a political philosophy (corporatism). This line of thinking viewed society as an organic whole: Individuals belonged naturally to a variety of functional social groups (e.g., craft guilds, clergy, aristocracy). Although each of these groups may have dissimilar interests, all are needed for the harmonious operation of society. It stands to reason that the interests of the entire "body politic" should come before the interests of any particular component. Politically speaking, the needs of the state take precedence over the specific desires of any single group or individual within the state; groups exist to serve the state, not vice versa.

The institutional impact of this worldview was a statist, patrimonial style of government. For the body politic to function properly, so the argument ran, a centralized entity needed to mediate any potential conflict between social groups. The most effective way to do this is to have the state determine which interest groups are socially vital and then regulate their operation. Rather than allowing for the autonomous, grassroots organization of individuals with distinct interests, the state itself organizes, grants legitimacy to, and absorbs these groups into the decision-making apparatus of society. It also has a tendency to promote rigid class distinctions while downplaying the possibility of social mobility.

Corporatism, in the Mexican context, reflects a "top-down" strategy of interest aggregation, a process directed by the state, in contrast with the "bottom-up" approach of classic liberalism, in which spontaneously formed interest groups emerge and function autonomously. This latter philosophy, a product of the English Enlightenment, emphasizes individual (not group) rights and views competition among autonomously organized interests as healthy for the economy and polity. The fact that Spain tried to keep its colonies isolated from such ideological influences had a long-term impact on Mexico's political identity and institutional design. Yet despite the predominance of this corporatist ideology, Mexican politics could not remain completely immune to liberal ideas. The struggle between the corporatist and liberal worldviews is an ongoing theme in Mexican political history and is still playing itself out today.

In terms of social interests, the primary motivation driving colonization was the enrichment of Spain, particularly in relation to its European rivals. Although mineral wealth (e.g., silver) was highly prized, the Spanish crown also taxed other economic production (e.g., cotton and sugar), with the goal of increasing royal wealth. Given the distance between the crown and the colonies, ensuring the proper amount of revenue flow back to Madrid was a difficult task. Colonists had a competing interest in keeping as much wealth as possible for themselves, and thus they tried to hide their wealth from royal tax agents. The political institutions established to govern the colonies reflected an attempt to minimize the problem of wealth extraction for Spain.

The colonies were also governed with an eye toward ensuring that local officials remained strictly loyal to the crown. Only individuals born in Spain were appointed to the highest levels of colonial government. Each official served a specified term and then returned to Spain. Inasmuch as poor administration was punished on return, the rotation of colonial officials in this manner ensured a high degree of loyalty. To enhance it further, the monarchy conducted regular audits of colonial administrators. The Catholic Church was also under the control of the king and was used to keep watch over both colonial officials and citizens (specifically by the Holy Office of the Inquisition). Although relatively complex in nature, the system of colonial administration was far from perfect. The social structure of the community often dictated that even high-ranking officials court the favor of the colonists. Because it was difficult to supervise the behavior of colonial officials completely, corruption was common and, up to a point, even tolerated by Spain.

Despite tight control by Spain, colonists were granted a limited degree of self-governance. Municipal councils (**cabildos**), staffed primarily by individuals born in the colonies, administered the day-to-day activities of town life (e.g., issuing building permits). These local councils later became the locus for the independence movement. However, it is important to note that the *cabildos* were relatively isolated from one another and were in no position to provide unified national leadership. Therefore, when Spain eventually did withdraw from Mexico, no strong centralized institutions existed to replace the colonial administration. The inevitable result was that the post-independence period would be one of substantial political uncertainty and instability.

The final consequence of the colonial period for the contemporary era relates to the pattern of land tenure and the resulting social-class relations. To encourage the conquest and settlement of New Spain in the mid-1500s, the Spanish monarchy had granted large tracts of land to conquistadors and the Catholic Church. These land grants typically included access to the labor and tribute of indigenous communities. The result of this pattern of land tenure and labor relations was the creation of a rigid class structure and a serious maldistribution of wealth that closely paralleled racial cleavages: **criollos** (individuals of pure-blooded Spanish descent) typically have occupied the upper classes, *indigena* the lowest classes, and mestizos (mixed blood) in between. As the indigenous population has tended to be concentrated in southern Mexico, economic and political tension has had a strong geographic component to it. Under such conditions, trying to construct a fair and just governmental system that represents the interests of all Mexicans and creates a common national identity has proven to be an enormous challenge. With criollos claiming higher economic status than the *indigena*, interest-based conflict has frequently inspired clashes over cultural identity.

From Independence to Revolution

INDEPENDENCE AND THE ERA OF THE CAUDILLOS

Comparative political scientists understand that seemingly distant international events can have very important effects on domestic political arrangements. Mexican decolonization is a prime example. Both material interests and ideological influences emanating from abroad provoked the separation of Mexico from Spain. The seeds of Mexican independence were sown during the seventeenth-century decline of Spain. With the Spanish fleet unable to seal off New Spain from foreign ships (primarily French and British), contraband trade increased. Colonists began to get a taste for economic life beyond Spain's exploitative system. In 1700, a new royal dynasty (the Bourbons) attempted to reverse Spain's imperial decline. The central goal of the Bourbon Restoration was to rebuild Spain's influence in European affairs. Achieving this meant extracting greater amounts of revenue from the Americas. To this end, Charles III (1759–1788), the most influential Bourbon monarch, initiated a series of economic and political reforms. He promoted intracolonial trade, which spurred economic activity and increased Spain's colonial tax revenue. The king also tightened administrative control over the colonies by introducing a more rigorous bureaucratic arrangement borrowed from

France. The plan was an overall success, and the colonial economy boomed. Despite their resentment over the effective collection of higher taxes, most colonists benefited economically from the reforms. Nonetheless, political tensions erupted as many of the Spanish bureaucrats sent to administer the king's affairs replaced or marginalized local administrators. Just as in the U.S. War of Independence, "taxation without representation" stirred discontent with Spain among the Mexican populace.

The final series of events that sparked the drive toward independence had their origins in Europe. In 1808, French troops invaded Spain and imprisoned Charles IV (1788–1808). Confusion reigned as to who had final authority in the colonies: The deposed king? The king's colonial administration? The local *cabildos*? A small number of criollos influenced by European liberalism and the U.S. and French revolutions declared independence. Colonists loyal to the crown immediately quashed this liberationist movement and arrested all involved. A more significant challenge came in 1810 from two renegade Catholic priests – Padres Miguel Hidalgo and José María Morelos. Following a severe economic crisis in 1809, they rallied a significant peasant army around the symbolic banner of the **Virgin of Guadalupe** – an apparition of the Virgin Mary seen by an indigenous man in 1531. Given the dark, indigenous complexion of the Virgin, this apparition became one of the most important symbols of Mexican nationalism, reflecting the country's unique blending of European (Catholic) and indigenous cultures. The lower-class rebellion inspired by Hidalgo and Morelos, who were eventually captured and executed, lasted nearly five years. Many landholders and urban criollos, fearing a radical peasant rebellion, allied with the royalists. This caused independence to be delayed by a decade.

The path toward independence followed a circuitous route. Once French troops had withdrawn from Spain, Ferdinand VII (reigned 1808, 1814–1833) took the throne and increased military assistance to New Spain in a relatively successful effort to extinguish lingering separatist forces. However, just when it appeared that the independence movement had been defeated, events in Spain intervened to turn the tide. Under pressure from the Spanish Parliament, Ferdinand VII endorsed a liberal-inspired constitution in 1820. Frightened that similar liberalizing tendencies would infect New Spain, many conservative, pro-royalist forces abandoned their support of the king and opted for Mexican sovereignty. Mexico's independence thus had a decidedly conservative, antiliberal tinge. Instead of a liberationist movement promoting the democratic ideal, the newly separated Mexican state declared itself a constitutional monarchy under the reign of Emperor Augustín de Iturbide (who abdicated in 1823, returned to the throne in 1824, and was assassinated in 1824).

The monarchy did not last long. Several events conspired to bring it to an end in 1823. First and foremost was a serious economic crisis facing the new nation. Eleven years of war had destroyed most of the revenue-producing assets in Mexico, including mines, livestock, and cropland. The financial capital and entrepreneurial skill needed to restart the economy had fled to a safer haven in Spain. War casualties had depleted the source of skilled labor. Lacking a strong economy and tax base, the government found itself bankrupt. Even if the economy had been able to jump-start itself, the state lacked the institutional capacity to collect taxes. Because central administrative authority was largely in the hands of Spaniards at the turn of the nineteenth century, this bureaucratic capacity vanished when those officials fled. The paucity of internal transportation networks further meant that centralizing control over an expansive territory would be an impossible task. Attempts to reign in autonomous localities met with fierce resistance. Unable to raise revenue, the new regime could not finance basic governmental functions, including the salaries of military officers and troops. Criticism of the monarch grew rapidly, forcing him to resign in 1823 under the threat of a military coup and civil war.

Iturbide's abdication marked the beginning of a cycle of political instability known as the "era of the caudillos." (**Caudillos** were independent military leaders who commanded localized armies.) The most famous (perhaps notorious) was **Antonio López de Santa Anna**, who ruled Mexico directly nine times and manipulated the choice of the presidency on numerous other occasions. The pattern of political instability during this period followed a typical cycle: A sitting president would discover the government was bankrupt and be forced to cut back on military expenditures, including salaries and troop levels. With a stagnant economy, unemployed soldiers and officers were unable to find work. Discontent spread rapidly among the military, provoking a coup d'état. The new president would find himself in the same situation as the previous one and the cycle would be repeated.

All told, there were roughly 50 separate administrations from 1821 to 1860. This was hardly the environment for any single model of government, let alone democracy, to flourish. Nor was this a suitable context for the forging of a national identity, although the long-term effect of this chaos was a preference for more corporatist (in contrast with liberal) forms of government. The anarchic nature of this period allowed for the rise of local political bosses (**caciques**), who firmly resisted attempts to centralize national authority in any meaningful sense. To this day, the "culture" of the caciques persists, as current administrations have difficulty implementing policies without first considering the interests of local power brokers.

International pressures aggravated Mexico's political chaos. Foreign powers could easily take advantage of the country's weakened domestic position. Primary among these foreign interlopers was a young, expansionist United States. Settlers from the United States began occupying the Texas region in 1821, the year of Mexico's independence. Although Texans were technically citizens of Mexico, efforts by Mexican authorities to make them accountable to central rule led the settlers to call for secession. Tensions escalated as U.S. settlers quickly outnumbered native Mexicans. Domestic U.S. pressure to annex Texas eventually provoked a war in 1846. With Mexico in political disorder, the United States won the war and roughly half of Mexico's national territory (extending from present-day Texas to California and Washington State).

The United States was not the only foreign power to play a role in complicating Mexico's political development. Several European powers, most notably France, also intervened. Financial interests were at the heart of the conflict. With the national treasury essentially empty from the first days of independence, various Mexican administrations had found it difficult to make restitution for damage done to foreign property during the wars of independence. Nor could the government repay foreign loans used to fund day-to-day administrative operations. In 1861, the Mexican government, facing a serious fiscal crisis, suspended payment on foreign debts owed to Britain, France, and Spain. These three powers responded by occupying Mexican ports to collect customs duties as repayment. French ambitions, however, extended beyond this action. Emperor Louis-Napoléon Bonaparte opted for an all-out invasion of the country and installed an Austrian aristocrat, Ferdinand Maximilian Joseph, as president. The French intervention lasted for three years (1864–1867) until Mexican armed forces prevailed in ousting Maximilian. Such intervention only aggravated the country's political instability, retarding the creation of viable political institutions.

THE ASCENDANCY OF LIBERALISM

Foreign occupation and war were not the only international influences to shape the Mexican polity. An ideological "invasion" also proved decisive in Mexico's political history. Along with increased contraband trade in material goods during the latter half of the eighteenth century, new ideas began to filter into the region. Increased contact with Britain, France, and the United States following independence further exposed many Mexican elite to new streams of political thought. The philosophies of the English Enlightenment and French Revolution, with their emphasis on citizens' liberties and rights, contrasted with conservative, corporatist thought that gave primacy to the state over the individual. Throughout the nineteenth century and for the first several decades of the twentieth, the struggle for a national political identity involved the efforts of liberals to graft their ideological beliefs onto a culture heavily influenced by medieval Catholicism.

The conflict between liberalism and corporatism resulted, during the 1800s, in a bloody contest between two factions – **Liberals** and **Conservatives**. The former sought to build a political system based upon many of the same precepts as the U.S. Constitution. Mexico's first constitution (1824) divided national government among three branches – legislative, executive, and judicial. A bicameral legislature further balanced the geographical interests of states (two senators per state) with representation based on population (one deputy per 8,000 people). The document also promoted a federalist system that distributed power away from the capital, Mexico City, and toward local governments. Subsequent constitutions of 1836, 1857, and 1917 were based on this earlier document and kept a preference for liberal political institutions. Liberals also favored moving Mexico toward a more secular society and pursued anticlerical reforms to restrict the Catholic Church's cultural, political, and economic power. Conservatives, alternatively, preferred centralized government based upon a strong executive. Their philosophical identity owed more to the corporatist thought of medieval Catholicism than to the English Enlightenment. It was their defense of the Catholic Church that most differentiated Conservatives from their Liberal counterparts.

Although the political instability of the 1800s took on the veneer of a great battle between competing worldviews, the ideological basis for conflict during this period should not be overestimated. Interest-based struggles over personal power prompted constant turnover in presidential administrations. Politics became a "winner-take-all" game; daily survival in office took precedence over achieving long-term philosophical goals. Over time, Liberals and Conservatives became virtually indistinguishable in their economic policy preferences, with both favoring export-oriented growth and trade relations with Europe and the United States. Politically, Liberals abandoned their federalist pretensions and opted for centralized government, which allowed them to rule a large territory more effectively. This was most evident during **La Reforma** (1855–1876), when Liberals finally dominated their Conservative rivals. Dominance did not imply political stability, however. This period included a major civil war (1858–1861) and the French occupation of 1864 to 1867. The most prominent politician during this period was **Benito Juárez,** a pure-blooded Zapotec Indian who demonstrated that although upward mobility was very difficult for the indigenous, it was not impossible. (Juárez's heritage is often championed as evidence of the strong indigenous influence in Mexico's cultural identity.) Juárez, a Liberal, realized that Mexico needed a strong, centralized government to end the internecine warfare that had torn the country apart since independence. He concentrated power in the presidency against his own liberal principles calling for a strong legislature. In doing this, Juárez became the first president to complete a constitutionally prescribed term in office (1867–1871) and provided the country with its most stable governance to date. This lesson was not lost on future leaders. Ruling Mexico meant maintaining centralized political institutions. Under Juárez's presidency, business investment became a reasonably safe activity and the economy began to show signs of growth.

THE PORFIRIATO

President Juárez's successful completion of his presidential term raised the hope that a stable rule of law had finally arrived in Mexico. Unfortunately, personal hostilities erupted during Juárez's next term in office, which ended prematurely with his natural death. The resulting succession crisis gave way to a harsh dictatorship under Porfirio Díaz from 1876 to 1911, a period known as the **Porfiriato**. Although ruthless, the dictatorship did have a beneficial side. For 35 years, Mexico experienced unprecedented political stability and economic growth, bolstered by a favorable global context. Industrial growth in Europe and the United States fueled demand for raw materials. Rising commodity prices boosted Mexico's domestic economy and helped fill state coffers. Government tax revenue, along with U.S. and British foreign investment, was used to build Mexico's infrastructure. Railroads were built, ports modernized, and the national bureaucracy expanded. Because Britain had no interest in expanding its empire into the Americas, and the United States was pursuing a policy of relative isolation, direct foreign intervention in Mexican affairs was minimal. Expansionary desires of other countries were kept in check by the Monroe Doctrine, a U.S. policy designed to prevent European encroachment into the Americas.

Porfirio Díaz also left his mark on Mexico's political landscape. He was the first of Mexico's rulers to unify Mexico effectively under central authority for any extended period. He accomplished this by means of shrewd manipulation of military appointments, the buying off of local political bosses (caciques), and the creation of a separate police force directly loyal to his authority. Despite ideological loyalty to the liberal constitution of 1857, which provided for a strong legislative branch, Díaz further concentrated institutional power in the executive branch. Since that time, the Mexican president has enjoyed political power above and beyond what is legally prescribed.

The Porfiriato's final legacy was to establish a style of rule that has been used to guarantee political stability to the present day – ***pan o palo***, the rule by "bread or club" – meaning the dual use of patronage and coercion. With increased revenues flowing into the treasury during the economic boom, Díaz bought the loyalty of various towns and constituencies. Important members of the elite received lucrative positions in the governmental bureaucracy in exchange for their support. Hence, Díaz earned his legitimacy not by appealing to the will of the majority but by being able to "deliver the goods." The liberal goal of popular sovereignty gave way to the corporatist manipulation of political support. Alternatively, those individuals or groups not willing to cooperate with the policy directives of the president were dealt with by the heavy hand of the police.

Although dissent was not permitted, it could not be entirely prevented. The economic prosperity of the late 1800s gave rise to a new set of middle-class interests. Although generally pleased with the economic management of the country, middle-class professionals began demanding greater political participation, something that their brethren in other Latin American countries were enjoying at that time. With Díaz nearing his eightieth birthday, many anticipated that the dictatorship would soon end and lead to a liberalization of Mexican politics. Díaz himself heightened these expectations by announcing in 1908 that he would not run for office in 1910. Positioning began in earnest for the upcoming presidential campaign, with Francisco Ignacio Madero as an early favorite. As the election neared, Díaz changed his mind and Madero found himself in prison for mounting an effective opposition campaign. Díaz's rigged electoral victory in 1910 unleashed the **Mexican Revolution**.

Politics in the Twentieth Century: Revolution and Institutionalized Rule

THE MEXICAN REVOLUTION

The Mexican Revolution began as another conflict over presidential succession, something to which Mexicans had grown accustomed. The ideological rhetoric of the initial rebellion mirrored the liberal leanings of the 1800s, with a call for representative democracy coupled with checks and balances on executive power. Early on, revolutionary leaders attempted to institutionalize the classic liberal tenets contained in the 1857 constitution. However, the Mexico of 1910 was much different from what it was just 30 years earlier. New social classes, such as urban labor, had arisen, and existing ones (especially the rural peasantry) had grown politicized. These groups brought to the political arena a new set of interests – a desire for higher wages, better working conditions, social welfare, and access to arable farmland – that political institutions needed to capture. A new global ideological climate also shaped the course of the revolution; in Europe, socialist ideals began to challenge the underlying logic of liberal capitalism. The Russian revolutions of 1905 and 1917 provided further examples that the peasantry and urban labor were becoming a major force for social change and could not be ignored in any new political arrangements. Many of those participating in the revolution wanted not only liberal political institutions but also major social reforms aimed at bringing the lower classes into a ruling coalition. Such demands radicalized the revolution and gave form to the resulting **Constitution of 1917** and the corporatist institutions it would spawn.

With the disappearance of Díaz's effective system for holding the country together, internal chaos again reigned. The initial coalition that brought Madero to power began unraveling. Accusing Madero of failing to carry out his promised social reforms, a rebel from southern-central Mexico, **Emiliano Zapata**, declared war on the Liberal administration. An attempt to suppress this rebellion by relying on one of Díaz's former generals back-fired, and Madero was overthrown in a counterrevolution supported by the Catholic Church and the U.S. government. Another faction, led by Venustiano Carranza (northern Mexico's governor and a landholder), top-pled this counterrevolutionary regime with the help of Zapata. Unhappy with Carranza's reluctance to implement progressive policies, Zapata's forces marched on Mexico City and forced a number of radical reforms that resulted in the drafting of a constitution in 1917. This new constitution included provisions for workers' rights to unionize, exclusive national ownership of mineral wealth, and communal land redistribution. These provisions represented a step beyond classical liberalism's preference for individual rights and established a basis for a modern corporatist system that gave the state enhanced powers in regulating social conflict. Much of the contemporary political strife in Mexico relates to efforts by recent presidents to rescind these social duties and move the country back to a more liberal framework.

The consolidation of the modern Mexican state began in 1920, the year typically viewed as the end of the revolutionary transition. That year marked the beginning of the peaceful transfer of power between presidential administrations and the return of political stability. The decade from 1924 to 1934 saw the emergence of another presidential strongman, Plutarco Calles. Calles became the first president to implement the revolution's most radical promises, including the distribution of nearly eight million acres of land to communal farms (***ejidos***) and the organization of labor into government-sponsored unions. Other social policies, including increased wages, better sanitation, and health programs, were also implemented. All of this was made possible by a relatively strong global economy that allowed Mexico to increase its exports of raw materials and attract foreign investment.

Despite the progressive social policies undertaken by Calles, the actual political working order that emerged was far from the liberal-democratic ideals contained in the 1917 constitution. Dissidents were jailed and the press censored. Calles's governing strategy closely resembled the *pan o palo* methods of Porfirio Díaz. Indeed, the heavy reliance on patronage networks by a centralized presidency to win social support and legitimacy is one of the main reasons Mexico's political system remained stable and free from military intervention from the 1920s to the present. Coercion (*palo*) became less needed as time wore on because rapid economic growth guaranteed that the patronage strategy (*pan*) would work effectively. In effect, the legacy of the revolutionary era was the forging of a new mode of governance for Mexico – one that synthesized the basic political elements of liberalism (e.g., elections, popular sovereignty) with the corporatist mode of operation (i.e., top-down social organization, increased political centralization). Although corporatism came to dominate liberalism, the blend of these two forms of government represented a political system that was uniquely Mexican.

THE REVOLUTION INSTITUTIONALIZED

The figure most credited with shaping the Mexican political system into what it is today is **Lázaro Cárdenas**. As president from 1934 to 1940, he institutionalized the corporatist philosophy of government. However, the revolutionary process had radically transformed the philosophic basis of corporatism. The corporatism of the nineteenth century was inherently conservative and exclusionary, seeking to preserve the socioeconomic organization of a bygone colonial era. Political participation by those other than the landed elite was strictly forbidden, and class relations remained static. The corporatist philosophy underlying Cárdenas's political arrangements, on the other hand, was progressive and inclusionary. It sought to transform Mexico into a modern industrial nation by organizing, coordinating, and controlling the social groups that would build the nation. Government would be pro-worker and pro-peasant. The state would try to tame the ravaging effects of "raw capitalism" and build a nation free from foreign influence. Under Cárdenas, Mexico had finally achieved a strong national identity based on a unique blend of liberalism, corporatism, and socialist ideas.

Economically, Mexico's international position prescribed a more state-centric approach to development rather than the Anglo-American model of capitalism. Being an industrial latecomer placed several constraints on the country's ability to achieve a modern economy. Most of what Mexico wanted to produce domestically was already being produced more efficiently in the United States and Europe. Mexican entrepreneurs were at an inherent disadvantage because domestic consumers would invariably prefer less costly, higher-quality goods manufactured abroad. No incentive existed to engage in entrepreneurial activity unless the state stepped in to guarantee businessmen domestic markets (via protective tariffs) or to subsidize their production costs. It is ironic that providing business with domestic markets meant creating a consumer base for manufactured goods because this, in turn, meant promoting higher wages for urban and rural workers, a situation that businesses try to avoid in order to protect their profits.

The political tumult that ravaged the country for nearly a century meant that there was little private capital to provide the impetus to build factories. Given the high start-up costs of building heavy industry in the mid-twentieth century, few Mexican citizens had the financial capacity to invest in large-scale industry. As in other cases of late development, such as Russia and China, the state would become the main vehicle for raising and investing capital. Mexico's industrialization was promoted extensively by a combination of state-owned enterprises and state subsidization of preferred industries. Overall, this general economic strategy was known as **import-substituting industrialization (ISI)**. The component parts of ISI included high import tariffs on manufactured consumer goods, financial subsidies to private business, overvalued exchange rates (to reduce the costs of producer imports), and state ownership of industries with high capital costs (e.g., electrical power and steel). Unionization and higher wages were promoted and a welfare system created to provide a consumer base for domestically produced goods. Import-substituting industrialization was common throughout Latin America and other parts of the developing world (e.g., Iran) during the mid-twentieth century and was largely a reaction to the Great Depression and World War II, when these countries were cut off from the manufactured goods traditionally provided by Europe and the United States. Although ISI policies were designed essentially to promote autarkic development, the lack of domestic capital inevitably meant courting foreign investment.

The Revolutionary Party, created under President Calles, became Cárdenas's institutional vehicle for achieving political stability and industrialization. The Mexican Revolutionary Party – later renamed the **Institutional Revolutionary Party** (Partido Revolucionario Institucional, known by its Spanish acronym, PRI) – was created as an autonomous entity to mobilize the population in support of Cárdenas's reformist agenda. Cárdenas structured the party around three organizational pillars, each representing an important social sector: (1) the Mexican Workers' Confederation (CTM), representing urban industrial labor; (2) the National Peasant Confederation (CNC), representing rural workers and the *ejidos*; and (3) the National Confederation of Popular Organizations (CNOP), composed of white-collar professionals, government bureaucrats, and small entrepreneurs. Each of these organizations was given representation in the policy-making apparatus of the party and, hence, the government. (The PRI was the only party to hold national office from 1934 to 2000.) However, because the party's top leaders chose the officials of these organizations, the PRI became the epitome of inclusionary corporatism. The ruling party organized societal interest groups from the top down, and political loyalties were based on "corporate," not geographic, identities. Autonomous groups that arose over the years were absorbed into the corporatist structure, ensuring that the government maintained tight regulatory control over popular interests.

A fourth organizational body, representing the armed forces, was also created. Cárdenas's early incorporation of the military into the party proved crucial to ensuring his immediate political survival. By currying the favor of officers and troops with substantial pay raises, educational opportunities, and other benefits, he prevented his rivals from using the army to plot against him. More importantly, these actions institutionalized civilian control over the armed forces, something historically rare in Latin America. In large part, Cárdenas's actions during the 1930s prevented Mexico from falling prey to the intermittent coups and military dictatorships that plagued South America for most of the 1960s and 1970s. The military reforms proved so successful that when the PRI disbanded the official organization representing the military in 1940, no military revolt ensued.

The institutionalization of labor, the peasantry, and the middle class into the ruling party became the crucial defining feature of Mexican politics for the next six decades. By connecting each social sector to the party, Cárdenas ensured enormous popular support for the PRI and set the stage for a single-party state. Relying more on "pan" (patronage) than "palo" (coercion), Cárdenas won the long-term loyalty of the Mexican lower classes. He dramatically improved urban working conditions and promoted the unionization of more than a million workers. During his presidency, roughly one in three Mexicans benefited from land reform involving nearly 50 million acres. The majority of land went to communal *ejidos*, which received privileged loans and technology from the government, further ensuring their political support. Finally, the incorporation of government bureaucrats, teachers, and lawyers into the PRI meant that the state and Revolutionary Party would become virtually indistinguishable.

Cárdenas also instituted many of the political practices that became standard fare over the next several decades: He extended the presidential term to six years. The president, as head of the PRI, would nominate his successor. Patronage benefits to privileged groups, controlled almost exclusively by PRI officials, increased in the months preceding a national election. Government-organized labor received higher wages, business groups were granted subsidies, and public works projects sprang up in rural communities. This increased spending prompted a period of inflation leading up to the election. Following national elections, the outgoing president would undertake deflationary policies so that the new president could begin his term with the task of rebuilding the economy. In many respects, this pattern represented a classic "political business cycle" of inflation and recession, determined by the electoral calendar.

Cárdenas also institutionalized a number of other political practices that made the Mexican system uniquely stable. Retiring presidents left office quietly and avoided interference in political matters. Power continued to be concentrated in the presidency; the Senate and Chamber of Deputies served as a rubber stamp for the policies of the executive. Although the CNOP, CTM, and CNC were supposed to be involved in the policy-making process, they fell under the increasing dictate of party leaders. Government and party officials decided when and where labor could strike or make demands on employers. Assistance to rural communities was conditioned on unswerving support of the PRI. Reasonably fair elections were held, but real political competition was minimized. All of this combined to ensure the electoral dominance of the PRI and gave the state a "quasi-authoritarian" flavor. Although outsiders may be quick to criticize the lack of effective democracy in Mexico, it should be remembered that the institutionalization of one-party rule in Mexico gave the country something it had long lacked – political stability. This in turn provided the basis for rapid and sustained economic growth until the 1980s.

The final legacy of the Cárdenas era was his reaction to the international political and economic environment. Mexico had always been at the mercy of foreign powers, either militarily or economically. This changed during the 1930s. The 1938 nationalization of 12 foreign-owned oil companies not only signaled a country seeking to control its own economic development but also was a high point in the creation of a Mexican national identity. Antiforeign (particularly anti-U.S.) sentiment increased noticeably. The economic policies of ISI were a natural extension of this growing nationalism as Mexico sought to become industrially self-sufficient. Despite being located adjacent to the world's foremost superpower, the Mexican government exercised a substantial degree of autonomy in its economic and foreign policy. Mexico became a leading member of the nonaligned, developing nations during the Cold War and frequently criticized U.S. foreign policy in Latin America.

The reforms of the Cárdenas era were politically and economically successful, and they benefited from a favorable international climate. When manufactured imports from Europe and the United States slowed to a trickle during the Great Depression and World War II, Mexican industry developed to fill the supply gap. The war also created a high demand for oil and other primary commodities in the world market. Political stability further boosted the domestic economy, and the country entered an era of unprecedented growth known as the "**Mexican Miracle**" (ca. 1940–1980). Gross domestic product grew at an average annual rate of over 6 percent, an unprecedented feat in Latin America. Accounting for population growth, per capita income increased approximately 3 percent per year. Within two short decades (1950–1970), living standards doubled.

Presidential succession continued peacefully for the next six decades, and the PRI held onto the major institutions of power. Although much of the PRI's dominance can be attributed to its control over important government resources and manipulation of patronage to loyal constituents, the party's popularity was also due to the nation's strong economic performance. The Mexican single-party system maintained a high degree of popular legitimacy. This is not to say that economic gains were distributed evenly. Over time, the actual policies of the government began to deviate from its revolutionary rhetoric and the redistributive legacy of Cárdenas. Large private industries not included in the 1930s corporatist arrangement gained an increasingly privileged position among policy makers. Contrary to the nationalist intentions of ISI, Mexico increasingly depended on foreign investment to fuel economic growth. Nonetheless, economic growth and political stability became mutually reinforcing. As long as the economy stayed healthy, the PRI was able to "buy" the support of most major social groups, and a politically dominant PRI ensured a stable social environment that was attractive to domestic and foreign investors. Despite outward appearances of durability, however, the corporatist system built under Cárdenas was fragile. If either the economy or the PRI faltered, the political system as a whole would become vulnerable to crisis. This is exactly what happened during the 1980s and 1990s. Fortunately, unlike the collapse of other civilian regimes throughout Latin America that ended in military dictatorships from the 1960s to the 1980s (Chile, for example), Mexico managed to deal with its political and economic crises with a peaceful transition to an opposition party in the year 2000.

THE FORMAL INSTITUTIONAL STRUCTURE OF MEXICAN POLITICS

At this point, it is worthwhile to review the general institutional structure of Mexican politics in the late twentieth century. These institutions were largely laid down in the 1917 constitution, although they have undergone some modifications since the 1970s. As noted earlier, Mexican politics between the 1920s and the late 1990s was determined by the informal politicking that went on within the dominant PRI. With single-party rule and the president and his close advisers controlling the party, most of the formal constitutional rules of politics held little sway. The Mexican Congress was largely a "rubber stamp" for presidential decrees, and the judiciary served to bolster executive dominance by posing little challenge. However, with the breakdown of the corporatist control of the PRI and the rise of real electoral competition, the rules establishing these governing institutions will undoubtedly take on greater importance.

The 1917 constitution provided Mexico with a federalist and presidential form of government similar in structure to the U.S. Constitution, although with important procedural differences. First, in keeping with the historical regional fragmentation of the country, Mexico is divided into 31 states, and each state has a relative degree of autonomy in setting policy relevant to regional interests. Second, political power was divided among three branches – executive, legislative, and judicial – each of which was to retain institutional autonomy from the others. The president initially was to be elected by popular vote every four years, although this provision was modified under President Lázaro Cárdenas to extend to a six-year term. The memory of Porfirio Díaz dominating the presidency for an extended period of time created a strong desire to impose a strict, one-term limit on the president. Unlike the case in the United States, the Mexican political system does not have a provision for a vice president. In the event that the president is unable to fulfill his term in office, the national legislature (Congress) is empowered to appoint an interim president, with a call for a new general election if the president is incapacitated during the first two years of his term. If the president's incapacitation occurs in the final four years of his tenure, the appointed interim president will serve the remainder of the term.

The national legislature, known as the Congress, is divided into two chambers – the Chamber of Deputies (lower house) and the Senate (upper house).

Members of the former are elected for three-year terms via two methods of election. Three hundred members of the Chamber of Deputies are elected via plurality rule in single-member districts. The remaining seats are selected via proportional representation with a provision guaranteeing seats to any party able to garner at least 2.5 percent of the vote. Initially, only 100 seats were to be selected in this manner, but bowing to increased pressure for representation by minority parties, the number of seats allocated by this method was expanded to 200 in 1986. The Senate originally consisted of two senators from each state and an additional two from the federal district of Mexico City. A 1993 constitutional reform doubled the number of senators to 128. This reform again represented a concession to minority parties who were calling for greater representation in a system dominated by the PRI. Currently, three of the senators from each state are elected via plurality rule, and the fourth seat is guaranteed to the minority party receiving the highest number of votes. Both Deputies and Senators are restricted to serving only one term in office.

Finally, the judicial branch of government was designed originally to be an autonomous check on the legislative and executive branches of government. Twenty-six judges, appointed by the president and confirmed by the Senate, sit on the Supreme Court and serve lifetime terms. Despite this guaranteed tenure, a norm developed wherein all Supreme Court justices would proffer their resignation following a presidential election, allowing the new president to retain the justices he desired and appoint any new people from his political coterie. A series of federal circuit courts exist below the Supreme Court, and judges within these courts are appointed by the Supreme Court. Not surprisingly, the courts did not function according to institutional design; instead of being a check on government abuses, the judicial system only served to strengthen and legitimize a top-heavy presidential system.

The Crisis of Corporatism during the Late Twentieth Century

Mexico's political development since the 1980s, defined by the historical tension between liberalism and corporatism, has been a battle of interests as well as identities. Following decades of social turmoil, top-down corporatist institutions proved best at reducing political conflict and promoting rapid industrialization. In turn, the Mexican Miracle financed the corporatist system. But miracles rarely last forever. Political stability and economic growth gave rise to new social interests and demands for a liberalized political system. Addressing these demands was easy when the economy was strong and government resources plentiful. However, changes in the world economy during the 1970s seriously limited state access to the resources needed to keep patronage-based corporatist arrangements intact. With the PRI finding it financially difficult to fulfill its corporatist obligations, groups that were once loyal constituents began organizing independently and seeking help from new political parties. The ruling party's rule is no longer guaranteed, and corporatism is giving way to demands for political liberalization. How Mexico negotiates its transition from a single-party, corporatist state to a liberal-pluralist democracy, if it does so at all, is the central problem facing the country today.

ORIGINS OF THE CRISIS

Mexico's political foundation began to show cracks during the late 1960s. Just as economic growth during the late 1800s gave rise to new social interests that prompted the Mexican Revolution, the Mexican Miracle created new social interests that demanded reform of the country's corporatist institutions. Among these new demands were greater autonomy for local governments, the ability to organize groups independent of government ties, and alternative (non-PRI) political representation. Such demands appeared first in the wealthy industrial and ranching states of northern Mexico. The central government's corporatist policies worked against northern interests by directing patronage resources away from them and toward the more populous central and southern regions. Defending their economic interests meant promoting electoral competition; if PRI power were challenged in the region, the central government would be required to respond to northern interests. In 1965, candidates from the center-right National Action Party (Partido Acción Nacional, PAN) won two mayoral elections in the prosperous state of Baja California, Norte. The ruling PRI, unfamiliar with such a challenge, nullified the elections, marking the first time that fraudulent tactics were used openly to retain power. Political liberalization might favor the industrial north, but it was not in the interests of the ruling party. Corporatism still trumped liberalism.

University students also began to call for political change. A booming economy created an expanding middle class; more youths were attending college and expecting professional careers. However, the closed political and economic system of the time could not adapt to meet these heightened expectations of a rapidly expanding population. Frustration among students ensued. Inspired by campus unrest in the United States and Europe, they began to agitate for expanded civil liberties. These protests boiled over just before the opening of the 1968 Olympic Games in Mexico City. The spark was a brawl among high school students that prompted local government officials to call riot police in a massive show of force. Police overreaction enraged students, who then demanded police reform and expanded civil liberties. The well-organized student protesters eventually mobilized the largest antigovernment rally in Mexican history, involving some 500,000 people. Un-fortunately, a two-month series of protests ended with government troops firing on demonstrators in the **Tlatelolco** district of Mexico City, killing more than 100 civilians (and perhaps upward of 400). The Tlatelolco massacre showed that popular support for the corporatist political system was waning.

By the early 1970s, the economy also began to show signs of stress. Import-substitution industrialization encouraged inflation, currency overvaluation, and a serious balance-of-payments crisis. Inflation ate away at the real wages of most Mexicans. More importantly, the corporatist institutions designed to give workers and small farmers a voice in government (e.g., the CTM and *ejidos*) increasingly became a way to repress their demands. The government discouraged workers from striking and implemented policies favoring business interests. The government also promoted large-scale, capital-intensive farming for export, which markedly slowed the pace of land redistribution between 1940 and 1970. Disaffected peasants responded by invading private lands. Contrary to nationalist rhetoric, foreign investment gained a notice-able presence in the economy, causing resentment among local workers and small businesses.

The social unrest of the late 1960s challenged Mexico's corporatist system but did not break it. President Luis Echeverría (1970–1976) responded to this discontent by increasing wages, distributing more land to the rural poor, and permitting the autonomous organization of labor. His administration also allowed limited civil protests. Bowing to pressure for increased political representation, Echeverría's successor, José López Portillo, enacted legislation in 1977 that guaranteed opposition parties 100 seats in the Chamber of Deputies based on proportional representation. These reforms represented a limited "democratic opening" and raised expectations for future liberalization.

The corporatist system survived due in large part to the oil crisis of the 1970s. Mexico, an oil-exporting nation, benefited from the dramatic rise in petroleum prices beginning in 1973. Revenue from the state-owned petroleum industry flowed into the national treasury, where it was used to alleviate economic hardship caused by a global economic slowdown. Addi-tionally, the flood of Middle East "petrodollars" on world financial markets allowed the Mexican government to borrow abroad. Increased government revenue prompted more state intervention in the economy as the state be-gan to nationalize hundreds of firms. In turn, the expansive economic reach of the government provided more avenues for distributing patronage in the form of jobs, preferential loans for favored businesses, and subsidies to im-portant rural clientele. Because Mexico's political stability was built upon the PRI's extensive patronage networks, oil revenue and foreign loans bol-stered the survival of the corporatist system during a time of growing popular discontent.

POLITICAL CHALLENGES IN THE 1980s AND 1990s

The same global economic system that provided the financial liquidity to keep corporatism afloat during the 1970s served to undo the system during the 1980s and 1990s. Relying upon oil revenue and foreign loans to buy domestic political support was at best a temporary solution for Mexico's socioeconomic ills. Loans required repayment, and reliance on petroleum for the bulk of government revenue was an inherently risky strategy. Two international events during the late 1970s and early 1980s made this strategy unworkable and sent shock waves through Mexico's political system. First, to combat soaring inflation at home, the U.S. Federal Reserve raised interest rates between 1979 and 1982. Rates on international loans followed suit, dramatically increasing Mexico's debt obligation. Concurrently, the world market experienced an unexpected oil glut and prices dropped precipitously. With roughly two-thirds of Mexico's foreign revenue coming from petroleum exports, government income fell sharply just as international financial obligations increased. Facing a massive outflow of economic resources, Mexico devalued its currency, reducing the value of the peso relative to other currencies, announced it was suspending payment on its international debt, and nationalized the country's banking system.

Business and consumer confidence disintegrated rapidly. International loans dried up and domestic investment slowed to a standstill. Mexico, like many countries in the developing world, entered its worst economic recession in more than a century. Total domestic production declined by 4.2 percent in the year following the devaluation and debt moratorium. Real wages tumbled by over 25 percent between 1980 and 1987. Unemployment and underemployment soared. With the economy in decline, government revenue (collected from taxes as well as oil) shrank noticeably. Although halting payment on international loans would seem a reasonable response to the domestic crisis caused by a shortage of government revenue, this solution was not feasible. Defaulting on its loans would have entailed severe economic sanctions from the world community, including the denial of loans in the future. Over the next several years, Mexico renegotiated repayment of its foreign debt, thus averting a major default and restoring partial confidence in the economy.

Part of the debt-negotiation agreement required the implementation of a series of "austerity measures" designed to control inflation and reduce the fiscal deficit. A radical reduction in government spending ensued. Jobs and wages in the government bureaucracy were trimmed. The government privatized hundreds of state-owned enterprises, which were used in the past to reward union supporters with high-paying jobs. Making these firms competitive meant slashing salaries and positions. Privatization thus struck at the heart of one of the central institutional pillars of corporatism – industrial labor. The peasantry felt the pinch of austerity as well. In order to generate foreign exchange with which to pay back foreign loans, the PRI began to promote agricultural exports. Government policy favored the most efficient, export-oriented farmers, typically those with large, capital-intensive plantations. *Ejidos* typically did not meet this need, and policy turned against their interests. Again, a traditional clientele of the corporatist system felt the brunt of the international economic crisis. A Mexico that had once tried to gain independence from the vagaries of the world market was now more than ever at its mercy.

THE POLITICAL CONSEQUENCES OF ECONOMIC CRISIS

Events in the economy profoundly affected the Mexican political sphere. The loss of government revenue placed severe restrictions on government spending. This undermined the ability of the PRI to manipulate patronage networks to ensure popular support. Discontent that had been brewing since the late 1960s erupted during the mid-1980s. A strong civil society began to emerge at the grass roots, a trend contrary to the corporatist philosophy of "top-down" organization. The growth of civil society received an unlikely push from a series of major earthquakes in 1985 that killed more than 10,000 residents of Mexico City. The massive destruction left a cash-strapped government paralyzed. Foreign assistance poured in, but what really mattered most was the autonomous creation of thousands of small community organizations that assisted in rescue and cleanup efforts. These organizations sowed the seeds from which independent political-action groups took root. For the first time since the modern corporatist system was constructed, a complex network of nongovernmental social groups emerged to challenge the hegemonic authority of the PRI.

The self-assertion of an autonomous civil society affected electoral politics. In 1983, members of the opposition National Action Party (PAN) won a significant number of municipal posts in the northern states of Chihuahua and Sonora. It is interesting to note that whereas one would expect leftist parties to make the greatest gains from labor discontent, PAN occupied the center-right and advocated an economic platform similar to the PRI's current neoliberal policies. National Action Party candidates won these elections because they were the only opposition party with significant organizational strength to mount an independent attack aimed at loosening the PRI's hold over the government. Most left-wing parties had been previously co-opted by the PRI through links to labor unions. Officials in those parties accepted this situation in exchange for token positions at various levels of administration. In other words, the leftist leadership owed its existence to the PRI and thus had little incentive to challenge the ruling party's authority. Only PAN had sufficient leadership that remained independent of the PRI.

PAN's electoral success went beyond organizational strength. It also signaled growing dissatisfaction with the PRI. Because northern Mexico is wealthier and more industrially developed than the central and southern states, PAN's success made it apparent that business interests were becoming increasingly unhappy with a PRI-dominated government. Furthermore, the preference for PAN indicated that there was more to the electoral discontent than strictly pocketbook matters; the electorate wanted real political choice and a greater say in government. The top-heavy corporatist model was facing a serious challenge from the grass roots.

The extent of popular unhappiness became clear during the presidential election of 1988. The handpicked PRI candidate, Carlos Salinas de Gortari, won the presidency with only 50.5 percent of the vote, a slimmer margin than for any previous PRI candidate. Cuauhtémoc Cárdenas, son of the former president and the representative of a loose coalition of left-wing parties, came in second with 30.9 percent. The PAN candidate, Manuel Clouthier, finished third with 16.7 percent. This in itself signified a substantial defeat for the one-party state. In reality, Salinas may have actually lost the election. Electoral irregularities marred the election, including a power outage that affected the computerized ballot counts. As political competition grew throughout the 1980s, the PRI increasingly resorted to electoral fraud to retain important seats. Although the true totals from the 1988 election may never be known, it is enough to say that this election had a lasting impact on the Mexican polity. The Mexican corporatist framework that had brought an era of unprecedented political stability for Latin America could no longer be sustained in its present form. The 1990s thus initiated a transitional period for the Mexican state.

INTERESTS, IDENTITIES, AND INSTITUTIONS AT THE END OF THE TWENTIETH CENTURY

As the 1990s came to a close, Mexico found itself struggling with one of the central political themes of its past – the tension between liberal and corporatist forms of government. Whereas this conflict was resolved for most of the century in favor of a corporatist one-party state, the crises of the 1980s and the rise of an autonomous civil society made liberal-pluralism a viable contender as the organizing principle of Mexican political life. Economic globalization and the collapse of the socialist model of development have pushed economic policy in the direction of laissez-faire policies. President Carlos Salinas de Gortari (1988–1994) stepped up the pace of privatization begun by his predecessor, Miguel de la Madrid (1982–1988). Under pressure to attract foreign capital and cultivate new export markets, Salinas also gave the central bank greater autonomy and entered into an expansive free-trade agreement (NAFTA) with the United States and Canada. His successor, **Ernesto Zedillo**, continued on the same economic path, although Zedillo was more adventurous when it came to introducing liberalizing political reforms. Salinas's policy of economic liberalization under a one-party state was reminiscent, in some ways, of similar reforms undertaken by Mikhail

Gorbachev in the Soviet Union – so much so that the Mexican reforms were given the name "Salinastroika." But as Gorbachev found out, economic liberalization unleashes powerful forces in society. New interests are created, institutions transformed, and identities reshaped.

The economic crises of the 1980s and the resulting laissez-faire (**neoliberal**) policies remade political interests in ways not seen since the Mexican Revolution. Definite winners and losers emerged. The most extreme example has been in the southern state of Chiapas, where a guerrilla insurgency burst onto the scene in 1994. With land becoming increasingly concentrated in the hands of a few large-scale farmers, *ejidos* found it exceedingly difficult to sustain a living, and grievances against the government grew. In 1992, President Salinas revised Article 27 of the 1917 constitution, which was the cornerstone for earlier land-redistribution programs. The new article made privatizing *ejido* lands easier. Peasants seeking to have their concerns addressed were frequent targets of violent attacks by the state police and private paramilitary groups supported by large landholders. The implementation of NAFTA in 1994 further threatened the interests of *ejido* farmers, as it favored large-scale agricultural exporters over small-scale communal farms. With their economic livelihood at risk, many peasants found it worthwhile to join the Zapatista National Liberation Army (EZLN). As of this writing, the EZLN and the Mexican government remain deadlocked over a variety of issues that affect peasant interests, including land redistribution, human rights, effective political representation, and electoral fraud.

The Zapatista movement is not only about economic interests. Because many of the peasants in Chiapas are of direct Mayan ancestry, the movement has asserted strong indigenous claims. Mexican nationalism plays little, if any, role. In fact, the insurgency in Chiapas has demonstrated the difficulty in forging a single Mexican identity. In societies where economic class divisions map closely onto racial and ethnic cleavages, ethnic identity is bound to be closely associated with interest-based politics. How the central government treats the descendants of pre-Columbian inhabitants has become a central policy issue in a country that has largely ignored such concerns for nearly five centuries. Indigenous communities are now identifying themselves as distinct groups within the Mexican polity and demanding to have their voices heard in the central government. This implies a greater respect for civil liberties (e.g., freedom of association) and the ability of indigenous groups to freely elect government officials who represent their interests. The rise of a strong indigenous identity thus creates pressures for political liberalization.

The political legacy of the 1990s has been the emergence of real electoral competition, one of the central features of a liberal-democratic polity. With the PRI losing its ability to deliver patronage to its core constituencies because of fiscal restraints on state spending and an ambitious program of privatization and government downsizing, many of those interests tied tightly to the party in the past have sought new avenues of representation. Non-governmental organizations have appeared as a new force in society. Political participation also has been channeled into two major opposition parties – the National Action Party (PAN) and the **Democratic Revolutionary Party (Partido Revolucionario Democrático, PRD)**. The latter was forged from a coalition of leftist parties and disaffected members of the PRI in the early 1990s. It has attracted mostly members of the urban and rural working class and poor, although significant portions of lower-income voters remain tied to the traditional patronage networks of the PRI. Political infighting has also weakened the PRD. During the 1994 presidential elections, the PRD candidate – Cuauhtémoc Cárdenas (a former member of the PRI) – won only 17 percent of the vote in a reasonably clean election. Nonetheless, by the late 1990s, the PRD had scored a number of important victories at the local level, including winning the mayoral seat of the nation's capital.

The PAN has been the most consistent threat to the PRI's political hegemony. Representing upper-income interests, the PAN has tapped into domestic business disapprobation with many of Salinas's and Zedillo's economic policies. Although it seems odd that domestic businesses would be dissatisfied with laissez-faire policies, it must be remembered that many of these businesses benefited from the high tariffs and government subsidies of the 1960s and 1970s, and these businesses were not prepared to compete internationally. Neoliberal policies took many of these benefits away, although overall they have helped to create a friendlier environment for foreign investment. It is ironic that the PAN champions many of the same neoliberal policies as the PRI. In this respect, much of the support for the PAN can be viewed more as a search for an alternative political voice than as a desire to shift the economic policies of the state. This voice has found a forum, as PAN candidates have won numerous local offices and captured key gubernatorial positions in several northern states.

The increase in electoral competition affected two of the country's primary political institutions – the national legislature and the PRI. Power still remains highly concentrated in the presidency, and the executive branch remains under the control of the PRI. However, in 1997 the PRI lost majority control of the Chamber of Deputies (equivalent to the U.S. House of Representatives). Previously, the PRI had enjoyed majority representation in both the Chamber of Deputies and the Senate, making the Congress a "rubber stamp" for executive decisions. This pattern was reinforced by the fact that the PRI Party leadership chose each legislator, which meant that the president had a strong influence over the career paths of politicians. In some respects, this resembled "parliamentarianism in reverse" – the leading party executive chose legislators rather than vice versa. Results from the 1997 midterm elections earned opposition parties a combined majority in the Chamber of Deputies for the first time in the twentieth century. Although the PRI still controls the Senate and can play "divide and conquer" among the deputies to ensure a winning legislative coalition, the presence of a majority opposition in the lower house has forced the PRI to engage in negotiation and compromise, both steps toward more pluralistic interest representation. With opposition parties in general agreement on the need for further electoral reforms, this environment bodes well for continued political liberalization. Political liberalization, in turn, raises the prospects for greater representation for opposition parties in the Congress and for a stronger legislative branch. Although it is still too early to tell, the classic liberal notion of checks and balances may become a reality in the near future.

Increased political competition and social pluralism have shaken the dominant party itself. Within the party elite, a debate rages over how to manage the economic and political turmoil engulfing Mexico. The faction that emerged as dominant since the 1980s represents a more reformist line of thinking. Known as the ***técnicos*** (technocrats), they hearken from the bureaucratic side of the PRI. Presidents Salinas and Zedillo are members of this faction. Both were educated in U.S. universities and earned their political stripes by working their way through the Mexican bureaucracy rather than by winning seats in local and regional government. The *técnicos* began occupying high-level offices during the 1980s, when the economic crisis called for policymakers with specific expertise in managing domestic and international macroeconomic affairs. The ascendance of *técnicos* gave rise to a competing faction within the PRI called the ***dinosaurios*** for their hard-line, traditional corporatist stance.

The split within the PRI created an interesting and fluid pattern of alliances. The primary intraparty cleavage related to economic policy. Whereas the *técnicos* favored neoliberal economic reforms to modernize Mexico's economy, the *dinosaurios* preferred the old formula of state-directed growth and opposed both the privatization of industries and NAFTA. This put the *dinosaurios* in policy agreement with the PRD. The *técnicos* found policy allies among the center-right PAN. Despite their differences, both the *técnicos* and *dinosaurios* strongly desired that the PRI hold onto political power. Political survival tended to take precedence over economic policy disagreements, and both factions were involved significantly in vote tampering during the 1980s. The transparency of electoral fraud, especially at the local level, only fueled further dissatisfaction with the ruling party and intensified public cries for electoral reform.

Whereas President de la Madrid (1982–1988) represented a transition between the hard-line *dinosaurios* and the *técnicos*, Carlos Salinas de Gortari firmly identified himself with the latter. Following his narrow electoral victory in 1988, Salinas surprised many analysts by charting a course independent of the *dinosaurios*. It was believed that this would be a dangerous strategy for a man who needed as much internal party support as he could muster. Nonetheless, his institutional reengineering had a lasting impact on the

Mexican polity, and he most likely will be remembered as a pivotal character in Mexico's political history. Salinas was credited with disassembling many of the PRI's traditional patronage networks. Realizing that *dinosaurio* power rested in those channels, he cut funds for favored programs and dismissed important union officials. Still needing social support for his presidency, however, Salinas created the Solidarity Program, a new set of patronage networks that circumvented many of the local political bosses who remained loyal to the *dinosaurios*. President Zedillo continued this tradition through a similar set of programs. The end result was to destroy almost completely the traditional pillars of support holding up Mexico's corporatist system, which had ensured political stability in the past.

Constitutional reforms undertaken in 1992 further changed Mexico's political landscape by removing some of the most radical elements of the revolutionary constitution. Without recourse to the revolutionary ideals of the past, a new legitimating formula needed to be found. Although Salinas and the *técnicos* hoped that economic growth would boost support for the PRI, they realized that economic restructuring would pay dividends too far off in the future. Discontent with the country's economic situation was increasing, especially among the traditional corporatist allies of the PRI – labor, the peasantry, and middle-class bureaucrats. Both presidents Salinas and Zedillo sought to restore the PRI's legitimacy by championing political reform. Salinas began the process of promoting electoral reforms that would allow opposition parties a fair chance at winning office. Secret balloting was guaranteed to prevent voter intimidation, and ballot counts came under greater scrutiny. Salinas further cracked down on local PRI officials who engaged in electoral fraud, although enforcement of this policy typically favored the PAN, not the PRD. Given that the *técnicos* and PANistas shared a similar economic policy agenda, capitulating to their electoral victories was a more palatable solution than allowing PRD victories. Fraud continued against PRD candidates, leading to violent clashes between protesters and police. Despite ideological disagreements, however, leaders of the PAN and PRD found it in their mutual interest to cooperate and press for more electoral reforms. The PRI still controlled access to state financial resources and public media outlets, giving it a significant electoral advantage.

Political reform was put to the test in 1994. The growing rift within the PRI erupted in violence. In March, Luis Donaldo Colosio, a *técnico* and Salinas's handpicked presidential successor, was assassinated on the campaign trail. Although the crime was pinned on a young garage mechanic, it was widely suspected that members of the PRI's *dinosaurio* faction had masterminded the plot. Several months later, the secretary-general of the PRI (and brother-in-law of the president) was gunned down. Salinas's own brother was arrested as the prime suspect. Such high-level political violence had a profound effect on Mexican politics. To ensure free and fair elections and deflect further accusations of fraud, an independent electoral commission was established to monitor voting practices. International observers also were invited to oversee national balloting. As a result, Mexico's 1994 presidential elections were the most honest in nearly two decades, a triumph for liberal-pluralism.

The PRI's Ernesto Zedillo, another young *técnico*, won the election with a plurality of the vote (48.8 percent), and the ruling party hung onto a narrow majority in the Chamber of Deputies. The victory came at a severe cost for the country, however. To win popular support amid growing political turmoil, the PRI inflated the Mexican economy throughout most of 1994, making it easier to pay off needed constituents with government projects and providing a general feeling of economic prosperity in the country. The government also issued a large quantity of short-term government bonds to boost the confidence of foreign investors, who were growing increasingly nervous about the spreading political violence (including the Zapatista uprising). However, faced with rapidly declining foreign currency reserves, the incoming Zedillo administration was forced to devalue the Mexican peso. Traditionally, hard economic choices had been made by the outgoing president, thereby allowing the incoming president to avoid public hostility. Former President Carlos Salinas de Gortari, however, was pursuing a bid to become the president of the newly created World Trade Organization, based on his success in negotiating NAFTA. He refused to devalue the peso, knowing that such action would reveal weakness in his administration's monetary policy. When Zedillo finally attempted a controlled devaluation, speculator pressure pushed the currency into a spiraling freefall. Inflation soared and government actions to stem rising prices plunged the economy into another major recession, just as it had a decade earlier. Salinas further challenged the informal norms of Mexican political life by criticizing the Zedillo administration's handling of the economic crisis. Zedillo countered by investigating the former president's financial dealings. In a unique turn of fate for a former Mexican president, Salinas exiled himself abroad, fearing arrest should he return to Mexico. Such an unprecedented situation clearly signals that the Mexican political system is no longer operating as it has in the past, although the future shape of the polity is still unclear.

Pressured by a severe recession, a stalemated guerrilla insurrection, and growing international skepticism about Mexico's business climate, Zedillo was forced to speed up the political reforms begun under Salinas. The centerpiece of these reforms was an electoral reform package implemented in 1996. Among its many provisions, the new laws provided for greater public financing of campaigns and media access for all parties. The plan also eliminated party membership based upon group ("corporate") affiliation. This measure effectively eliminated the basis for corporatist interest representation that had been the bedrock of Mexico's political system for most of the twentieth century. Perhaps more important was the strengthening of the

Federal Electoral Institute and the Federal Electoral Tribunal in 1996. The former institution, composed of an independent citizen advisory board, is charged with the duty of monitoring all federal elections to minimize fraud. The Tribunal serves as a court to investigate all electoral irregularities and prosecute individuals engaged in electoral malfeasance. Initially created in 1990, both entities were given full independence and a permanent footing by President Zedillo in 1996. Since introducing these reforms, most observers of Mexican politics agree that the incidence of fraud, although still present, has been greatly reduced. Finally, President Zedillo departed from the traditional practice of the *dedazo*, the selection by the president of a successor. Instead of the sitting PRI president naming his successor, an open primary would be held to determine the presidential candidate of the party. This move was geared largely toward ensuring that the PRI's candidate would be vetted by the voting public and, hopefully, possess greater popular appeal and legitimacy during the general election.

Implementing these reforms has not been easy. Regional PRI caciques continue to manipulate local politics, subverting the implementation of the new laws. A once hegemonic party facing real political competition for the first time can be expected to bend or break rules in order to stay in power. Nonetheless, the reforms have shown some success in guaranteeing a more open political process. The 1997 midterm elections for the national legislature gave opposition parties their first combined majority in the Chamber of Deputies. Both the PAN and PRD made substantial gains in local elections, culminating in the historic victory of Vincente Fox in the 2000 presidential election. Despite his rather unassuming personality, overshadowed by the controversial Carlos Salinas de Gortari before him and the animated Vincente Fox who followed, Ernesto Zedillo should really be remembered as one of the most influential Mexican presidents of the twentieth century, perhaps rivaling Lázaro Cárdenas in importance. Ironically, his being perceived initially as a weak president who was not threatening to entrenched interests in the PRI may have granted him the political space in which to undertake these bold political reforms. And as the tumultuous twentieth century came to a close, he could rest assured that his decisions helped to initiate a new era in Mexican politics.

THE 2000 PRESIDENTIAL ELECTION AND ITS AFTERMATH

Just as January 1, 1994, will be remembered in Mexican history for its high political drama, so will the date of July 2, 2000, when the PRI went down to defeat in presidential elections. Polls just weeks before the election showed a dead heat between the PAN's candidate, Vincente Fox Quesada, and the PRI's candidate, Francisco Labastida. Although no one assumed that the PRD's candidate, Cuauhtémoc Cárdenas, would win the election, his presence certainly represented a wild card in the race. Mexican citizens held their breath as election results came in. It was feared that a narrow victory by the PRI would raise doubts about the integrity of the electoral process and might provoke social chaos. Alternatively, some feared that if the PAN (or PRD) won by a slim margin, the military might intervene and declare a coup. Although in hindsight such fears appeared overblown, they were nevertheless real at the time. Fortunately, Vincente Fox emerged as the clear victor in the contest, winning 42.5 percent of the vote compared with Labastida's 36.1 percent.

Fox's success at the ballot box certainly resulted from two decades of growing pressure for political change and the liberalizing political reforms championed by Ernesto Zedillo. But an interesting question still presents itself: Why, with the Mexican economy struggling for more than two decades, did the citizenry decide upon a candidate who represented a continuation of the neoliberal economic policies of the new *técnicos* (such as Salinas and Zedillo) instead of the PRD's candidate, who promised a return to a more statist/corporatist approach to economic policy? If anything, the results of the 2000 election signaled that the Mexican populace was hungrier for political change than economic change, and Vincente Fox – as a dynamic campaigner – represented the most viable option for an opposition victory. Moreover, there is no reason to suspect that greater state intervention will be demanded by a population in times of economic crisis. The Reagan and Thatcher revolutions were enormously popular among the working classes in the United States and Britain, and more recently neoliberal reforms in New Zealand have garnered widespread support. Even in Chile, the privatization of the social security system has proven to be a political winner. Although academics have often assumed that the identity of economically distressed populations would naturally favor increased state intervention of the nature that the PRD was promising, the results of the Mexican election may prove otherwise.

But the reasons for Fox's victory may go beyond the policy preferences of voters. At a time when popular support for the PRI was rapidly eroding, the PAN had the strongest political organization and a historical identity that crossed various socioeconomic barriers. Founded in the 1920s, the original aim of the PAN was not so much to win elections as it was to educate Mexicans about civic engagement. This approach represented a long-term strategy in influencing the political landscape and made perfect sense after it was realized that the PRI was the overwhelmingly dominant player in the electoral arena. The PRI initially appealed to an odd mix of socially conscious Catholics and small and medium-sized business owners. Both of these groups were excluded from the corporatist pillars established under the Cárdenas regime. As the Mexican Miracle provided a robust economy wherein even small and medium-sized businesses thrived, the latter group drifted away from the PAN, leaving a number of Catholic lay intellectuals in charge of the party. Influenced by the socially progressive thinking of Pope Pius IX (1846–1878) and the Second Vatican Council (1962–1965), the PAN had a noticeable leftist identity during the 1950s and 1960s. However, as the economy soured during the 1970s and the more interventionist policies of President Echeverría alienated the business community, small-business owners began returning to the PAN, moving the party leadership in a more rightward direction in terms of economic policy. Moreover, with the PRI's support beginning to erode among the middle class, the PAN began to focus on a strategy of winning local elections. Focusing primarily on a platform of greater political liberalization, the PAN managed to create a somewhat broad-based ideological umbrella that was comfortable both for the progressive Catholics and neoliberal business interests. The PAN developed an extensive grassroots campaign network that was rather unified in its purpose and, as noted earlier, paid off during the 1980s and 1990s with some significant electoral victories in local elections.

One could contrast this institutional organization with the PRD, which did not come together as a formal political party until the late 1980s and consisted largely of a splintered coalition of leftist parties, each with their own separate organizations, personalities, and ideologies. Although Cuauhtémoc Cárdenas, as the son of the famous Mexican president and a high-profile defector from the PRI, presented a figure to rally around in the 1988 elections, the organizational inexperience and disparate interests within the PRD did little to help them build national momentum. Granted, the PRD was capable of winning local elections (particularly in the southern states that were home to the poor and the indigenous peoples), where their organization was more cohesive, but translating these successes to a national level proved more elusive.

The PAN also benefited enormously from the vibrant personality of Vincente Fox. His story as a self-made business executive, moving from delivery driver for Coca-Cola, through the ranks of the company's sales force, and eventually to become the CEO of Coca-Cola's Mexican subsidiary, gave him the aura, rightfully deserved, of economic success. His towering height and polished speaking skills also added to his reputation as a strong leader. Finally, and perhaps most ironically, Fox apparently fell victim to electoral fraud at the hands of the PRI while running for the governorship of Guanajuato in 1991. This case made Fox a national celebrity and guaranteed his election as governor of the state in 1996. His national profile, combined with his political ambition, made Fox the ideal candidate for the PAN in the 2000 presidential campaign. His optimistic energy contrasted greatly with the more dour and pessimistic campaign style of Cárdenas and, in a new era where opposition candidates were granted greater access to the popular media, this enhanced the electoral edge of both Fox and the PAN Party in general.

The peaceful transition of power to Vincente Fox certainly represented a major step toward competitive multiparty democracy in Mexico. Most observers would now argue that this one election bodes well for future elections in Mexico at all levels of government. Indeed, the 2003 midterm elections for the Chamber of Deputies were once again hailed as being reasonably free from corruption. Although the PAN lost a substantial number of seats in the Chamber of Deputies and the PRI and PRD gained seats, all of this represents the normal vagaries of democratic politics. With an economy in recession, it was normal to expect that the party holding the presidency would lose seats. The importance of the 2003 elections is that the electoral process is functioning as it should and the main political parties are adjusting to a new political environment.

Nonetheless, the political future is not unequivocally promising for Mexico. Several problems remain, many of which are directly related to the institutional structures that were developed during the twentieth century to deal with problems of the nineteenth century. Preeminent among the institutional problems facing Mexico is the term limit placed upon the president and members of Congress. In the past, with one dominant party and a system that gave the greatest power to the president, the president was able to get his legislative agenda passed quickly. Concerns over a single-term limit were ameliorated by the fact that the president would choose his successor and determine the political fortunes of others within the party, making almost all legislators willing to give the president what he wanted. Although one could rightly argue that this system was too dictatorial and could lead to bad policy outcomes, it also allowed for rapid government decision making in times of crisis. The situation in the early twenty-first century is much different. With a president highly restricted in his ability to name his successor, legislators have less incentive to cooperate on policy making with the president. This problem has been exacerbated by the specific relationship that Vincente Fox has with the PAN Party. Being a relative newcomer to the political arena, only getting involved in politics in the decade before he was elected president, Fox had very few loyal connections to PAN Party members, and many of his initial policies were not to the liking of PAN legislators. Attempts to negotiate a settlement with the Zapatistas by demilitarizing Chiapas early in his administration were met with resistance not only by the PRI but members of his own party as well. A similar situation arose when Fox tried to reform Mexico's complicated and rather archaic tax structure. In general, the first several years of the Fox administration have been characterized by policy gridlock.

This policy gridlock also results from the mixed electoral system that chooses the national legislature. Although plurality voting in single-member districts tends to push the political system to a two-party outcome, the presence of plurality rule in deciding a significant portion of the Chamber of Deputies still encourages minority parties. This has resulted in there being no clear majority party in the legislature since 2000. Riding the coattails of Vincente Fox in 2000, the PAN picked up a substantial number of seats but ended up in a virtual dead heat with the PRI, the latter winning 208 seats while the former held 207. Only by forming a fragile coalition with members of the PRD and Green parties was the PAN able to obtain a majority in the Chamber of Deputies. In the 2003 elections, the situation reversed. The PRI won more seats than the PAN but could only sustain a majority with help from the Greens. Even if the PAN were able to win a legislative majority and work amicably with President Fox, they would be facing a large administrative bureaucracy that is still staffed by partisans loyal to the PRI. With administrative staffers owing little allegiance to the president, there has been a noticeable increase in administrative corruption in recent years, a problem that is difficult to combat.

Conclusion

The Mexico that we see today is an artifact of its past. The legacy of political violence during the 1800s and early 1900s paved the way for a quasi-authoritarian, corporatist regime. Foreign intervention in Mexican affairs complicated the country's search for political stability and gave the country's policies a decidedly nationalist and autarkic tone. But the world economy could not be ignored. Despite attempts to free itself from dependency on the world economy, Mexico found itself more dependent upon the good graces of the international financial community by the late 1970s. The economic crisis of the 1980s prompted Mexicans to rethink not only their economic development strategy but also their political system. Grassroots demands for greater political representation prompted a movement away from a one-party corporatist state and toward a multiparty pluralist democracy.

All of this history has shaped the interests and identities found within Mexico today. Moreover, Mexico's position in the international arena has combined with these interests and identities to shape its current political landscape. Mexico's long-standing tradition of corporatism has created strong interests in society that expect government patronage. Unionized labor has come to expect job security and wages that support an increasing standard of living. Rural campesinos (farm laborers), particularly in the south, have come to expect a certain level of stability that the constitutionally mandated *ejido* system provided. And both small and big businesses (in both the industrial and agricultural sectors) have demanded subsidies and tariff protection to shield them from international competitors. Meeting these basic economic interests was possible when the Mexican economy was growing by leaps and bounds.

Those days ended in the early 1980s when Mexico became saddled with an expanding international debt and a sharp loss in export revenues. Although the international economy changed, societal interests in Mexico did not. The PRI could no longer meet the societal demands that had become part of the institutional and ideological fabric of Mexican society. With a shrinking economy, the various sectors (labor, agriculture, and industry) found their demands in direct competition with one another. Mexico's corporatist identity – the ability to develop economically based on the harmonious balance of competing social interests – was also torn apart. Recognizing that the PRI could no longer deliver upon past corporatist privileges, citizens began to demand more organizational autonomy from the government and a greater say in political decision making.

This conflict of interests also appeared to tear at another aspect of Mexico's national identity. Whereas Mexican heritage had often been presented as a distinct mix of two cultures – Spanish and indigenous (Aztec and Mayan) – it has become increasingly apparent since the 1980s that economic inequity closely mirrored racial and ethnic divisions within society. Criollos maintained their historic position at the top of the socioeconomic ladder, whereas indigenous populations languished at the bottom. As noted at the beginning of this chapter, this long-standing problem became evident to the world on January 1, 1994, when a guerrilla insurgency composed mainly of impoverished indigenous farmers placed a damper on the festivities of a New Year's Eve party attended mostly by criollos and well-to-do mestizos. These insurgents proudly identified themselves as being of Mayan ancestry, and far from simply demanding reintegration into past corporatist arrangements, they announced their desire for greater political independence and the ability to freely choose their political representatives. It is interesting to note that these demands demonstrated that the struggle between corporatism and liberalism was not just a historical artifact but a present reality.

At the dawn of the twenty-first century, Mexico finds itself on the verge of a new era of liberal democracy with competitive multiparty elections. Demands for greater political participation during the early 1800s resulted in independence from Spain, although many among the governing elite sought to keep the top-down political arrangements of the colonial era. Similar cries for political reform were heard during the Mexican Revolution a century later. Although significant changes did result in a general rise in economic well-being, governing structures continued to leave little room for popular participation at the grass roots of society. The changes taking place today are reminiscent of those earlier eras. However, the contemporary world in which Mexico operates is, in many ways, smaller than it was before. With international investors demanding a liberalized economy, and with labor and capital mobility more fluid than ever, the Mexican government has less leeway in determining its economic policy. Yet the urgency to rekindle economic growth will affect the country's social stability. The new neoliberal course pursued since the 1990s will undoubtedly affect the interests of important political players and reshape the national character of Mexican society. As in previous centuries, the new shape of politics will play out over time. Interests and identities are not set in stone. Although it is too early to predict what the political outcomes will be, this ever-shifting global environment offers a wonderful opportunity to understand the complexities of comparative politics.

BIBLIOGRAPHY

Bulmer-Thomas, Victor. *The Economic History of Latin America Since Independence*. Cambridge: Cambridge University Press, 1994.

Camp, Roderic Ai. *Politics in Mexico: The Democratic Transformation*. Fourth edition. New York: Oxford University Press, 2002.

Cardoso, Eliana, and Ann Helwege. *Latin America's Economy: Diversity Trends and Conflicts*. Cambridge, MA: MIT Press, 1992.

Chand, Vikram K. *Mexico's Political Awakening*. Notre Dame, IN: University of Notre Dame Press, 2001.

Cothran, Dan A. *Political Stability and Democracy in Mexico: The "Perfect Dictatorship"?* Westport, CT: Praeger, 1994.

Eckstein, Susan. *The Poverty of Revolution*. Princeton, NJ: Princeton University Press, 1988.

Eisendstadt, Todd A. *Courting Democracy in Mexico: Party Strategies and Electoral Institutions*. Cambridge: Cambridge University Press, 2004.

Fuentes, Carlos. *A New Time for Mexico*. Berkeley: University of California Press, 1997.

Gill, Anthony. "The Politics of Regulating Religion in Mexico: The 1992 Constitutional Reforms in Historical Context." *Journal of Church and State* 41, no. 4 (1999): 761–794.

Gill, Anthony and Arang Keshavarzian. "State Building and Religious Resources: An Institutional Theory of Church–State Relations in Iran and Mexico." *Politics and Society* 27, no. 3 (1999): 430–464.

Grayson, George W. *Mexico: From Corporatism to Pluralism?* Fort Worth, TX: Harcourt Brace, 1998.

Hamilton, Nora. *The Limits of State Autonomy*. Princeton, NJ: Princeton University Press, 1982.

Hansen, Roger D. *The Politics of Mexican Development*. Baltimore, MD: Johns Hopkins University Press, 1971.

Meyer, Michael C., and William L. Sherman. *The Course of Mexican History*. Fourth edition. New York: Oxford University Press, 1991.

Middlebrook, Kevin J. *The Paradox of Revolution: Labor, the State, and Authoritarianism in Mexico*. Baltimore, MD: Johns Hopkins University Press, 1995.

Morris, Stephen D. *Political Reformism in Mexico: An Overview of Contemporary Mexican Politics*. Boulder, CO: Lynne Rienner, 1995.

Ruvio, Luis, and Susan Kaufman Purcell, eds. *Mexico Under Fox*. Boulder, CO: Lynne Rienner, 2004.

Skidmore, Thomas E., and Peter H. Smith. *Modern Latin America*. Fourth edition. Oxford: Oxford University Press, 1995.

Wiarda, Howard J. "Toward a Framework for the Study of Political Change in the Iberic-Latin Tradition: The Corporative Model." *World Politics* 25 (1973): 206–235.

Womack, John, Jr. *Zapata and the Mexican Revolution*. New York: Vintage Books, 1970.

TABLE 9.1. Key Phases in Mexican Development

Time Period	Regime	Global Context	Interests/Identities/ Institutions	Developmental Path
1521–1821	colonialism – strict control of Spanish America by crown; Spain discourages autonomous government in colonies, although some local control granted	rise and decline of the Spanish Empire. Napoleonic Wars and occupation of Spain, combined with growth of liberalism in Spain, prompt independence movement.	strong landed elite (*latifundistas*)/ monopolistic Catholicism and mestizo culture develops (Virgin of Guadalupe represents fusion of European colonial culture and indigenous culture)/colonial authoritarian control.	mercantilism – raw material exports from colonies to Spain; finished goods imported to colonies from Spain. Tight regulation over domestic colonial economy. Colonial manufacturing discouraged.
1820s– 1876	era of the Caudillos – period of political uncertainty, instability, and internecine warfare punctuated by foreign economic and military intervention; battles between Liberals and Conservatives	growth in European economic influence (primarily British and French); U.S. territorial expansion leads to war and loss of Mexican territory.	geographically located strongmen seek power/weak nationalism develops and grows/ intermittent authoritarianism at national level; local caudillos rule regionally	economic chaos – political instability discourages economic investment and fosters government fiscal crises. Export-led growth based on primary goods in latter period
1876–1911	Porfiriato – "liberal dictatorship" of Porfirio Diaz; expansion of middle class.	direct foreign economic and military interference wanes.	export agriculture and mining/growing liberal sentiment/ centralized authoritarian rule	export-led growth – economic stability and growth prompts initial industrialization

(continued)

TABLE 9.1 (continued)

Time Period	Regime	Global Context	Interests/Identities/ Institutions	Developmental Path
1910–1920	Mexican Revolution – begins as succession crisis, but radicalized by lower-class social movements and leftist political ideologies. General political chaos.	general non-interference in Mexican affairs, U.S. isolationist, and Britain's presence in Western Hemisphere waning.	geographic strongmen seek power. Rise of peasantry and working class as political force/ growing socialist/ redistributive sentiment/ intermittent dictatorial rule.	economic chaos – economic activity severely limited by political chaos.
1920–1982	state-led corporatism – one-party rule based on incorporation of social groups into government structure. Creation of extensive patronage networks.	growing U.S. influence in Latin America; Great Depression and movement toward economic openness among industrialized nations.	labor, peasantry, and large business closely integrated with state/ corporatism/highly centralized state and one-party rule.	"Mexican Miracle" and import-substitution industrialization (ISI) – Restriction of imports of manufactured finished goods; increasing government intervention in economy.
1982–2000	decline of corporatism – movement toward greater political openness and party competition. Rise of civil society. New model of governance still uncertain.	third world debt crisis and end of Cold War.	rise of bureaucratic *técnicos* and decline of influence of labor and peasantry/ disillusionment with one-party rule and corporatism/ gradual decay of one-party rule. Opposition parties begin to win local elections.	neoliberalism – promotion of free trade (NAFTA) and less government regulation of economy.

IMPORTANT TERMS

cabildos town councils established during the colonial period that served as the basis for the independence movement.

caciques political bosses who control local government and are relatively autonomous from the federal government. Co-opting these individuals has been a main concern in the centralization of political authority in Mexico.

Lázaro Cárdenas president of Mexico from 1934 to 1940. He was responsible for institutionalizing the corporatist form of government and bringing labor, agricultural workers, and industry under the control of the state.

caudillos political strongmen during the 1800s who frequently controlled their own armies and dominated local politics. Their presence made centralized political authority difficult to establish during the nineteenth century and led to decades of political instability.

Conservatives loose-knit political party during the 1800s that represented the interests of the agricultural sector while being opposed to industrialization and democratic reforms.

Constitution of 1917 constitution of the Mexican Revolution that promoted radical agrarian reform and workers' rights. It would become the legal basis for Lázaro Cárdenas to redistribute land and nationalize Mexico's oil industry.

corporatism (Mexican) an ideology derived from medieval Catholic thought that sees the polity as an organic whole and seeks to minimize social conflict via central government organization of competing interests in society. In its institutionalized form, the government organizes and directs urban and rural labor unions as well as professional organizations.

criollos individuals of pure-blooded Spanish heritage born in Mexico. The economic and political elite tend to be from this racial class.

Democratic Revolutionary Party (PRD) a leftist political party formed after the 1988 presidential election by defectors from the PRI in order to offer an electoral alternative to the dominant party.

dinosaurios a faction of the ruling PRI Party in the last two decades of the twentieth century. Its members want to maintain corporatist forms of economic and political organization.

ejidos communal farms that originated in pre-Columbian indigenous societies and were promoted in the 1917 constitution. Lázaro Cárdenas established a number of them during the late 1930s as a way of distributing land among indigenous populations and poor farmers (found mostly in southern Mexico).

Vincente Fox victor of the 2000 presidential election from the PAN Party and a former businessman. The first candidate from an opposition party to win the presidency since the Mexican Revolution.

import-substituting industrialization (ISI) the dominant economic policy of Mexico from the 1930s to the early 1980s, designed to industrialize the nation. According to this general economic strategy, high import tariffs are imposed to stimulate domestic production of consumer goods.

Institutional Revolutionary Party (PRI) the dominant ruling party of Mexico since the 1920s. Although it originated as a center-left party, it has drifted toward the center-right since the 1980s.

Benito Juárez a liberal reformer in the mid-1800s who sought to promote land reform, centralize political authority, and modernize Mexico.

La Reforma a period in Mexican political history (ca. 1855–1876) during which liberal political forces predominated over their conservative rivals and began implementing economic and political reforms designed to bring Mexico closer to the policies and forms of government of the United States and Northern Europe. This represented the first time since the end of colonialism that a consistent governmental plan appeared, even though this era was beset by civil war and a foreign occupation.

Liberals a loose-knit political party during the 1800s that represented urban interests and promoted increased trade ties with Northern Europe and the United States.

Antonio López de Santa Anna the most important caudillo in Mexico during the nineteenth century and who intermittently served as president.

mestizos individuals of mixed Spanish and indigenous heritage. They represent the mingling of two different cultures into a distinct Mexican identity.

Mexican Miracle a period from the 1940s to the 1970s (with the apogee from 1950 to 1970) wherein rapid industrialization promoted high levels of economic growth and improved living standards. This era gave rise to a new middle class with rising expectations that were restricted by the government's inability to satisfy these demands during the last two decades of the twentieth century.

Mexican Revolution the period from 1910 to 1920 wherein a major civil war among various factions eventually led to a set of radical social programs, namely labor rights and land reform, being included in the constitution of 1917 and eventually implemented under Lázaro Cárdenas during the 1930s.

National Action Party (PAN) a center-right party established in the mid-1900s as a challenge to PRI dominance. It won some critical local elections during the 1980s and 1990s that pushed Mexico toward greater political liberalization.

neoliberalism a policy that emphasizes free trade, privatization of industry, and a reduction in government intervention in the economy. This strategy was pursued by Presidents Salinas and Zedillo during the 1980s and 1990s.

North American Free Trade Agreement (NAFTA) an international treaty that lowered trade barriers among Mexico, the United States, and Canada. The centerpiece of President Salinas's neoliberal economic strategy, it was implemented on January 1, 1994, the same day that the Zapatista National Liberation Army initiated its guerrilla insurgency.

pan o palo literally meaning "bread or club," the phrase that refers to two common forms of political power in Mexico. *Pan* (bread) denotes the use of political patronage to buy political support, whereas *palo* (club) implies the use of coercion.

Porfiriato the period from 1876 to 1910 during which caudillo and dictatorial President Porfirio Díaz ruled Mexico. This was the first time since colonial days that Mexico was unified under central rule for a significant period; it was also a time of strong economic growth that gave rise to new social classes and, eventually, the Mexican Revolution.

Carlos Salinas de Gortari Mexican president from 1988 to 1994. He reversed decades of corporatist and ISI policies in favor of a neoliberal economic agenda. His economic liberalization prompted calls for political liberalization at the end of the twentieth century.

técnicos a faction within the ruling PRI that rose to prominence in the 1980s by promoting neoliberal economic reforms. Typically trained in U.S. and European universities, the members are in conflict with the *dinosaurios*, who favor corporatist policies.

Tlatelolco site of a massacre in 1968 where more than 100 protesters were killed by state police. The protest signaled that the long-standing legitimacy of the PRI's corporatist rule was wearing thin, especially among students and the middle class.

Virgin of Guadalupe a symbol of Mexico's unique national identity that blends European Catholicism with indigenous images. It represents the appearance of the Virgin Mary before an indigenous boy during the colonial period and has since been used as a rallying point for Mexican nationalism.

Emiliano Zapata the leader of a revolutionary army during the Mexican Revolution. He demanded greater rights for indigenous rural workers in southern Mexico, including a substantial land reform that eventually became a centerpiece of the 1917 constitution.

Zapatista National Liberation Front (EZLN) a guerrilla army that appeared in the southern Mexican state of Chiapas in 1994 following the implementation of NAFTA. Like their earlier revolutionary namesake, Emiliano Zapata, the Zapatistas, as they are known, demanded land reform, economic justice, and freer political representation for the poor indigenous communities.

Ernesto Zedillo president of Mexico from 1994 to 2000. He oversaw an extension of neoliberal reforms and promoted greater political liberalization, including the first-ever presidential primary election in Mexican history.

STUDY QUESTIONS

1. Mexico has prided itself on its unique blend of Spanish and indigenous heritages. Not only did the Spanish conquistadors adopt a number of indigenous traditions and symbols, but Spaniards and indigenous people also physically intermingled, forming a mestizo (mixed-blood) ethnic group. Nonetheless, economic and political power remains highly stratified along class lines, with criollos holding the most powerful positions, the indigenous population inhabiting the lowest economic classes, and the mestizos falling in between these two groups. Tensions among these groups spilled over most recently during the Zapatista uprising in southern Mexico, with the guerrillas being composed mostly of indigenous, non-Spanish-speaking individuals. How might this ethnic/racial stratification affect the ability of Mexicans to craft a single national identity? As long as this stratification exists, is it possible to speak of "one Mexico"? What actions might the government take to alleviate the problems created by these socioeconomic and ethnic divisions?

2. Political instability was one of the main features of Mexico during the 1800s. What factors led to and exacerbated this political instability? (Consider a comparison with the United States, which won its independence from colonial powers four decades earlier.) What were the short- and long-term consequences of this era of political instability? Consider how this era both shaped the interests of various actors in society and affected the nation's political consciousness.

3. A common problem faced by political rulers during the colonial and postcolonial periods was how to govern distant geographic regions that had incentives not to obey central authority. Even today, the Mexican president has difficulty implementing policies in isolated regions, such as the state of Chiapas. Local political bosses (caciques) retain a great deal of power over local populations. How have political leaders dealt with this problem throughout Mexican history? What types of policies could the current Mexican government develop to bring local caciques in line with national policy?

4. The revolutionary constitution of 1917 promised radical changes in land tenure and workers' rights. Many of these proposals were implemented by Lázaro Cárdenas during the late 1930s, but enthusiasm for continuing these programs has since waned. Why has this been the case? Is it possible to maintain policies that support communal farms (*ejidos*) and government-sponsored labor unions in an increasingly globalized world economy?

5. Consider the name of the Institutional Revolutionary Party. Looking at Mexico's history, why do you think this name was chosen? To what extent can a revolution be institutionalized? To what extent has the PRI remained a revolutionary force in Mexican society? Now consider the name of the Democratic Revolutionary Party. Why do you suppose this name was chosen? If the PRD gains power, do you expect to see it evolve similarly to the PRI? Discuss.

6. Mexican corporatism brings various social actors (e.g., labor, business professionals) into an officially sanctioned ruling coalition. While guaranteeing certain privileges for these groups (e.g., job security for unionized labor and subsidies for businesses), it also limits such freedoms as choosing when to strike or how to allocate capital. Discuss the advantages and disadvantages of such arrangements. Since the 1980s, there has been a move by some groups to obtain greater autonomy from the government. Why? Consider the role of the economic crisis in the 1980s and its effects on government revenue.

7. Mexico's general economic strategy from the 1930s to the 1980s (known as import-substituting industrialization) was to isolate itself from the world economy by imposing high tariffs on imported consumer goods and limiting foreign investment in the economy. Although it was successful in generating rapid economic growth in the short term, this plan has created some long-term problems. Discuss. To what extent is it possible for Mexico to isolate itself from the world economy today? What possible effects might increased economic integration (e.g., NAFTA) into the global economy have on domestic politics?

8. There is a popular saying in Mexico that describes the country as follows: "So far from God; so close to the United States." What role has the United States (and other foreign countries) played in shaping Mexican politics? How has this role changed over the past 200 years? What does NAFTA have to say about changing relationships among the countries of North America? Is the relationship between the United States and Mexico only a "one-way street," or has Mexico influenced the domestic politics of its northern neighbor?

9. Both Presidents Salinas and Zedillo faced the difficult task of promoting economic growth and political democracy while maintaining the PRI in political power. What are some of the difficulties in balancing these competing interests? How has the pursuit of these different goals affected the PRI itself? To what extent does the pursuit of economic liberalization and liberal democracy conflict with Mexico's long-standing identification with a corporatist philosophy?

10. Many observers of Mexican politics argue that Mexico's transition to a liberal democracy will not be complete until there is a new party in charge of the executive branch. Consider the results of the 2000 presidential election. Would you agree that Mexico has made a successful transition to a stable democracy?

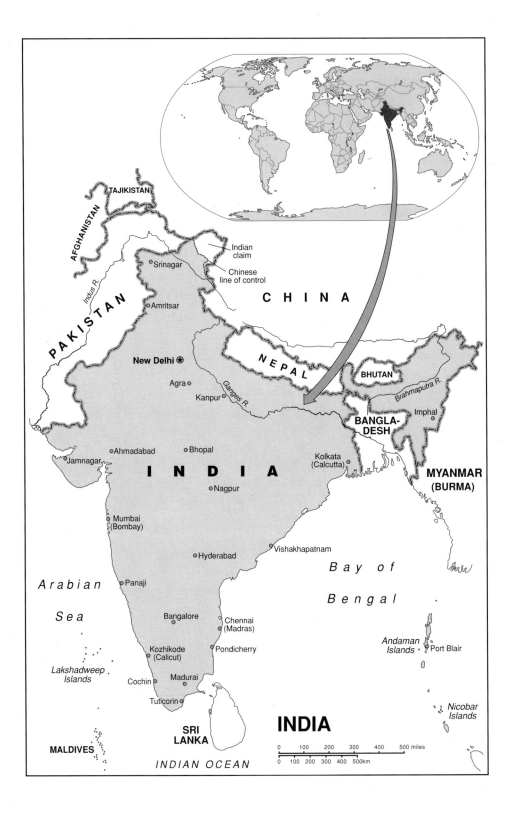

TAJIKISTAN

AFGHANISTAN

PAKISTAN

Indus R.

Srinagar

Amritsar

Indian
claim

Chinese
line of control

CHINA

New Delhi ⊛

Agra

Kanpur

NEPAL

Ganges R.

BHUTAN

Brahmaputra R.

Imphal

BANGLA-
DESH

Ahmadabad

Bhopal

Jamnagar

INDIA

Nagpur

Kolkata
(Calcutta)

MYANMAR
(BURMA)

Mumbai
(Bombay)

Hyderabad

Vishakhapatnam

Arabian

Sea

Panaji

Bay of

Bengal

Bangalore

Chennai
(Madras)

Kozhikode
(Calicut)

Pondicherry

Andaman
Islands

Port Blair

Lakshadweep
Islands

Cochin

Madurai

Tuticorin

SRI
LANKA

INDIA

Nicobar
Islands

MALDIVES

INDIAN OCEAN

0   100   200   300   400   500 miles
0   100 200 300 400 500km

CHAPTER TEN

India

Rudra Sil

Introduction

For most of the first four decades after its independence, India was led by the **Congress Party**, which descended from the independence movement once led by **Mohandas K. (Mahatma) Gandhi** and was committed to a vision of a modern, industrialized, secular state. The party that led India into the twenty-first century, however, was the **Bharatiya Janata Party** (BJP, or the "Indian People's Party"), which descended from political and social organizations committed to redefining Indian national identity in terms of *Hinduttva* (Hindu culture and civilization). Under the leadership of the BJP, India held a series of underground nuclear tests in 1998 and proclaimed itself a member of the nuclear club, setting off joyous celebrations throughout the country and prompting rival Pakistan to launch its own nuclear tests. The following year, Indian troops ousted Pakistani-backed militants from Kargil in Indian-held Kashmir (the Himalayan region claimed by both India and Pakistan), spurring another round of celebrations accompanied by emotional tributes to the "Kargil martyrs." Soon after, India's population passed the one billion mark, triggering still more national euphoria as India closed in on China for the dubious distinction of being the world's most populous country. Following the terrorist attacks of September 11, 2001, in the United States, given Al Qaeda's stated support for Muslim insurgents in Kashmir, India became a key player in the international war on terror, but it also reaffirmed its independent posture by refusing to join the U.S.-led coalition that invaded Iraq. And, with its huge pool of scientific talent and an economic growth rate surpassing 8 percent in 2003–2004, India began to receive international recognition as an emerging global economic power and a new hub for high-tech research and development.

Given this string of achievements, it did not come as a surprise when the BJP's leaders called for early elections in 2004 and initiated a public relations campaign triumphantly dubbed "India shining." What did come as a surprise was the result of the election. The BJP and its allies saw their share of seats in the Parliament drop dramatically from 56 percent to 35 percent, whereas the Congress Party raised its share from 25 percent to 40 percent, forming a new government with the backing of leftist parties that had garnered an additional 11 percent of the parliamentary seats. In retrospect, it is clear that the BJP had underestimated the economic frustrations of India's large pool of poor voters, especially in the rural areas where nearly two-thirds of the country's population still reside. It is to this pool that the Congress Party and the leftist parties had appealed, attacking the BJP for catering to the wealthy and neglecting the plight of the poor. It was true that the Congress Party had given economic liberalization momentum during the early 1990s, and it was equally true that a Congress government was not about to abruptly shift economic policies that were generating high growth. But, the fact remains that the party that lost power in 2004 did so at a time of impressive economic growth and rising international stature, whereas the new ruling coalition came to power by appealing to poorer voters, including many former BJP supporters, whose economic frustrations were only magnified by the "India shining" campaign.

What does this turn of events tell us about the evolving interplay of identities, interests, and institutions in postcolonial India? How can India's economic liberalization and growing significance in the high-tech sectors of the global economy be sustained in a parliamentary democracy featuring over six hundred million potential voters, the majority of whom are engaged in agriculture? What accounts for the continued political salience of identities based on **caste**, region, and religion even as new kinds of interest groups and social movements have proliferated rapidly? Why did Hindu nationalism suddenly become a powerful force during the 1990s, and why did its salience decline in 2004? And, more broadly, what do the political, economic, and social transformations in India since the early 1900s tell us about the challenges and opportunities facing post-colonial developers in a changing global order?

This chapter will help you make sense of these questions in the course of tracing the shifts in India's developmental path from the arrival of colonialism through the post–Cold War era. The first section will discuss the emergence of a South Asian civilization comprised of numerous social identities, the arrival and effects of British colonial rule, and the rise of Indian nationalism. The second section will examine the developmental path taken by India during the 1947–1984 period when, in the midst of the Cold War, India's leaders sought to define a "third way" that combined democratic political institutions and a state-led program of autarkic economic development. The third section will trace the shifts in India's developmental path accompanying the end of the Cold War, including the arrival of a new era of coalition politics, the evolving significance of long-standing cultural identities, India's experience with economic liberalization, and the emergence of new kinds of interest groups and social movements.

Pre-independence India: Civilization and Empire to Colonialism and Nationalism

The term "India" has its origins in one of the world's great ancient civilizations that developed in the Indus Valley region to the northwest of present-day India (in the southern part of present-day Pakistan). The Indus Valley civilization, which is thought to have emerged as early as 4000 B.C., flourished around 2500–2000 B.C., developing its own system of culture, language, irrigation, municipal administration, and even intercity communications networks. This civilization seems to have gone into decline by 1500 B.C., just as a distinct population of Indo-Aryans arrived on the Indian subcontinent, ushering in a new era in the making of South Asian civilization.

CIVILIZATION AND EMPIRE: THE SOURCES OF IDENTITY AND UNITY IN SOUTH ASIA

One of the great divides in Indian society has its roots in the settlement of the lighter-skinned Indo-Aryans in the northern and central plains of the Indian subcontinent. The newly transplanted population spread across the subcontinent, developing a series of languages that were loosely related through their common roots in ancient Sanskrit. The darker-skinned Dravidians, who were native to the subcontinent, became concentrated in the southern part of India. Although the physical differences between Indo-Aryans and Dravidians have been exaggerated by British anthropologists and historians, the descendants of Dravidians continue to constitute a distinct ethnic group, encompassing one-quarter of the population of present-day India. As we shall see, this ethnic divide has played a significant role in Indian electoral politics and center-periphery relations.

The shared identity of Dravidians is reinforced by the fact that they speak languages that are not derived from Sanskrit, upon which most northern Indian languages are based. Each of the four main Dravidian languages today serves as an official state language in the south (e.g., Telegu in Andhra Pradesh and Tamil in Tamil Nadu). Most other languages spoken in India have common roots in ancient Sanskrit, but no single language can be identified with a majority of India's population. The official languages of several states in northern India are not spoken much outside of those states (e.g., Bengali in West Bengal and Punjabi in the Punjab). Of the languages spoken by significant populations in different states, the most common is Hindi, the main indigenous official language. Constructed by standardizing popular local variants, Hindi is spoken by 36 percent of the population spread over the north-central states called the "Hindi" belt (e.g., Bihar, Uttar Pradesh, and Haryana). Other significant languages include English, which has the status of an official language and is regularly used for government documents as well as in several major newspapers. Although spoken by only about 5 percent of the total population, the proportion is much higher in urban areas and has been increasing steadily since the time of independence. Also spoken commonly across regions is Urdu, the primary language for nearly half of the Muslims in the country. The use of Urdu dates back to the arrival of Central Asian Islamic groups and combines most of the vocabulary of Hindi with an Arabic script. As we shall see later, these linguistic differences have acquired a political significance given the nature of state boundaries in India.

In spite of the formation of diverse linguistic communities, from the time of the Indo-Aryan settlement of the Indian subcontinent, a common civilization began to take shape in the northern and central plains. This process was intensified through the formation of empires under powerful princes who managed to conquer several regional kingdoms in different parts of the subcontinent. Soon after Alexander the Great's invasion stalled in India, the first major empire in South Asia was founded by Chandragupta Maurya in 326 B.C. His empire eventually stretched from the Indus Valley region to all but the most southern part of the subcontinent. Subsequent rulers (e.g., the Gupta kings, A.D. 320–550, and King Harsha Vardhana, A.D. 606–647) would also establish large empires that contributed to the expansion of administrative bureaucracies as well as closer economic and political ties among the diverse regions of the subcontinent. In addition, the tributary relationships established between the emperor's court and the regional provinces provided a model for later empires, including the British colonial empire.

These periods of dynastic rule also contributed to the flowering of a recognizable Hindu culture throughout much of the Indian subcontinent. The main beliefs, deities, rituals and spiritual philosophy identified with Hinduism can be traced back to the writing of two major texts (the *Vedas* and the *Upanishads*) in northern India between the eighth and fifth centuries B.C. With the formation of progressively larger empires from the fourth century B.C. onward, an increasingly recognizable set of religious beliefs and practices – such as the belief in reincarnation and the rituals of *puja* (the worship of gods and deities) – came to be manifested among Hindus across the Indian subcontinent. This process gained momentum during the fourth and fifth centuries A.D., when priests and scholars under the patronage of the Gupta dynasty rulers helped to mold a more standardized expression of Hinduism. By the eighth century, the process spread to the southern regions of India as Dravidian princes, poets, and religious scholars began to accept and promote Hindu beliefs and practices. The result was not a unified religious doctrine upheld by a central religious authority (as in the case of Catholicism), but in everyday life, many of the beliefs and practices associated with Hinduism were recognizable across different regions throughout the Indian subcontinent.

Caste is another key aspect of social life that was recognizable across South Asia. As a way of organizing work and ordering social life, the Indian caste system was not fundamentally different from social hierarchies prevalent in Europe during the Middle Ages. What made the Indian caste system distinctive was the fact that families associated with different traditional occupations were ranked on a hierarchical scale of "purity." Those who were able to read Hindu scripts (written in Sanskrit) and perform Hindu rituals came to be regarded as a higher-status (more "pure") category of **Brahmins** (priests). Rulers, court officials, and soldiers constituted the second category in the caste hierarchy. They were followed by merchants and traders, peasants and artisans, and, finally, "untouchables," who performed menial tasks considered "unclean" or "impure." These categories, however, were too broad to serve as sources of shared identity across regions. What really counted was membership in one of the specific subdivisions (*jati*) of the five general caste categories *within a given region* (usually a cluster of nearby villages). In everyday life, it was one's *jati* that marked one's inherited occupational and social status; it is *jati* that determined the rules, habits, and obligations of individuals; and it is *jati* that defined the pool of eligible marriage partners within a region. Although the tasks, rules, obligations, and relative positions of a given *jati* varied across regions, in all cases, work and society were organized in terms of a fixed hierarchy within which there was no opportunity for upward mobility or intermarriage.

Many Indian leaders and scholars (including Mahatma Gandhi) have not viewed the caste system as an intrinsic feature of Hinduism. However, the fact that social organization and religious practice were so thoroughly fused for so many centuries contributes to the perception – both in India and abroad – that the caste system is inseparable from Hinduism. This also accounts for the fact that caste communities have remained an important source of identity and division throughout contemporary India even after the caste system was formally abolished by the Indian constitution after independence. At the same time, this source of division paradoxically facilitated the crystallization of a South Asian civilization by making the social structures of diverse communities recognizable throughout India. In fact, the basic structure of the caste system later influenced the social organization of many Muslim and **Sikh** communities in India.

Now, we turn to the origins of the religious cleavage between the Hindu majority, which accounts for more than 80 percent of the Indian population, and the significant Muslim minority, which accounts for about 11 percent. (The remainder consists of Sikhs, Christians, Buddhists, and members of other religions.) The Hindu–Muslim divide has its origins in raids carried out by Muslim groups from the Arabian peninsula and Central Asia into the northern plains of India. Some of these groups attempted to convert local populations and eventually settled down. A more significant and lasting Muslim presence in India came about with the arrival of an Afghan Muslim prince named Babur, founder of the Moghul Empire (1526–1757). Babur's grandson, Akbar (1556–1605), followed in the footsteps of the Mauryan and Gupta empires, extending Moghul control through most of the Indian subcontinent. As in the case of earlier empires, a centralized administrative machinery coexisted with tributary relations with several layers of provincial and regional rulers who retained their titles and some autonomy as long as they paid tribute to the emperor in Delhi. Under Akbar, Islam gained a permanent foothold in South Asia and led to the establishment of new Muslim settlements as well as a spate of conversions. At the same time, Akbar adopted aspects of Hindu political thought, included Hindus in his court in Delhi, treated Hindu scholars with respect, and abolished many policies that discriminated against Hindus. In this tolerant atmosphere, Akbar won the respect of Hindu princes while Muslim artists and scholars came to be appreciated by Hindu cultural elites. This period of relatively peaceful coexistence between Hindus and Muslims suggests that the relationship between the two groups is not inherently a conflictual one, and that the outbreaks of Hindu–Muslim violence during and after colonialism have many complex causes.

In sum, between 1500 B.C. and A.D. 1700, a number of sociocultural cleavages emerged throughout the Indian subcontinent: between northern Indo-Aryans and southern Dravidians, between different linguistic communities, between different caste groups, and between the majority Hindus and religious minorities such as Muslims and Sikhs. Yet, it is important to remember that for all the emphasis placed on social divisions in India, there was a centuries-old civilization that had evolved and spread through most of the Indian subcontinent well before the establishment of British colonial rule. The use of Sanskrit as a common language for priests and literati, the spread of recognizable religious beliefs and practices across regions, the emergent similarities in social organization across diverse communities, and the establishment of tributary rule and bureaucratic administration during various empires all provided a common frame of reference for people in different parts of South Asia. Although this may not have been sufficient to preempt every kind of social conflict, it did serve to distinguish South Asian civilization from the tribally based local communities scattered across sub-Saharan Africa, giving India's future leaders more of a foundation for building a modern nation-state.

THE ENCOUNTER WITH THE WEST: BRITISH COLONIAL RULE, 1757–1947

Although contact with "foreign" cultures (e.g., Persians and Afghans) was nothing new to South Asia, the arrival of British traders marked South Asia's first significant encounter with the West. As the Moghul Empire went into decline during the seventeenth century, the British East India Company, a large trading company officially backed by the British government, began to establish trading stations in coastal towns such as Bombay (now Mumbai) in the west and Calcutta (now Kolkata) in the east. The regional rulers in these areas signed agreements with the British East India Company partly to enhance their own political and economic position vis-à-vis neighboring provinces and the Moghul court in Delhi, but they could not foresee the long-term consequences of the trading concessions that they gave the British. Eventually, a Bengali prince realized that the agreements were giving the British increasing economic control over his region and he set out to evict the British. However, his troops were decisively defeated by British troops at the Battle of Plassey (1757). Partly as a result of disunity among India's provincial rulers and partly as a result of superior military technology, the British rapidly proceeded to defeat dozens of other regional armies and by 1840 had established their own colonial empire throughout the subcontinent.

Initially, British colonialism proceeded through "indirect rule." This system functioned through a series of alliances with regional princes who kept their titles, possessions, and local authority in exchange for supporting British administrators and their economic interests. This informal colonial empire would become a more formalized system of "direct rule" after a major 1857 rebellion launched by Indian guards trained by the British. The Sepoy Mutiny began as a spontaneous reaction to the discovery that animal grease from pigs (hated by Muslims) and cows (sacred to Hindus) was being used in rifle cartridges, but it soon became an organized campaign supported by some Indian princes to end Britain's political and economic control in their regions. After violently suppressing the mutiny, the British established direct rule over most of India (but maintained indirect rule in a few of the less troublesome provinces such as Kashmir). Direct rule still depended on cooperation from Indians serving as soldiers and administrators, but now Queen Victoria was crowned the ruler of India, a viceroy was appointed to rule India directly on her behalf, and British governors and local officials were appointed to maintain local order. During the next ninety years (1857–1947), the impact of British rule became more pronounced as India became "the jewel in the crown" for an expanding British empire that stretched from Hong Kong to East Africa.

The *political* legacy of British colonialism was twofold: the establishment of institutions that would be adapted by a postcolonial Indian nation-state and the heightening of mistrust among groups identifying with different castes, regions, and religions. With regard to political institutions, one of the most important bodies created by the British was the civil service, which assisted in the administration of the colony and would later provide the foundation for the Indian Administrative Service (IAS), the backbone of modern Indian bureaucracy. After World War I, the British also proceeded to establish national and regional assemblies consisting of elected representatives in order to create a semblance of legitimacy for the colonial administration. Of course, these assemblies had no real legislative power and had little say over the most important policies and laws introduced by the British viceroy. However, they did provide an institutional basis for parliamentary democracy in post-colonial India. Also, as part of direct rule, the British systematized the division of labor between central and provincial administrations, providing a bridge from the tributary system set up by various empires to the institutions of modern Indian federalism. Although these institutions were not set up with an independent nation-state in mind, they did provide a foundation for the political system that is still in evidence in contemporary India.

A more problematic political legacy of British colonialism is its differential treatment of various groups, which is most clearly evident in the deliberate strategy of "divide and rule." Even during the period of indirect rule, the British had taken advantage of the fact that native elites in different regions could be made to compete with each other for status or influence. During the period of direct rule, upper-caste Hindus (especially Brahmins), because of their relatively high level of literacy, were recruited into the colonial administration in disproportionate numbers. This left the much larger lower-caste groups with fewer opportunities for upward mobility and made some suspicious of political leaders drawn from upper-caste backgrounds. But the most divisive legacy of colonialism stems from the manipulation of tensions between the Hindu majority and Muslim minority in order to justify British colonial administration in South Asia. The best example is the 1905 partition of Bengal in eastern India into a predominantly Muslim eastern half (today the nation of Bangladesh) and a predominantly Hindu western half (today the eastern Indian state of West Bengal, which borders Bangladesh). Although Hindus constituted 40 percent of the population in the east and Muslims constituted 20 percent in the west, and although the populations in both parts spoke Bengali, the British claimed that the partition was necessary to administer the region more efficiently. Although many Muslims may have welcomed the opportunity to constitute a majority in a separate province, the partition was consciously designed to stifle a nationalist movement that was gathering steam in Bengal and causing great concern for the British viceroy at the time, Lord Curzon. Ironically, the partition had the unintended effect of spurring greater activism across India and giving more impetus to the budding independence movement.

British *economic* policies had a more profound and widely felt impact on the interests and identities of different segments of the Indian population. Karl Marx once wrote that British colonialism was a progressive force in India because it helped to dismantle feudalism and expedite the formation of capitalism (which had to precede socialism). Indeed, throughout British India, colonial economic activities contributed to new mining and construction, the building of new factories and machinery, and the construction of an extensive network of transportation and communication, including what is today one of the world's largest railroad systems. This led to the first sustained exposure for thousands of Indians to industrial production and factory life. A small Indian middle class and a somewhat larger working class also emerged as a result of the increase in British economic activities in India, setting the stage for class divisions that would cut across preexisting cleavages based on caste, region, and religion.

These were significant changes for a society that was overwhelmingly agrarian, but Marx may have underestimated the negative effects of British colonialism on Indian economic development. Throughout the two centuries of colonial rule, the original motives that had brought the British East India Company to the subcontinent remained very much in play. Much of the infrastructure set up by the British was designed not to boost native industrial growth but to facilitate the extraction of valuable resources and the transportation of British-manufactured goods to distant markets. The participation of the native Indian middle class in production and distribution was controlled and restricted; for example, the British imposed limits on textile production by Indian-owned factories because their products were in competition with the more expensive textiles imported from British factories. The nascent working class was severely exploited as the British took advantage of cheap labor as part of their continuing industrial expansion. The expanded production of cash crops took away land and labor from subsistence agriculture, intensifying poverty and hunger among the rural population. The British also established monopolies on the production of key necessities (even salt) in order to make the native population dependent on the colonial economic apparatus. Thus, although the British did help to create a new infrastructure for industrial production in India, they also contributed to "misdevelopment" because the economic institutions of colonialism were intended to facilitate the exploitation of resources and markets rather than to support India's industrialization. Post-colonial India's economic problems would have many and complex causes, but the economic legacy of colonialism is certainly one of them.

The *social* impact of colonialism affected far fewer people but proved to be most significant in the eventual weakening of British rule. This social impact was mainly evident among educated, urban, mostly Hindu intellectual elites who attended British schools and universities in increasing numbers. These elites encountered new literature and new social movements, as well as Western political ideologies such as nationalism, liberalism, and socialism. The effect of this exposure came to be evident toward the end of the nineteenth century in vigorous debates among Indian intellectual elites in response to British social reforms aimed at institutionalizing English common law and eliminating certain egregious local customs (such as the practice in Rajasthan of wives throwing themselves on the funeral pyres of their husbands). Also worth noting is the use of the English language, which not only provided an alternative medium for communication among elites from different regions but also enabled these elites to express themselves articulately to foreign audiences. The significance of these changes for the development of Indian nationalism cannot be understated. In fact, one of the ironies of British colonial rule is that its dependence on an English-speaking Indian elite paved the way for the emergence of a new political class that would lead the movement for Indian independence.

THE RISE OF NATIONALISM AND THE MOVEMENT FOR INDEPENDENCE

The organization that led India to independence, the **Indian National Congress** (**INC**), was established in 1885. The founding members, the majority of whom were educated Brahmins from relatively wealthy families, did not initially challenge British rule. Their two original purposes were to expand the representation of Indians *within* the British colonial administration and to debate the merits of various Hindu traditions in light of social reforms initiated by the British. However, the British rejection of even the most moderate demands, together with the outcry over the aforementioned partition of Bengal, spurred the INC to embrace the goal of independence (*swaraj*) in 1906.

The evolution of the INC into a mass nationalist movement, however, did not happen until the arrival of Mohandas Karamchand Gandhi (referred to as "Mahatma," or "Great Soul"). Gandhi had gone to Britain to be trained as a lawyer and then spent several years challenging discriminatory British policies in South Africa. Upon his return to India in 1915, Gandhi quickly became a popular leader of the INC. Most significantly, Gandhi managed to attract the attention of lower-caste Indians in the countryside. To demonstrate to India's mostly rural population that the INC was more than an exclusive club of educated upper-caste urbanites, Gandhi chose to live as most villagers did and traveled throughout the countryside to document economic difficulties and social injustices brought about by colonialism.

Gandhi focused on the points that united Indians from different religions, regions, castes, and classes. He emphasized the power of a universal inner truth that all human beings shared, while appreciating the distinctive spirituality shared by all *Indians* despite their diversity. He also emphasized the more universal aspects of Hindu philosophy, such as its spiritualism, while attacking specific beliefs and practices that served to divide communities by caste or religion. This was not an easy synthesis for many Indians to grasp. Some Hindus worried that Gandhi was diluting the core tenets of Hinduism, whereas Muslims saw his philosophical positions as relevant mainly for Hindus. Nevertheless, by emphasizing the negative economic and cultural consequences of British colonial rule for members of all castes, regions, and religions, Gandhi was able to draw millions of previously apathetic South Asians into the campaign for independence.

It was Gandhi's strategy of nonviolent noncooperation that did the most to attract the attention of the rural masses as well as the international community. This strategy, which was later replicated by Martin Luther King, Jr., during the U.S. civil rights movement, served two purposes. First, it directly disrupted British colonial administration and its economic activities, which depended on the cooperation of the native population. Second, it demonstrated to the Indian masses that their strength lay in their numbers and their will rather than in the acquisition of arms. For example, Gandhi and the INC orchestrated a major nationwide boycott of British cloth in 1920–1921 during which millions of Indians burned cloth manufactured in Britain and began to wear white homespun cotton; in just one year, the value of foreign clothes imported into India was cut nearly in half. Even today, most Indian politicians continue to wear white homespun in public as a sign of their patriotism. Similarly, Gandhi's "salt march" caught the attention of Indians everywhere as he led hundreds of his followers on a 200-mile trek to the sea to make salt on the beaches; this was in defiance of a British law prohibiting Indians from manufacturing salt and requiring them to pay taxes on salt manufactured in factories. Also noteworthy are two campaigns that began in Bengal but spread rapidly to other parts of the country: a student boycott of British-run schools and colleges and a boycott of British-run courts by scores of well-known lawyers who gave up lucrative practices (including Motilal Nehru, the father of India's first prime minister).

Most INC members followed Gandhi, renouncing violence in favor of continued reliance on the tactic of nonviolent noncooperation. The one leader who opted for more direct action, Subhas Chandra Bose, was elected president of the INC for a brief period in 1938 but left to organize the Indian National Army (with German and Japanese assistance) to fight British rule. Whether this army might have eventually become an effective instrument for ending British colonialism is not clear given the outbreak of World War II. Nor is it clear whether colonial rule would have ended when it did in the absence of the impact of World War II on Britain's own economy and infrastructure. What is clear is that the INC campaign of nonviolent noncooperation made it increasingly difficult and costly for the British to maintain the existing system of colonial administration.

On August 15, 1947, British colonial rule formally ended, and two independent nations emerged: India and Pakistan. Gandhi himself had hoped for a unified nation that would include all Hindus and Muslims, but now that independence was at hand, the unity of the nationalist movement was giving way to competing interests. Although some Muslims supported the idea of a unified India, others simply did not trust the Hindu-dominated INC, fearing that their interests as a minority would be ignored. Mohammad Ali Jinnah, an INC member who helped found the Muslim League in 1920, insisted on a separate Pakistani nation and would become its first leader. On the other side, several Hindu organizations that had supported the INC campaign for independence now devoted themselves to promoting traditional Hindu ideals and symbols that they felt had been diluted by Gandhi's efforts to court Muslims. Fearing civil war, Gandhi agreed to a plan that would form a separate nation, Pakistan, in parts of the subcontinent where Muslims constituted a majority: a western part corresponding to the borders of present-day Pakistan and an eastern part corresponding to eastern Bengal (which would secede in 1971 to form the present-day nation of Bangladesh). During the partition, millions of people left their old homes to migrate to find new homes, while thousands died in bloody clashes between frustrated Hindus and Muslims. Eventually, the violence subsided, and in India the INC leaders set out to draft a new constitution. The Indian constitution, based on principles of democratic federalism and English common law, went into effect on January 26, 1950.

India's "Third Way": Political and Economic Development in the Cold War Era

The global context within which India emerged as an independent nation helped to shape India's self-image in world affairs, its political system, and its development program. The influence of Western political doctrines and institutions, the appeal of the Soviet model of rapid industrialization, and the Cold War between the two superpowers all contributed to a distinctive developmental path Indians proclaimed to be a "third way." This path was identified with neutrality in the Cold War, a steadfast commitment to secularism, and a "mixed" strategy of development that combined elements of both capitalism and socialism. This "third way" came to represent an appealing mixture for the dozens of new nations becoming independent in the 1950s and 1960s, most of which joined India in forming the "nonaligned movement" to proclaim their neutrality in the Cold War. It is true that few of the new nations were able to remain neutral given their security concerns in an era of superpower competition; indeed, India would later sign a "treaty of friendship" with the Soviet Union as Pakistan sought closer ties to the United States. However, India's generally independent foreign policy and its conscious effort to balance elements of capitalism and socialism made it a model for many developing countries and gave Indians a sense of identity and pride within the international order during the years of the Cold War. But what distinguished India from most other newly independent countries was a set of stable political and legal institutions that has now remained more or less intact for over five decades.

THE MAKING OF A SECULAR NATION: POLITICAL AND LEGAL INSTITUTIONS

After independence, the Indian National Congress (INC) reconstituted itself as the Congress Party but was without many of its most distinguished former leaders. Gandhi was assassinated in 1948 by a Hindu fanatic. Bose, who had advocated armed confrontation with the British and had envisioned a centralized one-party Indian state, is thought to have died in a plane crash after his anti-colonial army was disbanded. Sardar Patel, a prominent Congress Party leader who envisioned an industrialized India in which Hindu traditions would be preserved, died of natural causes. Thus, **Jawaharlal Nehru** found himself to be the party's undisputed leader and the nation's first prime minister (1950–1964). Much more so than Gandhi or Patel, Nehru embraced an unequivocally modern worldview. This included a commitment to science and technology, a faith in the capacity of technocratic planning to deliver both economic growth and social justice, and, above all, a belief that a secular, democratic nation-state could function for all citizens regardless of caste, region, and religion.

"Secularism" generally implies that public life should be governed by the rule of law as evident in a written constitution and legal codes (and not by traditional customs, religious texts, or hereditary privileges). As such, the term applies both to the United States and the Soviet Union. In the Indian context, however, secularism acquired a more specific meaning in opposition to "communalism." Aside from the formal equality of all citizens before the law, secularism in India implies that politics should revolve around the interests of individuals rather than of groups identified by the communal ties of caste, region, or religion. Significantly, this understanding of secularism incorporates the principle that minorities and previously disadvantaged groups should be granted special privileges until the playing field becomes more level for all citizens. Thus, the caste system was abolished by law. A system of "**reservations**" (India's version of affirmative action) was instituted to help members of the lowest caste groups gain entry into educational institutions and employment, and India's Muslims and other religious minorities (but not the Hindu majority) were granted the special right to observe certain religious laws and attend religious schools.

India's parliamentary democracy was based mainly on the British Westminster model. This system has remained more or less unchanged since India's independence and continues to function in an orderly fashion. The legislative branch is bicameral. The focus of national politics is the lower house of the Parliament, the Lok Sabha. Elections for the lower house are held every five years unless the ruling party chooses to call early elections or unless defections from the ruling coalition result in no party being able to command a majority. Of the 545 members in Parliament, 543 are candidates winning a plurality of votes in single-member districts (a "first-past-the-post" system),

TABLE 10.1. Government Leaders of India, 1950–present

Prime Ministers*	Presidents (Heads of State)
1950–1964: Jawaharlal Nehru, Congress[a]	1950–1962: Rajendra Prasad
1964–1966: Lal Bahadur Shastri, Congress[b]	1962–1967: Sarvapalli Radhakrishnan
1967–1977: Mrs. Indira Gandhi, Congress-I	1967–1969: Zakir Hussain[h]
1977–1979: Morarji Desai, Janata Party	1969–1974: Varahagiri Venkata Giri
1979–1980: Chandra Shekhar, Janata Party	1974–1977: Fakhruddin Ali Ahmed[i]
1980–1984: Mrs. Indira Gandhi, Congress-I[c]	1977–1982: Neelam Sanjiva Reddy
1984–1989: Rajiv Gandhi, Congress-I[d]	1982–1987: Giani Zail Singh
1989–1991: V. P. Singh, Janata Dal	1987–1992: Shri R. Venkataraman
1991–1996: N. P. Narasimha Rao, Congress-I	1992–1997: Shankar Dayal Sharma
1996–1997: Deve Gowda, Janata Dal/UF[e]	1997–2002: Shri K. R. Narayanan
1997–1998: Inder Gujral, Janata Dall/UF	2002–present: A. P. J. Abdul Kalam
1998–2004: Atal Behari Vajpayee, BJP/NDA[f]	
2004–present: Manmohan Singh, Congress/INC[g]	

* Selected by party forming government after Parliament elections; prime ministers in office for less than one month are not included.
[a] Died in office 1964.
[b] Died in office 1966.
[c] Assassinated while in office 1984.
[d] Lost elections, but assassinated during campaign for next elections in 1991.
[e] Janata Dal and allies renamed "United Front" (UF) in 1996–1998.
[f] BJP and allied parties also called "National Democratic Alliance" (NDA).
[g] Congress-I now renamed Indian National Congress (INC).
[h] Died in office 1969.
[i] Died in office 1977.

and two special members are appointed by the president. The upper house of the Parliament, the Rajya Sabha, consists of 250 members elected for fixed six-year terms, with one-third standing for elections every two years. Most members are elected by the parliamentary assemblies of the states and territories constituting India, but 12 are appointed by the president on the basis of special considerations or expert knowledge. Like the British House of Lords (but not the U.S. Senate), the primary function of the upper house is not to independently make laws but to approve existing laws and provide continuity and stability through changing governments; given these functions, the upper house can never be dissolved.

The prime minister is usually the leader of the party or coalition that holds a majority in the lower house of the Parliament. He or she serves as the head of the government and is the focal point of national politics, being responsible for appointing cabinet ministers, launching new initiatives or programs, and making important decisions with regard to key domestic and foreign policy issues. The president, the head of state, is usually a nominee of the victorious

TABLE 10.2. Congress Party's Parliamentary Majorities, 1952–1984

Year	Popular Vote (%)	Seats in Parliament (%)
1952	45	74
1957	48	75
1962	46	73
1967	41	54
1971	44	68
1977*	35*	29*
1980	43	67
1984	48	79

* 1977 elections held after ending of "emergency rule" declared by Indira Gandhi in 1976; Janata Party coalition forms government 1977–1980.

party in Parliament but is formally elected to a five-year term by an electoral college that gives votes to each member of Parliament and weighted votes to all members of the state assemblies (to ensure reasonable representation of each region). The president often is not a career politician but an individual with significant personal accomplishments (for example, in science or literature) who is thought to stand above political conflicts as a symbol of unity and order throughout the republic. At the state level, the triad of the national parliament, prime minister, and president are replicated in the triad of the state assembly, the chief minister (leader of the ruling majority in the state assembly), and a governor appointed by the Indian president (often at the behest of the prime minister) to ensure that public order, the rule of law, and the constitution are upheld at the state level. Table 10.1 lists the prime ministers and presidents of India to date.

The first-past-the-post electoral system used at both the national and state levels means that a larger, better-organized party can convert narrow margins in popular votes into a disproportionately large share of seats in the Parliament or the state assembly. In the course of the system's first four decades, only the Congress Party was sufficiently large and organized to be able to benefit from this. In the first three elections (1952, 1957, and 1962), for example, the Congress Party managed to capture more than 70 percent of the seats in the national parliament without once gaining a majority of the popular vote (see Table 10.2). During this period, the Congress Party also controlled the state assemblies in most states. This led to the characterization of India's political system as a "**dominant-party system**," with the Congress Party holding sway over national politics and several smaller national or regional parties acting as "parties of pressure" to lobby Congress Party leaders or mobilize public opposition to particular Congress Party policies.

A "dominant-party system," however, is a far cry from one-party rule (as with the PRI in Mexico). Elections were fairly contested by parties espousing vastly different platforms, leadership transitions were generally orderly, and the rule of law was upheld for most of India's existence as an independent republic. More telling is the fact that the "parties of pressure" as well as a host of new regional parties eventually became better organized during the 1960s–1970s, cutting into the Congress Party's share of parliamentary seats and taking control of several state assemblies. And, when the era of Congress Party dominance in national politics came to an end in the late 1980s, this was not the result of any electoral reform or external pressure; it was simply the predictable result of the growth of other parties and the reduction in the Congress Party's size and unity. These facts suggest that the "dominant-party system" was mainly a result of the initial advantages that the Congress Party had in the form of the leadership, reputation, and organizational base inherited from the independence movement once led by Mahatma Gandhi.

India's founders also adopted an independent judiciary headed by a national Supreme Court. This body consists of a chief justice and 25 justices who are formally appointed by the president but are usually chosen by the prime minister in consultation with sitting members of the court. As in the United States, the Indian court's main purpose is to interpret the constitution and ensure civil liberties. However, its prerogative of judicial review has been hampered at times by numerous constitutional amendments introduced in Parliament, notably Amendment 42 (1976), which prohibits the court from reviewing changes introduced by constitutional amendment. The court also suffered a temporary loss of reputation for failing to oppose the suspension of several constitutionally guaranteed rights during the eighteen-month period of "**Emergency**" rule in the mid-1970s. Compared with courts in other postcolonial settings, however, India's courts have generally functioned in a fair, nonpartisan manner and have been able to safeguard the basic spirit of the constitutional and legal order.

THE MAKING OF INDIAN FEDERALISM AND CENTER–PERIPHERY RELATIONS

To deal with India's diverse regions, a federal republic was set up, with a central government in New Delhi sharing powers with the governments of each of the 14 states and 6 territories existing at that time (now 28 states and 7 territories). Certain policies are primarily in the jurisdiction of state governments (for example, rural policy, municipal projects, and educational curricula), whereas others are primarily in the jurisdiction of the central government (for example, defense, foreign policy, and national economic planning and related budget transfers to states). Although this division of labor between center and state is essentially similar to that found in federal systems elsewhere, other features of Indian federalism emphasize the primacy of the center and the integrity of the nation as in unitary states (states in which power is concentrated in the center and not shared with other levels of government) such as France or Japan.

Consistent with the views expressed by James Madison and Alexander Hamilton in *The Federalist Papers*, India's founding leaders (notably Nehru and B. R. Ambedkar, the chair of the committee that drafted the constitution) were seeking to balance the imperatives of states' rights and state-level governance with the preservation of national unity in the face of conflicts within or among states. In the case of India, however, the latter challenge took precedence given the Hindu–Muslim riots that accompanied independence, the conflict with Pakistan over Kashmir, and fears of destabilizing secessionist movements. As a result, the Indian constitution was more explicit in asserting the unity and primacy of the central government than in the U.S. Constitution. For example, India's constitution treats the union as indestructible but allows the national parliament to alter the boundaries of its constituent units. Moreover, in contrast with the United States, the Indian national government (and not the state governments) retains the residual powers of legislation and can preempt any state legislation that contradicts a parliamentary act or federal law. In addition, Article 356 establishes "**President's Rule**" when serious disturbances are reported by a state's governor. Since independence, the article has been invoked on dozens of occasions, sometimes for valid reasons but sometimes on shaky grounds for the purpose of ousting uncooperative state legislatures.

Another distinctive feature of Indian federalism is the manner in which state boundaries are defined. The 1956 States Reorganization Act established 14 states and 6 territories (now 28 states and 7 territories) with boundaries corresponding to populations predominantly speaking a particular regional language. Prime Minister Nehru did not wish to encourage the provincialism of the Congress Party's regional leaders, but he encouraged the nation to adopt the States Reorganization Act in the interest of stability. In any case, he expected the central government to play the dominant role in India's development as a unified modern nation. Yet, by institutionalizing differences between linguistically defined regions, the States Reorganization Act ended up establishing a principle that has since been invoked to carve out a number of new states. Thus, in contrast with the United States, conflicts in center–periphery relations and competition among states are reinforced by the identities shared by members of the linguistic groups corresponding to respective state boundaries.

India's distinctive brand of federalism has produced three patterns of center–periphery politics in India. First, the most complicated cases involve the very few states or territories where a non-Hindu group constitutes a majority. In these cases, dramatic, even violent, social movements have sprung up at various points with the aim of securing autonomy. This is evident in the state of Punjab (where Punjabi-speaking Sikhs constitute 51 percent of the population), the state of Jammu and Kashmir (which is the only Indian state with a Muslim majority and encompasses the disputed area of Kashmir), and the northeastern territories (which are economically underdeveloped and inhabited by tribal populations that are ethnically distinct). Although there are also political parties that have sought to gain control of a state assembly on behalf of the non-Hindu majority (for example, the Akali Dal in the Punjab), violence has been evident in all three regions since the time of Nehru. The threat posed by this violence has varied, however. Conflicts in the Punjab largely subsided after reaching a peak during the 1980s; conflicts in the northeast have been sporadic and relatively small-scale; and conflicts in Jammu and Kashmir have been an ongoing problem since the time of independence, a situation that has been complicated by Pakistan's support for Muslim militants in Kashmir.

A second pattern of center–periphery politics involves the emergence of regional political parties that claim to represent the distinctive interests of the dominant majority in a linguistically defined state. This pattern is most common in the southern states, where much of the population is identified as Dravidian and where the main state languages are distinct from those with roots in Sanskrit. For example, two major parties have dominated politics in the state of Tamil Nadu since the 1960s: the Dravida Munnetra Kazhagam (DMK) and its splinter party, the All-India Anna DMK (AIADMK). These parties can be traced back to a powerful regional movement during the 1940s and 1950s that aimed at reducing the influence of northern (Indo-Aryan) culture in southern India and even called for an autonomous state of "Dravidastan." Rather than continue to press for autonomy, however, these parties have participated within the framework of Indian federalism, focusing on controlling their respective state assemblies and capturing a block of seats in the national Parliament.

The third pattern of center–periphery politics involves the operation of national parties as de facto regional parties. Such parties have platforms that publicly outline national priorities rather than promote the interests of any one state, but the fact that they come to power in one state makes them behave much like the regional parties in the south in the course of center–periphery bargaining. The best example is the dominance of the **Communist Party of India (Marxist)**, or CPI-M, in the state of West Bengal. Although formally dedicated to Marxist ideology, which regards class divisions as more significant than national or ethnic ones, this party took over the West Bengal assembly from the Congress Party in the 1960s. Although it originally focused on working-class interests and land reform in gaining power, the CPI-M has proven remarkably flexible in adapting to changing times, with much of its continuing appeal resulting from its role as a steadfast defender of Bengali interests. Long after the fall of communism in Eastern Europe, the CPI-M stands as a rare example of a Communist Party that has been able to gain and maintain power in one state within the framework of democracy and federalism. With the decline of Congress Party dominance in national politics, this pattern has become more prevalent, with some parties splitting off from national parties to seek influence among some large bloc of voters in a particular state (e.g., the Samajwadi Party in Uttar Pradesh).

THE INDIRA GANDHI ERA: POPULISM, PATRONAGE POLITICS, AND THE "EMERGENCY"

After Jawaharlal Nehru's death in 1964, Lal Bahadur Shastri emerged as the new leader of the Congress Party and the next prime minister of India. Shastri had not been a unanimous choice to begin with, and his untimely death just two years into his term (in 1966) left the Congress Party scrambling once again to reach consensus on a new leader who could lead it to victory in the 1967 elections. That leader turned out to be **Indira Gandhi** (daughter of Nehru and not directly related to Mahatma Gandhi), primarily because her lineage was seen as an asset to the Congress Party's public image in the upcoming elections. Given her inexperience, however, she was expected to essentially serve as a figurehead for the more established party bosses. In the 1967 elections, the Congress Party's popular support declined to a low of 41 percent, but it was able to capture a majority of seats in the Parliament. Indira Gandhi was named prime minister, becoming one of the first women to head a national government.

Once in power, Indira Gandhi surprised the party bosses by announcing her own policy agenda and elevating individuals personally loyal to her at the expense of the older party elites. The rift between Indira Gandhi and the old bosses became so deep that the Congress Party split into two distinct parties: One, following Mrs. Gandhi, reconstituted itself as Congress-I, (henceforth referred to as Congress), inherited the bulk of the old Congress Party's grassroots membership, and is considered the main successor to the original Indian National Congress. The other, Congress-O (for "organization"), was formed around several of the old party bosses who now joined the opposition. As the successor to the independence movement, the Congress Party had been able to build an extensive organizational framework that cut across national, state, and local levels. Given the split with some of the party bosses, Indira Gandhi now had to find ways to shore up her own base of support.

One strategy was evident in a concerted effort to mobilize the masses directly by means of populist appeals to the economic interests of peasants and workers, who had not seen their positions improve much during the first two decades after independence. In areas where Mrs. Gandhi no longer had reliable local allies to deliver "**vote banks**" (blocs of votes obtained by a candidate as a result of deals made with leaders of a local caste or village community) during critical elections, she needed a new message that she could take directly to a new, larger vote bank – the hundreds of millions of impoverished lower-class and lower-caste voters, especially those in the rural areas. This message took the form of a national antipoverty campaign with promises to boost agricultural production while not giving in to the interests of large foreign companies. This message resonated with India's lower classes and castes, enabling Mrs. Gandhi's Congress Party to capture over two-thirds of the seats in Parliament during the elections of 1971. Also worth noting is that Mrs. Gandhi began to rely more heavily on appeals to Indian national pride to buttress her populist posture. This was evident not only in the framing of her protectionist policies (economic nationalism) but also in the cultivation of nationalistic fervor accompanying the 1971 war with Pakistan (in which India provided military support to successfully aid the secession of Bangladesh).

A second strategy that Mrs. Gandhi used to offset the loss of the former Congress Party bosses had to do with building a new base of Congress-I cadres through a distinctive brand of patronage politics. With her demonstrated ability to capture a parliamentary majority and her popularity soaring after the victory over Pakistan, Mrs. Gandhi had no trouble attracting new recruits to Congress-I while regaining the support of former Congress Party activists who had initially joined Congress-O. But what became strikingly apparent during this process was Mrs. Gandhi's active personal involvement in the appointment and promotion of key party leaders. Increasingly, these personnel decisions were based not on demonstrated competence or loyalty to the Congress Party as a whole but on the basis of *personal* loyalty to Mrs. Gandhi in exchange for her political patronage. She and her advisers regularly reviewed personnel files to identify and reward politicians who were loyal to Mrs. Gandhi, while taking note of those who might challenge her authority. Although patronage politics was nothing new to India, Mrs. Gandhi's emphasis on personal loyalty resulted in a more hierarchical web of patron–client networks centered on the prime minister and her closest advisers.

During the mid-1970s, this approach served to further alienate Mrs. Gandhi's opponents and led to a serious crisis that almost undermined India's political and legal institutions. During 1974, some of the older Congress Party bosses (Congress-O leaders) and other opposition leaders joined together to accuse Mrs. Gandhi of corruption and campaign violations. One of these leaders, J. P. Narayan, once a devout follower of Mahatma Gandhi, organized frequent protests and even called upon the army to oust the prime minister. The Indian army, noted for its noninterference in civilian politics, did not intervene. Mrs. Gandhi, however, felt that her opponents had gone too far, and she responded by declaring a national emergency. The next eighteen months (1976–1977), referred to simply as "the Emergency," represented the only period during which postcolonial India appeared to function more like an authoritarian regime than a parliamentary democracy. Many of the opposition leaders were arrested for their part in the campaign against Mrs. Gandhi, selective censorship was introduced, and some parts of the constitution were temporarily suspended. At the same time, in contrast with typical dictators in authoritarian regimes, Mrs. Gandhi had come to power via the electoral process rather than through a military coup, she did not seek to dismantle opposition parties or rewrite the constitution, and she promised and called a new round of national elections, stepping aside when her party lost in those elections.

In the 1977 election, Mrs. Gandhi hoped that the voters would understand her actions and that her Congress Party would retain its power, given its sheer size. However, these elections marked the first time that the Congress Party was unable to gain a parliamentary majority. Instead, the new government was formed by the Janata Party, an umbrella organization composed of a wide array of opposition parties, including the Congress-O. Just as the "first-past-the-post" electoral system had previously enabled the Congress Party to convert pluralities of popular votes into a majority of seats, the Janata Party managed to convert 43 percent of the popular vote into 55 percent of the seats in Parliament. The result demonstrated that the Congress Party's previous electoral dominance was partly a result of a fragmented opposition that, when united, proved capable of unseating it. At the same time, the "dominant-party system" remained intact because the Janata Party was little more than a hastily formed coalition of parties with quite different interests and ideologies, with no *single* party capable of defeating Congress in national elections. Opposition to Mrs. Gandhi proved sufficient to enable the Janata Party to engineer a victory following her controversial actions during "the Emergency," but it was not sufficient to enable it to stay in power for a full term. The diverse elements constituting the Janata Party found little common ground when it came to specific policies for reducing central planning or attacking the problems of poverty and inequality. Moreover, the two Janata prime ministers (Morarji Desai, 1977–1979, and Charan Singh, 1979–1980) had neither the reputation nor the personal appeal of Mrs. Gandhi. As a result, the 1980 elections saw Indira Gandhi stage a spectacular comeback, with her Congress capturing two-thirds of the seats in the national parliament.

Following her return to power, Mrs. Gandhi sought to consolidate her political base by more frequently invoking Hindu nationalist themes, although still officially committed to the secularism of her father, Jawaharlal Nehru. This tactic was intended to boost her personal popularity by appealing to as large a segment of the Indian population as possible. Predictably, however, this also triggered fears among India's religious minorities, sparking a militant movement for greater autonomy in the Punjab (where there was a Sikh majority). In her efforts to quell militants seeking an independent "Khalistan," Mrs. Gandhi ordered the army to storm the Sikh Golden Temple at Amritsar (where the militants had holed up). This sparked violent Hindu–Sikh riots and provided the main motivation for her assassination at the hands of her own Sikh bodyguards on October 31, 1984.

INDIA'S "MIXED" STRATEGY OF ECONOMIC DEVELOPMENT, 1950–1984

India's development strategy was set in motion under Jawaharlal Nehru and was influenced by the global context in which it was conceived. National economic priorities were influenced by the level of wealth and technology evident in the West. The program for achieving those goals was simultaneously influenced by the vitality of entrepreneurship evident under Western capitalism and by the dramatic achievements engineered by socialist planners in the USSR during the 1930s and 1940s. This led to the emergence of another component of Nehru's "third way": a "mixed" strategy of economic development.

As part of this strategy, the principle of private property was respected, and private economic activity was encouraged in some sectors. However, half of the gross domestic product (GDP) was supposed to be accounted for by a large public sector managed according to Soviet-style "five-year plans." This public sector, consisting of thousands of large state-owned factories, mainly concentrated on heavy industry (i.e., the large-scale production of major industrial goods along with major infrastructure projects such as coal mining, power stations, railroads, and so forth). Private firms were selectively authorized to participate in heavy industrial production, but most tended to be concentrated in the production of agricultural and light industrial (or consumer) goods. Moreover, the public and private sectors were protected and regulated by the Indian government so that they could contribute to the expansion of industrial production while being shielded from competition against firms from more advanced industrial countries. The assumption was that because colonialism and economic backwardness had made the playing field uneven, a postcolonial economy could not hope to catch up to that of its former colonizers without state protection and coordination of domestic industry and without tight restrictions on foreign imports. The Indian government also upheld laws that prevented public-sector workers from being fired, provided generous welfare benefits for public-sector employees, guaranteed protection for trade-union members, and established a progressive system of taxation.

Under Nehru, this "mixed" development strategy did enable native industrialization to take off but did not make any significant strides toward closing the gap between India and the advanced industrial economies of the West. In addition, some serious problems with the strategy became evident during Nehru's last few years in office. In spite of Nehru's personal commitment to improving the lot of the lower classes, his fixation on rapid industrialization and the priority given to heavy industry neither helped to reduce poverty and socioeconomic inequities nor brought tangible benefits to the masses whose expectations had been ratcheted up after the euphoria of independence. Even more problematic was the continually low level of investment in the agricultural sector, which left millions of villagers perilously close to the threshold of subsistence. As a result, when severe droughts struck during the early 1960s, there was not enough of a cushion to prevent famine in many parts of the countryside. In light of these problems, Nehru's successors would have to make some adjustments, albeit within the framework of India's "mixed" strategy of development.

First, a new consensus emerged on the importance of addressing chronic food scarcity for India's rapidly growing populace. Nehru's successors believed that one key reason for the famines of the early 1960s was the inadequacy of channels for distributing surplus grain. To remedy this, in 1965 the government set up the "public distribution system," a network of thousands of shops through which surplus grain from high-yield agricultural regions would be redistributed throughout the country at controlled prices to be monitored by state governments. The other part of the solution was India's "**green revolution**." Under Indira Gandhi, the government encouraged the use of new varieties of seed, new methods of fertilization, and new techniques of crop rotation. Although the green revolution targeted regions with good soil and irrigation and tended to benefit relatively wealthy farmers, the total increase in agricultural production was dramatic and made India self-sufficient for the first time. While the green revolution and the public distribution system did not put an end to poverty and malnutrition, the combination of the two measures did help to bring an end to starvation-related deaths by sharply raising food production and guaranteeing access to cheap foodstuffs for poorer citizens nationwide.

A second set of changes was evident in increased state control over the economy, manifested in greater protectionism and greater regulation of the private sector. With developing countries becoming a dominant majority in the United Nations by the early 1970s, India joined a group of 77 such countries that passed a United Nations resolution calling for a "new international economic order." Although it was not enforceable, the document reflected the proponents' common view that free trade would effectively perpetuate the exploitation of former colonies unless protectionist measures were allowed to boost native manufacturing capabilities and create a level playing field. In keeping with the spirit of this movement, Indian banks and some key firms were nationalized, and new restrictions were imposed on multinational corporations, prompting many to leave. Moreover, the domestic private sector came to be more thoroughly regulated through the expansion of the "**license raj**," the requirement that private firms with assets above a certain threshold secure a government license to manufacture, export, or import goods in several key sectors. These measures were designed to protect Indian firms from foreign competition and boost native industrial production, but it also increased the government's leverage over large private-sector firms, benefiting some while stifling others.

On the whole, India's strategy of "mixed" development during the 1950–1984 period did not generate anything resembling the rapid economic growth seen in the East Asian newly industrialized countries (NICs) during the same period. Given its burgeoning population, India's per capita growth rate remained low, and comparatively little progress was made in reducing the rate of poverty. With economic pressures mounting, corruption became a more serious problem. Bribery became a part of everyday life, and government funds for special programs often ended up in the pockets of local officials. The license raj also contributed to the growth of corruption, enabling those who were politically connected or willing to offer bribes to obtain licenses more expeditiously, while others faced endless delays caused by bureaucratic red tape. The licensing system also conferred certain benefits on established firms – many of which became inefficient in the absence of competitive pressures – while stifling the growth of newer firms that were potentially more efficient. Among the working class, organized workers in the public sector had secure jobs and little incentive to be productive, whereas most of India's workers (including a sizeable contingent of child laborers) continued to toil under poor working conditions for low wages. Poverty was still widespread, with nearly half the rural population officially considered below the poverty level. Sharp differences also emerged between states and regions in the levels of growth, poverty, and literacy.

Yet, it is important to bear in mind that the economic legacies of colonialism and the initial advantages held by advanced industrial countries in the world economy combined to make it difficult for most postcolonial nations to achieve any dramatic results during the first decades after independence. Against this background, India's "mixed" economy did make some important strides that should not be ignored. Between 1950 and 1984, the real gross domestic product gradually tripled. Over this period, total food-grain production also tripled, with wheat production growing nearly sixfold. In industry, coal production went up fourfold, steel production went up more than sixfold, electricity generation rose more than twentyfold, and India developed indigenous automobile and airplane manufacturing facilities. There were also significant improvements in health and literacy, as average life expectancy rose from just 30 years at the time of independence to nearly 55 by 1984, while the rate of adult literacy rose from under 20 percent to nearly 50 percent over the same period. Although India continued to depend on substantial foreign aid, the per capita rate of borrowing was much lower than in other developing countries, and foreign debts were generally repaid as scheduled. Given the more rapid growth accompanying liberalization since the early 1990s, one might argue that much more could have been achieved during the 1950–1984 period with less government intervention and more open markets; at the same time, India's growth since the early 1990s may not have been possible at all without first establishing a secure base for domestic industrial manufacturing, without solving the problem of food scarcity, without the marked improvements in basic health and literacy, and without keeping foreign debt from spiraling (as it did in Latin America).

India Shining? Institutional Dynamics, Resilient Identities, and Evolving Interests in the Post–Cold War Era

The end of the Cold War coincided with a marked shift in the development path that India had been following for four decades since independence. With the decline of communism as a viable alternative model, the significance of, and pride associated with, being a leading nation of the developing world began to decline. Suddenly, dozens of countries were scrambling to redefine their national interests, identities, and strategies within an increasingly interdependent global economy that was clearly dominated by the advanced industrial capitalist countries. Within this changing global context, India's democratic institutions and federal system remained stable and have enjoyed a measure of legitimacy that is uncommon in postcolonial nations in the Middle East or Africa. However, the political dynamics within these institutions became more fluid and more "decentered" as more local actors found new ways to influence political outcomes. Core identities related to caste or religion remained politically salient, but the way in which they influenced politics became more subtle. India cautiously embarked upon economic liberalization, progressively becoming a more significant actor in the global economy. In response to these changes, the interests of different groups became varied, and new social movements began to tackle such problems as women's rights and environmental degradation.

STABLE INSTITUTIONS AND COALITION POLITICS IN THE WORLD'S LARGEST DEMOCRACY

Following Indira Gandhi's assassination in 1984, her elder son, Rajiv, reluctantly agreed to lead Congress (his younger brother was being groomed for this role but had died in a plane crash). **Rajiv Gandhi** led his party to a landslide victory in the 1984 elections as it captured 79 percent of the parliamentary seats. The results appeared to point to the continuing appeal of both the dominant-party system under Congress and the Nehru dynasty (which had now provided three generations of leadership spanning Jawaharlal Nehru, his daughter Indira Gandhi, and his grandson Rajiv Gandhi). As it turns out, however, the election outcome was heavily influenced by the wave of sympathy following Mrs. Gandhi's death. In the six national elections held over the following two decades, Congress remained an important player but was never again able to secure a majority in Parliament without the aid of other parties. In fact, the 1984 elections marked the beginning of a transition to a new, more fluid era of coalition politics in which it has become commonplace for leading parties to form a government with allies and coalition partners. ("Allies" refers to parties that campaign alongside a leading national party and agree in advance to support its agenda in the parliament; "coalition partners" refers to parties that offer outside support to a leading party and its allies to help construct a ruling majority but without subscribing to the party's political agenda.) This has forced larger parties to broaden their appeal while generating new opportunities for dozens of smaller parties to join coalitions and bargain for greater influence. Table 10.3 provides an overview of the performance of the leading parties in each of the national parliamentary elections held between 1989 and 2004.

Upon becoming prime minister in 1984, Rajiv Gandhi set out to fulfill a campaign promise to uproot corruption in the government. However, his own administration soon became ensnared in a corruption scandal involving accusations of officials accepting bribes in exchange for offering contracts to a Swedish defense firm (Bofors). The Congress Party's huge majority in Parliament allowed Rajiv Gandhi's administration to serve out the full five-year term, but the fallout from the Bofors scandal and the growing trend toward coalition politics caused Congress's share of parliamentary seats to plummet from 79 percent to 38 percent during the 1989 elections. Although no other single party won more seats, Congress's opponents banded together once again under the umbrella of the Janata Party (this time using the Hindi term Janata Dal) and managed to form a ruling coalition with the backing of several smaller parties, including an emerging Hindu nationalist party called the Bharatiya Janata Party (BJP, or Indian People's Party).

The new Janata Party government came to be led by Prime Minister **V. P. Singh**, an ardent critic of Rajiv Gandhi's administration. Singh is noted for his support for the work of a national commission, the **Mandal Commission**, that identified several new caste-based categories for consideration under an expanded system of reservations. However, the Singh government was not able to do much beyond approving the report because its unwieldy coalition broke up by the end of 1990 under the strain of the different interests and ideologies of its members. Especially significant here was the coalition's dependence on support from the BJP, which was led by upper-caste Hindus and was on a campaign to mobilize public support for its distinctive agenda of promoting *Hinduttva*. In 1990, a key BJP leader (future Home Minister **Lal Krishna Advani**) was arrested for exhorting his countrymen to take down a mosque and rebuild a Hindu temple that had supposedly stood at the same

TABLE 10.3. Election Results during the Era of Coalition Politics, 1989–2004

Year	Party	Popular Vote (%)	Seats in Parliament (%)
1989	Congress	39	38
	Janata	18	28 (forms government)
	BJP	11	16
	Others**	32	18
1991	Congress	37	45 (forms government)
	BJP	20	24
	Janata	11	11
	Others**	32	20
1996	Congress	29	26
	Janata and allies (UF)*	29	32 (forms government)
	BJP & allies	24	34
	Others**	19	8
1998	BJP and allies*	36	46 (forms government)
	Congress & allies*	26	26
	Janata & allies (UF)*	21	18
	Others**	17	10
1999	BJP and allies (NDA)*	41	55 (forms government)
	Congress and allies*	34	25
	Others**	25	20
2004	Congress and allies (INC)*	35	40 (forms government)
	BJP and allies (NDA)*	35	35
	Left parties***	8	11
	Others**	22	13

* UF refers to the "United Front" alliance formed around the Janata Party in 1996. ND refers to the "National Democratic Alliance" (NDA) set up by the BJP and its allies in 1999. INC refers to the "Indian National Congress," the name of the former independence movement taken by Congress and its allies in 2004.

** "Others" include regional parties winning national parliamentary seats as well as national parties or splinter parties that are not part of alliances and that individually receive less than 10% of parliamentary seats. For 1999 and 2004, this includes former members of the Janata-led alliance that did not join the alliances formed by the Congress Party or BJP.

*** The two largest "left parties" are the Communist Party of India-Marxist (CPI-M) and the Communist Party of India (CPI), but there are dozens of other communist or socialist parties, including the Revolutionary Socialist Party (RSP) and the All-India Forward Block. These are counted among "others" in 1989, 1991, and 1999 and as part of the United Front coalition in 1996 and 1998. They are listed separately for 2004 because they independently won 11% of the contested seats and offered crucial outside support to form the new Congress-led government.

spot to honor the Hindu demigod Rama. Given Singh's own secularism and his full support for Advani's arrest, the BJP withdrew its support from the government, leaving the Janata Party without a majority in the Parliament. New elections were temporarily staved off because Congress was willing to offer outside support to the Janata coalition but only after a new prime minister was named in place of Singh, who had been a long-time thorn in Congress's side. However, this coalition proved to be short-lived, as Congress used the time to prepare for fresh elections that would be called as soon as it withdrew its support of the Janata coalition in 1991. The Janata-led government of 1989–1991 demonstrated that the new era of coalition politics would prove to be a complicated one, requiring careful negotiations among parties of different sizes that represented the interests of different regions, classes, castes, and religious groups.

Congress began campaigning during the 1991 elections with hopes that it would return to its dominant position after its rule had been temporarily interrupted by a fragile coalition. But, unlike Mrs. Gandhi's triumphant return to power in 1980, there would be no second term for her son. On May 21, 1991, as Rajiv Gandhi left behind his security cordon to go into the crowds as part of a more open campaign strategy, a young woman set off a massive bomb strapped to herself. The group involved in Rajiv Gandhi's assassination was linked to an organization operating in Sri Lanka with the intention of establishing greater autonomy for the Hindu Tamil minority there. During the 1980s, rather than side with the Tamils in the name of Hindu solidarity, Rajiv Gandhi had offered troops to help the Sri Lankan government maintain stability. He did so because he viewed the Tamil separatists' demands in Sri Lanka as analogous to unacceptable demands for regional autonomy by militant separatists in India (e.g., Sikh militants pursuing an autonomous "Khalistan"). Thus, although Rajiv Gandhi's assassination was orchestrated by a group operating in Sri Lanka, he essentially fell victim to the same dynamic that had claimed his mother's life six years earlier: Both sought to uphold the principle of a unified nation-state in the face of separatism, and both were assassinated by members of separatist groups.

After a brief respite to allow for Rajiv Gandhi's funeral, the elections resumed and another wave of sympathy helped the Congress Party to form the new government under **Narasimha Rao** (1991–1996), the first Congress Party prime minister to come from outside the Nehru dynasty in nearly a quarter of a century. Significantly, however, Congress was unable to secure a majority of seats in the Parliament and found itself in the unfamiliar position of having to woo coalition partners. Anyone paying attention to the other parties' performances, however, might have been surprised that the party finishing second in the 1991 elections was not the Janata Party but the BJP, the Hindu nationalist party that had forced the collapse of Singh's cabinet and now held nearly one-quarter of the seats in Parliament. The coalition under Rao, led by Congress, proved stable enough to serve out its full five-year term. However, when the next election was held in 1996, it was the BJP that won the largest bloc of seats (34 percent) in Parliament. The more loosely organized Janata-led alliance finished second with 32 percent of the seats. Congress ended up with its worst finish ever, totaling just 26 percent of the seats in Parliament.

The BJP's rise and the politics of identity are examined in more detail later, but what is worth noting here is how the BJP's emergence as a powerful new national party further increased the fluidity of coalition politics in India. To prevent a BJP-led coalition from forming the new government in 1996, the Congress Party agreed to offer outside support to the alliance led by the Janata Party. Given the history between Congress and Janata, however, the so-called "United Front" coalition government collapsed after going through two prime ministers (Deve Gowda and Inder Gujral) in as many years. This paved the way for fresh elections in 1998, and this time, the BJP and its allies won a decisive victory with 46 percent of the seats in Parliament and managed to form a majority coalition by courting several smaller parties. When new elections had to be called after the defection of a key coalition partner, the BJP and its allies, referring to themselves as the "National Democratic Alliance" (NDA), went on to control 56 percent of the parliamentary seats, while Congress's share dropped to a new low at 25 percent. Unlike Congress, which was not used to coalition politics and had only courted a handful of allies, the BJP aggressively set out to strike deals to make regional parties not just coalition partners but integral members of the ruling alliance. One of the most significant of these was the Telegu Desam Party, from Andhra Pradesh, which had historically attacked the central government for favoring the interests of the "Hindi belt" states in northern India. Now, ironically, Telegu Desam found itself in an alliance with the BJP, which had owed its rise to the same Hindi belt states.

Without having to depend on outside support from uncommitted parties, the BJP was able to remain in power until 2004 under the leadership of Prime Minister **Atal Behari Vajpayee**. Initially, given the BJP's assertive brand of Hindu nationalism, the Vajpayee cabinet was viewed with some anxiety. This was understandable given the strident nationalist rhetoric that some BJP leaders continued to embrace publicly. For the most part, however, Vajpayee and the BJP's national leadership proved to be pragmatic in their approach and did not break sharply with what previous governments had done. Although there was some talk of amending the constitution, the dynamics of alliance-building and coalition politics made it obvious that this effort would be a waste of time. The BJP's economic policies essentially continued along the path of liberalization initiated during the late 1980s. The BJP's decision to launch nuclear tests in May 1998 shocked many, but these tests were only possible then because the preparations had been well under way during the previous Congress government. The BJP's decision to join the U.S.-led war on terror in the aftermath of the 9/11 attacks was consistent with past leaders' efforts to secure international backing for the suppression of militants in Kashmir, and the decision *not* to join in the U.S.-led coalition's invasion of Iraq was consistent with India's fiercely independent foreign policy posture since independence. And the common threat posed by Islamic militants and terrorists even provided new momentum toward the normalization of relations with Pakistan and China. On the whole, as we saw in the introduction to this chapter, the BJP's rule at the center came to be associated not with ardent fundamentalism but with a sober approach in domestic and foreign policy that helped to produce high economic growth and increase India's stature as an emerging global power. These achievements were the basis for the BJP's triumphant "India shining" public relations campaign.

Thus, the verdict of the 2004 elections came as a surprise to many. Many had expected a small reduction in the BJP's share of parliamentary seats as a result of communal riots that broke out in BJP-controlled Gujarat in 2002. But few had expected that the populist appeals to the rural poor by Congress would enable it to capture 40 percent of the parliamentary seats and form the new government. The Congress victory was unusual in two regards. First, it was being led by the Italian-born widow of Rajiv Gandhi, **Sonia Gandhi**, whose foreign birth did not seem to trouble millions of rural voters as much as the BJP thought it would. Second, Sonia broke with tradition in that, although remaining party leader, she declined the post of prime minister in favor of the internationally respected economist **Manmohan Singh**. Also surprising was that Congress's ruling majority came to depend on outside support from leftist parties, which pulled off one of their strongest showings to date by capturing 11 percent of the parliamentary seats. All in all, this was Congress's best performance in over a decade, and it occurred when its chief nemesis, the BJP, appeared so confident of its performance that it had called for elections several months early. The Congress Party not only managed to attract a much wider range of allies than before but also garnered significant support in BJP strongholds such as Gujarat and Maharashtra (where the BJP had thoroughly defeated Congress in 1999). These results showed that the BJP leadership failed to anticipate how its "India shining" campaign would serve to magnify the social inequities and economic hardships still afflicting India's poor. At the same time, just as it would have been a mistake to deem Congress irrelevant after its defeats in the previous three elections, so, too, would be any premature dismissal of the BJP, which, after all, managed to finish dead even in popular votes with the alliance led by Congress.

Thus, the 2004 elections revealed that the decline of Congress dominance is not the same thing as the demise of the party, and that, even in defeat, the BJP showed that it was here to stay. The Janata Party, although it provided a common front for Congress opponents and played a role in ending Congress dominance, was never a unified organization to begin with, and its constituent elements increasingly began to be run as independent parties or as allies of the BJP or Congress. As a result, it appears that Indian politics is now dominated by two well-organized national parties, Congress and the BJP. Even without allied parties, the candidates from these two parties accounted for nearly half the seats in 2004. At the same time, it would be a mistake to see this as a two-party system in the making, as neither party is likely to be in a position to form a government without allies and coalition partners. In 2004, Congress's 40 percent share of parliamentary seats and the BJP's 35 percent share both depended on dozens of allies, most of which individually received less than two percent of the seats in parliament but without which Congress's and the BJP's share of seats would have been just 26 percent and 21 percent, respectively. This means that regional parties and smaller national parties, far from receding, now have even greater reason to focus on local constituencies to ensure some representation in Parliament given their value as potential allies and coalition partners. This also means that, whatever their ideological commitments, both Congress and the BJP will have to be pragmatic in their approach in order to attract a wide range of voters, allies, and coalition partners.

THE EVOLVING POLITICS OF CASTE AND RELIGION IN CONTEMPORARY INDIA

In light of the resilience of identities that emerged centuries ago on the Indian subcontinent, it is worth taking a closer look at the role that caste and religion have continued to play in the post–Cold War era. Ironically, although India's secular political institutions do not recognize caste practices or Hindu religious institutions as having any legal standing in public life, the efforts to institutionalize special considerations for lower-caste groups and religious minorities have had the effect of giving cleavages based on caste and religion a new political significance as electoral politics has become more competitive in a changing international environment.

During the last quarter of the twentieth century the link between occupational structures and caste hierarchies has been steadily weakened. India's Hindu political elites, once dominated by the upper castes, are now from a much more varied background, with several lower-caste politicians rising to national prominence. India's business elites now extend beyond the Hindu merchant caste and include members of other caste groups and non-Hindu minorities. Also, India's laboring classes are comprised of members of all caste groups. Nevertheless, caste-based identities are still relevant in everyday social relations, as is evident in the still high rate of within-caste marriages, the formation of community associations, and the continuing role of Brahmins in the performance of Hindu rituals. Within the context of contemporary politics, the significance of caste continues to be manifested in two ways.

First, there is the mobilization of electoral support through local caste communities. In the past, regional Congress Party candidates often received an entire block of votes from members of local caste communities in exchange for promises to advance the interests of these communities. With the rise of coalition politics, such "vote banks" are no longer clearly bounded because there are now multiple candidates promising varied social goods and because electoral preferences reflect not only caste-based interests but also a variety of class-based, regional, or individual interests. Nevertheless, caste-based identities remain available as an important basis for political mobilization, especially because many of the regional and splinter parties, whether they officially claim to represent certain caste groups or not, have been focusing on strengthening their standing among particular castes in a given state. Moreover, many candidates have been making direct appeals to members of their own caste communities. These trends have had an especially significant impact in boosting the political relevance of the more numerous lower-caste communities, catapulting several low-caste leaders into national prominence.

Second, the politics of caste is evident in responses to the government's efforts to expand the system of "reservations" for lower castes. It will be recalled that reservations refer to quotas in education and employment to enable the upward mobility of lower-caste groups. This includes the "scheduled castes" (encompassing the 20 percent of the population labeled "untouchables" and a number of marginalized tribal groups), which are eligible for a wide range of special privileges, including access to education, government, and public-sector employment. In addition, various strata of peasant or artisan caste groups (roughly 25 percent of the population) are considered "other backward castes" and receive a somewhat narrower range of privileges with smaller quotas in education and employment. As in the case of "affirmative action" in the United States, India's system of reservations has been the subject of much debate, with many upper-caste Hindus voicing concerns about the utility and fairness of the reservations system. This opposition has become even more vocal as a result of the release in 1990 of the Mandal Commission Report, which identifies a lengthier list of caste groups to be considered for some form of preferential treatment under the label of "other backward castes." Implementing the recommendations of this report would result in nearly half the jobs in the government or public sector being set aside for members of certain castes, but given that upper-caste Hindus represent less than one-fifth of the population, this would have only had a slight impact on opportunities for most upper-caste groups. Nevertheless, the government's approval of the Mandal Report in 1990 provoked some stunning reactions, ranging from the suicide of several upper-caste students to large numbers of upper-caste individuals changing their names to acquire lower-caste surnames. These dynamics suggest that the reservations system, although contributing to the upward mobility of lower-caste individuals, has ended up making Indians simultaneously more conscious of caste distinctions and more calculating in terms of the impact of caste-related social policies on their individual interests. As we will see, tensions over caste-based "affirmative action" would also play a role in strengthening the BJP's appeals to Hindu nationalism during the 1990s.

The BJP, formally established under that name in 1984, had its roots in the immediate post-independence period, when a small political party, the Jan

Sangh, was formed with the support of the **Rashtriya Seva Sangh (RSS)**. The RSS itself was a key Hindu social organization that was created in 1925 to preserve and promote Hindu traditions. Although it joined the INC's struggle against British colonialism, after independence it steadfastly opposed the Congress Party's secular vision in favor of the revival of pride in *Hinduttva*, the values and ideals of a centuries-old Hindu civilization. The RSS criticized Congress-led governments for disregarding the values and interests of India's Hindu majority while granting special privileges and considerations to Muslims, Sikhs, and Christians. The RSS became especially strong in Hindi-speaking states across northern and western India, cultivating ties to various social and political organizations and holding weekly meetings devoted to discussions of nationalist–religious ideology. In the 1970s, the RSS began to coordinate its activities with the **Vishva Hindu Parishad (VHP)**, which was also promoting *Hinduttva* among Hindus worldwide. With the emergence of the BJP in 1984, the RSS and VHP teamed up to put their organizational and financial resources at the disposal of the party in the hopes of eventually overcoming Congress Party dominance. At the time, however, the BJP's appeal was primarily limited to upper-caste groups who embraced the idea of *Hinduttva* for its own sake. This was not a particularly large social base for a party aspiring to one day lead a country as diverse as India.

The BJP's subsequent rise to power during the 1990s would be the result of three intersecting factors. First, the BJP was able to expand its core constituency of upper-caste Hindus by empathizing with the latter's anxieties over the Mandal Commission's recommendations for expanded quotas for lower-caste groups. An increasing number of upper-caste communities, whether or not they had given much thought to the place of *Hinduttva* in India's national identity, came to see the BJP as a viable alternative to secular parties that seemed to be going too far to accommodate the lower castes at the expense of upper castes. With the BJP's visibility rising, the 1991 elections brought it 20 percent of the popular vote. This made the BJP a significant national party, but two other factors were necessary for the BJP to build a broad enough base of support to form a government.

The second factor was the BJP's ability to fill the need for redefining India's national identity in the post–Cold War era. With India's place in the international system no longer tied to being a leader of the developing world, the BJP was prepared to offer a compelling substitute: the renewal of a millennia-old Hindu civilization that would retain its distinctiveness while propelling India's ascent in a new world order. The Congress Party's continued emphasis on secularism held some appeal for many cosmopolitan citizens, but without the aura of the independence movement and the status as a leader among postcolonial nations, Congress had difficulty constructing an inspiring vision of India's place in the world. For a newly emerging class of self-confident professionals, both in India and abroad, the BJP was able to provide such a vision.

The third factor was the most significant: The BJP was able to attract the attention of a large segment of lower-caste voters throughout rural India by drawing attention to the privileges accorded to religious minorities at the expense of the majority Hindu population. Severing the historical association between Hindu civilization and caste hierarchies, the BJP's leaders focused public attention on the imbalance between the rights of Hindus and religious (mostly Muslim) minorities, pointing out that members of other religious groups were accorded special privileges (such as Muslim citizens' right to selectively follow Islamic law and attend Islamic schools). These issues were driven home by the drama surrounding the destruction of the Babri mosque in Ayodhya at a site where a temple honoring the demigod Rama had been razed by Muslim invaders five centuries ago. Although the BJP's General Secretary Advani had been arrested in 1990 for exhorting Hindus to take down the Babri mosque, in December 1992, BJP supporters and cadres from the RSS and VHP did just that. This sparked a huge uproar and resulted in several days of Hindu–Muslim rioting in cities throughout India while catapulting the issue of *Hinduttva* into the national spotlight and capturing the attention of Hindu lower castes. In the 1998 elections, the BJP managed to win 40 percent of the lower-caste vote while also garnering substantial support from big business, urban workers, student groups, and educated professionals working in high-tech sectors.

While these dynamics suggest that communal identities were mobilized in different ways during the era of coalition politics, it is also important to note that the BJP's share of the popular vote never exceeded the total share held by Congress and other parties committed to secularism. Moreover, the challenges of maintaining alliances and coalitions gave impetus to the pragmatic wing of the party, led by Atal Behari Vajpayee (prime minister from 1998 to 2004). In its profile of former prime ministers, the Office of the Prime Minister of India refers to Vajpayee as a leader who is at once a "champion of women's empowerment and social equality" *and* a leader who "stands for an India anchored in 5000 years of civilizational history, ever modernizing, ever renewing, ever re-engaging itself." Vajpayee, perhaps to the chagrin of hardcore RSS activists, managed to craft a formula that linked the unifying aspects of Hindu civilization to modern India's national greatness and international standing, which, in turn, were linked to further progress in economic liberalization and scientific and technological advancement. This message resonated with India's ambitious business elites, students, and white-collar professionals, and even enabled Vajpayee to recruit a few Muslim political leaders into the BJP alliance.

At the state and local levels, however, BJP leaders' often strident rhetoric of Hindu revivalism has often drowned out the more inclusive themes emphasized by the party's pragmatic wing. This has tended to generate anxiety among religious minorities, sometimes fueling communal riots between Hindus and Muslims. The most troubling event in this regard occurred in the state of Gujarat in 2002. Hundreds of Hindus were returning from a trip to Ayodhya (where they had gone to show support for the building of the Rama temple) when the train they were on was set afire in the state of Gujarat, killing dozens. For the next several days, Hindus went on a rampage, attacking Muslims and burning their homes and shops. Even after the rioting had subsided, sporadic attacks continued for weeks. In the end, hundreds of Hindus and nearly two thousand Muslims were dead, and ten thousand people were left homeless. The Chief Minister of Gujarat, the BJP's Narendra Modi, was seen by some as either failing to act quickly to end the violence or consciously exploiting the riots to consolidate Hindu support ahead of his reelection. (He went on to win the election decisively.) Although Vajpayee condemned the violence as an isolated incident that needed to be investigated, the BJP as a whole lost credibility among some groups for its poor handling of the Gujarat riots, giving more ammunition to Congress and other secular parties during the 2004 election.

However, although the BJP's victories in 1998 and 1999 should not be viewed as evidence that the forces of communalism were on the rise, the 2004 election results should not be interpreted as evidence that secularism has now prevailed. It is true that the BJP lost some support as a result of its handling of the Gujarat riots, but the BJP did win 35 percent of the seats in Parliament and matched Congress in terms of the popular vote. It is also worth noting that Congress's populist campaign not only unseated the BJP but also ousted a once popular regional incumbent party in Andhra Pradesh (Telegu Desam). Although formally an ally of the BJP in national politics, this party's appeal had rested not on *Hinduttva* but on its emphasis on boosting Andhra Pradesh's position within India through faster liberalization and promotion of the information technology sector. This suggests that Congress's successes in 2004 had less to do with its secularism and much more to do with its populist appeal to the frustrated urban underclass and the rural poor. In fact, taken together, the elections since the mid-1990s suggest that the salience of the battle between communal and secular forces can vary significantly depending on the immediate concerns of voters at the time of a particular election. In the turbulent years immediately following the end of the Cold War, perhaps the need to redefine India's place in the world amplified the BJP's emphatic elevation of *Hinduttva*. Subsequently, however, the BJP's trumpeting of economic achievements without acknowledging the continuing difficulties facing hundreds of millions of voters gave the edge to Congress's message of poverty alleviation and social justice.

ECONOMIC LIBERALIZATION IN A GLOBAL AGE: ACHIEVEMENTS, PROBLEMS, AND PROSPECTS

During the 1980s, under the pressure of mounting foreign debt, many countries throughout the developing world abandoned import-substituting industrialization and opted for market-oriented reforms, partly as a condition for new "structural adjustment" loans from the World Bank and the International Monetary Fund. Following the demise of communism in Eastern Europe, the push for market reforms accelerated worldwide and was marked by the liberalization of trade, privatization of many state-owned enterprises, and increased foreign investment. Although a major borrower, India had maintained a low level of per capita foreign debt and had consistently managed to service the debt in a timely manner. Thus, economic liberalization in India began without the same sense of crisis or the same level of external pressure that accompanied economic reforms elsewhere in the developing world.

Under Rajiv Gandhi's leadership (1984–1989), although there was no dramatic initiative to indicate that India had embarked upon a new developmental path, a new consensus began to take form among India's economic bureaucrats and business elites. With the Soviet Union and China both reconsidering the efficacy of central planning, and with other developing countries adopting reforms to make their economies more competitive, it was time to consider more fundamental changes to the Nehruvian model of a state-managed "mixed economy." The clearest signal of this emerging consensus came in the form of changes in the licensing system by: (a) raising the asset threshold that determined whether a company needed a government license, and (b) permitting companies with licenses to manufacture certain products to manufacture upgraded versions of those products without procuring a new license. In effect, this meant that there were now fewer "barriers to entry" for new firms and that a wider range of existing companies could now expand their activities without going through the long and corrupt process of obtaining a license. These changes were modest, but they marked the beginning of a new era of economic development that has proceeded steadily along the path of liberalization through several changes of government.

The V. P. Singh (1989–1991) government, although an ardent critic of Congress, continued to support further economic liberalization, linking the attack on corruption to a critique of the government's role in the economy. When the Congress Party returned to power, the cabinet of Narasimha Rao (1991–1996) was able to engineer further steps to accelerate economic liberalization. Licensing requirements were relaxed even further to allow for the growth of the private sector, and imports were liberalized more significantly as new incentives began to attract more foreign investment to India. Even state governments under leftist parties (e.g., Kerala and West Bengal) had to embrace market-oriented policies in order to attract investment and keep up with expanding economic opportunities and activities in neighboring states. The process of reform was still quite gradual and featured many obstacles. There remained what some refer to as "barriers to exit" in that it was still illegal to shut down state enterprises, even if they were insolvent, and that several laws still protected major firms from going bankrupt despite mounting losses. With fears of a backlash from public-sector employees, most state-owned enterprises were not privatized right away. In sectors with significant workforce reductions, the government's effort to retrain laid-off state workers through the National Renewal Fund proved to be costly. And import tariffs, although declining, still remained relatively high, prompting foreign multinational companies to invest in countries where liberalization and privatization had occurred more rapidly. But the progress in liberalization made during the early 1990s was significant, building momentum for increasing rates of economic growth without triggering any major social catastrophes such as a spike in unemployment or hyperinflation.

After Congress lost the election in 1996, the Janata government of 1996–1998 and the BJP government of 1998–2004 continued to move forward along the course of liberalization. Under these governments, the central administration pursued unpopular reform measures by strategically coordinating with international financial institutions. In contrast with countries on which the World Bank and the IMF imposed specific conditions for further loans, India's central government actually worked with these organizations to identify conditions that corresponded to policies it wanted to enact. This enabled the government to characterize unpopular policies as unavoidable steps that were necessary to secure the cooperation of international financial institutions. Under the BJP, the government took one of the boldest steps to date in seeking to revise labor laws to remove restrictions on employers in relation to the dismissal of redundant workers and the signing of short-term contracts. The BJP also continued to court foreign investors and support the development of the high-tech sector. Thus, although often portrayed as a party preoccupied with India's past, the BJP showed that it was willing to take the necessary steps to accelerate economic growth and promote science and technology, viewing these as essential to India's ascendance in the international arena.

These policies, engineered in an incremental fashion over more than a decade, have begun to pay dividends. The average rate of economic growth during the 1990s climbed to six percent per year, nearly double the rate of annual growth seen during the 1970s. In the 2003–2004 fiscal year, India recorded eight percent annual GDP growth, becoming one of the world's fastest-growing economies. And, unlike economies that have depended on particular sectors for growth, India's GDP growth has come from all sectors, ranging from agriculture and manufacturing to services and information technology. Not surprisingly, foreign companies have come to recognize that the Indian middle class, no matter how small it is relative to the population as a whole, represents a huge market compared with most other national markets worldwide. Past investments in higher education have also begun to pay off in the form of a huge pool of highly educated English-speaking professionals whose scientific training and computer skills are now in high demand. This is most clearly evident in the rapid expansion of the high-tech sector of the economy, which regularly exports software programs to the West, and in the proliferation of research and development centers established by such global corporate giants as IBM, Intel, Nokia, and Google.

Critics, however, point to a number of problems. One is the growth of social inequalities, as is evident in the wide income differential between urban and rural residents, increasing disparities among states, and a greater concentration of national wealth in the hands of the richest segments of the population. Poverty remains a serious problem, with 250 milion people below the official poverty line established by the government, and this figure does not include the hundreds of millions who are not counted as poor but are close to the poverty line. Especially worrisome is the fact that the poverty is extreme among some segments of the population. In light of significant cutbacks in the government's public distribution system and rural development programs, extreme poverty has led to the first reports of starvation-related deaths in nearly two decades, along with a spate of suicides among desperate farmers burdened by rising debt.

At the same time, when considering the ramifications of economic liberalization elsewhere in the developing world, the picture in India is not so bleak (see Table 10.4). The official poverty rate of 25 percent of the population, even if it understates the real magnitude of the problem, reflects a significant drop from the 40 percent poverty rate of the 1980s. This reduction in the poverty rate offers cause for some hope, especially when contrasted with the current 40 percent poverty rate in Mexico and Iran and the 50 percent poverty rate in South Africa. Inequality may be rising, but the overall level of social stratification in India is comparatively low. The richest 20 percent of India's population controls six times the share of national income controlled by the poorest 20 percent, which is lower than in the United States (where the ratio is nine) and much lower than in Mexico (where the ratio is seventeen) and South Africa (where the ratio is thirty-four). Moreover, new strategies are becoming apparent for coping with rural poverty without having to put the brakes on the growth of the high-tech sector of the Indian economy. In the state of Karnataka, for example, hundreds of computer kiosks have been set up throughout rural areas where farmers previously lacked access to crucial services because of poor roads and inadequate communication links. These kiosks allow farmers to access computerized databanks where millions of land deeds have been recorded, helping to reduce the incidence of land fraud. For those without access to sophisticated medical facilities, these kiosks help local medical providers obtain updated medical information and send data to urban doctors who can run laboratory tests. And, farmers can now directly purchase seed and fertilizer at wholesale rates online rather than going through middlemen who may charge exorbitant fees for their services. Of course, it remains to be seen whether such initiatives can be replicated in other states, whether they can boost the standard of living for the 250 million

TABLE 10.4. Economics and Social Development Indicators, ca. 2001–2003

Category	India	Selected Countries
GDP / rank out of 175 (purchasing power parity, billion U.S.$), 2003	3002/4	U.S.: 10308/1; China: 5861/2; Japan: 3425/3; Iran: 438/22; Mexico: 905/12; Russia: 1186/10; S. Africa: 457/18
GDP per capita / rank out of 175 (purchasing power parity, U.S.$), 2003	2900/115	U.S.: 34320/2; China: 4020/102; Japan: 25130/14; Iran: 6000/78; Mexico: 8430/58; Russia: 7100/66; S. Africa: 11290/47
Share of labor force in agriculture (%) in 2000	60	U.S.: 2; Japan: 5; China: 50; Iran: 30; Mexico: 20; Russia 12; S. Africa: 30
Human development indicator rank (175 countries ranked, based on trends in life expectancy, infant mortality, poverty, inequality, literacy, etc.)	127	Norway: 1; U.S.: 7; Japan: 9; Mexico: 55; Russia: 63; China: 104; Iran: 106; S. Africa: 111
Life expectancy at birth 2003 [1970–1975 average]	64 [50.3]	U.S.: 76.9 [71.5] Japan (highest): 81.3 [73.3] China: 70.6 [63.2] Russia: 66.6 [69.7] South Africa: 50.9 [47.7]
Population below poverty line (%) (based on official government data)	25	U.S.: 12.7; China: 10; Iran: 40; Mexico: 40; Russia: 25; S. Africa: 50
Ratio of richest 20% to poorest 20% (by share of national income or consumption)	5.7	U.S.: 9.0; Japan: 3.4 (best); Iran: 9.7; Mexico: 17.0; Russia: 10.5; S. Africa: 33.6
Literacy of adults over 15 (%), 2003 [and ratio of female to male literacy]	60% [0.82]	U.S., Japan, Russia: > 99 [1.0]; China: 86 [0.98]; Mexico: 91 [0.99]; Iran: 77 [0.95]; S. Africa: 86 [0.98]
Public spending on debt servicing (as percentage of GDP, 1998–2000)	1.9%	China: 2.1; Iran: 4.4; Mexico: 7.9; Russia: 5.6; S. Africa: 3.8
Annual population growth rate (%) projected for 2001–2015 [and average rate, 1975–2001]	1.3 [2.0]	U.S: 1.0 [1.0]; Japan: 0.0 [0.5]; China: 0.6 [1.3]; Mexico 1.2 [2.0]; Iran: 1.4 [2.7]; Russia: −0.6 [0.3]; S. Africa: 0.0 [2.1]

Sources: World Bank, *World Development Indicators 2003* (Washington, DC); United Nations, *Human Development Report 2003* (New York); *CIA World Factbook 2004* (Washington, DC).

Indians living in poverty, and whether they can help bridge the widening gaps in living standards across classes, regions, and sectors.

THE DIVERSIFICATION OF SOCIAL FORCES: LABOR, WOMEN, AND ENVIRONMENTAL GROUPS

The growing fluidity of electoral politics and the liberalization of the economy have propelled an increasingly diverse array of interest groups that cut across long-standing cleavages based on caste, region, and religion. Several of these groups are at the forefront of India's integration into the global economy. India's business elites are sophisticated, well-educated, attentive to international trends, and strategic in their pursuit of new opportunities both within India and abroad. India's economic reformers rely heavily on the advice of native scholars who are well trained in macroeconomics and thoroughly familiar with the dynamics of international trade and global financial markets. Younger members of the urban middle class are hooked into satellite television, carry cell phones, and regularly surf the Internet, absorbing certain common topics of discussion, lifestyles, and consumption patterns found worldwide. However, these groups, although more visible to outside observers, constitute only a small fraction of India's huge population. Hence, to understand the challenges facing the country in the coming century, it is necessary to consider the evolving interests of some of the less visible segments of Indian society: the laboring classes, women, and grassroots environmentalists.

India's working class represents a heterogeneous social category with significant variation across different segments. The 10 percent of the workforce that is organized into trade unions is primarily concerned with maintaining the level of job security, workplace benefits, and social recognition of workers in larger firms, especially in the public sector. Historically, Indian trade unions have been fragmented because they are joined together in federations that subscribe to different ideologies and are allied with competing political parties. The unions that support the BJP, for example, reject the socialist principles embraced by unions linked to the leftist parties. However, the increasing fluidity of coalition politics, together with the common threat of workforce reductions in the public and private sectors, has given rise to increasing coordination across union bodies. This has been evident in strikes and protests to challenge the privatization of certain enterprises and to preserve the job security, wage levels, and social benefits associated with public-sector employment. However, given the challenges facing unions worldwide and the very small segment of the Indian workforce that is unionized, there is little reason to expect that India's unions will emerge victorious in their confrontation with business.

For the hundreds of millions of laborers in the "informal sector" who are not organized, the challenges are quite different. The informal sector includes millions of workers in agriculture, industry, and the service sector who are employed without formal contracts on a casual basis. Although some work-ers in the informal sector have made the most of their opportunities, for the majority, the lack of contracts and adequate legal protection has translated into long working hours, low hourly wages, and miserable working conditions. The World Bank and the International Monetary Fund still insist that aggre-gate economic growth will *eventually* bring about the alleviation of poverty and inequality, but for those facing extreme poverty, waiting may not be an option. Thus, it is not surprising that the most impoverished segments of the laboring classes have been responsive to populist criticisms of incum-bent politicians accused of representing the wealthy and neglecting the poor. Some have even looked to radical social movements – some organized around revolutionary ideologies (e.g., the radical socialist Naxalite movement), oth-ers around the predicaments of specific tribal or lower-caste groups (e.g., the Telengana movement in Andhra Pradesh). Although still confined to the mar-gins of political life, such groups may quickly grow in size if no public action is taken to alleviate the hardships of the poorest segments of the workforce. As a whole, workers in the informal sector constitute a large underclass of have-nots that has a far more pressing interest in eradicating poverty and reducing inequality than in basking in India's growing importance in the high-tech sector.

The majority of India's women, too, are facing new challenges as a group. India has traditionally been a patriarchal society, with men dominating the de-cision making in most communities and women often confined to the domes-tic sphere. Today, the gender gap in India, although smaller than before, re-mains significant, with men continuing to be disproportionately represented in higher education, public office, and the organized workforce. Neverthe-less, in comparison with other postcolonial developers, it is noteworthy that women's participation in the Indian political system has been steadily growing over the past century. Women's involvement in the nationalist movement, the arrival of universal suffrage in connection with parliamentary democracy, the increase in the literacy rate for women and girls, and the rise of Indira Gandhi and other women to prominence in national politics all helped to gradually increase the visibility of women in the public sphere. This is evident in the in-creasing number of female voters and candidates in electoral politics, in femi-nist movements spearheaded by urban middle-class women who have set out to challenge patriarchal attitudes, and in the proliferation of nongovernmental organizations (NGOs) that provide credit to support women's independent economic activities or campaign to end violence against women (especially physical abuse or murder related to dowry disputes). Since the 1990s, India's integration into the global economy has brought new challenges for women, especially those in poorer families, who have been negatively impacted by reduced public spending on programs targeting women. At the same time, the social dimension of globalization has enabled Indian women's groups to form transnational alliances as they seek to expand their political clout and create new opportunities for themselves in the public realm. The diverse forms of women's activism in India may not evolve into a Western-style feminist movement, but nor can it be expected to given the distinctive experiences of Indian women. What is more important is that increasing numbers of Indian women, regardless of their religion, caste, or language, are coming together to challenge practices that restrict their options, limit their upward mobility, or endanger their lives.

Environmental activists also have become more visible in the public sphere, with growing fears that the quest for economic growth will further accelerate environmental degradation. In the 1970s and 1980s, environmental movements were made up of relatively poor people focused on the protection of their own communities and habitats in the face of particular developmental projects. The "Chipko" ("Embrace the Trees") movement, for example, was launched in the early 1970s when a group of poor hill people in northern India stood between trees and loggers' saws in order to prevent the loggers from destroying the forests that constituted their habitats. During the late 1980s, several communities in western India banded together to form a campaign to protest against the construction of a massive dam on the Narmada River; the protest gained enough international attention to get the World Bank to withdraw financial support for the project and led the Indian government to change the original blueprint for the dam. These movements have gained national and international attention, providing the impetus for a rapid proliferation of environmental activism that features NGOs such as the Green Future Foundation as well as cross-regional citizens' groups such as the National Alliance of People's Movement. The environmental movement in India today is now a heterogeneous one, with some groups coordinating with environmental advocacy groups worldwide and others continuing to focus on the immediate concerns of local communities.

Conclusion

Under Prime Ministers Nehru and Mrs. Gandhi, India's national identity remained secular and tied to its self-conception as a leader of the developing world on the international stage. India's political institutions functioned well compared with those in many other experimental developers, but the Congress Party's initial advantages produced a "dominant-party system" in which other "parties of pressure" could not yet compete on the national stage. A "mixed" economy with a large public sector became firmly entrenched. Mrs. Gandhi introduced her own distinctive brand of politics and her own economic initiatives, but these took place within the institutional framework and program of development initiated by Nehru during the 1950s. During this period, many scholars and leaders – indeed, Nehru himself – thought that preexisting sources of collective identity were atavistic, and the national political elite maintained a secular vision of modern India.

Since the mid-1980s, however, the changes in the global order have been accompanied by a fundamental shift in India's developmental path (see Table 10.5). India's political system has remained stable, but with the growth of new parties and platforms, a more fluid era of coalition politics is now under way. With the growth of the BJP, Congress no longer dominates, and both parties depend on alliances or coalitions involving dozens of regional and splinter parties. In the process, new interests and strategies have emerged, while preexisting identities linked to caste and religions have taken on a new significance as a basis for political mobilization. This has been accompanied by a move away from a "mixed" economy, with economic liberalization accompanied by greater integration into the global economy. This shift has, in turn, produced new groups of "winners" and "losers," with the latter thus far being a more significant portion of the electorate. These transformations mean that India's leaders in the twenty-first century will have to demonstrate considerable political skill if they wish to maintain the delicate balance between social forces pulling in different directions – between cosmopolitan secularists and those identifying with centuries-old civilizational ideals; between a majority Hindu population and Muslims and other religious minorities; between upwardly mobile lower-caste groups and anxious upper-caste groups fearful of losing access to educational and employment opportunities; between an urban elite that is seizing new opportunities in the information technology sector and a rural population that constitutes over 60 percent of the population but accounts for just one-quarter of India's GDP; and between those trumpeting India's achievements in science, technology, and industry and those concerned with environmental degradation, labor standards, and the gender gap in economic opportunities.

India's leadership will also have to be nimble in balancing the interests of their domestic and international constituencies. Immediately following the 2004 elections, the Bombay Stock Exchange, the country's largest stock market, initially experienced a sharp drop because of fears of a retreat from market reforms. The fears soon subsided, and the stock market stabilized with the naming of former Finance Minister Manmohan Singh as the new prime minister. However, these fluctuations reveal the challenge of managing a nervous international audience in a fast-moving global economy. Had foreign investors continued to flee India, they would have been effectively penalizing hundreds of millions of voters for casting their ballots in line with their interests and values. They would also have been triggering an economic downturn on the basis of unsubstantiated assumptions: Many of those who were concerned over a Congress victory in 2004 had also worried when the the BJP gained power in 1998. In 1998, some of these foreign investors did not see the link between the BJP's vision of *Hinduttva* and its ambitious hopes

TABLE 10.5. Key Phases in Indian Development

Time Period	Regime	Global Context	Interests/Identities/ Institutitions	Developmental Path
Pre-1757	empires, kingdoms	invasion and settlement	emergence of race, caste, religious, and regional identification, tributary systems, local autonomy, competition between localities	diffusion of some shared administrative, social, and cultural practices
1757–1947	British colonialism	European imperialism	indirect rule with princely states, but more direct rule from 1857, nascent urban commercial interests, Parliament and courts established, spread of national identity led by Indian National Congress	early industrialization with "misdevelopment" (promotion of cash crops and limits on local capital)
1947–1984	Congress Party dominance	Cold War and nonaligned movement	caste-based "vote banks," peasant and working-class interests, federalized democracy, with residual powers left to center	state-dominated import-substitution industrialization, with 1970s Green Revolution
1984– present	coalitional politics with two major parties	post–Cold War globalization, with entry into "nuclear club"	rise of Hindu nationalism (BJP), lower-caste mobilization grows, business interests gain ground, new social movements emerge, political institutions stable, but with more subnational units and regional parties	incremental process of liberalization, with selective privatization (accelerated after 1991)

for elevating India's place in the world; in 2004, they did not consider that the victorious party, although it had embraced a populist platform, was the same party that had set economic liberalization in motion. Thus, in marked contrast with leaders in authoritarian countries such as China or "superpresidential" political systems such as Russia, leaders in parliamentary democracies such as India must constantly balance the threat of exit by foreign investors (if they seek to appease voters clamoring for social justice) with the threat of electoral defeat at the hands of the voters (if they adopt policies perceived as catering to business elites and foreign investors). Thus far, Indian politicians have proven themselves up to the task, but whether they can continue to handle this challenge over the long run remains to be seen.

Finally, it is worth noting that, in the face of adversity and skepticism, India's institutions have proven to be durable, enjoying a measure of legitimacy not often seen in postcolonial countries. This legitimacy is most clearly evident in voter turnout, which is considerably higher than in the United States. It is also evident in the behavior of all kinds of political parties, ranging from Hindu fundamentalists to Marxist-Leninists, who have generally behaved responsibly once in power. Thus, without minimizing the social problems and conflicts that continue to plague India today, it is necessary to acknowledge the robustness of the institutions that have somehow managed to reconcile the complex web of identities and interests that has emerged across India. The real test for these institutions, however, may still lie ahead as this nation of over one billion people continues to grow in population while its leaders simultaneously attempt to combat poverty, preserve its rich cultural heritage, and elevate its position in a changing global order.

BIBLIOGRAPHY

Basu, Amrita. *Two Faces of Protest: Contrasting Modes of Women's Activism in India.* Berkeley: University of California Press, 1992.

Bayley, Susan. *Caste, Society and Politics in India.* Cambridge: Cambridge University Press, 1999.

Bose, Sugata, and Ayesha Jalal. *Nationalism, Democracy and Development: State and Politics in India.* New York: Oxford University Press, 2003.

Brass, Paul. *The Politics of India Since Independence.* Cambridge: Cambridge University Press, 1994.

Carras, Mary C. *Indira Gandhi: In the Crucible of Leadership.* Boston: Beacon, 1979.

Chanda, Asok. *Federalism in India.* London: Allen and Unwin, 1965.

Chhibber, Pradeep. *Democracy without Associations: Transformation of the Party System and Social Cleavages in India.* Ann Arbor: University of Michigan Press, 1999.

Chibber, Vivek. *Locked in Place: State Building and Late Industrialization in India.* Princeton, NJ: Princeton University Press, 2003.

Cohen, Stephen. *India: Emerging Power.* Washington, DC: Brookings Institution Press, 2002.

Dalton, Denis. *Mahatma Gandhi.* New York: Columbia University Press, 1993.

Das, Gurcharan. *India Unbound: The Social and Economic Revolution from Independence to the Global Information Age.* New York: Anchor/Doubleday, 2002.

Dasgupta, Jyotirindra. *Language, Conflict and National Development.* Berkeley: University of California Press, 1970.

Echeverri-Gent, John. "Politics in India's Decentered Polity." In A. Ayres and P. Oldenburg, eds., *India Briefing.* Armonk, NY: M. E. Sharpe, 2002.

Frankel, Francine. *India's Political Economy, 1947–2004: The Gradual Revolution.* New Delhi: Oxford University Press, 2005.

Galanter, Marc. *Competing Equalities: Law and the Backward Classes in India.* New Delhi: Oxford University Press, 1984.

Ganguly, Sumit. *The Crisis in Kashmir: Portents of War, Hopes for Peace.* Woodrow Wilson Center Press Series. Cambridge: Cambridge University Press, 1999.

Gopal, Sarvepalli. *Jawaharlal Nehru: A Biography.* New Delhi: Oxford University Press, 1984.

Guha, Ramachandra. *The Unquiet Woods: Ecological Change and Peasant Resistance in the Himalaya.* New Delhi: Oxford University Press, 1991.

Hardgrave, Robert, and Stanley Kochanek. *India: Government and Politics in a Developing Nation.* Fifth edition. New York: Harcourt Brace Jovanovich, 1993.

Jaffrelot, Christophe. *The Hindu Nationalist Movement and Indian Politics, 1925–1993.* New York: Columbia University Press, 1998.

Jaffrelot, Christophe. "The Subordinate Caste Revolution." In A. Ayres and P. Oldenburg, eds., *India Briefing.* Armonk, NY: M. E. Sharpe, 2002.

Jalal, Ayesha. *Democracy and Authoritarianism in South Asia.* Cambridge: Cambridge University Press, 1995.

Jenkins, Rob. *Democratic Politics and Economic Reform in India.* Cambridge: Cambridge University Press, 1999.

Jha, Raghbendra. *Indian Economic Reforms.* New York: Palgrave Macmillan, 2003.

Kohli, Atul. *Democracy and Discontent: India's Growing Crisis of Governability.* Cambridge: Cambridge University Press, 1990.

Kohli, Atul, ed. *The Success of India's Democracy.* Cambridge: Cambridge University Press, 2001.

Kothari, Rajni. *Politics in India.* Boston: Little, Brown, 1970.

Lewis, John. *India's Political Economy.* New York: Oxford University Press, 1995.

Müller, Anders Riel, and Raj Patel. *Shining India? Economic Liberalization and Rural Poverty in the 1990s.* Oakland, CA: Food First/Institute for Food and Development Policy, 2004.

Nehru, Jawaharlal. *An Autobiography.* New Delhi: Oxford University Press, 1980.

Parekh, Bhikhu. *Gandhi.* New York: Oxford University Press, 1997.

Perkovich, George. *India's Nuclear Bomb.* Berkeley: University of California Press, 2001.

Robb, Peter. *A History of India.* New York: Palgrave, 2002.

Rudolph, Lloyd, and Susanne Rudolph. *In Pursuit of Lakshmi: The Political Economy of the Indian State.* Chicago: University of Chicago Press, 1987.

Sengupta, Bhavani. *Rajiv Gandhi: A Political Study.* New Delhi: Konarak Publishers, 1989.

Srinivas, M. N. *The Dominant Caste and Other Essays.* New Delhi: Oxford University Press, 1987.

Subramanian, Narendra. *Ethnicity and Populist Mobilization: Political Parties, Citizens and Democracy in South India.* New York: Oxford University Press, 1999.

Talbot, Ian, and Gurharpal Singh. *Region and Partition: Bengal, Punjab and the Partition of the Subcontinent.* New York: Oxford University Press, 1999.

Van der Veer, Peter. *Religious Nationalism: Hindus and Muslims in India.* Berkeley: University of California Press, 1994.

Varshney, Asutosh. *Democracy, Development and the Countryside: Urban–Rural Struggles in India.* Cambridge: Cambridge University Press, 1995.

Varshney, Asutosh. *Ethnic Conflict and Civic Life: Hindus and Muslims in India.* New Haven, CT: Yale University Press, 2003.

Wolpert, Stanley. *A New History of India.* Fifth edition. Chicago: University of Chicago Press, 1997.

IMPORTANT TERMS

Lal Krishna Advani leading figure in the BJP, who served as the home minister in the 1998–2004 BJP government. He was noted for his public advocacy of the destruction of the Babri mosque in Ayodhya, for which he was once arrested.

Bharatiya Janata Party (BJP) the "Indian People's Party," a political party that has its roots in past Hindu fundamentalist organizations and gradually became a major political force during the 1990s on the strength of its glorification of *Hinduttva* (see term).

Brahmins Hindu priests, considered to be the most "pure" of the caste groups and uniquely qualified to read scriptural texts and perform Hindu religious ceremonies.

caste the generic term employed to mean a fivefold occupational and social hierarchy ranging, in decending order of "purity," from Brahmins (see term) and warriors to merchants/traders, peasants/artisans, and "untouchables." Should be distinguished from the term "jati," which is used to identify groups of families belonging to a subcategory of a caste within a particular region or community.

Communist Party of India – Marxist (CPI-M) the most significant leftist party in India, notable as a rare case of a communist party that gained power through elections. It has maintained continuous control over the state assembly of West Bengal since the 1960s.

Congress the political party that grew out of the Indian National Congress (INC) and held power for most of the first five decades after independence. Later referred to as Congress-I (for Indira Gandhi), which split with the less significant Congress-O (for "organization") in 1967. Since the 1990s, Congress and its allies have been using the original pre-independence appellation (INC).

dominant-party system the term employed to characterize India's political system as a result of the Congress Party's steady control over Parliament for all but one election between 1952 and 1984. Not an authoritarian system but rather the combined result of India's "first-past-the-post" electoral system and the initial advantages inherited by the Congress Party.

Emergency an eighteen-month period from late 1975 to early 1977 when Indira Gandhi suspended parts of the constitution and arrested opposition leaders in response to her opponents' calls for the army to remove her from power for alleged campaign violations.

Indira Gandhi daughter of Jawaharlal Nehru, and prime minister of India (1967–1977, 1980–1984). Identified with the rise of patronage politics, the green revolution, a populist antipoverty campaign, the "Emergency" (see term), and the assault on Sikh militants in the Punjab. Assassinated by Sikh bodyguards in 1984. No direct relation to Mohandas K. Gandhi.

Mohandas K. Gandhi (Mahatma, or "Great Soul") British-educated   lawyer who became the de facto leader of the Indian nationalist movement. Noted for his opposition to the caste system and for nonviolent civil-disobedience campaigns that helped to mobilize grassroots support for independence. Assassinated in 1948 by a Hindu fanatic.

Rajiv Gandhi elder son of Indira Gandhi, who became prime minister of India (1984–1989) following Indira's assassination. His administration took the first steps toward economic reform. Following the Congress Party's defeat in 1989, Rajiv was assassinated while campaigning for the 1991 elections.

Sonia Gandhi Italian-born wife of Rajiv Gandhi. Initially stayed out of politics, but then led the Congress Party to victory in 2004, although declining the post of prime minister.

green revolution the campaign during the early 1970s to promote the use of new seeds and new methods of fertilization and crop rotation in order to boost agricultural production. Helped to make India self-sufficient in food production.

Hinduttva a term popularized by the BJP and some Hindu nationalist social organizations to emphasize the distinctiveness and greatness of Hindu civilization and to make this civilization the basis for defining India's national identity.

Indian National Congress (INC) an organization that emerged in 1885 and became the main force for the independence movement. Turned into the Congress Party after independence.

Janata Dal a loosely organized party that includes several diverse components that claim to share a common platform that emphasizes reduced planning, local self-reliance, poverty alleviation, and redistribution of wealth. Originally called the "Janata Party," this party has formed three separate coalition governments (1977–1979, 1989–1991, and 1996–1998), none of which has lasted a full term.

license raj an aspect of India's statist economy in which private-sector firms above a certain asset threshold had to obtain a government license to produce, import, or export goods. Has been steadily scaled back since the mid-1980s as part of economic liberalization.

Mandal Commission Report a report approved in 1990 that identifies a long list of groups as "other backward castes" that would qualify for preferential treatment through India's system of "reservations" (see term).

Jawaharlal Nehru leading figure in the Indian National Congress and India's first prime minister. He is identified with a "third way" of development that rejected alliances with the superpowers while combining aspects of Western-style capitalism and Soviet-style planning.

Narasimha Rao prime minister of India (1991–1996) who led the Congress Party after Rajiv Gandhi's assassination. His cabinet sped up the pace of economic liberalization.

President's Rule the rule stipulated in Article 356 of the Indian constitution whereby the president can authorize intervention by the central government in states thought to be experiencing extraordinary political or social unrest.

Has sometimes been invoked on shaky grounds to oust uncooperative state assemblies.

Rashtriya Seva Sangh (RSS) a Hindu social organization created in 1925 to preserve and promote Hindu traditions. Together with the VHP (see term), it helped mobilize support for the BJP.

reservations the term used by Indians to refer to India's "affirmative action" system for increasing the representation of lower-caste groups in educational institutions and the public sector.

Sikhs followers of the Sikh religion, who constitute a slim majority in the state of Punjab. Sikh militants waged a struggle for a separate "Khalistan" nation during the 1980s, but the conflict has since subsided.

Manmohan Singh prime minister of India following the Congress Party's surprising electoral victory in May 2004. Formerly minister of finance in the 1991–1996 Congress government.

V. P. Singh prime minister of India under the Janata government of 1989–1991. Noteworthy for efforts to check corruption and expand system of "reservations" (see term).

Atal Behari Vajpayee BJP leader who served as prime minister of India from 1998 to 2004. Identified with pragmatic wing of the BJP.

Vishva Hindu Parishad (VHP) a worldwide organization of Hindus committed to promoting *Hinduttva* (see term). Constitutes a major social base and source of funding for the BJP.

vote bank a bloc of votes for a particular candidate delivered by members of a given community (usually a local caste group or a village) as a result of deals brokered between the candidate and the community's leaders.

STUDY QUESTIONS

1. What were the various sources of collective identity in South Asia prior to British colonialism? Why have these cleavages generated less collective violence than we find in postcolonial Africa?

2. In what ways did British colonial administration affect the prospects for political and economic development in postcolonial India?

3. Why was Mahatma Gandhi's leadership important to the success of the Indian National Congress? What were the strengths and limitations of his strategy of nonviolent noncooperation?

4. What institutional characteristics distinguish Indian democracy and federalism from democracy and federalism in the United States?

5. In what respects did Nehru's India represent a "third way" of political and economic development? How did successors modify his approach from the 1960s to 1970s?

6. What were the sources of the Congress Party's dominance between the 1950s and early 1980s? What trends characterize the transformation of India's electoral politics since the late 1980s?

7. In what ways have long-standing identities based on caste or religion affected Indian politics since the end of Congress Party dominance?

8. What do the BJP's electoral victories in 1998–1999 and the Congress Party's victory in 2004 suggest about the dynamics of coalition politics and about the salience of the debate over secularism and communalism?

9. How would you characterize the pace and effectiveness of India's approach to economic liberalization since the late 1980s? Which groups appear to be the main "winners" and "losers" in the process?

10. How have global economic, social, and political processes affected the interplay of identities, interests, and institutions in post–Cold War India?

RUSSIA
GEORGIA
ARMENIA
AZERBAIJAN
AZERBAIJAN
TURKEY

Caspian
Sea

TURKMENISTAN

o Tabriz

⊛ Tehran

Mashhad o

o Qom

o Kermanshah

AFGHANISTAN

Tigris R.

o Dezful   o Esfahan   Birjand o

I   R   A   N

o Yazd

o Ahvaz

Abadan

o Kerman

Zahedan o

PAKISTAN

KUWAIT

o Shiraz

o Bandar-e Bushehr

Persian

Gulf

Bandar-e 'Abbas

SAUDI

BAHRAIN

OMAN

ARABIA

QATAR

Gulf of
Oman

IRAN

Euphrates R.

IRAQ

0   100   200   300 miles
0   100   200 300km

UNITED ARAB EMIRATES   OMAN

CHAPTER ELEVEN

Iran

Vali Nasr

Introduction

At the turn of the twentieth century, Iran embarked on a path to development that was typical of many late developers. Iran's experience, however, has proved to be unique. Development was accompanied by ideological conflicts that culminated in a religiously inspired revolution in 1979. In the process, a modernizing monarchy gave place to the theocratic and revolutionary politics of the **Islamic Republic of Iran** (the official name of Iran since the revolution). As populism changed the character of the economy and **Islamic ideology** (a political doctrine based on **Islam**) transformed Iranian society, its norms, institutions, and, for a time at least, pursuit of its interests were subsumed under preservation of identity. Since the revolution, the nature of development has been complex, revealing modernizing impulses tempered by the pressures of Islamic ideology. Beyond its ideological and institutional particularities, the Islamic Republic shares many of the characteristics and problems of populist authoritarian regimes elsewhere in the developing world: a bloated public sector, mismanagement, and corruption.

There are three distinct and yet interrelated periods in Iran's modern development: the early and later **Pahlavi** (the dynasty that ruled Iran from 1925 to 1979) periods; those of **Reza Shah Pahlavi** (1925–1941) and **Muhammad Reza Shah Pahlavi** (1941–1979); and the Islamic Republic (1979–present). There is greater continuity between the first two periods, under the Pahlavi monarchs, although there are notable differences as well. The Reza Shah period coincided with the rise of the modern Iranian state and started the process of development. The Muhammad Reza Shah period continued in the footsteps of the first period but accelerated the pursuit of modernization. Development under the second Pahlavi monarch was, moreover, conditioned by different global influences and domestic sociopolitical identities and interests. The Islamic Republic has been distinct from the earlier periods in its ideological orientation and in many aspects of its economic policies and political characteristics. Above and beyond their differences in ideological orientation or policy choices, the three periods are similar in the dominant role of the state in development. The basis of Iran's path in the modern world is to be found in the historical circumstances in which Iran first embarked on development.

The Global Context and the Rise of the Modern Iranian State

Iran is among the handful of developing countries to escape direct colonialism but not the impact of imperialism. Throughout the nineteenth century, the ruling Qajar dynasty (1796–1921) was unable to resist Western imperialist penetration; nor could it stave off the gradual loss of territory and control over national assets to foreign powers. This provided the context for the rise of the modern Iranian state and the path to development that it would follow (see Table 11.1).

Also important was the pivotal role of the monarchy during the nineteenth century. The monarchy was important to imperial powers who wished to maintain a captive and weak center in Iran. As a result, imperial powers provided strategic support to the monarchy and helped thwart significant challenges to its authority. The broader powers of the monarchy were rooted in the dominant social position of the feudal aristocracy and tribal leaders, who sustained monarchical authority at the center, even as they resisted taxation and defended their autonomy. Of equal importance was the role of the religious establishment. Throughout the nineteenth century, the clergy resisted domination by the monarchy and defended the rights of the nation before imperialist interests that often worked through the monarchy. Still, at a more fundamental level, the clergy defended the sociopolitical position of the monarchy, just as the monarchy protected the socioeconomic interests of the clergy. The nature of relations among the state, the elite, and the religious establishment would change over time, with important consequences for Iran's pattern of development.

Concentration of power in the monarchy occurred at a time of weakening of the ruling political establishment as a whole, in large part caused by pressures that were brought to bear on Iranian society and Iran's body politic by imperialism. The concentration of power in a decaying central government led to circumstances in which neither the state nor social forces enjoyed countrywide domination. This, in turn, produced a crisis for monarchical absolutism. Eventually the monarchy found itself on the defensive against a strong constitutionalist movement that included the intelligentsia – who were the conduit for European constitutionalist ideals – elements of the religious establishment, the urban poor, and aspiring members of the bureaucracy and the emerging middle classes. The Constitutional Revolution, as this movement and the resultant 1906 Constitution came to be known, placed limits on the power of the monarchy and vested much of its authority in a parliament. This would be the first serious attempt to alter the balance of power between the state and society. It produced a period of democratic rule in Iran, which proved to be short-lived. By the end of the first decade of the twentieth century, Iranian democracy had begun to lose ground to authoritarian tendencies.

The rise of democracy did not produce stable governing coalitions or well-organized and effective political parties. Democracy intensified political competition in the central government, just as it weakened the hold of the central government over the country, leading to palpable fears of the country's disintegration. This, along with the collapse of law and order, rampant corruption, and deteriorating economic conditions, limited the prospects for democratic consolidation. Elected governments proved to be just as pliable in the face of imperialist pressure as had absolutist monarchs before 1906. It had further become evident that democracy would not produce rapid modernization. Hence, those social forces that supported the Constitutional Revolution with the hope of bringing both political and economic modernization to Iran were confronted with a zero-sum choice – democracy or socioeconomic modernization. Many opted for the latter, believing that a strong central state would better protect fundamental rights to life and property, the integrity of national borders, and national rights before imperialist demands.

In the meantime, the Anglo-Russian rapprochement of 1907 made the division of Iran between the two world powers a distinct possibility, placing greater pressure on the democratic order. This possibility would continue to haunt Iranians until the Bolshevik revolution of 1917 drove a wedge between Russia and the West. Thenceforth, the British would once again take an interest in strengthening the central government in Iran. However, by then, the democratic order had been seriously damaged. Consequently, the domestic and foreign efforts to shore up the central authority and the increasing demands for effective modernization and development within Iran – which had first been pursued through the Constitutional Revolution – would now lead to a regime change. The result would be a new political order that would draw heavily on the institutional framework of the absolutist era. Iran would thus embark on its path to development by reconstituting the pre-1906 political institutions.

The Reza Shah Period and the Beginnings of Development, 1921–1941

The crisis of democracy ended with a military coup in 1921 that was led by Reza Khan (later Reza Shah Pahlavi) in alliance with dissident civilian politicians and intellectuals. Reza Khan quickly consolidated power and in

1925 ascended the throne. The coup ushered in a new period in Iran's history, during which national boundaries became institutionalized, the country committed itself to development, and its interests, identity, and institutions became defined and entrenched. In many ways, the fundamental characteristics of the modern state and the defining elements of its path to development were outlined during this period.

Reza Shah's monarchy was concerned with two separate but interrelated objectives: first, to assert the power of the central government and limit regional autonomy – that is, to ensure law and order and guarantee the territorial integrity of the country; and second, to develop Iran, understood at the time to mean social modernization and industrialization. The first objective required the establishment of a strong military, and the second objective required the construction of modern bureaucratic institutions. The realization of both objectives required an increase in state revenue and the mobilization of financial resources through taxation, greater regulation of the economy, and attempts to increase the proceeds from oil production and export. Both objectives would in time broaden the state's ability to formulate and implement coherent policies and to reach into society. The two objectives were the most important examples of the state's provision of "public goods" (that is, things that people want but that no individual or group of individuals can provide) in a society where such a concept was largely absent. The provision of these public goods had popular support and helped the state to expand its role in the society and economy and to organize resources and people effectively. In fact, reshaping identities and value systems in order to better provide those goods became central to the state's conception of its own function.

Reza Shah was largely successful in realizing both objectives. His military campaigns defeated separatist movements and subdued autonomous regions and rebellious warlords. In the process, he asserted the primacy of the central government and laid the foundations for strong centralized control of the country. Still, this did not end the obsession with territorial integrity, which at key junctures would translate into xenophobic nationalism but would otherwise further serve to strengthen state control and nudge Iran in the direction of absolutism. Historically, military-bureaucratic absolutism in Europe had facilitated the mobilization of resources in the face of threats to borders. The same process was evident in Iran as well. Hence, early on, the modern Iranian state developed authoritarian tendencies in response to international and domestic military threats and the need to mobilize resources to respond to them.

The goal of economic development led the state to extend its control over the economy to mobilize resources for industrialization. Following the examples of Germany and Japan during 1921–1941, the state established the first industries, invested in infrastructure, and tightened its hold over customs, banking, and foreign trade. The result was a form of state-led capitalism in which the state would see to industrialization, just as it would manage the day-to-day affairs of the economy, although it would provide a role for the private sector.

The objective of economic development both required and promoted administrative and social reform. Reza Shah supported the rise of modern bureaucratic institutions, a new judiciary, and the reform of public health and education. Students were sent abroad, and modern educational institutions were established in Iran. In addition, new administrative procedures and secular civil and penal codes were adopted.

Reza Shah was convinced that making Iran strong and fostering its economic development would require fundamental changes in the country's identity and social relations – an ambitious project of cultural engineering that required a coherent state ideology. The state secularized the judiciary and the educational system, and it restricted the powers of the clergy. It mandated the change of traditional dress to Western dress and promoted secular values. In so doing, it hoped to make popular culture compatible with the requirements and goals of development. In place of Islam, the state promoted nationalism, defined in terms of pre-Islamic Iranian identity. Such an identity would be secular and would provide an ideological foundation for both monarchical power and rapid development. The change in identity was also intended to inculcate discipline in the population as a prelude to development. It was then believed, largely because of imperialist propaganda, that Iranian cultural beliefs could not promote discipline and the values that are necessary for a modern society. Secular nationalism would remedy that problem. In all of this, Reza Shah was deeply influenced by the examples of Germany and Japan, and of **Kemalism** (a model of development based on secularism, nationalism, and state dominance in socioeconomic matters) in Turkey. Global context thus shaped interests, identities, and the relation between the two.

The concern with identity as a necessary prerequisite for successful development would become a hallmark of state–society relations in Iran. In Iran, the two dominant markers of identity are Islam and Iranian nationalism. The two have at times reinforced one another and at other times have represented different political ideals. Iranians became Muslim pursuant to the Arab invasion of Iran in the seventh century. As such, Islam has always been viewed by Iranian nationalists as the invader's faith. Iranians are unique among the early civilizations that converted to Islam in that they did not adopt the Arabic language and culture. This has created tensions between Iran's nationalism and its faith. Iranian **Shia** Islam is a minority sect in Islam that is distinguished from the majority Sunnis in that it believes that the descendants of the Prophet (whom Shias refer to as *Imams*) were the legitimate successors to the Prophet and that today the clergy (*ulama*, the highest-ranking among whom the Shias call **Ayatollah**) serve as their representatives and as such exercise authority over the Shias. The Shias were always a suppressed community, and they did not exercise power until 1501, when a Shia monarchy made the faith the official religion of Iran. Shias differ from Sunnis in matters of faith much as the Eastern Church differs from the Western Church in Christianity. That Iran became the seat of Shi'ism gave the country its own unique attachment to Islam, which has always distinguished it from the Arab world and as such underscored the uniqueness of Iranian identity – setting it apart from the rest of the Muslim world.

Islam and Shi'ism have always played an important role in defining Iranian identity. However, with the advent of the modern state, emphasis was placed on secularism, which demanded separating Islam from Iranian nationalism. In place of Islam, Iranians were to identify themselves with their ethnicity and language, which as secular concepts were seen to be more compatible with modern nationalism and developmentalism. Iranian nationalism never replaced Islam, nor were the complex relations between the two ever completely resolved. Rather, from Reza Shah's regime to that of the Islamic Republic, identity featured importantly in state policy. The preoccupation with questions of identity – and hence issues such as music, dress, popular beliefs, and the cultural outlook of the individual – became important in defining the public good and setting the agenda for development. The legacy of the state's cultural policies continues to influence state–society relations in Iran to this day, and hence debates about development begin with struggles over identity.

Giving the state the means to govern effectively was expensive. In fact, how it dealt with financial needs shaped, to a significant degree, the nature of state power. Since the beginning of the twentieth century, Iran received royalties from the Anglo-Iranian Oil Company, a British company that managed oil production in southern Iran. Efforts to increase royalty payments to the Iranian government proved futile, which forced the state to rely more on tax revenue. Tax farming – a system in which local officials' incomes are tied to the amount of taxes they manage to collect – and other forms of unsystematic revenue collections were replaced with a centralized taxation system. The state also turned to foreign advisers to streamline Iran's financial system. Foreign expertise helped the state to extract resources from society and develop plans for economic development; it did not, however, altogether resolve the financial problems confronting the state. Financial constraints encouraged the state to monopolize power in order to increase its ability to extract resources from society and to negotiate more effectively with foreign commercial interests over royalties.

That a strong state did in fact rise in Iran at this time and that it did so despite significant financial constraints and resistance to central control, and in contravention of foreign interests, is noteworthy. It has been generally accepted that the rise of states is directly correlated with war making, and that societies that experience wars or significant social dislocation are more prone to produce strong states. The rise of the modern Iranian state during the 1920s was closely tied to the military campaigns that consolidated the central government's hold over the country and occurred amid the significant hardships – for example, economic hardship, famine, disease, social strife, and civil war – that Iranians endured during the first two decades of the twentieth century. The campaign to centralize power and defend the territorial integrity of the country had broad support among many social groups, notably those who had also been the main support for democracy. This allowed Reza Shah to tie the defense of the integrity of state borders to his own consolidation of power. It also allowed his regime to avoid compromises with various social actors – the feudal elite, tribal leaders, and merchants – in order to mobilize resources for the military campaigns.

During the 1920s, local power in Iran was strong but unorganized. It was, moreover, dissociated from politics at the center, and in some cases was supported by, and integrated with, foreign interests. It therefore did not serve as a source of support for the Parliament during the turbulent years of the democratic period or during the period of regime change in the 1920s. The subsequent weakening of democratic institutions such as the Parliament during the period of regime change meant minimal oversight by the Parliament of the administrative and financial activities of state leaders. Consequently, power accumulated at the center, and absolutist tendencies grew unbridled.

The growing dominance of the monarch combined with the social changes that development entailed created tensions in Iranian politics. In the first place, Reza Shah had been prevailed upon by the clergy to become a monarch, whereas in reality his regime was a "republican monarchy." No sooner had Reza Shah become king when he embarked on secularization and modernization and also abolished the hereditary titles of the aristocracy. In addition, his campaign to assert centralized control over the country pitted the state against local leaders. He thus moved away from those elite groups and social classes that had until then served as the pillars of the monarchy – the elite, the religious establishment, and tribal leaders – and was looking instead to the new middle classes to bolster his regime. The Reza Shah period thus changed the social base of the ruling order. In the economic arena, the same trend was evident. Traditional tradesmen and commercial interests became alienated from the state as it extended its control over the economy. The change in the social base of the monarchy would prove consequential. Disenchanted elite groups, the religious establishment, and small merchants and traders would form the basis of the anti-Pahlavi oppositional coalition. This coalition would eventually serve as the backbone of the revolution of 1979.

Initially, Reza Shah allied himself with the new middle classes to take on the elite, local leaders, and the clergy. The new middle classes were then receptive to modernization, secularization, and the nationalist identity that Reza Shah promoted in lieu of Islam. The alliance between the new middle classes and the monarchy, however, failed to provide the state with a countervailing base of support because these classes were not ideologically committed to the monarchy. As the pace of modernization increased, tensions in the monarchy's relations with the new middle classes grew. By the 1930s, many in these classes were joining pro-democracy and various leftist organizations.

Development spearheaded the rise of modern bureaucratic agencies. At the outset, the bureaucracy supported Reza Shah. Over time, however, he became wary of the rising power of the bureaucracy and purged it of its principal leaders. By exercising more control over the bureaucracy, Reza Shah precluded the possibility that the bureaucracy would develop as a legal-rational institution independent of the control of the monarchy. The Iranian state from this point forward would display many characteristics of what comparativists sometimes term *patrimonialism*, in which power is concentrated in the ruler, whose exercise of authority is only partially influenced by legal and administrative procedures.

In sum, during this period, the global context – in the form of imperialism and the German-Japanese model – combined with the state's need to safeguard territorial integrity and pursue development to shape interests, identity, and institutions in a manner that empowered the state and hence ensured its domination over Iranian politics.

The Democratic Interregnum, 1941–1954

The pattern of development that began in 1921 was interrupted by World War II. The Reza Shah state fell victim to changes in the broader international environment. The western Allies were keen to use Iranian territory for supplying the Soviet Union against Germany, and for this it was imperative that they maintain control over Iran. Reza Shah's constant bickering with British oil companies, combined with Iran's reliance on Germany for a number of public projects, had made the British wary of him. The Allies demanded that Iran declare neutrality and expel all German citizens, that Reza Shah abdicate, and that the Iranian military disarm. In 1941, Reza Shah was replaced on the throne by his son, Muhammad Reza Pahlavi (known in the West as "the **Shah**"). Foreign intervention thus ushered in a new era in Iranian politics that was characterized by greater openness and new possibilities for state–society relations. Still, foreign intervention did not decisively reshape Iranian politics – rearranging its institutions and altering the balance of power among them – in the manner that the United States would do in Germany and Japan after the war. The British retained the monarchy and did not change the country's constitution or the balance of power among the various social and political actors. That the monarchy would in later years emerge once again as a dominant force in an all-powerful state was therefore not very surprising.

Still, Reza Shah's departure opened the political process and created alternate developmental paths. During the war, political groups that had been suppressed by Reza Shah – liberals, leftists, and the clergy – organized and established a place for themselves in the political arena. The Parliament, which since 1921 had steadily lost ground to the monarchy, was empowered and once again occupied center stage. The political opening suggested that Iran could develop along democratic lines and that power might permanently shift from the monarchy to the Parliament, devolving in the process from state institutions to a broader spectrum of social and political actors. By 1954, however, domestic problems combined with changes in the global context to end the democratic opening.

The 1941–1954 period witnessed an intense struggle over the definition of political identity in Iran. The outcome of that struggle would be important for the fate of democracy. Some of the political forces that became dominant during the 1941–1954 period were illiberal. Communist, fascist, and religious groups and parties operated in the open political process but were not committed to democracy. In fact, their activities would serve as the pretext for once again vesting the state – and the institution of the monarchy – with greater powers.

Most important in this regard was the communist Tudeh (Masses) Party. Closely allied with the Soviet Union, the Tudeh Party posed a strong challenge to the ruling order and Western interests in Iran. The party was active among the middle classes, labor, intellectuals, and students, mobilizing these social groups in defense of social justice. It subscribed to the cult of Stalin and did not favor democracy. The Tudeh Party's ambiguous role in the Soviet Union's attempt to separate two provinces in northern Iran after World War II helped create both popular and Western support for strengthening the political center, which ultimately weakened the Tudeh Party and, in the process, the budding democracy.

The resurgence of religion in politics was equally significant. Religious forces were keen to roll back the secular policies of the Pahlavi state and to institutionalize their role in society and politics. To this end, they became active in the political arena, but not with the aim of strengthening democracy. Both the communists and religious forces weakened democracy by engaging in agitational politics: demonstrations, strikes, and sit-ins in the case of the Tudeh Party, and political assassinations in the case of religious activists. By creating political uncertainty, disruptions, and social tensions, the two groups made the task of democratic consolidation difficult and helped the monarchy enlist foreign support for its campaign to consolidate power.

Most damaging to democracy was the oil crisis of 1951–1953 and its link with Cold War politics. The dispute over royalties with the **Anglo-Iranian Oil Company**, which had begun during the 1930s, eventually culminated in an impasse during 1951–1953. As the British company refused to accommodate Iran's demands for higher royalties, nationalist feelings were aroused and they dominated Iranian politics. The monarchy, the military, and some in the business community favored a low-key approach, believing that a confrontational attitude would not favor Iran. Because of British intransigence, however, Iranians demanded more. The popularly elected nationalist prime minister, **Mohammad Mossadeq**, and his National Front Party capitalized on the public mood and nationalized the assets of the Anglo-Iranian Oil Company in Iran in 1953. The decision was widely popular within Iran and was supported by the Tudeh Party and religious activists as well.

Britain responded by cutting Iran out of the oil market. The Iranian economy collapsed, causing social tension and political radicalism. The palpable fear of a communist takeover changed the political alignment that had dominated Iranian politics. The clergy, worried about communism, switched sides, as did key segments of the middle classes, commercial interests, and elements of the nationalist elite. This political realignment facilitated concerted action between the monarchy and the Iranian military in close cooperation with the United States and Britain. The result was a military coup that toppled the National Front government, ending the democratic interregnum and restoring the monarchy to power. The 1941–1954 period had seen the possibility of alternate identities – Islamic, secular, democratic – shaping state–society relations and Iranian politics developing along a different path. By 1954, however, those possibilities were no longer present. Foreign intervention first interrupted and then led to the resumption of the state's development in the direction first instituted by Reza Shah. Interests, identities, and ultimately institutions were reshaped by the changing global context.

Resurrection of the Pahlavi State, 1954–1963

The 1954–1963 period was one of consolidation of monarchical power. Relying on the military, and with crucial financial and technical assistance from the United States, the monarchy went on the offensive against its opponents. The National Front Party and the Tudeh Party were banned. The military and bureaucracy were purged of their sympathizers. The campaign also weakened the institutions of civil society and ultimately the Parliament, dimming the prospects for democracy. Cold War considerations led the United States to support these developments in Iran and to help train Iranian military and intelligence agencies to protect the state, which was viewed as a bulwark against communism and the southward expansion of the Soviet Union. Financial aid helped buoy Iran's economy and generated support for the ruling order. The consolidation of power under the monarchy would commit the state to a largely economic vision of development. The spirit of this posture was captured in the Shah's statement: "When the Iranians learn to behave like Swedes, I will behave like the king of Sweden."

The single-minded pursuit of development – the public good whose provision would justify state authority from this point forward – required further streamlining the organization of resources and people, the imperatives that had also propelled the expansion of state authority under Reza Shah. This led the state to reformulate its relations with agrarian elites, who had to this point remained close to the monarchy; the religious establishment, with which the monarchy had only a tenuous alliance; and the middle classes, which were the main agents and beneficiaries of development, although they were not committed to the monarchy. The consequences of these reformulations would determine the course of Iran's subsequent development.

Economic Growth and Authoritarianism, 1963–1979

Between 1959 and 1963, the Pahlavi state had to weather a number of challenges, the resolution of which both necessitated redoubling its commitment to development and created greater room for pursuing it. The political rumblings occurred at a time when the United States began to waver in its unconditional support of the Pahlavi state and viewed some form of reform in Iran as necessary to limit communist influence in the country. The change in the U.S. attitude was parlayed into momentum for wide-scale reform.

In the meantime, an austerity package prescribed by the International Monetary Fund, which included a cut in government spending and devaluation of the currency to discourage imports, brought on a severe recession during the 1960–1962 period. The perceived threat to the ruling order convinced state leaders that they could not afford prolonged economic crises. Oil revenue, even despite modest increases ($555 million [U.S.] in 1963–1964, comprising 12 percent of the GNP), would not remedy the crisis or satisfy development needs. Hence, reform would have to go hand in hand with, as well as help spur, economic growth. The state began to see its objective of development as integral to sociopolitical reform. This vision culminated in the "White Revolution" of 1963, the term coined to upstage the Left and its promise of "red" revolution.

The White Revolution was a package of sweeping reforms that aimed to change the structure of societal relations in Iran and to enable more effective resource mobilization in the service of development. The most important initiatives were land reform, the enfranchisement of women, and the provision of greater rights and a greater share of industrial profits to industrial labor. Through the White Revolution, the state was hoping to institutionalize its hold over the middle classes and among those social groups that might serve as the base of support for an effective communist movement, including the poor, the peasantry, and industrial labor. These reforms, so the argument ran, were necessary for effective development. They would modernize Iranian society, changing it in ways that would help industrialization.

The White Revolution was a risky venture because the principal losers in the reforms – the landed elite and the clergy – had in the past served as sources of support for the monarchy, whereas the support of the modern middle classes for monarchy had at best been tenuous. The Shah was falling into the same trap that his father had, vesting his political fortunes in a social class whose loyalties ultimately would not rest with the monarchy. In addition, given the Pahlavi state's pro-industry bias, it did not cultivate a base of support among the peasantry that it was enfranchising. Industrial labor, meanwhile, did not as yet possess sufficient power to act as a significant source of support for the monarchy; and if they were to become a force, the monarchy was unlikely to claim their allegiance for long. More immediately, however, the state would rely on the rising power of the bureaucracy, which itself was being modernized from within. The bureaucracy was committed to development and to that end joined in a ruling alliance with the monarchy. In effect, the state reformulated its links with society and also defined the shape of its opposition. The landed elite, the clergy, and the "liberal Left," all of whom opposed the White Revolution or viewed it as the means through which the state might devour their base of support, gravitated toward a united antistate stance. The restoration of power to the monarchy thus reconstituted the oppositional alliance that had first surfaced during the earlier Reza Shah period.

The first expression of this opposition was the protest movement led by the cleric **Ayatollah Ruhollah Khomeini** in 1964. The protest was strongly antistate, but its immediate concern was with the White Revolution. Khomeini characterized the enfranchisement of women as "un-Islamic." He also rejected land reform as a violation of Islamic protection of property rights. The protest movement brought together the landed elite, the religious establishment, and the liberal Left. The first two groups opposed specific points of the White Revolution, whereas the liberal Left viewed the entire reform package as a threat to its political position and had a vested interest in its failure. The White Revolution sought to change the social structure, in opposition to which the liberal Left had mobilized support, and to render the Left's political programs obsolete.

The protest movement failed. The state's agenda of social reform and rapid economic development thus unfolded unencumbered. Still, the protest movement had the effect of committing the state to a greater use of force in contending with the opposition. This in turn led to the consolidation of the anti-Pahlavi forces into a more coherent alliance under the unified leadership of the clergy and the liberal Left. Such thinkers as **Ali Shariati** actually began to formulate a socially conscious religio-ideological perspective that could consolidate an anti-Shah alliance. This opposition would in time become increasingly violent and would, in turn, face greater violence from the state. From this point forward, the security apparatuses of the state, most notably the secret police, **SAVAK**, would use repressive measures, including detentions and torture, to subdue the opposition. The opposition produced radical communist and Islamist urban-guerrilla organizations, escalating antistate

activities to the level of armed conflict and acts of terror. The radicalization of the opposition and the state's use of violence in suppressing it polarized Iranian politics and gradually concentrated power in a limited number of state institutions – most notably its security apparatuses – and in the
monarchy.

Economically, however, the 1960s was a period of relative success. Land
reform, the overhaul of the bureaucracy, and the weakening of the Parliament
allowed economic managers to pursue growth aggressively and with greater
freedom from outside influence. The result was an industrial transformation,
producing growth rates that were unmatched in Iran's history. The gross domestic product (GDP) for this period grew at an average of 9.2 percent per
year, and industrial growth rates averaging 15 percent per year were among
the highest in the developing world. At the same time, the central characteristics of the economy changed as it acquired medium and heavy industries
and a modern private sector.

Economic development in Iran during the 1960s was based largely on
import-substituting industrialization (ISI). Although ISI produces rapid
growth rates early on and helps kick-start industrialization, it also poses political and economic challenges down the road. As we saw in the chapters
on Mexico and India, ISI places emphasis on capital-intensive industries and
hence leads to the neglect of small-scale production and the agricultural sector. It can lead to uneven development, overurbanization, and income inequality. It also puts pressure on government finances and the balance of
trade, just as it augments state control of the economy. It was partly to address problems born of ISI that Iran decided to support the oil-price hikes
of **OPEC** (the Organization of Petroleum Exporting Countries) during the
1970s.

The rise in oil prices ($958 million [U.S.] in 1968–1969, comprising
18 percent of Iran's GNP, in contrast with $20 billion in 1975–1976, rep-
resenting 35 percent of the GNP) removed financial pressures from the state
and allowed it to spend more freely on various industrial and social projects.
It is interesting to note, however, that higher oil prices augmented the challenges before the Shah. They adversely affected the pattern of economic development as the state deepened ISI, but did so with decreasing efficiency.
Although the Iranian economy performed well during the 1970s, it veered
off the path toward viable industrialization and market development and
eventually faced serious crises.

The oil boom created bottlenecks in the economy and led to wasteful spending on grandiose projects. Iran spent billions of dollars on infrastructure and
industrial projects. It also spent huge sums on war matériel and public enterprises of questionable economic value. All of this eroded trust in the management of the economy. The rapid pace of growth also created social dislocation, cultural confusion, and new political demands with which the state

was unequipped to contend. In addition, the newfound wealth encouraged corruption and speculative financial activities. This adversely affected public morale and skewed popular perception about the meaning and intent of entrepreneurial activity. The oil wealth also raised expectations – so much so that the state not only was unable to gain political support for acquiring the new wealth but also found itself falling short of fulfilling growing expectations.

The Iranian state began to face political problems associated with "**rentier states**"; that is, states in which income that is external to the productive capacity of the economy accounts for the lion's share of state revenue. Rentier states are generally politically weak because the state derives little if any of its income from the population and, as a result, does not devise ways to increase revenues through taxation. Nor does it negotiate with the population in order to increase society's contribution to state revenue. Instead, rentier states invest in distributive mechanisms and, having developed a relationship of distribution and patronage with their populations, do not develop meaningful links with society. The population does not credit the government for the generation of wealth, although it expects more from the government in terms of distribution of wealth. Popular support remains contingent on a continued flow of "rent."

As oil income came to dominate the Iranian economy, the Pahlavi state began to face a serious political crisis. On the one hand, its developmental agenda had concentrated power in the state and the monarchy and isolated both from other social groups. On the other hand, the state justified its course of action in terms of provision of a public good: development. Between 1946 and 1979, the state had changed the character of the economy in a fundamental fashion from agriculture to industry. Public planning, urbanization, industrialization, diversification, and infrastructural and human capital investments had produced sustained change and growth. The increase in oil wealth, however, denied the state the ability to claim credit for its economic achievements. It undermined the state's developmentalist claims as it depicted development as synonymous with oil revenue, rendering redundant the political apparatuses that the Pahlavi monarchs had argued were necessary for realizing development. All of this pushed an already narrowly based state to the brink of collapse. The resultant political tensions erupted in 1977, culminating in the Islamic Revolution of 1979 that toppled the Pahlavi state.

The global context proved important at this juncture as well. The revolution unfolded at a time of change in Iran's relations with the United States. Jimmy Carter, the U.S. president, was unwilling to provide unconditional support to the Shah's regime and instead strongly advocated political reform in Iran. The new U.S. approach created confusion in the Iranian state and emboldened the opposition.

The opposition to the Pahlavi state consisted of liberal and pro-democracy forces, the Left, and religious activists, but it increasingly adopted a strongly

Islamic character, especially after Ayatollah Khomeini – then in exile in Iraq – assumed its leadership. Khomeini used his position of authority to put forward a particularly revolutionary and antistate reading of Islam and used its symbols to mobilize the masses. Khomeini also built on the traditional role of Shia clerics, arguing that given their knowledge of religion, they must rule politically if the society was to be Islamic, just, and prosperous. His religio-political crusade was therefore directed at constructing a theocratic form of government.

Khomeini's arguments – which were published as *Islamic Government* – were part of a broader movement of revolt against secularism, and the state institutions that represented and promoted it, that was defining politics in the Muslim world at the time. Across the Muslim world, thinkers such as Khomeini were rejecting the modern state as a failure. They argued that it had failed to bring about genuine development or resolve regional crises such as the Arab-Israeli conflict, and most importantly it had failed to reverse the palpable decline of Muslim worldly power before that of the West. These thinkers captured the frustration of those whom development had left behind and those who lamented the weakness of Muslim states on the world stage when they argued that, rather than empower Muslims, the modern state had merely trampled on their culture by promoting secularism and marginalizing Islam in public life. These thinkers argued that the problem in the Muslim world was secularism and its protector and promoter, the modern state. Far from being the solution to sociopolitical problems and agents of positive change, the modern state had cut Muslims off from the roots of their power – their religion. Therefore, it would be by dismantling the secular state and erecting in its place an Islamic state that Muslims would find the path to development. For these thinkers and activists, Islam provided the blueprint for a perfect government that would be built on Islamic law and the model of the Prophet of Islam's rule during the religion's early years in the seventh century. Their vision of the Islamic state was revolutionary and utopian, rejecting the existing social and political systems and promising a perfect order in their place. Their challenge to the state was not only socioeconomic – as was the case with the Left – but also cultural. The Shah's regime – with its pro-Western secularism – and Khomeini's challenge to it in many regards epitomized the politics of Islamic activism and served as the opening battle between Islamic activism and the secular state that has defined Muslim politics since 1979.

The success of Islamic activism in Iran was not entirely a matter of ideology. In promoting his cause, Khomeini strengthened the alliance between the religious establishment and the Left that had been in place since 1964. Khomeini successfully managed to keep the opposition focused on overthrowing the Shah, while postponing the resolution of ideological disagreements and cultural tensions between the religious and secular opposition to the Shah to the postrevolutionary period. His presence on the political scene, however, made religious identity central to politics. In so doing, Khomeini and the revolutionary forces rejected the developmentalist secularism of the Pahlavi state. The revolution owed its success, in large part, to the fact that this stance did not create tensions in the ranks of revolutionary forces, segments of which were politically at odds with the Pahlavi state but shared in its secularism and were themselves products of the Pahlavi state's social engineering. As a result, the revolutionary movement in Iran in 1979 was politically uniform but culturally and socially eclectic in that it had both Islamist and secular-liberal and leftist elements in it.

The revolution itself unfolded rather rapidly over the course of a mere 18 months. It fed on a set of cascading events that converged to overwhelm the Shah's regime, which failed to react adroitly to the challenge before it. These events were: wide-scale street demonstrations, the mobilization of religious institutions and activists, labor strikes, the disappearance of the democratic middle, and the collapse of the military. The first three events had the effect of including larger numbers of people in the revolution, producing a degree of popular mobilization that overwhelmed state institutions. The latter two events ensured that the state would not respond effectively to the mobilization, guaranteeing the success of the revolution.

Throughout 1977 and 1978, a growing number of Iranians joined street demonstrations to ask first for political reform and later for regime change. The Shah's government proved unable to contend with the demonstrations either through a show of force in the streets or by giving in to demands for reform. The growing religious tenor of the demonstrations that was facilitated by the growing political importance of a network of mosques, seminaries, and religious organizations soon provided a backbone to the demonstrators and helped tie their demands to the larger ideological arguments that were put forth by Khomeini. The popular mobilization reached a critical stage when it led to labor strikes, which included not only government workers but also employees of critical industrial sectors such as oil and electricity, whose walkouts were of more than symbolic importance and impacted the economy directly.

There were then two forces capable of dealing with the mobilization: the first were the pro-democracy politicians who were associated with the National Front Party of the 1950s; and the second was the military. The first could contain and manage the mobilized social force, and the second could have suppressed them. The democratic middle failed to play its historic role, partly because it would not reach an agreement with the Shah on how to deal with the mobilization and partly because it decided not to challenge Khomeini or the Left. The military was not deployed in an effective way during the early months of the agitations when it could have changed the outcome. It was not until the Shah had left Iran in February 1979 that the military decided to flex its muscles, only to find that its window of opportunity had already been closed.

In the end, the Shah's failure to divide the opposition along ideological and cultural lines precluded the possibility of negotiations between the monarchy and the liberal Left over a transfer of power. The result was that the political situation continued to radicalize in favor of the religious element in the revolutionary coalition. This did not bode well for democratic development in Iran in 1979. In the end, the Pahlavi state collapsed because of the Shah's inability to contend with political challenges at a critical juncture. The Pahlavi state had in effect become reduced to the Shah, and his inaction meant that despite the broad coercive power available to the state, it would not survive.

With the fall of the Shah in 1979, the evolution of state authority and function took a new turn. However, despite significant changes in the way in which the state and the economy work in the Islamic Republic, the balance of power between state and society, and the role of the state in socioeconomic change, cannot be understood separately from what occurred during the Pahlavi period. Despite the regime change, ideological shift, and radical social transformation, the path down which the Pahlavi period set Iran continued to shape its subsequent development.

The Revolutionary Era, 1979–1988

The collapse of the monarchy in February 1979 ushered in a new era in Iranian politics. The ideological force of the revolution suggested that the working of the state, the role of interests, and the centrality of identity in development were all likely to change. The revolution promised an axial shift in Iranian politics that would occur in a changing global context.

The immediate aftermath of the revolution was a period of great fluidity during which the old order was dismantled and revolutionary forces began to leave their imprint on the state and society. Revolutions destroy certain social classes, alter state bureaucracies, and thus make other paths of development possible. In Iran, however, the revolution did not produce a strong state but took over an existing one and adapted it to its ideology. The central role of the state in development thus remained unaffected. As a result, the postrevolutionary state displayed continuity with the past as well as change from it.

Revolutionary forces purged supporters of the old order from various state institutions, public and private organizations, and economic enterprises, and the revolution quickly produced institutions of its own. Revolutionary courts and committees and the **Revolutionary Guards** were organized to serve the functions of the judiciary, the police, and the military. Just as the rise of the Pahlavi state had been closely associated with the creation of the Iranian military, the rise of the new revolutionary state was closely tied to the emergence of these new institutions. Although initially formless and disorganized, the new institutions wielded a great deal of power. In time, their presence would create confusion in the state, as the purview of activities of the old military, police, and judiciary would overlap with those of the newly formed revolutionary committees, guards, and courts.

The liquidation of the old order, however, was only a prelude to larger struggles over defining the new order. With the success of the revolution, Ayatollah Khomeini became the undisputed leader of Iran. His supremacy only thinly disguised the intense conflict that was being waged over the definition of the new order. With the triumph of the revolution, the political concord of the disparate groups in opposition to the Shah began to unravel. The liberals, the Left, and the clergy now competed to determine Iran's future.

In March 1979, Iranians voted in a referendum to replace the monarchy with an "Islamic Republic." The term was coined by Khomeini, but it symbolized the struggle among the various factions of the revolutionary alliance over the identity of the regime that was to rule Iran. Throughout 1979, the struggle became more pronounced in the debates over the new constitution. The resulting document envisioned the Islamic Republic as a modern state with all of the constitutional and organizational features of such a state. It provided for a parliament, a judiciary, and an executive branch. It delineated the powers of each through a system of checks and balances. But the constitution also made Islamic law supreme. It furthermore recognized Khomeini's position as that of the supreme leader of the revolution (office of **Vali-e Faqih**, or "supreme guardian-jurisconsult"), an office whose occupant would not be elected, would not be accountable to any authority, and would have total veto power over all government decisions and policy making. This arrangement subjugated the political to the religious in state affairs. It also made identity central to the question of state authority, above and beyond economic and social interests.

The outcome of the constitutional process suggested that the religious element, led by Khomeini, had gained the upper hand. His domination became more apparent as the revolutionary regime demanded greater popular observation of Islamic strictures, especially those concerning women's dress. Religious elites also mobilized support among the lower middle classes and the poor – groups with close ties to the religious establishment – to marginalize the modern middle classes, who served as the social base of the liberal Left. With the victory of the religious hard-liners in this conflict, the number of clerics in high political offices grew dramatically.

The final consolidation of power in the hands of the religious element came in 1981–1982. Although Islamic activists had already gained the upper hand, it was the global context in the form of the "**hostage crisis**" in 1979–1980 (when a group of militant "students" took over the U.S. embassy in Tehran and held its American personnel hostage for months on end) and the **Iran–Iraq**

War (1980–1988) that facilitated their complete domination. These events diverted popular attention in Iran, and international attention abroad, from domestic power struggles. In addition, both events created a siege mentality that bolstered the popularity of the religious leadership, who could claim to be defending Iran from American and Iraqi aggression. In this climate, the liberal Left was portrayed as U.S. stooges, and resistance to a greater role for Islam in society was depicted as a Western ploy to destabilize the revolution.

With the purge of the liberal Left, the revolution became a distinctly Islamic affair. Revolutionary zeal and concern with identity would henceforth define the nature and function of the state. As in the formation of the Pahlavi state under Reza Shah, the Islamic Republic likewise justified its power in terms of the provision of a public good, except that the public good presented by the Islamic Republic was to be greater Islamization of society and politics rather than economic development. The Islamic Republic was not interested in rolling back the state's control over society or its ability to penetrate and control it. It, too, believed in a domineering state. In fact, the leadership of the Islamic Republic aimed at expanding rather than contracting the state's control of society.

As in the early Pahlavi state, the Islamic Republic engaged in social engineering as a prerequisite for the realization of its public-policy agenda. It, too, became directly concerned with the dress, music, and cultural outlook of Iranians. It instituted tight control of both the public and private arenas, and viewed social engineering as central to successful policy formulation and implementation. The state's understanding of its function and powers, in some respects, reflected significant continuities with the Pahlavi period.

The centrality of Islamic ideology to state policy made identity and revolutionary fervor central to the flow of politics and the relations between the state and society. That fervor, in turn, continued to unfold in the context of the Iran–Iraq War during the 1980s. The war, caused by border disputes and Iraqi leader Saddam Hussein's expansionism, was one of the most costly and devastating of the latter part of the twentieth century. During the course of the eight-year war, some 1 million Iranians lost their lives. Iran temporarily lost control of parts of its oil-rich province of Khuzestan and incurred significant damage to its urban centers, agriculture, and industrial infrastructure. It was able to turn the tide of the war only at a tremendous human cost. The need to mobilize support and resources for the war pushed the state to emphasize ideology and the revolutionary values that are associated with it. The successful use of ideology in mobilization for war helped entrench revolutionary zeal and identity in lieu of socioeconomic interests in Iranian politics. Consequently, throughout the 1980–1988 period, the workings of the state remained closely tied to the pursuit of Islamization. This, in turn, committed Iran to a confrontational foreign policy and shifted power to the more radical elements in the state leadership. Khomeini supported this trend because it bolstered his power in Iran and served his ambitions to influence regional and international politics.

Ideological zeal also shaped politics and economics in the Islamic Republic. The Islamic Republic has been different from the Pahlavi state in that despite greater state domination of society, it has avoided personalized rule. Even when Khomeini was at the helm, power was spread among the clerical leaders, who were unified through a patronage network that connected the religious leadership at the center to clerical power brokers. The clerical establishment was committed to the Islamic Republic and to Khomeini's leadership. In fact, Khomeini quickly inculcated group interest in a politically active clergy, thus tying their political ambitions and social position to the fortunes of the Islamic Republic. The clerical leadership ruled collectively – acting as a dominant class – distinguished from the general population by dress and education. The uniform commitment to the Islamic Republic and Khomeini's ideology, however, did not eliminate struggles for power, differences over policy, and disagreements over ideological interpretation among the religious activists and the clerical leadership.

The clerical leadership did not produce a satisfactory way of managing these political debates and conflicts. Before the revolution, there had existed no dominant revolutionary party, as had been the case in Russia or China before their communist revolutions. Iran's revolutionary movement was not ideologically and culturally uniform, further limiting the development of a dominant revolutionary organization either before or immediately after the revolution. This revolution, then, turned out to be the first modern revolution to lack a **"vanguard" party**.

In the absence of a formal organization to manage struggles of power and debates over policy among state leaders, factional politics came out into the open. In the 1980s, three notable factions emerged within the Islamic Republic. The first favored a relaxation of revolutionary vigilance and stabilization of economic relations. Its members came to be known as the "moderates." Those identified with the second faction favored a continuation of revolutionary fervor but at the same time wished to promote a mercantile economy and the right to private property. They came to be known as the "conservatives." The third faction favored a strong anti-Western policy and the export of the revolution, as well as state control of the economy and limited rights to private property. It came to be known as the "radical" or "hard-line" faction and was responsible for much of the excesses of the Islamic Republic in foreign policy and for the expropriation of private property during the first decade of the Islamic Republic. The Iran–Iraq War and Iran's confrontational foreign policy helped the radical faction, whose members were closely allied with the Revolutionary Guards and oversaw Iran's support for revolutionary activism in the Muslim world. The revolutionary fervor espoused by this faction served the aims of mobilizational politics. Although the hard-liners had only a small base of support, mainly in the Revolutionary Guards and in the lower-middle and lower classes, they wielded much power in the government and were supported by Ayatollah Khomeini throughout the 1980–1988 period. The hard-line faction owed its power to its role in mobilizing support for the war and for the Islamic Republic's foreign policy. That power, derived from the global context in which Iran found itself, worked to increase state domination of the economy and promoted centralized economic planning.

The three factions existed only informally. There has been no actual organization, charter, rules, or platforms to define membership; nor are there any grassroots movements or party structures. The factions have functioned as informal circles within the revolutionary elite, with ill-defined and often changing boundaries. The factions have, however, become protoparty structures, especially because they have shaped electoral results directly.

Struggles for power among these factions occurred for the most part in the Parliament, in various consultative forums, in government agencies, in **Friday Prayer** sermons, and in the media. Whereas debates over foreign policy were restrained, in economic matters the differences were pronounced and the debates were acrimonious. Most notably, the radical faction clashed with the two other factions over the right to property and the legal protection of mercantile activities, both of which were eventually accepted by the revolutionary government.

Factionalism dominated politics in Iran throughout the 1980s. It greatly influenced the distribution of power between the president and prime minister on one side and the Parliament on the other. It also influenced the state's relations with society. More importantly, it influenced the working of the economy and determined the extent to which interest or identity would shape the state and its policies.

The revolution changed the course of economic development in Iran significantly. The political turmoil of the revolution (1977–1979), subsequent domestic political crises, legal uncertainties following the collapse of law and order, the meting out of revolutionary justice, debates over property rights, "the brain drain" (the exodus of educated people), the war with Iraq, and international isolation after the hostage crisis all acted to retard the rate of growth. The revolution also radically altered the perceptions of socioeconomic interest and the nature of development. The leftist elements in the revolution viewed economic development under the Pahlavi state as misguided, capitalistic, and, hence, doomed to failure. The religious element was uninterested in development as such and favored replacing it as a national goal with Islamization. Khomeini set the tone in this regard when he commented that "economics is for donkeys" – that is, only Islamization matters. The pursuit of interest, he maintained, should be made subservient to identity.

After 1979, therefore, economic development occupied a less prominent place in the priorities of state leaders. To the extent that there was an economic policy in the early years, it was heavily influenced by Marxist models that had been tried in a number of developing countries. Hence, soon after the revolution, the government nationalized the financial institutions, major industries, and business ventures of those who had been close to the Pahlavi state. By 1998–1999, the state owned 80 percent of the Iranian economy, relegating the private sector to small-scale economic activities.

The expansion of the state's control of the economy in time served political ends because the state could distribute jobs to its most ardent supporters. The growth of the public sector also produced new avenues for corruption in the bureaucracy and the political leadership. The net result of this was significantly reduced efficiency. Between 1978 and 1988, the GDP fell by 1.5 percent per year. Put differently, in 1988, the GDP stood at 1974 levels. Industry experienced six years of negative growth. Rapid population growth produced high levels of unemployment, which in 1988 exceeded 30 percent. The weak private sector was unable to create enough jobs to absorb the surplus labor. The government throughout the 1980s addressed the problem by providing employment in the public sector, which by 1988 accounted for one-third of all jobs. In the meantime, oil income fell. The share of oil revenue as a percentage of GDP fell from 30–40 percent in the 1970s to 9–17 percent in the 1980s as production levels fell from 5.6 million barrels per day to between 2.2 and 2.9 million. The government increased the rate and scope of taxation, but the economy depended on oil revenues, which continued to account for 85 percent of hard-currency earnings.

By 1988, the economic impact of the war with Iraq, international isolation and economic sanctions, and a growing population and declining production presented the Iranian economy with a serious crisis. Shortages in consumer goods had produced a thriving black market that skewed economic interests and the distribution of resources, further reducing efficiency. In addition, the growth of the public sector did not eradicate poverty. By weakening the private sector, it did reduce income inequality. But standards of living, especially of the urban poor, did not improve substantially. Inflation and unemployment had effectively undermined the radicals' populism.

Although during the 1980–1988 period economic hardships could be blamed on the Iran–Iraq War, the conclusion of the war denied the state that excuse. The scope of the economic crisis facing the state now posed serious political challenges. Interests could no longer be easily made subordinate to ideological concerns and the rhetoric of identity politics. Change thus became imperative.

The Post-Khomeini Era, 1988–Present

In 1988, the Iran–Iraq War ended with Iraq's unequivocal victory. The following year, Ayatollah Khomeini died. These two events had a profound effect on politics in the Islamic Republic. The defeat in the war was a psychological blow to the revolutionary elite. It diminished their legitimacy and reduced the utility of their ideological politics. The population became less tolerant of sacrifices demanded of them, especially because eight years of such sacrifices had ended in an ignoble military defeat. Khomeini's passing from the scene made it more difficult for the ruling order to resist change. As the state began to yield to pressure for change, its policy making became more pragmatic, reflecting a greater concern for interests over identity.

After Khomeini died, the president, **Ayatollah Ali Khamenei** (a member of the conservative faction), became supreme leader, and the speaker of the Parliament, **Ayatollah Ali Akbar Hashemi-Rafsanjani** (a member of the moderate faction), became president (1988–1997). The ascendance of the two suggested an alliance between the conservative and moderate factions to marginalize the radical faction. The immediate consequence of Khamenei's and Rafsanjani's assumption of power was the streamlining of the workings of the offices of supreme leader and president. These changes were followed by constitutional reforms that, among other things, integrated revolutionary committees and courts and the Revolutionary Guards with the police, judiciary, and the military, respectively. The Rafsanjani administration also vested greater powers in the bureaucracy and reduced the influence of ideological politics in its day-to-day work. These efforts once again made economic development a central concern of the state and a justification for its power. The post-Khomeini era thus saw the revival of the Pahlavi conception of the state. These changes did not, however, altogether resolve problems of governance in the Islamic Republic. Most importantly, the position of the supreme leader limited the power of the president and continued to tie the political system to ideological politics.

The Iranian legislature wields extensive power and limits the scope of the presidency. This is because of the complexities of the political relations of the ruling elite. From the outset, the Islamic Republic did not have the institutional means to distribute power among its various elements and factions. The function that should have been performed by internal party elections was thus performed by general elections. As such, the Islamic Republic itself functions as a party with regular and free elections among "Islamic" candidates. The ruling order has viewed the voters as party members, mobilized through mosque networks and ideological propagation, and the Parliament as a "**Central Committee**" of sorts. Still, the regularity of general elections has helped institutionalize the place of the Parliament, the Islamic Consultative Assembly, in the Islamic Republic. Hence, the requirement of deciding over the distribution of power within the ruling regime, and the absence of institutional mechanisms to do so outside of the public arena, by default introduced electoral politics and parliamentary behavior to Iran.

General elections and parliamentary practices, despite all their limitations, have brought about a certain degree of pluralism in the essentially theocratic structure of the Islamic Republic. This means that although Iran is an authoritarian state, far more of its political offices are distributed on the basis of elections – albeit limited elections – and its Parliament wields far more effective power than comparable bodies in the Arab world. In fact, one observes two contradictory tendencies working themselves out in the Islamic Republic: on the one hand, the concentration of supreme power in an ideological state; and on the other, democratic practices that are being given significant, if limited, scope for expression within a power structure governed at its apex by a clerical leadership.

It is important to note that elections in the Islamic Republic have not been entirely open in that there are strict limits on which candidates are allowed to participate. However, once the list of candidates has been set, the elections have been generally free. This has to do with the combination of the institutional restriction and procedural freedom that characterizes the structure of the Islamic Republic. The state possesses an authoritarian control over society, but the state itself is complex and made up of powerful factions that continuously vie with one another for control. Although the state has been successful in eliminating from the electoral process all those who challenge its fundamental ideological vision, it has not been able to eliminate those who, while sharing this vision, nonetheless challenge various aspects of policy making. Elections are therefore real insofar as they determine the relative influence of the various power centers at the top. They are less than real, however, in that they do not allow for any genuine change in the distribution of power within society nor alter the composition of the leadership of the state.

The importance of the elections and the Parliament increased in the post-Khomeini era because Khomeini's passing from the scene intensified factional rivalries. Khomeini's death also increased interest in electoral politics, which reached its climax in the presidential elections of 1997. The intensification of the factional rivalries has in effect nudged the Islamic Republic in the direction of electoral politics and vested greater powers in its representative institutions.

Also important in this regard has been the growing role of economic considerations and, more generally, interests in policy making. Rafsanjani assumed his presidency at a time of economic crisis in Iran. He proposed to reform the Iranian economy and also change the policy-making environment to better reflect economic interests and pragmatic considerations. His government proposed an extensive privatization program, investment in infrastructure, introduction of free-trade zones, relaxation of currency restrictions, and the attraction of expatriate entrepreneurial talent. The proposals were designed to generate growth through effective state management of the economy, an interesting return to the Pahlavi state's developmentalist approach.

The reform initiative enjoyed some success. Investment in infrastructure increased, management became more efficient, and as a result, the economy began to grow again. In this regard, the institutional and industrial developments of the Pahlavi period were greatly useful to the economic policies of the Islamic Republic. Nevertheless, more fundamental reforms proved difficult. The government faced stiff resistance to privatization from the bureaucrats and the myriad quasiprivate foundations that manage state-owned enterprises, as well as from labor – and the power brokers who had used public-sector jobs for patronage – who feared the loss of jobs. As a result, privatization meant the transference of the ownership of public-sector industries to state-controlled foundations and cronies of the regime. In this way, the state retained control of the industries, even though technically it had privatized them.

The bureaucracy's attempt to assert its autonomy in economic policy making also faced resistance, as it would have reduced kickbacks and patronage, along with profits made by merchants and black-marketers. This resistance translated into support for the conservative faction in subsequent elections and pressure to prevent Rafsanjani from running for a third term in 1997.

In the end, Rafsanjani's economic initiative suffered as a consequence of the tightening of Western sanctions against Iran. New efforts to isolate Iran internationally and stop its support of terrorism during the 1990s led to a collapse of the Iranian currency and a decline in the rate of economic growth. The consequence of change in the global context was a heightened debate over Iran's future. Should economic interests continue to be sacrificed in the pursuit of ideological goals, or should Iran subordinate its commitment to identity politics in favor of economic growth? Although there is strong support for continuing Iran's commitment to Islam and the values of the revolution, the scope of economic crises facing the state has prevented complacency in the economic policy-making arena. By 1998, 65 percent of Iran's population was under 21 years of age, the unemployment rate stood at 40 percent, inflation was at 300 percent, and the GDP growth rate lagged behind the population growth rate. Without ending Iran's international isolation as well as undertaking domestic economic reform, Iran could face a political crisis, which could threaten the ruling order and its revolutionary values more seriously than would pragmatism.

By the mid-1990s, revolutionary values and ideological politics came under attack from an unexpected quarter – a resurgence of the secular values of the Pahlavi period. The Islamic Republic has enforced a strict cultural code in Iran. The "Islamization" of society has extended beyond the public sphere and has sought to transform the private lives of Iranians as well. Women's dress, music, public programs, school texts, publications, and all manners of cultural, social, and educational activities have been subject to state control. This state policy has generated unhappiness and opposition.

The Pahlavi state, too, had sought to transform its citizens, secularizing as well as modernizing them as a prelude to development. Its collapse in 1979, however, has diverted scholarly attention from the extent to which it was successful in transforming Iranian society. In 1979, there existed a peculiar circumstance wherein the Pahlavi state was weak politically but quite strong culturally. The fact that its secular subjects did not have the same political outlook as the rulers weakened the state. The new Islamic Republic, on the other hand, enjoyed far more political appeal among the middle classes than it did cultural support. The Islamic movement in Iran triumphed politically in large measure because it was able to divide secular Iranians along political lines. The Pahlavi state's political failure, however, should not be read as evidence of its cultural irrelevance because the underlying cultural impact of Pahlavi policies continues to be a major force in Iranian society. Its continued salience is attested to by the inability of the Islamic Republic to establish uncontested cultural hegemony in Iran two decades after the revolution and also by the fact that prerevolutionary cultural attitudes have increasingly served as the starting point of important dissenting tendencies in the political arena. Those social groups that continue to live by the norms of the past may be out of power but they remain nonetheless potential contenders for power.

The Islamic Republic was never able to win over the secular social stratum or eliminate it. It could merely suppress it. Islamic clerics imposed new laws and regulations on the population, largely by force. For instance, new attire for women was imposed after several large demonstrations, one of which drew more than a million woman protesters into the streets in 1979. Since then, the strict women's dress code has been enforced brutally by the Revolutionary Guards.

The "**Cultural Revolution**" in 1980 "cleansed" educational institutions of all those who did not subscribe to Islamic ideology. As far as the liberal Left element within the revolutionary movement itself was concerned, the Islamic Republic eventually resolved that inherent anomaly in the alliance that brought it to power. After an open struggle for power in 1979–1981, the Islamist element in the revolutionary alliance purged the secular liberal Left element.

Secular Iranians, among them prominent professionals and intellectuals, were forcibly marginalized, but they remained important as they shifted their activities to the private arena and the important sphere of civil society. In fact, this social stratum has acted in a fashion similar to those groups who spearheaded the uprising in the name of civil society against Eastern European communist states. The refusal to abide by state ideology at the popular and even personal levels has challenged the domination of Islamic ideology and is forcing changes on the ruling regime. The cultural influence of the Pahlavi era has continued and remains dominant at the personal level among the middle classes. Since the early 1990s, economic crises and problems of isolation have constricted the ruling regime and weakened its hold over society. Creeping pragmatism in policy making has, moreover, made the secular middle classes and the values they espouse the vanguard force for a decisive movement of political resistance. That economic growth both needs and will empower this social stratum has made it difficult for the Islamic Republic to resist its influence.

The Presidential Elections of 1997

All of these factors coalesced to determine the outcome of the presidential elections of 1997. These elections were the first to involve a transfer of power at the level of the presidency during the post-Khomeini era. Given the debates over the relative importance of identity and interests in state policy, the elections were viewed as decisive. Early on in the election campaign, the nominee of the conservative faction emerged as the front-runner. The faction had a strong base of support among small businessmen and in the political apparatus of the Islamic Republic, and it also had the backing of Ayatollah Khamenei. In addition, the conservatives posed as a force for continuity, and to some extent retrenchment, of the values and norms of the Islamic Republic. They held to a conservative line on social and cultural issues and supported the thrust of Iran's anti-Western foreign policy. In this way, they differed from President Rafsanjani, who had favored easing the strictures that govern social and cultural practices, and who had tried – albeit with little success – to reduce tensions between Iran and the Western powers.

What appeared to be the conservatives' unchallenged march to the presidency, however, soon became a closely contested race with Ayatollah Mohammad Khatami. Khatami did not represent any of the rival factions but appealed to the moderate faction and its followers. In addition, his promise of relaxing the state's ideological vigilance also gained him a following among women, youth, and the secular elements. In many regards, Khatami's platform and following greatly resemble those of Gorbachev in the Soviet Union. Khatami, too, believes in the promise of the revolutionary ideology and hopes that once that ideology is freed from the authoritarian control of the state through reform measures, it will fulfill its promise of progress and prosperity. Many who followed Khatami (again, similar to Gorbachev in Russia) did not share his belief in the promise of revolutionary ideology but liked the implications of his reform proposals.

The intensity of the factional rivalry guaranteed the openness of the elections and paved the way for greater freedom of expression in the media. The election itself, held in May 1997, proved to be nothing short of an earthquake in Iranian politics. Most observers had expected Khatami to do well but thought that in the end the conservatives would win. This did not come to pass. Khatami won the elections with an overwhelming majority of the vote – 70 percent (some 20 million votes). The defeat of the conservative faction was total and humiliating. Iranians had taken the elections seriously and had voted convincingly in favor of fundamental changes in the nature, structure, and workings of the Islamic Republic. Many saw the elections as a referendum on the Islamic Republic and, at the very least, as a referendum on how its existing leadership ought to understand its mission and relations with society. The vote was also one for interests over identity in the workings of the state.

The election results had important implications. First, this was a unique case in the Middle East: A head of state stepped down from power at the end of his term of office and peacefully handed over power to a successor elected through constitutional means. The transition of power from Rafsanjani to Khatami has therefore been of tremendous significance in itself. Second, the large turnout – some 30 million, an overwhelming majority of the eligible voters – meant that Iranians of all political persuasions had taken the elections seriously and decided to voice their views and demands within the political process rather than outside of it. This means that the electoral process has become institutionalized in the Islamic Republic and has become the most important means of integrating various social groups into the political system. It is no longer an artificial appendage to the Islamic state but is very much part of the fabric of its politics.

Khatami's campaign speeches were peppered with references to "democracy," "civil society," "women's status," "rule of law," and "dialogue between civilizations." He in particular emphasized "civil society" and championed the cultural freedoms and legal protections that empower it. As such, Khatami gave new direction and energy to the demand for reform. The decision by so many to use the ballot box to promote change has also strengthened the Islamic Republic, as those who have been unhappy with its achievements have chosen to participate in it rather than opt out of it. The elections and the transition of power have the potential to include greater numbers of Iranians within the Islamic Republic. However, to do so successfully, the Islamic Republic must accommodate a broader set of sociopolitical demands, and most notably move farther away from ideological politics and the values of the revolution. This generated democratic expectations on which Khatami now had to deliver.

The elections of 1997 had caught the leadership of the Islamic Republic off-guard. This led to a short-lived "Prague Spring" in Iran during which significant freedom of expression in the press and certain relaxations in control of social behavior gave new impetus to demands for change. These demands began to take an increasingly secular orientation as the new cultural opening mobilized the Iranian middle class, which now became a new force in Iranian politics. This new political constituency was no longer merely satisfied with debating Islam and began to demand fundamental political reforms.

Khatami's campaign promised to address those demands and by so doing create a bridge between reformers inside the regime – who were attached to its ideological foundations – and the larger constituency for reform. His ideal of "Islamic civil society" captured this objective. His success in this endeavor would have transformed the Islamic Republic but would have kept it in control of the process of change. However, his failure has instead created a rift between reformers within the Islamic Republic's ideological fold and political reformers in the larger society, and clearly pitted the latter against the Islamic Republic.

Within a year after Khatami assumed office, the supreme leader, Ayatollah Ali Khamenei, began to use the judiciary and the Council of Guardians (a watchdog institution that is dedicated to protecting the ideological foundations of the Islamic Republic), and his allies in the media, the Parliament, and various government agencies, to stifle reform. Khatami repeatedly lost ground to these conservative forces in showdowns over legislation, freedom of the press, the rule of law, and individual rights. His more reform-minded ministers were pushed out of government, and some were tried and incarcerated. From the time that Khatami assumed office in 1997 until January 2004, the Council of Guardians has vetoed 111 of his 297 legislations. Faced with strong resistance to change, Khatami and his lieutenants and supporters began to speak about instituting limits to theocracy and advocated the rule of law and the protection of individual rights.

These developments shifted the focus from calls for rational government to demands for democratization. However, Khatami shied away from openly breaking with the theocratic core of the Islamic Republic. He would not endorse fundamental constitutional changes and proved unwilling to openly challenge Khamanei's authority. On a number of occasions, he threatened the supreme leader with resigning, and on one occasion with not running for reelection in 2001; but each time he backed away from an open breach with Khamanei and his conservative allies.

More importantly, Khatami continued to declare fealty to the theocratic constitution of the Islamic Republic, which runs counter to his support for "civil society" and the "rule of law." As such, at the end of the day, Khatami's rhetoric went no further than advocating better management of government. Khatami's capitulations to Khamanei have attested to his reluctance to step beyond the bounds of the constitution of the Islamic Republic. This in turn has severely limited his ability to continue to lead the popular demand for democracy that his own electoral success had unleashed.

Khatami's dilemma has, however, had a cathartic effect on the democracy debate. By failing to reconcile the demands for change with the reality of the Islamic Republic, Khatami relinquished control of the democracy debate to voices outside the regime. The debate moved to the streets, where, for instance, student demonstrations became a leading voice in demanding fundamental changes to the structure of the Islamic Republic. Student demonstrations during the summer of 1999 to protest the closure of some reformist newspapers, in November 2002 to protest against a death sentence for alleged blasphemy imposed on a university lecturer, and in 2003 to demand greater political rights have not only posed direct challenges to theocracy but also confirmed the shift in focus of the struggle for reform from the high circles of power to the society and to those who want constitutional change and secular democracy. Popular demands for change have further mobilized secular intellectuals and activists associated with civil-society institutions and universities as well as journalists, who initially rallied in support of Islamic reform.

The ideal of the reformists is not Islamic democracy but secular democracy. This involves placing limits on the exercise of state power and creating legal institutions and a system of checks and balances that guarantee individual and social rights. This trend found greater impetus when the 2003 Nobel Peace Prize was awarded to a leading advocate of individual rights, Shirin Ebadi. However, the democracy movement in Iran today lacks clear leadership. The Khatami presidency has failed to provide that leadership, and secular political activists and the students have yet to fill the void.

In the meantime, the ruling establishment has a different path of development in mind. The supreme leader and the conservative leadership look to the Chinese model of reform: economic change and opening to the world with little or no political reforms. They believe that the Soviet transition to democracy under Gorbachev was not a success; rather, it is the Chinese path to change that holds true promise. The conservative leadership is now looking to roll back gains made by pro-democracy forces under Khatami – following a "Putin" strategy, referring to the creeping authoritarianism in Russia under Vladimir Putin. With that aim in mind, the conservative Council of Guardians prevented many pro-reform candidates from participating in the parliamentary elections of 2004, producing a conservative Parliament ahead of the presidential elections of 2005, in which a conservative victory can give the conservatives complete domination over the political power structure as well as the scope and extent of political reforms.

Looking back at developments since 1988, one can conclude that greater pragmatism has restored the state to its central role in the management of society, politics, and the economy in the name of economic development, as in the earlier Pahlavi era. Nevertheless, the possibility of greater democratization of politics suggests that beyond restoration of power to the state and greater attention to the pursuit of economic growth and development, Iranian politics may be developing along a new trajectory. Whether elections will evolve beyond settling struggles for power among ruling factions into a broad-based democratic system or whether the state will be able to regain control will depend on changes in the relative power of the state and society as well as the relative importance of interests and identity in shaping institutions and, ultimately, Iran's developmental path. The pace and scope of economic reform will influence those changes in turn. These considerations have already spurred much thinking about the role that civil-society institutions, the private sector, and other foundational features of democracies must play in the political maturation of the Iranian state. The relations of power that have defined Iranian politics over the course of much of this century will most likely also influence the process of change.

Conclusion

At the beginning of the twentieth century, there existed little in the form of interests, identity, or institutions in the Iranian polity to provide an impetus for development or to chart a path for that process. It was the global context at the time that imbued the Iranian political process with interests and set the country on its path to development. Those interests, in turn, influenced identity and shaped institutions to give form to the modern Iranian state. Iran looked to Germany and Japan – and also Turkey – as models to follow, and so invested in strong state institutions and promoted a secular national identity. As state institutions expanded, they defined interests and identity in order to serve the state's objectives in the economic and the political arenas. Thus, early on in the process of development, the global context and interests that emerged from it shaped Iran's identity and institutions, guaranteeing the central role of the state in that process.

A changing global context in subsequent years, along with crises that are inherent in development, altered the state in important ways but would not change the state's dominant role in society and politics. Even the Iranian revolution did not reverse this trend. The revolution placed more importance on identity – articulated in Islamic terms – in charting the country's developmental path. It changed some old institutions and produced some new ones, but it did not change the role of the state in economic development. The case of Iran shows that the interaction among interests, identity, and institutions – as militated by changes in the global contexts and imperatives of the domestic scene – is more fluid early on in the development process but becomes increasingly less so over time. As institutions grow in size and reach, they become more rigid. Although institutions continue to respond to the global context and reflect the influence of interests and identity, they do so with greater infrequency and seldom in major ways. The size and power of the state thus become more important in determining the course of development than do interests and identity, the impact of which must now happen through institutions rather than separate from them.

In many ways, the domination of institutions that emerged through Iran's experiment with development – producing a strong and centralized state – accounts for the fact that Iran has been unable to achieve the end goal of democratic capitalism. Still, in major and minor ways, the global context has shaped interests, and through them identity and institutions, to present Iran with new development possibilities. At the dawn of the twenty-first century, Iran has yet to arrive at democratic capitalism. However, history has shown that even strong institutions – such as the eighteenth-century French monarchy, nineteenth-century Meiji Japanese feudalism, and the twentieth-century Soviet Union – change in response to global pressures. Given the changes in economic and political life in Iran during the early years of the twentieth century, the possibility of realizing that goal is not as remote as it may have been only a short while ago.

BIBLIOGRAPHY

Abrahamian, Ervand. *Iran Between Two Revolutions*. Princeton, NJ: Princeton University Press, 1982.

Akhavi, Shahrough. *Religion and Politics in Contemporary Iran: Clergy–State Relations in the Pahlavi Period*. Albany, NY: SUNY Press, 1980.

Amuzegar, Jahangir. *Iran's Economy Under the Islamic Republic*. London: I. B. Tauris, 1993.

Arjomand, Said A. *The Turban for the Crown: The Islamic Revolution in Iran*. New York: Oxford University Press, 1988.

Azimi, F. *Iran: The Crisis of Democracy*. New York: St. Martin's Press, 1989.

Bakash, Shaul. *The Reign of the Ayatollahs: Iran and the Islamic Revolution*. New York: Basic Books, 1984.

Bakhtiari, Bahman. *Parliamentary Politics in Revolutionary Iran: The Institutionalization of Factional Politics*. Gainesville, FL: University Press of Florida, 1996.

Dabashi, Hamid. *Theology of Discontent: The Ideological Foundation of the Islamic Revolution in Iran*. New York: New York University Press, 1993.

Ehteshami, Anoushiravan. *After Khomeini: The Iranian Second Republic*. New York: Routledge, 1995.

Elm, Mostafa. *Oil, Power, and Principle: Iran's Oil Nationalization and its Aftermath*. Syracuse, NY: Syracuse University Press, 1992.

Ertman, Thomas. *Birth of Leviathan: Building States and Regimes in Medieval and Early Modern Europe*. Cambridge: Cambridge University Press, 1997.

Ghani, Cyrus. *Iran and the Rise of Reza Shah: From Qajar Collapse to Pahlavi Rule*. London: I. B. Tauris, 1998.

Karshenas, Massoud. *Oil, State and Industrialization in Iran*. Cambridge: Cambridge University Press, 1990.

Katouzian, Homa. *The Political Economy of Modern Iran, 1926–79*. New York: New York University Press, 1981.

Kurzman, Charles. *The Unthinkable Revolution in Iran*. Cambridge, MA: Harvard University Press, 2004.

Looney, Robert. *Economic Origins of the Iranian Revolution*. New York: Pergamon Press, 1982.

Migdal, Joel S., Atul Kohli, and Vivienne Shue, eds. *State Power and Social Forces: Domination and Transformation in the Third World*. Cambridge: Cambridge University Press, 1994.

Schirazi, Asghar. *The Constitution of Iran: Politics and the State in the Islamic Republic*. London: I. B. Tauris, 1997.

Skocpol, Theda. "Rentier State and Shi'a Islam in the Iranian Revolution." *Theory and Society* 11, no. 3 (May 1982): 265–283.

TABLE 11.1. Key Phases in Iranian Development

Time Period	Regime	Global Context	Interests/Identities/ Institutions	Developmental Path
1921–1941	autocratic monarchy	European imperialism	authoritarian institutions	state-building
	foreign occupation	World War II	landed and tribal elite, ethnic and regional forces, and authoritarian forces	state collapse
1941–1954	constitutional monarchy and parliamentary democracy	European imperialism	democratic, Islamic, and communist force and authoritarian institutions	democratic institution-building
1954–1963	autocratic monarchy	Cold War	landed elite, authoritarian institutions	state-building
1964–1979	autocratic monarchy	Cold War	bureaucratic and industrial elite; authoritarian institutions	state-building and centralized economic development
1979–1988	revolutionary theocracy	Cold War	lower classes and revolutionary institutions	state important
1988–1997	autocratic republican and theocracy	globalization	revolutionary institutions, mercantile and bureaucratic forces	state-building and economic development
1997–present	autocratic theocracy and reformist presidency	globalization/ war on terror	authoritarian institutions, civil society, mercantile forces	state-building, economic development, and democratic institution-building

IMPORTANT TERMS

Anglo-Iranian Oil Company the British company that owned the concession to excavate, process, and export Iran's oil until 1954.

Ayatollah literally meaning "sign of God," the title of the highest-ranking religious leader in Shia Islam. He has the authority to interpret religious law and to prescribe proper personal, social, and political behavior.

Central Committee the central decision-making body in a communist party structure.

Cultural Revolution attack by the revolutionary forces on Iranian universities and intellectuals in 1980 in order to purge them of liberal and leftist elements and to force conformity with revolutionary values. This term originated in China during the purges of the 1960s.

Friday Prayer congregational Muslim prayer on Fridays. In the Islamic Republic, it has been used as a political forum to propagate government views and mobilize the masses in support of government policies.

Ayatollah Ali Akbar Hashemi-Rafsanjani revolutionary leader, speaker of the Parliament and president between 1988 and 1997. He introduced the first efforts to reform the Islamic Republic.

hostage crisis the crisis initiated in November 1979 when radical students took U.S. diplomatic personnel hostage at the U.S. embassy in Tehran, demanding the handover of the Shah to Iran and recognition of Iran's grievances against the United States for its role in the 1953 coup and support of the Shah. The hostages were released in January 1981 after 444 days.

import-substitution industrialization (ISI) a strategy for industrialization that became popular in the developing world after World War II. It advocates beginning industrialization by producing finished goods and then expanding the scope of the process by moving to intermediary and primary industrial goods and using protectionism to favor the young industries. It has been associated with several economic and political problems.

Iran–Iraq War an intense war between Iran and Iraq between 1980 and 1988 during which Iraq first occupied parts of Iran but then was compelled to defend its own territory against Iranian offensives. The most bloody and costly war since World War II, it ended with Iran's defeat.

Islam a monotheistic religion and the world's second-largest faith, with more than one billion followers.

Islamic ideology a political doctrine with views on society and government that are drawn from a puritanical understanding of Islam. Advocating that politics should be subservient to religion, it was the guiding ideology of the religious faction of the revolution.

Islamic Republic of Iran the official name of Iran after the revolution. It attests to the centrality of Islam to statecraft since 1979.

Kemalism a model of development that emerged in Turkey during the 1920s. Named after the Turkish president Mustafa Kemal, its most important features were secularism, nationalism, and a domineering role for the state in socioeconomic change.

Ayatollah Ali Khamenei revolutionary leader, president, and currently supreme leader of Iran. He has been associated with the anti-reform faction since 1997.

Ayatollah Mohammad Khatami Iran's president since 1997. He has spearheaded efforts to liberalize the Islamic Republic.

Ayatollah Ruhollah Khomeini the chief architect and leader of the revolution of 1979, who ruled Iran as supreme leader between 1979 and 1988.

Mohammad Mossadeq the nationalist prime minister at the time of the 1953 coup. He nationalized Iran's oil industry and led the drive for limiting foreign influence in Iran and for instituting democracy in the country.

OPEC Organization of Petroleum Exporting Countries, a cartel formed in the late 1960s to strengthen the position of oil producers in the international market. It pushed for higher oil prices during the 1970s.

Pahlavi the name of the dynasty that ruled Iran between 1921 and 1979.

Muhammad Reza Shah Pahlavi the second Pahlavi monarch, who ruled between 1941 and 1979.

Reza Shah Pahlavi the founder of the Pahlavi monarchy and the initiator of Iran's development during the twentieth century. He ruled between 1921 and 1941.

rentier state a state that earns an overwhelming proportion of its income from sources outside of its domestic economic activity. Such states become autonomous from the society and rely on distributive mechanisms to assert authority. That, in time, will erode their legitimacy.

Revolutionary Guards an ideologically committed militia that was formed after the revolution to perform the functions of the police and the military.

SAVAK Iran's intelligence agency between 1954 and 1979. It was responsible for contending with the opposition and was associated with the Pahlavi monarchy's human-rights violations.

Shah "king" in Persian.

Ali Shariati an intellectual who blended Marxist ideology with Islamic teachings to produce a potent ideology of revolutionary change in Iran during the 1970s.

Shia a branch of Islam that is dominant in Iran. It places great authority in its religious leaders and values sacrifice in the path of justice.

Vali-e Faqib literally meaning the "supreme guardian-jurisconsult," it is a position that was put forward by Ayatollah Khomeini to embody his belief that it is religiously mandated for Shia clerics to rule in the political arena. This view justified the religious nature of the revolution and the constitutional setup of the Islamic Republic.

vanguard party a party that spearheads a revolution.

STUDY QUESTIONS

1. How has change in identity influenced Iran's development?

2. How has the revolution altered prospects for democratic capitalism?

3. What are the most important turning points in Iran's development?

4. Was there a greater chance for democratic development in 1977 or in 1997?

5. Has identity been important in Iranian institutional change? If so, how?

6. Does the pursuit of interests produce a more sustainable development path than pursuit of identity?

7. Can religious identity sustain secular state institutions and serve developmental goals?

8. How important is the location of Iran to its path of development?

9. In what ways can the global context influence Iran's development from this point forward?

ZIMBABWE

Messina

BOTSWANA

Pietersburg

✪ **Pretoria**

Johannesburg

MOZAMBIQUE

SWAZILAND

NAMIBIA

Upington

Kimberley

Ladysmith

Bloemfontein

Pietermaritzburg

LESOTHO

Durban

De Aar

SOUTH AFRICA

INDIAN

OCEAN

ATLANTIC OCEAN

Saldanha

East London

Cape Town

Port Elizabeth

Mosselbaai

SOUTH AFRICA

0	100	200	300	400	500 miles
0	100	200	300	400	500km

CHAPTER TWELVE

South Africa

Michael Bratton

Introduction

As one of the world's youngest democracies, South Africa seeks to escape a bitter political legacy. During the second half of the twentieth century, its white-minority government systematically built a powerful, militarized state around institutions of racial oppression. Even earlier, the discovery of minerals had enabled the development of an industrial economy, which thrust Africans and the descendants of European settlers into close contact in the country's burgeoning urban areas. Predictably, political conflicts erupted between blacks, who provided labor, and whites, who benefited from economic growth. Because the old regime was dead set against political change until the late 1980s, the struggle over **apartheid** (as extreme racial segregation was called in South Africa) seemed destined to end in a cataclysm of violence.

That a bloodbath was averted was one of the most remarkable stories of an eventful interlude of global democratization. Against the odds, political leaders from both sides (but especially the visionary **Nelson Mandela**, president of the **African National Congress**) came to recognize that the long-term interests of South Africa's deeply divided black and white communities were inextricably intertwined. Through tough negotiation and painful compromise, hardheaded opponents forged an elite pact, albeit against the backdrop of popular mobilization, that allowed the country to hold an open election and to install in 1994 the country's first democratic government (see Table 12.1). The world welcomed this transition as marking both the end of colonial rule in Africa and the burial of the last twentieth-century government based on myths of racial supremacy.

The years that followed have seen a flurry of political creativity in South Africa. New institutions and policies have been designed to redress the exclusions and inequities of the past. But difficult questions remain about the viability of the new order. Do South Africans from different social backgrounds acknowledge their interdependence? Can the government redistribute wealth to blacks without inducing white flight? Does the government have the independence and capacity to deliver the benefits promised in South Africa's expansive new constitution? And, perhaps most importantly, given the absence of a democratic heritage and the omnipresence of crime and HIV-AIDS, what are the prospects for consolidating democracy?

The Global Historical Context

The southernmost tip of Africa, a dry region rich in mineral resources, has supported small hunting and gathering communities from the time that humans first trod the Earth. Beginning about 2,500 years ago, the indigenous Khoisan peoples were gradually joined by **Bantu**-speaking African migrants from the north, who introduced herding, crop cultivation, and iron production. As these groups intermingled, they formed a succession of small-scale chieftaincies that, because of the relative abundance of land, had little need to establish standing armies or other state institutions.

Southern Africa became less isolated from the rest of the world during the late fifteenth century when – at about the same time that Spain was dispatching Columbus to the Americas – Portuguese mariners rounded the Cape of Good Hope in search of an eastward route to India. Succeeding the Portuguese as the world's top trading power during the seventeenth century, the Dutch founded the first permanent European settlement there. From the beginning, the **Cape Colony** was run along lines that established the foundations for modern South Africa: the forced annexation of land and the coercion of labor. This economic system, together with sexual liaisons among white burghers, Malay slaves, and native blacks, gave rise to a complex society stratified along racial and class lines.

The ascendancy of Britain as a global power was marked in Southern Africa by its annexation of the Cape Colony in 1806 and the arrival of English settlers on the frontier of the eastern Cape in 1820. At this time, the colony remained predominantly rural, although its economic importance to Britain remained as a waystation for trade rather than as an agricultural exporter. The population clustered into four main groups: the English, the **Afrikaners** (Dutch descendants who had developed their own Africanized culture and dialect), the so-called Cape **Coloureds** (an emerging community of mixed-race people), and the indigenous **Xhosa** (on the eastern frontier). Political conflicts among these groups over land rights gave rise to demands for government. At the same time, agitation against slavery by English missionaries drove many Afrikaners to trek northward in an effort to escape the reach of regulation.

The first colonial administrations were autocratic: Former military officers drawn from the ranks of the English aristocracy were appointed as colonial governors. An important political precedent was set in 1853, however, when Britain allowed the establishment of an elected legislative council. Henceforth, the country's political evolution would diverge from that of India, whose elected institutions were not set up until almost a century later. Instead, the Cape Colony came to more closely resemble Canada (and later Australia and New Zealand), where Britain gradually granted self-government to a small but dominant group of white settlers. Although the first franchise was color-blind – it granted the vote to any adult male who owned property or earned a salary – Africans and Coloureds were effectively excluded from political life because they were poor.

As in other settler colonies (including the United States), contacts with white immigrants were devastating for indigenous peoples. Even during the rule of the Dutch East India Company, the Khoisan hunters and herders of the western Cape had been decimated by European diseases such as small-pox and measles. By the mid-nineteenth century, Bantu-speaking groups as far north as the Limpopo River had lost their land, crops, and livestock to European invaders. Foreign conquest was not achieved by strength of num-bers (blacks have always greatly outnumbered whites in South Africa) but by the technological superiority of a metropolitan industrial economy that could mass-produce firearms. This is not to say that conquest occurred easily; in-stead, it was punctuated by hard-fought wars of resistance launched by the Xhosa in the eastern Cape during the 1840s, the **Zulu** in Natal during the 1850s, and the Sotho, the Venda, and the Pedi in the interior highlands during the 1860s. The Zulu, who themselves had earlier brutally repressed neighboring groups, managed to retain the identity and organization of a warrior nation throughout much of the nineteenth century.

Initially, four separate settler states were formed in the territory now known as South Africa. Apart from the Cape, the British controlled Natal, a second colony on the eastern seaboard, to which they imported laborers from colo-nial India (mainly Hindu but also Muslim) to develop sugar plantations and railways. Christian missionaries were particularly active in Natal, establish-ing schools and hospitals that attracted displaced Africans into modernized lifestyles. On the high-altitude savanna, Afrikaner stock-farmers set up two agrarian republics based on the institutions of individual land title and an armed citizenry. The Orange Free State was a constitutional republic run by an elected assembly of white males under a semblance of legality, whereas the Transvaal was a much more rough-and-ready state held together by rov-ing commandos. The political and religious leaders of these republics con-structed a historical mythology of the Afrikaners as a chosen people who had thrown off the bonds of the British Empire and founded their own promised land.

Although the British colonies and Boer (Afrikaner farmer) republics had distinct origins, they nonetheless shared a patrimonial ideology that reduced the relations between the races to those of master and servant. For their part, the African peoples of the region ultimately proved more resilient than the aboriginal populations of the Cape. Shunted into crowded rural areas, they adjusted to an emerging capitalist economy by growing crops for sale to the settlers (both on their own land and as sharecroppers), providing labor on white commercial farms, and adopting not only Christianized religions but tastes for Western consumer goods. The presence of missionaries, labor recruiters, and tax collectors in the African territories further reduced the influence of hereditary chiefs, whose authority already had been undermined by conquest and colonization.

The Path of Development

The economic growth of the region reached a major turning point in 1870 with the discovery in South Africa's interior of the world's richest deposits of gold and diamonds. The resultant mining boom generated glittering profits for investors in Britain, Europe, and North America, and, by the turn of the century, firmly integrated Southern Africa into a global capitalist economy. Industrialization was accompanied by urbanization. Waves of English-speaking immigrants from around the world and African migrant laborers from as far north as modern-day Mozambique, Tanzania, and Zambia converged on the boom towns of Kimberley and Johannesburg. From the outset, the industrial economy was constructed on racial lines. Whites were awarded skilled jobs with high wages and supervisory responsibilities, whereas black laborers were poorly paid and housed in spartan, male-only barracks. The joint stock companies that dominated the mining sector found common cause with the colonial governments in controlling the flow of labor by introducing "pass" laws, which ruled that no unemployed African could stay in an urban area without a valid identity document.

Political conflicts intensified over the country's newfound wealth. Despite deep differences between Boers and Britons, the colonists united to crush the last remnants of African resistance. Aided by intelligence reports from the Afrikaners and by factionalism in the Zulu royal family, an armed British expedition finally subdued the region's most powerful African kingdom in 1879 – but not without significant military losses. The Zulu monarchy was abolished, and Zululand was divided into 13 weak parts under appointed chiefs. At the same time, Britain was determined to wrest political control of the goldfields from the Afrikaners in the Transvaal; after several unsuccessful attempts at annexation, it resorted to all-out war to guarantee imperial supremacy. The South African War (1899–1902) pitted an orthodox British army of almost half a million soldiers against a mobile guerrilla force. A British victory was achieved only when Boer farms were burned to the ground and families were herded into disease-ridden camps, humiliations that rankled long after the war was over.

A postwar peace settlement unified the region politically and gave birth to the modern state of South Africa. The constitution of the **Union of South Africa** of 1910 contained several principles that profoundly shaped the course of subsequent events. First, the constitution adopted a British Westminster model in which Parliament was supreme within a unitary state (that is, with a single center of power rather than a federation). In the absence of a separation of powers, the political party that controlled Parliament enjoyed considerable latitude. Second, the plural culture of the new state was acknowledged when English and Dutch (later supplanted by Afrikaans) were recognized as official languages of equal status. Finally, and most importantly, blacks (that is, Africans, Indians, and Coloureds in the local lexicon) were denied a share of political power. The franchise laws of the former colonies remained in place, entirely excluding blacks from government in the new provinces of Transvaal, Orange Free State, and Natal. Voting rights for blacks were protected in the relatively more liberal Cape Province; in practice, however, blacks never accounted for more than one-seventh of the electorate and never elected one of their own to parliamentary office.

Instead, white settlers set about consolidating control of a large and potentially affluent African state whose autonomy from the mother country was further strengthened when the British Parliament abandoned legislative oversight in 1934. The period of the white-run Union (later Republic) of South Africa can be divided conveniently into two periods: first under anglicized Afrikaners (1910–1948) and later, momentously, when Afrikaner nationalists took over (1948–1994). Public policies during these periods differed in degree rather than kind; both aimed at racial segregation. The post-1948 apartheid regime, however, extended the separation of the races to a deranged extreme by drawing biological distinctions between people and institutionalizing them in the structure of the state.

These political developments were offset by two countervailing forces. On the one hand, the expansion of the industrial economy required the creation of a stable urban workforce, which brought the races into close economic interdependence. At the same time, the enactment of discriminatory laws was matched at each stage by the emergence of new and gradually more militant forms of black resistance, starting with the formation in 1912 of the organization that became known as the African National Congress (ANC).

One of the first steps of the Union government was to pass the Native Lands Act (1913), which prohibited Africans from buying or leasing farms designated for whites. The effect of this legislation – and of accompanying "hut" taxes – was to force peasants into wage labor as farm workers or miners.

As for the urban areas, the state gave legal effect to customary color bars; for example, the Industrial Conciliation Act (1924) denied Africans the right to engage in collective wage bargaining, and in 1936, the Natives Representation Act removed Africans from the ordinary voter rolls in the Cape Province even as white women were being enfranchised nationwide. These indignities fueled campaigns for legislative reform by a small elite of educated Africans – clergy, lawyers, and teachers – who had begun to rally under the ANC banner. They also prompted strikes led by the Industrial and Commercial Workers Union (formed 1928), even though labor actions had been ruled illegal. Indeed, despite segregation, Africans continued to pour into towns, surrounding the prim, white, middle-class suburbs with proletarian squatter settlements that teemed with violent discontent.

The Second World War (1939–1945) divided the white community. Many Afrikaners were distressed that South Africa entered a European conflict on the side of Great Britain, leading extremists in their midst to openly express sympathy for Nazi ideas of racial purity. For their part, most English-speakers welcomed a chance to mobilize South Africa's resources in support of the Allied war effort, which resulted in the rapid buildup of the country's coal, iron, and garment-manufacturing industries. Seeking to extend economic expansion after the war and recognizing the economy's growing reliance on black labor, the moderate United Party government of Jan Smuts, a minister of the Dutch Reformed Church who was first elected to Parliament in 1918, suggested modest reforms to improve African wages and working conditions. But even these timid steps prompted a right-wing backlash. In the 1948 election, the electorate swung to the **National Party** (a right-wing party supported largely by Afrikaners), which won a narrow victory in part because rural voting districts were overrepresented. The government of D. F. Malan, prime minister from 1919 to 1924 and from 1939 to 1948, came to power at a time when ideas about apartheid (literally, apartness) were gaining currency in the Afrikaner churches and secret societies. A monstrous social experiment to create a government of racial institutions was about to begin.

The Apartheid Experiment

The National Party government began by packing the state apparatus – the army, the police, the civil service, and the publicly owned railways – with its own supporters. It ensured that Afrikaners became the prime beneficiaries of agricultural and educational subsidies and of public construction contracts. Thus was state power used to enable social mobility for a population that had always resented the greater economic wealth of the English-speakers. These developments, along with the duplication of public services for segregated communities, meant that the state in South Africa became large, interventionist, and riddled with patronage.

As the basis for apartheid, the government classified every citizen under the **Population Registration Act** (1950) into one of four racial categories: African, Coloured, Indian, or white. New laws were introduced to prohibit sex and marriage between people of different races; the authorities even went so far as to break up existing mixed-race families. Under the Group Areas Act (also 1950), black urban neighborhoods such as Sophiatown in Johannesburg and District Six in Cape Town were bulldozed and their inhabitants dispersed. Every public facility was segregated (from bus and train stations and drinking fountains to parks, cinemas, and beaches) by means of demeaning "Whites Only" signs. A Bantu Education Act (1953) effectively abolished mission schools for Africans, replacing them with substandard public institutions. Bent on removing every vestige of political rights for people of color, the National Party did to Coloured voters in 1956 what the United Party government had earlier done to African voters: removed them from the common electoral rolls.

But the architect of apartheid, Hendrick Verwoerd (prime minister, 1958–1966), had an even grander vision that called for the complete geographical partition of the races. Under the Bantu Homelands Constitution Act (1957), Africans were stripped of citizenship, expelled from the choicest parts of the country (and from 87 percent of its total land area), and consigned to 10 scattered ethnic "**homelands**." The implementation of this scheme – which included nominal political independence for unviable entities such as Transkei and Bophutatswana – amounted to the largest forced movement of population anywhere in the postwar world. Because the impoverished homeland administrations could neither generate employment nor deliver basic services, relocation exacted a harsh toll of malnutrition, disease, and death.

The government's policy of "separate development," however, flew in the face of the reality that South Africa had become an economically integrated society. By 1980, at the peak of apartheid's ethnic cleansing, more than half of the nonwhite population continued to reside in towns, where blacks – 6.9 million Africans, 2 million Coloureds, and 700,000 Indians – together outnumbered 4 million whites.

Urban dwellers rejected the official fiction that Africans belonged in rural backwaters under the tutelage of "tribal" chiefs. Instead, a new generation of young leaders, such as Walter Sisulu, Oliver Tambo, and Nelson Mandela, recommitted the African National Congress (ANC) to multiracial democracy. In 1955, the ANC's Freedom Charter declared that South Africa belongs to all who live in it, black and white, and that no government can justly claim authority unless it is based on the will of the people. The Charter's mix of liberal values (equality before the law, freedom of speech, and the right to vote) with more socialist ideas (free education and health care and the public ownership of mines and industry) reflected the ANC's openness to various political tendencies. Other liberation movements – such as the South African Communist Party (SACP, formed in 1921), the Pan-Africanist Congress (PAC, formed in 1959), and the black consciousness movement (which coalesced during the 1970s around the ideas of Steve Biko) – sounded more radical or Africanist themes.

Resistance to apartheid started out peacefully in civil disobedience: Modeled on Gandhian principles of nonviolence, the anti-apartheid movement first took the form of the burning of identity "passes" or the defiance of other discriminatory laws. In response, the police gunned down 67 demonstrators at **Sharpeville** in 1960 and banned the ANC and PAC. Deprived of all opportunity to organize peacefully, resistance leaders had little choice but to take up arms. The military wings of the PAC and ANC – later known as the Azanian Peoples Liberation Army (APLA) and Umkhonto we Sizwe (MK, or the Spear of the Nation) – embarked on bombing campaigns against state installations such as electricity switching stations and post offices. Convicted for authorizing such attacks, Mandela and Sisulu were incarcerated under life sentences on Robben Island in 1964. There followed a long hiatus while the resistance movement gathered strength again, punctuated by a wave of strikes led by increasingly militant black workers' organizations in 1973 and by a courageous youth uprising in Soweto (South Western Townships) in 1976. The schoolchildren employed black consciousness ideas to challenge the use of Afrikaans as a medium of instruction. Within a year, however, the police had arrested, beaten, and killed their hero, Steve Biko.

By the 1980s, apartheid entered a crisis born of its own contradictions and of new pressures emanating from a changing world. Internally, the economy suffered from recession, currency inflation, and the excessive costs of administering a maze of oppressive social controls. As white professionals began to emigrate and blacks bore the brunt of a second-rate education system, the country encountered shortages of the skills necessary to operate its increasingly sophisticated economy. Then the National Party was rocked by a scandal over misappropriated public funds that forced the resignation of Prime Minister John Vorster. His successor, P. W. Botha, pursued a mixed strategy of repression and reform. On the one hand, he enhanced the powers of the presidency at the expense of the cabinet, drew military men into government through a State Security Council, and used the police as agents of local government. On the other hand, he tried (unsuccessfully) to co-opt Indians and Coloureds into their own separate legislatures and local government councils under a revised 1984 constitution. By 1986, Botha even authorized the repeal of selected "petty" apartheid laws in recognition of the fact that blacks now lived permanently in the heart of all major metropolitan areas.

Botha's strategy did not work because it continued to ignore the political aspirations of the majority. It was overtaken by events as Africans in the urban townships and industrial workplaces took matters into their own hands. By the end of the 1970s, trade unions had won the right to organize legally, and strikes were occurring at unprecedented rates. In 1983, the **United Democratic Front (UDF)**, a coalition of trade unions, churches, civic organizations, and women's and youth groups, coalesced to protest the new constitution. The UDF, considered by many to be a front for the banned and exiled ANC, completely disrupted urban local government through an orchestrated campaign of service and consumer boycotts, although too often the resultant void of authority was quickly filled by intimidation and violence. Faced with open popular resistance (symbolized by the *toyi-toyi* dance performed en masse at political funerals), the Botha government had no answer except to deploy the army in a nationwide state of emergency in June 1986.

Internationally, South Africa was becoming increasingly isolated. Long gone were the halcyon days of the 1960s and 1970s when international investors were attracted by a stable business climate. Gone also was the political support of U.S. President Richard Nixon, who earlier had concluded on the advice of Secretary of State Henry Kissinger that white settlers had a long-term future in Southern Africa and were a valuable bulwark against communism. The fall of settler regimes in Mozambique, Angola, and Rhodesia (now Zimbabwe) on South Africa's northern borders removed the country's buffer from black Africa.

In place of these allies, South Africa faced an increasingly hostile Organization of African Unity (the international body of black African states) and British Commonwealth (the association of former British colonies, many from Asia and Africa, from which South Africa had withdrawn in 1961 when it declared itself a Republic). The United Nations was clamoring for South Africa to surrender its mandate over neighboring Namibia, to withdraw its troops from Angola, and to immediately dissolve apartheid. The administration of U.S. President Jimmy Carter in the United States came out openly for majority rule and, in 1986, the U.S. Congress overrode a veto by President Ronald Reagan in order to impose comprehensive economic sanctions against South Africa. The inflow of investment capital turned into an outflow. Not only at home, but also abroad, the South African state had become a pariah.

An Unexpected Transition

As political attitudes hardened on all sides, a race war seemed inevitable. Yet nothing that had gone before prepared South Africans for what was to follow.

Recognizing that further violence would devastate Africa's most productive economy, the leaders of the country's opposing political forces stepped back from the brink. Driven by their own intertwined interests, they unexpectedly forged a peaceful passage that granted black majority rule in return for a continued place for whites in South Africa's bright economic sun. Against the backdrop of the end of the Cold War, South Africa made a sudden transition to multiracial democracy in the mid-1990s.

Events during the 1980s created the climate for negotiation and compromise. Cut off from flows of international capital, the economy began to shrink, driving the South African government to seek rehabilitation from the Western world. The collapse of communism in the Soviet Union and Eastern Europe deprived the ANC of its main sources of political, financial, and military support. Because both sides therefore lacked the means to win an outright military victory, each began to see virtue in coming to terms. Thus, political contacts were initiated: openly among white businessmen, Afrikaner intellectuals, and the ANC leaders in exile, and, secretly, between government officials and political prisoners within the country. These encounters reassured the government that Nelson Mandela would not insist on a winner-take-all solution and would respect minority (i.e., white) rights. Soon after acceding to leadership of the National Party, **Frederick Willem (F. W.) de Klerk** decided to gamble on political reform while Afrikaners still enjoyed a measure of control over the political situation. On February 2, 1990, he announced that Mandela would be released, banned parties could resume political activities, and negotiations for an inclusive new political order would begin. Nine days later, in the glare of global television coverage, Mandela walked free.

Negotiations over the country's political future began at the end of 1991 when delegates from the government, the ANC, and 17 other political organizations, including leaders from the ethnic homelands, gathered in the **Convention for a Democratic South Africa (CODESA)**. Some political parties held back: Leftist black-power movements such as the PAC continued to favor armed struggle ("one settler, one bullet"); and conservative groups, such as **Inkatha** and its political party, the Inkatha Freedom Party (IFP), which appealed to Zulu traditionalists, launched attacks on ANC supporters with the covert connivance of the South African security forces. CODESA and the multiparty forums that followed were "on-again, off-again" affairs, regularly breaking down in the face of violent incidents (such as the massacre of shack-dwellers at Boipatong in 1992 and the 1993 assassination of the popular Communist Party Secretary General, Chris Hani). Ironically, however, the ever-present specter of escalating disorder repeatedly helped to drive the parties back to the negotiating table.

At issue in negotiations was the shape of the new political order. The two major parties could agree on a few basic points (one person, one vote; an independent judiciary; and the reintegration of the homelands) but on little else.

Whereas the ANC insisted on a unitary state, the National Party (at first) and the IFP (throughout) favored federalism. Whereas the ANC wanted majority rule, their opponents called for a rotating presidency and minority vetoes. These differences were ultimately resolved through a series of behind-the-scenes pacts: a political pact to share power in a **Government of National Unity (GNU)** for five years; an economic pact to guarantee property rights and civil-service positions and pensions; and a military pact to extend amnesty to individuals on all sides who confessed to politically motivated crimes. Although these deals were struck largely as a result of the self-regarding calculations of South African elites, the international community kept nudging the peace process forward with promises of diplomatic recognition, aid, and investment.

The multiparty negotiating forum of 1993 eventually produced a transitional government, an interim constitution, and a timetable for the country's first open elections. The interim constitution was modeled on a variety of sources – German, American, and Indian, among others – but, more than anything, it reflected the art of the possible in South Africa's complex society. It was a quasifederal document with a strong central government that provided for nine provincial legislatures and eleven official languages. It imported conventional ideas from abroad such as proportional representation, according to which seats were allocated in the national and provincial assemblies on the basis of the share of the electoral votes won by each political party. But it was original in its provisions for a GNU, whereby parties also obtained seats in a coalition cabinet based on their share of the vote.

The election was scheduled for April 27, 1994. From the outset, the campaign was fraught with uncertainty. Inkatha and the far-right Conservative Party announced that they would not take part because the new constitution did not provide autonomy for either a Zulu kingdom or an Afrikaner republic. As a result of growing armed clashes between supporters of the IFP and the ANC, a state of emergency was declared in Natal Province. Chief **Mangosuthu Buthelezi**, the leader of rural Zulus, was effectively sidelined from negotiations by Mandela and de Klerk. In return, he appeared willing to risk civil war and to sacrifice South Africa's transition to democracy in pursuit of personal political ambitions and his people's regional interests. Eventually realizing that the transition would occur without him, however, Buthelezi ended his brinkmanship barely one week before the election by announcing that the IFP would take part.

The 1994 election in South Africa was a celebration, both solemn and jubilant, of a momentous historical shift. For the first time ever, South Africa's diverse peoples participated as political equals in the democratic ritual of choosing their own leaders. The election brought an end to 350 years of settler colonial rule and, with it, the perverse idea that the right to self-government was the preserve of some races but not others.

To be sure, South Africa's founding election did not run entirely smoothly: Voters had to wait in long lines to cast their ballots, some for several days; and the result in the Zulu heartland probably owed as much to an elite political bargain as to a valid vote. Nevertheless, the high voter turnout (86 percent of all adults) and the peacefulness of the polls throughout the country enabled the Independent Electoral Commission to declare the election substantially free and fair. The ANC won a solid majority (63 percent of the vote), followed by the National Party and the IFP (20 percent and 11 percent, respectively), each of which secured control of at least one provincial legislature (in the Western Cape and Kwazulu-Natal, respectively). These three parties formed a Government of National Unity with Nelson Mandela as president and F. W. de Klerk as his second executive deputy. Against all expectations, these farsighted and level-headed leaders – who deservedly shared the 1992 Nobel Peace Prize – had averted revolution, created a culture of compromise, and – unexpectedly – pulled democracy out of the hat.

The Socioeconomic Structure

Despite the drama of the democratic transition, change in the political sphere was offset by socioeconomic continuities. South Africa's first elected government inherited a society and economy whose population was mutually estranged, not only in terms of race but also wealth and well-being. The economy had never been designed to serve a black majority that included a vast, impoverished underclass – that now clamored for jobs, houses, and education. Could South Africans from different social backgrounds emerge from a bitter political conflict and put old divisions behind them? Whereas whites tended to see the democratic transition as the end of a difficult process of change, blacks saw it as just a beginning.

South Africa has always been a predominantly African country, although official policies acknowledged this only after 1994. According to the 1996 census, the total population was just over 40 million people, of whom some 77 percent classified themselves as African, 11 percent as white, 9 percent as Coloured, and 3 percent as Asian. The most common mother tongues were Zulu (23 percent), Xhosa (18 percent), and dialects of Sotho (17 percent), followed by Afrikaans and English (14 and 9 percent, respectively). Although South Africans are relatively literate and unusually multilingual, many people have received poor-quality schooling and remain uncomfortable using English, the country's main language of government and business. Yet, over one-half live in towns (at least 54 percent), and the urban areas are growing at more than twice the rate of the nation as a whole (5 percent versus 2 percent).

With the largest and most complex economy on the African continent and a gross national product (GNP) of 6,854 rand per person in 1994 (then about $1,950 U.S.), South Africa is a middle-income country. It features bustling cities with gleaming skyscrapers, modern highways filled with fancy German and Japanese automobiles, and vast irrigated farms employing the latest agricultural technologies. Indeed, the country's stock of physical infrastructure (roads, railways, harbors, power grids, and water networks), financial institutions (banks, insurance companies, and a stock market), and business and technological skills is solid. After stalling during the late 1980s and early 1990s, the economy revived after 1994: Over the next three years, the GNP grew at a rate exceeding population growth for the first time in two decades. Foreign debt was low, and inflation was under control. Importantly, because the South African economy was capable of financing socioeconomic development from domestic resources, the government had little need for aid or loans from international donors.

Set against these advantages, however, are poverty and inequality. At least one-third of economically active South Africans lack a formal job, with unemployment being highest among young people, women, and Africans. The average monthly wage of an employed African (about $300 U.S.) is barely above the amount needed for the subsistence of a low-income household. Thus, poverty haunts not only the unemployed but also many families with wage earners. Among the African population, one-quarter lack access to safe drinking water, almost one-half have only minimal sanitation, and three in ten (more in rural areas) are without electricity. The most common living conditions for the poor are either a single-roomed hut in an isolated rural backwater or, more commonly, a homemade shack in a garbage-strewn, periurban, informal settlement.

Thus, grinding poverty coexists alongside brazen displays of wealth. Among countries that keep reliable records on the gap between the "haves" and the "have-nots," South Africa ranks as one of the most unequal societies in the world, second only to Brazil. The poorest 20 percent of households earn just 3 percent of the country's income, whereas the richest 20 percent earn 63 percent. According to the Human Development Index of the United Nations, the lifestyle enjoyed by white South Africans is equivalent to that of New Zealanders, whereas black South Africans live under conditions similar to their counterparts in Congo-Brazzaville. Asians and Coloureds fall somewhere in between.

HIV, the virus that causes AIDS, has spread alarmingly in South Africa. By the end of 2001, 20 percent of adults aged 25 to 49 were living with the virus or the disease, a higher proportion than for any country in the world at that time. Although all classes of society are affected, the poor and women are disproportionately stricken. An average South African's life expectancy fell by ten years (from 63 to 53 years) between 1991 and 2002 and is projected to fall much further (to 38 years) by 2010. Some 13 percent of South African children have already lost one or both parents.

Severe deprivation and inequality, combined with a legacy of brutal politics, have bred crime and social violence. South Africa's murder rate – 65 deaths per day in 1997 – leads the world; other manifestations include gang warfare, organized cash-in-transit heists, and illegal international trade in drugs, guns, and diamonds. The government claims that it has reduced crime, but the facts are mixed: Whereas some offenses, such as murder, may be falling, others, such as residential burglary, continue to climb. Conventional wisdom connects crime with joblessness, but this economic interpretation does not explain the link between crime and violence. Here it is necessary to remember that South Africa's seemingly smooth political transition was actually very turbulent. Both the security forces and some anti-apartheid activists adopted tactics of intimidation and vigilantism. A gap in authority opened up between a repressive state and an ungovernable citizenry, into which large numbers of weapons have continued to flow as a result of conflicts elsewhere in the region. Fear of crime is pervasive among South Africans both black and white.

Scholars have engaged in heated debates about whether South African politics are better understood in terms of social identities such as ethnicity (including race) or with reference to the interests of economic classes. What is important, however, is that race and class significantly overlap in South Africa; in social science terminology, social and economic cleavages tend to reinforce rather than cross-cut. To the extent that apartheid was an integrated system that used racial classification not only to exert political control (over blacks) but also to accumulate wealth (for whites), it resulted in particularly deep and lasting divisions.

Thus apartheid's legacy of race-based material inequality remains the starting point for any analysis of the dynamics of the country's contemporary politics. The inherited socioeconomic structure has profoundly shaped the design of political institutions in the country's new constitution. Inequality between the races remains a potentially explosive source of political instability that could still turn South Africa into yet another failed multiethnic state. And the capacity of elected governments to deliver social justice has already become the standard by which many South Africans evaluate the merits of democracy.

Contemporary Political Identities

To what extent, then, are contemporary South African politics shaped by social identities, particularly race, but also other aspects of ethnicity? Is it possible to build a shared sense of nationhood in this deeply divided, multicultural society?

Nelson Mandela staked his political career on the proposition that the country belongs to all of its people. He used his considerable moral authority to promote a vision of "reconciliation" in which South Africa's diverse groups forgo revenge and live peacefully side by side in a "rainbow nation." To this end, the first GNU cabinet was truly multiracial, being made up of sixteen Africans, eight whites, and six Indians or Coloureds. The transition spawned new symbols of national unity such as a multicolored flag and an anthem that melds the favorite hymns of the old and new regimes. In this sports-mad country, citizens of all races demonstrate their patriotism by enthusiastically embracing these symbols at national soccer and rugby matches. And, in public-opinion surveys, more than 90 percent of respondents say they feel proud to call themselves South Africans.

Nevertheless, the same surveys show that most citizens still also identify with narrow subcommunities. Even as they profess newfound commitments to non-racialism, South Africans still behave politically as if they belong to racial and language blocs. In important respects, for example, national elections are a kind of "ethnic census": In 1994, fewer than 3 percent of whites cast ballots for the (black-led) ANC, and fewer than 5 percent of Africans chose the (white-led) National Party. The fact that two-thirds of Coloured and Indian voters sided with white-led parties suggests that these communities also felt racial distance from Africans and were concerned about the consequences of majority rule. These concerns center on the potential for monopolization of the electoral process by one demographic group. Because black Africans constitute some 69 percent of the electorate, and because about 75 percent of them vote for the ANC, the ruling party would seem to enjoy a permanent, built-in majority. With a dominant ruling party and a fragmented opposition, it is difficult to see how South Africa can attain a turnover of governments in the near future. This aspect of democracy would require the realignment of voter support away from its present racial structure.

Indeed, the salience of race in South African politics has hardly declined since 1994. The government ordered that racial categories be restored in the collection and reporting of official data, arguing that this was necessary to address existing inequities. Also introduced were policies of affirmative action to create job opportunities for disadvantaged groups, which, although encouraging the much-needed transformation of institutions throughout society, also helped to keep a consciousness of ethnicity alive. Race relations are marred by harsh stereotypes: Many South African whites believe that their black counterparts lack the technical capacity to operate a complex economy and government; aware of these prejudices, many blacks are overly sensitive to criticism, tending to dismiss even constructive dissent as racism. Thus have debates between the government and the opposition – especially in Parliament and in the press – too often lapsed into a defensive exchange of epithets.

To South Africa's advantage, however, the industrial economy long ago brought blacks and whites together in workplaces across the country and now, increasingly, into residential proximity in the major cities. Economic integration therefore continues to dissolve the mutual isolation of the two main racial communities. Some minority groups, however, remain clustered in their own areas: For instance, 83 percent of the Coloureds live in the Cape provinces, especially around Cape Town, and 78 percent of Asians live in Kwazulu-Natal, especially in Durban. In these cases, geographical concentration has probably helped minorities to avoid being shut out from politics entirely. In the long run, however, any party that wishes to govern at the national level in South Africa must attract black votes.

Ethnic interpretations of South African politics should not be pushed too far, however. The struggle over the allegiance of the Zulu people is not a simple tribal conflict. Instead, the Zulus are internally split; whereas rural folk have been attracted to the Inkatha Freedom Party (which borrows Zulu cultural symbols such as assegais, shields, and leopard skins), many urban Zulus support the ANC. Political killings in the countryside have usually arisen when ANC adherents have sought to mobilize support back home, only to invoke a counterreaction from Inkatha traditionalists who perceive a threat to the power and status of the *amakhosi* (chiefs). Although the level of political violence between the IFP and ANC declined in Kwazulu-Natal after 1994, it rose again as the 1999 elections approached. Persistent clashes prompted the top leadership of the two parties to reopen negotiations, including talk of a governing alliance. To ease tensions and demonstrate trust, Mandela appointed IFP leader Buthelezi not only as minister of home affairs but as acting president during the former's absences from the country.

Both Zulu and Afrikaner nationalists now seem to recognize that their communities' separation from the South African state is both undesirable and impractical. Instead, they have turned their attention to preserving languages and cultures. Under the interim constitution, Afrikaans was downgraded from one of two official languages and, when the terms of a permanent constitution were being negotiated in 1996, language rights became a critical issue. Afrikaner leaders sought to portray the ANC's multicultural project as an effort to subjugate linguistic minorities (including Zulu-speakers and Afrikaans-speaking Coloureds). Thus were racial and ethnic differences bridged by shared cultural concerns. Again, Mandela bent over backward to accommodate differences, recognizing that extremists among cultural minorities could constitute a threat to the stability of the political system if they were not incorporated within it.

Other potential bases for political identity include religion and gender. As elsewhere in Africa, religious movements that combine Christian and indigenous beliefs have strong popular appeal. The largest voluntary association in the country is the **Zion Christian Church**, which has more active members than the ANC or the trade-union confederation. This independent religious movement advocates traditional African values such as *ubuntu* (community) and its positions differ from those of the governing party in that it opposes abortion and favors the death penalty. Here, religion serves not so much to mobilize people into politics as to encourage withdrawal from a secular world that is seen as excessively materialistic, corrupt, and competitive. The social conservatism of many South Africans also expresses itself in the suppression of women. Whether in Afrikaner, Zulu, or Xhosa families, the older males dominate and try to confine women to the domestic sphere. Disrespect for females is expressed in disturbingly frequent incidents of domestic violence and rape, the latter an especially frightening prospect in a society where HIV-AIDS is rampant. Encouraged by guarantees against sexism in the South African constitution but set back by weak implementation, women in South Africa have yet to make a reality of gender equality.

Finally, although overt racial discrimination is no longer socially acceptable, new forms of exclusion are arising. Even as a new South African identity takes shape, nationalism reveals a darker side. Xenophobia (fear of the "other") is on the rise as hundreds of thousands of political refugees and economic migrants from other parts of Africa (especially unstable Zimbabwe) have streamed into the country since the democratic transition. In the context of an economy that cannot generate enough employment for local entrants into the labor market, foreigners are too often blamed for job shortages, diseases, and criminal activities for which they are not responsible. Attacks on strangers are on the rise. And political tolerance – both within South Africa's diverse citizenry and between citizens and outsiders – remains in short supply.

Contemporary Political Interests

The development of an industrial economy helped to dissolve divisions between the races, but it also helped to create social classes. At the same time as South Africans have tried to shrug off the ethnic labels imposed by apartheid, they have devised new forms of political solidarity based on economic interests. As in other capitalist economies, class conflict in South Africa revolves mainly around the divergence of interests between business and labor.

Under apartheid, the government and private companies got together to prohibit African workers from joining trade unions, engaging in collective bargaining, or going on strike. But a vast semiskilled industrial workforce with the power to bring economic production to a halt could not be contained indefinitely. Escalating "wildcat" (i.e., unauthorized) strikes in the metal, textile, and chemical industries forced government and employers alike to officially recognize African trade unions in 1979 and to acquiesce to the formation of a federated **Congress of South African Trade Unions (COSATU)** in 1985. By 1990, COSATU's 14 affiliated unions represented 1.2 million workers. At first, the unions focused on securing better wages and working conditions, refusing to align themselves with any political movement. With the advent of COSATU, however, organized labor entered the "national democratic struggle" under the leadership of the ANC.

As in Poland and Zambia, the labor movement was a key actor in South Africa's late twentieth-century transition to democracy. In 1991, COSATU successfully pushed for amendments to the Labor Relations Act that established mediation procedures for settling industrial disputes. When political negotiations over the country's future began to break down in 1992, COSATU orchestrated the "rolling mass action" (marches, stoppages, and stay-aways) that backed up the ANC's bargaining positions. And, in 1994, when the ANC announced lists of candidates for national and provincial parliaments in the GNU, the names of 70 COSATU leaders were included.

Because the labor movement played a crucial role in building support for the ANC's electoral victory, COSATU expected the new government to adopt labor-friendly policies. In practice, however, worker interests were not always protected, in part because the ANC had also developed close ties with private capital. Contacts grew from tentative overtures between business and political leaders during the late 1980s to substantial corporate contributions to the ANC's election campaigns after 1994. In the intervening period, entrepreneurs had set up projects to uplift the poor, brought together diverse interest groups to discuss options for the future, and sponsored research on policies for the post-apartheid era. By the time Mandela put together the Government of National Unity, it seemed only natural that he would seek guidance from Harry Oppenheimer – former chairman of Anglo-American Corporation, South Africa's largest conglomerate – about appointments to key economic portfolios in the cabinet.

Although learning occurred on both sides, contacts with business interests – both domestic and international – transformed the ANC's approach to economic policy. The party had long preferred a socialist strategy based on the "seizure" of the "commanding heights of the economy," such as land, industries, and banks. Even as Mandela was released from prison in 1990, he reiterated the movement's commitment to nationalization of the means of production and the redistribution of wealth. But moderate voices within the ANC began to question whether it was advisable to grab property and raise taxes in an era of mobile international capital. By late 1991, on a visit to the United States, Mandela reassured corporate executives, the World Bank, and U.S. President George H. W. Bush that nationalization was no longer in the cards. Instead, the ANC declared that economic growth was the best means for addressing poverty, which in turn was only possible if private companies – local and foreign – felt confident enough to invest.

In revising its economic strategy, the ANC did not completely jettison a role for the state. After all, the new government announced a **Reconstruction and Development Program (RDP)** that envisaged socioeconomic transformation through public investments in education, housing, health care, electricity, and other basic amenities. The fact that the RDP was originally a COSATU blueprint is evidence that popular, working-class interests remained critical in shaping ANC thinking. But the RDP never really addressed and was unable to satisfy citizens' (and the unions') most pressing demand: jobs. To this end, the government introduced an orthodox macroeconomic policy framework in 1996 known as GEAR (for Growth, Employment, and Redistribution). Following market principles and reflecting fiscal discipline, GEAR sought to accelerate South Africa's annual economic growth rate to 6 percent by reducing budget deficits, deregulating the economy, and selling off selected state-owned enterprises.

The South African government thus finds itself at the fulcrum of class conflict. It must perform a delicate balancing act between rival political interests. How can it satisfy the expectations of the downtrodden for improved living standards without at the same time driving away the capital and skills needed to make the economy grow? In search of solutions, the government built on the country's experience with negotiation and compromise. It established a bargaining forum called the **National Economic Development and Labour Council (NEDLAC)** in which workers, employers, and the state discuss proposed legislation before Parliament enacts it. NEDLAC represents what political scientists call corporatism: an institutional arrangement that channels conflicting interests into a process of cooperative decision making. Because corporatism allows giving extra weight to groups who are more powerful than their mere numbers would indicate, it has led to economic policies in South Africa that are more business-oriented than most ANC supporters would like. At first, COSATU showed restraint at this departure from its interests, but a rising tide of strike actions suggests that the patience of workers is wearing thin.

The government can make economic adjustments without losing too much political support, however, in part because the class structure is changing. As race barriers weaken, a black middle class is emerging. In the decade before 1994, the personal disposable income of Africans increased by more than 35 percent, whereas the disposable income of whites dropped slightly. Since 1994, a new African elite has eagerly embraced moneymaking and American-style consumption, perhaps because private enrichment was so long denied them. In response to legislation requiring "employment equity" and "economic empowerment," the private sector has created new opportunities for blacks to advance rapidly in their careers and to purchase stocks, partnership shares, and even entire companies. As a result, income inequality has risen to almost the same level within the black community as for the society as a whole.

Even the working class is not immune from the allure of the market. COSATU's member unions have established profit-making companies and invested worker retirement funds in the stock market. Trade-union leaders now sit on the boards of major corporations, including those in the deeply conservative mining sector. These movements in the class structure have unsettled relations within the trade unions and between unionized workers and the unemployed. Labor leaders face charges that they have "sold out" to capitalism, and calls have started for a new political party of the Left. The more militant members of COSATU see their own organization as the vehicle for such a party, openly urging the unions to split from their alliance with the ANC.

As South Africans come to reject ethnic labels in favor of class identities – in a 2002 survey, just as many people saw themselves in terms of occupation as of race – a foundation is being laid for civil society. Voluntary associations and social movements have always thrived in South Africa, as has an independent press. Whereas, in the past, dissenters organized resistance outside the bounds of conventional politics, today they partake in the democratic process as forceful advocates on a range of single-issue policies, especially employment, land reform, and HIV/AIDS. In 2001, for example, protests by the Treatment Action Campaign (TAC) forced reluctant pharmaceutical firms to reduce the price of antiretroviral drugs and the government to begrudgingly begin a drug-distribution program.

Democratic Political Institutions

The purpose of government institutions is to provide authoritative decisions that resolve political conflicts among opposing identities and interests. To govern ("rule") is to issue decisions ("rulings") that must be obeyed by everyone. Under an authoritarian regime (such as the old apartheid system), citizens reluctantly comply with the commands of government institutions because they fear that the state will unleash violence against them if they do not. Under a democratic regime (such as South Africa since 1994), citizens grant compliance more willingly because they regard elected institutions as having been legitimately installed. Ideally, a good government is both responsive to popular demands and effective at enforcing its own policy decisions.

Several key institutions are essential to a democracy. These include a constitution with a bill of rights, a separation of governmental powers, a regular cycle of open elections, and a vibrant and autonomous civil society. Each of these (sets of) political institutions is examined in the section that follows. And special mention is made of two bodies – the **Constitutional Court** and the **Truth and Reconciliation Commission (TRC)** – that have made distinctive contributions to South Africa's development as a democracy.

The **South African Constitution** of 1996 is both liberal and social-democratic. Widely praised internationally, it was produced by the GNU's Constituent Assembly and is the jewel of the first government's political accomplishments. In addition to a full gamut of civil and political liberties (e.g., freedom of speech and association and the right to vote), the constitution's bill of rights also includes wide guarantees of access to food, water, education, health care, and social security. Certain offsetting provisions reflect South Africa's unique history: freedom of expression is qualified with prohibitions on hate speech; rights to cultural heritage are allowed only to the extent that they do not infringe the rights of others; and property rights do not preclude the possibility of redistribution (for example, through affirmative action and land reform). Adopted by an overwhelming parliamentary majority, the constitution has won broad acceptance throughout society. Given the generosity of its promises, however, it has yet to prove fully enforceable.

As in other countries, the constitution of South Africa lays the foundation for the rule of law. It requires a measured separation of central government powers, assigning these conventionally to the legislative, executive, and judicial branches of government. It is unconventional, however, in the relative balance ascribed to the executive and legislative branches, resulting in a democratic system that is neither presidential nor parliamentary but a hybrid of the two. On the one hand, the constitution (rather than Parliament) is supreme. And the constitution provides for an executive president who enjoys extensive powers of appointment and decision making. On the other hand, the president is not elected directly (but by the National Assembly from among its own numbers), and he or she must select cabinet members from the Assembly and dissolve the government if faced with a "no confidence" vote. Because of these formal limitations, the South African chief political executive looks more like a Commonwealth prime minister than the unconstrained "super-president" commonly found in other African republics.

In practice, however, the ANC's large working majority in Parliament has enabled the executive branch to control the legislature. In South Africa, the Parliament is bicameral, meaning that it has two houses, the National Assembly and a National Council of Provinces, both currently based in Cape Town. Parliament has been active, passing an average of over 100 laws in each of its sessions, which together have reversed the thrust of apartheid legislation. All bills originate from the president's office or from other departments in the executive branch. Major decisions on economic policy – such as the shift in emphasis from service delivery under the RDP to job creation under GEAR – are made within the executive branch and without consultation with members of Parliament (MPs). Nor are parliamentary checks effective. For example, the ANC blocked an effort by Parliament's Standing Committee on Public Accounts to investigate a massive corruption scandal in the Ministry of Defense over a $5 billion (U.S.) arms deal during 2001.

So far, the judiciary has been more independent than the legislature. A Constitutional Court, which has final say on fundamental legal matters, rejected the draft constitution until provisions were included to strengthen the rights of individuals, the autonomy of provincial governments, and public oversight by watchdog agencies. Although being careful to frame its judgments narrowly, the Court has already tilted the scales in favor of social justice: In landmark rulings in 2001 and 2002, it directed that the state must provide drugs to combat mother-to-child transmission of HIV and that the homeless have a right to state-provided housing. Even while dragging its feet on implementation, the executive branch has ultimately respected these rulings of the judiciary. This commitment to a rule of law is all the more remarkable given that elderly judges held over from the previous regime continue to serve on the higher courts. Compared with the nonracially constituted legislature and executive branch, the judiciary is the least transformed branch of government.

Because South Africa's recent past was marred by gross violations of human rights, the new order included special institutions to deal with this legacy. Again to international acclaim, the new government established a Truth and Reconciliation Commission (TRC) under the supervision of Archbishop Desmond Tutu, another Nobel Peace Prize winner. The TRC was charged with three tasks: to uncover the truth about the abuses of apartheid; to offer amnesty to those who confessed to politically motivated crimes; and to make reparations to victims. The Commission sought to resolve South Africa's past problems of political violence without causing an escalating spiral of punishment and revenge. Armed with the stick of subpoena power and the carrot of amnesty, it was easily the most powerful commission of its kind ever created.

Several thousand victims testified before the TRC's public hearings, which provided a chance for those who had suffered in silence to be heard at last. A stream of low-level apartheid functionaries also came forward to admit, in chilling detail, how they served as the covert hit men of the old order. The commission also delved into the misdeeds of the liberation movements, including torture in former ANC training camps and the alleged involvement of Winnie Madikizela-Mandela (then Nelson's wife) in several murders during the late 1980s. The TRC's extraordinary achievement was to cast a spotlight on the inner secrets of the apartheid years, making denial difficult and reducing the likelihood that its horrors can ever recur.

By the time the TRC issued its final report in 2003, however, it faced criticism from across the political spectrum. Unconfessed perpetrators from all political parties cried foul. Because senior figures such as former

Prime Minister P. W. Botha and IFP leader Gatsha Buthelezi refused to testify, the truth about state-sponsored killings and the civil war between the
ANC and IFP in Kwazulu-Natal remained obscure. The families of victims
also expressed anger at a process that opened old wounds and offered minimal compensation and little succor afterward. Indeed, the TRC confirmed
that truth does not always lead to reconciliation. The graffiti scrawled on
an underpass in the administrative capital of **Pretoria** – "Tutu has made
them confess, now we will kill them!" – surely represents an extreme view,
but it nonetheless captures the missing element: justice. For many South
Africans, the righting of wrongs will require more than criminal justice for
official perpetrators; it also requires a meaningful measure of social justice
that involves broad sacrifices by apartheid's beneficiaries.

In the context of persistent social divisions, the political institutions of
democracy, including multiparty elections, offer one way forward. In both
the interim and new constitutions, South Africans chose an electoral system
based on proportional representation (PR), which seemed like an appropriate choice. In contrast with the previous constituency-based, winner-take-all
system that had helped the (Afrikaner) National Party rise to power, rules
of proportionality now ensure that all voices are heard. In practice however,
PR has also created new problems in South Africa. Because candidates for
legislative office are not chosen by local districts but are selected by their
parties to run on a national electoral list, citizens have found it difficult to
hold MPs accountable. A "representation gap" has quickly grown between
voters and political elites.

By 1999, the government was no longer constitutionally bound to share
power with minority parties, although the ANC again chose to offer cabinet
seats to the IFP in 1999 and the New National Party (NNP) in 2004. The
second national elections in that year marked the completion of the country's
transition to a multiparty democracy, which now featured a government in
office and an out-of-power opposition. With each passing election, the majority party's hold on the electorate has grown ever more secure: The ANC
increased its share of votes to 66 percent in 1999 and 70 percent in 2004. In
so doing, it virtually eliminated the NNP from Parliament, gained outright
control of eight out of nine provincial legislatures, and cemented a two-thirds
majority in the national legislature, a number sufficient to change the constitution. The ANC's nearest competitor, the white-led Democratic Alliance,
won just 12 percent of the vote in 2004.

Rather than regarding these lopsided developments as an unwelcome
harbinger of one-party rule, however, many citizens apparently see the ANC
as the country's best bet for reducing the gap between the "haves" and the
"have-nots." To be sure, voter turnout was down in 2004 (to about 75 percent of registered voters, and a smaller percentage of all eligible adults),
perhaps because supporters of opposition parties stayed home, thinking

that their vote would not count. But the ANC, having delivered in good part on promises to improve access to housing, electricity, water, health care, and pension services, can convincingly portray itself as the representative of the impoverished majority. Indeed, for the moment, South Africans seem to judge the consolidation of democracy in terms of the satisfaction of material expectations, an issue to which we return at the end of this chapter.

Bureaucratic State Institutions

When South Africans refer to "government" (or "Pretoria," the city where most government offices are found), they usually mean the executive branch. The executive branch is charged with running the country between elections. It comprises the president, the deputy president, the cabinet, and all government ministries and departments. The Department of Finance (in consultation with an independent Financial and Fiscal Commission that oversees the distribution of revenues to provincial and local governments) is responsible for drawing up the national budget.

From the outset, President Nelson Mandela concentrated on solving high-profile political problems and performing the presidency's ceremonial duties; he delegated policy making and routine administrative decisions to Deputy President **Thabo Mbeki**. In a smooth leadership succession in 1999, the ANC prepared the country and the world for Mandela's retirement and ensured Mbeki's ascent to the presidency. Although South Africans may never love the technocratic Mr. Mbeki as much as they do the charismatic Mr. Mandela, the former has proved a capable steward of the economy, presiding over a reduction in the government's budget deficit and the restoration of a measure of growth. But Mbeki has played a less sure hand in political and social affairs. By pulling power into the president's office and appointing loyalists in the provinces (techniques for sidelining rivals), he has often alienated rank-and-file members within the ANC. And by disputing whether HIV causes AIDS and supporting dictator Robert Mugabe in neighboring Zimbabwe, he has caused citizens and outsiders alike to question his judgment.

Much like the legislature, the executive branch of government in South Africa is strongly influenced by the majority political party. The top organs of the ANC – its National Congress, National Executive Committee (NEC), and National Working Committee (NWC) – lay down the policies for the government to follow. The NEC is the party's highest policy-making body between party congresses, and the NWC is responsible for the day-to-day running of the organization. Most importantly, because almost all cabinet ministers also serve as ANC officeholders, party ideas regularly find their way into government policy. But, whereas ANC activists aim to blur the line between the executive branch and the party, senior civil servants seek to define it clearly. The directors-general (DGs) of government departments – the senior civil servants who provide professional advice and management – are often able to influence policy in their own right. Similarly, insofar as government programs are funded by foreign aid, international donors insist on technical requirements that counterbalance the party's political weight.

Precisely because modern governments control considerable resources – such as budgets, expertise, and coercion – the potential for the abuse of power always exists. This threat increases to the extent that the ANC government aims to accumulate and centralize power in order to radically transform society. Certainly, South Africa's previous National Party government was highly secretive, an impulse that still guides bureaucrats today; and a culture of corruption took deep root in the former "homeland" governments that have been incorporated into current provincial administration. A 2002 public-opinion poll revealed that 70 percent of South African citizens see the new government as equally or more corrupt than the one it replaced. A string of corruption cases reported in the national press – not only the spectacular arms scandal but more mundane violations such as the illegal sale of drivers' licenses, nonexistent "ghost workers" on the state payroll, and violations in contract-tendering procedures – suggests that there is substance behind popular perceptions.

On paper, South Africa's constitution provides plentiful antidotes to the abuse of executive power. A Human Rights Commission is charged with redressing violations and educating the citizenry; a Public Protector receives citizen complaints about lax or unfair administration; and an Auditor-General reports to legislatures on executives' use of taxpayer money. At first, the ANC sought to expand these ample provisions for public oversight, for example by passing a model code of conduct for parliamentarians. With the passage of time, however, the ANC has backed off from early commitments to transparency, for instance by stalling on an open democracy bill that would provide freedom of information about the work of government. And, in practice, the operations of all public watchdog agencies have been limited by budgetary constraints imposed by the Ministry of Finance; none functions comprehensively at the provincial or local levels, where most abuses occur. If such institutions cannot be sustained, executive accountability may be difficult to obtain in this new democracy.

At the heart of executive authority is the coercive power of the state. Under apartheid, the South African government used the state security apparatus – the army, the police, and the intelligence services – not only against neighboring countries but against its own people. Since 1994, the role of the army has been redefined (it is now charged to guard against external threats and to keep peace in regional conflicts), and the defense budget has been slashed in favor of social spending. A smaller South African National Defense Force (SANDF) has been built by combining selected elements from the old regular army and the armed wings of the guerrilla movements. Although not entirely eliminating racial tensions over promotions and salaries, the merger helped the executive branch establish civilian control over the military, greatly reducing the possibility of an illegal coup (seizure of power).

More troublesome are the intelligence services and the police, which still contain elements uncommitted to the new political order, some of whom have indulged in disruptive "dirty tricks." Citizens have not forgotten that the South African Police Services (SAPS) were used as paramilitary shock troops to impose order during the township uprisings of the 1970s and 1980s. The police are widely distrusted by South Africans of all races because they lack professional training (for example, in crime control and community relations) and because their ranks have not been fully purged of racists, torturers, and criminals. This lack of public confidence is not alleviated by a justice system that regularly fails to convict offenders. Instead, prosecutors are overworked, witnesses are inadequately protected, hearings are endlessly postponed, and many badly prepared cases are thrown out of court. As such, the government is widely regarded as soft on crime.

This brings us to the biggest challenge faced by the new South African government: building institutional capacity. As stated earlier, governments must be effective at implementing their own policies and at eliciting citizen compliance. In short, they must govern. The first decade of the new South Africa was a productive interlude of progressive reform in which popular policies were enacted in almost every governmental sector. But amid the welter of policy papers, a nagging question remains: Is the executive branch equipped to ensure proper implementation?

The task of building institutional capacity in South Africa is complicated by the complex structure of its government. In order to accommodate the country's social diversity, the constitution established three tiers of government: the national, the provincial, and the local. Each tier has responsibility for particular public functions. Whereas the national government is responsible for tasks such as defense and most taxation, the provinces take the lead on health and education, among other things; for their part, local governments must deliver a range of municipal services such as street cleaning, road maintenance, and waste disposal. Each tier has a legislative body (a provincial parliament or local government council) and an executive body (a provincial executive council or a municipal/district administration). Simply staffing all of these units of government when the majority population lacks relevant education and experience is only the start of the capacity-building challenge.

Generally speaking, the state apparatus tends to perform less well as one moves from well-established institutions at the political center to new and untested structures in the locality. And yet, South Africa's great social needs arise primarily among poor populations at the grassroots level. The new government therefore is trying to take on an expanded range of services to mass populations at the same time as it is revising public policies and constructing new delivery institutions, often from scratch. As one politician put it, this is akin to moving the furniture into a new house before you have finished building the house.

Even in the central government, civil servants sometimes lack the management and technical skills necessary to run a modern state, leading to a heavy reliance on external consultants. The South African Revenue Service (SARS) has shown improvement in collecting income, corporate, and sales taxes, for example, by meeting revenue targets in 2004. But customs control at international airports and harbors leaves much to be desired. Basic middle-management skills are scarce at the provincial level, where 57 percent of the public budget is actually expended. As a result, provincial ministries responsible for education and health have been unable to meet goals of providing universal service coverage ("education and health for all"). Although many previously disadvantaged South Africans have obtained school places or preventive health care for the first time, the quality of such services is falling. In the localities, life goes on much as before: Established suburban areas enjoy a full range of modern services, but too many informal settlements endure without paved roads, running water, and electricity.

On the surface, the problems of institutional capacity would appear to be financial. In about one-third of urban townships and rural areas, the local authorities cannot collect enough revenues to cover the costs of delivering basic services. Provincial governments are unable to fully spend their annual budgets or to adequately monitor the use of funds that they do actually disburse. But, the vacuum of governmental authority is fundamentally political, originating in unresolved struggles from the apartheid era. For example, many township dwellers still continue to resist payment of fees and taxes for services delivered by local councils, even though these bodies are now democratically chosen. And in some rural areas, traditional leaders and their followers refuse to recognize the authority of elected councilors, whom they regard as interlopers in the jurisdiction of chiefs. Thus, among South African citizens, the legitimacy of democratic institutions is far from universally accepted.

Conclusion: Consolidating Democracy?

The long-term challenge in South Africa is to consolidate recent achievements of peace, prosperity, and democracy. Even though the country's transition from authoritarian rule was led by bold political initiatives, the health of its

fragile new institutions will hinge on subsequent economic and social developments. Satisfying the material interests of disadvantaged identity groups in
the context of an AIDS crisis is the key to the country's future. As President
Mandela stated when opening Parliament in 1998, "Our performance should
be judged above all on whether our programs are positively affecting the lives
of the most vulnerable sections of society."

In this task, the South African government faces several knotty dilemmas.
By way of conclusion, we will consider just five, and the ways in which the following questions are addressed will determine the kind of economy, society,
and polity that South Africa will attain in the future.

First, can the economy grow fast enough to enable redistribution? South
African political leaders are bound to be preoccupied with the economy,
which must generate enough jobs to ease chronic black impoverishment. Yet
the formal (as opposed to the "underground") sector's ability to create employment has slumped, with mining, manufacturing, and agriculture all experiencing net job losses since the 1990s. Foreign investment has been slow to
arrive in South Africa, and capital is only now returning to emerging markets
following the Asian financial crashes of 1997–1998. These events undermined
the government's strategy for rapid economic growth and strengthened the
hand of critics (such as COSATU and the Communist Party) who called for
the state to play a larger role in job creation. Ironically, however, the more the
state intervenes in the economy, the less competitive South Africa becomes
in attracting essential private investment both from domestic and international sources. Such are the narrow policy options available to a government
whose economy reentered the world marketplace at a moment when capital
had become thoroughly mobile.

Second, can public institutions be deracialized while effectively delivering
services? The South African government is trying to "downsize" a bloated
bureaucracy while also "transforming" it (i.e., making it more socially representative and responsive). Some ministries and departments have been virtually paralyzed by clashes between old-order officials and new civil-service
recruits, often in disputes over affirmative action. Such logjams contribute
to the crisis of institutional capacity (the ability of state agencies to deliver
services in a timely and effective manner) that has slowed South Africa's post-
transition development. Malaysia's experience suggests that preferences for
formerly disadvantaged groups can be implemented with little conflict within
the context of a rapidly growing economy. But where job opportunities are
shrinking, affirmative action implies real losses to the formerly advantaged,
leading those with marketable skills to seek opportunities abroad. Already,
South Africa has lost too many doctors, accountants, and engineers, whose
talents are vital to the country's progress.

Third, can the government fight crime and respect human rights at the same
time? Because democratization imposes limits on the use of state power, it

relaxes controls over society. People who previously feared state repression are freed to engage in new pursuits, both legal and illicit. In South Africa, evidence is rising that former combatants from the apartheid conflict (both regular soldiers and guerrillas) are applying their war skills to careers in violent crime. Criminals of all types are taking advantage of the ANC's progressive policies, such as the abolition of the death penalty and guarantees against arbitrary arrest and detention. Lacking confidence that the state will punish wrongdoers, citizens in South Africa are increasingly taking the law into their own hands. The response varies across social groups: In the wealthy enclaves, people retreat behind the protection of private security guards; in poorer communities, they are more likely to resort to vigilante action. Regardless of whether the government cracks down, crime threatens to undermine many of the gains of democratization.

Fourth, can political and economic progress continue to be made if HIV/ AIDS is not controlled? Because the pandemic strikes young people in the prime of their lives, it strips valuable human capital from the workforce and the electorate and weakens the capacity of today's generation to pass on skills and knowledge to the next. The South African Bureau for Economic Research predicts that HIV will reduce the country's economic growth rate by one-half percent each year at least through the second decade of this century. And the Independent Electoral Commission, among many other political and economic institutions, recognizes that it will have to replace many of its experienced staff while still continuing to provide a high-quality service. Although we do not know for sure that declining electoral turnout is attributable in part to AIDS, it stands to reason that sick people, caregivers, and young people disillusioned with the government for delaying treatments are unlikely to be enthusiastic voters.

Finally, can democracy ever be consolidated in the absence of a supportive political culture? Observers have hailed the impressive array of democratic institutions embodied in South Africa's new constitution. But the behavior of citizens reveals low levels of political tolerance among competing social groups and strong popular attachments to antidemocratic political traditions. Certainly, there is little in South Africa's political history – whether in Zulu chieftaincy, the apartheid state, or exiled liberation movements – that nurtured democratic commitments. We should therefore not be surprised that South Africans do not value democracy as an end in itself: Just one-quarter of respondents in a national survey associate democracy with civil and electoral rights. Instead, South Africans tend to regard democracy as a means to other ends: Almost one-half associate it with jobs, education, and housing. And a similar proportion of citizens say they would be willing to give up elections in return for a leader who would provide these material goods.

Thus, South Africa has a distance to travel before its formal political institutions are transformed into a living, breathing democracy. Those who expect democracy to deliver social and economic equality may be sorely disappointed. All that democracy bestows is political equality. It does not guarantee that disparities of social and economic status will be redressed, although, comparatively, empirical studies indicate that democracies have a slightly better track record at redistributing wealth than do authoritarian regimes. This does not mean that a culture of democracy is a lost cause in South Africa. There are at least two hopeful signs. The first is that South Africans are likely to remember that democratization restored to people of all races the human dignity that apartheid denied. This they will not surrender easily. The second is that, when push came to shove, South Africans of widely differing backgrounds resorted to negotiation and compromise to find their way out of the country's deepest political crisis. One must therefore be confident that, in building democratic institutions, South Africans will recognize afresh that, however divided their identities, their interests are inexorably connected.

BIBLIOGRAPHY

Bhorat, Haroon, Murray Liebbrandt, and Muzi Maziya. *Fighting Poverty: Labour Markets and Equality in South Africa*. Cape Town: Juta Press, 2004.

Butler, Anthony. *Contemporary South Africa*. New York: Palgrave Macmillan, 2004.

Cling, Jean-Pierre. *From Isolation to Integration: The Post-Apartheid South African Economy*. Pretoria: Protea Book House, 2001.

Friedman, Steven, and Doreen Atkinson, eds. *The Small Miracle: South Africa's Negotiated Settlement*. Randburg: Ravan Press, 1994.

Gibson, James, and Amanda Gouws. *Overcoming Intolerance in South Africa: Experiments in Democratic Persuasion*. Cambridge: Cambridge University Press, 2003.

Johnson, R. W., and Lawrence Schlemmer, eds. *Launching Democracy in South Africa: The First Open Election, April 1994*. New Haven, CT: Yale University Press, 1996.

Lodge, Tom. *South African Politics: From Mandela to Mbeki*. Cape Town and Johannesburg: David Philip Publishers, 2003.

Mandela, Nelson. *Long Walk to Freedom: The Autobiography of Nelson Mandela*. Boston: Little Brown, 1994.

Mattes, Robert. "South Africa: Democracy Without the People?" *Journal of Democracy* 13, no. 1 (January 2002): 22–36.

Nattrass, Nicoli. *The Moral Economy of AIDS in South Africa*. Cambridge: Cambridge University Press, 2004.

Price, Robert. *The Apartheid State in Crisis: Political Transformation in South Africa, 1975–1990*. New York: Oxford University Press, 1991.

Thompson, Leonard. *A History of South Africa*. New Haven, CT: Yale University Press, 1995.

TABLE 12.1. Key Phases in the Development of South Africa

Time Period	Regime	Global Context	Interests/Identities/ Institutions	Developmental Path
Until 19th century	small-scale chieftaincies, European outposts	European trade with Asia; slavery and forced labor	access to plentiful resources/ emergence of mixed races/limited institutional reach	imperial trade
1806–1853	Cape Colony (authoritarian, colonial)	colonial annexation; seizure of land; wars of conquest and resistance	struggles over land/construction of racial identities/British governors	early state-building and expansion
1853–1910	self-government by white settlers (authoritarian, oligarchic)	Industrial Revolution; discovery of minerals; influx of migrant populations	control of gold and diamond fields/ racial and ethnic warfare/elected legislative councils for whites only	consolidation of settler states
1910–1948	Union of South Africa (authoritarian, segregated)	World Wars I and II; globalization of industrial production	capitalist firms versus African workers/English- versus Afrikaner-speakers/exclusive parliamentary democracy	political unification; economic integration but social segregation
1948–1994	Republic of South Africa (authoritarian, apartheid)	United Nations; liberation wars; decolonization	growing labor unrest and organization/ Afrikaner versus African nationalism/ separate unequal institutions, police state	ethnic cleansing; state capitalism
1994–present	Republic of South Africa (democratic)	globalization of capital markets; global wave of democratization	persistent economic inequalities/ interdependence of racial groups/liberal constitution, majority rule	multiparty democracy; market capitalism

IMPORTANT TERMS

African National Congress the political party that led the struggle for majority rule in South Africa.

Afrikaners people of mainly Dutch extraction who comprise a distinctive linguistic subculture within the white community.

amakhosi traditional tribal chiefs, such as those of the Xhosa and Zulu.

apartheid an oppressive system of racial segregation that denied political and economic equality to blacks.

Bantu a language group that includes Zulu and Xhosa, it was formerly used by the apartheid regime as a general designation for Africans.

Mangosuthu Buthelezi president of the Inkatha Freedom Party, whose supporters are mainly rural Zulus.

Cape Colony the first outpost of white settlement, located in the southwest of present-day South Africa.

Coloureds the South African term for persons of mixed race, an identity group in their own right.

Congress of South African Trade Unions (COSATU) the national confederation of trade-union organizations, politically affiliated with the ANC.

Constitutional Court the supreme court, charged with deciding constitutional issues.

Convention for a Democratic South Africa (CODESA) a multiparty forum convened in 1991 to negotiate the political future of the country.

F. W. de Klerk the last Afrikaner president, known for releasing Nelson Mandela and negotiating a handover of white power.

Government of National Unity (GNU) the government formed as a coalition of the parties who won the most votes in the founding election of 1994.

homelands impoverished rural areas to which Africans were banished under apartheid, supposedly to govern themselves.

Inkatha a movement of Zulu traditionalists, represented by its own political party, the Inkatha Freedom Party.

Nelson Mandela president of the African National Congress and first national president of majority-ruled South Africa. Widely respected as the father of racial reconciliation in South Africa.

Thabo Mbeki Mandela's successor as national president, who took office in July 1999.

National Party right-wing political party, supported mainly by Afrikaans-speakers, that came to power in 1948 and proceeded to implement apartheid.

National Economic Development and Labour Council (NEDLAC) a bargaining forum for discussion of policy proposals among the business, labor, and governmental sectors.

Population Registration Act the legislative foundation of apartheid, by which the South African people were classified into racial groups.

Pretoria administrative capital of South Africa; shorthand for "government."

Reconstruction and Development Program (RDP) the 1994 initiative that envisaged rapid socioeconomic "transformation" of the lives of poor people.

Sharpeville site of a massacre of peaceful protesters in 1960 and a commemorated landmark of anti-apartheid resistance.

South African Constitution ratified in 1997, this document promises a wide range of long-denied political, social, and economic rights to the citizens of South Africa.

Truth and Reconciliation Commission (TRC) the commission (established 1995) charged with investigating the human rights abuses of apartheid.

Union of South Africa formed in 1910, this confederation of former colonies defined the geographical boundaries of the modern South African state.

United Democratic Front (UDF) a social movement of community organizations that confronted apartheid policies during the 1980s.

Xhosa an African language group concentrated in the Eastern Cape province.

Zion Christian Church a mass-based, socially conservative, independent religious movement.

Zulu a centralized African kingdom found in Kwazulu-Natal province.

STUDY QUESTIONS

1. What were the historical origins of South Africa's identity groups? When, where, and how did they first come into mutual contact?

2. Describe the new political interests that emerged as a consequence of industrial development in South Africa. On whose terms, and how, were differences of interest first resolved?

3. Apartheid has been described as a "system of institutionalized racism." What were its key institutions?

4. Trace the course of political resistance to racial segregation in South Africa from its beginnings to the release of Nelson Mandela in 1990.

5. What explains the failure of apartheid and the unexpected success of the democratic transition? Consider both socioeconomic developments within South Africa and influences from abroad.

6. In South Africa's deeply divided society, which are more important: political identities based on race or the economic interests of social classes?

7. In what sense do elections in South Africa take the form of an "ethnic census"? How does this tendency square with an emerging popular attachment to "South African" identity?

8. How are the divergent interests of business and labor addressed in contemporary South Africa? Identify key institutions.

9. From a comparative perspective, what is new and distinctive about the political institutions created in South Africa since 1994?

10. How are South Africa's current challenges – creating jobs, building state capacity, and controlling disease and crime – derived from its past?

STOP AND **COMPARE**

EARLY DEVELOPERS, MIDDLE DEVELOPERS, LATE DEVELOPERS, AND EXPERIMENTAL DEVELOPERS

Taken together, the chapters you have just read underscore the importance of domestic political responses to international political challenges. In fact, a different title for the book might well have been *Liberal Democracy and Its Challenges*. As we have seen, Britain and France developed first, each with its own institutional variation on the liberal-democratic theme. This development, as positively as we may now evaluate it from our own perspective, made these two states powerful and ultimately threatening to Europe and the rest of the world.

Still, because of British and French successes, other countries sought to emulate the experience of the initial developers. In terms of our five-step framework: (1) Although middle developers Germany and Japan reacted to British and French development, devising variations on the initial British and French innovations, they were never actually able to replicate them for the simple reason that they were trying to catch up from behind. (2) As middle developers, middle-class interests were weaker, nationalist identity more pronounced, bureaucratic state institutions stronger, and democracy weaker. (3) These different circumstances of development ultimately weakened liberalism in Germany and Japan, which paved the way for the Nazi and fascist responses. It therefore makes sense to speak of a fascist path to the modern world. (4) The Nazis and the Japanese launched World War II, which ultimately led to occupation by the core liberal powers and a recasting of domestic identities, interests, and institutions. (5) In contemporary democratic Germany and Japan, interests, identities, and institutions grapple with the economic and political legacies of their distinctive authoritarian path to the modern world.

The late developers in this book are the (post-) communist giants Russia and China. In terms of our five-step framework: (1) Both tried to industrialize

467

their societies in a global order dominated by liberal-democratic and fascist capitalist states. (2) As late developers, middle-class interests were even weaker, nationalist identity more pronounced, bureaucratic state institutions even stronger, and democracy even weaker. (3) These different circumstances of development cut off both the liberal-democratic and fascist paths and paved the way for communism – the twentieth century's third main contender for a path to the modern world. (4) After an initial flirtation with global dominance, both the Soviet Union and China settled into an effort to legitimate their specific response to liberalism with superior economic performance under communist economic institutions. (5) Both failed. After desperately trying to repair a basically unworkable communist economic and political model in the decades after Stalin's death, the Russian response was to give up communism and introduce democracy and markets in the hope of rejoining the democratic-capitalist world system. Neither democracy nor markets have been terribly successful in Russia, however. China, on the other hand, shed its communist economy but not its Communist Party. Under the influence of the other successful semiauthoritarian capitalist states in East Asia, the Chinese response was to introduce markets into their society while attempting to maintain Communist Party dominance. Whether either country will be able to succeed in its newfound flirtation with a complete or partial reintegration with the international liberal order remains to be seen.

During the Cold War, the countries that we have called "experimental developers" tried to develop by seeking a path between the two surviving paths – liberal democracy and communist totalitarianism. They searched for a political middle way between democracy and authoritarianism and an economic middle way between markets and central plans.

EXPERIMENTAL DEVELOPERS: MEXICO, INDIA, IRAN, AND SOUTH AFRICA

Our final group of countries thus has a distinctive global historical heritage and shares common links. Most often, this commonality is colonial. Mexico, India, Iran, and South Africa experienced the impact of European colonial power. All now confront the cultural, institutional, and economic pressures of the global economy. Despite these similarities, each of these countries has distinctive, if modal, kinds of political problems that are of great interest to comparativists.

South Africa and India, respectively, conduct democratic politics in countries with very high levels of ethnic and racial diversity. Both have developed an innovative set of institutional arrangements for adjudicating conflicting ethnic and racial interests and identities within the parameters of what we normally think of as democratic institutions. Their experiments with multicultural democracy may even provide lessons, both positive and negative, for more industrialized Western societies. Furthermore, both confront the problem of sustaining democracy in environments of economic scarcity.

Iran experienced decades of steady Westernization under a dictator, the Shah. After an Islamic revolution in 1979, it sought to reshape its society and live under the rules of political Islam. It thus stands as a fascinating case of the religious reaction to global cultural influences, economic competition, and international political pressure. The on-again, off-again turn to more moderate leadership in Iran since the death of Ayatollah Khomeini illustrates vividly the power of the homogenizing forces of global liberalism. It remains unclear whether these latest developments signal a gradual return to the modernizing path taken before the Islamic revolution or whether it is a sign that the Islamic revolution is now institutionally stable and has indeed carved out a viable alternative to the liberal-democratic and global capitalist order that it consciously rejected.

Finally, Mexico has taken precisely the opposite route of Iran, choosing to integrate itself economically as closely with the United States as it can. Integration into the global trading system, however, has created both new political elites that are supportive of this move and new social movements that oppose it. Until the year 2000, Mexico was steadily (if somewhat corruptly) ruled by one party (the PRI). The election of Vincente Fox in 2000, however, turned a new and important page in Mexican history. Whether the new political elites and social movements that have emerged as a result of rapid economic change will contribute to the consolidation of liberal democracy remains an open question.

In sum: four countries, four experiments. Mexico's grand experiment is independence: Is it possible for a country to be autonomous when its northern neighbor happens to be the most powerful nation in the world? Iran's grand experiment is Islam: Is it possible for a country to be economically and politically powerful when it has had an Islamic revolution that creates an Islamic state? India's grand experiment is nonrevolutionary democracy: Is it possible for a large postcolonial country to be a democracy when it has had a major independence movement but not a social revolution? And South Africa's grand experiment is multiracial democracy: Is it possible for ethno-constitutional democracy and markets to survive in a country that made a relatively peaceful transition from colonialism and apartheid?

More generally: ten countries, ten experiments. The closer we look at our ten countries, the more we discover that there were ten developmental paths to the modern world. States made their own development choices and evolved local institutional variations of globally dominant political economies. In the words of our framework: (1) The constant of global context influences (2) the types of domestic interests, identities, and institutions that produce (3) the variables of developmental paths to the modern world that, in turn, generate (4) international-relations feedback effects on the global context and (5) comparative-politics feedback effects on domestic interests, identities, and institutions.

Index